THE RISING COST OF STATE GOVERNMENT, CORRECTED FOR THE VALUE OF THE DOLLAR

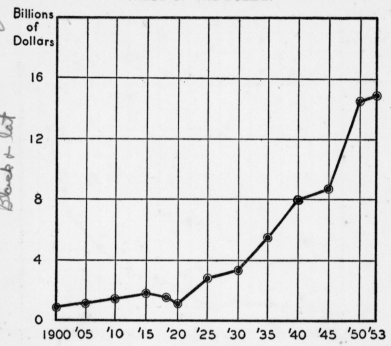

THE RISING COST OF CITY GOVERNMENT, CORRECTED FOR THE VALUE OF THE DOLLAR

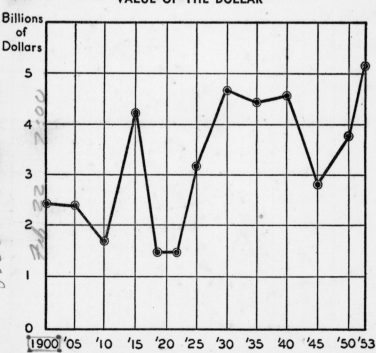

State and Local Government
in the United States

STATE *and* LOCAL GOVERNMENT
in the United States

AUSTIN F. MACDONALD
Professor of Political Science
University of California

THOMAS Y. CROWELL COMPANY • NEW YORK

MANUFACTURED IN THE UNITED STATES OF AMERICA
BY THE VAIL-BALLOU PRESS, INC., BINGHAMTON, N. Y.

Preface

Many persons have asked whether *American State Government and Administration,* now in its twenty-second year and fifth edition, could not be rewritten to place considerably greater emphasis on local government. Such a change might well prove advantageous for those who cover the combined fields of state and local government in a single term. On the other hand, it would hold few attractions for those who offer one course in state government and another separate course in municipal or local government.

The best solution of the problem, therefore, seems to be two separate books to meet these diverse needs. So *American State Government and Administration* retains substantially its original form, but a new volume, *State and Local Government in the United States,* is offered for those who prefer the combined treatment. This new work devotes approximately equal space to state and local problems. Nine of the thirty-one chapters deal exclusively or primarily with local government, and thirteen other chapters contain substantial sections on various aspects of local government and administration. There are two chapters on the organization of city government, one of the government of counties, and one on towns, townships, villages, and special districts. The relations of the federal government and the local units are given a separate chapter; so, too, is the government of metropolitan areas. There are chapters dealing with such primary local matters as housing and recreation.

The material on state government has been substantially compressed, in order to avoid a final product of unwieldy proportions. The new book, therefore, is no longer than *American State Government and Administration.* But this result has been achieved without sacrificing any of the essentials of state government. All the major problems—and virtually all the minor ones, for that matter—still receive enough space to permit adequate treatment. Extensive use has been made of charts and tables. It is hoped that *State and Local Government in the United States* will fit the needs of many colleges.

AUSTIN F. MACDONALD

Berkeley, California
January 10, 1955

Contents

PART ONE
Intergovernmental Relations

1 Federal-State Relations   **3**
Units of Government in the United States   3
Overlapping and Competition   4
The Division of Powers between the Nation and the States   4
Powers of the Federal Government   5
Powers of the States   20
Admission of New States   28

2 Interstate Relations   **32**
Diversity of State Legislation   32
Interstate Co-operation   34
Suits against a State   42

3 State-Local Relations   **46**
State Authority over Local Governments   46
Municipal Home Rule   51
Expansion of State Control   57

4 Federal-Local Relations   **62**
Indirect Federal Services   62
Direct Federal Services   63
Direct Aid to Local Communities   68
Federal Restrictions on State's Power over Local Governments   70

PART TWO
The Organization of State Government

5 State Constitutions   **77**
Organization and Subject Matter of State Constitutions   77
Constitutional Conventions   88
Constitutional Revision Commissions   91
Increasing Length of State Constitutions   92

6 State Executives   **96**
Restrictions on the Governor   96
The Administrative Reorganization Movement   98
The Office of Governor Today   106
The Lieutenant Governor   115

The Secretary of State   116
The Attorney-General   118
The Treasurer   119
The Auditor   120
The Superintendent of Public Instruction   121
Other Administrative Officers and Agencies   122
An Executive Cabinet   122

7   State Legislatures   124
    Size of Legislatures   124
    The Members of the Legislatures   125
    Underrepresentation of Cities in Legislatures   130
    Bicameral or Unicameral?   131
    Legislative Sessions   132
    Constitutional Restrictions on the Power of the Legislature   137
    The Legislature's Nonlegislative Functions   139
    Organization of the Legislature   140
    Procedure in Enactment of Legislation   147
    Legislative Reference Bureaus   153
    The Lobby   154
    Legislative Recommendations by the Governor and Heads of Admin-
        istrative Agencies   156
    Reform of the Legislature   157

8   State Courts   160
    Civil and Criminal Cases   161
    Organization of the Courts   161
    Selection of Judges   168
    Removal of Judges   169
    Need for Court Reform   171
    Judicial Review   179
    Advisory Judicial Opinions   181

PART THREE
The Organization of Local Government

9   City Government: Mayor and Council   187
    History of the Mayor's Office   187
    Types of Mayor-Council Government   189
    American Mayors   193
    American City Councils   197

10 City Government: The Newer Forms   203
    Beginning of Commission Government   203
    Rise and Fall of Commission Government   204
    Nature of Commission Government   204
    Arguments for Commission Government   206
    Defects of the Plan   207
    Dayton's Adoption of the Manager Plan   208

Business Organization in Government   208
Growth of the Manager Plan   209
Operation of the Manager Plan   210
Appraisal of the Manager Plan   214

11 Government of Metropolitan Areas   219
    Consequences of Congestion   219
    Difficulties of Co-ordinating Metropolitan Services 220
    Solutions of the Metropolitan Problem   223

12 County Government   236
    Organization of County Government   236
    Defects in County Organization and Administration 244
    County Consolidation   251
    Functional Realignment   251

13 Towns, Townships, Villages, and Special Districts   254
    New England Towns   254
    Townships   260
    Villages   264
    Special Districts   265

PART FOUR
The Political Process

14 Nominations and Elections   273
    The Caucus System   273
    The Convention System   274
    The Direct Primary   276
    Elections   285
    The Ballot   289
    Who May Vote   295
    Registration of Voters   299
    Absent Voters   301
    Nonvoters   302
    Compulsory Voting   303

15 Parties and Politics   306
    Definitions of a Political Party   306
    Rise of the Party System   308
    The Function of Political Parties   309
    Dominance of National Parties in State and Local Elections 312
    The Two-Party System   313
    One-Party Dominance in the South   314
    Organization of the Major Parties   315
    Sources of Revenue for State and Local Machines   320
    Boss Control   323

16   Direct Legislation and the Recall   327
     The Initiative and Referendum   327
     The Recall   334

PART FIVE
The Protective Services

17   Safety   343
     The National Guard   343
     State Police Forces   346
     Municipal Police Forces   349
     The Sheriff   354
     The Public Prosecutor   356
     Defense Counsel   358
     The Coroner   359
     The State Fire Marshal   361
     Municipal Fire Department Organization   361
     Treatment of Criminals   362

18   Welfare   370
     Substandard Incomes   370
     The Forced Shift from Private to Public Poor Relief   372
     Indoor versus Outdoor Relief   374
     The Old-Age Problem   378
     The Care of Homeless Children   382
     Aid for Mothers of Dependent Children   385
     Help for the Blind and the Disabled   387
     The Able-bodied Unemployed   387
     Administrative Organization   388

19   Health   392
     Establishment of State Health Organizations   392
     Federal Participation in Public Health Activities   394
     Organization of the State Health Department   394
     Local Health Organization   395
     Communicable Disease Control   399
     Mental Diseases   401
     Vital Statistics   404
     Public Health Laboratories   404
     Sanitary Engineering   405
     Child Hygiene   406
     Public Health Nursing   408
     Industrial Hygiene   409
     Educational Activities of the State Health Department   409
     Socialized Medicine   411

20   Housing   415
     Unsatisfactory Housing Conditions   415
     Municipal Housing Laws   417
     The Slum Problem and Low-cost Housing   420

PART SIX
Education and Development

21 **Education** 431
Shift from Private to Public Education 431
Division of Responsibility for Public Education 431
Local Units of School Administration 433
Unified State School Administration 438
State Administrative Organization 441
Improved Standards for Teachers 443
Compulsory School Attendance Laws 445
State Control of Other Educational Matters 447
Special Schools and Classes 449
Higher Education 449

22 **Recreation** 453
Parks 453
Playgrounds 457
Community Centers 459
Municipal Camps 461
Divided Control of Recreational Policies 461

23 **Highways** 463
Road Building in the United States 463
Highway Administration 466
Federal Aid for Highways 472
Means of Financing Highway Construction 475
Measures to Decrease Motor Car Accidents 479

24 **Natural Resources** 486
State Conservation Agencies 486
Forestry 488
Fish and Game 492
Soil Conservation 495
Agricultural Extension Work 496
Agricultural and Mining Experiment Stations 499
Oil and Gas 499
Water Power 501

PART SEVEN
Business and Labor

25 **Regulation of Business** 507
Corporation Charters 507
Anti-trust Laws 510
Pure Food and Drug Acts 511
Protection from Fraud 512

Regulation of Interest Rates on Loans   514
Regulation of Businesses Affected with a Public Interest   515
Handicaps to Effective Utility Regulation   523
Public Ownership of Utilities   528
Regulation of Professions and Trades   529

26 **Regulation of Labor**   **533**
Promotion of Safety in Industry   533
Workmen's Compensation   535
Protection of Health   538
Restriction of Hours of Labor   539
Wage Legislation   544
Prevention of Racial Discrimination   547
Collective Bargaining   548
The Right to Strike   549
Open versus Closed Shop   553
Compulsory Settlement of Industrial Disputes   556
Regulation of Union Activities   556
Public and Private Employment Agencies   558
Unemployment Insurance   559

PART EIGHT
Staff Activities

27 **Personnel**   **565**
Gradual Abolition of Spoils System   565
Civil Service Commissions   568
Strikes by Public Employees   575
Pension Systems   576

28 **Expenditures**   **581**
Causes of Upward Trend   581
Major Items of Expenditure   582
State Payments to Local Governments   583
Budget Systems   584
Preparation of the Budget   588
Legislative Budgetary Appropriation and Revenue Bills   591
Central Purchasing   594

29 **Revenues**   **599**
Tax Conflicts between the Federal Government and the States   600
Taxes—the Chief Source of Revenue   600
The Canons of Sound Taxation   601
The General Property Tax   603
The Income Tax   610
The Inheritance Tax   611
Business Taxes   612
Other Taxes   616

Use of Taxation for Regulatory Purposes   617
Special Assessments   618
State Tax Commissions   619

30 Indebtedness   **622**

The Nineteenth Century to the Civil War   622
The Civil War and Reconstruction   625
The Twentieth Century   626
Municipal Indebtedness   630
Borrowing Practices   631

31 Planning   **635**

Growth of the State Planning Movement   635
Activities of State Planning Agencies   637
Organization of State Planning Agencies   639
Growth of the City Planning Movement   640
Activities of City Planning Agencies   641
Organization of City Planning Agencies   643
Regional Planning   644
Civil Defense   645

Table of Cases   **653**

Index   **657**

Charts and Graphs

Federal Grants-in-Aid to the States, 1915–1953   13
Purposes of Federal Grants-in-Aid to the States, 1953   15
Uniform State Laws Enacted by 36 or More States   36
Government under a Typical State Constitution   99
Government under the Model State Constitution   101
Growth of State Legislative Council Movement   135
Weak Mayor Government   189
Strong Mayor Government   191
Commission Government   205
Relation between the Voters, Council, City Manager, and Administrative
    Personnel   211
Local Governments, Population and Area, of the 168 Metropolitan Areas
    of the United States   221
Organization of an Urban County (Alameda) in California   245
Model County Government   249
New England Town Government   256
A Long, Long Ballot   291
A Short, Short Ballot   294
The Voter's Burden in California   333
Growth of State Police Forces   347
Growth of Municipal Police Forces   351
State Expenditures for Public Welfare   375
Per Cent of United States Population 65 Years of Age and Over   379
Distribution of State Public Welfare Expenditures, 1953   383
State Expenditures for Health   393
City Expenditures for Health   397
Patients in Hospitals for Mental Disease   403
Construction of Nonfarm Homes   423
Number of School Districts, 1932–1952   435
Municipal Expenditures for Recreation   455
Motor Vehicle Registration in the United States   465
State Expenditures for Highways   477
State Expenditures for Natural Resources   487
Distribution of State Expenditures for Natural Resources, 1953   495
Functional Distribution of State Employees, 1953   570
Functional Distribution of City Employees   573
How the States Spend the Public's Dollar   582
How the Cities Spend the Public's Dollar   583
State Payments to Local Governments   585

The State Purchasing Agency   596
Sources of State Revenue   601
Sources of Municipal Revenue   602
Per Cent of Total State Revenue Represented by General Property Tax   605
Trend of State Indebtedness   627
Trend of Municipal Indebtedness   629

PART ONE

Intergovernmental Relations

CHAPTER 1

Federal–State Relations

UNITS OF GOVERNMENT IN THE UNITED STATES

Within the United States there are nearly one hundred and seventeen thousand units of government below the national level. In addition to the forty-eight states there are slightly more than three thousand counties, nearly seventeen thousand cities and villages, another seventeen thousand towns and townships, sixty-seven thousand school districts, and about twelve thousand other special districts of various kinds. The number of units of local government varies greatly from state to state, and even from county to county within the same state. Minnesota has nine thousand local governments, whereas Virginia has fewer than four hundred, despite its larger population. Cook County, Illinois, which includes Chicago, has four hundred and twenty-seven local governments, all operating more or less independently of one another. Another Illinois county—Edwards—manages to get along with only ten local governments. Neither rhyme nor reason determines the number or kind of local governments within any state or county. In fact, reason would seem to suggest a drastic reduction of the total. There has been a marked reduction in recent years—twenty-five per cent in the last decade. Some local governments have consolidated with one another. Others have lost their various functions, and finally their identity, to the counties in which they are situated. The trend, therefore, is in the right direction. Perhaps another few decades will witness additional consolidations and absorptions, until the number of local governments in the United States is brought within reasonable limits. It should be noted, however, that recent reductions have been brought about almost entirely by school district reorganizations. Other types of local governments are still multiplying.[1]

[1] *Governments in the United States in 1952,* a publication of the United States Bureau of the Census.

OVERLAPPING AND COMPETITION

There is a great deal of overlapping among the local governments of the United States. Counties, cities, townships, and special districts often handle different aspects—or even the same aspects—of the same activity within the same area. They jostle one another and step on one another's toes. Even the states compete with one another, and with the federal government, for tax revenues or control of natural resources. The inevitable result is inefficiency and waste. Competition may be the life of trade, but co-operation is the life of government. American experience shows clearly the need for co-operation among the different units of government, and also the difficulty of obtaining it. Yet there can be no doubt that the picture has changed somewhat in recent years. Public officials have begun to join with taxpayers' groups and private research agencies in an effort to find ways of making government more efficient, whether by consolidation of existing units, increased co-operation, or other means. This quest for efficient government will doubtless continue for many years, and along many paths. No simple panacea for waste and inefficiency will ever be found. Modern government is a complex process demanding the best thought, the most constant labor, and the most co-operative spirit that this or any other nation can provide.

THE DIVISION OF POWERS BETWEEN THE NATION AND THE STATES

The government of the United States is federal in form—that is, the powers of government are divided between the nation and the states, and neither the nation nor the states may disturb the balance that has thus been established. This does not mean that the original apportionment of authority is perpetual, and may never be altered to meet changing conditions. It means, instead, that every reallocation of power must be the result of agreement between the nation, as represented by Congress, and the states, as represented by their legislatures or by conventions chosen for that purpose.

In order to set up a government of the federal type it is necessary to establish, by means of a written constitution, the line of demarcation between federal and state powers. Otherwise there would be no basis for settling the disputes that might arise between the states and the nation as to the exact scope of their authority. Experience has shown that such controversies are frequent.

Outside of the United States the federal type of government has not proved very popular. It is used by a few other nations,[2] but most countries prefer the unitary form. Under the unitary plan of government, all power is vested in the national authorities. Some of this power they may delegate to local agencies of government; in a large country they usually find it necessary to do so. Thus the central government in England permits the county and municipal boroughs to handle many important matters; and even in France, the classic land of centralization, the communes are given a certain measure of local self-government.

But this distribution of authority in England or in France does not indicate a trend toward federalism, for the essence of power still remains in the hands of the national government. It may reapportion authority at any time, and in any way it sees fit. It may even abolish all the agencies of local government—counties, municipal boroughs, or communes—at a single stroke. For under the unitary plan the local governments are merely creatures of the nation, and possess only such measure of authority as the nation may care to bestow. The federal form, on the other hand, makes provision for a national government and for state governments as well, each independent of the other within its own sphere of action.

POWERS OF THE FEDERAL GOVERNMENT

After a federal scheme of government has been decided upon, there are two practicable methods of preparing a dividing line between state and national authority. One plan is to make a careful list of state powers, and then specify that the remainder of governmental authority shall vest in the nation. That was the procedure followed in establishing the present Dominion government of Canada in 1867. But it did not appeal to the men who met in Philadelphia in the spring of 1787.

Most of the delegates to the Convention had taken a more or less prominent part in the Revolution, and had long been accustomed to regard local self-government as the cornerstone of liberty. Their experience under the Articles of Confederation had prepared them for a stronger and "more perfect union," but they still agreed that the rights of the states must be carefully protected. Not unnaturally, therefore, they enumerated the powers of the federal government, and assumed that all authority not dele-

[2] The list includes four Latin American republics: Argentina, Brazil, Venezuela and Mexico; two British dominions: Canada and Australia; and one European nation: Switzerland. The Soviet Union is also included by some writers, but its government is not truly federal. Argentina and Venezuela seem almost to have abandoned their federalism, at least temporarily.

gated to the nation would continue to reside in the states. In 1791 this arrangement was made emphatically clear by the adoption of the Tenth Amendment to the federal Constitution. The amendment did not in any way alter the original plan; it simply recorded an existing fact. Its exact form follows:

The powers not delegated to the United States by the Constitution, nor prohibited by it to the States, are reserved to the States respectively, or to the people.

Delegated Powers

The federal government, therefore, is a government of *delegated* powers. It may exercise those powers that are conferred upon it by the Constitution, and no others. The test of federal authority over any activity of government is not the importance of the activity, nor the extent or manner of its control by state officials, but whether it has been included among the federal powers listed in the Constitution.

Implied Powers

The federal government, however, is not limited to those powers *expressly* conferred upon it. The Constitution authorizes Congress "to make all laws which shall be necessary and proper for carrying into execution" [3] the powers expressly granted, and this clause has been interpreted quite liberally.

Thus, under the power "to establish post-offices and post roads," [4] Congress has arranged for the transportation of mail by railroad, boat, and airplane; it has placed armed guards in railway mail cars as a protection against robbery; it has prohibited interference with the United States mails, and has prescribed suitable penalties; it has provided for federal supervision of the construction of a great national highway system, and has even authorized road building directly by the federal government; [5] it has excluded seditious, salacious, and fraudulent matter from the mails; and in 1912 it established a federal express business under the name of parcel post.

The power "to lay and collect taxes, duties, imposts, and excises" has also proved capable of broad interpretation. It has been the basis of Congressional action, not only in imposing taxes for the purpose of raising revenue, but also in building up a system of protective tariffs, regulating

[3] Art. I, Sec. 8, Cl. 18.
[4] Constitution, Art. I, Sec. 8, Cl. 7.
[5] The Cumberland Road, which played an important part in the early development of the Middle West, was built by the federal government. For many years it was under federal control, and was known as the Great National Pike.

the distribution of narcotics, establishing a comprehensive scheme of unemployment insurance, and controlling the sale of certain foodstuffs. The implied powers of the federal government, therefore, are quite as important as those granted to it in express terms.

Transfer of Power to National Government

Ever since the adoption of the Constitution there has been a tendency to increase the authority of the federal government at the expense of the states. National prestige and influence have grown steadily, while the importance of the states has declined. This transition has been especially noticeable during two periods in American history. Immediately after the Civil War there was a great wave of nationalism—a reaction against the extreme states' rights view of the South; and the powers of the federal government were materially increased.

And during the thirties and forties of the present century—the emergency years of depression and war—a similar expansion of national authority took place. A striking example of this trend was the Fair Labor Standards Act of 1938, which established minimum wages and maximum hours of labor for millions of American workers. This law applied not only to businesses engaged directly in interstate commerce, and obviously subject to federal regulation, but also to manufacturing enterprises, which had always been regarded as properly under state control. Yet the Supreme Court of the United States unhesitatingly discarded long-established precedents [6] to rule that manufacturers must accept federal regulation if they obtained their raw materials from sources outside the state or sold their finished products across state boundaries.[7] Other laws increased the scope of federal activity in various additional ways. Thus many powers formerly vested in the states were transferred to the federal government; the balance of power shifted to the nation.

In December, 1941, came the Japanese treachery at Pearl Harbor, and the immediate aftermath of this attack was a veritable deluge of statutes, decrees, and orders designed to strengthen the position of the federal authorities, in order to subordinate every aspect of American life to the war effort. There was general agreement that nothing must be permitted to interfere with complete victory at the earliest possible moment. Therefore the national government assumed control of rents, prices, wages, profits, and hours of labor, with virtually no regard for the traditional limits of its authority. It rationed gasoline, tires, shoes, and even food. It established prices for innumerable categories of goods regarded as necessary to the

[6] Hammer v. Dagenhart, 247 U.S. 251 (1918).
[7] United States v. Darby Lumber Co., 312 U.S. 100 (1941).

conduct of the war.   It ordered the removal from the Pacific Coast of thousands of persons of Japanese ancestry, many of whom were American
citizens.   But these drastic steps did not represent a deliberate attempt by
the federal government to secure permanent control of local affairs.   State
officials recognized this fact, and co-operated heartily with the national
authorities in carrying out the vast war program.   State laws were amended
to conform to federal specifications.   Most of the actual work of rationing
gasoline and other articles was performed by local boards.   The care of
evacuated Japanese-Americans became the joint responsibility of the nation, the states, and the counties.   At the end of the war the national government abandoned most of its newly acquired powers without undue delay.

A Slight Countertrend

Today a slight countertrend is evident, as many public officials, from
the president of the United States to the mayors of tiny villages, express
concern over the rapid expansion of federal power.   In August of 1953
President Eisenhower declared to the Conference of Governors that he had
accepted its invitation to speak "because of my indestructible conviction
that unless we preserve in this country the place of the state government—
its traditional place, with the power, the authority, the responsibilities and
the revenues necessary to discharge those responsibilities, then we are not
going to have America as we know it." [8]   The Eisenhower administration
has taken some steps to make these words effective.   It has appointed a distinguished commission to study the whole problem of federal-state relations.   It has heartily endorsed a new law giving the states title to oil resources in the submerged lands along their coasts.   But no informed person
believes that these fragile straws indicate more than a mild breeze of reaction
to the headlong expansion of federal power.   The process of centralization
may be slowed down, but certainly it will not be reversed.   It is a trend
that continues decade after decade, in war and in peace.

Increase in Power through Constitutional Amendments

The transfer of authority from the states to the nation has been accomplished in part by means of formal amendments to the Constitution.   Thus
the Sixteenth Amendment, proclaimed in 1913, made possible an effective
system of federal income taxation.[9]   But if constitutional amendment were

[8] *New York Times,* August 5, 1953.
[9] For a discussion of the argument that the ordinary process of amendment is not
sufficient to alter federal-state relations, see National Prohibition Cases, 253 U.S.
350 (1920).

the only method of changing federal-state relations, the process would be difficult and tedious.

In more than a century and a half the Constitution has been amended but twenty-two times, and ten of those twenty-two amendments were virtually a part of the original document. So cumbersome is the amending process that only proposals of the greatest importance have even a slight chance of adoption, and the opposition of a substantial minority is sufficient to prevent favorable action. First, a proposed amendment must be approved by a two-thirds vote in each house of Congress. Almost invariably this means that it must be acceptable to both major parties, for neither Republicans nor Democrats can hope to control two thirds of the Senate and the House of Representatives, except at rare intervals. Then it must be ratified by three fourths of the states. Small wonder that few amendments are adopted!

Broadening Power through Judicial Interpretation

But there are other ways of broadening the sphere of federal authority. One of these is commonly known as judicial interpretation. Every year the courts are called upon to determine the exact significance of some word or phrase of the Constitution, and their decisions have a profound effect upon the scope of the nation's powers.

Take, for example, the control of the federal government over interstate commerce. "Congress," declares the Constitution, "shall have power to regulate commerce . . . among the several States." [10] It would seem that nothing could be clearer than this simple statement, or less likely to cause disagreement as to its meaning, yet it has produced an astounding amount of litigation. As early as 1824 the Supreme Court was asked to define commerce. The contention had been advanced that commerce comprised only "traffic—buying and selling, or the interchange of commodities," and did not include navigation. Had this narrow view prevailed, the authority of Congress would have been seriously restricted. But the Court refused to accept any such interpretation. Speaking through Chief Justice Marshall, it said: "All America understands, and has uniformly understood, the word 'commerce' to comprehend navigation. . . . The word used in the Constitution, then, comprehends, and has been always understood to comprehend, navigation within its meaning; and a power to regulate navigation, is as expressly granted, as if that term had been added to the word 'commerce.' " [11]

[10] Art. I, Sec. 8, Cl. 3.
[11] Gibbons v. Ogden, 9 Wheaton 1 (1824).

Half a century later another issue was raised that threatened to restrict the sphere of national power. The Pensacola Telegraph Company, denying the right of Congress to interfere with its affairs, argued that the framers of the Constitution could not possibly have intended to include telegraphy within the meaning of *commerce*, since telegraphy was not known until many years afterward. Had this contention been upheld, it would subsequently have prevented the federal government from regulating the interstate movements of automobiles and airplanes, in fact, all the newer agencies of communication. But the Supreme Court took a broad, statesmanlike view. "The powers thus granted . . . are not confined to the instrumentalities of commerce, or the postal system known or in use when the Constitution was adopted," declared Chief Justice Waite, speaking for the Court, "but they keep pace with the progress of the country, and adapt themselves to the new developments of time and circumstances. They extend from the horse with its rider to the stagecoach, from the sailing vessel to the steamboat, from the coach and the steamboat to the railroad, and from the railroad to the telegraph, as these new agencies are successively brought into use to meet the demands of increasing population and wealth. They were intended for the government of the business to which they relate, at all times and under all circumstances." [12]

In 1837 the Supreme Court of the United States stated that persons were not the "subject of commerce," and therefore could not be controlled under the interstate commerce clause of the Constitution.[13] Subsequently, however, it ruled otherwise in a number of far-reaching decisions, thus broadening materially the scope of national authority. Upholding an act of Congress that prohibited the transportation of women from state to state for immoral purposes, the Court said in part: "Commerce among the States . . . consists of intercourse and traffic between their citizens, and includes the transportation of persons and property. There may be, therefore, a movement of persons as well as of property; that is, a person may move or be moved in interstate commerce." [14]

As recently as 1944 the Supreme Court expanded the authority of the nation by declaring that insurance contracts made across state lines are interstate commerce and therefore subject to congressional regulation. In reaching this conclusion the Court abandoned a contrary rule that had stood for three quarters of a century.[15] The nineteenth-century judges had been

[12] Pensacola Telegraph Co. *v.* Western Union Telegraph Co., 96 U.S. 1 (1877).
[13] New York *v.* Miln, 11 Peters 102 (1837).
[14] Hoke *v.* U.S., 227 U.S. 308, 320 (1913). See also Gloucester Ferry Co. *v.* Pennsylvania, 114 U.S. 196, 203 (1885).
[15] Paul *v.* Virginia, 8 Wallace 168 (1868).

primarily concerned with the attempts of insurance companies to escape state regulation, and had thwarted such attempts by decreeing that insurance was primarily a local business.

By 1944, however, the circumstances were very different. The insurance companies had adjusted themselves to the necessities of state regulation, and were trying to avoid prosecution under the federal anti-trust laws. Their contention, of course, was that the federal statutes could not be applied to their business, which was essentially local in nature, *according to the Supreme Court's own words*. Without hesitancy, therefore, the Court proceeded to eat its own words, although not specifically overruling its earlier decision. "A nation-wide business is not deprived of its interstate character," it declared, "merely because it is built upon sales contracts which are local in nature." [16]

These liberal decisions have been a vital factor in the growth of federal prestige and the expansion of federal power. They have obviated the necessity of amending many essential features of the Constitution. Of course, the courts have not invariably looked with approval upon the acts of Congress. In a number of instances they have set aside important legislation on the ground that it exceeded federal authority. But the general effect of court decisions, from Marshall to Warren, has been to uphold or increase the power of the nation.

Expansion of Power through Federal Aid

The growth of federal influence has not been solely the product of constitutional amendment and judicial interpretation, however. In recent years Congress has discovered a very effective means of securing a measure of control over matters not mentioned in the Constitution, and therefore presumably reserved to the states. The plan has worked so well that it is now an established part of federal administration. Its essential features are quite simple. Congress offers a sum of money to the states for agricultural extension work, forest fire prevention, or some other activity, *provided they will match the federal grant dollar for dollar, or in some other ratio, and agree to accept federal supervision of their work*. This offer is in no sense a club. It is an inducement, and the states are free to accept or reject it as they see fit. But the inducement is so powerful that acceptance follows almost as a matter of course.

CONDITIONS GOVERNING GRANTS. Under the terms of a typical subsidy law the actual details of administration remain in the hands of state officials. They formulate policies, prepare plans, choose subordinates, spend the com-

[16] United States *v.* Southeastern Underwriters Association, 322 U.S. 533 (1944).

bined federal-state money. The federal government merely acts in an advisory and supervisory capacity. But state budgets, policies, plans, and even personnel must receive federal approval. They must at least measure up to minimum federal standards, though the states are free to exceed the minimum in any way they desire.

When a state legislature accepts the provisions of a federal grant, it is required to establish a state agency to co-operate with federal officials, or else designate an existing state agency for that purpose. The state agency prepares a detailed plan showing exactly how the money is to be spent. Although this plan must conform to certain specifications of the federal government, state officials are given considerable leeway. No attempt is made to impose exactly the same conditions on all states, without regard to local conditions. The state plan is supposed to reflect local needs, even though it must measure up to the prescribed minimum.[17]

Federal suggestions frequently cause a modification of state plans, although only minor details are involved in most instances. Once federal approval has been given, a state is free to proceed with its program. It can be absolutely certain of receiving its allotment of federal funds—provided, of course, that it respects its part of the agreement. But when a state fails to carry out a plan that its own officials have prepared, the result is likely to be a withdrawal of federal aid.

RESULTS OF FEDERAL AID. Federal funds are granted to the states in support of a wide variety of different activities—construction of highways, vocational education, school lunches, re-education of physically handicapped persons, financial assistance to the blind, the aged, the physically disabled, and dependent children, promotion of maternal and child welfare, control of tuberculosis and venereal diseases, maintenance of public employment offices, administration of unemployment compensation, extension work in agriculture, forest fire prevention, upkeep of state agricultural colleges and experiment stations, development of public airports, and miscellaneous services to war veterans. Even this long list is not complete.

However, some of the laws offering grants to the state deviate from the standard pattern by requiring little or no federal supervision of state activities. The earliest subsidy laws enacted by Congress omitted all reference to federal approval of state plans, and some of the more recent statutes—especially those relating to the federal government's social security program—leave matters almost exclusively in state hands.

The total of annual federal appropriations to the states has risen almost steadily. Today it is nearly four times as large as it was ten years ago, and

---

[17] See, for example, the Federal Highway Act, 42 Stat. L. 212.

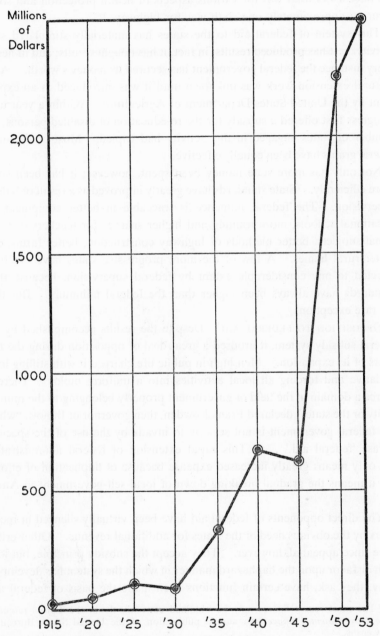

Based on figures of the United States Bureau of the Census.

more than twenty-five times as large as in 1930. The accompanying chart indicates the rapid growth of federal grants-in-aid. Nearly two thirds of the huge 1953 total was for various aspects of health protection and social security; approximately one sixth was for highways.[18]

This system of federal aid to the states has materially stimulated state activity. It has produced results; in fact, it has bought results; and in nearly every instance the federal government has secured its money's worth. Agricultural extension work was unknown until it was introduced as an experiment by the United States Department of Agriculture. Within a year after Congress first offered a subsidy for the re-education of disabled persons, the number of states engaged in this activity had tripled. Most of the other federal grants have been equally effective.

Not only has more state money been spent, however; it has been spent more efficiently. State standards have greatly improved as a result of federal supervision. The federal influence is traceable in better equipment for vocational schools, more training and higher salaries for teachers of vocational subjects, better methods of highway construction, better farms, and better rural homes. A few of the more progressive states have not been affected to any considerable extent by federal supervision, because their standards have always been higher than the federal minimum. But they are rare exceptions.

OPPOSITION TO FEDERAL AID. Despite the results accomplished by the federal subsidy system, it aroused a great deal of opposition during the first years of its expansion. Men high in public life charged it with stifling local initiative and forcing all local activities into a uniform mold. "There is scarce a domain in the field of government properly belonging to the municipality or the state," declared Frank Lowden, then governor of Illinois, "which the federal government is not seeking to invade by the use of the specious phrase 'federal aid.' . . . This rapid extension of federal administration not only means greatly increased expense because of duplication of efforts, but it means the gradual breaking down of local self-government in America." [19]

The direct opponents of federal aid have been virtually silenced in recent years by the obvious need of the states for additional revenue. Other critics have since appeared, however. They accept the subsidy principle, but look with disfavor upon the haphazard manner in which the system has developed. Why, they ask, have certain functions been made the basis of federal aid,

---

[18] The most recent figures may be obtained conveniently in the *Compendium of State Government Finances,* an annual publication of the United States Bureau of the Census.

[19] Convocation Address, University of Chicago, June, 1921.

while other equally important functions have been denied such treatment? Why should the states be required to match some grants, but not others? Why should federal funds be apportioned on the basis of population or area or similar factors, when other factors may be much more significant in determining the needs of the states and their ability to support themselves? These questions cannot readily be answered. Every thoughtful student of the federal subsidy system deplores the lack of settled policy in these matters. Careful planning was less important when the grants-in-aid totaled less than

PURPOSES OF FEDERAL GRANTS-IN-AID TO THE STATES, 1953

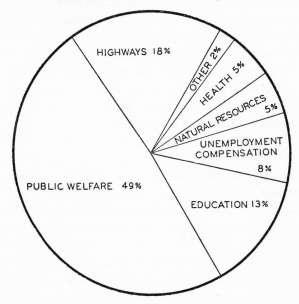

Based on figures from *Compendium of State Government Finances, 1953,* a publication of the United States Bureau of the Census.

one hundred million dollars. Today, however, they have grown to more than twenty times that amount, and represent nearly one seventh of all state revenues. Obviously, therefore, the time has come to consider the subsidy system with some care. A joint committee of congressmen and state governors, which recently studied the problem, made two significant recommendations: first, that federal grants to the states be reduced at least twenty per cent; and, second, that a co-ordinated program of future grants be developed after further detailed investigation.[20]

[20] See the report submitted by Frank Bane, executive director of the Council of State Governments, to the board of managers of that organization. This report is published in the January, 1949, issue of *State Government,* pp. 4–8. For a detailed considera-

The question of the subsidy system's constitutionality was presented to the Supreme Court of the United States in 1923 in two separate cases.   The Court dismissed both cases for want of jurisdiction, pointing out that no justiciable issue was presented; but in handing down its decision it took occasion to brush aside the constitutional objections to federal aid.   The chief argument against the system, that it was "an effective means of inducing the states to yield a portion of their sovereign rights," the Court answered by saying: "Probably it would be sufficient to point out that the powers of the States are not invaded, since the statute imposes no obligation, but simply extends an option which the State is free to accept or reject.   But we do not rest here. . . .   What burden is imposed upon the States, unequally or otherwise?   Certainly there is none, unless it be the burden of taxation, and that falls upon their inhabitants, who are within the taxing power of Congress as well as that of the State where they reside.   Nor does the statute require the States to do or yield anything.   If Congress enacted it with the ulterior purpose of tempting them to yield, that purpose may be effectively frustrated by the simple expedient of not yielding." [21]

Reasons for the Expansion of Federal Power

And so the scope of federal power has gradually broadened—by formal amendments to the Constitution, by judicial interpretation, by grants from the federal treasury to the states.   It is worth while, therefore, to make inquiry concerning the causes of this expansion of national authority.   In part, at least, the greater efficiency of the federal government as compared with that of state governments has been responsible.   Though the methods of administering national affairs have at times been open to serious criticism, they have usually been far ahead of current state practices.   Some persons contend that this greater efficiency has been due to the relatively narrow scope of national activities—that the federal government has been more efficient because it has had less to do.   And it must be admitted that the record of the war years added force to this argument.   The marked expansion of federal activities, expenditures, and personnel apparently caused a deterioration of federal standards—at least, in certain fields.   But today federal efficiency contrasts favorably with the relative inefficiency of many states.   As long as this situation continues, many men will doubtless favor federal assumption of every task that has proved difficult for the state governments.

Nor must it be forgotten that those who are interested in improving social

---

tion of federal aid to the states, see *The Fiscal Impact of Federalism in the United States,* by J. A. Maxwell.

[21] Massachusetts *v.* Mellon and Frothingham *v.* Mellon, 262 U.S. 447 (1923).

and economic conditions turn naturally to the federal government. They welcome federal control over matters that seem to need correction, for they know that the task of influencing Congress, difficult though it may be, is as nothing compared with the burden of bringing sufficient pressure to bear upon forty-eight state legislatures.

But the chief reason for the expansion of national power has been the broadening scope of modern civilization. Present-day industry pays scant attention to state boundaries. Present-day commerce crosses them at will. The United States is bound together by a network of railways, highways, and airways. Giant corporations and super-corporations extend their activities to the nation's boundaries and beyond. Labor unions operate on a national scale. Time and distance have lost much of their former significance. Small wonder, therefore, that national power has been increased to meet this rapidly changing situation!

Arguments against Excessive Centralization of Power

To a certain extent this expansion of federal authority *is* natural and almost inevitable. But it should not be permitted to continue indefinitely, lest it prove a menace to popular government. Excessive centralization is quite as dangerous as excessive decentralization, and quite as likely to become an inefficient method of control. This principle is fundamentally sound, regardless of the nation or the century to which it may be applied; but it has an especial significance for present-day America.

The United States has a population of more than one hundred and fifty million and an area equal to three fourths of all Europe; it has great metropolitan centers, rich farm lands, vast stretches of trackless desert, mountain peaks where the snow never melts, and valleys where the snow never falls. Among the people of the nation there are differences of color, custom, and creed. The forty-eight states are too diverse to be fitted into an absolutely uniform mold. No central government, however efficient, can solve all their problems. While it can scarcely be disputed that the nation should have authority over national affairs, this principle should not be distorted to justify federal control over matters of purely local concern.

It must be remembered, also, that an overburdened national government may become top-heavy and unresponsive to the wishes of the people. Federal bureau chiefs, seated at their desks in Washington, may be entirely out of touch with local conditions and entirely ignorant of local needs. However proficient they may be in their chosen professions, they may lack the personal touch that is so essential to successful administration. Overwhelmed by the complexity of their task, they may take refuge behind a set of rules poorly suited to meet every possible contingency.   Thus government may cease to be a personal matter and may become instead an arbitrary routine.

There is still another reason why excessive centralization is undesirable: it prevents local experiments in government.   The states are sometimes characterized as "experiment stations."   They afford an opportunity to try new plans, new theories, new dogmas, without involving the entire nation. If a state is convinced of the advisability of adopting any new reform, from the short ballot to the single tax, it may do so without hindrance.   Its experience may induce other states to follow its lead, or instead may save them from costly error.   In either case the experiment has been worth while.   But if all authority were centered in the national government, the opportunity to try new schemes on a small scale would disappear.

Striking a Proper Balance

One of the most perplexing problems of American government, therefore, is to strike a proper balance between the powers of the states and the nation. It is easy to say that the federal government should confine its attention to national matters, whereas the states should limit their activities to state affairs.   Virtually everyone assents to this statement of principle.   But when it becomes necessary to apply the principle in specific cases—in other words, to classify the functions of government according to their local or national character—the difficulties are at once apparent.   Men may agree in principle, but with regard to specific functions they almost invariably differ.

Importance of Co-operation

There is one matter, however, on which agreement is practically unanimous: the need for a full measure of co-operation among the various units of government.   The nation and the states—and also the counties and cities, for that matter—must work together harmoniously in many fields in order to produce satisfactory results.   The need for co-operation may be especially obvious in time of war, but it is scarcely less urgent in peacetime. Public officials at all levels of government are gradually recognizing this fact, and therefore are working together more closely than ever before.   Some of this co-operation, of course, has been purchased by the federal government through its system of financial aid to the states, but a great deal has arisen without such direct inducements.   Sometimes state officials take an active part in carrying out national policies.   State and local police aid in the apprehension and arrest of persons who have violated federal laws; state courts naturalize aliens in accordance with the rules established by Congress; state regulatory agencies achieve a considerable degree of uniformity by requiring residents who desire to engage in certain activities—the piloting of airplanes, for example—to hold federal licenses. The federal government, for its part, makes available to the states and local communities the results of its research on many important problems. Sometimes Congress makes its own statutes directly dependent on state action. Thus it has prohibited the transportation of prison-made goods in violation of state law, and has forbidden the shipment of oil in interstate commerce in excess of state quotas. Three decades ago many persons talked glibly of "the twilight of state government," and predicted that the states would soon collapse from sheer inertia, giving way perhaps to large administrative units controlled directly from Washington. Today, however, much less is heard about the decline of state government. The states have proved their value as partners of the nation in a great variety of co-operative enterprises.[22]

Concurrent Powers

The delegation of certain powers to the federal government is not necessarily a denial of those powers to the states. In some cases both the states and the nation may have jurisdiction over the same matter—that is, they may exercise *concurrent* authority. The concurrent powers of the states are not very numerous, however. They may borrow on their own credit, while the federal government may borrow on the credit of the nation. They may impose taxes on commodities, incomes, and the like, even though those commodities and incomes have already been taxed by the federal government. From 1919 until 1933 they had concurrent power to enforce the prohibition against the manufacture and sale of intoxicants, by virtue of a specific provision of the federal Constitution.[23] Control over the state militia is divided between the nation and the states.

State Authority in Federal Sphere

In addition, the states may even invade the sphere of national authority to some extent for the purpose of protecting the welfare of their inhabitants, provided Congress has not acted in the matter. Thus reasonable state laws concerning safety appliances on interstate railroads will be upheld in the absence of Congressional legislation, despite the fact that Congress is vested

---

[22] See the special supplement to the January, 1949, issue of *State Government*. This supplement is entitled "Are We Maintaining Our Federal System?"

[23] Eighteenth Amendment, Sec. 2. "The Congress and the several states shall have concurrent power to enforce this article by appropriate legislation."

with control over commerce among the states.[24]   Reasonable anchorage and pilotage rules will also receive judicial approval, even when applied to vessels from other states and other nations,[25] unless Congress sees fit to supplant state regulations with regulations of its own.

When Congress acts, however, its decisions are final within the sphere of national authority.   Any conflicting state legislation becomes inoperative at once.[26]   For long periods in American history there was no federal legislation on the subject of bankruptcy, though this matter was specifically placed under the control of Congress.[27]   Each state, therefore, controlled bankruptcy in such a manner as it saw fit, and these state laws remained in force until the passage of a national bankruptcy law.[28]

It must be understood, however, that a state may not under any circumstances exercise control over a matter prohibited to it by the Constitution. For example, it may not enter into treaties with foreign nations.[29]   Nor may it regulate matters of an exclusively national character, such as naturalization, even in the absence of an express constitutional prohibition.

POWERS OF THE STATES

It has already been pointed out that the federal government is a government of delegated powers.[30]   The state governments, on the other hand, are governments of *reserved* or *residual* powers.   To them is reserved, generally speaking, all the authority not specifically or impliedly given to the nation. They possess the residue of power.   Therefore it is not necessary to search the federal Constitution for specific grants of power in order to determine the scope of state authority.

The distribution of powers between the nation and the states has left the states supreme in many fields.   State governments—and local governments operating under state authority—are primarily responsible for the maintenance of the public school system and the protection of the public health. State and local authorities enforce most of the laws against crime and maintain most of the prisons.   State courts are the places where most alleged criminals are tried and where most litigants in civil suits bring their com-

---

[24] New York, New Haven and Hartford Railroad *v.* New York, 165 U.S. 628 (1897).

[25] Cooley *v.* Port Wardens of Philadelphia, 12 Howard 299 (1851).

[26] Pennsylvania Railroad *v.* Pennsylvania, 250 U.S. 566 (1919).

[27] Constitution, Art. I, Sec. 8, Cl. 4.

[28] Congress enacted a bankruptcy law as early as 1800, but repealed it three years later.   Subsequently it passed and repealed two other bankruptcy statutes, and did not permanently occupy the field until 1898.

[29] Constitution, Art. I, Sec. 10, Cl. 1.

[30] See page 6.

plaints.   State and local officials have a principal part in constructing and repairing streets and highways, enforcing the housing laws, providing recreational facilities, furnishing water supplies, and maintaining public sanitation. State commissions supervise the rates and standards of most public utilities and play a major role in the regulation of other businesses.   Even today, therefore, after more than a century of expanding federal power, the state governments have an important part in the lives of the people of the United States.

Due Process of Law versus Police Power

Unless clearly prohibited from doing so, a state may make any reasonable regulations to promote the health, safety, morals, convenience, or comfort of its people.   This right to take reasonable action for the general welfare is known as the police power of the state.   It is the legal justification for a vast quantity of social legislation that has been enacted by the states during the last few decades.

Such laws have not always been upheld by the courts, however; in many instances they have been declared void as contrary to the Fourteenth Amendment to the federal Constitution.   That Amendment declares that no state shall "deprive any person of life, liberty, or property, without due process of law." [31]   This phraseology should be noted carefully.   A state is not prohibited from depriving a person of his life, liberty, or property, but only from doing so *without due process of law*.   If due process of law is observed, nothing more can be demanded.   It becomes necessary, therefore, to know the meaning of the phrase *due process of law*.

According to the courts, *due process* includes the idea of *reasonableness*. The powers of the state must be exercised "within the limits of those fundamental principles of liberty and justice which lie at the base of all our civil and political institutions." [32]   Thus the due process clause of the Fourteenth Amendment and the police power of the state are always in potential conflict.

A single illustration may suffice to show how readily this conflict arises. A state may limit the hours of work in mines to five a day.   By so doing it deprives men of their liberty—that is, their liberty to work more than five hours daily if they feel so disposed, for *liberty* includes more than mere freedom from imprisonment.   It includes "the right of a citizen to be free in the engagement of all his faculties; to be free to use them in all lawful ways; to live and work where he will; to earn his livelihood by any lawful calling; to

[31] Sec. 1.
[32] Hurtado *v.* California, 110 U.S. 515, 535 (1884).

pursue any livelihood or avocation; and for that purpose to enter into all contracts which may be proper, necessary, and essential to his carrying out to a successful conclusion the purposes above mentioned." [33]   But is the limitation imposed by this statute reasonable, and likely to improve the welfare of the people of the state?   If so, it is constitutional, as falling within the state's police power.   If it is simply an arbitrary enactment, however, it is contrary to the due process clause of the Fourteenth Amendment, and void for that reason.

Some person or group of persons must decide, therefore, whether the statute is reasonable or arbitrary.   Since this is a question of policy, and not of law, it would be natural to assume that final judgment would rest with the legislature.   The legislature's primary function is to determine policy, and the mere fact of enacting a law is sufficient evidence that it considers the law reasonable.   But the courts refuse to accept this viewpoint, and so they declare unconstitutional any such statute that seems to them unreasonable. Thus the Fourteenth Amendment, as judicially interpreted, may operate as a serious limitation upon the police power of the states.

Constitutional Limitations

Although the federal Constitution reserves to the states a large measure of authority, it specifically limits state power in a number of ways.   Some of these restrictions are virtually self-explanatory, and need little or no comment:

No State shall enter into any treaty, alliance, or confederation; grant letters of marque and reprisal; [34] coin money; emit bills of credit; make anything but gold and silver coin a tender in payment of debts; pass any bill of attainder, [35] ex post facto law, [36] or law impairing the obligation of contracts, or grant any title of nobility. [37]

No State shall, without the consent of Congress, lay any imposts or duties on imports or exports, except what may be absolutely necessary for executing

[33] Allgeyer v. Louisiana, 165 U.S. 578 (1897).

[34] Letters of marque were commissions issued by a belligerent state to vessels owned and manned by private persons, either its own citizens or neutrals, authorizing them to carry on hostilities at sea against the enemy.   Such commissions are no longer issued by civilized nations.

[35] In English law a bill of attainder was a bill introduced into Parliament convicting a person, without trial in an ordinary court of justice, of a high crime, and prescribing the penalty of death and the forfeiture of the estates of the person accused.   For two centuries, at least, this was the usual English method of dealing with influential political offenders.

[36] A retroactive criminal law is known as an ex post facto law.   Under this heading would come legislation which provided a penalty for an act that was not a crime at the time it was committed, or which increased the penalty for an offense already committed.

[37] Constitution, Art. I, Sec. 10, Cl. 1.

its inspection laws; and the net produce of all duties and imposts, laid by any State on imports or exports, shall be for the use of the Treasury of the United States; and all such laws shall be subject to the revision and control of the Congress.[38]

No State shall, without the consent of Congress, lay any duty of tonnage, keep troops or ships of war in time of peace, enter into any agreement or compact with another State [39] or with a foreign power, or engage in war, unless actually invaded or in such imminent danger as will not admit of delay.[40]

The right of citizens of the United States to vote shall not be denied or abridged . . . by any State on account of race, color, or previous condition of servitude.[41]

The right of citizens of the United States to vote shall not be denied or abridged . . . by any State on account of sex.[42]

Privileges and Immunities

Then there are a number of other constitutional limitations upon the power of the states that require at least a few words of explanation. Article IV specifies that "The citizens of each State shall be entitled to all privileges and immunities of citizens in the several States," [43] and the Fourteenth Amendment extends this guarantee:

No state shall make or enforce any law which shall abridge the privileges or immunities of citizens of the United States; nor shall any State deprive any person of life, liberty, or property without due process of law; nor deny to any person within its jurisdiction the equal protection of the laws.[44]

The "privileges and immunities" clauses just quoted might seem to be a guarantee that privileges granted by one state could be carried into every other state. If the citizens of each state are "entitled to all privileges and immunities of citizens in the several States," what is to prevent a man from securing the privilege of practicing medicine, or driving a motor car, in some state where such privileges are easily secured, and insisting upon his constitutional right to do likewise in every other commonwealth?

The barrier that effectually prevents such action, with its resultant destruction of state standards, is the attitude of the United States Supreme Court. Interpreting the "privileges and immunities" clauses, it has said that "special privileges enjoyed by citizens in their own States are not secured in other States by this provision. It was not intended . . . to give to the laws of

[38] Constitution, Art. I, Sec. 10, Cl. 2.
[39] There are many examples of interstate agreements made with the approval of Congress.
[40] Constitution, Art. I, Sec. 10, Cl. 3.
[41] Fifteenth Amendment.
[42] Nineteenth Amendment.
[43] Sec. 2.
[44] Sec. 1.

one State any operation in other States." [45]   Therefore special privileges granted by one state—exemption from certain taxes, permission to practice law, medicine, or any other profession, and the like—are not recognized in other states unless as a matter of comity.   No obligation to recognize them exists.

What, then, are the "privileges and immunities" guaranteed by the Constitution?   The Supreme Court has refused to make a complete enumeration,[46] but it has said that they include the right "to pass into any other State of the Union, for the purpose of engaging in lawful commerce, trade, or business, without molestation, to acquire personal property, to take and hold real estate, to maintain actions in the courts of the States, and to be exempt from any higher taxes or excises than are imposed by the State upon its own citizens." [47]   To this list the Court added, in 1935, the right to make a lawful loan of money in any state other than that in which the citizen resides.[48]   It should be noted, however, that a corporation is not a citizen [49] and that its creation by one state does not give it the right to enter other states for the purpose of doing business.   Other states may exclude it, or may admit it on such terms as they choose.[50]

EQUAL PROTECTION OF THE LAWS.   As already indicated, no state may deny to any person within its borders the equal protection of the laws.[51] Even aliens are entitled to this protection; so are corporations, which are artificial persons.[52]   This clause does not mean that all persons must be treated alike, however.   Distinctions may be made by the state, which has a wide scope of discretion in this regard.   It is necessary only that the distinctions have a reasonable basis.   Thus taxes may be imposed upon certain trades, and not on others; special assessments may be levied against specially benefited property, while other property is permitted to escape this burden.   But the classification of persons or property for the purpose of according them different treatment must be reasonable—in other words, it must bear some relation to the purpose to be accomplished.[53]

[45] Paul v. Virginia, 8 Wallace 168, 178 (1868).
[46] Conner v. Elliott, 18 Howard 591, 593 (1856).
[47] Ward v. Maryland, 12 Wallace 418, 430 (1871).
[48] Colgate v. Harvey, 296 U.S. 404 (1935).
[49] Paul v. Virginia, 8 Wallace 168, 178 (1868).
[50] Pembina Mining Co. v. Pennsylvania, 125 U.S. 181, 189 (1888).   A corporation may not be excluded, however, if it wishes to enter for purposes of interstate commerce (because control over interstate commerce is given to Congress by the Constitution); or if it desires to enter for the performance of some "governmental or quasi-governmental" functions of the federal government.   Hooper v. California, 155 U.S. 648, 652 (1895).
[51] Fourteenth Amendment, Sec. 1.
[52] Santa Clara County v. Southern Pacific Railway Co., 118 U.S., 394, 396 (1886).
[53] Barbier v. Connolly, 113 U.S. 27, 31 (1885).

The guarantee of equal protection of the laws was written into the Constitution in 1868 for the purpose of insuring equal treatment to the former slaves. Until recently, however, it failed to obtain even approximately equal treatment for Negroes, especially in the Southern states. But conditions have changed in the last few years, partly as the result of Supreme Court decisions defining and expanding the meaning of the "equal protection" clause. In 1948 the Supreme Court of the United States ruled that agreements among home owners to exclude Negroes from residential neighborhoods could not be enforced in federal or state courts.[54] Two years later the Court decided that Negroes, quite as much as white persons, were entitled to seats in railroad dining cars.[55]

Education provides an important area of interracial friction. In 1896 the Supreme Court of the United States held that separate schools established for Negro boys and girls must be of approximately the same quality as those provided for whites. This "separate but equal" doctrine did not immediately revolutionize the educational systems of the South, where racial segregation was the rule. Inferior schools for colored children continued to be inferior, without any serious effort to bridge the gap in the quality of black and white education. But the years immediately following the Second World War witnessed substantial changes. School buildings and equipment for Negroes were improved, and better-trained teachers were employed. Many Southerners were fearful that prolonged failure to provide substantially equal educational facilities for both races might lead eventually to abolition of the principle of segregated education. In this fear they were fully justified, but they acted too late, for the Supreme Court of the United States swept away the "separate but equal" doctrine in the spring of 1954. In a far-reaching decision it ruled that separate educational facilities, regardless of their quality, were inherently unequal. Said the Court: "We come then to the question presented: Does segregation of children in public schools solely on the basis of race, even though physical facilities and other 'tangible' factors may be equal, deprive the children of the minority group of equal educational opportunities? We believe that it does." [56]

FULL FAITH AND CREDIT. The Constitution specifies that "Full faith and credit shall be given in each State to the public acts, records, and judicial proceedings of every other State." [57] Included under this heading are records of deeds, mortgages, marriages, and the like, kept in public offices. But this does not mean that the acts of one state are necessarily binding upon

[54] Shelley v. Kraemer, 334 U.S. 1 (1948).
[55] Henderson v. United States, 339 U.S. 816 (1950).
[56] Brown v. Board of Education of Topeka, 347 U.S. 442 (1954).
[57] Art. IV, Sec. 1.

other commonwealths. It does not, for example, indicate that a divorce issued in one state must be honored by every other state of the Union.[58] The only effect of the "full faith and credit" clause of the Constitution is to establish a binding rule of evidence, so that the facts properly determined in one state need not be judicially redetermined in another commonwealth.[59]

ARREST AND DELIVERY OF FUGITIVES. "A person charged in any State with treason, felony, or other crime," states the Constitution, "who shall flee from justice, and be found in another State, shall, on demand of the executive authority of the State from which he fled, be delivered up, to be removed to the State having jurisdiction of the crime." [60] The meaning of this clause is unmistakable. It has been supplemented by Congressional legislation which imposes upon the state governor the duty of arresting and delivering fugitives on demand.

The question may well be raised, however: What means is provided for enforcing this command? If the governor of a state refuses to give up fugitives when properly requested to do so, is there any way of coercing him? When this question was presented to the Supreme Court of the United States, it answered that the governor's obligation was merely moral, and not legal. Said the Court: "The performance of the duty, however, is left to depend on the fidelity of the State Executive to the compact entered into with the other States when it adopted the Constitution of the United States, and became a member of the Union. It was so left by the Constitution. . . ." [61] Despite this decision state governors have generally recognized their "moral duty," and only occasionally is a request for the return of a fugitive refused.

REPUBLICAN FORM OF GOVERNMENT. The Constitution also specifies that "The United States shall guarantee to every State in the Union a republican form of government." [62] Since *republican government* is guaranteed to the states, it necessarily follows that every other form of government is prohibited.

But the Constitution provides no means for enforcing this clause. It establishes no test by which a republican form may be clearly distinguished from all others. Nor will the Supreme Court undertake to define the meaning of the term. It has said that the determination of whether a state has a republican form of government is a political rather than a judicial matter, and therefore within the control of Congress.[63] Actually, Congress has

---

[58] Williams *v.* North Carolina, 325 U.S. 226 (1945).
[59] Virginia *v.* Tennessee, 148 U.S. 503 (1893).
[60] Art. IV, Sec. 2, Cl. 2.
[61] Kentucky *v.* Dennison, 24 Howard 66 (1861).
[62] Art. IV, Sec. 4.
[63] Pacific States Telephone Co. *v.* Oregon, 223 U.S. 118 (1912); Mountain Timber Co. *v.* Washington, 243 U.S. 219, 234 (1917).

never attempted to pass upon the question. It could do so, no doubt, by refusing to admit Senators and Representatives to its membership on the ground that their state government was not republican in form; and it might even use the armed forces of the United States to eject an unrepublican government.

DENIAL OR ABRIDGMENT OF VOTING RIGHTS. The Fourteenth Amendment provides, among other things, that any state denying or abridging the right to vote to "any of the male inhabitants of such State, being twenty-one years of age and citizens of the United States, . . . except for participation in rebellion, or other crime, . . ." shall suffer a proportionate reduction in the number of its Congressmen. But this section of the Constitution has never been enforced, for reasons that are considered in a subsequent chapter.[64]

STATE TAXATION OF NATIONAL GOVERNMENT. Another limitation on state power, not found in the exact words of the Constitution but long regarded by the Supreme Court as an inherent part of the American federal system, is the rule that no state may tax the federal government or its agencies. This rule originated in the fear that the states might otherwise impose such heavy taxes on the national government as to impair its functions or even drive it out of existence. "The power to tax," declared Chief Justice Marshall in 1819, speaking for a united court in the famous case of McCulloch v. Maryland,[65] "involves the power to destroy." Half a century later the converse of this principle—that the national government might not tax the state or its agencies—was also affirmed by the Supreme Court of the United States, in Collector v. Day.[66]

In the spring of 1939, however, the Court specifically reversed its earlier stand, and permitted state taxation of the salaries of federal employees.[67] It is now assumed that non-discriminatory federal taxation of state salaries is permissible, also, and such taxation has been accepted by the states without further protest. At last the Supreme Court has rejected Marshall's "power to destroy" dictum in favor of the words of Holmes: "The power to tax is not the power to destroy while this court sits." [68]

[64] See page 296.
[65] 4 Wheaton 316 (1819).
[66] 11 Wallace 113 (1870).
[67] Graves v. New York, 306 U.S. 466 (1939).
[68] Dissenting opinion in the case of Panhandle Oil Co. v. Knox, 277 U.S. 218 (1927).

ADMISSION OF NEW STATES

The Constitution empowers Congress to admit new states into the Union.[69] The first step is usually a petition from the people of a territory to Congress, requesting admission as a state.   If Congress approves this petition it passes a so-called *enabling act,* authorizing the people of the territory to frame a constitution and specifying the exact manner in which this is to be done. After the constitution has been framed and has been ratified by the people, it must receive the approval of Congress before the territory is admitted to statehood.   In some instances the people of a territory have framed their constitution before receiving the sanction of Congress, but subsequent Congressional approval has remedied this irregularity.

Since the federal government has absolute power to determine whether a territorial petition for admission to the Union shall be granted or denied, it is able to impose any conditions that it may see fit, and to insist upon those conditions as a *sine qua non* of statehood.   In a number of instances federal restrictions have actually been inserted in enabling acts.

Utah, for example, was admitted in 1896 on condition that polygamy be prohibited.   Because of the insistence of President Taft, Arizona and New Mexico were not permitted to enter the Union until clauses providing for the recall of judges had been deleted from their new constitutions.

Oklahoma, admitted in 1907, was required to agree that its capital would not be removed from the City of Guthrie prior to 1913.   In 1910, however, the Oklahoma legislature violated this pledge by moving the state capital to Oklahoma City, and thereby created a serious legal problem.   Granted that the federal government may impose conditions when admitting a territory into the Union, does it have any means of enforcing those conditions after statehood has been acquired?   Or is the new state's duty to respect its agreement merely a moral obligation, unenforceable by any federal agency?

The Supreme Court decided the matter in the case of Coyle v. Smith [70] and ruled that the federal government possessed no authority to rob the states of a portion of their control over local affairs by forcing burdensome restrictions upon them.   As territories they might agree to the terms of Congress, but as states they could not be compelled to keep their promises.   Otherwise Congress might impose all sorts of unreasonable conditions, and establish different classes of states with varying degrees of power.   Such an arrange-

[69] Art. IV, Sec. 3, Cl. 1.   This clause continues: "but no new States shall be formed or erected within the jurisdiction of any other States; nor any State be formed by the junction of two or more States or parts of States, without the consent of the legislatures of the States concerned as well as of Congress."

[70] 221 U.S. 559 (1911).

ment, said the Court, would clearly be contrary to the Constitution, for the Union "was and is a union of States, equal in power, dignity, and authority, each competent to exert that residuum of sovereignty not delegated to the United States by the Constitution itself."

It must be clearly understood, however, that by admitting a territory to statehood Congress does not in any way surrender its control over national affairs, even within the boundaries of the new state. Therefore it may include in the enabling act a provision concerning some matter within the scope of national authority, and such a provision is enforceable even after the territory has become a state.

This principle was made clear in the case of Ervien v. United States.[71] The enabling act for the admission of New Mexico had granted national lands to the state government and had specified how the proceeds from their sale were to be used. In defiance of federal requirements the New Mexico legislature subsequently authorized the expenditure of some of this money for the purpose of advertising the natural resources of the state, but the federal Supreme Court unanimously ruled that the conditions imposed by Congress must be respected. "The United States, being the grantor of the lands, can impose conditions upon their use, and has the right to exact performance of the conditions," it declared.

While it is true, generally speaking, that the states are "equal in power, dignity, and authority"—to use the exact words of the Supreme Court—there are two respects in which the states are quite unequal in power, dignity, and authority. State representation in the federal House of Representatives is on the basis of population, so that the states with large numbers of inhabitants have proportionately greater voting power than the less populous commonwealths.[72] And state voting power is roughly equivalent to state population in selecting the president of the United States.[73] In the United States Senate, on the other hand, the legal equality of the states is recognized by giving equal representation to every state.[74]

PROBLEMS

1. Prepare a list of the factors that seem to indicate a further expansion of federal power at the expense of the states, and also a list of the factors that may check this trend. Do you believe that further federal expansion is inevitable?

[71] 251 U.S. 41 (1919).

[72] Constitution, Art. I, Sec. 3, Cl. 3, and the Fourteenth Amendment, Sec. 2.

[73] The Constitution specifies that "Each State shall appoint . . . a number of electors, equal to the whole number of senators and representatives to which the State may be entitled in the Congress." Art. II, Sec. 1, Cl. 2.

[74] "The Senate of the United States shall be composed of two senators from each State. . . ." Constitution, Art. I, Sec. 3, Cl. 1.

2. In what respects are the present methods of apportioning federal aid among the states unsatisfactory? What bases of apportionment would you suggest?

3. Write a paper on the legal aspects of the removal from the Pacific Coast of persons of Japanese ancestry.

4. Prepare a brief history of the extradition of fugitives in the United States.

5. Should the federal government be permitted to tax the income from state and municipal bonds? Discuss this question in detail.

6. Select one of the states admitted into the Union since 1875, and trace the history of its transition from territory to state.

SELECTED REFERENCES

Anderson, William, *Federalism and Intergovernmental Relations; a Budget of Suggestions for Research*, 1946.

Benson, G. C. S., *The New Centralization; A Study of Intergovernmental Relationships in the United States*, 1941.

Bittermann, Henry J., *State and Federal Grants-in-Aid*, 1938.

Blough, Roy, and Others, *Tax Relations among Governmental Units*, 1938.

Clark, Jane P., *Rise of a New Federalism*, 1938.

Council of State Governments, *Federal Grants-in-Aid*, 1949.

———— *Handbook of Interstate Crime Control*, rev. ed., 1949.

———— *State-Local Relations; Report of the Committee on State-Local Relations*, 1946.

Green, Thomas S., Jr., *Liquor Trade Barriers*, 1940.

Heinberg, John G., *Manual on Federal-State Relations for the Missouri Constitutional Convention of 1943*, Columbia, 1943.

Hughes, Charles E., *The Supreme Court of the United States*, 1928.

Johnsen, Julia E., comp., *Interstate Trade Barriers*, 1940.

Johnson, Byron L., *The Principle of Equalization Applied to the Allocation of Grants-in-Aid*, 1947.

Kallenbach, Joseph E., *Federal Cooperation with the States under the Commerce Clause*, Ann Arbor, Mich., 1942.

Key, V. O., Jr., *Administration of Federal Grants to States*, 1937.

Macdonald, Austin F., *Federal Aid*, 1928.

Maxwell, James A., *The Fiscal Impact of Federalism in the United States*, Cambridge, Mass., 1946.

Mort, Paul R., and Others, *Principles and Methods of Distributing Federal Aid for Education*, Washington, D.C., 1939.

Quattlebaum, Charles A., *Federal Aid to the States for Education*, 1944.

Raup, Ruth, *Intergovernmental Relations in Social Welfare*, Minneapolis, 1951.

Reed, Thomas H., *Federal-State-Local Fiscal Relations*, 1942.

Ribble, Frederick D. G., *State and National Power over Commerce*, 1937.

Rourke, Francis E., *Intergovernmental Relations in Employment Security*, Minneapolis, 1952.

Studenski, Paul, and Mort, Paul R., *Centralized versus Decentralized Government in Relation to Democracy*, 1942.

Talbott, Forrest, *Intergovernmental Relations and the Courts*, Minneapolis, 1950.

Tax Institute, *Tax Barriers to Trade*, Philadelphia, 1941.

White, Leonard D., *The States and the Nation*, Baton Rouge, 1953.

Williams, Mrs. Juanita K., *Grants-in-Aid under the Public Works Administration; A Study in Federal-State-Local Relations*, 1939.

Wyatt, Lawrence, *Intergovernmental Relations in Public Health*, Minneapolis, 1951.

CHAPTER 2

Interstate Relations

The Constitution of the United States sets forth in great detail the relationships of the states to the nation and carefully draws a dividing line between state and national powers. It is not greatly concerned, however, as to the dealings of the states with one another. Not only does it make no attempt to establish interstate co-operation, but, instead, it forbids the states to make mutual agreements except with the approval of Congress. As a result, interstate co-operation has developed slowly. Only a few years ago disagreements were much more numerous than agreements, every state tending to regard its neighbors with suspicion, instead of working with them for the common good.

DIVERSITY OF STATE LEGISLATION

For many years the wide diversity of state legislation on matters requiring uniform treatment has produced very unfortunate results. Some states have tried to discourage divorce by making it a difficult proceeding; others have made a strong bid for the divorce business of the nation by reducing the necessary residence period to six weeks and at the same time legalizing gambling in order to provide for the recreation of those awaiting divorce decrees. An act regarded as a felony in one commonwealth may be treated simply as a misdemeanor in another; in still another state it may not even be illegal. Murder, robbery, burglary, and larceny are words whose meanings vary greatly from state to state. Tax laws, labor laws, statutes regulating trade and industry, laws concerning the ownership and operation of motor vehicles —these are just a few examples of diverse state legislation in fields where uniformity is urgently required. Numerous laws have been enacted to protect local manufacturers, merchants, and farmers against competition from other states. Trade barriers have been erected by the states against the products of their neighbors, and the result has been a large crop of retaliatory legislation.

The Constitution of the United States specifically authorizes Congress to regulate interstate commerce, but the state governments have found numerous ways to evade the letter of the fundamental law. Sometimes they impose special taxes and license fees on "foreign" corporations (that is, corporations from other states); sometimes they tax "foreign" trucks and buses at excessive rates; sometimes they impose heavy tax burdens on local products manufactured from out-of-state raw materials. In many instances discriminations against the goods of other states are accomplished by means of quarantine and inspection measures allegedly enacted for the protection of the public health or safety. A minimum standard for "fresh" eggs may be set so high that it can only be met by domestic hens. Some of the competing agricultural products of other commonwealths may be excluded, or made to bear exorbitant inspection fees—and such legislation may be justified as a health measure.

During the last few years, however, there has been some evidence to indicate that the states are wearying of their cutthroat competition. Apparently they are beginning to realize that no commonwealth can hope to sell its commodities to other states unless it accepts their products in exchange. This realization has led to a gradual reduction of trade barriers in the more progressive states, even though some of their neighbors have failed to reciprocate. The Second World War hastened the process of good neighborliness. The War Department had already approved uniform size and weight requirements for trucks, and all forty-eight states adopted these requirements as their own, thus eliminating many of the legal difficulties encountered by heavy trucks on interstate journeys.

Even when the states insist on enacting or retaining discriminatory legislation, however, it is sometimes set aside by the courts. Some years ago the Supreme Court of the United States was asked to pass upon the validity of a 1937 Florida statute requiring inspection of all imported cement and imposing an inspection charge of fifteen cents per hundred pounds.[1] This measure was alleged to protect the public from some of the dangers of faulty construction; its preamble declared that "it is of paramount importance to the public safety that only cement measuring up to a minimum standard should be offered for sale, sold, or used in the State of Florida." The highest court of the state upheld the law,[2] but the Supreme Court of the United States, intent upon safeguarding interstate commerce, refused to follow suit. "The scheme for inspection and for the inspection fee," declared Mr. Justice Frankfurter, speaking for the Court, "applies only to cement imported or brought into the State of Florida from any foreign

[1] A. B. Hale *et al. v.* Binco Trading Co., Inc., 306 U.S. 466 (1939).
[2] State *v.* Hale, 129 Fla. 588 (1937).

country. . . . The statute thus renders the seventy per cent domestic cement immune from its requirements of inspection and its attendant fee. . . . So far as public safety demands certain standards in the quality of cement, such safety is dependent on assurance of that quality by appropriate inspection no less of the seventy per cent domestic cement than of the thirty per cent obtained from abroad. That no Florida cement needs any inspection while all foreign cement requires inspection at a cost of fifteen cents per hundred weight is too violent an assumption to justify the discrimination here disclosed. . . . No reasonable conjecture can here overcome the calculated discrimination against foreign commerce. . . . It would not be easy to imagine a statute more clearly designed than the present to circumvent what the commerce clause forbids." [3]

The Twenty-first Amendment to the federal Constitution, which repeals the prohibition amendment, specifically authorizes the states to impose such restrictions as they may see fit upon liquor imported from other commonwealths. "The transportation or importation into any state, territory, or possession of the United States for delivery or use therein of intoxicating liquors, in violation of the laws thereof, is hereby prohibited." This clause was obviously designed to protect "dry" states from the activities of their "wet" neighbors, but it has served equally well to protect liquor-producing commonwealths from unwelcome competition. In 1935 the State of Minnesota prohibited the importation for sale of non-registered liquors, and applied this rule to unregistered intoxicants brought into the state by an Illinois corporation before the enactment of the law. The corporation, alleging denial of the equal protection of the laws, turned to the Supreme Court of the United States for relief. But the Court held the "equal protection" clause of the Fourteenth Amendment inoperative in this case, because of the words of the Twenty-first Amendment conferring upon the states plenary power to regulate the liquor traffic.[4]

INTERSTATE CO-OPERATION

Serious efforts have been made to promote greater uniformity of state legislation. Some of these efforts were begun well over half a century ago. The National Conference of Commissioners on Uniform State Laws, for example, was established in 1892. It is composed of representatives of the several states and territories—usually three commissioners from each state and territory, appointed by the governor. They are united in a perma-

[3] A. B. Hale *et al. v.* Binco Trading Co., Inc., 306 U.S. 466 (1939).
[4] Mahoney *v.* Joseph Triner Corp., 304 U.S. 401 (1938).

nent organization and come together for four or five days every year to consider the work of their standing committees.[5]   The commissioners are prominent members of the legal profession—judges, practicing attorneys, and law school professors.   They serve without compensation and usually pay their own expenses.   They have at various times drafted and recommended to the states about one hundred "model" acts, in addition to approving a few standard statutes drafted by other organizations.   But the states have been discouragingly slow to adopt the statutes thus prepared. Only eight of the recommended laws have received anything like unanimous state approval.[6]

Every year the governors of the several states hold a conference, normally of three days' duration, for "an exchange of views and experiences on subjects of general importance . . . the promotion of uniformity in state legislation and the attainment of greater efficiency in state administration."[7]   The first conference of governors was called by President Theodore Roosevelt in 1908, with such satisfactory results that it was decided to hold annual meetings.   But subsequent sessions have not always lived up to their early promise.   Sometimes the governors of important states are absent, and frequently the speakers deal in platitudes.   The governors' conferences are not without political significance.   They offer a convenient opportunity for governors of the same political faith to discuss party strategy, and they provide a sounding board for governors whose eyes may be fixed longingly on the presidency of the nation.[8]

Occasionally the chief executives of a number of states sharing some common problem, such as the regulation of the oil industry or the control of flood conditions in a river basin, meet less formally to discuss possible solutions.   These conferences have no regular meeting dates; instead, they are called when actual crises arise.   They have proved much more effective than the formal annual conferences of all the governors—largely because of the more limited scope of the agenda, the greater need for immediate action, and the increased likelihood of representation from all the interested states.

The American Legislators' Association

In 1925 the American Legislators' Association was formed.   The idea of such an association was conceived by Henry W. Toll, a Colorado state

[5] An interesting volume, *The Handbook of the National Conference of Commissioners on Uniform State Laws*, is published annually by the Conference.

[6] That is, approved by forty or more states.   Seven other proposed laws have been enacted by at least thirty states.   See the accompanying chart.

[7] *Articles of Organization of the Governors' Conference*, Art. III.

[8] See the annual volume of *Proceedings* published by the Governors' Conference.

UNIFORM STATE LAWS ENACTED BY 36 OR MORE STATES

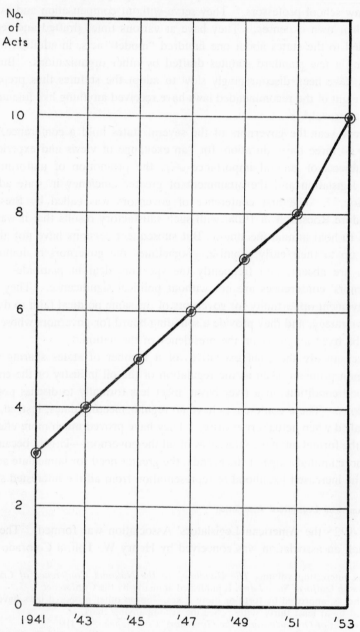

Based on information from *The Book of the States, 1954–55,* and previous volumes.

senator, who sent letters to seventy-five hundred state legislators inviting them to participate in the task of organization.   Many accepted the invitation, and shortly afterward legislators from ten states met in the senate chamber at Denver.   The Association was formally established, and a program of activity approved.   But interest in the movement soon lagged, and lack of funds proved a serious handicap.   When, therefore, Mr. Toll called a second meeting in 1927, only five persons appeared at the appointed time and place.   Four of them were newspaper reporters; the fifth was a lobbyist.   It seemed that the American Legislators' Association had ceased to be more than a name.

But new interest arose in 1929.   A number of state legislators contributed substantial sums, and shortly afterward a private foundation made a large grant for the expansion of existing activities and the establishment of new projects.   The Association then began publication of an official monthly magazine, *State Government,* which replaced a small leaflet that had previously been circulated.   Association headquarters were moved from Denver to Chicago, and membership increased rapidly.   More recent developments have swept away all doubt as to the success of the movement. The Association has now received the formal endorsement of the legislatures of all forty-eight states.

Impressed with the need for a united attack by state legislatures upon common problems, the American Legislators' Association organized a convention of state legislators in 1933.   Approximately one hundred legislators from thirty-two states met in the national capital in February of that year and devoted a number of busy days to questions of overlapping and conflicting taxation, and the like.   This gathering was known officially as the First Interstate Legislative Assembly.   Other conventions have since been held at two-year intervals; they now include administrators as well as legislators.

The legislators attending the First Interstate Assembly were handicapped in their study of tax conflicts by lack of information concerning existing conditions.   Few members were familiar with the proposals already made by various groups for improving the nation's tax structure.   It was obvious, therefore, that conventions of legislators must be supplemented by permanent research staffs and that legislators' resolutions must be based on expert fact-finding and analysis.   So the members of the convention directed the presiding officer to appoint an Interstate Commission on Conflicting Taxation—a permanent body consisting of ten representatives and seven senators. This commission promptly appointed an expert research staff, which presented a scholarly report on tax conflicts to the Second Interstate Assembly

(1935).   By this time it was generally understood that the tax difficulties of the states involved not only interstate complexities, but also conflicts of authority between the states and the nation; therefore a Tax Revision Council was set up, with members representing the federal government as well as the states and the local communities.

Interstate Compacts

For more than a century after the adoption of the national Constitution the states seldom made agreements to co-operate with one another.   During the 1920's, however, state officials began to realize that such agreements might provide a satisfactory basis for the joint solution of many of their common problems.   They signed a number of compacts dealing with a wide variety of subjects, and Congress gave its formal approval.   During the 1930's the movement seemed to lag, but since the end of the Second World War the trend toward co-operation by interstate compact has been quite marked.   Today there are about one hundred and ten interstate agreements, though only one—regulating the interstate supervision of paroled convicts and probationers—has been accepted by all the states. Many of the compacts affect only certain parts of the nation, and therefore are not of universal interest.   Thus the Colorado River Compact, which provides for the equitable distribution of the river's waters, has been signed by all seven affected states.   The Tri-State Pollution Compact, designed to control the pollution of the waters of New York Harbor, has been accepted by New York, New Jersey, and Connecticut, the three states directly concerned.   The Interstate Oil Compact, which aims to conserve oil and gas, has received the approval of all the major oil-producing commonwealths. There are agreements among the states concerning such diverse matters as flood control, forest fire prevention, park and parkway improvements, development of port facilities, better utilization of marine fisheries, and mutual aid for civil defense.

Many of the agreements among the states are administered by specially created interstate agencies.   The Ohio River Valley Sanitation Compact, for example, sets up a commission with fairly extensive regulatory powers. Representatives of all eight participating states [9] are included in the commission's membership.   Similarly organized are the Port of New York Authority (representing both New York and New Jersey), the Pennsylvania–New Jersey Toll Bridge Authority, and the Interstate Commission on the Delaware River Basin (New York, New Jersey, Pennsylvania, and Dela-

[9] Illinois, Indiana, Kentucky, New York, Ohio, Pennsylvania, Virginia, West Virginia.

ware).   Some interstate agreements, however, are administered within each state by state agencies, rather than by specially created interstate commissions.   The Probation and Parole Compact, for example, is enforced quite well without an interstate commission.   The governor of each state appoints an official administrator, whose duty is to carry out the agreement within the state's borders and to co-operate with his fellow administrators in other states for the purpose of establishing necessary rules and regulations.[10]

When two or more states have signed an agreement to make a joint attack upon some common problem, they normally submit the pact to Congress for its approval.   Sometimes, however, Congress gives its consent in advance of state action, as it did for the Ohio River Valley Sanitation Compact.   Indeed, interstate agreements can become operative without any action by Congress.   The Supreme Court has said that the constitutional requirement of congressional approval does not apply to all understandings among the states, but only to agreements "tending to increase the political power of the states, which may encroach upon or interfere with the just supremacy of the United States." [11]   Whenever the slightest doubt exists, however, as to the exact nature of an agreement among the states, the wisest course is to obtain congressional consent.

In 1950 the system of interstate compacts was menaced by a decision of West Virginia's supreme court of appeals.   The state auditor had refused to honor a requisition for West Virginia's share of the expenses of an interstate commission, and the court upheld his refusal.   State power, it said, resided in the officials of the state, and could not be transferred to an interstate commission.   Moreover, the state legislature could not agree to support any agency for an indefinite future period, because of the restrictions on borrowing in the state constitution.[12]   The case was appealed to the Supreme Court of the United States, which promptly reversed the decision of the state court.   "What is involved," said the federal tribunal, "is the conventional grant of legislative power.   We find nothing in that to indicate that West Virginia may not solve a problem such as the control of river pollution by compact and by the delegation, if such it be, necessary to effectuate such solution by compact."   The Court went on to say that state constitutional restrictions on borrowing were not applicable, because the

---

10 See *The Interstate Compact since 1925,* by Frederick L. Zimmermann and Mitchell Wendell.

11 Virginia *v.* Tennessee, 148 U.S. 503 (1893).

12 State *ex rel.* Dyer *v.* Sims, 58 S.E. (2nd) 766 (1950).   For a brief discussion of the significance of this case, see "The West Virginia Compact Decision," by Leonard A. Weakley, in the December, 1950, issue of *State Government,* pp. 273–275.

West Virginia legislature still possessed the final power to appropriate or withhold funds for the work of the interstate commission.   But what of the generally accepted rule that the highest court of each state shall be the final interpreter of the state's own constitution?   Would not the Supreme Court of the United States exceed its authority if it reversed the opinion of the West Virginia tribunal concerning the precise meaning of some of the state constitution's clauses?   No, said the United States Supreme Court, not if the rights of the nation or other states are involved.   Then the meaning of the state constitution becomes a federal question.[13]

The system of procuring interstate co-operation by means of formal compacts has serious disadvantages.   It is both slow and clumsy.   State legislatures often take a long time to ratify necessary agreements, and sometimes they take even longer to approve necessary amendments.   Delays in a single state can jeopardize a co-operative program involving a number of commonwealths.   In many instances, therefore, less formal and less complicated methods of obtaining joint action are to be preferred.   But the interstate compact cannot be dismissed as a totally inadequate device. One careful student of the problem concludes that it is "well adapted to serve some purposes and ill adapted to serve others." [14]

The Council of State Governments

Most of the agencies concerned with co-operation among the states have been united as branches or affiliates of a sort of "holding company" of interstate co-operation—the Council of State Governments.   The plan for such a council was first broached at a meeting of the planning board of the American Legislators' Association early in 1935.   Administrators as well as legislators were to be included in the council's membership, and authority was to be derived from forty-eight commissions on interstate co-operation— one in each of the states.

New Jersey was the first state to establish such a commission.   On March 12, 1935, the governor signed the necessary legislation, and appointed five administrative officers—the attorney-general and the tax commissioner, among others—to serve as the commission's administrative members.   Five members from the state senate were appointed by its president, and five members from the lower house were chosen by its presiding officer.

[13] West Virginia *ex rel.* Dyer *v.* Sims, 341 U.S. 22 (1951).   This case is discussed by George G. Bogert in a brief article, "Decision of the Supreme Court in the West Virginia Compact Case," *State Government,* June, 1951, pp. 162–164.

[14] Vincent V. Thursby, *Interstate Co-operation: A Study of the Interstate Compact,* p. 143.

Colorado followed New Jersey's example a few weeks later. Before the end of the year commissions on interstate co-operation had been established in nine states. Others promptly fell into line, bringing the total number to thirty-seven in 1937. Today every state has such a commission.

Most of the state commissions on interstate co-operation follow the original New Jersey pattern—five members from each house of the legislature, and five administrators. One of the administrators commonly serves as chairman. Some commissions are fully organized, and have been equipped with offices and permanent secretaries. Other commissions, however, maintain no regular staffs for clerical work and meet infrequently. The more progressive commissions frequently invite their neighbors to conferences on common problems, ranging from banking practices to highway safety; and take the lead in promoting uniform legislation and uniform administrative practices.

The Council of State Governments is the central agency of the state commissions on interstate co-operation. Each commission contributing to the Council's work is entitled to one representative on its board of managers, which meets semiannually to review past activities and formulate future policies. The central secretariat of the Council, located in Chicago, maintains separate divisions for publications, research, organization, and public relations. During the last few years the work has been facilitated by the establishment of an office in the national capital, as well as regional offices in New York and San Francisco.

The Council maintains closest relations with other agencies that are working for interstate co-operation. It operates clearing house services for the Governors' Conference, the American Legislators' Association, the National Association of Attorneys-General, and the National Association of Secretaries of State. The executive director of the Council serves also as director of the American Legislators' Association and as secretary-treasurer of the Governors' Conference. These affiliated organizations are all represented on the Council's board of managers. Numerous other organizations, such as the American Society of Planning Officials, the American Public Welfare Association, the Civil Service Assembly, and the Governmental Research Association, maintain offices in the same building as the Council of State Governments and share some of its research facilities.

It should, perhaps, be emphasized that the Council of State Governments and its affiliated organizations are concerned primarily with research. They have no authority to shape the policies of any agency of state government. Instead, they make studies of state and interstate problems and publish their findings in various bulletins and periodicals and in an official reference work, the biennial *Book of the States;* they maintain consultant services for scores of state agencies and for private citizens; they sponsor regional and national conferences on dozens of important public questions.   But no administrative officer is required to heed their advice; no legislature is bound to accept their recommendations.   Their influence arises solely from the fact that they are expert, impartial agencies, completely unconcerned with the ebb and flow of politics.   And it must be confessed that even yet the machinery created for interstate co-operation is more impressive than the results achieved.   But the movement is still young and represents one of the first intelligent, large-scale attempts to co-ordinate the activities of the forty-eight states.[15]

SUITS AGAINST A STATE

The framers of the federal Constitution realized that disputes involving the state governments would inevitably arise, and they made provision for the settlement of such disagreements.   "The judicial power of the United States," declares Article III,[16] "shall extend . . . to controversies between two or more States; between a State and citizens of another State. . . . In all cases . . . in which a State shall be a party, the Supreme Court shall have original jurisdiction."

The Doctrine of Non-suability

It was generally assumed, when the Constitution was adopted, that these clauses did not confer upon any private citizen the right to sue a state. The British king was not suable,[17] and this immunity was thought to inhere in the states of the American Union.   In 1793, however, the Supreme Court of the United States took a contrary view and upheld a private action against the State of Georgia.[18]   So firmly entrenched was the doctrine of states rights in those days that the Eleventh Amendment to the Constitution was promptly adopted, depriving the federal courts of jurisdiction over such disputes.   Therefore a state cannot be sued without its consent by a citizen of another state, by one of its own citizens,[19] or by a citizen of any foreign

---

[15] This description of the Council of State Governments and its affiliated organizations is drawn largely from the several volumes of the *Book of the States.*

[16] Sec. 2.

[17] This legal fiction has become a mere technicality in England, however.

[18] Chisholm *v.* Georgia, 2 Dallas 419 (1793).

[19] Hans *v.* Louisiana, 134 U.S. 1 (1890).

nation.   But it can be sued by another state of the Union, and such suits are not infrequent.   The nation cannot be sued without its consent, and this limitation applies even to actions brought by a state.[20]

Settlement of Claims

Since a state may not be sued by private citizens against its will, it may readily escape legal responsibility for the acts of its officials and employees. Merely by refusing to hear the claims of individuals under any circumstances, it may avoid the inconvenience and expense of such lawsuits.   Such a policy is manifestly unjust, however.   Many persons have legitimate claims against the state—perhaps because they have been improperly dismissed from the state service, or have been unable to obtain payment for work performed under a contract with some state department, or have been injured in a highway accident involving a state-owned vehicle.   There are hundreds of reasons why damages may properly be asked.   And if the state absolutely refuses to permit its judges or administrators to pass upon such claims, regardless of the circumstances, then the injured parties are without legal remedy.   Their only recourse is to persuade the state legislature to pass a special law indemnifying them for the losses they have received.   Special laws of this kind are still common.   State legislative committees spend many hours of their valuable time considering such questions as whether Farmer Smith should receive compensation of five hundred dollars for his cow, which was killed by a Department of Public Works truck.

In more than one third of the states the legislature is the sole judge of the merit of claims against the state government.   In these states, therefore, the individual's chances of collection are influenced by such irrelevant matters as the generosity of the legislature, the pressure of legislative business, and even partisan politics.   A majority of the states, however, have attempted to find some more satisfactory way of settling legitimate claims. Some commonwealths have established boards of claims,[21] which hear cases and make awards—subject, in some instances, to legislative approval of large payments.   In some states claims are handled by a designated officer —the auditor, or secretary of state, or attorney-general.   Four states [22] have adopted a common-sense solution by creating special courts of claims,

[20] Kansas v. United States, 204 U.S. 331 (1907).   The non-suability of the United States is not expressly stated in the federal Constitution but is declared by the Supreme Court to be a fundamental principle of government.

[21] The board of claims usually consists of three persons named ex officio.   The three officers most commonly appointed are the state auditor, the attorney-general, and the secretary of state.

[22] Illinois, Michigan, New York, West Virginia.

and thus transferring the matter from the field of politics to the field of law, where it properly belongs.   In two of these commonwealths,[23] however, the constitution specifically forbids suits against the state, so that the court of claims is unable to make any binding awards.   In theory it is merely a body created to advise the legislature.   Its recommendations have been followed so consistently by the legislative branch, however, that they are now recognized as virtually the equivalent of final judgments.   There is a noticeable trend in state government toward a more liberal attitude concerning lawsuits by individuals, but the movement is slow, for many states are loath to abandon their old ways.

PROBLEMS

1. Prepare a brief report on the evils of diversity in state legislation and state administrative practices.
2. Describe the organization and activities of the National Conference of Commissioners on Uniform State Laws.
3. Summarize the reports and recommendations of the Interstate Commission on Conflicting Taxation.
4. What has been done by your state to promote the movement for interstate co-operation?
5. Write a brief history of the National Association of Secretaries of State or the National Association of Attorneys General.

SELECTED REFERENCES

Bird, Frederick L., *A Study of the Port of New York Authority,* 1949.
Buell, Raymond L., *Death by Tariff; Protectionism in State and Federal Legislation,* 1939.
Governors' Conferences, *Proceedings,* 1909—(published annually).
Graves, W. B., *Uniform State Action,* Chapel Hill, N.C., 1934.
Green, Thomas S., Jr., *Liquor Trade Barriers,* 1940.
Interstate Commission on Conflicting Taxation, Research Staff of the, *Conflicting Taxation,* Chicago, 1935.
Johnsen, Julia E., comp., *Interstate Trade Barriers,* 1940.
Melder, Frederick E., *State and Local Barriers to Interstate Commerce in the United States,* Orono, Me., 1937.
National Conference of Commissioners on Uniform State Laws, *Handbook,* Washington, D.C., 1892—(published annually).
Raup, Ruth, *Intergovernmental Relations in Social Welfare,* Minneapolis, 1951.
Rourke, Francis E., *Intergovernmental Relations in Employment Security,* Minneapolis, 1952.

[23] Illinois and West Virginia.

Talbott, Forrest, *Intergovernmental Relations and the Courts,* Minneapolis, 1950.

Tax Institute, *Tax Barriers to Trade,* Philadelphia, 1941.

Thursby, Vincent V., *Interstate Cooperation—A Study of the Interstate Compact,* Washington, D.C., 1953.

White, Leonard D., *The States and the Nation,* Baton Rouge, 1953.

Wyatt, Lawrence, *Intergovernmental Relations in Public Health,* Minneapolis, 1951.

Zimmermann, Frederick L., and Mitchell Wendell, *The Interstate Compact Since 1925,* 1951.

Biery, Hudson, "Intergovernmental Plans for Pollution Control: Ohio River Valley," *State Government,* October, 1948, pp. 210–213.

Ellis, William J., "The Interstate Parole and Probation Compacts," *State Government,* March, 1945, pp. 40–42.

Short, John A., "Co-ordinated Planning in the Missouri Valley: The Osage Basin," *State Government,* October, 1948, pp. 207–209.

CHAPTER 3

State–Local Relations

A city, in law, is defined as a municipal corporation. It possesses a charter granted by the state, conferring upon it certain rights and privileges and also imposing certain obligations. To some extent, therefore, it resembles a private corporation, which is also chartered by the state and given certain rights and duties. But the resemblance between municipal and private corporations is only superficial, for private corporations receive a measure of protection against arbitrary state action that is commonly denied to cities.

STATE AUTHORITY OVER LOCAL GOVERNMENTS

The courts have said repeatedly that municipalities are merely the creatures of the state, called into being for the express purpose of doing the state's will and exercising such powers as the state may choose to confer. Therefore the state possesses broad authority over the structure and functions of municipal government; and, in the absence of constitutional provisions to the contrary, this authority is exercised mainly by the legislature. While it is undoubtedly true that cities have been given considerably broader powers of self-government in recent years and that to this extent the state legislature has relinquished its control, these recent changes have not altered the fundamental proposition that in most states, and for most purposes, the legislature molds the destiny of every city within the state boundaries.

Counties and townships are in an even less fortunate position. They, too, are regarded as creatures of the state, subject to the will of the legislature, but they are not accorded even the status of municipal corporations.[1] Instead, the courts commonly describe them as quasi-corporations and declare in no uncertain terms that their rights and privileges—and, in fact, their very existence—are subject to the pleasure of the legislature, except so far

[1] Some exceptions must be made to this statement, however. The counties of a number of states, including Indiana, New York, Oklahoma, Texas, and Wyoming, are specifically designated as municipal corporations by constitutional provision or judicial decree.

as constitutional provisions limit legislative control. "Municipal corporations," said the Supreme Court of Illinois in an important decision, "are those called into existence either at the direct request or by consent of the persons composing them. Quasi-municipal corporations, such as counties and townships, are at most but local organizations, which are created by general law, without the consent of the inhabitants thereof, for the purpose of the civil and political administration of government, and they are invested with but few characteristics of corporate existence. They are, in other words, local subdivisions of the state created by the sovereign power of the state of its own will, without regard to the wishes of the people inhabiting them. A municipal corporation is created principally for the advantage and convenience of the people of the locality. County and township organizations are created in this state with a view to carrying out the policy of the state at large for the administration of matters of political government, finance, education, taxing, care of the poor, military organization, means of travel and the administration of justice." [2]

Legislative Control

In the early days of American independence the state legislatures were given complete freedom to manage municipal affairs as they saw fit. Constitutional restrictions on legislative control of cities were practically unknown. At first there was a tradition of local self-government that prevented excessive state interference with local matters, but this tradition disappeared with the passing of years, and then state legislatures proceeded to regulate every minute detail of municipal activity.

Sometimes their interference was prompted by a sincere desire to protect the people of the cities against the machinations of scheming municipal politicians; sometimes, in fact, it came as a direct result of requests made by the "better" elements of the urban population, who were disgusted with municipal inefficiency and corruption and desired state protection from further excesses; but in most instances the chief motive was the desire of the state legislators to seize for themselves greater power, prestige, and patronage.

Whatever the motives for state interference with municipal affairs, the results were almost invariably bad. State legislators soon proved that they were as inefficient and corrupt as city councilmen and far less familiar with city needs. Almost everywhere the legislature was dominated by the voters of the rural sections—a condition of affairs that has continued

[2] Cook County v. City of Chicago, 142 N.E. 512 (1924).

to the present day, despite the stupendous growth of American cities.[3] Therefore control of cities by the state legislature meant control by the country districts. Every agency of city government was forced to pass in review before the critical and somewhat unfriendly view of the farmers' representatives, and requests by city officials for additional authority to deal with pressing problems were frequently denied without serious consideration.

The legislature seemed to consider itself the keeper of the municipal pocketbook and the municipal conscience. It specified the exact number of administrative officers and employees that each city might have; it prescribed their powers and duties, stating precisely how each power should be exercised and each duty performed; it imposed rigid limits on municipal taxing and borrowing. Some of these restrictions appeared in the charter, as framed by the legislature; others took the form of special laws, which were enacted at every legislative session. In either case, the members of the legislature habitually displayed little or no regard for local sentiment.

Reaction against Special Legislation

Such arbitrary use of power inevitably produced a reaction against state control. The people of the cities began to demand a larger share in the management of their local affairs. Having learned from bitter experience that the legislature could not be trusted to use its authority wisely, they united to secure the adoption of constitutional amendments restricting that authority. At the outset this movement took the form of an attack upon special legislation. In every state the legislature had acquired the habit of dealing separately with each municipality, and each additional grant of power was made the subject of a special law. No two cities were treated alike.

This differential treatment might have been advantageous if it had borne some relationship to the widely different problems and needs of the cities affected. Actually, however, such a relationship seldom existed. State legislators had neither time nor inclination to acquire a reasonable understanding of municipal affairs, and in many instances they voted additional grants of power or additional limitations of power for individual cities with only the faintest notion of what they were trying to accomplish. Sometimes they acted because of the insistence of interested local groups; sometimes because of a hazy belief that cities should be restrained; and many times because of mere caprice.

So those who favored a larger measure of municipal self-government naturally pointed to the evils of special legislation. They urged that all cities

---

[3] The various methods by which the rural sections maintain their supremacy in the state legislatures are discussed in a later Chapter. See pages 130–131.

should be treated alike.   All men were equal before the law; why, they asked, should not cities also be placed on an equal footing?   Although this change would not entirely prevent legislative interference, it would probably put an end to the worst abuses of legislative power.

If properly enforced, it would compel the legislature to impose its will in general terms, and leave the cities free to determine all the details of their government and administration.   For general laws, applying alike to cities of five thousand population and cities of five hundred thousand population, could not possibly be made to cover more than the broad outline of legislative policy.   They could not specify, for example, the size of the police force or the salary of the police chief; if designed to meet the needs of the large metropolitan centers, they would prove unenforceable in small communities.

Prohibition of Special Legislation

Ohio was the first state to prohibit special legislation.   In 1851 it adopted a new constitution which provided that "the general assembly shall pass no special act conferring corporate powers." [4]   This clause was not the product of the movement for municipal self-government, however; on the contrary, it was designed especially to secure equal treatment for *private* corporations, and the inclusion of municipal corporations was largely a matter of chance.   But other state constitution makers, copying the Ohio provision, were directly concerned with the protection of cities.   Thus the framers of the Illinois constitution of 1870, after specifying that all corporations must be created by general law, then proceeded to forbid the enactment of local or special laws "incorporating cities, towns, or villages, or changing or amending the charter of any town, city, or village." [5]

Somewhat similar restrictions, applying directly or indirectly to cities, have now been written into the constitutions of forty states.   Usually they take the form of an unqualified prohibition of special legislation, but in some instances they permit the exercise of legislative or judicial discretion. Thus the constitution of Michigan declares that "The legislature shall pass no local or special act in any case where a general act can be made applicable, and whether a general act can be made applicable shall be a judicial question." [6]

Popular resentment against state interference with local affairs has been limited almost entirely to the cities, especially until the last few decades. The demand for local self-government, as previously indicated,[7] has been

[4] Art. XIII, Sec. 1.
[5] Art. IV, Sec. 22.
[6] Art. V, Sec. 30.
[7] See pages 46–47.

made chiefly by the people of the urban centers.   In nearly every state the counties have been judicially recognized as state agencies peculiarly subordinate to the legislative will, and this attitude of the courts has aroused no widespread opposition.   Constitutional prohibitions against special legislation for corporations do not apply to counties as a rule because of the generally accepted doctrine that counties are not corporations.   Yet a number of state constitutions have been amended to forbid special legislation for counties as well as for cities.   The constitution of Kentucky, for example, specifically declares that special laws may not be enacted for "any city, town, district, or county," [8] and several other constitutions use substantially the same phraseology.

Methods of Evasion

Even the most absolute prohibitions against special legislation, whether for cities or counties, have proved rather easy to evade and therefore have afforded a much smaller measure of protection against legislative abuses than their language would seem to indicate.[9]   One very effective method of evasion, regularly employed by most state legislatures, is to classify the cities of a state on the basis of population, and then enact laws applying to all the cities *within a single class*.   This is general legislation, according to the legislatures; and the courts of every state except Ohio agree.

There is, in fact, a great deal to be said for the principle of classification. It is a recognition of the differences in local needs arising from the very fact of differences in size.   Great metropolitan centers have little in common with small, semi-rural municipalities.   Therefore, if all cities of approximately the same size are treated alike, the result should be substantial justice.

Once the principle of classification has been accepted, however, difficulties immediately arise.   What is to prevent the legislature from setting up fifty or one hundred classes—or as many classes as there are cities? And, with every city in a separate class, what is to prevent the enactment of different laws for every class—that is, for every city—under the guise of general legislation?   Solemn humbuggery of this sort has been practiced more or less extensively in many states, and still serves a useful purpose for legislatures intent upon defeating the spirit of the constitution.

Classification is the most common method of evading the requirement that state regulation of affairs shall be by general law, but it is not the only

---

[8] Sec. 60.

[9] See A. C. Breckenridge's article, "The Mockery of Classification," in the November, 1947, issue of the *National Municipal Review,* pp. 571–573.

way.   Sometimes laws can be so phrased as to be general in form, though in fact they apply only to a single municipality or county.   Often the plain purpose of the constitution can be nullified by the creation of special districts, such as school or highway districts, charged with a single function of government.   Such districts can be multiplied indefinitely, and each district accorded separate treatment, in the absence of an express constitutional provision to the contrary.   Thus the legislature that is prohibited from passing special laws concerning the educational systems of counties may often regulate the educational systems of school districts in any way that it pleases, even though county and school district boundaries are practically identical.

MUNICIPAL HOME RULE

Even under most favorable circumstances, constitutional prohibitions against special legislation are merely a protection against the worst abuses of legislative control.   They do not assure any substantial measure of local self-government.   Therefore the people of the cities have been forced to seek other devices to secure control of their own affairs.

Its First Constitutional Establishment

Before the close of the Civil War it was suggested that municipal charters should be home-made, instead of coming as a gift from the legislature; but this proposal did not bear fruit until 1875.   In that year Missouri adopted a new constitution that contained an epoch-making clause: "Any city having a population of more than one hundred thousand inhabitants may frame a charter for its own government . . ."   Thus the principle of municipal home rule was recognized for the first time.

Spread of the Movement

In 1879 California became a convert to the new gospel of municipal home rule.   At the outset San Francisco was the only city authorized to establish its own framework of government, but subsequently this privilege was extended to all municipalities with populations of more than ten thousand.

For more than a quarter of a century after California's adoption of home rule the movement lagged.   Only three states made the necessary changes in their constitutions during this period,[10] and popular agitation for local self-government was not widespread.   Between 1906 and 1915, however,

[10] Washington (1889), Minnesota (1896), and Colorado (1902).

municipal home rule became a vital force.   It was adopted by Oregon in 1906, by Oklahoma and Michigan in 1908, and by Arizona, Ohio, Nebraska, and Texas in 1912.   In 1915 Maryland adopted county home rule and extended the provisions of this amendment to the City of Baltimore.   Since that time there have been but five adoptions—New York in 1923, Wisconsin in 1924, Utah in 1932, West Virginia in 1936, and Rhode Island in 1951, bringing the total number of municipal home-rule states to eighteen.[11]   It should be noted, however, that two thirds of the fifty largest American cities [12] are in these eighteen states.

Division of Authority between States and Municipalities

The problem of maintaining a reasonable degree of state control over cities in matters of state concern, while giving them a free hand in the management of their purely local affairs, has always been difficult to solve. Every home-rule amendment has required numerous judicial interpretations to make clear its meaning.

To some extent, of course, this uncertainty might have been avoided by the use of more explicit language; but it has arisen in part from the natural complexity of the subject.   For any division of authority between state and city, involving municipal control over municipal functions and state authority over matters of state-wide importance, necessarily implies a more or less clear-cut recognizable distinction between state and local functions. And such a distinction, while it does actually exist, is neither clear-cut nor readily recognizable.   Virtually every governmental activity within municipal boundaries affects the residents of the municipality and also affects the people of the entire state to some extent.   When a state constitution specifically provides, therefore, that cities shall have authority to exercise all powers of local self-government or all municipal powers—and such clauses are typical of home-rule amendments—the courts must decide what matters are in fact matters of local concern.

Variations in Autonomy

The measure of self-government actually enjoyed by so-called "home-rule" cities varies considerably from state to state.   In California and

---

[11] This list includes Utah, although no Utah city has ever exercised its right to adopt a charter of its choosing.   Pennsylvania is not included, despite a provision in the state constitution authorizing the legislature to grant home rule, because the legislature has never seen fit to do so.   Mention should be made, however, of a 1947 Pennsylvania law conferring broad tax powers on the cities of the state.

[12] Excluding Washington, D.C., which is under the jurisdiction of the federal government.   The residents of the national capital have no voice in their governmental affairs.

Michigan, for example, the cities manage their own affairs, largely free from state interference, whereas in Ohio and Washington the control of the legislature over municipal matters is almost as complete as before the adoption of home rule.[13]   These differences are due partly to variations in the phraseology of the home-rule clause of the state constitution and partly to variations in judicial interpretation.   The supreme court of Ohio has ruled that so-called home-rule cities may not create municipal courts, provide day nurseries for working mothers, establish their own retirement systems for firemen, or even prescribe qualifications for the members of their police forces.

The attitude of the legislature is important, also.   If the legislature of a home-rule state desires to obey the spirit as well as the letter of the constitution in matters of local self-government, the cities have no cause to fear the loss of their autonomy.   If, on the other hand, the legislature is determined to retain control of municipal affairs, it can find ways to evade more or less completely the home-rule section of the constitution, just as it has commonly found ways to defeat the purpose of the prohibition against special legislation.   In recognition of this fact, the constitutions of a few states make the grant of home rule dependent on legislative action.

Legislative Grants of Local Self-government

The legislatures of seven states,[14] in the absence of definite constitutional authorization, have conferred upon cities more or less extensive power of self-government.   Iowa took this step in 1858—seventeen years before the beginning of constitutional home rule.   Most of these "home-rule" laws have proved virtually worthless because of legislative hesitancy to renounce a single important power.   The Mississippi statute, however, vests broad authority in the cities of the state and shows that home rule by legislative grant need not be a contradiction in terms.   In a few states, when the legislatures have attempted to grant municipal home-rule powers, they have been blocked by adverse court decisions.[15]   Otherwise this method of increasing municipal powers might have acquired a considerable degree of popularity.

[13] In 1949 Rodney L. Mott prepared a study of municipal home rule for the American Municipal Association.   This study has been published under the title: *Home Rule for America's Cities.*

[14] Connecticut, Florida, Georgia, Iowa, Louisiana, Mississippi, South Carolina.

[15] See, for example, Elliott *v.* City of Detroit, 121 Mich. 611 (1899); and State *ex rel.* Mueller *v.* Thompson, 149 Wis. 488 (1912).

Steps in Adoption of Home Rule Charter

Municipal home-rule procedure, as established by constitutions and laws, follows the same general lines in all states, though varying somewhat in certain details. The city charter is framed by a commission especially chosen for this purpose.[16] Usually the members of this commission are chosen by the voters, but in Minnesota they are appointed by the district court. When the commission's work is finished, the charter goes to the voters, and must be approved by them—a bare majority usually sufficing for this purpose.

Three states—Arizona, Michigan, and Oklahoma—specify that every home-rule charter must receive the approval of the governor before taking effect; and California requires the assent of the state legislature. But these restrictions on local self-government are not serious, because California's legislature and the governors of the other three states regularly give their assent to charters that have received popular approval. Amendments to home-rule charters are proposed by city councils, or by the people through initiative petitions.

Arguments for and against Municipal Home Rule

The municipal home-rule movement is opposed as a matter of course by those rural politicians who consider it a direct menace to their control of city patronage. It is opposed, also, by some students of government who urge that the field of strictly municipal affairs is too narrow to deserve serious consideration, and that, even within this narrow field, cities need the firm hand of the state to protect them from the corruption and inefficiency of their own officials. These arguments are scarcely worthy of rebuttal.

The list of governmental functions in which the local interest is paramount cannot fairly be called narrow or unimportant. It includes the structure of city government, the salaries, terms, and qualifications of city officials, the methods of awarding contracts, ordinance procedure, the enforcement of charter and ordinance provisions, street cleaning and lighting, fire protection, recreation, water supply, ownership and operation of municipal utilities, zoning, housing, and the construction and maintenance of local streets.

The assertion that state control is needed, even in matters of local concern, is a flat denial that local self-government is possible. Although it is true that city officials are sometimes inefficient and corrupt, the assumption

---

[16] A few states permit city councils to frame new charters, provided the voters approve this arrangement.

should not be made that state officials are always efficient and incorruptible. State legislatures sometimes prevent city councils from using city property and funds for unwise or dishonest purposes, but at other times state control becomes a dangerous instrument of oppression in the hands of unwise or dishonest legislators.   Honors—and dishonors—are probably about even.

There are many arguments for municipal home rule, but the strongest point in its favor is that it is based upon the generally accepted principle of self-determination.   The people of the cities have many interests that they do not share with the people of the rural districts, and simple justice would seem to demand that they be given the right to control those interests in such manner as they may see fit.

The opponents of home rule for cities contend, with some force, that the principle of self-determination can readily be abused—that it can be used to justify the establishment of a separate government for every dissatisfied ward within a city, or every precinct within a ward.   But this danger of abuse does not in any way invalidate the principle.   Almost every desirable reform would prove undesirable if carried to extremes.

Cities are "natural" units for the exercise of governmental functions— "natural" in the sense that they have commonly been created by the play of economic forces.   They are legal entities, too—municipal corporations, as they are designated by law; and sometimes the boundaries established by charter are quite different from the boundaries of the economic area.   But, all things considered, the city is an important unit for the solution of local problems and the satisfaction of local needs, and its right to control its own affairs should not be denied or abridged.

Arguments against County Home Rule

County home rule is sometimes advocated as a desirable reform.   The sponsors of this movement usually reason by analogy: municipal home rule is a proper recognition of the right of local self-government; therefore county home rule is also a proper recognition of that right.   But such an argument ignores the fundamental differences between counties and cities.

Counties are not natural units created by economic forces, nor is the legislature's demarcation of their boundaries merely a recognition of existing fact.   Instead, counties are local areas established by the state for the performance of state functions.   Their boundaries have been fixed more or less arbitrarily.   Their purely local functions have been assigned largely as a matter of convenience.   Therefore the home-rule argument loses a great deal of its force when applied to counties.

Perhaps this consideration has retarded county home rule.   At any rate, it has been adopted by but eight states—California in 1911, Maryland in 1915, Ohio and Texas in 1933, New York in 1935, Missouri [17] and Georgia in 1945, and Washington in 1948. A constitutional amendment conferring a measure of local self-government upon Arkansas counties was invalidated by the supreme court of the state in 1925.

Even in the so-called "home-rule" states local self-government means less freedom for counties than for cities. Thus the section of the California constitution conferring home rule on counties—a section of about four thousand words—specifies a number of matters that must be included in every county charter and even prescribes certain details of organization and procedure.

The Optional Charter Plan as a Substitute

A device for permitting the people to take some part in their local government, without an actual grant of home-rule powers, is known as the optional charter plan. The legislature offers to the cities or counties of the state a certain number of charters, ranging from three to six, which generally include the more important forms of governmental organization. Thus, for cities, the choice may lie among commission government, council-manager government, the weak-mayor plan, and the strong-mayor plan. Each of these charters is fully drawn, and the people of the city or county have no discretion beyond designating the charter that they desire. In New Jersey the law authorizes the people of any city to elect a charter commission, and the commission then decides which of several different types of ready-made charters shall be submitted for popular approval. All states using the optional charter plan have specified that amendments to city charters must be made by act of the legislature—the customary procedure when home rule has not been granted.

The first state to offer a reasonably complete list of municipal charters from which the people of the cities might choose was Ohio, in 1913. Several other states promptly followed suit—New York in 1914, Massachusetts in 1915,[18] Virginia and North Carolina in 1917, and New Jersey in 1950. As early as 1907 Iowa had extended the option of commission government to its first-class cities,[19] and a number of other states have since adopted the optional principle in part for certain cities or classes of cities. In 1951 Illinois extended the option of adopting the manager plan to all cities in the state except Chicago.

---

[17] The county home-rule provision of Missouri's constitution applies only to those counties having more than eighty-five thousand inhabitants.

[18] The provisions of the Massachusetts optional charter law were not extended to Boston.

[19] That is, cities whose population exceeded fifteen thousand.

WEAKNESS OF THE PLAN FOR CITIES. Clearly this scheme is a poor substitute for home rule—at least in cities, where home rule is a vital need. The plan affords an opportunity for each community to determine its structure of government, but nothing more. Local powers and duties are prescribed by the legislature, often with little regard for local sentiment.

SUITABILITY FOR COUNTIES. In the field of county government, however, the optional charter plan still serves a definite purpose. It conforms to the specifications set up long ago by two careful students of local government—that any grant of power to counties "should stress their freedom to elect the form of governmental organization rather than freedom in the exercise of governmental powers." [20]   Seven states [21] have adopted the optional charter plan for counties, and the constitutions of a number of other states permit its use.

Veto by Cities of Special Legislation

In 1904 Illinois amended its constitution to confer upon the people of Chicago the right to veto special legislation relating to that city. "No [special] law . . . affecting the municipal government of the City of Chicago," declared the amendment, "shall take effect until such law shall be consented to by a majority of the legal voters of said city voting on the question at any election." [22]   New York had adopted a somewhat similar plan ten years earlier, but the power of veto had been vested in municipal officials instead of the people, and the legislature had been authorized to override the local veto by a simple majority vote. In Illinois, of course, the people of Chicago were given the final word.

This "Illinois plan," as it is sometimes called, was heralded as a sure way to end the constant wrangling between Chicago and the farm-controlled state legislature, but it has failed to meet early expectations. The legislature seldom submits proposals that are acceptable to the metropolis; Chicago voters seldom accept the measures that are offered by the legislature; and the result is usually a deadlock.

EXPANSION OF STATE CONTROL

Reasons for the Movement

During the last few years the movement for a greater degree of local self-government has run counter to a more recent movement for extending the scope of state supervision and control of local affairs. One state restricts

---

[20] Fairlie, J. A., and Kneier, C. M., *County Government and Administration,* p. 76.
[21] Georgia, Illinois, Missouri, Nebraska, North Carolina, North Dakota, Virginia.
[22] Art. IV, Sec. 34.

the sphere of city or county authority while another expands it. Even within a single state cross-purposes are at work.

The reasons for the comparatively new development of interest in state supervision are fairly obvious. First, many governmental functions are outgrowing municipal boundaries and require some larger unit of control. The county is seldom properly equipped to assume additional responsibilities; moreover, even county boundaries may be restricted too narrowly to permit adequate performance. Therefore the state must take charge unless it can place complete responsibility in some agency specially created for regional government.[23]

To some extent, at least, the movement for state control has arisen from the desire of local property owners to escape from the crushing tax burden on real estate. As pointed out in a subsequent chapter, the general property tax—essentially a tax on real property, because most forms of personalty escape—is still the mainstay of local governments, whereas the states have developed many new sources of revenue.[24] Therefore a transfer of control from city or county to state, provided it involves a transfer of financial responsibility as well, is likely to lead to a rearrangement of the tax system and some reduction of property taxes. Tax relief has been the avowed goal of the proponents of a number of recently adopted constitutional amendments increasing state control over certain functions.

While it is doubtless true that general property bears an unreasonably heavy share of the total tax burden, this fact should have no weight in deciding the important question of the proper distribution of governmental powers. Tax relief for real estate could be accomplished equally well by unconditional distribution of state-collected funds in greater amounts among the local units of government. This suggestion does not imply elimination of state supervision over such local functions as are generally conceded to require such supervision; it is merely a proposal to separate two logically unrelated subjects—tax relief and state control.

In many instances state control of city and county finances has been established to counteract the more disastrous effects of excessive local borrowing and local mismanagement of public funds. State legislatures have been unwilling to permit the weakening of state credit by insolvent local units, and have taken some drastic steps to forestall such a development.

In North Carolina a local government commission, created in 1931 for the primary purpose of exercising control over local debts, has greatly facilitated the task of refinancing local bond issues. Kansas has a state

[23] For a discussion of such agencies, see pages 229–233.
[24] See page 603.

municipal accounting board, set up in 1935, which controls the auditing of accounts in the larger cities.   In 1937 Iowa adopted the plan—long established in Indiana—of permitting state review of local budgets.   The same year Maine established an emergency municipal finance board and authorized it to take over the fiscal management of virtually bankrupt cities. Kentucky set up a county debt commission in 1938.   In New Jersey a state department of local government has been created, with broad general powers of supervision over city and county finances and additional authority to regulate defaulting local governments.

Many of these laws authorizing state financial control were the product of the economic depression; some of them were said to be temporary.   But there has been no general tendency to repeal them since the end of the depression.   On the contrary, state control has been strengthened in a number of states.

Increase in Administrative Control

Probably the most important reason for the recent development of state control is the improvement of control technique.   Authority to supervise and direct local affairs is being vested increasingly in administrative departments or boards, rather than in the state legislature, though legislative control is still the rule.   Under the plan of administrative control the legislature prescribes merely the broad outlines of policy, leaving the determination of details to administrative officers who presumably possess special qualifications for the task.

Advantages of Administrative Control

The advantages of administrative control are obvious.   First, it supplies an element of flexibility that is urgently needed in state control of local affairs.   It permits separate consideration of each local problem, rather than general treatment under a general law.   Local variations may be approved on the basis of differing local needs.   The other important advantage of administrative control is that it is—potentially, at least—control by experts.   Local health matters are passed upon by the state board of health; local educational programs are scrutinized by the state board of education. In other words, the power of supervision is vested in those persons who ought to be most competent to use it properly.

The widespread use of legislative control in the relations of American states with their local units is often contrasted with the virtual disappearance of such control in Europe.   The nations of Europe, without exception, rely almost entirely upon administrative control of local activities.   The central government grants broad powers to the cities—and usually to the local rural areas; but it appoints its own representatives to supervise local affairs, and make certain that these broad powers are not misused.   Even in England, where Parliament is supreme and grants of power to the boroughs are made piecemeal, the actual responsibility for passing upon borough activities rests with administrative officers of the national government.

In the states of the American Union, though legislative control is still generally used, it has already lost considerable favor.   The pages of this volume are filled with examples of supervision of city and county functions by state boards, commissions, or administrative departments, and this type of supervision may completely replace the legislative variety some day.   But reforms move slowly—especially administrative reforms that lack the dramatic quality of great moral issues.

PROBLEMS

1. Trace the movement for local self-government in some state that has not yet adopted municipal home rule.   What measure of control do the cities of the state exercise over their own affairs?

2. Give five instances of legislative control of cities and five instances of administrative control of cities in your state.

3. What has been the attitude of the courts of your state or of a neighboring state toward classification of cities by the legislature?   Examine the decisions of the state supreme court.

4. What evidences of increasing state centralization can you find in your state? Do you think that this movement is likely to prove stronger than the movement for local self-government?

5. Study the relations of some nearby large city with the county in which it is situated.   Do you find instances of unnecessary duplication or conflicts of authority?

SELECTED REFERENCES

Anderson, William, and Lehman, Bryce E., *An Outline of County Government in Minnesota,* Minneapolis, 1927.

Barclay, Thomas S., *The Movement for Municipal Home Rule in St. Louis,* 1943.

Betters, Paul V., ed., and Others, *State Centralization in North Carolina,* Washington, D.C., 1932.

Brannon, Victor D., *State Auditor and Fiscal Control in Missouri Counties,* Columbia, 1940.

Carr, Robert K., *State Control of Local Finance in Oklahoma,* Oklahoma City, 1937.

Committee on Intergovernmental Fiscal Relations, *Federal, State and Local Gov-*

ernment Fiscal Relations, Senate Document No. 69, Washington, D.C., 1943.

Council of State Governments, *State-Local Relations,* 1947.

Crouch, Winston W., *State Aid to Local Government in California,* Berkeley, 1939.

Dickerson, Milton B., *State Supervision of Local Taxation and Finance in Michigan,* East Lansing, 1944.

Fairlie, John A., and Kneier, Charles M., *County Government and Administration,* Part II, Chaps. IV, V, VI, 1930.

Ford, Robert S., and Goodrich, Kenneth S., *State Supervision of Local Borrowing,* Ann Arbor, Mich., 1942.

Hebden, Norman, and Smith, W. S. *State-City Relationships in Highway Affairs,* New Haven, Conn., 1950.

Jacoby, Neil H., and Others, *State-Local Fiscal Relations in Illinois,* 1941.

Keith, John P., *City and County Home Rule in Texas,* Austin, Texas, 1951.

Kilpatrick, Wylie, *State Supervision of Local Budgeting,* 1939.

———, *State Supervision of Local Finance,* 1941.

Leland, S. E., ed., *State-Local Fiscal Relations in Illinois,* 1941.

MacCorkle, Stuart A., *State Financial Control Over Cities in Texas,* Dallas, 1937.

McBain, H. L., *American City Progress and the Law,* 1918.

———, *Law and Practice of Municipal Home Rule,* 1916.

McGoldrick, Joseph D., *Law and Practice of Municipal Home Rule, 1916–1930,* 1933.

McQuillin, Eugene, *Law of Municipal Corporations,* 2nd ed., 1947.

Mott, Rodney L., *Home Rule for America's Cities,* 1949.

Pontius, Dale, *State Supervision of Local Government; Its Development in Massachusetts,* Washington, D.C., 1942.

Reed, Thomas H., *Federal-State-Local Fiscal Relations,* 1942.

Rhyne, Charles S., ed., *Municipalities and the Law in Action; a Record of Municipal Legal Experience,* Washington, 1949.

Schulz, Ernest B., *Effect of the Contract Clause and the Fourteenth Amendment upon the Power of the States to Control Municipal Corporations,* Bethlehem, Pa., 1938.

Shavely, Tipton Ray, Hyde, Duncan Clarke, and Biscoe, Alvin Blocksom, *State Grants-in-Aid in Virginia,* 1933.

Stout, Randall S., *Recent Trends in State Grants-in-Aid and Shared Taxes,* State College, Pa., 1948.

Tharp, Claude R., *State Aid in Michigan,* Ann Arbor, 1942.

Van de Woestyne, Royal S., *State Control of Local Finance in Massachusetts,* Cambridge, 1935.

Wager, Paul W., *County Government and Administration in North Carolina,* Chapel Hill, 1928.

Wallace, Schuyler, *State Administrative Supervision over Cities in the United States,* 1928.

CHAPTER 4

Federal–Local Relations

Until recent years American cities and counties had few direct contacts with the federal government.   As political subdivisions of the states, created by state law and subject to state control, they turned naturally to their respective state governments for assistance in solving problems that seemed beyond the scope of local authority or the limit of local resources.   During the last few years, however, the direct contacts of the federal government with cities and counties have multiplied rapidly.   This has been especially true in municipal affairs.   In 1875 only fourteen services were performed by the national government for urban communities.[1]   By the turn of the century, however, the number had risen to thirty, and during the next two decades thirty other services were created.   Seventeen more were added to the list by 1930; during the depression years of the 1930's forty-two new activities were begun; and since 1940 dozens of other relationships have been established.   Nor have the old services been abandoned save in a few instances, most of which are relatively unimportant.   There are now more than one hundred agencies of the national government—bureaus, boards, and independent establishments—that maintain direct contacts with the cities, or perform important services that materially affect municipal activities.

INDIRECT FEDERAL SERVICES

Some federal contacts with cities are relatively indirect.   They involve no formal agreements, nor even informal understandings.   In this category are the activities of many national agencies, which collect information concerning local problems and make it available to all interested persons—including, of course, local officials.   Thus the Bureau of the Census publishes an annual volume entitled *Compendium of City Government Finances,* as well as other reports giving preliminary figures or covering certain groups of cities.   The Bureau of Standards, with the aid of representatives of related professional organizations, has prepared a comprehensive series of reports on planning

[1] National Resources Committee, *Urban Government*, pp. 63–64.

and zoning. Its technical specifications have been widely adopted by city purchasing departments. And the school studies and surveys of the Office of Education have proved invaluable to local school officials.

In other federal agencies the story is similar. The Public Roads Administration is continuously engaged in studying street construction methods. The investigations of the Bureau of Mines form the basis for numerous activities of local health departments. Even more significant, in this field, are the studies of the United States Public Health Service. The Bureau of Fisheries and the Bureau of Dairy Industry conduct a surprisingly large number of researches that affect various aspects of local administration. Indirect federal assistance to cities and counties includes flood control by the Army engineers and fire fighting and policing by the Coast Guard.

There are other ways, also, in which the federal government indirectly aids local governments. It has frequently assumed responsibilities that otherwise must have fallen to the lot of state and local officials. During the depression years of the early 1930's, for example, it adopted an extensive program of relief for the able-bodied unemployed. Not only were the states and local communities given direct grants and loans for construction jobs involving relief labor, but in addition they were spared the necessity of caring for millions of workers employed on emergency federal projects.

DIRECT FEDERAL SERVICES

Law Enforcement

Far more important than these indirect relationships, however, are the direct federal contacts with local governments. Thus the Federal Bureau of Investigation of the United States Department of Justice maintains an elaborate file containing the fingerprint records of millions of known criminals. The facilities of this identification system are available to all local law enforcement officers. Local requests for the identification of arrested persons are acknowledged within thirty-six hours, and produce results in most cases. Agents of the F.B.I. (the much-publicized "G-men") co-operate with local police departments in identifying handwriting, firearms, bits of clothing, blood stains, and the like. Closer federal co-operation in kidnaping cases has been assured by the enactment of a law making kidnaping a federal crime if it involves interstate conspiracy or the transportation of the victim across state lines. And similar legislation has extended federal jurisdiction in a number of other fields. It is now a federal offense to rob a federally insured bank (which means, in practice, virtually any public banking institution) or to flee from one state to another to avoid arrest on serious criminal charges.

Since 1930 the F.B.I. has served as a central clearing house for the collection, compilation, and publication of police and crime statistics. Its *Uniform Crime Reports,* a semi-annual bulletin, is based on the information supplied by local police departments.

Co-operation in Many Local Activities

The Library of Congress gives advice to local officials on every phase of library administration, and stresses such technical services as card cataloguing, indexing, and the interchange of books. Bibliographies on a wide variety of subjects are available to local librarians. Several bureaus of the United States Department of Agriculture distribute technical supplies, serums, plants, and trees to cities, and even aid in stocking municipal zoos. Federal-municipal co-operation is involved in surveys of ports and terminals, joint use of ports, and construction of terminal facilities. State and local employment agencies work with the United States Employment Service to reduce the volume of unemployment; in fact, during the Second World War the federal, state, and local employment services were combined. Other examples of co-operation, involving dozens of federal services and practically every aspect of local administration, might readily be added to this list.

Attention to Public Personnel

PERSONNEL STANDARDS. The improvement of local personnel has received the attention of many federal agencies. The United States Civil Service Commission, for example, has studied the requisite qualifications for certain positions in the local service, and has prepared standard tests for the use of city and county officials. It furnishes personnel information to all communities on request, and even conducts examinations for certain cities at infrequent intervals. Many of the federal bureaus charged with the administration of grants to the states demand trained state and local personnel as a prerequisite of federal assistance.

Thus the United States Public Health Service insists that every local government benefiting directly from public health funds must have a properly trained full-time health officer, and an adequate number of assistants possessing at least the minimum requirements of training and experience. These requirements were set up by the Public Health Service in collaboration with the Conference of State and Provincial Health Officers, and assure at least the irreducible minimum of technical competence. Federal grants to the states—and, through them, to the communities—for vocational training and the re-education of disabled persons, are conditioned upon the acceptance of federal personnel standards. The Public Roads Administration, which administers the huge federal grant for state and municipal highway construction, makes no direct effort to control local personnel, but it achieves substantially the same result by passing upon the quality of local construction and maintenance. And some of the federal supervising agencies merely recommend personnel standards, without attempting to enforce their suggestions. The Children's Bureau, for example, suggests that local staffs co-operating in the child health program adopt the standards of their recognized professional organizations, but it continues to co-operate with agencies that ignore this recommendation. Although the Social Security Board is specifically forbidden to deal with the selection of state and local personnel, it can and does require the states to set up suitable qualifications for officers and employees in this field.

FEDERAL TRAINING PROGRAM. In recent years the federal government has greatly improved public personnel standards by providing facilities for the advanced training of certain groups already in the employ of states, cities, and counties. These "in-service" training programs were established, in most instances, for the benefit of federal personnel, but their widespread popularity soon suggested the desirability of permitting local officials and employees to enroll.

In 1934 the courses of the National Police Academy, a training school maintained primarily for the further education of agents of the F.B.I., were opened to a limited number of municipal police officials. Advanced training is now offered in practically all aspects of police work—fingerprint identification, scientific crime detection, use of firearms, report writing, and the like. Several thousand local police officers have completed the general course, and hundreds of others are on the Bureau's waiting list. Only a small percentage of the local law enforcement officers desiring federal training in the National Police Academy can be accepted as students, because of limited facilities. But the Bureau of Investigation assists cities in preparing local in-service training programs, and even assigns its own agents for this work. The Social Security Board offers courses of training for state and local personnel, partly to provide a sufficient background in the general field of welfare and partly to emphasize the necessary special technique. Many other federal agencies hold periodic conferences with local officials, using these opportunities to stress latest developments in their respective fields. And some of the federal bureaus, in training their own personnel, offer courses specially designed to fit staff members for closer co-operation with local communities. Federal funds have been available to cities and counties since 1931 for personnel training.

"CLEAN POLITICS" LAW. In 1940 Congress passed a so-called "clean politics" law, sharply restricting the political activities of those state and local employees who were paid wholly or partly with federal funds.   This statute has been attacked as an unnecessary restriction on the civil rights of public employees, but there is no reason to suppose that it will prevent any legitimate activity.   And it may well reduce the evil effects of partisan politics in local administration.

Financing Street Construction

Federal funds have been made available on a large scale for the construction of city streets.   As early as 1916 the national government inaugurated a policy of aiding the states in highway building, and the annual grant for this purpose had been increased to one hundred and twenty-five million dollars before the worst years of the Great Depression.   But the law specifically stated that not one dollar of federal funds—or of state funds used to match the federal grant—might be used for the construction of city streets.   When, however, Congress made large emergency grants to the states for highway building in 1932, it omitted the usual prohibition against street construction within city limits.   Two years later it permanently removed this restriction; and the reversal of federal policy was made complete when an executive order decreed that one fourth of the emergency highway grants *must* be used for municipal street construction.   Cities now regularly receive slightly more than one fourth of the federal highway subsidy, using most of the money for streets that are connecting links in the state's primary highway system. Several thousand miles of city pavements have been financed, at least in part, with federal funds.

Civil Defense

The part played by cities in the national program of civil defense is discussed in a subsequent chapter.[2]   Reference should be made at this point, however, to the federal grants that are available to cities for various aspects of civil defense.   City officials may request federal assistance in purchasing warning devices, improving their communication systems, obtaining medical equipment, and conducting programs of public information and volunteer training.   It is important, of course, that every city's civil defense plans be co-ordinated with the state program.   The Federal Civil Defense Administration tries to accomplish this result by specifying that municipal requests for federal assistance must be routed through the state civil defense agency.

[2] Chapter 31.

Armory Construction

The local militia known as the National Guard is essentially an aggregation of state forces. State officials are responsible for its organization and for the administration of its affairs, within the fairly rigid limits imposed by Congress. In some cities, however, municipal officials take the initiative in constructing armories or improving existing armory facilities. They may obtain federal financial assistance by providing the land and assuming responsibility for at least twenty-five per cent of the cost of construction. First, however, they must submit each project to state officials and receive their approval. Final action is then taken by the federal government, which makes certain that the local project fits into the general scheme of national defense.

School Lunch Program

Every local school system that is providing lunches for its pupils on a nonprofit basis may receive federal aid. The amount of such assistance varies with the number of meals served and the ability of the local community to pay its own way. At least three state or local dollars must be spent on the school lunch program for every dollar of federal funds. The federal contribution may sometimes take the form of surplus commodities distributed through the United States Department of Agriculture. Arrangements between the nation and the local communities are made through the state department of education.

Federal Adjustment of City Debts

Nearly nine hundred cities defaulted on their debt obligations during the depression of the 1930's. So, too, did large numbers of counties and special districts. They had borrowed heavily, and were totally unable to raise sufficient revenue to meet interest payments. A large majority of the creditors, in many instances, were willing to scale down the principal of the debt in order to prevent the total loss of their investment, but there was no way of forcing minority bondholders into line without impairing the obligation of contracts. In 1934, therefore, Congress enacted a so-called "municipal bankruptcy" act, authorizing insolvent cities and other local units to adjust their financial difficulties in the federal courts. The consent of the state was required in each instance, and also the consent of a certain percentage of the creditors. When, however, this act was tested before the Supreme Court of the United States, it was invalidated in a five-to-four decision, on the ground that it constituted an infringement of the sovereign authority of

the states over their local units.[3]   Justice Benjamin Cardozo, who prepared
the dissenting opinion, expressed his inability to see a limitation of state
sovereignty in a statute which depended for its validity upon the formal consent of every state involved; but the majority of the Court was unimpressed.
Thereupon Congress enacted another "municipal bankruptcy" law, somewhat similar in terms but designed to place greater emphasis on state control.
Many members of Congress who voted for the measure were frankly skeptical
of its constitutionality, but this time the Supreme Court nodded approval,
with but two justices dissenting.   Said the Court:

> Nor did the formation of an indestructible union of indestructible states make
> impossible co-operation between the nation and the states through the exercise
> of the power of each to the advantage of the people who are citizens of both.
> The state acts in aid, and not in derogation, of its sovereign powers.   It invites
> the intervention of the bankruptcy power to save its agency, which the state itself
> is powerless to rescue.   Through its co-operation with the national government,
> the needed relief is given.   We see no ground for the conclusion that the federal
> Constitution, in the interest of state sovereignty, has reduced both sovereigns
> to helplessness in such a case.[4]

The number of cities taking advantage of the "bankruptcy" act was never
very large, but many persons believe that the mere existence of the legislation
had value during the depression years in compelling municipal creditors to
adopt a reasonable attitude.

DIRECT AID TO LOCAL COMMUNITIES

Most federal-local contacts are made through the medium of the state.
Congress, as we have seen, appropriates federal funds to the states for highway purposes, and specifies that part of the money must be used for the construction of city streets.   Co-operative vocational training and public health
programs are prepared by representatives of the states and the national
government, and local officials are invited to participate.   Such arrangements illustrate the traditional pattern of federal-local relations.   There
are, however, numerous examples of direct aid to local governments.

Aid to Congested Areas

Some cities have faced serious problems in recent years because of the
concentration of federal defense activities within their borders.   They have
had to provide additional facilities for thousands of newcomers with virtually
no previous notice and with very little change in their normal sources of

---

[3] Ashton v. Cameron County Water Improvement District, 298 U.S. 513 (1936).
[4] United States v. Bekins, 304 U.S. 27 (1938).

revenue.   The situation first became acute during the Second World War. Many cities that had become centers for war industries experienced in four years the population growth that they might normally have expected in two or three decades.   The population of the San Francisco region, for example, increased forty per cent between 1940 and 1944.   In the same period Mobile had an increase of sixty-seven per cent, and San Diego's population more than doubled.   These communities, and others similarly affected, suddenly found their housing facilities totally inadequate.   Schools were overcrowded, medical and recreational facilities were insufficient, and local transportation systems groaned under the unaccustomed strain.   It was obvious that these war-swollen cities must have outside help in order to prevent a virtual collapse of some of the functions of local government.   Congress responded by authorizing an extensive war housing program in communities designated as congested production areas.   It also appropriated several hundred million dollars to supplement regular municipal funds in maintaining and expanding such regular municipal services as education, police and fire protection, and public health.

Today the situation is less dramatic than in wartime, but it is no less real in many communities.   Federal defense activities still place an unreasonable burden on housing accommodations and municipal services.   In cities thus affected the federal government is willing to lend a helping appropriation.   It pays a part of the cost of new waterworks, sewage disposal plants, streets, hospitals, libraries, and the like.   Under some circumstances it even helps to finance the day-to-day costs of local administration.   City officials who believe that their communities are entitled to such special consideration may apply directly to Washington, without consulting any state agency.

Airports

Congress has authorized the Civil Aeronautics Administration to deal directly with local communities in developing a comprehensive airport program.   Half a billion dollars have been set aside for this purpose, and local governments have been told that they may present plans for the construction and improvement of their airports.   Every local plan meeting federal standards and receiving federal approval will be financed in part with federal funds, though the federal share may not generally exceed one half of the total cost. Congress tried to forestall criticism of this new scheme of direct federal-local relationships by specifying, in the Federal Airport Act of 1946, that local communities might not participate if prohibited by state law from doing so. Over four hundred projects have already been completed, and nearly twenty-four hundred additional airport agreements between the local units and the nation have been signed. But Congress has been slow to appropriate the funds already authorized, and local officials have frequently complained of the stringency of the rules governing federal grants for airports. The future of the program is uncertain.

Housing

Since 1949 Congress has given financial aid to cities in the solution of their housing problems. The federal law provides that any municipality may apply for federal funds if it has a slum area and a master plan for the redevelopment of that area. The plan must include some arrangement for housing the displaced slum dwellers until the new homes are completed. Details of this housing program are considered in a subsequent chapter.[5]

Short-circuiting State Governments

We have already seen that Congress has not hesitated, in periods of emergency caused by war or depression, to make loans and grants directly to local governments for a variety of purposes. And local officials have eagerly welcomed this federal aid as a means of balancing their local budgets. Little by little, therefore, a pattern of direct federal-local relationships is being established. To some extent the state governments are being "short-circuited." Small wonder, therefore, that students of government are tempted to ask whether this newer policy may not prove the entering wedge for extensive federal regulation of local affairs by means of conditional grants from the federal treasury.

FEDERAL RESTRICTIONS ON STATE'S POWER OVER LOCAL GOVERNMENTS

In the preceding chapter it was pointed out that cities and counties are subordinate units of local government. The state may do with them what it pleases, subject only to such restrictions as may be found in the federal Constitution. So we may well inquire what limitations are imposed by this document. At first glance it might seem that the federal Constitution would have no bearing on the relations of the state and its local subdivisions. Every state, of course, is prohibited from passing a law impairing the obligation of contract, but the Supreme Court of the United States has ruled that the charter granted a city or county does not constitute a contract.[6]

[5] See Chapter Twenty.
[6] Mt. Pleasant v. Beckwith, 100 U.S. 514 (1880).

Due Process of Law Clause

There is, however, another clause of the federal Constitution more directly to the point. It is the oft-quoted Fourteenth Amendment, which declares that no state shall "deprive any person of life, liberty, or property, without due process of law." Now municipal corporations, like private corporations, are legal persons. They may own property, they may sue and be sued, they may enter into contracts. Virtually every city does, in fact, own a considerable amount of property. It owns public buildings, parks, and playgrounds, not to mention the public streets. It may own wharves, ferries, or an electric light plant. Is this property free from state interference? Is it covered by the guarantee that property shall not be taken without due process of law? May it be taken only for a public purpose, and with payment of just compensation? Or is it held by the city only at the pleasure of the legislature, to be handed over to state officials or to private interests without compensation, should the lawmakers be so minded?

A COMPLICATED PROBLEM. No simple, direct answer can be given, because the court decisions are neither simple nor direct. The problem is so complicated that perhaps a straightforward answer is impossible. Let us suppose for a moment that city-owned property is given exactly the same protection as privately owned property, and that it is equally beyond the control of the legislature. City streets at once cease to be parts of state highway systems. Anyone who uses them without the consent of the local authorities is a trespasser. City jails no longer fit into the state's correctional scheme. They may be used to house offenders against state law only if city officials are so minded. Such a condition of affairs would be intolerable. We cannot permit local whims to check the flow of commerce or delay the administration of justice, not to mention a score of other matters. Let us, then, go to the other extreme and declare that the state legislature has plenary power over all municipal property. Under such circumstances city waterworks and city parks, purchased with local funds and serving purely local needs, may be handed over to private interests by the state legislature without the requirement that a dollar of compensation be paid. Apparently we have come no nearer doing justice than before.

DISTINCTION BETWEEN PUBLIC AND PRIVATE PROPERTY. In an effort to reconcile the conflicting interests of city and state the courts have made a somewhat vague distinction between the public property and the private property of cities—between property held by a municipality purely as an agent of the state and property held by it in its "private and corporate" capacity. City streets are clearly in the first class; waterworks, gas and electric plants are generally recognized as belonging to the second. But what of parks, wharves, ferries? It must be admitted that the courts of the several states are not in harmony concerning these classes of property. In some jurisdictions they are regarded as public property, but in others they are classed as private. The practical importance of the distinction is that the private property of cities possesses a certain degree of immunity from state interference; their public property does not. A city-owned street railway, for example, may not be taken by the state without payment of compensation.[7] It may be regulated by the legislature as to rates and service, of course, but that would be true if it were privately owned. Streets, on the other hand, are held by cities in their public capacity, and therefore are entirely under state control.

All this is far from satisfactory. It is easy enough to make a distinction between public and private municipal property, but far from easy to apply the distinction. If the judges of the several state courts cannot agree as to the meaning of "property held in a private and corporate capacity," how can laymen hope to define the term? Only one fact stands out clearly—a great deal of city property, perhaps most of it, receives a considerably smaller measure of protection against state interference than is given to the property of private corporations or of individuals.

Equal Protection of the Laws Clause

Since cities are corporations, and therefore legal persons, it is sometimes contended that they are entitled to protection under the clause of the Fourteenth Amendment to the federal Constitution that prohibits every state from denying to any person within its jurisdiction the equal protection of the laws. The courts have ruled, however, that cities are not persons within the meaning of this guarantee. The equal protection clause was never intended to limit any state's control over its civil subdivisions.[8]

PROBLEMS

1. Examine the Bureau of the Census' annual volumes, *Compendium of City Government Finances,* and present a concise statement of the information that they contain.

2. What is the nature of *Uniform Crime Reports,* published by the Federal

---

[7] Exceptions have even been made to this general rule. See City of Boston *v.* Treasurer and Receiver-General, 237 Mass. 403; 130 N.E. 390 (1921). This decision was affirmed by the Supreme Court of the United States in 1922. See 260 U.S. 309 (1922).

[8] See Williams *v.* Eggleston, 170 U.S. 304 (1898), and Mason *v.* Missouri, 179 U.S. 328 (1900).

Bureau of Investigation? What is their value to municipal police departments?

3. Contrast the decisions of the Supreme Court of the United States in the first and second "municipal bankruptcy" cases. What reasons did the court assign for its altered point of view? Do you believe that the changed personnel of the court may have been partly responsible?

4. Write a concise account of the organization and work of the National Police Academy, stressing its services to local governments.

5. Prepare a brief summary of the more important problems that confronted the officials of your city as a result of the Second World War.

SELECTED REFERENCES

Blundred, Robert H., and Hanks, Donoh W., *Federal Services to Cities and Towns*, 1950.

Chatters, Carl H., and Hamilton, Randy H., *Federal Grants and Controls Affecting Municipalities*, 1952.

Civil Aeronautics Administration, *1950 Federal Aid Airport Problem*, Washington, D.C., 1949.

Committee on Intergovernmental Fiscal Relations, *Federal, State and Local Government Fiscal Relations*, Washington, D.C., 1943.

Hamilton, Randy H., and Deming, George H., *Congressional Legislation of Municipal Interest*, 1953.

Miles, Arnold, and Owsley, Roy H., *Cities and the National Defense Program*, Chicago, 1941.

Millett, John D., *The Works Progress Administration in New York City*, Chicago, 1938.

National Resources Committee, *Federal Relations to Research*, Washington, D.C., 1939.

National Resources Planning Board, *Federal Relations to Local Planning*, Washington, D.C., 1939.

Wells, Roger H., *American Local Government*, 1939, Chap. V.

Williams, Edward A., *Federal Aid for Relief*, 1939.

PART TWO

The Organization of State Government

CHAPTER 5

State Constitutions

Every state of the American Union has a constitution—a written document setting forth the fundamental principles by which it is governed. Here is set forth the structure of state government, together with a statement of basic individual rights. Trivial, inconsequential details and matters of a temporary nature may be included also, but always the fundamentals are there. For the constitution of a state is its supreme law, just as the federal Constitution is the supreme law of the entire nation.

Any state legislative act or administrative decree in conflict with the state constitution is therefore void and unenforceable, and the courts will set it aside when properly called upon to do so. Like the federal Constitution, which is above the power of Congress to change, the constitution of a state is beyond the reach of the legislature. It may be altered only by some special procedure, such as the action of an extraordinary majority in the legislature plus popular ratification at the polls.[1]

While the state constitution is supreme within its own sphere, it is necessarily subordinate to the Constitution of the United States within the realm of national authority. It must conform to the federal Constitution, and also to properly enacted federal laws and treaties. The restrictions imposed upon state power by the federal Constitution [2] cannot be swept lightly aside.

ORGANIZATION AND SUBJECT MATTER OF STATE CONSTITUTIONS

Lack of Originality

Among forty-eight state constitutions, designed for as many states whose local conditions and internal problems are widely different, one would naturally expect to find great variations in organization and subject matter. But even a cursory examination is sufficient to show that state constitutions closely resemble one another. The fundamentals are the same in every case;

[1] See pages 84–88.
[2] See pages 22–27.

only the details give any indication of originality. When the framers of a new state constitution begin their task, it seldom occurs to them to question the underlying principles with which they are already familiar. The popularly elected executive, the legislature of two houses, the independent judiciary, the nicely adjusted system of checks and balances—these things are commonly accepted as a matter of course.

Not only do the states borrow ideas from one another; often they copy the exact phraseology of constitutional provisions. Sometimes they do so for the purpose of securing clauses that have already been judicially interpreted, and are therefore comparatively free from the danger of troublesome litigation. In other instances they borrow simply because borrowing is easier than creating new terms. When they copy blindly, the result is almost invariably bad. Constitutional provisions that have proved unworkable in one state and are about to be discarded, sometimes become the model for similar clauses in other state constitutions.

Fortunately, however, such blind copying is becoming increasingly unfashionable. The delegates to nearly all recent constitutional conventions in the more progressive states have been supplied with up-to-the-minute, authentic information concerning the constitutions and governments of other commonwealths, and therefore have been in a position to know the probable effect of any clauses that they might see fit to borrow.[3]

Of course, it must not be assumed that similarity in fundamentals, and even in style, indicates complete uniformity in all details—far from it. Some of the superficial differences among state constitutions are so great that the underlying resemblances are nearly hidden. The governor may have virtually an absolute veto over certain types of legislation, or no veto power whatever. The legislature may meet annually or biennially. The means provided for amending the constitution may be very simple or very complex. The clauses dealing with labor, public utilities, and other matters may vary widely. But these differences do not affect the broad outlines of any state constitution. The fundamentals are accepted by nearly everyone as a matter of course.

It may well be asked, therefore, why the constitution-makers of forty-eight states have displayed so little originality in creating the framework of their governments. In part, at least, their conservatism is explained by the homogeneity of the American people. Possessing substantially the same background, the same culture, the same traditions of government, they have learned to regard the underlying principles as axiomatic. Knowing only one general plan of governmental organization, they have not thought to question

[3] See page 89.

it.   Nor is this at all surprising.   The people of every state read the same magazines, drive the same motor cars, smoke the same cigarettes, wear the same styles of clothing.   Why should they experiment with new fashions in government when the very foundations are involved?

The Preamble

Nearly every state constitution [4] begins with a preamble—a statement of reasons for drafting the document and objects to be attained.   This is almost invariably combined with the enacting clause.[5]   The preamble serves no real purpose, save that it sometimes furnishes the members of the constitutional convention with an opportunity to express their political philosophy.

The Bill of Rights

After the preamble comes the declaration or bill of rights, setting forth the fundamental guarantees designed to protect life, liberty, and the pursuit of happiness.   Every state constitution has its bill of rights, the length varying from fifteen to forty-five provisions.   Usually this part of the constitution is a curious mélange of old theories and new ideals.   Some of the statements most commonly found are lineal descendants of the Declaration of Independence and Magna Carta; others are a product of the modern era of gigantic corporations and quasi-monopolistic public utilities.   Some guarantees are phrased in such general terms that they have little or no significance; some are positively detrimental to the social development of present-day commonwealths; while still others deal with a wide variety of matters that cannot by any stretch of the imagination be classed as fundamental rights.

FREEDOM OF RELIGION.   Among the specific guarantees, freedom of religion has a very important place.   It is mentioned in every state constitution, though in language that varies considerably from state to state.   Thus Michigan specifies that "Every person shall be at liberty to worship God according to the dictates of his own conscience.   No person shall be compelled to attend, or, against his consent, to contribute to the erection or support of any place of religious worship, or to pay tithes, taxes, or other rates for the support of any minister of the gospel or teacher of religion." [6]

Clauses such as these are frequently coupled with other provisions designed to insure even more fully the complete separation of church and state.   Civil and political rights may not be denied on account of religious beliefs; no religious test may be required as a qualification for public office; jurors and

---

[4] There are three exceptions—New Hampshire, Vermont, and West Virginia.
[5] Delaware's constitution is the only exception.
[6] Constitution, Art. II, Sec. 3.

witnesses may not be disqualified because of their religious views.   Two states [7] even make ministers of the gospel ineligible to membership in the legislature.   Grants and donations to sectarian institutions are prohibited by the constitutions of twenty-four states.

On the other hand, some commonwealths provide transportation to parochial schools at public expense, or reimburse parents of Catholic children for school carfare already paid.   This arrangement has been challenged as a form of preferential treatment for Catholics, but the Supreme Court of the United States has said that it merely assures equality of treatment for all persons, regardless of their religious belief.[8]   Many state constitutions specifically prohibit religious instruction in the public schools.   Even in those states where no such prohibition exists, religious teaching in school buildings violates the provisions of the federal Constitution.   A few years ago, when the board of education of an Illinois school district made provision for the religious instruction of students in their classrooms, but only upon the written request of their parents, the Supreme Court of the United States ruled that this plan was an unconstitutional use of tax-supported property for religious purposes.[9]   Three years later New York City adopted a somewhat similar plan, but with the important difference that the religious instruction was given in churches or other private buildings.   The Supreme Court upheld this arrangement on the ground that it was not a use of public property for sectarian purposes but merely an adjustment of school programs to outside religious instruction.   Said the Court: "We cannot read into the Bill of Rights . . . a philosophy of hostility to religion." [10]

State constitutions still provide some curious examples of religious intolerance.   The preambles of the fundamental laws of Arkansas and Mississippi, for example, though specifying that no religious test shall be required as a qualification for public office, declare in subsequent clauses that no person who denies the existence of God shall serve as a public official.   Six other states [11] also require every officeholder to declare his belief in God, and two of these [12] demand in addition an expression of belief in a future state of rewards and punishments.   Eventually such clauses will doubtless be

---

[7] Maryland and Tennessee.

[8] Everson v. Board of Education of the Township of Ewing et al., 330 U.S. 1 (1947).

[9] Illinois ex rel. McCollum v. Board of Education of School District No. 71, Champaign County, Ill., 333 U.S. 203 (1948).

[10] Zorach v. Clauson, 343 U.S. 306 (1952).   See Frank Bowen's article, "The New York Released Time Program," in the Michigan Law Review, June, 1952, pp. 1359–1367.

[11] Maryland, North Carolina, Pennsylvania, South Carolina, Tennessee, Texas.

[12] Pennsylvania and Tennessee.

stricken from all state constitutions, but at present they still serve as a reminder of days when religious intolerance was everywhere accepted as a matter of course.

PROTECTION OF LIFE AND LIBERTY.   The bills of rights of state constitutions contain a large variety of provisions designed to prevent governmental interference with life and liberty.   Every person accused of crime shall be entitled to a speedy public trial; he shall have opportunity to confront witnesses against him and to summon witnesses in his own behalf.   He shall be permitted to obtain his release on bail unless a capital offense is charged, and if convicted he shall not be subjected to cruel or unusual punishment.   He shall not twice be put in jeopardy of life or limb for the same offense.   *Ex post facto* laws [13] are commonly prohibited; so, too, are bills of attainder.[14] The privilege of the writ of *habeas corpus* [15] may not be suspended.[16]   Protection against unreasonable searches and seizures, a guarantee that had no practical significance for a long period of years, subsequently acquired considerable importance during the most active period of prohibition enforcement.   Many state constitutions declare the right of jury trial to be inviolate and then violate the declaration by specifying in other clauses that jury trial may be dispensed with under certain circumstances.[17]

The constitutional provisions that afford protection to persons accused of crime have been subjected to a great deal of adverse criticism in recent years. It is frequently pointed out that they seriously handicap the state in its fight against professional criminals.   Broad guarantees designed to shelter the innocent from the arbitrary acts of capricious officials have become the means of escape for thousands of wrongdoers.   Murderers, thieves, bribe takers, racketeers have learned how to make effective use of constitutional and legal technicalities.   It seems clear that bills of rights should be so amended as to eliminate all unnecessary technicalities, while continuing to furnish the substance of necessary protection to persons wrongfully accused of crime.

PROPERTY RIGHTS.   State bills of rights also contain provisions intended to safeguard the ownership of property.   Private property may not be taken

[13] For a definition of an *ex post facto* law, see footnote 36 on page 22.

[14] Bill of attainder is defined in footnote 35 on page 22.

[15] A writ of *habeas corpus* is a writ, issued by a court of competent jurisdiction, directing that a prisoner be brought before it, in order that it may determine whether he is lawfully detained.   This writ is a safeguard against arbitrary imprisonment.

[16] Some of the more recent state constitutions make this prohibition absolute; the older constitutions generally follow the federal Constitution by adding "unless when in cases of invasion or rebellion the public safety may require it."

[17] For a discussion of recent modifications of the original rule of jury trial, see pages 176–177.

or damaged for public use without just compensation; private property may not be taken without due process of law. These guarantees have been strictly enforced by the courts. Sometimes it is said that the judiciary is more interested in upholding property rights than in preserving human liberty. At any rate, private property has received its full measure of protection under the terms of both federal and state constitutions.

THE RIGHTS OF FREE SPEECH AND A FREE PRESS. Clauses guaranteeing freedom of speech and of the press are found in all state constitutions. Like other rights, they are conditioned upon their proper use. They do not confer the privilege of slandering at will, nor do they assure freedom from libel suits. Yet the line between use and abuse of free speech is admittedly difficult to draw. In 1946 a man named Terminiello insisted upon addressing a public meeting in Chicago, despite the fact that hundreds of protesting pickets were gathered outside the building. While the police tried to hold the pickets in check, Terminiello hurled epithets at his opponents. "Filthy scum" was one of his mildest terms, and he used many other "fighting words." At last he was arrested for disturbing the peace, and found guilty by the courts of Illinois. On appeal, however, the Supreme Court of the United States reversed his conviction, on the ground that every man should be free to speak his mind, even if his words aroused fury in his listeners.[18] But three years later, in another Chicago case, the Supreme Court upheld the conviction for libel of a man who used extremely violent and fanatical language in his demands for segregation of Negroes.[19]

In wartime, when the undivided loyalty of all classes is urgently required, the guarantees of free speech and press are likely to receive a narrow interpretation. The important case of Schenck v. United States,[20] which was decided a number of years ago but never overruled, illustrates the viewpoint of the courts. "The most stringent protection of free speech," declared the Supreme Court of the United States, "would not protect a man in falsely shouting fire in a theatre, causing a panic. We admit that in many places and in ordinary times the defendants, in saying all that was said in the circular, would have been within their constitutional rights. But the character of every act depends upon the circumstances in which it is done. . . . When a nation is at war many things that might be said in time of peace are such a hindrance to its effort that their utterance will not be endured so long as men fight, and that no court could regard them as protected by any constitutional right."

[18] Terminiello v. Chicago, 337 U.S. 1 (1949).
[19] Beauharnais v. Illinois, 343 U.S. 250 (1952).
[20] 249 U.S. 47 (1919).

This and similar decisions have led some persons to declare that freedom of speech and of the press are merely peacetime rights, having no significance after the outbreak of war, but the courts have carefully pointed out that such is not the case. All the guarantees of individual liberty remain in force in time of war as in time of peace; their exact meaning may undergo a transformation, however, when war is declared.

IRRELEVANT PROVISIONS. The newer state constitutions include in their bills of rights many provisions that have no place in any recital of fundamental principles. There are clauses concerning lotteries, lobbying, dueling, pensions, slavery, contempt of court, tenure of office. Maryland, for example, sees fit to include in its declaration of rights a statement that Annapolis shall be the meetingplace of the legislature, and also affirms that "monopolies are odious, contrary to the spirit of a free government and the principles of commerce, and ought not to be suffered." [21] The inclusion of such provisions in a list of basic rights is sheer folly.

The Structure of Government

Following the bill of rights are found the clauses dealing with the structure of government. One article is commonly devoted to the legislature, one to the executive department, and one to the judiciary. In these sections are specified the officials of the state, how they are to be selected and how they may be removed, their terms of office, qualifications, powers, and duties. Some constitutions even fix the salaries of state officials, instead of leaving that matter to the legislature. Legislative procedure is commonly prescribed in considerable detail.

The doctrine of the separation of powers, inherited from a political theory long since discredited, is solemnly enunciated as a matter of course, the phraseology varying but little from state to state.

SEPARATION OF POWERS. In the closing quarter of the eighteenth century, when the first state constitutions were framed, men actually believed that the public business could best be administered by putting every branch of the government into a separate, power-tight compartment, so that power could not possibly flow from one to the other. With every public· official thus forced to adopt a policy of magnificent inaction, the danger of wrongdoing would be reduced to a minimum.

This theory proved unsound and unworkable, however, when put into practice. During the last century and a half Americans have gradually been learning that they must concentrate authority in order to prevent the diffusion of responsibility. They have rejected many of the implications of

[21] Arts. 11, 41.

the doctrine of the separation of powers, especially in the more progressive states. But the doctrine, in very explicit language, still has a prominent place in most state constitutions, even though, as one commentator remarked a number of years ago, it "is rapidly falling into a condition of harmless senility." [22]

OTHER PROVISIONS. After the structure of government has been covered in sufficient detail, the state constitution commonly devotes itself to a variety of other matters. As a rule there are articles dealing with finance, education, labor, corporations, local government. Since these matters are to be considered at length in subsequent chapters, we may pass on to the clauses dealing with constitutional amendment and revision. Amendment, in this connection, is used to indicate the making of specific changes without altering the general purport of the document; revision is the process of general overhauling. Amendments may be required at rather frequent intervals; revision should only occasionally be necessary.

Amendment

The men who framed the first state constitutions did not distinguish clearly between amendment and revision. They specified that all changes should be made by the legislature, as in Delaware, Maryland, and South Carolina; [23] or by constitutional conventions specially chosen for the purpose, as in Georgia, Massachusetts, and Pennsylvania; or else they failed to provide any method of altering the fundamental law, as in nearly half of the thirteen original states. At the outset there seemed to be no good reason to indicate more than one way of changing the constitution. [24]

TWO METHODS OF ALTERATION. After several decades, however, it became obvious that one method would not suffice. A constitutional convention could best accomplish the task of complete revision; but one or two specific changes, however urgent, would scarcely justify the calling of a special convention. As early as 1790 South Carolina recognized two methods of altering its constitution—convention and legislative action. Though Delaware did likewise two years later, no other state followed South Caro-

[22] James Q. Dealey, *Growth of American State Constitutions*, p. 264.

[23] The process of legislative amendment differed from ordinary lawmaking, however. Delaware required an extraordinary majority; so did Maryland; and South Carolina specified that "no part of this constitution shall be altered . . . without the consent of a majority of the members of the Senate and House of Representatives"— as distinguished from a mere majority of those present.

[24] A state employing the convention method of making amendments might, however, provide two ways of calling the convention. Thus the Pennsylvania constitution specified that a convention might be called by the legislature or by the council of censors—a body of men chosen every seven years for the primary purpose of determining "whether the constitution has been preserved inviolate in every part."

lina's example for nearly half a century. Then, about 1835, it became common practice to authorize both methods of constitutional change. More than half of the state constitutions adopted between the years 1835 and 1885 provided for amendment by legislative action and also by constitutional convention—the legislative mode to be used in most cases, and the convention reserved for those rare occasions when a few specific amendments would not suffice.

REVISION METHODS IN VARIOUS STATES.   Today thirty-five states authorize both types of change, and most of the others use both methods on occasion, though not explicitly empowered to do so.   In fact, there is now only one state—New Hampshire—that has no discretion as to the method of altering its constitution.   By express provision of its fundamental law it must rely on constitutional conventions; the legislature is given no authority to propose changes.   Rhode Island is one of eleven states whose constitutions make no reference to the calling of a constitutional convention.   In the other states of this group, however, conventions have been called from time to time without express constitutional sanction, and the absence of constitutional provisions on the subject has been regarded as immaterial, especially in view of the fact that the work of conventions must usually be submitted to the people for their approval.   But the Rhode Island supreme court ruled, in 1883, that a convention might not be held for the purpose of amending the state's constitution, so that Rhode Island was obliged to rely solely on legislative action until 1935, when the highest tribunal reversed its earlier stand.[25]

Frequent reference to amendment by action of the legislature must not lead to the assumption that the legislature has a final voice in the matter. In some of the earlier constitutions, it is true, the legislature was given complete power to frame and adopt amendments, although by some extraordinary procedure that would serve to emphasize the important distinction between constitutional provisions and ordinary legislation. Thus the Maryland constitution of 1776 specified that no change should be made "unless a bill so to alter, change, or abolish the same shall pass the general assembly, and be published at least three months before a new election, and shall be confirmed by the general assembly, after a new election of delegates, in the first session after such new election." *General assembly* was, and still is, the official designation of the Maryland legislature. The requirement of action by two successive legislatures was thought to be a satisfactory means of securing popular control. The intervening election would afford

[25] Following the court's change of front, the state legislature, in January, 1936, ordered a referendum on a call for a convention, but the proposal was defeated at the polls.

the voters an opportunity to elect senators and representatives who adequately expressed their views, so that the action of the new legislature might be considered the direct result of a popular mandate.

Popular ratification. This plan, or some modification of it, was adopted by a number of states; Delaware still uses it. South Carolina gives the people an opportunity to vote directly on amendments proposed by the legislature, but amendments approved at the polls do not go into effect without further legislative action.[26] The legislature, therefore, makes the final decision. But these commonwealths are exceptional. In forty-six states the vote of the people is conclusive.

As early as 1818 Connecticut introduced the plan of popular ratification of amendments. Every amendment, before adoption, must be passed at two successive sessions of the legislature and then approved at the polls. The next year Maine simplified this procedure by requiring the action of but one legislative session, followed by a popular vote. The Maine plan was not immediately popular, however. As the states in increasing numbers provided for popular ratification of amendments, most of them followed Connecticut's lead by requiring action at two sessions of the legislature prior to submission to the people.

Nor is this at all surprising, for the trend of the times was in the direction of a more difficult amending process. Until the latter part of the nineteenth century it was assumed, almost as a matter of course, that the sanctity of the fundamental law ought to be preserved by placing obstacles in the way of change. Clauses were adopted requiring the concurrence of three fifths or two thirds of the legislature, or specifying that an extraordinary majority of the voters must approve, or limiting the number of proposals that might be made at any one legislative session. State constitutions were the basis of the whole scheme of state government, and the statesmen of the mid-nineteenth century were determined that they should not lightly be altered.

Simplification of amendment procedure. Toward the end of the century, however, the increasing length and complexity of state constitutions made necessary easier methods of amendment. The so-called "fundamental laws" were rapidly degenerating into detailed manuals of legislative and administrative procedure—a movement that is still under way;[27] and all the details placed in the newer constitutions of that day could not well be left unchanged for long periods of years. So the amending process was simplified in many states.

The present trend is distinctly in the direction of an easy amending process.

[26] Constitution of South Carolina, Art. XVI, Sec. 1.
[27] See pages 92–94.

Fourteen states, led by Oregon in 1902, permit proposal of amendments by a certain percentage of the voters; such proposals then become part of the constitution when duly ratified at the polls, without the necessity of receiving the legislature's approval. This device is known as the *initiative*. Though its exact form varies somewhat from state to state, the underlying principle is everywhere the same.

The first step in initiating a constitutional amendment is to prepare a petition, together with the exact text of the proposal. The petition must then be signed by a portion of the electorate—either a specified number of voters, as in North Dakota, where twenty thousand signatures are required; or a certain percentage of the total vote cast for the governor or some other state officer at the preceding election, as in Nebraska, where the percentage is fixed at ten. California and Oregon require but eight per cent.[28] After the proper number of signatures has been obtained, the petition is presented to the appropriate state official—usually the secretary of state—who places the proposed amendment upon the ballot at the next election. A simple majority of those voting on the proposal is sufficient for adoption in most states that use the initiative for amending their constitutions.[29] The merits and defects of the initiative as a method of changing state constitutions need not be discussed at this point, since the entire problem of direct legislation is considered at some length in a subsequent chapter.[30]

Retention of cumbersome methods in some states. Although the tendency of the times is to simplify the procedure of constitutional amendment, there are still many states that insist on retaining the old, cumbersome forms. About one fourth of all the states require action by two successive legislatures before an amendment may be submitted to the people. About one fourth specify that the approving popular vote must be more than a bare majority of those voting on the amendment.

Some of these states, and some others also, limit the number, frequency, or character of proposals that may be submitted for popular consideration. Kansas, for example, prohibits the submission of more than three propositions to amend at any single election.[31] Tennessee forbids the legislature to propose amendments to the constitution oftener than once in six years.[32]

---

[28] Massachusetts restricts the use of the initiative in a number of ways. See the Massachusetts constitution, Art. XLVIII of the amendments.

[29] There are some exceptions, however. See, for example, the constitution of Nebraska, Art. III, Sec. 4, which requires for adoption of an amendment not only that a majority of the votes cast on the amendment must be favorable to it, but also that these favorable votes must be at least 35 per cent of the total number of votes cast at the election.

[30] See pages 330–334.

[31] Constitution, Art. XIV, Sec. 1.

[32] Constitution, Art. XI, Sec. 3.

New Mexico declares that certain sections of its constitution dealing with education and suffrage may not be amended except by a very large majority, both in the legislature and at the polls.[33]   Limitations such as these are found in the constitutions of ten states.   Most of them were adopted a number of years ago and will probably be amended or repealed when it is more generally realized that they serve only to hamper the work of the state.

CONSTITUTIONAL CONVENTIONS

State constitutions deal with many matters of transitory importance. They include numberless details that have no place in the fundamental law. Their text often indicates careless or inexpert draftsmanship.   It is not at all surprising, therefore, that complete constitutional revisions are necessary from time to time.   As already suggested, specially chosen conventions are well fitted for this purpose.[34]   Unhampered by the routine of ordinary legislation, they can bend all their energies to the single task of framing a satisfactory scheme of government.   Six state constitutions specifically declare that the question of holding a constitutional convention shall be submitted to the people at periodic intervals, ranging from seven to twenty years.   In the other states conventions may be called when necessary; but the legislature determines in the first instance whether such necessity exists. In a few states the legislature's decision is conclusive; much more commonly, however, the voters must also approve the suggestion that a convention be called.

Preliminary Steps

When a proposal to hold a constitutional convention is made and approved, numerous details must be agreed upon, unless they have been prescribed in advance by the constitution.   The number of delegates and the manner of their choice; their qualifications and compensation; the rules of procedure that are to guide their deliberations—these things cannot be left to chance.   Only three state constitutions, those of Michigan, Missouri and New York, cover these matters so completely that all need for supplementary legislation is eliminated, but the constitutions of a number of other states deal with one or more phases of the convention and its work.   Details

[33] Constitution, Art. XIX, Sec. 1.

[34] There have been a few instances, however, of practically complete constitutional revisions prepared by legislative action.   In 1928 the people of Virginia approved a new constitution framed in this manner.   The legislature of New Jersey, sitting as a constitutional convention by express authorization of the voters, drafted a new constitution in 1944, but this document was defeated at the polls.   Four years later the New Jersey voters accepted a somewhat similar constitution prepared by a convention.

not included in the constitution are commonly prescribed by law, though such matters as procedure may be left to the judgment of the convention itself.

Prior to the gathering of the delegates it is customary, in the more progressive states, to compile a considerable amount of necessary information: the present constitution of the state, clause by clause, together with judicial interpretations, governors' veto messages, and opinions of attorneys-general; constitutions of other states, with necessary comments; pamphlets dealing with important problems that are likely to occupy the time of the convention.[35] There are many states, however, in which no work of this sort has ever been attempted, so that the constitutional conventions called from time to time are seriously handicapped. The delegates cannot possibly take time from their deliberations to collect the comparative data on which their judgments should be based, and the lack of this essential information inevitably leads to unfortunate mistakes that could easily have been avoided.

The members of a constitutional convention are popularly elected. Usually they are chosen by districts, the districts established for the selection of state senators or state representatives being used for this purpose; but election at large, either for all the members or some of them, is not unknown. They may be chosen along party lines, or on a nonpartisan ticket. Elimination of the party ballot would seem to be desirable, for it is obvious that the constitution of a state should not be framed in the interest of any political party.

Committees

The convention varies in size from a membership of one hundred to three hundred or even more, the number usually bearing some relation to the number of members of the state legislature. Regardless of these variations, however, the convention is always too large to permit intensive examination of every proposal by all the members.

Committees, in which most of the work of the convention is done, are therefore necessary; and one of the first tasks of the convention, after it has chosen a president or speaker and other necessary officers, is to divide its membership into appropriate committees. Although there should be one committee for each important subject considered, which usually means a total of about twenty, the number, in actual practice, has varied from four to thirty-nine. Each member of the convention is usually assigned to two

[35] Among the states that have recognized the need for preliminary collection of information are Illinois, Massachusetts, Michigan, Missouri, Nebraska, New Hampshire, New Jersey, New York, and Ohio.

or more committees.   There is a general tendency to make committees too large; committees of twenty or even twenty-five members are not uncommon.   The inevitable result is an impairment of their efficiency.

The personnel of committees may be determined by the presiding officer, or by a specially selected committee on committees.   Each committee considers in detail its allotted subject—education, suffrage, the judiciary, or whatever it may be.   Many public hearings are held.   It is in committee meetings that most important decisions are made, and most of the provisions of the new constitution are welded into form.   The committees of a constitutional convention, however, are not usually given complete power of life and death over proposals, as are many legislative committees, but generally must make a report to the convention on every proposal.   As a result, committee members have no opportunity to dispose of suggestions that they dislike by the simple process of dropping them into the wastebasket.

CONSIDERATION OF COMMITTEE PROPOSALS.   As each proposed article reaches the floor of the convention it is considered in some detail and amended as many times as may seem necessary.   Adequate opportunity for discussion at this stage of the proceedings is desirable, and constitutional conventions usually begin their deliberations with virtually no restrictions on debate.   If the minority resorts to obstructive tactics, however, freedom of debate is likely to be limited.   At best a convention cannot hope to complete a thorough overhauling of the constitution in less than two or three months, and considerably more time may be needed.   Quite naturally, therefore, dilatory tactics are frowned upon.

EDITORIAL COMMITTEE.   At some time during the course of the proceedings every proposal that seems at all likely to receive the approval of the convention should be referred to an editorial committee, so that it may be drafted in proper form.   Though virtually every convention has such a committee, its importance varies.   In some cases it acts as a central clearing house for all suggestions, ruling out inconsistencies in thought as well as carelessness and awkwardness in phraseology.   In other instances its work is restricted virtually to proofreading.

Members of some conventions have expressed the fear that the editorial committee may seize too firmly the reins of power and mold the new constitution to its own desires under the guise of eliminating clumsy phrases and contradictory ideas.   Nevertheless, the experiences of a number of states demonstrate clearly that a convention without a powerful, well-organized, and well-informed editorial committee can seldom hope to produce a satisfactory constitution.

Popular Approval of Constitution

It has already been pointed out that the finished work of the convention is customarily submitted to the people for their approval, even though fewer than half of the state constitutions require this procedure.   In a number of the Southern states, it is true, constitutional revisions are still adopted from time to time without any formal expression of popular opinion; this was done in Louisiana in 1913 and again in 1921.   But such instances serve only to emphasize how nearly universal has become the practice of securing a vote of the people.   Usually the convention's work is submitted as a whole to the voters; sometimes, however, it is presented in the form of a series of amendments, so that an expression of popular opinion may be obtained on each separate proposal.

CONSTITUTIONAL REVISION COMMISSIONS

The complete revision of a state constitution by means of a constitutional convention is often a cumbersome process.   Several years may elapse between the first proposal for a convention in the state legislature and the final approval by the voters of the convention's handiwork.   Moreover, constitutional restrictions may prevent the prompt calling of a convention, even though the need for constitutional reform is obvious.   Under such circumstances the legislature or the executive, or both branches of the state government, may decide to create a commission for the purpose of studying the constitution and making recommendations as to needed changes.   Such commissions are not authorized by state constitutions—but, on the other hand, they are not forbidden.   And, since they are purely advisory bodies, there can be no legal objection to their activities.

A number of states have made use of constitutional commissions in recent years.   Commission members have been drawn from the legislature, the administrative departments, the courts, and even from private life.   Usually they have been chosen by the governor or the legislature.   In size the commissions have ranged from three members to thirty-eight.   Sometimes they have been told to recommend any desirable changes in the fundamental law; in other instances they have been instructed to limit themselves to a consideration of some one constitutional problem, such as judicial organization or city-state relations.   Their finished product has taken the form of reports, usually submitted to the legislature.   And there the matter has ended, of course, unless the legislature wished to take further action.

The principal value of the constitutional commission is its effect on public opinion.   If it conducts well-publicized hearings, and if its final report is widely circulated, it may be able

to inform the people of the need for amendment or revision, to develop a greater public understanding of constitutional issues, and to furnish suggestions that can serve as the basis for action by the legislature or even by a convention. One careful student expresses the opinion that if these educational services were not of considerable value, the record of the commission in recent years would merit a harsh judgment.   Persons seriously interested in thoroughgoing revision will do well to avoid the commission unless they have no alternative or unless they use it simply to prepare the ground for a constitutional convention.[36]

INCREASING LENGTH OF STATE CONSTITUTIONS

The men who framed the earlier state constitutions, and also the Constitution of the United States, clearly understood that the fundamental law should be restricted to *fundamentals,* and not choked with details.   Chief Justice Marshall stated the matter quite simply when he declared: "A constitution, to contain an accurate detail of all the subdivisions of which its great powers admit, and of all the means by which they may be carried into execution, would partake of the prolixity of a legal code, and could scarcely be embraced by the human mind.   It would probably never be understood by the public.   Its nature, therefore, requires that only its great outlines should be marked, its important objects designated, and the minor ingredients which compose those objects be deduced from the nature of the objects themselves." [37]   But this principle has long since been forgotten. Present-day constitutions have indeed acquired almost "the prolixity of a legal code."   They are filled with wearisome details that should be left to the discretion of the legislature.   Every decade they become longer and more involved.   And thus they become virtually unintelligible to all except the constitutional lawyers.

Transitory Nature of Many Provisions

To some slight extent the increasing length of state constitutions can be traced to the development of modern civilization.   The urgency of regulating new means of transportation, new businesses, new professions; the necessity of assigning to the state functions formerly performed by private initiative, or not at all—these things have led naturally to constitutional expansion. In some instances, also, new social policies have been written into the fundamental law to prevent the courts from declaring them unconstitutional.   But

[36] "Revision by Commission," in the April, 1951, issue of the *National Municipal Review*, p. 206.
[37] McCulloch *v.* Maryland, 4 Wheaton 407 (1819).

STATE CONSTITUTIONS

	Year Adopted	Estimated Length in Words	Number of Amendments Adopted
Alabama	1901	39,899	95
Arizona	1912	15,642	34
Arkansas	1874	21,500	42
California	1879	72,000	372
Colorado	1876	23,095	56
Connecticut	1818	6,741	47
Delaware	1897	13,409	20
Florida	1887	30,000	96
Georgia	1945	25,000	11
Idaho	1890	13,492	53
Illinois	1870	13,838	8
Indiana	1851	7,816	18
Iowa	1857	7,997	19
Kansas	1861	8,052	40
Kentucky	1891	21,500	15
Louisiana	1921	184,000	302
Maine	1820	10,302	75
Maryland	1867	23,300	70
Massachusetts	1780	28,760	81
Michigan	1909	14,055	52
Minnesota	1858	15,389	76
Mississippi	1890	15,302	32
Missouri	1945	30,000	4
Montana	1889	17,409	23
Nebraska	1875	11,677	65
Nevada	1864	16,657	50
New Hampshire	1784	10,900	94
New Jersey	1948	12,500	
New Mexico	1912	15,158	32
New York	1894	19,036	127
North Carolina	1876	8,861	28
North Dakota	1889	17,797	60
Ohio	1851	15,417	71
Oklahoma	1907	35,360	35
Oregon	1859	18,000	92
Pennsylvania	1874	15,092	53
Rhode Island	1843	6,500	32
South Carolina	1895	30,063	220
South Dakota	1889	34,337	57
Tennessee	1870	8,190	
Texas	1876	23,671	110
Utah	1896	13,261	29
Vermont	1793	5,759	40
Virginia	1902	23,101	87
Washington	1889	14,650	28
West Virginia	1872	14,928	24
Wisconsin	1848	10,517	56
Wyoming	1890	14,603	13

Reprinted, with permission, from *The Book of the States, 1954–55.*

the overwhelming majority of new articles, new sections, new clauses serve only to interfere with the normal functions of the legislature.   They deal with matters that are not fundamental and certainly not permanent.

It is not surprising, therefore, that state constitutions permitting of easy change have been altered with bewildering frequency.   The constitution of California, an extreme example, has been amended nearly four hundred times since its adoption in 1879.   In some states, of course, the amending process is so difficult that frequent change is practically impossible.   Proposals written into the constitutions of these commonwealths are therefore assured of some degree of permanence; but no assurance can possibly be given that they will continue to meet the need that led to their adoption. Many present-day constitutional provisions are simply reminders of conditions long past—ghosts whose fingers wrap themselves inexorably about the throat of progress until they choke it into insensibility.

As a rule the state constitution contains a schedule—an article making detailed arrangements for putting the new scheme of government into effect. This article is merely of temporary importance,[38] and for that reason it might seem advisable to place it after the ratification clause, so as to keep it entirely separate from those articles that deal with more permanent things. But instead it commonly becomes the concluding section of the constitution, thus burdening the fundamental law with additional matters of transitory concern.

PROBLEMS

1. Examine the constitution of your state, and make a list of the sections dealing with matters that might, in your judgment, be regulated more satisfactorily by the legislature.

2. If you were drafting a bill of rights for a present-day constitution, what rights would you include as essential to the welfare of the people of the state?

3. Compare the constitution of your state with the National Municipal League's model state constitution.   Note the outstanding differences.

4. How many times has the present constitution of your state been amended since its adoption?   Note the nature of the changes that have been made.

5. Contrast the policies of a number of states in gathering information for the use of constitutional conventions.   Note especially the careful preparations of Illinois (1920), Missouri (1943), New Jersey (1947).

6. Examine the debates of a recent state constitutional convention.   Can you discover economic motives for the attitudes of the various members?

[38] In some constitutions, however, permanent matters are improperly placed in the schedule.   Thus the schedule of the Illinois constitution provides (Sec. 18) that "All laws of the State of Illinois and all official writings, and the executive, legislative, and judicial proceedings, shall be conducted, preserved and published in no other than the English language."   Certainly this clause is intended to have more than temporary effect.

SELECTED REFERENCES

Bebout, John, *The Making of the New Jersey Constitution,* Newark, 1945.

Bridgmen, R. L., *The Massachusetts Constitutional Convention of 1917 . . . ,* 1917.

Council of State Governments, *Constitutional and Statutory Provisions of the States,* 5 vols., 1944–1946.

Dealey, J. I., *Growth of American State Constitutions,* 1915.

Dodd, Walter F., *Revision and Amendment of State Constitutions,* Baltimore, Md., 1922.

Erdman, Charles R., Jr., *The New Jersey Constitution of 1776,* Princeton, 1929.

Faust, Martin, *Manuals for the Constitutional Convention of Missouri,* Columbia, 1943.

Frothington, Louis Adams, *A Brief History of the Constitution and Government of Massachusetts,* 1925.

Green, Fletcher Melvin, *Constitutional Development in the South Atlantic States, 1776–1860; A Study in the Evolution of Democracy,* Chapel Hill, N.C., 1930.

Hicks, John D., *The Constitutions of the Northwest States,* University of Nebraska Studies, Vol. XXIII, Nos. 1 and 2, 1925.

Hoar, R. S., *Constitutional Conventions; Their Nature, Powers, and Limitations,* 1917.

Howe, Mark de Wolfe, *Cases on Church and State in the United States,* Cambridge, 1952.

Illinois Legislative Council, *Problems of Constitutional Revision in Illinois,* Springfield, 1942.

Illinois Legislative Reference Bureau, *Constitutional Convention Bulletins,* Nos. 1, 3, 15, Springfield, 1920.

Kettleborough, Charles, *Constitution-Making in Indiana: A Source Book of Constitutional Documents, with Historical Introduction and Critical Notes,* 3 vols., Indianapolis, 1916–1930.

———, ed., *State Constitutions,* Indianapolis, 1918.

McCarthy, Sister M. Barbara, *The Widening Scope of American Constitutions,* Washington, D.C., 1928.

O'Rourke, Vernon A., and Campbell, Douglas W., *Constitution-Making in a Democracy,* Baltimore, 1943.

Shambaugh, B. F., ed., *The Constitution of Iowa,* Iowa City, 1935.

Swisher, Carl Brent, *Motivation and Political Technique in the California Constitutional Conventions, 1878–1879,* Claremont, 1930.

CHAPTER 6

State Executives

The Constitution of the United States declares that "the executive power shall be vested in a president. . . ."[1] State constitutions do not go so far, however; they merely vest in the governor the *supreme* or *chief* executive authority. This distinction is more than a matter of terminology. It indicates a fundamental difference between the offices of president and governor. The president of the United States possesses all the executive power of the national government; he appoints the administrative officers, including heads of departments; he supervises their work to the extent that time and inclination permit; and he dismisses them at his pleasure. Although the confirmation of the Senate is necessary for most important appointments, it is not required for dismissals. Thus the president wields a tremendous influence over the conduct of national affairs. In administrative matters his word is law.

RESTRICTIONS ON THE GOVERNOR

In contrast with the president, the governor of a state finds the scope of his executive power narrowly restricted. He is commonly forced to share control over state administration with a number of other officials who, like himself, are popularly chosen. This group is generally composed of the secretary of state, the treasurer, the auditor or controller, the attorney-general, and the superintendent of public instruction. Sometimes others are also included, whereas in a few states the list of independently elected officers is materially reduced.

These officers are not responsible to the governor. They owe him no debt of gratitude for their selection; and they have no fear that he will remove them, since their tenure of office is fixed by the constitution. Occasionally they co-operate with the governor for the sake of party harmony or administrative efficiency, but much more commonly they disregard his wishes, and he has no way of compelling obedience.

[1] Art. II, Sec. 1, Cl. 1.

Some state constitutions authorize the governor to require regular reports from the heads of the independent administrative departments, and a few governors have tried to mold this power into a real instrument of control by demanding detailed statements of expenditures and complete accounts of activities.   In most cases, however, the reports received have been so vague that they have proved practically worthless from the standpoint of effective supervision.   Moreover, the few defects occasionally revealed by such reports have usually remained uncorrected, because the elected department heads have flatly refused to accept gubernatorial leadership.

Appointments

In recent years the appointing power of the governor has been materially increased.   Although the elective administrative offices have been retained in most states, a large number of additional departments, boards, and commissions have been created by constitutional amendment or, more commonly, by statute; and the power to fill these offices has usually been vested in the governor.   New activities of state government have led to new state agencies, so that the list of offices filled by appointment of the governor is now quite long.

Yet even this measure of appointing authority is subject to certain restrictions.   Senate confirmation of important nominations is required in most states, though not in all.   Fixed and overlapping terms, sometimes extending beyond the governor's own term of office, often make it impossible for him to appoint a majority of board and commission members.   Thus the governor is hampered at every turn, even in the selection of subordinates who are supposed to carry out his wishes.

Removal of Administrative Officers

With regard to the removal of administrative officers the governor is even more seriously handicapped.   He has no general power of removal, such as inheres in the office of president of the United States, but only the authority that may be vested in him by the state constitution or by statute.

Usually he is not permitted to remove the elective department heads; they may be removed from office solely through the cumbersome process of impeachment.   Officers appointed by the governor may be removed by him in many states, but often this power is so hedged with restrictions that its value is nearly destroyed.   Senate approval may be required, with the possibility of making a political issue out of every case; or officers and employees may be guaranteed the right of formal trial before dismissal, thus transforming every such incident into a public spectacle.

The limited removal power of the governor is one of the chief causes of his inability to control state administration. Lacking any effective means of getting rid of inefficient or disloyal subordinates, he must necessarily accept their half-hearted service.

The Results of Divided Responsibility

So restricted are the administrative powers of the governor that he cannot fairly be held responsible for the management of state affairs. Except in the few states that have thoroughly overhauled their administrative organization, only a part of the administrative machinery lies within his control. The remainder is under the direction of independent or semi-independent boards, commissions, and individuals.

The inevitable results of such hydra-headed administration are lack of co-operation, wasteful duplication, neglect or omission of necessary services —in a word, inefficiency; and also divided responsibility which makes it virtually impossible to fix the blame for unsatisfactory conditions. The natural tendency is to hold the governor responsible when things go wrong. He is declared by the constitution to be the *chief executive* of the state; he is the head of the government in name, but not usually in fact. Under such circumstances it is unreasonable to expect efficient state administration.

THE ADMINISTRATIVE REORGANIZATION MOVEMENT

The need for a thorough reorganization of state administration has been recognized, at least by informed persons, for nearly half a century. In 1909 a group of Oregon reformers, who called themselves the People's Power League and whose principal purpose was to fight the predatory activities of certain utility interests, proposed a rearrangement of state administration that would vest in the governor the power to appoint all administrative officers except the auditor. This plan was defeated by the voters of Oregon, but it is significant as a pioneer attempt to reorganize state administration. The next year Governor Hughes of New York proposed the consolidation of existing departments and the strengthening of the governor's power in the interest of greater efficiency.

Soon afterward it became the fashion to create committees or boards for the purpose of studying state administrative organization and recommending needed changes. Studies have now been made and reorganization plans submitted in almost all the states. Some state governments have been surveyed more than once. Many of these plans and surveys have fallen on barren ground. Sometimes they have encountered the opposition of the governor; occasionally they have been defeated by the voters, or have been declared unconstitutional by the courts. But in most cases they have not gone down to complete defeat. Instead they have been

GOVERNMENT UNDER A TYPICAL STATE CONSTITUTION

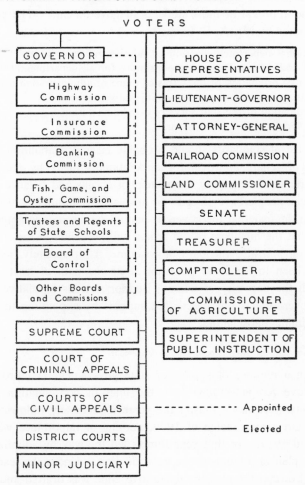

Based on chart prepared by Robert S. Bourn, The University of Texas, and published in the fifth edition (1948) of the National Municipal League's *Model State Constitution*.

whittled away by the opposition forces—usually in the legislature—until they have lost almost all resemblance to the brave reorganization plans originally made by enthusiastic commissions.

Standards of Administrative Reorganization

The suggestions for state administrative reform that have been made during the last three decades, and the discussions that they have aroused, have led to the development of certain standards of reorganization. These standards have been shaped into a definite reorganization program, which receives the approval of most students of government.[2] The program is concisely stated by Mr. A. E. Buck: [3]

1. Functional departmentalization of administrative agencies.
2. Fixed and definite lines of responsibility for all departmental work.
3. Proper co-ordination of the terms of office of administrative officials.
4. Boards undesirable as purely administrative agencies.
5. Co-ordination of the staff services of administration.
6. Provision for an independent audit.

To this list of standards should probably be added abolition of the requirement of senate approval for appointments made by the governor. This requirement is a part of the system of checks and balances in which the American people have placed—or misplaced—so much confidence. It is based on the fear that the governor may make wrong appointments, and the hope that the members of the senate will keep him in the straight and narrow path, and also the path of wisdom. Unfortunately, its principal result has been to force the governor along the path of least resistance. Faced with the necessity of winning support for his legislative program, many a governor has purchased that support by appointing to office the friends of influential senators.

Growth of the Administrative Reorganization Movement

Although a number of studies of state government and proposals for administrative reorganization along the lines of consolidation and fixed responsibility were made during the years immediately following the unsuccessful Oregon campaign of 1909, nothing of importance was accomplished until 1917. In that year Illinois led the way by adopting a comprehensive plan of administrative consolidation. Under the leadership of Governor Lowden the civil administrative code was drafted and adopted.

More than one hundred statutory offices, departments, boards, commissions, and agencies were abolished, and their functions consolidated under nine departments. Each department was placed in charge of a director

[2] There are some dissenters, however. See Marshall E. Dimock's article, "The Objectives of Governmental Reorganization," in the autumn, 1951, issue of the *Public Administration Review,* pp. 233–241.

[3] *Administrative Consolidation in State Governments,* 5th ed., pp. 5–6.

appointed by the governor, with senate approval, for a four-year term. A number of boards and commissions were created within the departments for the performance of quasi-judicial and quasi-legislative duties, but each

GOVERNMENT UNDER THE MODEL STATE CONSTITUTION

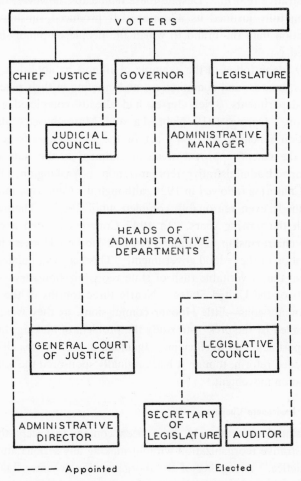

Based on chart published in the fifth edition (1948) of the National Municipal League's *Model State Constitution.*

board and commission was made a component part of the department to which it was assigned. Under the provisions of the administrative code the lines of responsibility were made to extend from the division and bureau chiefs through the heads of departments directly to the governor.

The Illinois reorganization of 1917 was epoch-making. It established a uniform and simplified administrative system.   This plan paved the way for the adoption of consolidation schemes by other states.   Yet it fell far short of the complete reorganization program desired by careful students of public administration and failed to measure up to the highest standards of administrative reform.   Despite these handicaps, however, the reorganization plan fully justified its adoption.   It produced substantially better administration than the brand to which the people of Illinois had become accustomed.

In 1919 Idaho followed the example of Illinois by abolishing more than fifty offices, boards, and commissions, and creating in their place nine consolidated departments.   New Jersey had already completed a partial reorganization.   During 1919 Nebraska and Massachusetts also adopted consolidation schemes, the 1919 act of the Massachusetts general court following the voters' approval of an amendment to the state constitution that authorized administrative reorganization.   Washington, Ohio, Michigan, and California followed in 1921, although the California reorganization was not made even reasonably complete until 1927.   Then came other states with the passing years.   In 1947 Congress created a commission, under the chairmanship of former President Herbert Hoover, to study the reorganization of the federal government.   This act so stimulated the public imagination that a veritable rash of state reorganization surveys broke out in all parts of the United States.   Nearly three fourths of the states soon created commissions—little Hoover commissions, as they were almost invariably called by the press—to study the problem of making state administrative departments more efficient.   Included in the list was Illinois, which clearly needed reform, though it had originally sponsored the administrative reorganization movement.[4]

Reasons for Inadequate Changes

Many states, unfortunately, have been content to accept the principle of administrative reorganization without making any serious attempt to put it into practice.   A number of the reorganization schemes finally adopted and now in effect are so complex—so far removed from the ideal of departmental consolidation and concentrated responsibility—that an understanding of earlier conditions is necessary in order to realize that progress has actually been made.[5]

COMPROMISE.   Not one of the states has adopted an entirely adequate

[4] See Samuel K. Gorie's article, "Reorganization in Illinois," in the November, 1953, issue of the *National Municipal Review,* pp. 502–506.

[5] See Ferrel Heady's article, "States Try Reorganization," in the July, 1952, issue of the *National Municipal Review,* pp. 334–338.

scheme of administrative reorganization.   Failure to go the entire distance along the path of reform is due in part to the need for compromise.   Every reorganization movement has a multitude of enemies.   Those who seem likely to lose prestige, positions, or patronage by the change combine with those who honestly believe that the proposed plan will not serve the public interest; the ultra-conservatives—the defenders of the sacred *status quo*— also join the ranks of the opposition.

These various groups, diverse in viewpoint but united by a common purpose, must be dealt with in some way.   Often it becomes necessary to purchase their partial support with partial abandonment of a carefully devised program.   Thus the plan of reorganization as finally adopted is usually a curious compromise—an amalgam of conflicting ideas.   Small wonder that it so frequently proves a disappointment to everyone!

STATUTORY INSTEAD OF CONSTITUTIONAL REFORM.   Another reason for the inadequacy of consolidation schemes is the general preference for statutory reform, instead of reform through constitutional amendment.   Statutory reform, it must be admitted, has marked advantages.   It is more easily accomplished, requiring only favorable action by the legislature and the approval of the governor.   Unlike an amendment to the constitution, it cannot be blocked by a persistent legislative minority.   No formal expression of approval by the voters is needed and, consequently, no expensive campaign of civic education.   Statutory reform can be put into effect more quickly—a matter of considerable importance to the governor who is trying to make an impressive showing before the expiration of his short term. Quite natural, therefore, is the tendency to rely on statutory changes.   Only a handful of states have changed their constitutions in order to facilitate administrative consolidation; the others have left the fundamental law unaltered.

This unwillingness to change the constitution may be good politics. Statutory consolidation may be an effective means of securing half a loaf of reform from an otherwise bare cupboard.   But the fact remains that thorough administrative reorganization is virtually impossible without constitutional amendment.   State constitutions, almost without exception, scatter the administrative functions of government among a number of independently elected offices, and nothing short of the elimination of those offices or their subordination to gubernatorial authority can produce a completely consolidated administrative system.

FEAR OF ONE-MAN CONTROL.   In the field of state government, *administrative reorganization* and *administrative consolidation* are commonly regarded as synonymous terms.   The only effective way to reorganize is to consolidate the many independent agencies into a few orderly departments under the control of the governor. Some states, however, still clinging to the belief that one-man control is dangerous, have attempted to reorganize without increasing the governor's authority by regrouping their administrative functions under the jurisdiction of a number of boards and commissions. New Jersey, which had gone further than any other state in this direction, relied almost entirely for many years on boards with overlapping terms. Virtually the only effective control over these boards was exercised by a so-called state house commission, of which the governor was merely a member. Then, in 1948, New Jersey completely abandoned its long-established policy, and regrouped the state's ninety-six administrative agencies into fourteen major departments, placing them largely under the governor's control.[6] But other states still use variations of the old-time "New Jersey plan," which New Jersey itself has discarded.[7]

A State Administration

In Minnesota, where two attempts at administrative reorganization have failed to produce entirely satisfactory results, the governor has been aided nonetheless by the creation of the office of commissioner of administration. The commissioner is appointed by the governor, and assumes some responsibility for supervising administrative agencies of the state government that have not been placed beyond the governor's control. Thus the governor has more time to devote to broad matters of policy, as well as legislative, political and ceremonial duties. The commissioner of administration has virtually no appointing power, and almost no authority over the departments whose work he is supposed to supervise. In this respect, of course, he is very different from a city manager, who appoints his department heads and exercises more or less complete control over their activities.[8] But successive governors of Minnesota have made clear that they will support the commissioner of administration, and as a result they have partially escaped the necessity of hearing a large number of appeals from his decisions. Michigan, Rhode Island,[9] and Kansas also have departments of administra-

[6] See C. Wesley Armstrong, Jr.'s article, "Administrative Reorganization in New Jersey," in the December, 1948, issue of *State Government*, pp. 244 ff.

[7] For a thoughtful discussion of some of the problems of the reorganization movement, see "Reflections on State Reorganizations," by John A. Perkins, in the *American Political Science Review*, June, 1951, pp. 507–516.

[8] See pages 212–213.

[9] See the article by John A. Perkins and Frank M. Landers, "Michigan Seeks Better Management," in the September, 1948, issue of *State Government*, pp. 184 ff. See also "Governor Sigler Wins Again," by Loren B. Miller, in the July, 1948, issue of the *National Municipal Review*, pp. 357 ff., and "Rhode Island's Department of Administration," in the February, 1952, issue of *State Government*, pp. 31–34.

tion, created respectively in 1948, 1951, and 1953, but they do not attempt to supervise all the other administrative agencies. Instead they merely assume responsibility for certain important fiscal matters, chiefly budgeting, purchasing, and accounting.[10]

Public Authorities

In many states the reorganization movement has been menaced, at least to some extent, by the spread of a device known as the public authority. This device is often regarded with favor when a state conducts public activities similar to business enterprises. A state may, for example, operate local transportation systems or port facilities or toll roads. Such services are commonly expected to pay their own way, and most people agree that they should be handled along business lines. So why not take them "out of politics"—in other words, remove them as far as possible from the state's regular administrative hierarchy? This result is achieved by placing them in the hands of specially created public corporations, now generally known as public authorities. A public authority is largely autonomous. It has the right to manage its own affairs with very little interference from other agencies of the state, and it even obtains necessary capital funds by selling revenue bonds to private investors, instead of turning to the legislature for appropriations. It is usually supposed to be self-supporting, so the law normally requires it to pay the principal and interest of its bonds from the revenues obtained in the course of its operations. The Montana Toll Bridge Authority, for example, borrows money to build bridges across the Missouri River, and then repays its indebtedness out of the tolls collected.

Public authorities have played a part in the organization of state government for more than half a century, but their extensive use is a development of the last ten years. Today they serve a wide variety of purposes, such as the construction and operation of toll roads and bridges, ports and harbors, terminal facilities, airports, marketing centers, recreational facilities, and power, water, and sewage systems. Some states have even set up public authorities to construct office buildings, schools, and hospitals. The public authorities established by the states are not unlike the special districts so widely used in local government,[11] and they have the same basic weakness —a tendency to cut across the regular lines of orderly administration, thus making the proper supervision and co-ordination of functions very difficult. In New Jersey, for example, the state's responsibility for highways is divided among the state highway department, the New Jersey Highway Authority, and the New Jersey Turnpike Authority. Yet it must be admitted that

---

[10] In Rhode Island the Department of Administration is the state's personnel agency.
[11] See pages 265–269.

public authorities have important advantages. They provide a convenient method of avoiding inflexible debt limits; they encourage the use of business methods in enterprises that are essentially commercial; and, in the case of undertakings involving a number of communities or states, they help to avoid boundary problems.

THE OFFICE OF GOVERNOR TODAY

Selection and Qualifications of the Governor

In virtually all the states the governor is now chosen by direct vote of the people.[12] A plurality vote is commonly sufficient, but Georgia, Maine, Mississippi, and Vermont provide that the winning candidate must receive a majority of all the votes cast. In these states, if no person obtains a majority, the governor is selected by the lower house of the legislature or by the two houses in joint session.[13]

Every state constitution establishes certain qualifications that the governor must possess. He must be a citizen of the United States, and usually he must have resided within the state for a period of years, varying from two to ten. A five-year residence requirement is most common. As a rule he must also have attained a certain age; thirty years is generally accepted, though the range is from twenty-five to thirty-five. In a few states the constitution is silent with regard to age and residence, but the omission has no practical significance, for custom decrees that the governor must be a resident and a person of maturity. Religious qualifications have largely disappeared, although eight states still deny to atheists the right to hold any public office.[14]

Tenure and Salary of the Governor

In recent years the governor's term of office has been materially lengthened. One-year terms, which were once the rule, have entirely disappeared. Massachusetts, the last state to elect its governor annually, made the change in 1918. At present there are twenty-nine states that elect for four years, and nineteen that favor the two-year term. The trend is toward the longer period. Twenty commonwealths impose restrictions of some sort on the number of terms a governor may serve. Most common is a prohibition

[12] Mississippi, the sole exception, has a peculiar arrangement that somewhat resembles the method prescribed by the federal Constitution for selecting the president of the United States.

[13] The two houses in joint session make the choice in Georgia and Vermont. The lower house selects in Maine as well as in Mississippi.

[14] See page 80.

GOVERNORS' TERMS AND SALARIES, 1953

	Length of Term in Years	Number of Previous Terms Served by Present Incumbent	Salary
Alabama	4		$12,000
Arizona	2	1	15,000
Arkansas	2		10,000
California	4		25,000
Colorado	2	1	17,500
Connecticut	4		15,000
Delaware	4		12,000
Florida	4		15,000
Georgia	4		12,000
Idaho	4		10,000
Illinois	4		25,000
Indiana	4		15,000
Iowa	2	1	12,000
Kansas	2	1	15,000
Kentucky	4		10,000
Louisiana	4		18,000
Maine	2		10,000
Maryland	4		4,500
Massachusetts	2		20,000
Michigan	2	2	22,500
Minnesota	2		15,000
Mississippi	4	1	15,000
Missouri	4	1	10,000
Montana	4		10,000
Nebraska	2		11,000
Nevada	4		9,100
New Hampshire	2		12,000
New Jersey	4		30,000
New Mexico	2	1	15,000
New York	4	2	50,000
North Carolina	4		15,000
North Dakota	2	1	9,000
Ohio	2	3	20,000
Oklahoma	4		15,000
Oregon	4		15,000
Pennsylvania	4		25,000
Rhode Island	2	1	15,000
South Carolina	4		12,000
South Dakota	2	1	9,500
Tennessee	4		12,000
Texas	2	1	12,000
Utah	4	1	10,000
Vermont	2	1	11,000
Virginia	4		17,500
Washington	4	2	15,000
West Virginia	4		12,500
Wisconsin	2	1	14,000
Wyoming	4		12,000

Based on information supplied by the Council of State Governments.

against two consecutive terms. Even in those states that have no such limitation, however, re-election is the exception rather than the rule.[15]

The salary of the governor ranges from forty-five hundred dollars a year in Maryland to fifty thousand dollars in New York. Only three other states pay less than ten thousand dollars,[16] and the average is about fourteen thousand. An allowance for expenses is sometimes added, and usually the state supplies an executive mansion for the governor's use.[17] Although the salaries of governors are large, as compared with the salaries of other officers in the state service, they seldom equal the expenses of the office.

A governor is the ceremonial head of his state; he must of necessity live in a rather expensive manner. He is expected to entertain frequently and lavishly. It becomes his duty to welcome distinguished visitors from other states and from foreign countries, and while he is their host he must furnish accommodations befitting their rank. Many a governor thus finds it necessary to supplement his official salary, either by drawing on his private resources or by taking advantage of some of the questionable opportunities for profit that are quite certain to come his way.

Removal of the Governor from Office

The governor may be removed by process of impeachment. It is customary, however, to use this power only when some very serious offense is charged—flagrant abuse of authority, for example, or downright dishonesty. Mere inefficiency is not enough to justify the presentation of charges. As a result, only four governors have been removed from office on impeachment charges since the troubled days of reconstruction following the Civil War.

One of the four—James E. Ferguson of Texas—was subsequently "pardoned" by the state legislature, and then announced his candidacy for the governorship, despite the specific provision of the Texas constitution that an officer convicted in an impeachment trial should be disqualified "from holding any office of honor, trust, or profit" under the state.[18] The Texas supreme court promptly declared the legislature's amnesty act unconstitutional.[19] This case is of more than local interest because most state constitu-

---

[15] On the basis of past experience, a governor's chance of re-election seems to be only slightly better than about one in three. Yet Governor Hunt of Arizona was elected for seven terms, Governor Smith served New York for four terms and Governor Lausche is now serving his fourth term in Ohio.

[16] Nevada and North and South Dakota.

[17] Three fourths of the states now provide their governors with official residences. The original outlay for these residences has ranged from six thousand dollars (North Dakota, 1893) to nearly two hundred thousand (Arkansas, 1950).

[18] Art. XV, Sec. 4.

[19] Ferguson v. Wilcox et al., 28 S.W. (2nd) 526 (1930).

tions similarly prohibit office-holding by persons who have been impeached and convicted. Removal of the governor by means of a recall election is almost unknown, as pointed out in a later chapter.[20]

Powers of the Governor

The powers of the governor, though much more narrowly restricted than the powers of the president of the United States, are extensive and important. In administrative matters the governor is most seriously handicapped; in the field of legislation, on the other hand, his authority and influence are considerable, and constantly growing.

Most of the governor's administrative powers have already been mentioned. He fills by appointment many important state offices, although his nominations must usually receive the confirmation of the senate. He is sometimes authorized by the constitution or by statute to suspend or remove from office persons whom he has appointed. He exercises at least a nominal power of supervision over the entire sphere of state administrative activity. The state constitution usually imposes upon him the duty to "see that the laws are faithfully executed." This clause means very little, however, except to the extent that the governor can make it effective through his powers of appointment, supervision, and removal.

HIS LEGISLATIVE PROGRAM. Although the voters have been loath to extend the administrative authority of the governor, they have looked with increasing favor in recent years upon his leadership in legislative matters. They have learned to expect a "governor's program" of legislation, and to judge the success of each governor on the basis of his ability to secure the legislature's support for his proposals. Quite naturally, therefore, the governors of most of the states have decided that the way to become a successful "chief executive" is to spend less time on executive affairs and more on legislation. Their legislative powers have been strengthened by constitutional amendment, by law, and also by custom; and these powers are usually exercised to the fullest degree.

The legislative program of the governor is usually embodied in his message to the legislature. If he belongs to the same party as a majority of the members of both houses, his road should be comparatively smooth. Some pressure upon party leaders may be necessary; some bargaining may be inevitable; but the governor can usually secure a reasonable degree of co-operation. An open break would benefit no one except the opposition. If the governor and the legislature are of different political faiths, however, it may be necessary to go directly to the people over the heads of the legisla-

[20] See page 338.

tors.   Some governors have done this very effectively.   They have supplemented formal messages to the legislature with widespread newspaper
and radio appeals, and have succeeded in arousing popular sentiment to
such a point that the members of the senate and house have deemed it wise
to fall into line.

HIS VETO POWER.   The governor's power to call special sessions of the
legislature will be discussed in the next chapter.[21]   So, too, will his veto
power,[22] but some reference to the gubernatorial veto should be made at this
point.   Except in North Carolina, where the veto power does not exist,
every bill passed by the legislature goes to the governor for his approval.
He has a certain number of days to make his decision; during the legislative
session this number varies from three to ten, but five days is most common.
Should the governor fail to act within the specified period, the bill becomes
law without his signature—*if the legislature is still in session.*   A bill on
which the governor has written the word *veto* (I forbid) is returned to the
legislature for further consideration.

But when the legislature adjourns before the governor has had time to
decide what his course of action will be, a different set of rules prevails.   In
three states [23] he is required to return every disapproved bill with his objections to the legislature at its next session; bills that are not approved and
not returned become law automatically.   Most of the other states place
a definite time limit, which varies from three to thirty days, upon the governor's post-adjournment deliberations.   During this period his veto is final.

But failure to act also defeats a bill in some states, whereas in the others
inaction is regarded as equivalent to approval.   Those commonwealths that
permit the governor to veto legislation by the simple process of ignoring it
follow the example of the federal government.   The federal Constitution
confers a similar power upon the president.[24]   A veto by inaction is known
as a "pocket" veto; the president or governor disposes of distasteful legislation by pocketing it.

If proposed laws flowed from the legislature to the governor in a steady
and fairly uniform stream throughout the legislative session, the governor's
absolute veto over bills received just prior to adjournment would not be
especially significant.   But the legislature's habit of procrastination, which
results in postponement of final action on nearly all important measures
until the last few days or hours of the session,[25] has greatly enhanced the

[21] See page 134.
[22] See page 151.
[23] Maine, Mississippi, South Carolina.
[24] Art. I, Sec. 7, Cl. 2.
[25] See pages 151–152.

governor's veto power.   Except in a few states it has given him absolute power of life and death over the major part of the legislative program.[26]

The president of the United States has no authority to veto portions of
bills; every bill must be vetoed outright, or not at all.   In thirty-eight of
the states, however, the governor is empowered to veto specific items of
appropriation bills.   He can thus eliminate excessive, wasteful appropriations without jeopardizing the safety of appropriations that are essential to
the proper conduct of state affairs.   Lacking this power, many a governor
would face the unpleasant alternative of vetoing entire appropriation bills
because of certain objectionable features, thus incurring the enmity of the
legislative leaders and probably necessitating an extra session of the legislature, or accepting the good with the bad and signing bills that did not have
his wholehearted approval.

In a few states the governor not only strikes out unwelcome appropriation
items but even reduces items that he deems excessive.   The amount of
the reduction rests entirely in his discretion.   Usually his action is final,
since the legislature has a habit of adjourning as soon as all necessary appropriations have been made.   This plan has worked badly in most states
where it has been adopted.   It has encouraged legislators to please their
constituents by voting for appropriations far in excess of total anticipated
revenues, thus forcing the governor to make the inevitable reductions and
incur the wrath of the interests adversely affected.[27]

In 1889, when Washington was admitted to statehood, its constitution
contained an interesting innovation: "If any bill presented to the governor
contains sections or items, he may object to one or more sections or items
while approving other portions of the bill." [28]   This was, in effect, an extension of the item veto principle to all legislation.   South Carolina adopted
a similar provision six years later.   Ohio, the only other state to try the plan,
abandoned it in less than a decade.

HIS EXECUTIVE BUDGET.   In recent years a substantial majority of the
states have placed upon the governor the responsibility for preparing an
annual program of state expenditures and revenues, and sponsoring his
program before the legislature.   This executive budget, as it is commonly
called, has greatly increased the governor's control over fiscal legislation,
and in some states has made him virtually a fiscal dictator.   The various

[26] See "The Governor as Legislator," by Samuel R. Solomon, in the November, 1951,
issue of the *National Municipal Review,* pp. 515–520.
[27] See M. Nelson McGeary's article, "The Governor's Veto in Pennsylvania," in the
October, 1947, issue of the *American Political Science Review,* pp. 941–946.
[28] Art. III, Sec. 12.

forms of the executive budget, and their effect upon state organization and activities, are discussed at length in a subsequent chapter.[29]

ORDINANCE-MAKING POWER. One of the important sources of the governor's influence is his ordinance-making power. Many of the laws that he is supposed to enforce require supplementary regulations to make them effective. The legislature has purposely left out many details and has authorized the governor to supply these omissions by means of executive orders. Such decrees, when issued, have all the force of law. They are called *ordinances* to distinguish them from the *statutes* or formal acts of the legislature, but statutes and ordinances are alike in their binding effect.

When the legislature enacts a law providing for the payment of state funds to local school districts, it may specify that state payments shall be conditional upon the maintenance of school standards to be established by the governor or one of his subordinates. When the legislature decides upon a policy of conservation of wild animal life, it may authorize the governor to prescribe from year to year the length of the hunting season, the animals and birds that must not be molested, and other related matters. Thereupon the governor—or more commonly, some officer acting in his name and with his approval—issues the necessary regulations. Frequently the executive ordinances supplementing a statute are much more voluminous than the law itself. In many cases they are much more important, because the law is phrased in general terms.

Many state legislatures have acquired the habit in recent years of enacting statutes that contain the barest framework of governmental policy—skeleton or outline laws, as they are often called. The governor or other administrative officers then fill in the details. This method of lawmaking has several marked advantages over the older and still generally used plan of detailed legislation. It conserves the time of the legislature; it insures more flexible administration, because ordinances can be changed to meet changing conditions or to recognize necessary exceptions much more readily than statutes; and it materially reduces the number of unworkable laws, since the details of each statute are fixed through administrative decree by the officer responsible for its enforcement. Yet the legislative assemblies of the states do not make the fullest possible use of the system. They still busy themselves with numerous minor matters that could be handled much more quickly and effectively by ordinance.

The courts have said repeatedly that the ordinance-making power of the governor and other administrative officers is not a power to legislate, but merely to determine the best means of enforcing the law. They have es-

[29] See pages 586–591.

tablished the constitutional principle that the legislature may not delegate its essential legislative function to any other branch of the government. Therefore if executive officers go so far as to determine broad outlines of policy, even when specifically authorized to do so by the legislature, their decrees are void and unenforceable because the legislature is without authority to delegate its lawmaking power. But if executive ordinances are issued merely for the purpose of applying principles that the legislature has established, they will be sustained by the courts. That is sound constitutional theory. In actual practice, however, it is virtually impossible to draw a clear line of demarcation between the establishment of principles and their application.

CONTROL OF THE MILITIA. In every state the governor is the recognized head of the state militia—the National Guard, as it is now known—unless these troops are temporarily in the service of the United States. He is not expected to take personal command, of course; the constitutions of Kentucky and Maryland specifically prohibit him from doing so without the consent of the legislature. Instead he merely exercises a measure of general supervision. He is authorized to call out the militia in order to execute the laws, suppress insurrection, and repel invasion; and for other purposes also in a very few states.[30]

In the early days of American independence state troops were frequently called into service to deal with Indian troubles, and as a result the governor's military power was of considerable importance. But the disappearance of frontier conditions has greatly reduced the need for military activities; today the militia is seldom used except to preserve public order during industrial disputes. Even when mobs of strikers threaten life and property the governor seldom acts until the local authorities admit their inability to handle the situation and appeal to him for aid. This is not invariably the case, however; the governor is the sole judge of the existence of a state of insurrection [31] and may order the militia to assume control despite the protests of local officials.

Occasionally a governor uses his position as commander-in-chief of the state's military forces for the purpose of exercising virtually dictatorial power. Governor Walton of Oklahoma, for example, called out the state militia in 1923 to prevent the members of the legislature from meeting in the state capitol.[32] In 1931 Governor Sterling of Texas and Governor

[30] See, for example, the constitution of Oklahoma, which authorizes the governor to call out the militia to protect the public health. Art. VI, Sec. 6.

[31] *In re* Moyer, 35 Colo. 159; 85 Pac. 190 (1904); Haley *v.* Cochran, 31 Ky. L. Rep. 505; 102 S.W. 852 (1907).

[32] As a result of this controversy the governor was subsequently impeached and convicted.

Murray of Oklahoma placed most of the oil wells of their respective states under martial law in an attempt to increase the price of crude oil.   And three years later Governor Long of Louisiana directed the state militia to seize and stand guard over the New Orleans voting lists, thus insuring the triumph of the Long political machine.   Other governors have used state troops for a variety of questionable purposes, such as the prevention of tax resales by county officers.   But such abuses of the military power are exceptional—and sometimes they fail to hurdle the barrier of constitutionality. Thus the Supreme Court of the United States invalidated Governor Sterling's use of the militia to raise oil prices.[33]

PARDONING POWER.   Until the middle of the nineteenth century the governor had virtually unrestricted power to pardon persons convicted of crime.   This prerogative of the English crown was given to the chief executives of the states and the nation as a matter of course.   Since 1850, however, the restrictions on the governor's pardoning power have become increasingly numerous.   In many states he has been compelled to share his authority with a pardon board; in others he has become merely a member of the board; and in a few he has lost all control over the granting of pardons.[34]

Previous Experience of the Governor

Most of the men who have been elected governors of American states have possessed considerably more than average ability and training.   In recent years, at least, more than half of them have been college graduates. Most of them have stood quite high in the occupational scale—as lawyers, educators, merchants, manufacturers.   It may fairly be said that they have been representative of the better class of business and professional men in their respective communities.

A large majority have held other public office before ascending to the governor's chair.   Most governors lack administrative experience, however, either in public or private life.   This is unfortunate, for it leads naturally to a neglect of administrative duties.   The last few years have witnessed an increasing recognition of the importance of efficient state administration, and it may be that governors of the future will be chosen with greater regard for their proved administrative capacity.   Indeed, the record seems to indicate a slight trend in that direction.[35]

[33] Sterling *et al. v.* Constantin *et al.,* 287 U.S. 378 (1932).
[34] The pardoning power is considered at greater length in a subsequent chapter. See pages 367–368.
[35] See Samuel R. Solomon's article, "U.S. Governors 1940–1950," in the April, 1952, issue of the *National Municipal Review,* pp. 190–197.

The Governor's Council

In four states—Maine, Massachusetts, New Hampshire, North Carolina—
the governor's council still exists as a relic of colonial days. It is composed of a number of persons, ranging from four to nine, whose duty is "to
advise the governor in the executive part of government." [36]   The functions
that it actually performs are not very important.   In the three New England
states its approval is required for certain appointments, and in addition it
deals with some judicial matters.   The North Carolina council of state, as it
is called, is a purely advisory body.   The members of the governor's council
are popularly chosen in Massachusetts and New Hampshire; in Maine they
are chosen by the legislature; and in North Carolina four state officials serve
ex officio.

THE LIEUTENANT GOVERNOR

His Duties

Thirty-seven states make provision for the office of lieutenant governor.[37]
The others do not, and the omission seems to occasion no inconvenience.
After all, the duties of the lieutenant governor are unimportant.   He
has been described as an administrative officer with legislative functions,
but even his legislative functions—which consist solely in presiding over the
state senate and casting a vote in case of a tie [38]—scarcely justify the maintenance of a separate office in the state government.   By far the most important duty of the lieutenant governor is a contingent one and seldom exercised.
It is the duty of serving as governor of the state in case of the governor's
death, disability, resignation, removal from office, or absence from the state.

The exact meaning of "disability," as used in this connection, is not easily
determined.   A few governors, with health shattered, have continued to exercise their authority through trusted subordinates instead of admitting their
infirmities and relinquishing the reins of power.   Nor is it certain, in most
jurisdictions, just how long a governor must be absent from the state before
the lieutenant governor may exercise gubernatorial authority.   Some lieutenant governors have seized upon a few hours' absence as an excuse for
signing bills and pardoning convicted criminals.   Only Alabama attempts

[36] Constitution of Maine, Art. V.
[37] The states that do not have the office of lieutenant governor are Arizona, Florida,
Maine, Maryland, New Hampshire, New Jersey, Oregon, Tennessee, Utah, West
Virginia, and Wyoming.
[38] See page 141.

to solve this problem by specifying exactly how long the governor may be out of the state without being temporarily out of office; under the provisions of its constitution the lieutenant governor acquires the power and authority of the governor's office if the governor is absent for twenty days.

Quite frequently the lieutenant governor is made an ex officio member of numerous boards and commissions; like most ex officio members, however, he usually contributes but little to the work of these bodies. Unless the office of lieutenant governor can be made to fill a more useful place in the general scheme of state government, it should be abolished. A successor to the governor in case of emergency could be provided in some other way. Most of the twelve states that have no lieutenant governors vest the succession in the secretary of state or the president of the senate.

His Qualifications and Tenure

The qualifications prescribed by state constitutions for the office of lieutenant governor are the same as for the office of governor—quite naturally, since the lieutenant governor may succeed to the governorship. The term of office is also the same. The lieutenant governor is elected by the people of the state on the same ballot as the governor and normally belongs to the same political party.

Factional rivalries, however, may result in the selection of a governor and lieutenant governor whose political tenets are greatly at variance, even though both men wear the same party label. Thus, if the conservative element of a party is sufficiently strong to dictate the nomination of its candidate for governor, it may gladly agree to the nomination of a liberal lieutenant governor for the sake of retaining liberal support. It is this possibility of discord between governor and lieutenant governor that has led some observers to suggest that the governor's successor, in case of death, disability or removal, should be an officer whom the governor has appointed.

THE SECRETARY OF STATE

The deep-rooted distrust of the governor, which was a prime tenet of American political life for many years, led naturally to the plan of choosing by popular vote most of the important administrative officials of state government. More recently the governor's prestige and influence have greatly increased, but he must still share with elective officers, in most states, the authority that should properly be concentrated in his hands. One of the most important administrative officers is the secretary of state, who is popularly elected in thirty-eight states, and chosen by the legislature in three others.[39]

His Duties and Selection

Aside from the keeping of state records and the countersigning of proclamations and petitions, there is no general agreement among the states as to what his duties should be.   Usually these duties are prescribed by statute rather than by the constitution, and in recent years they have increased rapidly.   Some states, whenever faced with the necessity of undertaking new activities, assign most of the routine work connected with these activities to the secretary of state.

As a result, this officer is now charged with a wide variety of duties, few of which bear any logical relationship to one another.   He may be the custodian of certain state buildings and grounds, responsible for their maintenance and repair.   He may be charged with the administration of the state's election system.   He may be the official who issues charters to cities and to private corporations, and he may be responsible for the enforcement of laws controlling the sale of securities.   He may supervise the issue of automobile licenses.   Almost certainly his office will involve ex officio membership on numerous boards and commissions.   In every state he performs some of these functions; in many states he performs them all.

His work involves little or no discretion; he merely complies with constitutional or statutory provisions.   It may well be asked, therefore, why the secretary of state should be popularly chosen.   The election of policy-determining officers can readily be justified on the ground that they are expressing the will of the people and therefore should be selected in a manner best calculated to secure a direct expression of the popular will.   But the secretary of state is not a policy-determining officer, no matter how this phrase may be stretched.   His only task is to execute state policy, and for that reason he should be made directly responsible to the state's chief executive—the governor.

His Tenure and Salary

In twenty-seven commonwealths the secretary of state has a four-year term; in the others his term is two years.[40]   His salary ranges from two

---

[39] The three states in which the legislature does the choosing are Maine, New Hampshire, and Tennessee.   In seven other states—Delaware, Maryland, New Jersey, New York, Pennsylvania, Texas, and Virginia—the secretary of state is appointed by the governor, with senate approval.

[40] Except in Delaware, where he serves at the pleasure of the governor.

thousand dollars a year in Maryland to sixteen thousand dollars in Illinois, with an average of about eight thousand.

THE ATTORNEY-GENERAL

His Duties and Selection

The attorney-general is the governor's legal adviser.   He also furnishes legal advice to other state officers and to the legislature and prosecutes or defends cases in which the state has an interest.   A few states give him a measure of supervision over the activities of the local prosecuting attorneys. He is an extremely important cog in the machinery of state administration, for his opinions on constitutional and legal questions often play a decisive part in determining the actions of the governor and other administrative officers.   Thousands of legal problems that are passed upon by the attorney-general never find their way into the courts; in such instances his judgment is conclusive.   Many state agencies—especially the semi-independent boards and commissions—prefer, however, to have their own legal counsel instead of relying on the attorney-general for advice and assistance.   While such an arrangement is sometimes necessary because of the volume of legal business handled by certain agencies, or the highly specialized nature of the problems involved, there can be no doubt that it is often carried to unjustifiable extremes.   The resultant duplication is unfortunate.

Equally unfortunate is the practice of electing the attorney-general, yet the constitutions of forty-one states provide for his selection in this manner.[41]   A former governor of Indiana forcefully stated the case for appointment when he declared: "The attorney-general is necessarily the legal arm of the executive; upon him must the governor depend for carrying forward many of the acts of his administration, and the appointment should be made by the governor. . . . I do not believe that we will be treading on dangerous ground if we give to the next chief executive of Indiana . . . the right to choose his own legal adviser, a right enjoyed by every citizen of our land, a right accorded the mayor of every city in our state and by every other executive officer from the president of the United States down to the most unassuming county commissioner." [42]

[41] Five states—Connecticut, New Hampshire, New Jersey, Pennsylvania, and Wyoming—provide for appointment by the governor, with the advice and consent of the senate.   In Maine the choice is made by the legislature, and in Tennessee, by the supreme court.

[42] Quoted in *Illinois Constitutional Convention Bulletins*, p. 694.

His Salary and Tenure

The compensation of attorneys-general is relatively high. Five states pay annual salaries of fifteen thousand dollars, and the average for all the states is about ten thousand. Terms of office are longer than for most administrative officers. Tennessee provides a term of eight years; New Hampshire specifies five years; and more than half of the others have established four-year terms.[43]

THE TREASURER

His Duties

The state treasurer is the custodian of state funds; he has no important policy-determining functions. He pays out state money from time to time, but only in accordance with law, and elaborate safeguards have been set up to prevent him from making improper disbursements. Every expenditure must be authorized by some administrative official, and in addition must be approved by the auditor or controller, who makes certain that a sufficient sum has been appropriated by the legislature for this purpose, that the appropriation has not already been spent, and that all necessary formalities have been observed. Thus the treasurer has no discretion in the matter; he merely pays out money from the state treasury when directed to do so by proper authority. Virtually his only opportunity to exercise discretion is in the selection of banks as depositories of public funds.

His Selection

Since the treasurer's duties are chiefly ministerial and routine, there seems to be little justification for his election by the people. The line of reasoning that justifies gubernatorial appointment of the secretary of state and the attorney-general applies with equal force to the state treasurer. If the governor is to exercise a reasonable measure of control over state administration, he must certainly be the dominant figure in the field of state finance, for administrative control without financial control is virtually a contradiction in terms.

Yet only two states—New Jersey and Virginia—authorize the governor to appoint the state treasurer. Three commonwealths—Maine, New Hampshire, and Tennessee—provide for selection by the legislature, and in New

[43] The information concerning salaries, terms and method of selection of attorneys-general, as well as many other state officials, is obtained from *The Book of the States,* 1954–55.

York a department of taxation and finance performs the treasurer's functions; elsewhere the treasurer is chosen by popular vote.

THE AUDITOR

His Duties and Selection

Some provision must be made for auditing the accounts of state officials, so as to reduce the likelihood of peculation and insure proper respect for the usual constitutional declaration that "no money shall be drawn from the treasury except in pursuance of an appropriation made by law." This task of auditing state accounts is commonly assigned to an officer known as the auditor or controller.

In most states [44] it is recognized that the auditor should be permitted a considerable degree of independence and that he should not be dependent for tenure or salary on the governor or other administrative officers whose records he must examine. After all, an audit of executive accounts by someone politically subservient to the chief executive would smack too strongly of self-audit. A large majority of the states have attempted to solve the problem of securing adequate independence for the auditor by providing that he shall be popularly chosen; in two states [45] his term of office is longer than that of the governor. Six states,[46] however, specify that the auditor shall be chosen by the legislature. In Great Britain and most of the countries of continental Europe the auditing officials hold office on the basis of judicial tenure, but no state of the American Union has been willing to go so far.

Administrative Functions

No valid objection to the auditor's freedom from gubernatorial control can possibly be made, if the auditor continues to devote his entire time and attention to his primary task of investigating accounts. His duties in this connection are inquisitorial rather than administrative, and their proper performance should not be endangered by the possibility of unreasonable interference.

In recent years, however, has appeared an unfortunate tendency to burden the state auditor with a number of additional functions that are quite clearly administrative. Thus some states make him responsible for the supervision of banks and building and loan associations, while others direct him

[44] The only exceptions are Georgia, Florida, Maryland, and Wisconsin.
[45] Minnesota and Ohio.
[46] Georgia, Maine, Nevada, New Jersey, Texas, and Virginia.

to administer the inheritance tax law, dispose of swamp and other undesirable public lands, and serve as an ex officio member of numerous administrative boards and commissions.

The governor has an interest in the proper performance of these additional functions of the auditor, because they are an integral part of the administrative activities of the state; yet he is denied the right of supervision on the ground that the auditor is an investigator whose independence must be protected. The remedy for this anomalous situation is not to place the auditor under gubernatorial control, but to take from the auditor his administrative duties and permit him to devote his entire time to his main task of inspecting public accounts.

Duplicate Auditing by Governor

A few states, recognizing the need for centralized financial control, have vested in the governor authority to make his own inspections of the accounts of state officials; these inspections necessarily duplicate the work of the auditor. Thus the State of Arizona has an examiner appointed by the governor with senate approval, in addition to the popularly chosen auditor. Montana, Washington, and Wyoming have also adopted this plan.

THE SUPERINTENDENT OF PUBLIC INSTRUCTION

Every state has an officer who is known as superintendent of public instruction, superintendent or commissioner of education, or something of the sort. Regardless of the title, his duties are always much the same— to administer the school laws of the state, apportion the state school funds among the local jurisdictions, and exercise a measure of supervision over local school authorities.

In twenty-six states he is chosen by the voters. Six states [47] provide for his appointment by the governor, and in the other sixteen [48] he is selected by the state board of education—a board whose organization and work are discussed in a later chapter.[49] The folly of permitting the electorate to select an officer whose work is chiefly advisory, supervisory, and clerical, and whose technical qualifications are of the highest importance, should be obvious; yet the superintendent of public instruction remains an elective officer in more than half of the states.

[47] New Jersey, Ohio, Pennsylvania, Rhode Island, Tennessee, Virginia.

[48] Arkansas, Colorado, Connecticut, Delaware, Idaho, Iowa, Maine, Maryland, Massachusetts, Minnesota, Montana, New Hampshire, New York, Texas, Utah, Vermont.

[49] See page 443.

OTHER ADMINISTRATIVE OFFICERS AND AGENCIES

Every state has a considerable number of administrative officers in addition to the secretary of state, the attorney-general, the treasurer, the auditor, and the superintendent of public instruction.   Among the more common are the adjutant-general, the director of public health, the director of welfare, the director of public works, and the director of agriculture.

The picture is further complicated by numerous boards and commissions dealing with virtually every phase of state activity.   These various agencies differ so widely from state to state with regard to organization, functions, and jurisdiction that no attempt will be made to describe them at this point. Some are appointed by the governor; many are not.   The general result is unco-ordinated, headless administration, woefully defective according to sound standards of organization and procedure.

AN EXECUTIVE CABINET

In the federal government, the heads of the major departments usually meet with the president at regular intervals for a discussion of important public policies.   This group—the president's cabinet, as it is called—is a purely advisory body, whose opinions the president is free to accept or reject; but its combined wisdom often proves valuable in the solution of complicated problems of government.

A similar gathering of state department heads at frequent intervals should be an outstanding feature of state government; in the majority of states, however, it cannot readily be arranged, because the heads of the most important departments are independent of the governor, and in many cases are not even on friendly terms with him.   A number of states have recently reorganized their administrative systems, vesting in the governor authority to select the heads of nearly all departments, and thus making possible a governor's cabinet.[50]   The governors of most of these states regard the cabinet idea with indifference, however, and scarcely ever call their department heads together for joint discussion.

PROBLEMS

1. How many bills have been vetoed by the governors of your state during the last twenty years?   In how many instances have these vetoes been overridden by the legislature?

2. Study the operation of the governor's power of item veto, as found in your state or a neighboring state.

[50] See pages 98–104.

3. What is the extent of the governor's removal power in your state? How freely does he exercise that power?

4. Does the governor of your state regularly act on the recommendations of members of the legislature in making appointments? To what extent does the senate refuse to approve nominations made by the governor?

5. How many times has the National Guard of your state been called into active service during the last twenty years? For what purposes has it been called?

6. Study the organization of the state auditor's office in your state. Does the present auditing procedure seem reasonably satisfactory?

SELECTED REFERENCES

Alexander, M. C., *Development of the Power of the Executive in New York,* Smith College Studies in History, Northampton, Mass., 1917.

Barth, Harry A., *Financial Control in the States with Emphasis on Control by the Governor,* 1923.

Black, Henry Campbell, *The Relation of the Executive Power to Legislation,* Princeton, N.J., 1919.

Cheek, Roma S., *The Pardoning Power of the Governor of North Carolina,* Durham, 1934.

Council of State Governments, *Emergency War Powers of the Governors of the Forty-eight States,* 1942.

———— *Public Authorities in the States,* 1953.

Faust, Martin L., *Manual on the Executive Article for the Missouri Constitutional Convention of 1943,* Columbia, 1943.

Friedman, J. A., *The Impeachment of Governor William Sulzer,* 1939.

Governors' Conferences, *Proceedings,* 1909—(published annually).

Illinois Legislative Reference Bureau, *Constitutional Convention Bulletin No. 9,* Springfield, 1920.

Jensen, Christen, *The Pardoning Power in the American States,* 1920.

Lipson, Leslie, *American Governor from Figurehead to Leader,* 1939.

MacMillan, Margaret B., *The War Governors in the American Revolution,* 1943.

Patterson, R. F., *The Office of Lieutenant Governor in the United States,* Vermilion, S.D., 1944.

Porter, Kirk H., *State Administration,* Chap. II, 1938.

Ransome, Jr., Coleman B., *The Office of Governor in the South,* University, Alabama, 1951.

Rohr, Charles James, *Governor of Maryland; A Constitutional Study,* Baltimore, 1932.

Ruscowski, Casimir W., *The Constitutional Governor,* 1943.

Scace, Homer E., *The Organization of the Executive Office of the Governor,* 1950.

Smith, Alfred E., *The Citizen and His Government,* Chap. IV, 1935.

United States Army Service Schools, Ft. Leavenworth, *Military Aid to the Civil Power,* 1925.

CHAPTER 7

State Legislatures

Every state has a legislature, which is almost invariably composed of two houses. During the early years of American independence three states experimented with single-chambered legislatures; but Georgia abandoned the unicameral plan in 1789, after using it for a little more than a decade, and Pennsylvania followed its example the following year. Vermont retained its unicameral legislature for nearly half a century, finally discarding it in 1836. The bicameral principle was not again successfully challenged until 1934, when Nebraska approved a constitutional amendment creating a one-house legislature.

SIZE OF LEGISLATURES

Wide differences are found in the size of the state legislatures. The senate varies from a membership of seventeen in Delaware and Nevada to sixty-seven in Minnesota; the lower house has an even greater range—from thirty-five in Delaware to four hundred in New Hampshire. The average membership is slightly less than forty for the senate, and about one hundred and twenty for the house of representatives. Most state senates, therefore, are small enough to be genuine deliberative bodies. In a group of forty or forty-five persons it is possible for everyone to participate in debate and take a reasonably active part in shaping group policies. But it can scarcely be said that the lower houses of the state legislatures are true deliberative bodies. Most of them are entirely too large to permit full expression of opinion by the rank and file of the members, and for that reason they possess some of the characteristics of a mob. Little cliques of seasoned veterans find it relatively easy to secure control and bend the majority to their will.

THE MEMBERS OF THE LEGISLATURES

Terms

In the early days of statehood, when the memory of English tyranny was still fresh, annual elections were considered essential, in order that government might be kept close to the people, and that elected representatives might be constrained at frequent intervals to remember the source of their authority.   The first constitutions of the thirteen original states provided, with only one exception,[1] that members of the lower house should hold office for but a single year, and several of them specified that state senators should also be elected annually.

Belief in frequent elections was so strong that the principle was written into several bills of rights and has not since been deleted from some of them. Thus the present constitution of Maryland declares that "elections ought to be free and frequent." [2]   New Jersey did not abandon annual elections for members of the lower house until 1947.   Four states [3] now provide four-year terms.   The other forty-three states [4] elect the members of the house of representatives or house of delegates—whatever it may be called —for two-year periods.   Terms of four years for state senators are now found in thirty-two states, while all the others fix the terms of senators at two years.   The old notion that annual elections are a necessary part of free government has practically disappeared.

Since state senators are commonly chosen for longer terms than the members of the lower house, and therefore are better able to familiarize themselves with the process of government, it is sometimes thought desirable to insure a measure of continuity in their service of the state.   This purpose is achieved by providing that only one fourth or one half of the entire membership of the senate shall retire at each election, instead of permitting the terms of all the members to expire simultaneously.   The plan has been adopted by nearly half of the states.

Although this arrangement acts as a check upon capricious and ill-considered reversal of public policy, it has the serious disadvantage of retaining in office men who may have lost the confidence of the people. Thus a newly elected house of representatives, with a fresh mandate from the voters, may find difficulty in carrying out its program because of the opposition of senators whose party has been severely defeated at the polls.

[1] South Carolina.
[2] Declaration of Rights, Art. 7.
[3] Alabama, Louisiana, Maryland, and Mississippi.
[4] Not counting Nebraska's one-house legislature, which is officially known as the senate.

LEGISLATIVE TERMS AND SESSIONS, 1953

| | Length of Term | | Sessions | |
	Senate	House	Time	Limit
Alabama	4	4	Bien.	36 days
Arizona	2	2	Ann'l	60 days
Arkansas	4	2	Bien.	60 days
California	4	2	Ann'l	120 days
Colorado	4	2	Ann'l	30 days
Connecticut	2	2	Bien.	5 months
Delaware	4	2	Bien.	None
Florida	4	2	Bien.	60 days
Georgia	2	2	Bien.	70 days
Idaho	2	2	Bien.	60 days
Illinois	4	2	Bien.	None
Indiana	4	2	Bien.	61 days
Iowa	4	2	Bien.	None
Kansas	4	2	Bien.	60 days
Kentucky	4	2	Bien.	60 days
Louisiana	4	4	Bien.	60 days
Maine	2	2	Bien.	None
Maryland	4	4	Ann'l	90 days
Massachusetts	2	2	Ann'l	None
Michigan	2	2	Ann'l	None
Minnesota	4	2	Bien.	90 days
Mississippi	4	4	Bien.	None
Missouri	4	2	Bien.	150 days
Montana	4	2	Bien.	60 days
Nebraska	2	..	Bien.	None

Qualifications

Every state constitution specifies that members of the legislature must be residents of the state, and of the district from which they have been chosen. The minimum period of state residence ranges from one to seven years; one or two years meets the district residence requirement. American citizenship is also required—sometimes in explicit terms, but more commonly by implication. Age limits vary from twenty-one to thirty years for members of both houses. Twenty-one years is the most common minimum for members of the lower house, however, and twenty-five years for members of the senate. Eight states exclude atheists.[5] Persons convicted of crime are commonly denied the right to hold any public office.

Salaries

The salaries of state legislators are ridiculously small. Seventeen states pay by the day, the compensation for each day of the legislative session rang-

[5] Arkansas, Maryland, Mississippi, North Carolina, Pennsylvania, South Carolina, Tennessee, Texas.

| | Length of Term | | Sessions | |
	Senate	House	Time	Limit
Nevada	4	2	Bien.	60 days
New Hampshire	2	2	Bien.	None
New Jersey	4	2	Ann'l	None
New Mexico	4	2	Bien.	60 days
New York	2	2	Ann'l	None
North Carolina	2	2	Bien.	90 days
North Dakota	4	2	Bien.	60 days
Ohio	2	2	Bien.	None
Oklahoma	4	2	Bien.	None
Oregon	4	2	Bien.	None
Pennsylvania	4	2	Bien.	None
Rhode Island	2	2	Ann'l	60 days
South Carolina	4	2	Ann'l	None
South Dakota	2	2	Bien.	60 days
Tennessee	2	2	Bien.	75 days
Texas	4	2	Bien.	120 days *
Utah	4	2	Bien.	60 days
Vermont	2	2	Bien.	None
Virginia	4	2	Bien.	60 days **
Washington	4	2	Bien.	60 days
West Virginia	4	2	Bien.	60 days **
Wisconsin	4	2	Bien.	None
Wyoming	4	2	Bien.	40 days

Based on information supplied by the Council of State Governments.
* Divided session—first part limited to 30 days.
** Session may be extended: in West Virginia by ⅔ vote in each house, in Virginia by ⅗ vote in each house for not more than 30 more days.

ing from four dollars in Tennessee to thirty dollars in Louisiana. Ten dollars is most common. In a few commonwealths even this small salary automatically diminishes, or stops altogether, after sixty or seventy days of the legislative session.[6] Sixteen states provide a fixed salary for the entire two-year period that normally represents a single session of the legislature. The other thirteen pay by the year or the month, but in six of them the legislature meets annually. Usually the compensation is two thousand dollars or less for the biennium; New Hampshire fixes the pay of its legislators at two hundred dollars, and Connecticut gives only six hundred. At the other end of the scale, however, are a few states whose legislators' salaries seem generous by comparison—California, with seventy-two hundred dollars for the two year period; Massachusetts, with nine thousand; and Illinois and New York, with ten thousand.[7]

[6] See page 133.
[7] Massachusetts and New York pay by the year, however, since their legislatures meet in regular annual session.

In addition to their salaries, members of the legislature are almost invariably given allowances for traveling expenses. The travel contemplated in this connection is between the legislators' homes and the state capital. Ten cents per mile is most common. A number of states also make modest provision for stationery, postage, or other supplies, and some states allow small sums for living expenses.

During the last few years there has been a definite trend toward higher legislative salaries. In most states, however, the increase has failed to match the rise in living costs, so that state legislators actually find themselves worse off than in 1940. It is not at all surprising that the most generous provisions are made in those states that leave the matter of compensation for the legislature itself to determine, instead of specifying in the constitution what the salaries of legislators shall be.

Pensions for Legislators

One way to make service in the legislature more attractive is to provide retirement pensions for legislators. Such pensions are now offered by fourteen states.[8] The usual plan is to draw legislators into the regular state pension system already established for civil service employees. Legislators must agree to become members of the state system and must contribute a part of their salaries to the pension fund. The state then matches the contributions of the legislators and pays them retirement benefits at the end of their public service. The amount of each legislator's pension depends on a number of factors, such as his age, the number of years he has served, and the sum he has accumulated to his credit in the pension fund. "Years of service" usually means all years spent in the public service, even though much of this time may not have been in the legislature. Obviously the attractiveness of these legislative pension systems depends on the measure of real security they can offer. In California and Illinois, which pay relatively large legislative salaries, the pensions have a substantial value after a number of years of service, whereas in Florida and Montana they are so insignificant that legislators do not bother to apply.[9]

[8] California, Florida, Illinois, Maryland, Mississippi, Montana, New Jersey, New Mexico, New York, Ohio, Pennsylvania, Rhode Island, South Carolina, Washington. Massachusetts and Nevada were formerly included in the list, but the Massachusetts system was abandoned in 1952 after a political fight, and the Nevada plan was dropped in 1953 after the attorney-general of the state ruled that legislators were ineligible to receive pensions.

[9] See *American State Legislatures*, pp. 80–86. This 1954 volume, edited by Belle Zeller, is a report of the Committee on American Legislatures of the American Political Science Association.

Selection of Legislators

The members of both houses of the legislature are popularly elected in every state. A state is divided into senatorial and assembly districts, and from each district one or more members are chosen. Many years ago—even before the end of the eighteenth century—it was discovered that districts could be laid out in such a way as to strengthen the influence of the dominant political party.

The plan was quite simple—to combine as many minority party voters as possible into a comparatively few districts, where they would do the least harm. Those districts, of course, would return landslide votes for minority party candidates at every election, but the other districts of the state would furnish comfortable majorities for the dominant party unless large numbers of voters deserted their normal party allegiance. When this scheme became general practice, the rearrangement of districts degenerated into a sort of jig-saw puzzle, with districts of every conceivable shape resulting from the attempt to concentrate, and thus waste, the strength of the minority.

Gerrymandering

Not until 1812, after it had long been in vogue, did the custom receive a name. In that year the general court (legislature) of Massachusetts passed an act revising the boundaries of state senatorial districts in such a way as to insure the retention of power by the Republicans. Elbridge Gerry, then governor of the state, was opposed to the measure and signed it with reluctance. He seems to have been blamed for the Republican trickery, however, for when a map showing the two distorted districts of Essex County was jokingly described as a salamander, someone instantly remarked: "Better call it a Gerrymander." [10]   The name stuck.

Today the practice is accepted as an almost inevitable incident of partisan politics, and everywhere it is known as *gerrymandering*. Attempts have been made from time to time to put a stop to it, but without much success. A number of state constitutions contain provisions designed to insure the creation of districts composed of "compact and contiguous" territory, and in some instances the courts have invalidated the legislature's redistricting.[11] Yet abundant examples of gerrymandering are still to be found—"shoe-string," "saddle-bag," "belt-line," "dumbbell" districts, into which large numbers of opposition voters have been crowded.

[10] Robert Luce, *Legislative Principles*, pp. 397–398.
[11] See, for example, the case of State *v.* Cunningham, 81 Wis. 400 (1892).

Contested Elections

State constitutions commonly provide in language that varies but slightly from state to state, that "each House shall be the judge of the elections and qualifications of its members." Therefore, every contested election of a member of the legislature is passed upon by the house concerned. Usually there is a committee on contested elections, and a great show is made of judicial impartiality. Actually, however, party feeling runs strong, and contests are almost invariably decided on a partisan basis unless the majority party is so strong that it can afford to be impartial.

UNDERREPRESENTATION OF CITIES IN LEGISLATURES

Throughout the entire course of American history there have been two conflicting viewpoints concerning the proper basis of representation in the state legislature. Some persons have held that representation should be strictly on the basis of population. One man—one vote; to many this proposition has seemed almost axiomatic. Others have urged, however, that *territory* as well as *population* should be considered in determining representation, and this opinion has generally prevailed. Today there are thirty states whose constitutions definitely recognize territory as a basis of representation.

Sometimes this is done by specifying that the senate shall be composed of one representative from each county, regardless of population, as in New Jersey. Sometimes it is accomplished by providing that every county or every town shall have *at least* one representative in the senate or the house, or both. Pennsylvania follows this plan. The constitution of New York declares that "No county shall have more than one-third of all the senators," [12] and a number of other state constitutions contain similar provisions. Still other devices, some of them highly complex, are used for the purpose of preventing representation strictly according to population. In California, where a proposal for more equitable representation of cities was presented to the voters in 1948, it was defeated after a campaign of systematic misrepresentation.

These clauses serve to neutralize the political effect of city growth, and enable the rural districts to retain control of state legislatures despite the decline of rural population. New York City's representatives, for example, are permanently in the minority in the state legislature, though the metropolis contains more than half of the state's population. Chicago, Philadelphia,

[12] Art. III, Sec. 4.

Cleveland, Baltimore, St. Louis, and most of the other large cities of the United States are the victims of similar discriminations.

Whatever the merits of territorial representation may have been in a day when great urban centers of population were almost unknown and differences in population were less marked, they seem to be unrelated to modern conditions.   Voting distinctions based on wealth have entirely disappeared; religious discriminations are regarded as a relic of the past; the suffrage is no longer denied because of race or color, except in a few Southern states—and there it is done in defiance of the federal Constitution.   The theory that every man's vote is as good as his neighbor's has won general acceptance, save only when urban and rural voters are compared.

BICAMERAL OR UNICAMERAL?

Early History of Bicameralism

It has already been pointed out that every state except Nebraska has a legislature composed of two houses.[13]   In the early years of American independence most states accepted the bicameral principle almost as a matter of course.   They had been accustomed to two-chambered legislative bodies during the colonial period and could see no good reason why the time-honored tradition should be abandoned.

It might have been argued, of course, that each house of a colonial legislature represented separate and distinct interests; the council was virtually the mouthpiece of the crown, while the assembly championed the cause of the people.   But the upper and lower houses of the first state legislatures were also the representatives of distinct and ofttimes conflicting groups. The senate represented aristocracy, wealth, privilege.   Relatively high property qualifications were established for senate membership, and also for the privilege of voting for senators.   The house, on the other hand, was the more democratic chamber.   Its members were the spokesmen of the masses, even more clearly than during the colonial era.

Present-day Conditions

This distinction, however, has long since passed into history.   Senate and house are equally democratic and equally responsive to manifestations of the popular will.   Members of both houses are chosen by the same electorate and represent the same groups and interests.   Though senators are commonly chosen for a somewhat longer period, and though the senate is a somewhat smaller body, these differences are unimportant.   To borrow

[13] See page 124.

a phrase from the jargon of photography, the house is merely an enlargement from the same negative. Most students of government are agreed, therefore, that one-house legislatures would prove more satisfactory than the present bicameral bodies.

Unicameralism in Nebraska

It is interesting to note that unicameralism has proved highly satisfactory in Nebraska, the only state to adopt it within the last century. It has produced legislators who are better equipped than their predecessors in ability, training, and legislative experience. Legislative procedure has been greatly simplified, and the time-honored device of manipulating the rules for political purposes has been virtually abandoned. Public hearings are mandatory for all bills, and measures are seldom enacted without adequate consideration. The number of bills introduced in each session has been reduced about 50 per cent since the establishment of the one-house legislature. The last-minute rush has been practically eliminated.

Most of the present criticisms of Nebraska's legislative body are directed at relatively unimportant details. It is sometimes said that committees should be smaller, that salaries should be larger, that a four-year term should replace the present term of two years. But very few impartial Nebraskans now challenge the unicameral principle. It has made many converts since its adoption.[14] In other states, however, it has made no headway. Constitutional amendments to establish one-house legislatures have been proposed in at least half of the states since 1936, but without success.

LEGISLATIVE SESSIONS

Curbs on Legislative Activity

The men who framed the first state constitutions were firmly convinced of the necessity for frequent meeting of the legislature. In colonial days the failure of royal governors to convene the provincial assemblies had been a source of much bitterness; and when England's political yoke was broken, the leaders in the revolutionary movement took care to provide for regular and frequent legislative sessions. The constitution of Massachusetts, adopted in 1780, declared that "The legislature ought frequently to assemble for the redress of grievances, for correcting, strengthening, and confirming the laws, and for making new laws, as the common good may require." In

[14] See Roger V. Schumate's article, "The Nebraska Unicameral Legislature," in the September, 1952, issue of the *Western Political Quarterly*, pp. 504–512.

most of the states annual sessions were held, and a few states provided for two sessions a year.

BIENNIAL SESSIONS.   In 1796, however, Tennessee specified that its legislature should meet at two-year intervals.   Its example was not generally followed at first, but after a time the biennial idea began to prove extremely popular.   Men had found to their sorrow that legislative assemblies could be guilty of tyranny and folly, not to speak of downright dishonesty.   They had learned that every legislative session was likely to be marked by the passage of unwise and unnecessary laws.   And so they reasoned, somewhat illogically, that the way to reduce the quantity of undesirable legislation was to cut in half the number of legislative sessions.   With only half as much time at its disposal, the legislature could do only half as much harm.   This was a counsel of despair, but it made a strong appeal to the popular imagination.   Even today it is generally accepted.   In thirty-eight states the legislature now meets in regular session at two-year intervals; the other ten states [15] have annual sessions.   In California, where biennial sessions had long been the rule, the constitution was amended in 1947 to provide for two kinds of sessions—general sessions in odd-numbered years, and budget sessions in even-numbered years.   The amendment specified that during the short budget session other matters might not be considered.   Colorado and Maryland have adopted somewhat similar schemes, but in Maryland the legislature is permitted not only to consider the budget during the so-called "budget" session, but also to deal with acute emergencies and enact laws "necessary for the public welfare."

OTHER RESTRICTIONS.   Not content with limiting regular sessions to alternate years, thirty states further restrict legislative activity by limiting the length of the session to a specified number of days, ranging from thirty in Colorado to one hundred and fifty in Connecticut and Missouri.   A sixty-day limit is most common.   Sixteen states endeavor to curb legislative enterprise by specifying that legislators' salaries shall be reduced, or stopped altogether, after a certain number of days.   Usually this wage restriction applies only to special sessions; sometimes, however, it refers to regular sessions as well.

Although it has been possible to limit the number of days in a legislative session, it has proved totally impossible to restrict the number of matters requiring legislative action.   Every year has brought additional governmental problems and increased need for governmental regulation; at the

[15] Arizona, California, Colorado, Maryland, Massachusetts, Michigan, New Jersey, New York, Rhode Island, South Carolina.

same time state legislatures have been compelled to complete their work in fifty, sixty, or ninety days.   Results have been highly unsatisfactory.

Attempts to Overcome Evils of Legislative Curbs

SPECIAL SESSIONS.   Since regular sessions of most state legislatures may be held but once in two years, and even then are narrowly restricted as to length, special sessions have inevitably become more numerous, though by no means the rule except in a very few states.   Even with regard to special sessions, however, popular distrust of the legislature is evident. Usually such sessions may be held only at the summons of the governor, and in some states they are limited to twenty or thirty days.   Arkansas has a fifteen-day limit.   Nine states permit the legislature to determine the necessity for a special session,[16] but six of them require an extraordinary majority for this purpose.[17]

In addition to permitting the governor to determine whether a special session shall be called, thirty states authorize him to specify the subject or subjects requiring legislative action.   The legislature, while in special session, is then prohibited from considering any other matter.[18]   Under this plan, therefore, the governor can prevent the enactment at special sessions of legislation that he dislikes; but he cannot compel acceptance of his own legislative program.

The constitutional prohibition against legislative consideration of matters not presented by the governor is generally considered to apply only to the function of lawmaking.   So it would be quite proper for a legislature summoned in special session for the express purpose of considering the problem of unemployment to turn its attention to the approval of appointments or the impeachment of state officials, since appointments are an executive matter, while impeachment is a judicial act.

LEGISLATIVE COUNCILS.   In 1933 Kansas attempted to overcome some of the evil effects of infrequent legislative sessions by creating a legislative council—a body of fifteen representatives and ten senators holding at least quarterly meetings after the legislature's adjournment—whose chief duty was declared to be the preparation of a lawmaking program for the succeeding legislature.   This council was also authorized to study problems of

---

[16] Arizona, Connecticut, Georgia, Louisiana, Massachusetts, Nebraska, New Hampshire, Virginia, West Virginia.

[17] Three fifths of all the members in Georgia, and two thirds of all the members in the other states.

[18] Alabama, Arkansas, and Florida, however, permit the legislature, by an extraordinary vote, to proceed to a consideration of other matters.   Mississippi expressly excludes impeachments from this limitation.

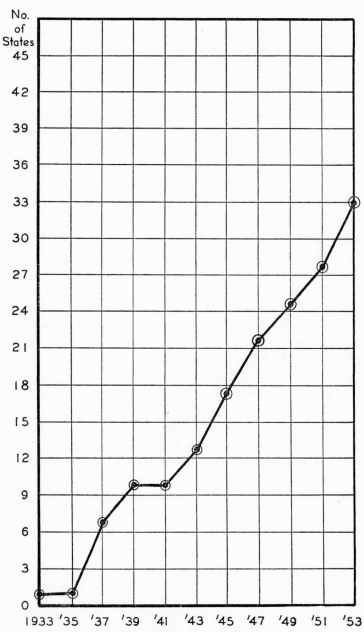

Based on figures from *The Book of the States, 1954–55.*

state-wide interest and to collect information on all pertinent subjects.   Before the close of 1933 Michigan also established a legislative council—a somewhat smaller body than the Kansas council, but organized in the same manner and vested with similar functions.   The act creating the Michigan council has since been repealed, but similar statutes have been enacted in thirty-two other states.   A few commonwealths have partially corrected a serious weakness of the legislative council plan—namely, its failure to recognize the important part played by the governor in formulating general policies—by naming the governor as chairman of its council.   Some of the councils include not only legislators but also the heads of certain administrative departments.   In Oklahoma, where the competition among state legislators for the honor of serving on the legislative council had grown to unreasonable proportions, the problem was solved in 1949 by expanding the legislative council to include all members of both houses of the legislature. Nebraska and South Dakota later adopted similar plans.   The legislative councils thus created have been too bulky to produce satisfactory results, so they have been obliged to assign many of their tasks to smaller executive committees.[19]

THE SPLIT SESSION.   Partly for the purpose of reducing the congestion and overcrowding that so generally mark the closing days of a legislative session and partly to secure a more careful examination of bills by legislators and the public, California adopted a scheme in 1911 that has since become known as the *split session*.   As its name indicates, the split session is a legislative session divided into two parts.

During the first part of the session [20] bills are introduced and referred to committees.   Some hearings are held.   A few bills may even be enacted into law, but the theory of the plan is that this period shall be used solely for the purpose of setting the legislative machinery in motion.   A recess of about thirty days is then taken.   Legislators returning to their homes should be able to give every proposal leisurely consideration and also learn the wishes of their constituents.   When the legislature reconvenes after this period of supposed meditation, the introduction of new bills is discouraged, though not absolutely prohibited.   In California no member may introduce more than two bills, and in order to introduce even one he must have the consent of three fourths of the members of the house to which he belongs.

West Virginia adopted the split session plan in 1920, but abandoned it

[19] See "They All Get into the Show," by Don L. Bowen, in the October, 1950, issue of the *National Municipal Review*, pp. 450–454.

[20] This arrangement applies only to the long session of the California legislature. The short or budget session is not divided.   See page 133.

eight years later. Since 1918 the constitution of Massachusetts has authorized split sessions, but the general court has preferred to carry on its business in the old way. The Alabama legislature, on the other hand, has occasionally split its sessions without express constitutional authorization, and in New Jersey the legislature regularly adjourns for about ten days immediately after organizing, in order to give the party leaders time to develop their legislative programs. Texas has divided the legislative session into three parts since 1930. The first thirty days are devoted chiefly to the introduction of bills; then comes a thirty-day period of committee hearings; and during the remaining sixty days bills are debated and passed. There is no legislative recess, however. In 1933 the constitution of Georgia was amended to provide for two sessions in each regular legislative year— a ten-day session in January and a longer session, limited to sixty days, beginning in July. In 1941 New Mexico adopted a plan similar to that of California, but later abandoned it.

The results of the split session system have been very disappointing. The mass of unfinished business has not been materially reduced, and bills still continue to pile up at the end of the session. Proposals introduced during the first part of the session are subsequently so amended that in many instances they become essentially different legislation. Very seldom do the people show any genuine interest in the measures they are supposed to examine during the legislature's recess; the layman who understands the exact nature of a single bill is probably exceptional.

CONTINUOUS SESSIONS. The National Municipal League's *Model State Constitution,* prepared by a committee of experts, proposes that the state legislature meet in regular session several times a year. It declares that "The legislature shall be deemed a continuous body during the biennium for which its members are elected. It shall meet in regular sessions quarterly or at such times as may be prescribed by law." [21] This recommendation was made in 1941, yet no state has given it serious consideration. The tradition of infrequent sessions, like all traditions, dies hard.

CONSTITUTIONAL RESTRICTIONS ON THE POWER OF THE LEGISLATURE

The powers of the state legislature have never been completely listed. In fact, they defy exact enumeration, for the legislature possesses residual authority. It may do anything that is not prohibited by the federal Constitution or the constitution of that state. In the first era of American

[21] Art. 307. See the 5th edition of the National Municipal League's pamphlet, *A Model State Constitution*

national life this principle of legislative supremacy was vitally important; it enabled the legislative body to control virtually every phase of state activity.

But the passing years have witnessed an ever-increasing number of limitations upon the power of the legislature, so that today it is almost impossible to enact a law on any important subject without regard to constitutional provisions that specify in great detail what may be included and what must be omitted; how the statute must be phrased and when it may go into effect; who may be included within its terms and who must receive exemption. So numerous and so minute have these restrictions become that the doctrine of legislative supremacy is now little more than a legal fiction.

State Finance; Special Legislation

One common type of limitation on the powers of the legislature relates to state finance.   Taxes must be uniform, or uniform within certain classes of property; exemptions from taxation shall not be made except in specified cases; state money shall not be appropriated to religious institutions; state credit shall not be loaned to private corporations; state loans may not exceed moderate limits, unless authorized by popular vote.   In the past, state legislatures have often been guilty of squandering public funds with little or no regard for the public welfare, and the financial limitations in state constitutions are designed to prevent a recurrence of such waste.

Another type of restriction on the legislature deals with so-called "special legislation."   A great deal of energy has been dissipated, and a great many unjust proposals have been enacted into law, as a direct result of the common legislative practice of passing laws affecting only one person, one corporation, or one community.   Obviously the legislature does not have time to give serious thought to the individual needs of every person, every corporation, and every community, and its attempt to do so has prevented the proper consideration of matters of more general importance.   Even worse, it has meant the passage of special laws on the recommendation of selfish vested interests or at the behest of uninformed zealots.   In order to prevent evils of this sort, most state constitutions prohibit the enactment of special legislation when general laws can be used instead, or in certain enumerated cases.   Restrictions on special legislation are rather easy to evade, especially if the state courts do not insist upon too literal an interpretation of the constitution; but they have unquestionably checked some abuses of legislative power.[22]

[22] For a more detailed consideration of the effects of special legislation as applied to cities, see pages 49–51.

Specific Grants of Power

Since the legislature may exercise all authority not prohibited to it by the constitutions of nation or state, it would seem unnecessary to confer upon it any specific grants of power.   Yet every state constitution makes particular mention of some matters that are declared to be within the scope of legislative power.   Some of these detailed grants have been inserted with no other purpose than to round out a phrase, or indicate the truly liberal spirit of the constitutional convention.

As interpreted by the courts, however, they have actually become limitations upon the authority of the legislature.   The courts have said repeatedly that any clause empowering the legislative body to act in a particular manner must be construed as a denial of its right to act in any other manner.   Thus an amendment to the constitution of California authorizing the legislature to enact a certain type of direct primary legislation was held to forbid the passage of any other kind of direct primary law.

Sometimes an explicit statement of certain powers of the legislature must be placed in the constitution to counteract the effect of unpopular court decisions.   For example, the courts may interpret the "due process" clause or the guarantee of free speech in a way never intended by the framers of the constitution or by the people.   The effect of their decision may be to restrain the legislature from exercising some power that it has long used as a matter of course.   Under such circumstances the only way to restore the legislature's prerogative is to amend the constitution, specifically bestowing upon it the power denied by the courts.   A considerable number of constitutional amendments containing particular grants of legislative authority have been adopted for this reason.

THE LEGISLATURE'S NONLEGISLATIVE FUNCTIONS

Although the legislature is primarily concerned with the enactment of laws, it often possesses various powers that are not directly related to lawmaking.   Judges of certain courts are appointed by the legislature in seven states,[23] and in six states [24] certain executive officials are similarly chosen. Most of the governor's important appointments must be ratified by the state senate, and in a number of commonwealths dismissal of state officers must also receive the senate's approval.   The legislature is often empowered

[23] Alabama, Connecticut, New Jersey, Rhode Island, South Carolina, Vermont, Virginia.
[24] Maine, Maryland, New Hampshire, New Jersey, Tennessee, Virginia.

to remove from office the judges of the state courts, a two-thirds or three-fourths vote generally being necessary in such cases. Virtually every state [25] vests authority in the legislature to remove executive and judicial officers by process of impeachment.

It should be noted at this point that impeachment is not the equivalent of conviction, but is merely the presentation of formal charges. The lower house nearly always has the sole right to impeach. Any member of that body may offer a resolution of impeachment, which is at once referred to an appropriate committee. The report of the committee, though not binding on the house, usually determines in large measure what action will finally be taken. If a majority of the members of the house indicate their belief that the accused official has been guilty of serious misconduct or neglect of duty, formal charges are thereupon prepared and adopted.

The senate sits as a court for the trial of these charges, and a specially chosen committee from the lower house prosecutes the case. The accused official is permitted to employ counsel and produce witnesses in his behalf, just as if he were on trial in an ordinary court of law.[26] Usually a two-thirds vote of the senate is necessary for conviction; the punishment does not extend beyond removal from office, or perhaps in addition disqualification from holding further office under the state or its civil subdivisions. Impeachment and conviction for a criminal offense, however, do not render the convicted official immune from subsequent arrest and trial in the criminal courts of the state.

ORGANIZATION OF THE LEGISLATURE

The first few days of a legislative session are commonly devoted to the task of organizing for business. Presiding officers must be chosen, rules adopted, committees named. Actually these matters do not require so much time as might be supposed. Usually it is known well in advance of the session who will occupy the speaker's chair. The rules of the preceding session are commonly adopted without debate. Certain well-recognized factors, such as previous service, factional allegiance, residence, and special

[25] Oregon is the only state that does not permit impeachment of its public officials. Its constitution provides (Art. VII, Sec. 6) that "incompetency, corruption, malfeasance or delinquency in office may be tried in the same manner as criminal offenses."

[26] In New York the judges of the state court of appeals sit with the senate in impeachment trials. The Missouri constitution of 1945 directs the supreme court to try impeachment cases, unless the governor or members of the supreme court have been impeached, in which case the trial takes place before seven eminent jurists chosen by the senate.

qualifications, determine committee membership to a very large extent. In a comparatively short while, therefore, the preliminaries are completed and the legislature is ready to begin its regular routine.

The Lieutenant Governor

Usually the lieutenant governor, the "fifth wheel of the coach of state," presides over the deliberations of the senate.[27] His powers are strictly limited; he is commonly though not invariably prohibited from participating in debate, and may vote only in case of a tie. Five states deny to him even this limited voting power.[28] He is presumed to be an impartial presiding officer, and as a rule he takes no active part in shaping legislation. In seventeen states, however, he appoints the regular standing committees and thus is a real factor in the legislative process.[29]

The senate chooses from among its own members a president *pro tempore,* who presides during the absence of the lieutenant governor in case of his elevation to the governorship. Ten states make no provision for the office of lieutenant governor, and in those states the senate selects its own permanent presiding officer. Regardless of the method of choice, the presiding officer of the senate is known as the "president" of that body in every state except Tennessee, where "speaker" is preferred.

The Speaker

In the lower house the regular presiding officer is invariably a speaker chosen by the house from its own membership. It is scarcely necessary to add that he is selected for this important post because he is the recognized house leader of the majority party. As speaker he wields a large measure of authority; his office is generally considered the second most important in the whole field of state politics, ranking next to the governorship.

Unlike the lieutenant governor, he is not supposed to preserve an attitude of judicial impartiality during the course of debate. On the contrary, he is expected to use the power of his office for the purpose of battering down the opposition and forcing the adoption of measures that have the support of his party. Speakers have not been slow to use the authority entrusted to them; quite frequently, however, they have given greater weight to the views

[27] In Nebraska the lieutenant governor presides over the single chamber of the legislature. A speaker, chosen by the legislature from its own membership, presides in his absence.

[28] Louisiana, Michigan, Minnesota, New York, Wisconsin.

[29] In three of these states—Idaho, Mississippi, and Washington—the lieutenant governor's committee appointments must be approved by the senate. In Mississippi and Washington special provision is made for the composition of the rules committee.

of a little clique of party leaders than to the opinions of a majority of the members.[30]

APPOINTMENT OF STANDING COMMITTEES. One of the important sources of the speaker's influence is his power to appoint the standing committees. Almost every state places this unrestricted power in his hands,[31] and thereby enables him to control to a very considerable extent the political career of every member of the lower house. The influence of a state legislator depends largely upon the committees to which he is assigned, and only a man who is supremely confident of his ability to play a lone hand or completely indifferent to the course of his political fortunes will dare to risk oblivion by deliberately and persistently ignoring the speaker's wishes.

RIGHT OF RECOGNITION. Another source of the speaker's power is his right of recognition. In some state legislatures the schedule of debate on each bill is arranged long in advance by the party leaders, a certain amount of time being assigned to each member who desires to speak. Under such circumstances the speaker does little more than follow the typewritten list before him and refuse to recognize any member who tries to speak out of turn or without first securing permission to express his views.

Much more commonly, however, the speaker is virtually free to recognize whom he will; he is thus in a position to guide the course of debate by recognizing his supporters and refusing to recognize those who dispute his rule. The leaders of the minority must be given adequate opportunity to express their views, of course; that is part of the unwritten law. But rebels within the ranks of the majority party need not be accorded a similar courtesy.

RULINGS ON POINTS OF ORDER. The speaker also passes on points of order, and in so doing he is sometimes able to interpret the rules of the house in such a way as to give his friends an unreasonable advantage. Bills that he favors may be hurried to a vote, and proposals that he dislikes may be prevented from reaching the stage of general discussion. He may twist and warp not only technical points of parliamentary law, but also questions of fact. Rulings of the speaker may be appealed to the house, but since the speaker is the chosen representative of a majority of the members, his decisions are not likely to be reversed.

---

[30] A somewhat similar development in the national House of Representatives led to the so-called "Revolution of 1911," in which Progressive Republicans united with the Democrats to deprive the speaker of some of his arbitrary power. In the states, however, the speaker of the house still retains his authority and prestige.

[31] The only exceptions are Kentucky, where committee appointments are made by a committee on committees; Oklahoma, where the speaker's appointments must be confirmed by the membership of the house; and, of course, Nebraska, where the lieutenant governor presides over the unicameral legislature.

REFERENCE OF BILLS TO COMMITTEES.   The other power of the speaker that is commonly cited as tending to give him absolute control over legislation in the house is his power to refer bills to committees.   A bill that has been introduced in the house finds its way to the speaker's desk, and from there is sent to some committee for detailed consideration.

Usually the assignment of bills to appropriate committees is a routine task; the subject matter of the bill determines in advance where it is to be sent. Some measures, however, are considered so important that the speaker feels justified in making purely arbitrary use of his power of reference.   He greatly facilitates their passage, or else condemns them to certain oblivion, according to his wishes, by referring them to committees that are considered "reliable."   The extent to which the presiding officers of state assemblies actually use their power to refer bills for the purpose of shaping legislation to their own desires varies from state to state.

VOTING AND DEBATING RIGHTS.   Unlike the lieutenant governor, the speaker is a member of the house over which he presides.   Therefore he has a right to vote on all measures.   He is not permitted to break a tie, however, by casting a second vote.   The speaker commonly refrains from participating in debate, though sometimes he takes part in the discussion when the house is sitting as a committee of the whole.[32]   In a few state legislatures the speaker even participates occasionally in the formal debates—leaving the chair for the purpose, of course; but this is not the rule.[33]

Other Legislative Officers and Employees

In addition to the speaker, each house of the legislature also chooses other officers and attendants, including a clerk, a chaplain, and a sergeant-at-arms.   A great deal of clerical, stenographic, and other help is necessary to handle the vast amount of business requiring the legislature's consideration, yet nearly always the number of senate and house employees greatly exceeds even the large number actually needed.   In some states every member of the senate and house is entitled to a private secretary, and the drain on the public treasury from this source is surprisingly heavy.

The Committee System

So great is the number of proposals placed before every legislature that some means must be found of sorting the wheat from the chaff—disposing

[32] For a discussion of the organization and purpose of the committee of the whole, see page 149.

[33] See Eugene C. Lee's monograph, *The Presiding Officer and Rules Committee in Legislatures of the United States,* published in mimeographed form in 1952 by the Bureau of Public Administration of the University of California.

of unwise, unnecessary, or unpopular bills as quickly and quietly as possible, and focusing attention upon those measures that should be enacted into law. The means invariably adopted is the committee system.

Both the senate and the house of every state legislature are organized on a committee basis, every member being assigned to several committees. Special committees are appointed from time to time to make special investigations and deal with special problems, but the normal routine of business is carried on by the regular standing committees.

NUMBER OF COMMITTEES.   The number of these standing committees is surprisingly large.   Twenty or more committees are usually found in the lower house,[34] the average being thirty-two.   Six houses of representatives each have more than fifty standing committees, while eight others have more than forty apiece.   In the senate the number of standing committees is somewhat smaller, though still very large.   There are ten state senates having at least thirty-five committees apiece, and only nine senates with fewer than twenty.

Many useless committees.   It may well be asked why so many committees are necessary.   Several partially satisfactory answers to this question can be given, but the answer that best explains the situation is that such a large number is entirely unnecessary.   In most state legislatures the total number of standing committees could be reduced at least one third without adversely affecting the process of lawmaking.   Many committees that seldom or never meet, and have virtually no business to transact, have been created chiefly for the purpose of rewarding ambitious party workers who have not yet earned the right to important assignments on the major committees.   A young man without powerful friends is usually glad to receive any sort of committee chairmanship, regardless of the committee's prominence.   It establishes his position among his constituents, to whom all committee chairmanships doubtless seem alike; and it entitles him to the clerical help —or, better still, allowance for clerical help—that accompanies the position.

Recent reductions in the number of committees.   Within the last four or five years there has been a slight but noticeable trend toward fewer legislative committees.   In 1952 Kentucky, for example, reduced the number of regular standing committees in the lower house of the legislature from seventy-one to forty-four.   At about the same time North Carolina cut its senate committees from fifty-two to twenty-eight.   When such reductions

[34] Alabama, with but fourteen standing committees in the lower house, is an exception.   So, too, is Rhode Island, with fifteen standing committees.

Kansas State Capitol

Oregon State Capitol

Louisiana State Capitol

California State Capitol

are made, all the newly organized committees are usually charged with responsibility for important and well-defined aspects of legislation.

SIZE OF COMMITTEES.   Not only are the committees of state legislatures very numerous; they are also very large.   Most careful students of government think that they are too large.   The average number of members assigned to senate committees varies from three in New Jersey to twenty-three in Illinois; in the lower house the range is from slightly less than five in Nevada to more than thirty-five in Georgia.   Extremes tell the story better than averages, however.   Illinois has seven senate committees and fifteen house committees whose membership exceeds thirty-five.   Ten committees of the lower house of the Georgia legislature have from fifty to seventy-five members apiece.

MAJORITY PARTY CONTROL OF COMMITTEES.   In most state legislatures it is customary to give the majority party control of every committee, although the minority party receives representation in every instance.   Almost invariably the chairman of a committee is a member of the majority party; usually he is the majority member who has served on the committee the longest time continuously.   This seniority rule has frequently been attacked on the ground that it keeps the younger men in subordinate posts, regardless of their ability or training; but state legislatures give no indication of abandoning it.

JOINT COMMITTEES.   Three New England states—Connecticut, Maine, and Massachusetts—conduct most of their business through joint committees, which are composed of both senate and house members.   House members usually outnumber senators on these committees, but only because the house is a larger body.   A few other states also make use of joint committees for certain purposes, such as investigations and ceremonies, but most of their legislative affairs are managed by separate committees of each house.   The merit of the joint committee system is that it eliminates some of the delays of the legislative process, and reduces the likelihood of disagreement between the two houses.   It is surprising that the plan has not found more widespread acceptance.

SELECT COMMITTEES.   Although the regular standing committees that have been described in the preceding pages carry on the bulk of every legislature's work, they are not the only committees of the legislature.   There are also select committees, specially created from time to time to perform specific tasks and discharged when the tasks have been completed.   For example, a select committee may be appointed to welcome a distinguished visitor, to investigate charges of fraud or inefficiency in one of the administrative departments, or to examine at first hand living conditions in a strike-ridden area.   The work of such committees is only temporary, and that is why they are not established on a permanent basis.[35]

PROCEDURE IN ENACTMENT OF LEGISLATION

Each house of the state legislature adopts its own rules of procedure. Some procedural details are quite commonly prescribed in the state constitution, but ways of evading these requirements are generally found without difficulty.   The rules, as adopted at an early meeting of each legislature, are practically certain to be the preceding legislature's rules without alteration of any kind.   Usually they are antiquated, cumbersome, needlessly detailed, and difficult to comprehend.

It might be supposed, therefore, that the older members who sponsor their adoption would propose instead a simpler and clearer method of procedure. The truth of the matter is that these veteran legislators who dominate senate and house activity actually welcome complex, verbose, ambiguous rules. Such rules may be called into service at will by the initiated, to the astonishment and discomfiture of the unwary.   It takes a long while for a newly elected member to learn all the tricks of the parliamentarian's trade; in the meantime he is at a serious disadvantage.

History of a Bill

Perhaps the best way to obtain a clear picture of the entire legislative process is to take a single bill and trace its history from the time it is first introduced until it is officially proclaimed a law by the secretary of state.   A bill may be introduced in either house by any member of the house or by any standing committee.   Since the standing committees scarcely ever initiate legislation, the vast flood of proposals that threatens to swamp most legislative sessions comes from the individual members.

FIRST READING.   A member introduces a bill by placing it in the hands of the clerk, who reads its title and thus gives it the official "first reading." Nearly every state requires three readings on three separate days for every measure enacted into law.

REFERENCE TO COMMITTEE.   After a bill has had its "first reading," it goes to the presiding officer for reference to a committee.   The extent to which the presiding officer's choice of an "appropriate" committee may determine the final fate of the measure has already been indicated.[36]   Many a state

[35] For an excellent discussion of the legislative committee system, see the American Political Science Association's previously cited report, *American State Legislatures,* pp. 95–103.

[36] See page 143.

assembly has a "graveyard" committee, whose chief purpose is to give decent burial to undesired proposals. Its true nature is always cloaked, however, by some imposing title such as *Special Committee on Judiciary* or *Committee on Legislative Procedure.*

An active committee receives so many bills in the course of a single session that it cannot possibly give them all serious consideration. Therefore it must select those proposals that deserve careful study. In making its selection it is influenced very largely by the wishes of the chairman, who normally acts as spokesman for the little group of "elder statesmen" controlling legislative affairs.

Although legislative rules do not require committee hearings, except in a very few states, hearings are usually held on all important measures. Taxpayers, lobbyists, experts, nonexperts, those who urge adoption and those who object—all are permitted to appear and express their views, subject to the narrow time limits necessarily imposed.

The next step is committee deliberation—usually behind closed doors, though Nebraska admits representatives of the press. Every bill that progresses this far is examined clause by clause, amended to any extent that may seem desirable, and finally adopted or rejected by committee vote.

RETURN OF BILL. The power of committees to suppress or pigeon-hole bills that fail to meet committee favor varies from state to state. The rules of some state legislatures make the committees virtually supreme in this respect; bills need not be reported, except on the demand of an extraordinary majority of the house. Fairly common is the provision for return upon a simple majority vote, but since every committee is dominated by the majority party its decision to bury a bill is not usually questioned. Some states place the power to recall a bill from committee in the hands of the author, or any member of the house, or a small part of the total house membership. Even more stringent is the requirement that all bills must be reported after a given number of days, or by a certain date, without the necessity of affirmative action by the house or any of its members. These provisions for automatic return of bills are found in the rules of one or both houses of twenty legislatures.

THE PARTY CAUCUS ON LEGISLATION. The Congress of the United States relies on caucus action to a very considerable extent to insure the enactment of important legislation. The caucus is a meeting of the Senate or House members of a party for the purpose of securing a united front on matters that vitally affect the party's welfare. Ostensibly it aims to discover the wishes of the members, so that the party leaders will know how to act. Actually it is a very effective device for forcing the leaders' views upon the rank and file, for the decisions of the caucus are usually forced upon it; and, once made, they become binding on all members.

In the state legislatures, however, the party caucus has never had a development corresponding to its growth in Congress. Barring the experience of a very few states, the caucus meets but seldom except at the beginning of the session for the nomination of officers, and its occasional decisions on legislative matters are not so seriously regarded as in Congress. Caucus measures are invariably given careful study, however, even if frequently denied united support.

SECOND READING. When the house proceeds to the consideration of a bill reported from committee, this stage is known as second reading. The bill is debated, amended, and finally voted on. It is common practice to supply every member with a printed copy of the bill before debate is begun. At least a dozen states, however, merely require the printing of a bill and its amendments *before final passage*—that is, in most cases, after the debate has been concluded; and a few commonwealths make no provision for printing bills unless specially authorized. Massachusetts, at the other extreme, is one of a small number of states that print every bill upon introduction.

Debate. The course of debate in every state legislature is necessarily very formal. Freedom of discussion is often narrowly restricted. Rules designed to save time and prevent obstructive tactics are rigorously enforced. In order to permit less formal consideration of bills and afford the average member somewhat greater freedom of expression, the rules of nearly all legislative bodies authorize the use of a procedural contrivance known as committee of the whole. A few state legislatures employ this device rather freely; the large majority, however, use it infrequently or not at all.

The committee of the whole, as its name indicates, is the entire membership of the chamber sitting as a committee. In appearance one of its sessions does not differ from a regular meeting of the house, except that the speaker's chair is occupied by one of the other members. But the regular rules are greatly relaxed, and debate is considerably freer. When the committee of the whole has discussed and adopted a bill, it immediately reports its action to the house—that is, practically speaking, to itself. The speaker resumes his place as presiding officer, and puts the question as to whether the action of the committee of the whole shall be made the vote of the house. This question is almost invariably answered in the affirmative, of course; but there have been instances of legislative bodies that reversed their informal opinions—and probably their honest convictions—when called upon for a formal vote.

Acceptance of committee recommendations.   The members of state legislatures are guided very largely by committee recommendations in making their decisions.   There are good reasons for this acceptance of committee leadership.   Committee control of legislation usually means control by the party leaders, and therefore it makes possible reasonably steady progress toward the legislative goal upon which the leaders have agreed.   Moreover, the members of a committee have—or are supposed to have—time to become familiar with the bills entrusted to their care.

THE FINAL DRAFT.   After a bill has been amended and passed on second reading, it is engrossed—that is, prepared for final passage.   A new copy is drafted, if necessary, so as to incorporate the changes that have been ordered by the house.   This task is commonly assigned to a committee on engrossed bills, whose duty is to present to the house an accurate draft of the original bill and its amendments.   On some occasions surprising additions and omissions have "accidentally" been made at this time; interested members find it well worth their while, therefore, to read the engrossed bill before casting their final vote.

THIRD READING.   When a bill comes before the house for its third reading it is frequently passed without debate.   To propose amendments at this stage requires unanimous consent, which is not commonly given; therefore the measure must be accepted or rejected as a whole.   A few states vary the customary procedure by making the second reading quite as meaningless as the first, and deferring opportunity for debate and amendment to the third reading.

A bill that has been passed on third reading is then sent to the other house, where the details of procedure already described must be repeated.   There must be reference to some committee, generally followed by committee hearings; three readings must be given, including the usual opportunity for discussion and amendment; and the final vote must be taken.

DISREGARD OF RULES OF PROCEDURE.   It may cause astonishment that such time-consuming procedure does not prevent the enactment of virtually all legislation.   That it has no such effect is quite evident, however; every legislative session witnesses a fresh deluge of laws added to the hundreds of thousands already crowded between the covers of the statute books. Forty or forty-five thousand pages of statutes are enacted by the legislatures of the states every biennium, and even yet legislators are not convinced that the point of diminishing returns in the field of lawmaking has been reached.

The chief reason why cumbersome rules of procedure do not decrease the legislative output to any considerable extent is that they are commonly ignored or evaded whenever short cuts seem necessary—especially during the closing days of the session.

Constitutional provisions concerning legislative procedure deserve greater respect than mere senate or house rules, but even they are often brushed lightly aside. In determining whether the legislature has obeyed the letter of the constitution the courts usually refuse to go further than the written record of the senate and house journals, so that violations can readily be concealed by appropriate entries.

CONFERENCE COMMITTEES. Unless a bill is passed by both houses in exactly the same form, the differences must be straightened out before it may be submitted to the governor. A compromise must be found that will be acceptable to the members of both chambers. To prepare such a compromise is the task of a conference committee, which usually consists of three senate members appointed by the president of that body and three house members appointed by the speaker. There are some variations, however. Occasionally conference committee members are chosen by one of the standing committees or by ballot. Conference committee recommendations may be rejected by one or both houses, but they are not likely to be.

When a bill has received the final approval of both houses, a new copy is made incorporating all changes. The preparation of this copy is known as enrollment. The signature of the presiding officer of each house is then affixed, and the bill goes to the governor for his consideration. In every state except North Carolina the governor has the power of veto, though his veto may be overridden in most cases by action of the legislature.[37] The vote required to overcome the governor's veto ranges from a mere majority of those present, as in Connecticut, to a two-thirds majority of the total membership of each house, as in half of the states.

Congestion at the End of the Session

Almost without exception is the tendency of state legislatures to postpone the enactment of legislation until the closing days of the session. The first few days are spent in organizing and getting down to business. Then committee meetings consume the serious attention of members for weeks at a time. The legislature may meet but a few hours each day, and only three or four days a week. Few significant decisions are made.

At last, with only a week or ten days of the session remaining and virtually no important measures enacted into law, the need for quick action

[37] The governor's veto power has already been considered in some detail. See pages 110–111.

becomes apparent. Committee reports pour in at the rate of fifty or one hundred a day, and the legislative calendars become hopelessly crowded. Some reports are purposely delayed by the leaders in the hope that the majority will give a hasty assent to proposals that could never pass if carefully examined, but in most cases committee tardiness is simply an indication of the natural tendency to procrastinate. Whatever the cause, the result is almost hopeless confusion. Many bills—especially those involving appropriations and administrative routine—must be passed in order to save the state government serious embarrassment. Many others must also be adopted if specific campaign pledges are to be fulfilled, and even campaign promises acquire some significance when it is remembered that election day is a day of reckoning.

Seldom is it possible, however, to give any measure the consideration it deserves. In most cases it is totally out of the question to follow the forms of procedure specified by the constitution or legislative rule, or both. So the rules are brushed aside, and the legislature sometimes enacts more laws in two hours than it did in two weeks at the beginning of the session. Under such circumstances the quality of the legislative product inevitably suffers. Many laws bear evidence of the haste with which they have been enacted. Crudely and ambiguously phrased, they sometimes defy the efforts of the administrative officials, the courts, and the public to determine their real meaning.

The experience of Massachusetts, and also of Wisconsin and Nebraska to a considerable degree, indicates that the last-minute rush so characteristic of state legislatures is totally unnecessary. In Massachusetts all committee reports must be submitted to the legislature before a specified date, well in advance of the probable close of the session,[38] and the introduction of bills is limited to the first few days of the session except under very unusual circumstances. In part, the success of Massachusetts in avoiding congestion at the end of the session is due to these excellent rules of procedure; in part, it is the result of sound legislative tradition.[39]

[38] This rule is scrupulously respected in some states. In Massachusetts, for example, a committee would not attempt to influence legislation by failing to make a report. But in many other commonwealths the rule is frequently disregarded.

[39] See the recommendations of the Illinois legislative council in its 1952 research report, *Scheduling Legislative Workloads*.

LEGISLATIVE REFERENCE BUREAUS

Unwise Legislation

Legislators are amateurs.   Most of them have no special qualifications as lawmakers, no special training for public service, no special knowledge of public affairs.   Few of them, prior to election, ever gave serious thought to government or its problems.   So it is not at all surprising that every session of every state legislature witnesses its share of freakish proposals.   From time to time legislative committees have been asked to consider bills forbidding school textbooks to be changed oftener than once in ten years, prohibiting locomotives from running backward, penalizing the exposure of bare legs on the stage, compelling every cigar store to display a wooden Indian.

Such suggestions are usually sidetracked without receiving serious consideration, but they indicate the low levels of legislative capacity.   Some foolish bills actually become law.   Thus one statute solemnly decreed that "when two trains meet at a crossing they shall both come to a full stop, and neither shall start up until the other has passed over."

Work of the Reference Bureaus

Increasing recognition of the very obvious fact that legislators are not experts, and need technical assistance of some sort, has led to the establishment of legislative reference bureaus or similar agencies in forty-seven states.[40]   Thirty-one of these states have separate divisions or departments whose time is devoted exclusively to legislative reference activities; the others merely increase the duties of some already existing agency—usually the state library.

Legislative reference work, in its proper sense, includes two main functions: to secure for members of the legislature such information as they may require for the performance of their duties, and to put the substance of legislators' proposals into form suitable for passage.   Some reference bureaus, however, are limited to one of these activities; while a few bureaus at the other extreme are charged not only with research and bill drafting but also with a considerable number of miscellaneous functions such as co-operation with legislative investigating committees, preparation for constitutional conventions, and assistance to universities and colleges.   In fifteen states the task of bill drafting for members of the legislature is assigned to the attorney-general's department.

The legislative reference bureau does not, as a rule, attempt to evaluate material collected for members of the state legislature.   It simply secures

[40] The only exception is Idaho.

requested information, permitting interested legislators to interpret this information in any way they desire.   With regard to bill drafting, also, the reference bureau is careful not to influence proposed legislation.   It merely considers questions of constitutionality, consistency with existing law, and probable interpretation by the courts.   Any other course would simply invite charges that the reference bureau was "playing politics"—charges that even now are not entirely unknown.

The first reference bureau was established in New York State in 1890 as a branch of the library at Albany.   Two years later the Massachusetts legislature first made an annual appropriation of one thousand dollars to the state library "for preparing an index to current events and other such matters contained in the newspapers of the day as may be deemed important by the trustees and the librarian."   But when Wisconsin adopted the reference bureau idea in 1901 it organized its new bureau so thoroughly and with such good results that it has generally been credited with stimulating other states to follow its example.

In 1931 the Interstate Reference Bureau, sponsored by the American Legislators' Association, was set up in Chicago.   It has prepared useful digests of important legislative problems and has aided some of the smaller and newer state bureaus to perform their functions in an adequate manner.   It is designed to become a central clearing house that will place the results of every reference bureau's research at the service of every other reference bureau, thus preventing needless duplication and wasted effort.

THE LOBBY

According to the express declarations of state constitutions, bills may be introduced only by the members of either house.   It must not be assumed, however, that every bill is the brain-child of some legislator.   On the contrary, many an important proposal owes its existence to persons or groups of persons whose contacts with the legislative body are at best extra-legal, and sometimes illegal.   The legislators who introduce such a bill in their respective houses can scarcely be called its authors, unless the customary meaning of the word is discarded.

In every state capital are large numbers of men and women, not connected with the state government in any official capacity, whose task is to influence legislation in behalf of the groups or interests they serve.   A few of them work without compensation; their fight for child labor laws, anti-cigarette legislation, or equal civil rights for all classes is a glorious adventure, tinged

with the religious fervor of a crusade.   But the large majority are paid, and
they command large salaries.   They have no illusions as to the nature of
their work.   They must accomplish the enactment of laws desired by their
employers, and the defeat of undesired proposals.   Fair means of producing
results are always preferred, but not used exclusively.   These men and
women swarm through the corridors of the state capitol, and even find their
way into the lobbies of the assembly chambers.   Thus they have come to be
known as lobbyists, and their activities have been given the name of lobbying.   So successful have the lobbyists been in their efforts to control legislation that they are frequently called the "third house" of the legislature.
Sometimes it seems that their influence is greater than that of the two regularly constituted houses.

Methods

The methods employed by lobbyists several decades ago were very crude,
though admittedly successful.   They consisted largely in spending money
"judiciously"—that is, purchasing for cash the support of the members of
the legislature.   When one vested interest had procured a dependable majority in this way, it often leased its control to others whose position was less
secure.   Millions of dollars changed hands secretly, without vouchers or
receipts.

Today, however, direct bribery is uncommon.   The methods now employed by lobbyists are more subtle, and no less effective.   They include
assistance to legislators in the preparation of bills—a service that is likely to
prove more thorough and complete than that of the legislative reference bureau; dinners and other social activities that draw new legislators into the exclusive inner circle of society at the state capital; and friendly gestures of
every sort that can be made without giving offense.   They include, also, such
indirect forms of lobbying as the publication of editorials and biased news in
friendly or controlled newspapers; personal work among the voters for the
purpose of inducing them to write or telegraph their wishes—that is, the
lobbyists' wishes—to their wavering representatives in the legislature; and
contributions to the campaign funds of favored candidates.

Need for Regulation

It is always a difficult task to distinguish between those lobbyists who use
questionable means to produce questionable results and those who merely
try in straightforward fashion to protect the legitimate interests of their employers.   There can be no doubt, however, that effective regulation of lobby-

ists and their activities is urgently needed. Laws designed to prevent the abuses of lobbying have been enacted in thirty-eight states,[41] but most of them have proved virtually worthless. Lobbyists are commonly required to register, giving the names of their employers, the term of their employment, and the special subjects, if any, to which their employment relates. In some states the employers are directed to submit itemized statements of their lobbying expenditures, such statements to be filed shortly after the close of the legislative sessions. The methods that lobbyists may properly employ, such as appearance before committees, newspaper publicity, and the like, are generally enumerated. Personal solicitation of members is forbidden. The penalties prescribed in the several state laws include fines, imprisonment, and disbarment from the lobbying service.

Although a few states, of which Wisconsin is the most notable example, have thus eliminated some of the most flagrant abuses of the lobbying system, their small measure of success should not be regarded as typical. Most of the states have accomplished little or nothing, and lobbyists continue to operate as before without molestation.

LEGISLATIVE RECOMMENDATIONS BY THE GOVERNOR AND HEADS OF ADMINISTRATIVE AGENCIES

Reference should be made in this chapter to so-called "administration measures." Every state constitution requires the governor to inform the legislature concerning the affairs of the commonwealth. This he does by sending a formal message, which usually contains specific recommendations as to necessary legislation. Many a governor, anxious to facilitate the adoption of his proposals, even has them drafted into proper form for legislative considerations. These bills are then introduced by friendly members of the legislature, and are known informally as administration measures. They receive prompt committee consideration and favored places on the calendar. Their enactment into law is by no means assured, however; much depends on the governor's ability as a political leader.

Reference should be made, also, to the part played by the numerous state administrative agencies in the process of lawmaking. The heads of these departments, bureaus, and offices are recognized as experts in their respective fields, and are frequently asked to testify before legislative committees. They supply individual legislators with information whenever requested to do so, and sometimes provide the arguments heard on the floor of the

[41] The ten exceptions are Arkansas, Delaware, Illinois, Minnesota, Nevada, New Jersey, New Mexico, Pennsylvania, Washington, and Wyoming.

assembly. When, therefore, they make suggestions concerning the context of proposed legislation, it is not at all surprising that their words should receive respectful attention.

Participation by department heads and bureau chiefs in the law-making process is not necessarily the same thing as executive leadership. The governor of the state is the chief executive; he supplies whatever executive leadership may be forthcoming. He may or may not consult his subordinates in the state administration before recommending the enactment of new laws. And, conversely, his subordinates may or may not secure his approval before placing their pet projects in the hands of friendly legislators. There is, of course, little likelihood that department heads or bureau chiefs will sponsor legislation directly contrary to the governor's announced program, but they may reasonably expect a free hand with regard to those matters that have never claimed the governor's attention.

REFORM OF THE LEGISLATURE

During the last few years the need for reform of the organization and procedure of state legislatures has received widespread attention. Official agencies in at least nine states, and private groups or individuals in a number of others, have made detailed investigations of existing legislative practices, together with recommendations for improvement. One of the most important of these studies is the report of the Committee on Legislative Processes and Procedures of the Council of State Governments. This report, published in December of 1948 under the title *Our State Legislatures,* makes twelve significant recommendations, which may be summarized as follows:

1. Restrictions upon the length of regular sessions of the legislature should be removed.

2. Legislators should receive annual salaries sufficient to permit service without financial sacrifice. Salaries should be fixed by statute rather than by constitutional provision.

3. Legislative terms should be lengthened and staggered.

4. Skilled and essential full-time legislative employees should be appointed on the basis of merit and competence, and should continue to serve without regard to changes in party control.

5. Legislative committees should be reduced in number wherever practicable, and organized with regard to related subject matter, equalization of work, and co-operation between the two houses.

6. Legislative committees should make provision for public hearings on all major bills, and should give advance notice of their time and place.

7. Provision should be made for legislative councils or similar agencies with adequate clerical and research facilities.

8. Legislative reference and similar services should be strengthened wherever necessary.

9. Legislative rules should limit the period of time during a session when new bills may be introduced.

10. Legislative rules should be reviewed and revised whenever necessary to expedite procedure, although with due regard for adequate deliberation and fairness to minority parties.

11. The legislature should make suitable provision, by means of a budget, for all its probable expenditures.

12. Special legislation should be avoided. Claims against the state should be handled by judicial or administrative agencies, and municipal affairs should be regulated by general or optional legislation, or by conferring home rule upon cities.

PROBLEMS

1. Write a brief history of the legislature of your state.

2. Study the unicameral legislature of one of the Canadian provinces. Describe its organization and work.

3. Make a list of important measures enacted by the legislature of your state during the last ten years, and note how the members voted on these measures, if their votes are recorded. Do you observe a sharp dividing line between urban and rural interests?

4. How many bills were introduced at the last session of your state legislature? Trace briefly the history of these bills—how many were reported from committee, how many actually received consideration on the floor of either house, how many were passed during the last forty-eight hours of the legislative session.

5. Note the number and duties of the committees of the two houses of your state legislature. How many of these committees could be eliminated without a reduction of legislative efficiency?

6. Study the work of the legislative reference bureau of your state or a neighboring state.

SELECTED REFERENCES

Buck, A. E., *Modernizing Our State Legislatures,* 1936.
Buehler, Ezra C., ed., *Unicameral Legislatures,* 1937.
Chamberlain, Joseph P., *Legislative Processes: National and State,* 1936.
Coigne, Armand B., *Statute Making,* 1948.
Commonwealth Club of California, *The Legislature of California,* San Francisco, 1943.
Council of State Governments, *Our State Legislatures,* 1948.
———, *State Regulation of Lobbying,* 1951.
Farmer, Hallie, *The Legislative Process in Alabama: Legislative Apportionment* (1944); *Local and Private Legislation* (1944); *Standing Committees* (1945); *Recess and Interim Committees* (1946); *Legislative Costs* (1947), University, Ala.

Geary, T. C., *Law Making in South Dakota,* 3rd ed., Vermilion, 1952.

Governor's Committee on Preparatory Research for the New Jersey Constitutional Convention, *Procedural Limitations on the Legislative Process in the New Jersey Constitution* (Monograph No. 14); *Lobbying* (Monograph No. 15), Trenton, 1947.

Greenfield, Margaret, *Legislative Reapportionment,* Berkeley, Calif., 1951.

Guild, F. H., and Snider, C. F., *Legislative Procedure in Kansas,* Topeka, 1946.

Illinois Legislative Council, *Legislative Broadcasting and Recording,* 1952.

———, *Scheduling Legislative Workloads,* 1952.

Johnson, Alvin W., *The Unicameral Legislature,* Minneapolis, 1938.

Laurent, Eleanore V., *Legislative Reference Work in the United States,* 1939.

Lee, Eugene C., *The Presiding Officer and Rules Committee in Legislatures of the United States,* Berkeley, Calif., 1952.

Leek, John H., *Legislative Reference Work: A Comparative Study,* 1925.

Luce, Robert, *Legislative Assemblies,* 1924.

———, *Legislative Procedure,* 1922.

———, *Legislative Problems: Development, Status, and Trend of Treatment and Exercise of Lawmaking Powers,* 1935.

Manning, J. W., *Unicameral Legislation in the States,* Lexington, Ky., 1938.

McKean, Dayton D., *Pressures on the Legislature of New Jersey,* 1938.

New York State Joint Legislative Committee on Legislative Methods, Practices, Procedures, and Expenditures, *Final Report,* Albany, 1946.

Plaisted, John W., *Legislative Procedure in the General Court of Massachusetts,* Boston, 1948.

Pound, Merritt B., *State Legislature, Two Houses or One?,* Athens, Ga., 1938.

Rousse, Thomas A., *Bicameralism vs. Unicameralism,* 1937.

Schriftgiesser, Karl, *The Lobbyists: The Art and Business of Influencing Lawmakers,* Boston, 1951.

Senning, John P., *The One-House Legislature,* 1937.

Shull, Charles W., *American Experience with Unicameral Legislatures,* Detroit, 1937.

Smith, T. V., *The Legislative Way of Life,* 1940.

University of South Carolina Bureau of Public Administration, *Aids for State Legislators,* Columbia, 1947.

University of South Dakota, Governmental Research Bureau, *Law Making in South Dakota,* Vermilion, 1947.

Walch, J. W., *A Complete Handbook on the Unicameral Legislatures,* 1937.

Walker, Harvey, *The Legislative Process,* rev. ed., 1948.

Willoughby, William F., *Principles of Legislative Organization and Administration,* 1934.

Winslow, C. I., *State Legislative Committees,* 1931.

Zeller, Belle, ed., *American State Legislatures,* 1954.

CHAPTER 8

State Courts

The courts are specialized agencies for the enforcement of law. They settle disputes between private persons, and also controversies between private persons and the state. They determine the innocence or guilt of persons accused of crime. They protect the rights of the individual, as guaranteed by federal and state constitutions. They prevent the executive and legislative departments from overstepping the bounds of their authority.

In addition to their judicial acts the courts commonly perform a number of essentially administrative functions that have been assigned by the constitution or by law. Thus they appoint and supervise certain public officers in a number of states, and in some instances they also have the right of removal. School boards, for example, are judicially appointed in several jurisdictions. The supreme court of Tennessee selects the attorney-general. Many city and county officials may be removed by court action.

Some control over elections is also exercised by the courts in a number of states, and occasionally they are empowered to pass upon applications for various kinds of business licenses. The estates of deceased persons are administered by the regular trial courts—or, in the more populous communities, by special probate courts; and this work differs in no essential respect from the activities of many administrative departments of the state government, which also handle a great deal of property. The courts appoint receivers to manage the property and affairs of bankrupt persons.

These various administrative duties, which are becoming constantly more numerous, consume a great deal of time, and tend to interfere with the primary function of the courts—the conduct of litigation. The suggestion is often made, therefore, that they be reduced to an absolute minimum, and that new administrative duties be assigned to administrative officers, wherever possible. But only a few states have acted on this principle.

CIVIL AND CRIMINAL CASES

The cases that come before the courts for adjudication may be divided into two classes—civil and criminal.   A civil suit arises when one person seeks legal redress from another person for an alleged private wrong or *tort,* such as the violation of a contract.   The state has no interest in the outcome of such a case, other than to insure fair play.   Its function is solely that of impartial arbiter.

A criminal suit, on the other hand, grows out of a public wrong—an offense against the state.   The laws of each state enumerate and define these public wrongs, and prescribe the penalties to be imposed upon guilty persons.   They also provide for public prosecution of persons whose probable guilt has been established by some formal process, such as indictment or information.   Most of the public wrongs or crimes defined by law are acts against persons, and to that extent they resemble torts.   Homicide, kidnaping, burglary, and arson, for example, are wrongs against individuals. But they are such serious matters that it has seemed wise to take them out of the category of private wrongs and declare them to be offenses against the state.

In many instances a wrongful act gives rise to a criminal prosecution and also to a civil suit.   Thus assault and battery may be a breach of the peace and, in addition, an invasion of the injured person's rights that leads naturally to civil action.   The criminal prosecution and the civil suit are separate proceedings, however, and are separately tried.   Frequently they go before the same court, but in such cases the court clearly indicates whether it is sitting in a criminal or civil capacity.   Or the court may have separate divisions, established by law, to handle the two classes of cases.

ORGANIZATION OF THE COURTS

Justices of the Peace

JURISDICTION.   At the base of the judicial pyramid, in the small towns and rural districts, are the justices of the peace.   Almost invariably they are popularly chosen, and their terms of office are short—usually two years. They are not required to be learned in the law, and as a result they seldom have any special preparation for their important work.   Their jurisdiction, though narrowly restricted by constitutional and legal provisions, extends to both civil and criminal matters.   In civil suits it is limited by the sum in controversy or the amount of damages demanded; thus the state law may fix fifty or one hundred dollars, or even five hundred dollars, as the maximum.

Suits involving larger sums may not be tried before a justice of the peace, but must go to a higher court.

In criminal cases the justices of the peace have two distinct functions. First, they exercise summary jurisdiction over minor infractions of the law, such as breaches of the peace, traffic law violations, disregard of health ordinances, and the like. With regard to such matters they issue warrants when necessary, hold hearings, determine innocence or guilt, and impose suitable sentences. But their power does not extend beyond the imposition of small fines and imprisonment for short periods. Moreover, their decisions may almost invariably be appealed to some court of superior jurisdiction. The second important function of the justices of the peace in connection with criminal matters is the preliminary hearing of serious complaints. They determine whether sufficient evidence exists to warrant holding accused persons for further action by the grand jury or other authorities; and, if bail is required, they fix its amount.

DEFECTS UNDER PRESENT-DAY CONDITIONS: *Lack of legal training.* To entrust these important duties to persons without legal training, whose chief qualification is their ability to control votes, is little short of absurd. In earlier times, when life was far less complicated, and the controversies of rural Americans could best be settled by a proper application of common sense, the justice of the peace system gave reasonably satisfactory results. The justice knew every man in the community; he understood the situations that give rise to lawsuits and breaches of the peace, and frequently he could give words of friendly advice that would be worth more than long citations from statutes and court decisions.

But that day is past. The justice of the peace is no longer a community patriarch, dispensing Solomon-like justice through his superior wisdom. He is an agent of the state for the enforcement of state law, and he cannot possibly hope to give reasonable satisfaction in the performance of his duties without adequate legal training. Even for laymen, according to the old maxim, ignorance of the law is no excuse. For justices of the peace such ignorance is utterly inexcusable.

The fee system. Some of the worst abuses of the justices' court arise in connection with the fee system. In more than half of the states justices of the peace receive no stated salaries, but instead rely on the fees that they are able to collect. Therefore their incomes bear a close relationship to the volume of business that they can attract to their courts. Within a single county there are usually several justices of the peace exercising concurrent jurisdiction, and each of them strives to secure a larger number of cases than his competitors. For this reason the decision in a civil case is likely to favor the plaintiff, regardless of the circumstances; the plaintiff's attorney is thereby encouraged to supply additional customers.

First steps toward reform. The justice courts have long been regarded as a defective branch of the American judicial system. More than a quarter of a century ago the New York State Crime Commission declared: "Probably the most unsatisfactory feature of the criminal law is the obsolete and antiquated institution known as the justice of the peace. Thoughtful students of the subject have for some years past realized fully that this was an unsatisfactory form of organization, and nothing but the expense of providing adequately trained lawyers to man these minor courts has prevented remedying the situation." [1]

This criticism is still generally valid. In some states, however, steps have been taken to correct the situation. Missouri has eliminated the justice courts and replaced them with magistrates' courts presided over by judges selected from the legal profession. Indiana has adopted a somewhat similar scheme, though retaining justices of the peace for certain minor purposes. California also has accepted the Missouri plan, except for its less populous areas, where the justices are required to be lawyers or to pass suitable examinations. Virginia and Maryland make use of legally trained justices of the peace, who are paid regular salaries.

Magistrates' Courts

In the cities the lowest tribunals are commonly known as police or magistrates' courts. The men who preside over these courts do not differ in any essential respect from the justices of the peace, except that they are commonly on a salary basis. They are chosen by the voters in most cities, which is merely another way of saying that they are selected by the dominant political machine. The salaries are low—so low as to attract only the poorer grade of politicians. They are constantly reminded that they owe their positions to the favor of the boss, and they are expected to retain this favor by using their authority for such purposes and in such manner as the boss may direct. Since they are not learned in the law, the intricacies of constitutions and statutes present no difficulties, and they can readily arrive at any conclusions that fancy or political wisdom may dictate. Of course, a right of appeal from their decisions exists in nearly all cases. But appeals are tedious, costly, and uncertain, so it usually happens that justice—or injustice—is finally done in the magistrates' courts.

[1] Annual Report, 1927, p. 44.

Special Police Courts

Many cities have attempted to solve some of their more difficult problems in the administration of justice by creating special courts—juvenile, domestic relations, small claims, traffic, and others. These courts are presided over by judges who are presumed to be specialists in the various fields to which they have been assigned.

The procedure is adjusted to the nature of the business at hand; usually the formality of the court room is swept aside in the interest of efficient justice. In a juvenile court case, for example, everything is done to put the boy or girl at ease and to ascertain all the facts without creating the impression that a trial is in progress. More important than the fact that a criminal act has been committed is the reason for that act, and the treatment that may be necessary to prevent the young delinquent from becoming a confirmed offender.

Other problems connected with the family—legal separation of husband and wife, divorce, support, the custody of children—also require special consideration and are generally handled in domestic relations or family courts. Here, too, the procedure is informal, since the purpose of the court is to bring about a reconciliation whenever possible and a friendly settlement when reconciliation is out of the question. It has been proposed that the juvenile and domestic relations courts be consolidated, on the ground that virtually every problem affecting the child is necessarily a family problem. This suggestion is logical, and its general adoption would eliminate many perplexing questions of conflicting jurisdiction.

Special court procedure is also necessary to handle small claims—perhaps for amounts less than twenty-five or fifty dollars. In such cases the sum in controversy is often but a fraction of the cost of an ordinary trial, including a lawyer's fee. Therefore some way must be found to give substantial justice simply and cheaply. It is absurd to declare—as the laws of every state did declare until a few years ago, and as most state laws still provide—that such matters as a twenty-dollar claim for unpaid wages or a bill of seven dollars for groceries cannot be adjusted judicially without an expenditure of approximately one hundred dollars. The small claims court offers the most satisfactory solution of this difficult problem. It eliminates all unnecessary formality, discourages the participation of lawyers, reduces court costs to a nominal figure, and narrowly restricts the right of appeal.

Traffic courts also deserve at least passing mention. Their function is to handle all cases of alleged violations of the motor vehicle laws, so as to secure prompt and uniform treatment of offenders. Poor organization, however, has prevented them from attaining maximum efficiency in most of the cities where they have been established.

The Unified Municipal Court

One of the most important reforms of recent years in the American judicial system is the unified municipal court.   Such a court, if properly organized, has complete original jurisdiction, both civil and criminal, over all matters arising under state law or municipal ordinance within the city's limits. Its work is divided among a number of branches—small claims, traffic, domestic relations, and the like—but complete responsibility is centered in the chief justice of the court, who assigns his colleagues to the divisions for which they are presumably best fitted.

To a large extent the municipal court determines its own organization and makes its own rules.   Thus it is able to modify its procedure whenever necessary to obtain greater efficiency.   Cases may be transferred from one judge to another, in order to distribute the work equally and prevent congested dockets.   This, then, is a unified municipal court—as properly organized.   But very few courts conform to this ideal pattern.   So-called "unified" municipal courts have been established in most of the great metropolitan centers of the United States.   Very commonly, however, they lack complete original jurisdiction or adequate rule-making power.

County or Circuit Courts

Above the justice and police courts, in every state, are the trial courts, where most litigation originates and most persons accused of crime are brought to trial.   These courts are called by various names.   In some states, where there is one such court in each county, they are known as county courts.   More commonly they are designated as district or circuit courts, since the laws of approximately two thirds of the states combine counties into judicial districts or circuits.   Under this plan two or three counties comprise a district, and in each county a session of the district court is held at regular intervals.   The number of judges assigned to a district varies with the population and the volume of litigation, but one judge to a district is generally regarded as a satisfactory arrangement, except for the larger cities.

The trial courts—by whatever name they may be known—have popularly elected judges in thirty-seven states.[2]   Four-year terms for these judges are most common.   The jurisdiction of the trial courts is very broad.   They

[2] The other eleven states are Delaware, Maine, Maryland, Massachusetts, New Hampshire, New Jersey, and Rhode Island, where the governor appoints; and Connecticut, South Carolina, Vermont, and Virginia, where the choice is made by the legislature.

THE STATE SUPREME COURTS

	Number of Judges	Term of Office in Years	Compensation*
Alabama	7	6	$12,000
Arizona	5	6	12,500
Arkansas	7	8	9,000
California	7	12	21,000
Colorado	7	10	12,000
Connecticut	5	8	15,000
Delaware	3	12	17,000
Florida	7	6	13,500
Georgia	7	6	14,000
Idaho	5	6	8,500
Illinois	7	9	20,000
Indiana	5	6	13,500
Iowa	9	6	10,000
Kansas	7	6	10,000
Kentucky	7	8	12,000
Louisiana	7	14	18,000
Maine	6	7	11,000
Maryland	5	15	16,500
Massachusetts	7	Life	18,500
Michigan	8	8	18,500
Minnesota	7	6	13,500
Mississippi	6	8	11,000
Missouri	7	12	17,500
Montana	5	6	9,000
Nebraska	7	6	9,100

usually handle all civil suits, without restriction as to amount.[3]   Such suits may be begun in the trial courts, or may come on appeal from the justice or police courts.   Original jurisdiction is exercised in virtually all criminal cases, other than the minor misdemeanor cases handled by the justices of the peace and the magistrates.   Separate courts may be established for civil and criminal matters, or, instead, there may be separate divisions of the same court.   It has already been indicated that the trial courts commonly perform a number of administrative duties, such as the management of the estates of deceased persons and the appointment and supervision of certain county officials.[4]

Appellate Courts

Above the trial courts, at the apex of the state's judicial pyramid, stands the state supreme court.   More than one fourth of the states have found it

[3] In a few states, however, a limit of one or two thousand dollars is imposed.
[4] See page 160.

	Number of Judges	Term of Office in Years	Compensation *
Nevada	3	6	15,000
New Hampshire	5	To age 70	12,000
New Jersey	7	7 (reappointment for life)	24,000
New Mexico	5	8	12,500
New York	7	14	35,000
North Carolina	7	8	16,000
North Dakota	5	10	10,000
Ohio	7	6	16,000
Oklahoma	9	6	12,500
Pennsylvania	7	21	25,000
Rhode Island	5	Life	17,000
South Carolina	5	6	12,500
South Dakota	5	6	8,700
Tennessee	5	8	15,000
Texas	9	6	12,000
Utah	5	10	9,000
Vermont	5	2	10,000
Virginia	7	12	13,500
Washington	9	6	15,000
West Virginia	5	12	12,500
Wisconsin	7	10	12,000
Wyoming	3	8	11,000

Based on data from *The Book of the States, 1954–55*.
* In twenty-one states the compensation of the chief justice is slightly higher than the figure given in the table.

necessary, however, to interpose courts of appeal between the trial courts and the supreme court, in order to lighten the burden of the highest tribunal. These intermediate courts are called by various names—courts of appeal, district courts of appeal, superior courts. Each court has from three to nine judges, who sit as a body and render decisions by a majority vote.

The intermediate courts vary almost as widely in jurisdiction as in nomenclature. In general, they handle cases that come to them on appeal from the trial courts. Their jurisdiction is final in some matters, but subject to an appeal to the supreme court in others. The laws of a few states confer original jurisdiction upon them for certain important subjects of controversy, such as contested elections.

The Supreme Court

Every state constitution, save that of New Hampshire, provides for a supreme court (though not always by that name), and in New Hampshire a supreme court has been created by act of the legislature. The number of members ranges from three to nine, and a majority vote is necessary in each case. State supreme court judges are generally chosen by the people.[5] Their salaries are relatively high,[6] and their terms of office fairly long. More than half of the states provide at least eight-year terms, and three New England states [7] have accepted the principle of tenure for life or during good behavior. Vermont, on the other hand, still retains a two-year term.

The chief function of the supreme court is to hear and decide cases from the lower courts. In eleven states it has only appellate jurisdiction,[8] and in thirty-three others its original jurisdiction is limited to the issuance of certain writs. The constitutions of the remaining four states [9] confer original jurisdiction in certain important cases—for example, cases in which the state is a party. The supreme court of a state is the final interpreter of the state's constitution and laws. No appeal from its decisions may be taken to the Supreme Court of the United States unless a so-called "federal question" is involved—that is, unless the case hinges upon the meaning of the federal Constitution or a federal law or treaty.

SELECTION OF JUDGES

Students of government and members of the bar are generally agreed that the judges of all courts should be appointed by the chief executive, and not forced to engage in the hurly-burly of an election campaign. "Popular election" is likely to be synonymous with "political selection"; therefore judges chosen by popular vote may reasonably be expected to be cogs in the dominant political machine. Judges should be experts—technicians of the highest order; but experts cannot be obtained by popular election, except at rare intervals and under unusual circumstances.

It is an axiom of public administration that appointment should be used when skill is desired, and that election should be employed only to secure representation. The more progressive states, in reorganizing their agencies

[5] The manner of selection is the same as for judges of the trial courts (see footnote on page 165) except in five states—California and Missouri, where the governor names judges of the supreme court, subject to eventual ratification by the voters; Rhode Island, where they are chosen by the legislature; and Illinois and Maryland, where they are popularly elected.

[6] Only two states—Idaho and South Dakota—pay less than nine thousand dollars a year. The average is slightly more than fourteen thousand. It is interesting to note that most states are as generous to their supreme court judges as to their governors.

[7] Massachusetts, New Hampshire, Rhode Island.

[8] Arizona, Connecticut, Georgia, Indiana, Kentucky, Maryland, Mississippi, New Hampshire, New Jersey, New York, Tennessee.

[9] Massachusetts, Nebraska, North Carolina, Pennsylvania.

of administration, have generally recognized this principle, at least to some extent.[10]   But election by the voters still remains the generally accepted method of choosing the judiciary.   Selection by the legislature seldom, if ever, gives better results than popular choice; it diffuses the responsibility for improper selections, and opens the way to secret deals.

For some years to come, at least, popular election is likely to remain the generally accepted method of choosing state judges in the United States. There are, however, some other plans that have been tried with excellent results.   In 1934 the voters of California approved a constitutional amendment permitting judges to run solely against their own records, instead of forcing them to campaign against rival candidates.   Under the provisions of this California plan any incumbent judge may, just prior to the end of his term, indicate his desire to retain his office.   His name is then placed on the ballot, and the voters are asked merely to decide whether he shall be retained —not whether they prefer him to a number of other candidates.   An unfavorable vote causes a vacancy, which is then filled by gubernatorial appointment.   The governor does not have a free hand in the matter, however; his selection must be approved by a commission on qualifications, consisting of the state supreme court's chief justice, another judge of a high court, and the attorney-general.   Moreover, the voters must give their approval at the next election.   If they again vote in the negative, another vacancy occurs; and so the process continues until general agreement is reached.

Missouri has had a somewhat similar plan since 1940.   Each judge is chosen by the governor from a list submitted by a nominating commission, which consists of lawyers and laymen, as well as a jurist serving ex officio. After the newly appointed judge has served for a year, his name is placed on the ballot—without rival candidates of course—and the voters are asked to decide whether he shall be permitted to complete his term.[11]   Such plans are a marked improvement over the ordinary scheme of popular election, but proposals for their adoption in other states have received little support.

REMOVAL OF JUDGES

Impeachment and Joint Address

Almost as important as the selection of judges is the matter of their removal.   Every state constitution provides that judges, as well as other civil

[10] See pages 98–104.

[11] See Jack W. Pelaston's monograph, *The Missouri Plan for the Selection of Judges.* See also "Missouri Provides New Methods in Improving the Administration of Justice," by Chief Justice Lawrance M. Hyde of the Supreme Court of Missouri, in the February, 1950, issue of *State Government,* pp. 28 ff.

officers, may be removed by process of impeachment.   In most states a two-thirds vote of the senate is necessary for conviction.   Moreover, state constitutions customarily limit the use of impeachment to very serious cases, in which criminal misconduct is charged.

Nearly half of the states authorize removal of judges by joint address of the two houses of the legislature—that is, by passage of a concurrent resolution.   This method does not partake of the judicial nature of impeachment; it is a purely legislative act and not suitable for determining the innocence or guilt of any person charged with an offense so serious as to warrant his removal from public office.   Fortunately, joint address has been hedged about with so many constitutional restrictions that it is scarcely ever used.

The Recall

It is obvious, therefore, that removal of judges by the ordinary processes of government is extremely difficult.   Impeachment—the means universally provided—is cumbersome, tedious, and suitable only for extreme cases. Therefore a judge may and sometimes does remain in office long after his period of usefulness is past.   He may suffer from physical infirmities that seriously interfere with his judicial duties, yet refuse to resign.   He may acquire an arbitrary and unreasonable attitude that prevents even-handed dispensation of justice in his court, yet continue in office because no ready way can be found to get rid of him.   Such cases have actually occurred, though infrequently, and have given rise to a demand for some easier way of removing judges who have become infirm, unreasonable—or unpopular. The scheme most commonly advocated is the recall.   The constitutions of eight states [12] now provide for the recall of judges, and in two other states judges have been exempted from the provisions of the recall by the narrow margin of a few votes.

Many leaders of the bench and bar believe, however, that the recall provisions of state constitutions should not be applied to judges under any circumstances.   They cite the usual arguments against the recall [13] and stress also the necessity of maintaining an independent judiciary.   Judges must be independent, because they must be free to enforce the law as they find it, without fear or favor.

[12] Arizona, California, Colorado, Kansas, Nevada, North Dakota, Oregon, Wisconsin.

[13] See pages 335–339.

NEED FOR COURT REFORM

Defects in the Judicial System

DELAY IN THE ADMINISTRATION OF JUSTICE.   For many years the American judicial system has been condemned as thoroughly unsatisfactory by statesmen, publicists, jurists—in fact, by virtually everyone qualified to express an opinion on the subject.   Delay is a common cause of complaint. A certain amount of delay is inevitable; it is, in fact, desirable.   It is inevitable because many things must be done in the preparation of a case. Facts must be ascertained, witnesses listed and subpoenaed, evidence assembled, and the case listed for trial.   Moderate delay is desirable because it materially lessens the likelihood of injustice.   It affords an accused person reasonable opportunity to prepare his defense.   As the supreme court of the State of Pennsylvania said in an important case: " 'The law of the land,' like 'due process of law,' requires timely notice and an opportunity to defend. It is vain to give the accused a day in court, with no opportunity to prepare for it, or to guarantee him counsel without giving the latter any opportunity to acquaint himself with the facts or law of the case." [14]   From time to time the newspapers carry stories of persons who have been arrested on serious charges, tried and convicted—all within the space of a few days. Such happenings are commonly cited as examples of speedy justice, despite the virtual impossibility of preparing a suitable defense in so short a time.

Injustice of delay.   At times, therefore, undue haste may produce very unfortunate results.   But when delay extends beyond a reasonable period, objection may well be raised.   Cases that drag on for months or even years before final settlement are productive of nothing but evil.   In many instances they amount to a substantial denial of justice.   Witnesses die, move away, or forget.   In a civil suit, attorneys' fees grow until they sometimes equal or exceed the amount of damages awarded.   A poor person, badly in need of money and impatient with the apparent procrastination of the courts, may finally agree to accept a small sum in full payment of a large debt, rather than undergo a further period of uncertainty.   In such cases, delay is a form of unfairness that should not be tolerated.

Causes of delay.   It may well be asked, therefore, why civil suits and criminal prosecutions are not handled more expeditiously.   The answer, at least in part, is that the courts are not properly organized to handle the large and increasing volume of business imposed upon them by the complexities of modern civilization.   Court dockets are congested.   In many jurisdictions new cases are placed on the calendar more rapidly than old cases

[14] Commonwealth *v.* O'Keefe, 298 Penna. 169; 148 Atl. 73 (1929).

can be disposed of, and every year the problem of delay becomes more serious. New discoveries, new inventions—in fact, a new world—have vastly broadened the field of human relationships, and therefore have made more litigation almost inevitable. Thousands of new laws dealing with hundreds of new subjects have defined as criminal many acts that were formerly regarded as beyond the scope of the law and in this way have increased the number of "criminals by definition." So it is not at all surprising that the judicial system, designed in another day to meet the requirements of a simple mode of life, should be unsuited to the tremendous task of dispensing justice swiftly and surely in this modern world.

A major cause of delay is the abuse of the right of appeal. This right must be preserved, of course; otherwise there would be no way of correcting the injustices that naturally result from human ignorance, indifference, carelessness—or worse. But it should be restricted within narrow limits. It should not be permitted to become a device for defeating the plain provisions of the law. Unfortunately, it has reached that low level in every American state.

UNCERTAINTY OF PUNISHMENT. One of the most serious defects of the American judicial system is the uncertainty of punishment. When a person commits a crime—anywhere in the United States—the chance that he will be apprehended, convicted, and punished is fairly remote. Crime may properly be listed among the safer vocations, provided one steers clear of murder. And even murderers, in this country, enjoy a comparative safety that is unknown in the progressive nations of western Europe. This state of affairs cannot be charged wholly against the judiciary. The police, who are primarily responsible for the apprehension of persons accused of crime, are often inefficient, and sometimes corrupt. Prosecuting attorneys, swayed by personal or partisan motives, frequently fail to press serious charges against politically powerful persons, preferring to make impressive records by forcing confessions from poor wretches who have neither money nor friends. But a great many miscarriages of justice in the United States can be traced directly to the obsolete judicial system. Their recurrence can be prevented only by thoroughgoing changes.

JUDICIAL REFORM PROPOSALS. Hundreds of reforms of the court system have been suggested. Some are highly conservative, amounting merely to slight changes in procedure. Others are extremely radical, contemplating a complete revision of judicial organization and methods. Many of the moderate proposals have already received more or less widespread acceptance. Many others, also, though not in actual operation, deserve serious consideration. In this volume, however, only a limited amount of space can be devoted to judicial reform; therefore attention will be centered on a few outstanding proposals.

Court unification. Most comprehensive, perhaps, is the plan of court unification advanced by a committee of the American Bar Association nearly half a century ago, and since indorsed by statesmen and publicists. According to this suggestion, the entire judicial power of each state, "at least for civil cases, should be vested in one great court, of which all tribunals should be branches, departments, or divisions. The business, as well as the judicial administration, of this court should be thoroughly organized so as to prevent not merely waste of judicial power, but all needless clerical work, duplication of papers and records, and the like, thus obviating unnecessary expense to litigants and cost to the public." [15]

The lowest courts would be known as county courts, and would have exclusive jurisdiction over all petty matters. Above them would be the superior courts, exercising original jurisdiction over controversies in which larger sums were involved and separated into appropriate divisions for the several types of business. At the top would be the supreme court—a single ultimate court of appeals with its necessary branches.

The chief justice of the supreme court, or a council presided over by him, would have power to assign judges to branches or communities as needed, to assign or transfer cases in order to equalize the amount of court work, and to establish court procedure within the limits fixed by law. Thus authority would be concentrated in one man, or a small group, and responsibility could readily be fixed if the court system failed to operate smoothly and efficiently.

This scheme is in marked contrast to the present organization—or disorganization—of the courts. If adopted, it would eliminate overlapping and conflicting jurisdiction, simplify appeal procedure, permit judges to specialize in particular classes of legislation, and produce a co-ordinated judicial system. It seems to have virtually no disadvantages worth mentioning. Yet it has not been written into the constitution of a single state. It is a sharp departure from present practice and therefore likely to be regarded with suspicion.

Judicial councils. Less ambitious than court unification, but also designed to improve court organization and procedure, is the judicial council movement. Ohio led the way in 1923. Its statute creating a judicial council was carefully drafted but the necessary appropriation was not made; therefore the council was able to accomplish virtually nothing. The next year, however, Massachusetts enacted suitable legislation and also provided

[15] American Bar Association *Reports,* 1909.

adequate funds.   Since 1924 the movement has grown steadily.   There are now judicial councils in thirty-two states, though three of them are inactive.

The primary function of judicial councils is to study the court system and recommend desirable changes.   For this purpose they conduct a continuous survey of the volume and condition of business in the various state courts and also observe the result of experiments in other jurisdictions. They devise ways of simplifying judicial procedure and handling cases more expeditiously.   Proposals for improved organization and methods are submitted to the legislature and occasionally to the judges of the courts.   Special investigations are made from time to time at the legislature's request.

In most instances, therefore, a judicial council merely investigates and recommends.   It is without power to compel the adoption of any of its suggestions.   It has no final authority.   But in a few states, of which California is the most notable example, it has a certain measure of control over the court system.   The California judicial council assigns judges to care for crowded calendars and also makes rules of procedure that supplement the rules established by state law.

Usually a judicial council is composed of nine or ten members, though the number varies from six in Rhode Island to fifty-two in Kentucky.   One or more members are chosen from the state supreme court and several from the lower courts.   In addition, it is customary to appoint one or two practicing attorneys who hold no public office.

Revision of rules of procedure.   One reason for excessive delays and congested court dockets is the antiquated set of rules under which virtually every state court is obliged to operate.   These rules, which prescribe judicial procedure in minute detail, have been enacted by the legislature and may not be altered except through legislative action.   Many of them serve chiefly to hamper the courts and prevent the efficient administration of justice.   In recent years, therefore, the suggestion has frequently been made that the courts be given authority, within broad limits, to establish their own rules and to make such changes from time to time as may seem desirable.   In defense of the proposal it is urged that cumbersome rules could be swept away with ease, that greater flexibility would inevitably result, and that the overburdened legislature would be relieved of a task for which it is poorly fitted.   The American Bar Association believes that the courts should make their own rules of procedure and has appointed a committee to foster the movement.   More than one fourth of the states have already conferred more or less extensive rule-making powers upon the judiciary, and several other states have given the matter serious consideration.

Increase of judge's authority.   The part played by the judge in the conduct of a trial varies somewhat from state to state, but not a single state of the American Union empowers him to assume a commanding position, like the judge of an English court, and guide the trial to a proper conclusion. Instead, the American judge, at least in the state courts, is merely an umpire, enforcing the rules of the game and unconcerned as to the result. The judicial codes of many states, though permitting him to instruct the jury as to the law applicable to each case, specify that the statement of law must be abstract. Therefore the jurors are utterly without guidance in their attempt to apply legal principles that they but half understand. In other respects, also, the judge is greatly handicapped. Usually he is forbidden to comment on the facts, or to express his opinion concerning the credibility of witnesses.

The effect of all these restrictions has been to reduce—almost to the vanishing point—the influence of the one disinterested person in the courtroom whose training and experience fit him to direct a search for justice. Thus a present-day trial in a state court becomes a sort of judicial duel, with the opposing attorneys as chief participants. The obvious remedy for this state of affairs is to increase the authority of the judge, so that he may direct the course of the trial with a firm hand. But the states seem disinclined to enact the necessary legislation.

Defects in the Jury System

Blackstone once declared that "trial by jury ever has been and I trust ever will be looked upon as the glory of the English law . . . and the most transcendent privilege which any subject can enjoy or wish for." [16] In present-day America, however, the "glory of the English law" shines less brightly, reflecting only the light of a time long past, and the ancient and honorable institution of jury trial has been subjected to a great deal of sharp criticism.

SELECTION OF JURORS. A number of factors are responsible for the present widespread dissatisfaction with the jury system. In the first place, modern conditions are not well suited to a scheme of fact-finding by twelve "good men and true, drawn from the vicinage." In urban communities, especially, men scarcely know their neighbors, and their slight familiarity with neighborhood happenings is valueless at a trial. Moreover, any prospective juror who has first-hand knowledge of the facts of a given case, or has given time and thought to the published accounts, is immediately challenged and declared ineligible to serve. Thus we find that the ancient practice has been completely reversed. Whereas jurors were once selected

[16] *Commentaries,* Book III, p. 379.

from the immediate vicinity so that their knowledge of local men and events might lead to a fair verdict, now jurors with pertinent knowledge of either men or events are excluded, and ignorance is made virtually a prerequisite of jury service.

Further, the methods commonly employed for the selection of jurors result in serious delays. Any prospective juror may be challenged by the prosecution or the defense "for cause"—that is, because of alleged prejudice or incompetence—and will be dismissed if the challenge is sustained by the court. In addition, the law always permits a certain number of challenges without assignment of cause—peremptory challenges, as they are called. But it is the abuse of the right of challenge for cause that chiefly produces delay. In a hotly contested case, with a judge who is disposed to allow virtually all challenges, an almost unbelievable amount of time is often wasted. The selection of the jury may take days or even weeks, and involve the examination of hundreds of prospective jurors.

Moreover, the jury laws of every state authorize presiding judges to relieve persons from jury service, if it appears that such service would impose a serious hardship. Judges usually grant exemptions liberally, for they realize that jury duty places a heavy burden on busy men and women who are engaged in important business and professional activities. Thus the better elements in the community are weeded out, and the only persons available for jury service are those who can find no better way of passing their waking hours.[17]

JURY VERDICTS. The mere fact that jurors are not trained in the law would seem to be a sufficient reason why they should not be permitted to determine the law under any circumstances. Yet in a number of states the jury is made the judge of both law and fact. The results are usually distressing to anyone interested in an impartial judicial system.

In some types of cases—complicated breach of contract suits, for example —the jury is not even a good judge of the facts. The exact meaning of abstruse documents, couched in formal legal terminology, must be determined, and the jurors are completely ignorant of the rules that should guide them. Even in less technical cases, where sound judgment is the chief requisite, juries are easily swayed by racial, religious, or class appeals. The stirring words of a clever attorney may prove more effective than unrefuted evidence.

PROPOSALS FOR CHANGES. Today, therefore, the jury system itself is

[17] For a somewhat more sympathetic view of the jury system, see Curtis Bok's article, "The Jury System in America," in the May, 1953, issue of the *Annals of the American Academy of Political and Social Science*, pp. 92–96.

on trial in the United States. Some persons maintain that it should be modified to meet modern conditions; others contend that it should be abolished root and branch. Virtually no one urges its retention without changes of some sort. A number of plans to improve the jury system have been proposed, and most of them have been tried in certain states.

It has been suggested that the size of the jury be reduced from twelve —the traditional number—to five, six, seven, or, at most, eight. A smaller number of persons should be able to reach an agreement more readily, with no greater likelihood of doing injustice. This plan has been adopted by twenty states for civil suits, and by eight states for criminal cases not involving the death penalty.

The usual requirement of a unanimous verdict is also under fire. Many persons believe that a verdict rendered by a substantial majority of the jury would often be much fairer than a so-called "unanimous" agreement. Real unanimity of opinion seldom exists, in juries or elsewhere, and constitutional provisions that fail to recognize this important fact simply place an unreasonable amount of power in the hands of one juror or a small minority. In recent years a number of states have amended their fundamental laws to permit jury verdicts by less than unanimous vote, especially in civil suits. Criminal cases are less frequently included, and no state has abolished the unanimity requirement for capital cases. A three-fourths vote is usually necessary for a verdict, though two-thirds suffices in Montana, and also in Idaho for minor offenses.

Striking at the very heart of jury inefficiency is the suggestion that persons accused of crime or engaged in civil suits be permitted to waive their right of jury trial if they so desire. The right to waive trial by jury in civil suits is now found in virtually all states, having been granted by constitutional amendment, statutory provision, or judicial action. Forty states permit waiver in misdemeanor cases. With regard to more serious offenses, however, only about one third of the states have abandoned the outworn custom of compulsory trial by jury without regard to the wishes of the accused. Moreover, in some of these states the right of waiver has no practical significance, since it is virtually never used by persons accused of crime. But in other commonwealths trial of felonies by the judge without jury has become the rule.

Three Widely Used Judicial Reforms

DECLARATORY JUDGMENTS. Three important judicial reforms remain to be considered. One of these, the declaratory judgment, is designed to provide a judicial interpretation of statutes, contracts, and the like before lawsuits actually arise. The persons involved are thus saved time and money, and the cost of administering civil justice is reduced. In order to produce this desirable result, however, it is necessary to modify the well-established rule that the courts will not pass upon any legal question until it is presented to them in the course of ordinary litigation. But modification is needed, for the rule often works hardship. It compels business men to guess at the exact meaning of a contract unless one of them breaks it and the other sues.

Quite naturally, therefore, practical men long ago wearied of such a method of interpreting the law, and asked why it would not be feasible to permit the courts to determine in advance of litigation, when requested to do so, the exact meaning of statute or ordinance, or a written instrument such as a contract, a will, or a deed. The only answer was that tradition and precedent would be seriously disturbed.

So in recent years "declaratory judgment" statutes have been enacted in nearly all the states, and the Conference of Commissioners on Uniform State Laws has drafted a model law on the subject which is urged for general adoption. Under the provisions of such an act, the courts are authorized to issue binding declarations of rights—declaratory judgments, as they are called—that will enable interested persons to determine their rights and duties under a written instrument or statute without the unpleasant necessity of engaging in litigation.

It must be clearly understood, however, that the courts cannot be compelled to issue declaratory judgments; they exercise a wide discretion in the matter. Therefore their time and energy are not dissipated.

CONCILIATION AND ARBITRATION. The two remaining judicial reforms —conciliation and arbitration—are so closely related that laymen frequently fail to distinguish between them. Both aim to settle disputes by less formal methods than the ordinary processes of litigation. But conciliation is an attempt by a third person—usually a court official—to induce the interested parties to settle their differences, whereas arbitration is the submission of a dispute by the interested parties to a third person whom they have jointly selected and whose award they agree to accept.

Conciliation has not been used in the United States to any extent until recent years. Since 1913, however, when Cleveland led the way, the municipal courts of many of the larger cities have established conciliation branches or have made provision for special conciliation procedure. In 1921 North Dakota adopted a state-wide conciliation act. The general features of conciliation are the same in all jurisdictions where it is employed. When a civil suit is begun, it may be taken first—usually at the discretion of the plaintiff—to the conciliation branch. Here the presiding judge attempts to find a way of satisfying both contestants. He points out the expense and trouble of prolonged litigation and suggests a reasonable settlement. His proposals have no binding effect, however, but depend upon the good will and good faith of the parties to the dispute. Yet many cases are quickly and cheaply settled by means of the simple process of conciliation.

Arbitration is much more common in the United States. In fact, arbitration laws are found in virtually every state, though most of these laws are inadequate and totally unsuited to modern conditions. A few commonwealths—especially California, Massachusetts, New Jersey, New York, and Oregon—have recently enacted effective, statewide arbitration acts, and therefore offer the best examples of satisfactory arbitration procedure.

When a dispute arises—perhaps as to the exact meaning of a clause in a contract—the parties select an arbitrator, and agree to abide by his decision. This arbitrator then studies every aspect of the case, and makes an award that may be enforced like any court judgment. An appeal from the arbitrator's award may be taken to the courts, but, in the more progressive states, only to determine whether the arbitration procedure was in accordance with the law. The civil codes of these states specify that the facts, once determined, may not again be challenged. In many jurisdictions, however, appeals are permitted on questions of fact as well as questions of law, so that arbitration necessarily loses much of its effectiveness.

JUDICIAL REVIEW

Invalidation of Laws

One of the fundamental principles of American government is the doctrine of judicial review. The need for review arises when the legislative body enacts a law that is alleged to conflict with the constitution. Some person or group must then determine whether the disputed law is actually contrary to a constitutional provision, or whether apparent differences can be reconciled. The decision might well be left to the legislature; in fact, most nations have solved the problem in this way.[18]

The United States, however, is a noteworthy exception. In this country the courts—both state and federal—will pass upon the constitutionality of any law if the question is properly presented to them in the course of or-

[18] In England, for example, the courts have no authority to invalidate an act of Parliament.

dinary litigation.   They will not consider the constitutional issue if the case
can be decided on some other point; nor will they accept an unconstitutional
interpretation of a law if a constitutional interpretation can be found.   But
when necessity arises they will invalidate any legislative act that, in their
judgment, violates the supreme law—the constitution.   It has already been
pointed out that the supreme court of a state is the final interpreter of the
state constitution.[19]   Disputes involving the federal Constitution, however,
may be appealed to the Supreme Court of the United States.

Proposals for Limiting Judicial Review

The courts have long declared that they will not invalidate properly enacted laws, however unwise or inexpedient such laws may seem to be.   This
is a proper point of view, for policy determination is a function of the legislature, and not of the judiciary.   Legislators decide what is to be done, and
the task of the courts is to enforce the law in specific disputes.   In recent
years, however, many cases have arisen in which the courts have adopted
the rôle of policy makers and have set aside legislative acts as "unreasonable"—that is, undesirable.   Most of these cases have been concerned with
"due process of law."

Judicial interpretation of the due process clause, as previously pointed
out,[20] has given to the courts a broad power to pass upon the wisdom of
legislation.   This power has sometimes been used to thwart the popular
will and to substitute the wishes of the judiciary for the wishes of the people,
as expressed through their chosen representatives.   Not unnaturally, therefore, considerable popular opposition to unrestricted judicial supremacy has
developed within the last few decades, and a number of proposals designed
to limit judicial power have received serious consideration.

Thus it has been suggested that an extraordinary majority—perhaps three-
fourths, or all but one or two—of the members of the supreme court be
required to declare a duly enacted law unconstitutional.   With such a rule
it would no longer be possible for a single judge to set aside the handiwork
of the legislature—a state of affairs that occasionally arises when a statute
is declared invalid by a four-to-three or five-to-four vote.   This plan has
been adopted by three states.[21]   The recall of judges should also be mentioned at this point, since it provides a means of getting rid of judges who
invalidate popular legislative enactments.[22]

Deserving of mention, also, is the recall of judicial decisions, a scheme ad-

[19] See page 167.
[20] See pages 21–22.
[21] Nebraska, North Dakota, Ohio.
[22] For a discussion of the recall as applied to judges, see page 170.

vocated by Theodore Roosevelt in 1912.   This novel plan, intended to make the people the final interpreters of the provisions of state constitutions, was adopted by one state—Colorado—but was set aside nine years later by the state supreme court as contrary to the federal Constitution.[23]

ADVISORY JUDICIAL OPINIONS

When a bill of doubtful constitutionality is introduced in the legislature, the natural tendency is to turn to the supreme court to learn whether the measure, if enacted into law, will be upheld.   The governor, also, may desire some specific assurance before he affixes his signature.   In the large majority of states, however, the courts refuse to give advance information; they insist that their function is merely the settlement of specific disputes. So the only way to determine whether a proposal is constitutional, in these states, is to put it on the statute books and then wait until some injured person challenges its validity.   Years may pass before a test case reaches the court; in the meantime no one really knows what the final outcome will be.

To obviate unsatisfactory conditions of this sort, nine states [24] have adopted constitutional or statutory provisions directing the justices of the supreme court to render advisory opinions upon all important questions of law presented to them by the governor or the legislature.   Except in Colorado,[25] an advisory opinion is merely a statement of the views of the individual justices, and therefore lacks the binding effect of a formal court decision resulting from ordinary litigation.   But it is commonly accepted by the governor and the legislature as the final word on any constitutional question, for experience has shown that the courts, as official bodies, are not likely to reverse the opinions of their individual members.   Advisory opinions have proved an effective means of reducing the uncertainties incident to law making, and of preventing many unnecessary lawsuits.   There seems to be no valid reason why they should not be authorized in every state.

[23] People v. Western Union Telegraph Co., 70 Colo. 90 (1921); People v. Max, 70 Colo. 100 (1921).

[24] Colorado, Florida, Maine, Massachusetts, New Hampshire, Rhode Island, and South Dakota have made provision in their constitutions for advisory opinions.   Two other states, Alabama and Delaware, rely on statute.   In Minnesota, however, a law directing the supreme court to render advisory opinions was declared unconstitutional; and in New York, Nebraska, Oklahoma and Pennsylvania, where advisory opinions were once given without constitutional or statutory authorization, the practice has long since been discontinued, but in North Carolina it persists.   The judges of the supreme court of that state average less than one advisory opinion a year.   See Preston W. Edsall's interesting article, "The Advisory Opinion in North Carolina," in the April, 1949, issue of the North Carolina Law Review, pp. 297–344.

[25] In Colorado, advance opinions have the authority of final court decisions.

PROBLEMS

1. Study the operation of the magistrates' courts in your city. What qualifications do the magistrates possess for their work? Is a real effort made to do substantial justice?

2. Prepare a chart showing the organization of the judicial system of your state.

3. Examine the organization and work of the judicial council in some state that has created such a body. What results has it accomplished?

4. How are members of the petit jury chosen in your community? Can you suggest ways to improve the present method of selection?

5. Select a state that has enacted a declaratory judgment statute, and find what results that statute has given. Compare the statute with the model declaratory judgment law prepared by the Conference of Commissioners on Uniform State Laws.

SELECTED REFERENCES

American Bar Association, *The Improvement of the Administration of Justice,* Washington, 1949.

Aumann, F. R., *The Changing American Legal System,* Columbus, Ohio, 1940.

Beattie, Ronald H., *A System of Criminal Judicial Statistics for California,* Berkeley, Calif., 1936.

Borchard, Edwin M., *Declaratory Judgments,* rev. ed., Cleveland, 1941.

Brownell, Emery A., *Legal Aid in the United States,* Rochester, N.Y., 1951.

Callender, C. N., *American Courts, Their Organization and Procedure,* 1927.

Council of State Governments, *State Court Systems,* rev., 1951.

Frank, Jerome, *Courts on Trial,* Princeton, 1949.

Fuller, Hugh N., *Criminal Justice in Virginia,* Charlottesville, 1931.

Haines, C. G., *The American Doctrine of Judicial Supremacy,* rev. ed., Berkeley, Calif., 1932.

Hannan, W. E., and Csontos, M. B., *State Court Systems,* 1940.

Harris, S. A., *Appellate Courts and Appellate Procedure in Ohio,* Baltimore, Md., 1933.

Haynes, Evan, *The Selection and Tenure of Judges,* 1944.

Hays, A. G., *Trial by Prejudice,* 1933.

Jensen, Christen, *The Pardoning Power in the American States,* 1922.

Lepawsky, Albert, *Judicial System of Metropolitan Chicago,* 1932.

Lou, Herbert H., *Juvenile Courts in the United States,* Chapel Hill, N.C., 1927.

Martin, Kenneth J., *Waiver of Jury Trial in Criminal Cases in Ohio,* Baltimore, Md., 1934.

Miller, B. R., *The Louisiana Judiciary,* Baton Rouge, 1932.

National Commission on Law Observance and Enforcement, Report No. 4, *Prosecution,* Washington, D.C., 1931.

Orfield, L. B., *Criminal Procedure from Arrest to Appeal,* 1947.

Osborn, Albert S., *The Mind of the Juror,* Albany, N.Y., 1937.

Pelaston, Jack W., *Missouri Plan for the Selection of Judges,* Columbia, 1945.
Pound, Roscoe, *Criminal Justice in America,* rev. ed., 1945.
————, *Organization of the Courts,* 1940.
President's Research Committee on Social Trends, *Recent Social Trends in the United States,* Vol. II, Chap. XXVIII, 1933.
Robinson, Edward S., *Law and the Lawyers,* 1935.
Seagle, William, *Law: The Science of Inefficiency,* 1952.
Sharp, Agnes A., *A Dynamic Era of Court Psychiatry,* 1944.
Ulman, J. N., *A Judge Takes the Stand,* 1933.
Vanderbilt, Arthur T., ed., *Minimum Standards of Judicial Administration,* 1949.
Warner, Florence M., *Juvenile Detention in the United States,* 1933.
Warner, Sam B., and Cabor, H. B., *Judges and Law Reform,* Cambridge, Mass., 1936.
Waite, John B., *Criminal Law in Action,* 1934.
Winfield, Charles H., *The Grand Jury,* 3rd ed., Newark, N.J., 1944.

The May, 1953, issue of the *Annals of the American Academy of Political and Social Science* is entitled "Judicial Administration and the Common Man."

PART THREE

The Organization of Local Government

CHAPTER 9

City Government: Mayor and Council

The history of American city government prior to 1900 is largely the story of the rising power of the mayor. In the early days of our independence the mayor was merely the presiding officer of the council, possessing little independent authority; by the close of the nineteenth century he had become a very influential person. He supervised municipal administration, though he did not always control it. He played an important part in shaping local legislation, and his powers of appointment and removal were broad. In name, and to some extent in fact, he was the head of the city government. More than any other person he could claim to represent all the people of the city. Unlike the members of the council, his viewpoint and his interests extended beyond the boundaries of a single ward.

HISTORY OF THE MAYOR'S OFFICE

The Mayor as the Center of Early Reform Movements

By the nineties of the last century even the dullest person could see that city government was woefully inefficient. The municipal reformers of that era, eager to improve the conduct of municipal affairs, pinned their faith on the mayor. Time and again they had seen the battle of mayor versus council, with the mayor usually protecting the public interest against the attacks of ignorant and corrupt councilmen. All too often they had witnessed the spectacle of a competent mayor handicapped and embarrassed by elected department heads. And they came to the conclusion that the solution of the municipal problem was to give the mayor complete control over administration, making him a sort of benevolent despot. Not that all mayors were benevolent in the nineties of the last century. Far from it. Many of them were not even honest. But as a class they better represented public opinion and more frequently opposed the forces of corruption than the members of the council and the other city officials. Generally they were men of higher caliber.

It is not at all surprising that the mayors of American cities were usually on a higher plane, both intellectually and morally, than their colleagues in the municipal service.   For one thing, the office was sufficiently prominent to attract men of ability.   An honest independent, well known and respected, might be induced by his independent friends to accept the reform party's nomination for mayor.   But what prominent business man would sacrifice his private affairs to run for coroner?   What leading attorney would give up his practice in exchange for the prospect of becoming a magistrate?   Of necessity the reformers concentrated on the office of mayor.   They hoped that the election of a good chief executive would insure good government— a hope too seldom fulfilled.   They exhorted the people to choose an independent mayor and usher in a new era of civic righteousness.   After the people had several times tried the experiment of electing an independent mayor, only to find him powerless because of hostile subordinates and a boss-controlled council, they began to lose interest in the whole matter. And the reformers were confirmed in their belief that the mayor's position must be strengthened.

Position of Mayor in Newer Forms of Government

With the turn of the century came a revolution in the theory and practice of city government.   Galveston adopted a form of government—the commission type—that reduced the mayor to a position of minor importance. He became merely the chairman of a board of five, possessing only the same voting power as his fellow commissioners and charged with the administration of but one of the city's departments.   The new idea proved immensely popular.   By 1914 four hundred cities and towns had followed Galveston's example.   Then came the council-manager plan, which took administrative control completely out of the hands of the mayor and made him nothing more than a presiding officer with some social duties, as he had been in colonial days.   A few manager cities have even abolished the office of mayor altogether.

These new forms of government are favorably regarded.   The manager plan in particular is gaining new converts every year.   Some day it may become the typical form of American municipal organization.   But as yet it has acquired no such widespread popularity.   The large majority of cities in the United States still trust their affairs to a mayor and council as they have always done.   In the largest and smallest cities especially mayor-council government retains its hold.   Of the fourteen largest American municipalities,[1] only two—Buffalo and Cleveland—have tried the newer

---

[1] Not counting Washington, the nation's capital, which is excluded from this discussion because it is controlled directly by the federal government.   The people of Washington have no voice in their own affairs.

forms.   In 1927 the people of Buffalo voted to return to the mayor-council fold, and in 1931 the people of Cleveland did likewise.   Nearly two thirds of the very small cities, with populations of five to ten thousand, still cling to the mayor-council plan.

WEAK MAYOR GOVERNMENT

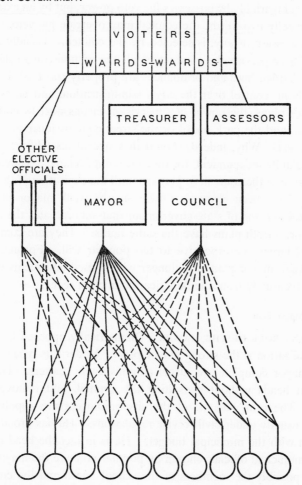

This chart and the chart on page 191 have been reproduced with permission from the National Municipal League's pamphlet, *Forms of Municipal Government.*

TYPES OF MAYOR-COUNCIL GOVERNMENT

The Weak Mayor Plan

DOMINANT ROLE OF THE COUNCIL.   Government by mayor and council, as it has developed in this country, takes two widely divergent forms.   One is the weak mayor type, so called because the mayor's powers are few and carefully restricted.   Under this plan most of the administrative departments are headed by boards or commissions whose members are elected by the people or chosen by the council.   The mayor makes but few important appointments, and those that are entrusted to him must be ratified by the council.   Almost invariably he possesses the veto power, but by an extraordinary majority, usually two-thirds, the council may override his veto.   The civil service commission, if any, is selected by the council.   Usually the mayor is directed to supervise the conduct of all the administrative departments and to see that the laws and ordinances are properly enforced; but since he has virtually no control over the city's administration, and no authority to carry out his plans, the power of supervision means next to nothing.   He may suggest, and the park board or the street commissioner may disregard his suggestions.   Why, indeed, should they accept his advice?   They can afford to be quite independent, for they owe him nothing.   They hold office at the pleasure of the council, or perhaps until the expiration of the terms for which they have been elected.   Obviously the weak mayor plan is very similar to the scheme of state government that subordinates the position of the governor.   Both plans have the same faults.   They are complex, inefficient, and largely unresponsive to the popular will.   Fortunately, however, the weak mayor plan is no longer widely used and seems destined to disappear eventually from the American municipal scene.

The Strong Mayor Plan

DOMINANT ROLE OF THE MAYOR.   Diametrically opposed to the theory of decentralization is the strong mayor plan.   Under this type of organization the mayor completely controls administrative matters.   He appoints department heads without consulting the council, and removes them at pleasure.   The rank and file of the city employees are appointed in his name, but usually under civil service regulations.   He has broad powers in connection with the municipal budget.   He is in fact the head of the city. The only municipal officials chosen by popular vote are the mayor, councilmen, and possibly the members of the school board and the controller or auditor.   New York, Boston, Detroit, and a few other cities have adopted the strong mayor plan.

Compromise Types of Government

In the matter of strong mayor versus weak mayor most American cities defy accurate classification.   Certainly very few belong to the strong mayor type.   Their charters still provide for the election of many administrative officials and the selection by the council of some others.   The mayor is commonly denied adequate authority.   Yet it seems scarcely fair to put them in the weak mayor list.   Many have changed their charters in recent years so as to permit a degree of concentration.   They have increased con-

STRONG MAYOR GOVERNMENT

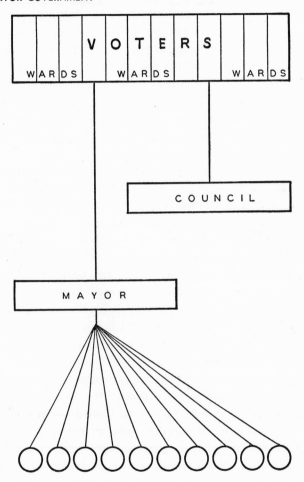

siderably the mayor's appointing power, but at the same time they have retained the requirement of confirmation by the council.   Important administrative officials are still chosen at the polls.

Sixty or seventy years ago virtually all our cities were of the weak mayor type, but since that time most of them have adopted certain features of the strong mayor plan.   They have given the mayor partial but not complete control over administration. They have shortened their ballots, but not enough. Today most American city governments closely resemble the weak mayor type, with a few strong mayor characteristics grafted on. That type of grafting has not proved popular with the professional politicians.

Evaluation of Strong and Weak Mayor Plans

THE WEAK MAYOR PLAN. In favor of the weak mayor plan no sound argument can be found. There are, however, a number of valid arguments against it. For one thing, it perpetuates the long ballot, with its tendency to weaken popular control and stifle popular interest. Then, too, administrative responsibility is scattered, which is only another way of saying that it is nonexistent. The government is so complex as to baffle all but the experts. Eventually the weak mayor type of city government will probably die a natural death. Today it finds very few converts among American cities.

THE STRONG MAYOR PLAN. Most of the defects of weak mayor government are sound reasons for the adoption of the strong mayor plan. Under the strong mayor type of organization government is made intelligible to the average citizen. Opportunities for shifting the blame are virtually eliminated. The council is given just one task—policy determination by means of legislation—and is not permitted to interfere with the technical details of administration. Concentration, simplicity, and confidence, principles of good government, are all embodied in the strong mayor plan.

There is, however, considerable reason to doubt that the city's chief executive should be elected. The very fact that the mayor is popularly chosen makes him inevitably a politician. He must depend on the political machine to produce the votes that will put him into office, and to reward him later for his party loyalty by making him governor or congressman. He spends his time advocating or opposing policies, instead of guiding the details of municipal administration. Usually he is not a trained administrator, for able technicians are seldom drawn into the public service by way of the ballot.

Because the executive in city government ought properly to have so much to do with the technical details of administration—police department organization, park and playground management, methods of street paving, and the like—and so little to do with deciding political issues, many careful students urge that he should be appointed by the council. Manager government is based on this philosophy. Since discussion of the manager plan is reserved for the following chapter, the relative merits of elected and appointed executives may be considered in greater detail at that point.

AMERICAN MAYORS

Methods of Selection

American mayors are almost everywhere elected by direct vote of the people. This method is in sharp contrast with European practice. In England the mayor is chosen by the councilmen and aldermen. The French *maire* is likewise selected by the municipal council. Even in the United States mayors have not always been elected. The early charters gave to the council the power of selecting the mayor, and it was not until 1822 that Boston led the larger cities by providing for a popularly chosen executive. In some respects the council-manager plan, with its appointed executive, is a return to the original form of municipal organization.

Removal by Governor

In France the mayor may be removed by the central authorities. Several American states have followed this European precedent, authorizing the governor to remove any mayor for cause. In New York, for example, the governor must prefer charges and hold a public hearing, but his decision is then final. There is a general tendency to limit this power strictly, so that it may not be used to settle personal differences or satisfy political grudges.

Qualifications

LEGAL. The mayor's legal qualifications vary widely from city to city. Always he must be a qualified voter, and occasionally he must be a taxpayer. Sometimes a minimum age limit is fixed—most commonly twenty-five or thirty years. Often there is a minimum residence requirement of from three to five years.

POLITICAL. There are other qualifications also, not mentioned in charters or ordinances. To be elected mayor of an average American municipality a man must usually be an important cog in the dominant political machine. He must have demonstrated time and again his ability and willingness to serve the organization. He must be acceptable to a wide variety of interests, for many groups have a veto on the selection of the mayor.

Terms of Office

Most American municipalities still cling to the two-year term for their mayors, but the larger cities—those with populations of fifty thousand or more—are almost equally divided between two- and four-year terms. In the great metropolitan centers the four-year term is easily the favorite. Three cities in the fifty thousand class fix the mayor's term at three years.

Annual election of the mayor, once so common, is now found in but a few cities. The trend of the last half century has been steadily toward longer terms. New charters frequently increase the length of the mayor's term, but virtually never shorten it.

Salaries

The range of mayors' salaries is from forty thousand dollars to nothing. Within a single state—New York—these variations occur. New York City tops the list of all American municipalities, whereas the mayor of Ithaca receives no compensation. In the larger cities the mayor is expected to devote his entire attention to the duties of his office, and his salary is large enough to make him financially independent. Most of the smaller communities, however, demand but a portion of his time and pay him accordingly.

Powers

The powers of the mayor may be classified conveniently under three main heads: legislative, judicial, administrative.

LEGISLATIVE: *Recommendations.* Although he is the city's chief executive, charged primarily with the enforcement of the laws, the mayor plays a very important part in shaping proposed legislation. In every city he is directed to make recommendations to the council—"suggestions for the protection and improvement of the city's government and finances," as the charter framers often put it. There is nothing except public opinion to prevent the council from ignoring his recommendations and following its own course. But a popular mayor with a reputation for fair dealing can often rouse popular sentiment to such a point that dallying councilmen will hasten to fall into line.

Veto power. The power to veto proposed ordinances is commonly given to the mayor. After a bill has been passed by the council it goes to the mayor for his approval or rejection. Should he disapprove, he returns it to the council with his objections, and unless it is then repassed by an extraordinary majority it fails to become law. The majority needed to override the mayor's veto varies from city to city; usually it is two thirds of those present.

Presiding officer of council. In the early days of our municipal history the mayor usually presided over the council. But the political thought of the early nineteenth century demanded a sharp division of powers, and as he became the administrative head of the city he commonly ceased to take part in the council's activities. In most American cities of the present day the council chooses its own officers. The mayor no longer presides. There are still a good many exceptions, however—mostly small communities and, oddly enough, the nation's second largest city. Chicago's mayor, who presides over council meetings, is given no vote except in case of a tie—and a tie seldom occurs. He may introduce bills only by petition to the clerk, as might any citizen. But the mere fact that he is always at hand, and that all debates must be conducted in his presence and under his chairmanship, greatly strengthens his influence.

JUDICIAL. The judicial powers of the mayor are no longer of any great practical importance. The colonial mayor devoted much of his time to judicial matters. He was a justice of the peace, presiding officer of the borough court, and often a member of the county tribunal. But the development of an independent court system and the multiplication of the mayor's administrative duties have combined to restrict his judicial authority. Usually he is a magistrate, and in some of the smaller cities he still exercises minor civil and criminal jurisdiction. No longer, however, is he the local fountainhead of justice. His judicial activities are little more than a relic of the past.

ADMINISTRATIVE: *Power to appoint.* Most important, of course, are the mayor's administrative powers. He is primarily an administrative officer, charged with the conduct of the city's day-to-day affairs. Most of the men and women in the municipal service are at least nominally responsible to him. He determines the manner in which the policies of the council are to be carried out. Nearly everywhere, therefore, he is given rather extensive powers of appointment. In a number of cities he names the heads of virtually all the important departments, while in others the charters still provide that some department heads shall be popularly elected. Usually his choices must be ratified by the council, although many cities now give him a free hand.

Power to remove. Quite as important as the power to appoint is the power to remove. Nearly everywhere the mayor has authority to dismiss all officials appointed by him—the consent of the council is unnecessary in some cities, and required in others. Even those cities that give the mayor a free hand usually establish a rather elaborate dismissal procedure. They provide that he must give his reasons in writing, that he must afford opportunity for a written reply, or that he must first hold a public hearing. After all these formalities have been observed his decision is final. The purpose of all this red tape, of course, is to prevent hasty or arbitrary action. Its actual effect in most cities has been to complicate the removal of incompetents.

Supervision of administration. The mayor supervises the work of administration. He is supposed to co-ordinate the city's services and to raise their standards of efficiency. Obviously this duty is only nominal unless he has authority to appoint and remove department heads. No man can fairly be held responsible for the actions of those beyond his control. In the larger cities that have adopted the strong mayor plan or some approximation of it there is a growing tendency to group the heads of departments into a cabinet, after the manner of the federal government. Once every week or fortnight they meet with the mayor and advise him as to matters of general policy. The mayor is not bound in any way by their suggestions, but he has the opportunity to secure different points of view.

Law enforcement. As the city's chief executive, the mayor is responsible for the enforcement of city ordinances and state laws. This is a power of the greatest importance, for it enables him to determine when and in what manner the laws shall be enforced. In theory, obedience to all laws should be compelled at all times, but as a matter of fact no government—city, state, or national—tries to enforce all its statutes twenty-four hours a day. To do so it would have to make every citizen a policeman. The number of laws that the average city is supposed to enforce is staggering. Every year its council enacts hundreds of local laws. The ordinances of former years are seldom repealed, and go to make up the total. Added to the list are the state laws, several hundred to a session, for the city is the agent of the state in executing its statutes. Obviously some person must determine which laws shall be rigorously enforced, for they cannot all be. The task usually falls to the mayor or to his subordinate—the chief of police.

Control of the budget. In connection with the municipal budget the mayor is usually given considerable authority. Some cities empower him to frame the budget and submit it to the council. In that case the estimates of expenditure are made originally by the department heads, and the mayor correlates them, balancing them against the estimates of revenue. The council's control over the budget is not everywhere the same. In most cities it may amend the budget in any way it sees fit, even to the point of discarding all the mayor's suggestions and substituting figures of its own. There are even some cities that vest the power of framing the budget in the finance committee of the council. But, on the other hand, some city charters specify that the council may do no more than reduce or eliminate items in the mayor's budget. The general tendency in American cities is to increase the budget authority of the mayor.

Public Relations of the Mayor

SOCIAL DUTIES. A large part of the mayor's time is occupied with social duties. Officially he is the head of the city government, and he is expected to welcome distinguished visitors, address civic gatherings, preside over chamber of commerce luncheons, and enlighten the women's clubs.   In the bigger cities these activities may easily take several hours a day.   And no mayor could afford to refuse all invitations to speak in public.   If he did, he would speedily acquire a reputation for coldness and indifference.   He may employ an "official welcomer" or a "municipal host," as is done in some cities, but most of the time he must appear in person.   The pleasure of his company is requested—and expected—every day at a vast number of functions.   Then there are the people who wish to see the mayor personally. They wend their way daily to the city hall.   Their business may be very trivial indeed.   It may require only the attention of a junior clerk.   But they wish to be sure that the mayor himself knows all about the matter, and if they are turned away after an interview with some underling they are apt to take offense.   They are unreasonable, of course, yet their votes may be needed to turn the tide of the next election.

POLITICIAN OR ADMINISTRATOR?   Every mayor must decide whether to emphasize the technical or the popular aspects of his office.   He must be either a good administrator or a good fellow.   He cannot be both.   The average mayor places popularity before administrative efficiency.   He is always ready to listen sympathetically to the troubles of others.   He never refuses to speak before the Kiwanis Club or the Women's Auxiliary.   He can call thousands of men and women by name, and he belongs to at least a score of fraternal orders.   To him these things are more important than efficient and economical government, and the reason is clear.   They undoubtedly contribute more to his advancement.   In a few years he must again go before the people, seeking re-election as mayor, or perhaps asking that he be made governor or United States senator.   He must be fondly remembered as the popular mayor with the sympathetic ear and the open hand.   Poorly paved streets or inadequate fire protection can readily be explained; the blame can easily be shifted to someone else.   But no amount of explaining will help the mayor who is a poor mixer, and no improvement in municipal standards will insure the support of the party organization.   The man who would go far in the political world must have the organization's backing, or else develop an organization of his own.

AMERICAN CITY COUNCILS

Reduced Authority of the Council

In the early days of American independence the council was virtually the city government.   It appointed the mayor, and supervised the nascent mu-

nicipal administration.   Subject to the overlordship of the state legislature
it enacted ordinances for the well-being of the townspeople.   Some of its
members—the aldermen—shared with the mayor extensive judicial power.
In the local field the council was supreme.   But all this has been changed
during the last century and a quarter.   In virtually every American city the
story has been the same.   The council has lost power and prestige steadily,
until it has come to be regarded by many as a necessary evil, sheltering the
misfits of the business and professional worlds.   Much of its authority has
been transferred to other agencies.

Since the early days the mayor has gained in power at the council's expense.   His veto and his power to make recommendations have given him
a considerable measure of control over proposed legislation.   The various
phases of administration have been placed in his care, or else entrusted to independently elected boards.   City charters contain all sorts of limitations
designed to curb the council's activities.   Bills may be passed only at certain times and in a certain manner; bonds may not be issued beyond a certain amount; for some matters the approval of state authorities must be
obtained.   In many respects the council is but a shadow of its former self.
Yet it is still the city's policy-determining body, and its present position
seems narrowly restricted only when compared with its former supremacy.
Even today its decisions affect every phase of municipal life.

Terms and Compensation

Annual election of councilmen was the rule for many decades.   The people had an abiding faith in short terms as a sure cure for all political ills.   In
recent years, however, two-year terms have become the rule, and in the
larger cities even longer terms predominate.   Approximately three fifths of
the cities with populations in excess of fifty thousand now elect their councilmen for four years.

With longer terms have come larger salaries.   The once popular theory
that every man should be prepared to give freely of his time and talent, with
no reward save the joy of public service, has now been definitely abandoned
by all but the very smallest communities.   The salaries of councilmen range
from nine thousand dollars a year in Philadelphia to a merely nominal fee
per session.   There are sound reasons why the smaller cities should pay their
councilmen merely nominal salaries, or even ask them to serve without compensation.   The duties of office are not arduous, and require only a few
hours each week or fortnight.   But in the great metropolitan centers all is
different.   A New York or Chicago councilman has an exceedingly busy
life.   In addition to council sessions there are committee meetings, which

occupy a considerable portion of his time. There are endless matters to be investigated and decided. Hundreds of persons come to make requests or present grievances, and they cannot be sent away unheard.

Size of the Council

Bicameral councils were popular in the early days of American independence, but they are now found in only a few small cities. Together with this reduction in the number of houses has come a marked decrease in the number of members. In more than two thirds of the larger cities of the United States—those with populations in excess of twenty-five thousand—the council now has a membership of from five to nine. Even a large city like Detroit, with a population of over a million and a half, has but nine councilmen, and nine is the number fixed by the charters of Boston, Cincinnati, Denver, Indianapolis, Pittsburgh, and Seattle. Many of the metropolitan centers, however, feeling that nine men cannot adequately represent all sections, have councils composed of about twenty-five members. Baltimore has twenty-two councilmen, New York has twenty-five, and Chicago has fifty.

Methods of Selection

Some years ago the ward plan of electing councilmen was extremely popular. Most cities were divided into wards or districts, with one or two members of the council chosen from each district. During recent years, however, the plan of election at large has steadily gained favor. Even in many of the largest cities, such as Detroit, Boston, St. Louis, Pittsburgh and San Francisco, every member of the council is chosen by the voters of the entire city without regard for ward boundaries. Most American municipalities now choose their councilmen at large. The Hare system of proportional representation, which is discussed in a later chapter,[2] is used by nine American cities. Other schemes—limited voting, combinations of the ward and at-large plans, and the like—have been adopted by a few municipalities, but are not sufficiently important to warrant separate consideration.

Powers of the Council

LEGISLATIVE POWERS. In every city the council has a wide variety of powers. The state courts hold that municipal powers not specifically assigned to other agencies are vested in the council, and this rule greatly increases the scope of its authority. First of all, the council is the local legislative body. Much of its time is spent in considering and passing ordinances for the government and welfare of the city. The charter may prescribe only

[2] See pages 281–282.

the outline of municipal organization. In that case the council fills in the details. It creates or abolishes bureaus within each department, prescribing the number of employees and the amount of their compensation. It makes certain actions misdemeanors, and provides for their punishment. It gives its official sanction to building codes framed by administrative officers and presented for its approval. It defines and abolishes nuisances. It makes regulations concerning the inspection of boilers, elevators, chimneys. All phases of public health, safety, and convenience are regulated to a greater or less extent. Franchises are granted to the city's utilities. In any large city hundreds of ordinances are enacted every year. Of course, the council is not given a free hand in all matters. The charter usually specifies in some detail what matters may be regulated and what procedure must be followed.

CONTROL OF ADMINISTRATION. Although the council is primarily a law-making body, its control over administration is by no means slight. In many cities its approval is still required for all the mayor's appointments, and in a few it actually appoints the heads of the administrative departments. Sometimes it passes upon the removal of administrative officers. Many matters of an essentially administrative nature come directly under its control. It regulates by ordinance hundreds of details that could be handled more quickly and satisfactorily by the chiefs of the city's bureaus. For example, exceptions to the tenement law may be necessary. Each exception is duly considered by the proper committee, and then passed by the entire council. The council is literally immersed in a labyrinth of trifling affairs that ought never to come to its attention. Seemingly it cannot learn that its part in administration should be limited to broad supervision.

Organization of the Council

THE PRESIDING OFFICER. The council usually chooses its presiding officer from among its own members. Occasionally the mayor presides, and in a few cases the task falls to a popularly elected vice-mayor. But such cases are exceptional. When chosen by the council, the presiding officer— president, as he is generally called—has broad authority. He usually appoints all committees, and frequently becomes a member of them all. If the council is large, he is practically free to recognize whom he pleases, and the councilman who stands in his bad graces is certain to find difficulty in obtaining the floor. Sometimes he appoints clerks and other minor employees; nearly everywhere, however, the clerk of council and the sergeant-at-arms are chosen by the council itself. The clerk of council usually functions as city clerk.

COMMITTEES. A city council, like a state legislature, does its work through committees. Every proposed piece of legislation must be referred to some committee, and the council is usually disposed to follow committee recommendations, though not bound to do so. In some cities committees are under no obligation to make reports to the council. As a result, a bill that chances to displease a majority of committee members is quietly buried in some obscure corner of the chairman's desk—or else committed to the waste basket. But the councils of nearly all the smaller cities, and of many large cities, also require committees to report on every bill entrusted to their care. Every proposal is certain, therefore, to see once more the light of the council chamber. But it may make its reappearance so amended that even its author can scarcely recognize it. The power of council committees is normally very great.

Sessions of the Council

In most cities the council meets regularly once a week, on a day prescribed by the charter. Usually special sessions may be called by a very few members—from one to five, depending on the size of the council. There is never the last-minute rush, therefore, so characteristic of state legislatures. Filibustering is infrequent, for a bill delayed by dilatory tactics at one session is virtually certain to come up for consideration a week or two later. Evening sessions are becoming increasingly popular, for they enable many business and professional men to sit in the city council who would not otherwise be available for public service. Most charters provide that all council sessions shall be public. The council can readily evade this requirement, however, by resolving itself into a committee of the whole. It is then no longer the council, but merely a committee composed of all the members of the council. There is no rule that committee meetings must be public. Moreover, it ought to be remembered that vital decisions on every important piece of legislation are usually made by some regular standing committee before the bill ever reaches the council floor. So the requirement of public meetings is less significant than it might seem.

PROBLEMS

1. Prepare a chart of the government of some city that is operating under a weak mayor plan, and also a chart of some city that is operating under the strong mayor plan.

2. Prepare a chart of the government of your city. How would you classify your city's government?

3. Make a comparative study of the men who have served as mayors of the ten largest American cities since 1910. Present all the facts that you can obtain. Most of these men are listed in *Who's Who in America.*

4. Watch your city council in action, and study its rules of procedure.

5. Write a concise report on the committee system as it operates in the council of your city.

SELECTED REFERENCES

Allen, Robert S., ed., *Our Fair City,* 1947.

Anderson, William, and Weidner, Edward W., *American City Government,* rev. ed., 1950.

Barnard, Chester I., *Functions of the Executive,* Cambridge, Massachusetts, 1938.

Blanshard, Paul, *Investigating City Government in the La Guardia Administration,* 1937.

Bright, John, *Hizzoner Big Bill Thompson: An Idyll of Chicago,* 1930.

Bromage, Arthur W., *Introduction to Municipal Government and Administration,* 1949.

Carey, Fred, *Mayor Jim,* Omaha, 1930.

Franklin, Jay (pseud.), *La Guardia: A Biography,* New York, 1937.

Griffith, Ernest S., *Current Municipal Problems,* Boston, 1941.

Harrison, Carter Henry, *Stormy Years; The Autobiography of Carter H. Harrison, Five Times Mayor of Chicago,* Indianapolis, 1935.

Hoan, Daniel W., *City Government, the Record of the Milwaukee Experiment,* 1936.

Ketcham, D., *A Manual of the Government of Detroit,* Detroit, 1943.

Macdonald, Austin F., *American City Government and Administration,* 5th ed., 1951.

National Municipal League, *A Guide for Charter Commissions,* 1952.

National Resources Committee, *Urban Government,* 1939.

Nolting, Orin F., *Management Methods in City Government,* 1942.

Pink, Louis H., *Gaynor; The Tammany Mayor Who Swallowed the Tiger,* 1931.

Story, R. M., *American Municipal Executive,* Urbana, 1918.

Whitlock, Brand, *Forty Years of It,* 2nd ed., 1925.

CHAPTER 10

City Government: The Newer Forms

For more than a hundred years the cities of the United States made use of the mayor-council form of government. Other schemes were not seriously considered, except by a handful of cities. But with the turn of the century came an era of experimentation with newer municipal forms—first, commission government, and then the manager plan. These newer schemes have had a marked effect upon the course of American municipal government.

BEGINNING OF COMMISSION GOVERNMENT

Commission government first attracted widespread attention in Galveston, though a few other cities had previously adopted somewhat similar plans. Disaster was directly responsible for the Galveston experiment. The city government had long been corrupt and inefficient, but no one had done very much to correct the situation. Then, on the eighth day of September, 1900, a tidal wave engulfed the city, killing nearly seven thousand people and destroying twenty million dollars' worth of property. It was a severe crisis, demanding brains and energy. The officials in charge of the city government could supply neither. Instead of pushing ahead with the work of reconstruction they proceeded to turn the tragedy to their personal profit.

The people of Galveston were thoroughly aroused by the spectacle of such inefficiency. The Deepwater Commission, an organization of business men previously formed to promote harbor interests, took over much of the relief work and appointed three of the city's prominent lawyers to frame a new charter. These three men met every evening for two months and drafted a charter that was at once sent to the legislature for its approval. The legislature gave its consent, and in September, 1901, just a year after the great storm, the new plan went into effect. It utterly ignored the conventional form of mayor-council government and set up instead an all-powerful commission of five members. The success of the plan was phenomenal.

RISE AND FALL OF COMMISSION GOVERNMENT

In 1904 the commission plan was adopted by another Texas city—
Houston.   Five other Texas municipalities fell into line in 1907, and also
two Iowa cities—Des Moines and Cedar Rapids.   After that, adoptions
came rapidly.   Twenty-eight cities discarded their mayor-council charters
in favor of commission charters during 1909, and the following year forty-
four municipalities became converts.   By 1911 the number of commission-
governed cities was one hundred and fifty-five; by 1917 it was nearly five
hundred.

Since 1917, however, there have been few new adoptions, and many cities
have abandoned commission government to return to the mayor-council
type of organization or, much more commonly, to accept the newer council-
manager plan.   Even yet, however, commission government is used by
several hundred American cities, including such large metropolitan centers
as New Orleans, Jersey City, St. Paul, and Portland, Oregon.   Newark,
Buffalo, and Oakland, formerly commission-governed cities, can no longer
be included in the list.

NATURE OF COMMISSION GOVERNMENT

When commission government first acquired wide popularity, many persons believed that the ideal form of municipal organization had at last been
found.   And, at a glance, the commission plan does seem to correct the
evils of excessive decentralization.   Without doubt it eliminates the complexities of weak-mayor government and greatly simplifies municipal organization.   In fact, simplicity is the essence of the commission plan.   Administrative and legislative authority are combined in a small commission, having
five members as a rule, but sometimes three or seven.   These commissioners are the city government.   As a body they enact necessary local legislation; individually they control the several administrative departments and
supervise the enforcement of the laws that they have made.   The number
of departments generally corresponds to the number of commissioners, and
each commissioner becomes responsible for the work of the department assigned to his care.

Commissioners are popularly chosen, usually for two-year terms, but
sometimes for four.   A few city charters provide for terms of one or six
years.   Salaries range from a few hundred dollars a year to several thousand.   One member of the commission is commonly designated as mayor,

but he possesses substantially the same authority as his colleagues, although representing the city on ceremonial occasions.

Because the members of the commission are chosen by the voters, it is unreasonable to suppose that they will possess the technical qualifications

COMMISSION GOVERNMENT

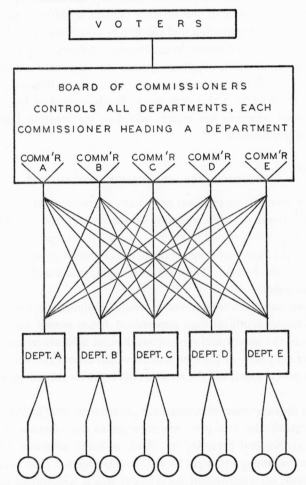

Reproduced with permission from the National Municipal League's pamphlet, *Forms of Municipal Government.*

necessary for the direct handling of administrative matters. Popular election does not produce technical skill, except by chance. The men who framed the Galveston charter of 1901 recognized this fact and made provision for appointive department chiefs to serve under the commissioners and be directly responsible to them.   The administrative duties of each commissioner, therefore, were to be purely supervisory.   But most of the cities that copied Galveston's charter promptly "improved" this part of the commission plan by eliminating the appointive department chiefs and making the elective commissioners the active heads of their respective departments.   Thus the efficiency of the commission plan was materially reduced.

Another modification of the original Galveston scheme, now found in many cities, is the nomination and election of commissioners to specific offices—commissioner of health, commissioner of finance, and the like—instead of the distribution of offices among the successful candidates after election.   This change is a logical result of the theory that members of the commission should be active department heads instead of lay supervisors. Its widespread adoption has merely added to the inherent inefficiency of commission government.

ARGUMENTS FOR COMMISSION GOVERNMENT

When the commission plan was new, many arguments were advanced in its favor.   Reformers urged its adoption on the ground that the old system of diffused responsibility would be swept away and that responsibility as well as authority would be concentrated in the hands of a small group of men directly responsible to the voters.   Thus, it was thought, praise and blame could be fairly apportioned.

Moreover, commission government would eliminate friction and needless delays.   Independently elected department heads would no longer flout the wishes of the mayor and make co-ordinated administration impossible. The greater simplicity of the new scheme would enable the voters to understand their government, and the result would be an awakened interest in civic affairs.

Many of the supporters of commission government were unduly optimistic, but undoubtedly the new plan was superior to the schemes of municipal organization that had preceded it.   And, in many instances, its adoption marked the beginning of an era of civic improvement.   The mainspring of the movement for commission government was a widespread popular demand for reform.   The voters were disgusted with the inefficiency and corruption of the professional politicians, and proceeded to sweep them out of office, replacing them with men of high caliber, many of whom accepted public office temporarily as a civic duty.

Such men could have produced satisfactory results with almost any form of organization; actually they produced results with commission government, and the commission plan received the credit.   Later, of course, the tide of public indignation receded, and in most cities the professional politicians again took control without serious opposition from the independents.   The defects of commission government then became glaringly apparent.

DEFECTS OF THE PLAN

Among the many weaknesses of the commission plan is its failure to concentrate responsibility sufficiently.   Its friends contend that concentration of responsibility is its chief merit; that it sweeps away a large number of independent boards, commissions, and departments, and puts in their place an all-powerful commission—usually having but five members.

Even the elimination of many independent agencies does not produce unity, however, if control is still divided among co-equal members of a commission.   Five men may disagree, and American experience with commission government has proved that they often do.   Five men may shift responsibility from one to another, and experience has further demonstrated the likelihood that such evasion will actually occur.   Commission government, therefore, stops short of its declared objective; it goes only part way along the path of administrative centralization.   Instead of concentrating authority in the hands of one man, it provides a five-ring circus with an all-star cast.

It has already been pointed out that commission government is necessarily government by amateurs.   The members of the commission are elected by the voters for relatively short terms, and their continuance in office depends upon personal popularity rather than technical skill.   In nearly every instance, therefore, they are masters of the art of winning votes.   Their spare time is usually devoted to additional vote-getting rather than additional study of public works or personnel programs, for they realize that the commission plan subordinates good administration to good politics.

Other defects of commission government should also receive at least passing notice.   The commission, usually composed of five members, is too small to serve as a legislative body, especially in the larger communities.   The many shades of opinion that inevitably divide the voters of a great city cannot be adequately represented.   On the other hand, the number of commissioners cannot be multiplied indefinitely, because of the necessity of assigning to each commissioner one of the departments of the city government.

Closely akin to this weakness is another defect: the arbitrary grouping of all municipal activities into five or some other specified number of departments, without regard to local needs.   The framers of a commission type of charter do not survey the administrative activities of a city for the purpose of determining how many departments are required and then fix the number of commissioners accordingly.   Instead they agree that the commission shall have five—or possibly three or seven—members, and then proceed to establish five, or three, or seven, administrative departments.   If this scheme of administrative organization happens to coincide with the city's activities, so much the better.   But no effort is made to insure such a result.

DAYTON'S ADOPTION OF THE MANAGER PLAN

Water-borne disasters have vitally influenced the course of city government in the United States.   A tidal wave virtually swept the commission plan into Galveston.   Thirteen years later a flood of the Miami River demonstrated the helplessness of Dayton's municipal authorities in the face of a grave crisis, and the people of Dayton eagerly welcomed the suggestion that the city council employ a manager to direct the affairs of the city, just as the board of directors of any private enterprise might hire a manager.   Dayton was not the first city to adopt the manager plan,[1] but it was the first large city to do so, and its experiment aroused nation-wide interest.

It did not require the flood to show that drastic reforms were needed in Dayton's government.   Many persons were disgusted with the waste and inefficiency of the old regime, and a committee had already been appointed by the chamber of commerce to draft a new charter.   But the flood that came in the spring of 1913, destroying one hundred and twenty-eight million dollars' worth of property and costing eighty-four lives, emphasized the committee's argument that the government of Dayton needed a thorough overhauling.   A new temporary government was sponsored by the businessmen of Dayton, and it deftly solved problems that would have paralyzed the professional politicians.   No wonder, therefore, that the demand for a "business" government became insistent.   The people were told that the new city manager plan was merely an adaptation of well-recognized principles of business organization; and when they were asked to pass upon the question of adopting it, they voted overwhelmingly in the affirmative.   The election was held in August, five months after the flood, and on the first day of January, 1914, the charter went into effect.

BUSINESS ORGANIZATION IN GOVERNMENT

It is quite correct to say that the manager plan borrows its method of organization from modern business.   The city council ceases to be a group of

[1] That honor goes to Staunton, Virginia, which adopted the manager plan in 1908.

department heads, as under commission government, and assumes the role of a policy-determining body—a board of directors, to use the analogy of corporate enterprise. This council or board of directors hires a manager, a technical expert who is placed in charge of every phase of municipal administration. Just so the board of directors of a private corporation employs a general manager to carry out its policies. Once chosen, the manager of a business has full authority to select his subordinates and direct their work. He is in complete control, though he is at all times responsible to the board of directors, and may be dismissed by them if he fails to give service. Similarly the city manager is given a free hand. In his own sphere of administration he is supreme. He is, however, responsible to the council. He may be removed by the council at any time if he fails to give satisfaction. To complete the analogy, the board of directors of a private corporation is chosen by the stockholders, and the council of a municipal corporation is selected by the voters.

GROWTH OF THE MANAGER PLAN

Trend of Popularity

Since its adoption by Dayton, council-manager government has attained widespread popularity. During 1915 and 1916 thirty-eight municipalities followed Dayton's example. By the end of 1920 the total number of manager cities had risen to one hundred and sixty-two. Today there are more than twelve hundred, and the number is growing at an ever-increasing rate. At first the manager plan made its appeal almost entirely to the smaller cities—communities of ten thousand or less. The great metropolitan centers were not interested. Prior to 1921 only three cities with populations in excess of one hundred thousand were numbered among the converts. Even today the large cities are inclined to stand aloof, but an ever-increasing number of them are adopting manager government. Since 1923 Cincinnati, Dallas, Des Moines, Fort Worth, Kansas City (Missouri), Oakland, Rochester (New York), San Diego, and Toledo have been added to the list.

Few Abandonments

Cleveland adopted the manager plan at the municipal election of 1923, but abandoned it eight years later after a partisan fight that had little or nothing to do with the efficiency of the city's government. Only a very few other municipalities have discarded the manager plan, and most of these did not give it a fair trial. They invited failure by adopting so-called manager charters that did not conform to sound principles of municipal organization;

they permitted the government to fall into the hands of professional politicians; or they used the manager plan as a scapegoat for unrelated economic or political difficulties.[2]

OPERATION OF THE MANAGER PLAN

The Council

MEMBERSHIP. Members of the council are popularly chosen, usually for terms of two or four years. Since the council is purely a deliberative or policy-determining body, there is no reason why it should be restricted to five members. The earlier charters, however, following the example of the commission plan, almost invariably provided for five-member councils, and even designated them as "commissions." For a time the new plan was generally known as commission-manager government. But the phrase "commission-manager" is unfortunate, for it suggests that the council-manager idea is merely a variation of the commission plan. Actually it is something very different. With the employment of a manager, the members of the council cease to be the directing heads of administrative departments. Their influence on administration is supposed to come only through their control over the manager. Therefore adequate representation properly becomes the determining factor in fixing the number of members. More than half of the larger manager cities, with populations in excess of one hundred thousand, have nine-member councils.

FUNCTIONS. The council is the city's lawmaking body, and it is directly responsible to the people for the condition of municipal affairs. Under the strict theory of the manager plan the council has just two functions. One is to pass necessary ordinances and resolutions; the other is to select the city manager and hold him responsible for the conduct of the municipal administration. All administrative matters are under his control. In practice, however, some manager charters vest rather broad powers of appointment in the council. Arrangements of this sort obviously hamper the manager, and make him something less than he is supposed to be—the directing head of the city's administrative affairs.

The Mayor

Under the manager plan the office of mayor is retained. As a rule, however, the mayor exercises no important powers. He presides over council

---

[2] For a concise discussion of the reasons why some cities have discarded manager government, see the 1949 edition of Arthur W. Bromage's pamphlet, *Manager Plan Abandonments*. See also the 1953 monograph, *Abandonments of the Manager Plan,* by Edwin O. Stene and George K. Floro.

sessions, and acts as the city's ceremonial head, relieving the manager of most of the bother connected with the reception of distinguished visitors, the unveiling of monuments, and a hundred other time-consuming activities of a

RELATION BETWEEN THE VOTERS, COUNCIL, CITY MANAGER, AND ADMINISTRATIVE PERSONNEL

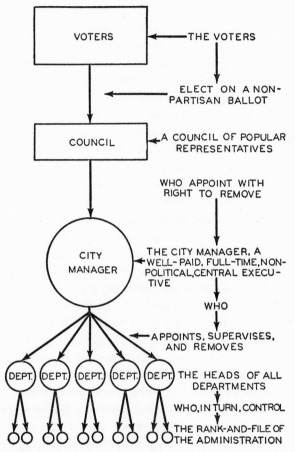

Reprinted with the permission of the University of Chicago Press, from Ridley and Nolting's *The City-Manager Profession,* p. 14.

similar nature.   He may be charged with the duty of preserving order in time of emergency.   Usually he is chosen by the council from among its own members, though in many cities he is elected as mayor by the voters.   His salary is generally higher than that of his fellow councilmen, and occasionally he is even given power to grant pardons.

The Manager

SELECTION AND QUALIFICATIONS. The central figure of the manager plan, of course, is the manager. He is chosen by the council, usually for an indefinite term. It is intended that he will remain as long as he gives satisfaction. Some charters provide that he may not be removed during the first six months, so as to give him a real opportunity to prove his worth. His responsibility is directly to the council, and only indirectly to the people of the city. He is a paid employee of the council—a glorified employee, directing all the city's administrative affairs, and more often in the public eye than any councilman, but an employee none the less.

The theory of manager government is based on the assumption that the council will choose an expert administrator, but very little is said in the charters about necessary technical qualifications. In several small cities the manager is required to be an engineer, and the charters of a few other small municipalities require experience as a city manager or assistant city manager. An outstanding feature of the manager plan is the common omission of any requirement that the manager be a resident of the city. Many charters expressly provide that residence is not necessary. The council is thus encouraged to find the right man for the job, even though it may have to go outside the limits of the city, or even the state.

SALARIES. The salaries of city managers are surprisingly high, judged by the general run of municipal salaries. In the ten largest cities operating under the plan, managers' salaries range from fifteen thousand dollars to twenty-seven thousand, five hundred, with an average of nearly eighteen thousand. For all manager cities, excluding small communities with populations of less than ten thousand, the average is about ninety-seven hundred dollars. Such salaries seem low when compared with the sums paid by private industrial enterprises to their executives. But in comparison with the salaries of elected mayors they appear remarkably generous.

POWERS AND DUTIES. The manager's powers are far-reaching. In fact, he is usually the most important municipal official. Everywhere he is the head of the city's administration, charged with the execution of the policies framed by the council. In the smaller communities he actually directs the work of one or more departments, serving perhaps as municipal engineer and thus reducing the total payroll. It is customary in the large cities, however, to provide for a skilled expert at the head of each department, and the manager is therefore free to devote his time to supervising and coordinating municipal activities. He selects his subordinates, from department chiefs all the way down the line, and the consent of the council is not required as a rule.

The manager is not shut off from all part in determining policy, for he is in a position to exercise considerable influence over the council. He attends all council meetings and makes such recommendations as seem desirable. He has no vote, of course, and the council is in no way bound by his suggestions. But in practice it is very likely to defer to his judgment, for he is an expert devoting all his time to the city's affairs. In all probability he knows more about community needs and community problems than anyone else. Council meetings are generally held in his office. Not infrequently he has the right to call special sessions. He frames the budget and submits it for the council's approval.

MANAGER-COUNCIL RELATIONS. Probably the most difficult problem facing every manager is the adjustment of his relations with the council. Under the theory of the manager plan the council alone determines matters of policy. The manager must be careful to keep hands off. He may suggest, advise, urge—but once the council has made up its mind he must abide by the consequences. He is only the council's employee, and he is expected to give loyalty to his employers. That is the theory, but time after time it has broken down in practice. The temptation to go directly to the people over the heads of the councilmen has proved too strong for some managers to resist. They have definite policies, and in their judgment it is essential that those policies be carried out. They prefer the willing co-operation of the council, but if that cannot be obtained, they resort to deliberate coercion by means of public appeals.

All this is a far cry from the original concept of the manager plan. The manager is supposed to be a technical administrator, not a political leader. Moreover, he must remain purely an administrator, for the moment he tries to shape public opinion in defiance of the council he plants the seed of his own destruction. He may win popular support at the next election, and secure a council composed of his own adherents. But sooner or later he will lose an election, and then he will inevitably be forced out of office. The manager who advocates policies must stand or fall with those policies. When the public withdraws its support from his ideas, he is honor bound to resign and permit the appointment of another manager whose policies are more to the public's liking. Thus he ceases to be a permanent, nonpolitical official. His ability as an administrator becomes less important than the popularity of his plans.

It is not easy for a manager to keep his lips sealed when the council overrides his cherished ideas, especially if he knows quite well that ignorance and prejudice have been determining factors.   Yet in no other way can he build the tradition of professional, permanent, non-partisan service. Fortunately, most managers recognize this important truth.   The revised code of ethics of the International City Managers' Association, adopted in 1952, declares: "The city manager realizes that the council, the elected representatives of the people, is entitled to the credit for the establishment of municipal policies.   The city manager avoids coming in public conflict with the council on controversial issues."

APPRAISAL OF THE MANAGER PLAN

Similarity to Modern Business

A number of advantages are claimed for the manager plan.   The fact that it is organized along the lines of modern business is constantly stressed. This fact is indeed important, for most of the work of city government is similar to the daily routine of thousands of private industrial enterprises. It consists of paving and repairing streets, purifying water and supplying it to homes and factories, collecting wastes and disposing of them, providing recreation of various kinds, from playgrounds to municipal opera.   These things involve no important questions of policy.   They are routine transactions of a highly technical nature, such as business men handle every day. In a word, they are administration.   It is safe to say that nine tenths of the work of our cities is administration.   Only at rare intervals does a vital issue make its appearance.   The greatest achievement of the manager plan has been to produce trained administrators, and to give American city government its first really professional touch.

Deterrent to Spoils System

The proponents of the manager plan frequently point out that it has been successful to a marked degree in freeing municipal administration from the baneful influence of partisan politics.   The average city manager is not interested in strengthening the dominant political organization.   To him the matter of improving municipal standards is vital, and he usually selects his assistants without regard for partisan considerations.   There are some managers, of course, who regularly and flagrantly play politics.   Even an efficient and conscientious manager may occasionally find the pressure too great, and permit the appointment of a henchman of the machine to some administrative post.   But it may be said conservatively that the spoils system has played a smaller part under the manager plan than ever before in the history of American city government.

Measuring by Results

A good way to test any theory is to put it into practice and watch the results. The results of the manager theory so far have been quite satisfactory. In some cities brilliantly successful administration has been achieved. Cincinnati, long known as one of the worst-governed cities in the country, adopted the manager plan in 1925, and almost overnight the new administration put municipal affairs on a high level of honesty and efficiency. Under manager government a large number of other municipalities have paralleled the experience of Cincinnati. The National Municipal League has characterized the manager plan as "America's chief contribution to municipal administration." [3]

Lack of Political Leadership under Plan

The most serious defect of the manager plan has been its failure to produce competent political leadership. Such leadership cannot properly come from the manager, of course; his business is administration, and not politics. It must, therefore, come from the council.

INCAPABILITY OF COUNCIL. The council is not accustomed to the responsibility of political leadership. For half a century it has looked to the mayor as the dominant figure in local political life, and has gradually settled down in comfort to the business of saying yes or no to his suggestions. And this arrangement has usually been satisfactory to the men who have served in American city councils. They have been small caliber persons for the most part, totally incapable of providing any real leadership. Unfortunately many of these men are still found in our city councils, and in some instances they have been joined by others of the same stripe. The manager plan has not materially altered the situation. It has not offered sufficient inducement to high grade men to seek service in the council. Yet it has placed on the council a new burden—the burden of guiding community thought. And the council has proved unequal to the job.

DANGER IN POWER OF MAYOR. It has sometimes been suggested that the mayor might fill the breach if he were given additional powers and recognized as the city's political head. Perhaps for this reason a number of manager charters entrust him with considerably more authority than his colleagues in the council. They make him an ex officio member of important boards, and sometimes they even give him extensive authority to make appointments. Such arrangements are probably unwise, for they contain a serious element of danger. The mayor is apt to consider himself

[3] *Forms of Municipal Government,* p. 12.

the head of the government in administrative matters as well as in questions of policy, and in a short time he may interfere with the work of the manager. Sound theory confines the mayor strictly to the field of policy determination, but in the rough and tumble of municipal politics there is little time for theory. The mayor may become a competitor of the manager for control of the city's government, and if a contest of that sort develops, the public is sure to be the loser, regardless of the outcome.

Undue Reliance on Local Talent

Manager government, as developed in the cities of the United States, has shown some unfortunate tendencies. Particularly discouraging has been the tendency to select local men as managers after the first appointment. In city after city the story has been the same. A thorough search, nation-wide if necessary, is made for the first manager. In their early enthusiasm the people are satisfied with no one less than the best man obtainable at their price. Then enthusiasm wanes. Local prejudices creep in. After a time the manager resigns—because he has received a more attractive offer, perhaps, or because the local politicians have made his position untenable. Whatever the cause of his resignation, a resident of the city is chosen as his successor. After that the local tradition holds full sway. There are many exceptions to this rule, of course. But it may safely be said, as a result of past experience, that when a municipality chooses its third or subsequent manager the chances are two to one he will be a local man. This does not necessarily imply that he will be incompetent, or that he will be merely a tool of the dominant political machine. It does mean, however, that his viewpoint is likely to be narrow, and that he is virtually certain to have friends clamoring for jobs in the municipal service. Worst of all, it indicates that his opportunity for advancement is seriously limited, regardless of the kind of service he gives.

Hazard of Overvaluation

It is sometimes said that the manager plan does not necessarily insure good government. Obviously this statement is true, for no type of organization can guarantee the selection of well-trained officials. Good men are quite as essential as good laws. Unfortunately, some friends of manager government have not realized this elementary fact. More than once they have made unqualified assertions that could not be proved, and promises that could not be fulfilled. In the heat of the campaign they have sometimes said that the manager plan would eliminate all graft, confound the professional politicians, and make the municipal administration one hundred per cent efficient. Then has come the adoption of the plan, together with the speedy return of the professional politicians to power; and the government has continued on about the same plane as before. When circumstances of this sort arise, good government cannot reasonably be expected. But the masses of the people do expect it, for they have been told that the manager plan will produce a civic millennium. The millennium fails to put in an appearance, and they blame the plan. Even at the expense of losing a few votes it would be better to say frankly that manager government cannot guarantee the honesty and efficiency of city officials. It is merely a scheme for simplifying the municipal framework and making easier the task of selecting good men.

Suitability in Large Cities

Some years ago, when Dayton and Norfolk were the largest manager cities, many people freely asserted that the plan would not work well in the great urban centers—communities with populations of one quarter of a million or more. Their contention was based chiefly on the fact that the large cities had made no move in the direction of manager government. This argument is heard less today, because Cincinnati, Dallas, Kansas City, Oakland, Rochester, San Diego, and Toledo have fallen into line. It ought to be discarded altogether, for it has no sound basis. Large cities need professional administrative service quite as much as their smaller neighbors. And they are in a better position to procure it. They can pay more attractive salaries with less effort. Should the City of Chicago adopt the manager plan, it could afford to hire administrative talent of a high order. A manager's salary of one hundred thousand dollars a year would impose a burden of but three cents on each person. But if Springfield, Illinois, became a convert, it would have to levy a tax of nearly seventeen cents per capita in order to pay the manager ten thousand a year. Moreover, the small town manager must be a Jack-of-all-trades. He must handle many administrative details himself, for lack of high-salaried subordinates skilled in the various phases of municipal administration. But in a great city every department can be headed by an expert technician. The manager need only be an administrator, supervising and co-ordinating. He has a better chance to succeed in the metropolis than in the village.

PROBLEMS

1. Prepare a description, with charts, of the government of Jersey City, New Orleans, or some other large municipality operating under the commission plan.
2. Trace the history of Cleveland's government from 1920 to date. Why

was the manager plan abandoned?   Consult the files of the *National Municipal Review*.

3. Prepare a description of the organization and work of the International City Managers' Association.   See the current issue of *The Municipal Year Book*.

4. Write a brief description of the manager plan in the cities of Ireland.   How does the Irish form of the manager plan differ from the American variety?

5. Trace the history of the adoption of the manager plan by some city near your home.   Examine the files of one of the city's daily newspapers.   What arguments were urged against the plan?

SELECTED REFERENCES

Bromage, Arthur W., *Manager Plan Abandonments*, 3rd ed., 1949.

Chamber of Commerce of the United States, *The City-Manager Plan of Municipal Government*, Washington, D.C., 1936.

Childs, Richard S., *Best Practice under the Manager Plan*, rev. ed., 1948.

Dow, Edward F., and Hormell, Orren, *City Manager Government in Portland, Maine*, Orono, Me., 1940.

International City Managers' Association, *Government in Small Council-Manager Cities*, Chicago, 1937.

————, *The Selection of a City Manager; Suggested Procedure to Aid City Councils in Appointing a Manager*, Chicago, 1937.

National Municipal League, *Forms of Municipal Government; How Have They Worked?* 1939.

————, *How Council-Manager Government Is Working*, 1940.

————, *Model City Charter*, rev. ed., 1941.

————, *The Story of the Council-Manager Plan*, rev. ed., 1948.

Overman, Edward, *Manager Government in Albemarle County, Virginia*, Charlottesville, Virginia, 1940.

Reed, Thos. H. and Doris D., *The Government of Cincinnati, 1924–1944: An Appraisal*, Cincinnati, 1944.

Ridley, C. E., and Nolting, O. F., *The City-Manager Profession*, Chicago, 1934.

Stene, Edwin O., and Others, *It Works in a Small City*, Lawrence, Kan., 1949.

Stene, Edwin O., and Floro, George K., *Abandonments of the Manager Plan: A Study of Four Small Cities*, Lawrence, Kan., 1953.

Stone, Harold A., *City Manager Government in the United States; A Review After 25 Years*, Chicago, 1940.

Stone, Harold A., and Others, *City Manager Government in Nine Cities*, Chicago, 1940.

Taft, Charles P., *City Management: The Cincinnati Experiment*, 1933.

Wells, Roger H., *American Local Government*, 1939, Chap. III.

White, Leonard D., *The City Manager*, Chicago, 1927.

The *Municipal Year Book*, published by the International City Managers' Association, contains a wealth of information concerning city government and administration.

CHAPTER 11

Government of Metropolitan Areas

It is difficult to say at just what point a city assumes metropolitan proportions. There is no hard and fast line between the mere city and the metropolis. Yet the distinction is well worth making, for the metropolitan center has problems peculiarly its own—problems that differentiate it sharply from smaller communities. A metropolis is something more than a small city grown large, with other cities clustering about it, for in the process of its growth it acquires new needs, new methods, a new viewpoint.

The Bureau of the Census uses a rather complicated formula in defining what it calls "standard metropolitan areas." But such areas are sure to have certain recognizable characteristics—congestion, a tenderloin, a considerable transient population, and at least the beginning of a cosmopolitan outlook.[1]

CONSEQUENCES OF CONGESTION

The most recent census figures show that more than one half of the people of the United States—fifty-six per cent, to be exact—are residents of the nation's one hundred and sixty-seven metropolitan areas. In other words, Americans have become not merely city dwellers, but big-city dwellers. This fact presents many serious problems, for congestion brings a host of consequences in its wake.

Need for Safeguards and Conveniences

When an area becomes congested, the volume of traffic becomes heavier, and new ways must be found to control it. Crime is likely to increase, and more effective steps must be taken to combat it. Contagious diseases are more readily communicated, and care must be taken to prevent their spread.

[1] For a detailed analysis of these metropolitan characteristics, see Don J. Bogue's 1949 monograph, *The Structure of the Metropolitan Community.*

High-pressure water systems are needed for proper fire protection; improved transit facilities must be provided for adequate transportation service.

High Cost of Government

Because of problems that increase with congestion it costs more per capita to run the government of a large city than the government of a small community. The largest municipalities in the United States are not only spending more than their less populous neighbors; they are spending considerably more per person. Moreover, this situation persists year after year. It is possible, therefore, to formulate a general law: *The per capita as well as the total cost of city government tends to increase with every increase in the population, other factors being equal.* It is necessary to add the final saving clause because other forces may tend to offset the operation of this law. But in general the rule holds, for nearly every municipal service in the metropolis involves a greater outlay. Even higher property values offer but a partial compensation in the form of increased taxable wealth.

DIFFICULTIES OF CO-ORDINATING METROPOLITAN SERVICES

Limitations of Political Boundaries

One of the more serious problems of large cities is their inability to control the development of their surrounding territory. Corporate boundaries are fixed by law, and for most purposes the jurisdiction of the city ends at the city line. But the problems of government show scant respect for city limits. Criminals cross the line at will; so do epidemics and conflagrations. So virtually every great city faces the problem of co-ordinating local services beyond its limits. Unless its boundaries have been recently extended they scarcely ever include the entire area that might well be called the economic city—the territory directly dependent upon the metropolis for its life and growth. In that territory are the homes of thousands who come every day to their work in the city. In it are factories drawing on the city's labor supply without paying the city's higher taxes. In it are farms that supply many of the city's needs. In it are smaller communities, perhaps cities in their own right, with governments and problems of their own, but after all merely satellites shining in the reflected splendor of the metropolis. The great trunk highways bearing the city's traffic must of necessity pass through this outer rim. The utilities that serve the city probably serve the outskirts also. The central airport probably lies beyond the main city's boundaries.

Duplication of Efforts

Officials of the metropolis and those of the surrounding cities and towns too often fail to co-operate.   They go about their tasks of testing milk supplies, arresting criminals, enforcing traffic regulations and building codes,

THE 168 METROPOLITAN AREAS OF THE UNITED STATES CONTAIN—

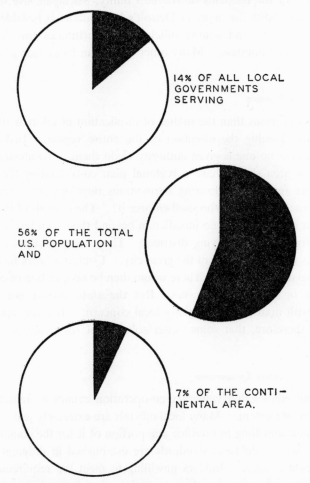

14% OF ALL LOCAL GOVERNMENTS SERVING

56% OF THE TOTAL U.S. POPULATION AND

7% OF THE CONTINENTAL AREA.

From *Local Government in Metropolitan Areas,* a 1954 publication of the United States Bureau of the Census.

fighting fires that may spread to other communities, with little or no regard for their neighbors.   And of course the same work is done time and again, when it might better be done once for the entire region.   Salaries are paid to an excessively large number of local officials.

Conflict of Authority

When a city grows to such a size that it dominates the county in which it is situated, paying most of the county's taxes and including within its limits most of the county's population, there is apt to be some duplication and a great deal of conflict between city and county officials. More than three fourths of the residents of Wayne County, Michigan, live in Detroit, yet the responsibility for many of Detroit's local affairs is bewilderingly divided between city and county officials. Opportunities for shifting the blame are almost limitless. Many other American cities face similar difficulties.

Lack of Regional Planning

Even more serious than the matter of duplication of effort is the neglect of problems claiming the attention of the entire region. Tasks are left undone because no one is given authority to do them. To illustrate, every metropolitan area should have a regional plan co-ordinating the facilities of the entire region and insuring harmonious development. But who is to prepare such a plan? Who shall enforce it? The officials of the metropolis? As a rule they have no jurisdiction beyond their own territory. The representatives of the outlying districts? They are powerless to enforce their rulings within the limits of the great city. Could the work be entrusted to state officials? Perhaps. There would then be no question of conflicting jurisdiction or inadequate powers. But the state should not be over-burdened with matters of essentially local concern. The conclusion is inescapable, therefore, that some better solution of the problem should be sought.

Inadequacy of Voluntary Co-operation

Experience shows that voluntary co-operation cannot be relied upon to any considerable extent. Many local officials are extremely jealous of their authority, and unwilling to sacrifice any portion of it for the common good. As a result widely different standards are established in different parts of the metropolitan area. Builders unwilling to meet the requirements of a rigid building code carry on their operations just beyond the city limits. Carefully planned programs of municipal development come to a dead halt at the boundary line. Fire hazards not tolerated within the city's borders are permitted just beyond. When two or more states are involved, however, any plan of activity *must* be based on friendly co-operation. There is no other way to get results.

SOLUTIONS OF THE METROPOLITAN PROBLEM

Territorial Annexation

In an effort to meet the needs of metropolitan regions a number of different plans have been tried. None has proved entirely satisfactory. Most commonly corporate limits have been extended. This is still the usual solution. When a city overgrows its boundaries new boundaries are created by law—not so soon as the need becomes apparent, perhaps not until the city has suffered from growing pains for a quarter of a century or more. But eventually the legislature shakes off its somnolence and traces a new boundary line more suited to changed conditions.

ADVANTAGES. Annexation has a number of advantages that cannot be ignored. For one thing, it gives city officials adequate control over the newly annexed territory. Their authority is as complete in the new sections of the city as in the old. The scheme is no half-way measure. It makes the region a political as well as an economic unit. Then, too, it simplifies the mechanism of government. One chief of police takes the place of a dozen or more. One council determines policies for the entire region. One local government replaces many. And since authority is concentrated in the hands of one set of officials they can be held responsible for results. Fewer opportunities are presented for evasion and quibbling.

UNFAVORABLE ASPECTS: *Unpopularity in suburbs.* Annexation is generally unpopular with the residents of the territory to be annexed. Almost any suggestion to extend city boundaries is virtually certain to receive its strongest opposition outside the city. Many a proposed consolidation has

NUMBER AND TYPES OF LOCAL GOVERNMENTS IN SELECTED METROPOLITAN AREAS

Metropolitan Area	Cities	Counties	Townships	School Districts	Other Special Districts	Total
New York	292	12	102	458	207	1,071
Chicago	192	6	108	419	235	960
Philadelphia	140	7	199	333	23	702
Los Angeles	58	2		171	67	298
Detroit	66	3	56	219	11	355
San Francisco– Oakland	51	5		160	156	372
St. Louis	143	4	46	165	62	420
Minneapolis– St. Paul	57	4	53	194	8	316

Based on figures from *Local Government in Metropolitan Areas,* a 1954 publication of the United States Bureau of the Census.

been defeated by the outlying districts.   People living just beyond the city limits feel, not without reason, that they already have most of the benefits of city life without helping to pay the city's bills.   They see no reason for assuming an additional tax burden, and it is difficult to convince them that they should.   When they are confronted with the prospect of a twenty cent increase in the tax rate, arguments about justice and increased efficiency seem rather weak.   Moreover, local pride plays a part.   Thriving small communities dislike the thought of casting aside their identity and becoming merely the numbered wards of a great metropolis.   And it must not be forgotten that local politicians are anxious to cling to their jobs.

State legislatures can ignore popular sentiment, of course, and consolidate local governments as they see fit.   In fact, city boundaries have often been extended without any attempt to ascertain local preference.   The more recent tendency, however, has been to emphasize the importance of local sentiment.   Virtually all recent annexation proposals contemplate an expression of opinion by the people of the districts immediately concerned. Certainly their preference ought to be ascertained, for democratic government is postulated on the consent of the governed.   But every referendum is another stumbling-block in the path of metropolitan development.   The people of the suburbs all too often do not wish to be absorbed; they consider absorption too expensive.[2]

Lack of permanence as a solution.   Another objection to a mere extension of city limits is that it does not permanently solve the metropolitan problem.   Boundaries suited to present needs may prove totally inadequate in another decade.   The cities are constantly expanding, constantly widening the sphere of their influence, and they are virtually certain to overflow any boundaries established by law.

INCLUSION OF UNRELATED INTERESTS.   If corporate limits are made so broad as to have any degree of permanence they must of necessity include a great deal of agricultural land, and perhaps even independent cities.   To permit a proper solution of the metropolitan problem they must be extended many miles beyond the outer rim of urban growth.   But state legislatures, not without reason, look upon cities primarily as urban communities.   They can seldom be induced to fix city boundaries fifteen or twenty miles beyond the limit of urban development, and perhaps they are right.   The blending of city and country under a single local government dominated by urban

[2] For an interesting discussion of the suburban attitude, see Ch. X of Victor Jones' excellent monograph, *Metropolitan Government*.   See also "Cities Urged to Reach Out," by Ben B. Ehrlichman, in the *National Municipal Review*, April, 1952, pp. 187 ff., and "Land Grabbing—Texas Style," by J. M. Claunch, in the *National Municipal Review*, November, 1953, pp. 494 ff.

interests might not be a happy experiment for the country folk directly affected.

City-County Consolidation or Separation

Sometimes it is possible to reduce duplication and simplify the structure of government by combining city and county.   As early as 1854 the Pennsylvania legislature gave the city of Philadelphia the same boundaries as the county, transferring to the city many county powers, including the power to lay and collect county taxes.   Philadelphia County continued as a separate government, however.   Two decades later the legislature of Louisiana partially combined the city and county governments of New Orleans.   Certain county functions are performed by the city government of Boston— an arrangement dating from 1821; and New York City has carried on important county activities since 1898, though the five counties originally comprising the area of Greater New York still remain as districts for the administration of justice.   In 1947 the city of Baton Rouge and East Baton Rouge County (or Parish, as a county is called in Louisiana) combined most of their functions.   City and county retained their separate identities, but unity of purpose was assured by specifying that the county council should consist of the seven members of the city council plus two other persons elected by the voters of the rural area of the county.   In a number of instances separation of city and county has been tried instead of consolidation. Baltimore, Denver, San Francisco, and St. Louis have been detached from their respective counties and given entirely independent governments of their own, with the status of counties.   In Virginia every city attaining a population of ten thousand is separated from its county, and made fully responsible for both city and county functions.

These schemes of consolidation and separation have accomplished a great deal, but they have proved vitally defective in a number of respects.   For one thing, though they strike at duplication of effort, they make no serious attempt to meet the need for regional co-ordination.   County boundaries may by chance conform to the limits of the metropolitan area, but there is little likelihood of such a happy circumstance.   And the result is that regional problems are left unsolved because local officials have no power to deal with them.   When city and county are separated, the people left in the old county often suffer a real hardship.   The plan of separation usually takes from them eighty or ninety per cent of the population and the wealth, leaving them eighty or ninety per cent of the territory.   The metropolis literally selects all the choice portions of the county, and then renounces its responsibility for maintaining what is left.

Federated City

GREATER NEW YORK. The creation in 1898 of Greater New York raised a number of serious problems. In all American history so large a territory and so many people had never before been consolidated into a single city.[3] It was freely predicted by the opponents of annexation that the scheme would fall of its own weight. The central government of the city, it was said, would be top-heavy. It would have too much work to do. It would be out of touch with local sentiment. All sections would not be adequately represented.

In order to meet objections concerning representation a certain amount of autonomy has been given to the five boroughs comprising the city.[4] Each borough has a president selected by its voters for a four-year term. Each has a number of locally appointed school board members, who are responsible only for minor matters. Each is charged with the construction and maintenance of streets and sewers, the care of public buildings, and the enforcement of building regulations. Most other phases of the city's administration are in the hands of city officials. The presidents of the five boroughs, together with the mayor, the city controller, and the president of the city council, sit as the board of estimate. This board has a large number of administrative functions. It passes upon matters connected with the organization of the municipal service, correlates local improvements, and manages the city's sinking funds. Through their membership on the board, therefore, the borough presidents are persons of considerable importance. Yet even when the five of them work together they are not sure of controlling the board's policies. A system of plural voting keeps them permanently in the minority.

This borough plan has been tried by no other American city. Local pride has been appeased instead by the use of local names or the retention of minor local offices. In Europe, however, London is organized along somewhat the same lines as New York. So was prewar Berlin. The details vary considerably, of course, but in both London and New York the work of administration is divided between the municipal and borough or district authorities.

ADVANTAGES OF FEDERATION. Federation has certain merits. For one thing, it satisfies local sentiment. Outlying communities are more easily persuaded to unite with the metropolis when they are permitted to retain a measure of their identity. Then, too, federation prevents overburdening

---

[3] Los Angeles, however, has since far outstripped New York in area.
[4] Manhattan, Brooklyn, Queens, the Bronx, Richmond.

of the central city government.   It reduces the number of centrally controlled activities by placing the boroughs in charge of certain local services.

New York's experience would seem to indicate, however, that the advantage of decentralization is of no great practical importance.   The governments of Manhattan, Brooklyn, and the other boroughs have in reality very little authority.   They control less than ten per cent of the city's total expenditures.

DISADVANTAGES OF FEDERATION.   A vital defect of federated city government is its tendency to foster unnecessary duplications.   Multiplication of authorities is apt to result in wasted energy and unnecessary expense. Moreover, conflicts of authority are almost certain to occur.   In London the disputes between county and borough officials are so numerous that at times they seriously interfere with the work of municipal administration. For most American cities, therefore, it may safely be said that the faults of federated city government outweigh its merits.   Other and less troublesome means of satisfying suburban pride should be found.

Extramural Jurisdiction

One way of meeting metropolitan needs is to give to the central city a limited jurisdiction beyond its boundaries.   Such a plan might seem at first thought a rather radical departure from the accepted order.   We are accustomed to think of the city line as a place where city power and city activity abruptly stop.   As a matter of fact, many municipal activities are carried on beyond the municipal boundary.   The legislatures frequently authorize cities to go beyond their corporate limits for a number of different purposes, such as water supply or parks.   These matters present no real problem.   The city is acting in its quasi-private capacity, and not as an agent of the state.   It holds hospital or park land in an adjoining city or a nearby township just as a private person might.   Its control over the land is no greater than that of any private owner.   Its hospital or park employees working beyond city limits must obey local village or borough ordinances.

In still another way a city may extend its authority over outlying areas. With the consent of the legislature it may exercise a limited amount of governmental power over the affairs of neighboring cities, towns, and villages. Some of the earliest instances of the extramural power of cities are found in connection with liquor regulation.   It was soon discovered that local option laws were worth little because saloons were so frequently opened just beyond the city line.   In order to correct this situation the legislatures of a number of states gave to the cities the right to determine whether dramshops might operate within a certain distance of their borders—one or two

miles or even five miles.   More recently municipalities have been authorized
to regulate or prohibit slaughter houses, hog farms, and other nuisances
found beyond their limits, but so close as to menace the health or comfort
of their residents.   Many cities pass upon the platting of land and laying
out of streets in the outer rim of territory adjoining their boundaries.   In
this way some of the problems of metropolitan government are partially
solved.   Matters affecting both the city and its satellites are placed under
the control of the city's officials.   Instead of extending the city's jurisdiction
for all purposes, as in the case of annexation, the legislature extends jurisdiction only for certain purposes.

ADVANTAGES.   The plan of meeting regional needs by granting extramural powers to the central city of the region has some marked advantages.   It can be put into effect with little trouble and with few formalities.
All it requires is a simple amendment to the existing law.   No new charters
are framed; no new agencies are created.   No radical changes in the structure of government are necessary.   Another merit of the scheme is that it
gives to the smaller communities of the region a wide range of independent
action.   Local governments continue as before, with most of their powers
unaffected.   Much greater emphasis is placed on local autonomy than under
the borough plan.   There is some doubt, however, whether the greater
freedom of the small communities should be listed as a merit or a defect.
If it proves a real barrier to regional unity it ought speedily to be limited.

DISADVANTAGES.   The central cities have generally found their extrater-
ritorial powers inadequate.   They have been denied the right to deal with
many of the most important regional problems.   Still more serious, they
have been permitted to go at most only five or six miles outside their boundaries.   And the limits of the region, as fixed by the forces of industrial and
social activity, may be twenty miles beyond.

Another grave disadvantage of the extramural plan is that it gives to
one unit of local government a measure of control over the territory and
people of another.   This is certainly contrary to the generally accepted
theory of democracy.   It means that suburban residents must obey ordinances of a council they have had no part in selecting, and that the use
of their land may be restricted without their consent.   When an outlying
section is annexed its people are given a voice in the affairs of the greater
city.   They vote at municipal elections, and their representatives help to
determine municipal policies.   But the extramural plan holds out no such
inducement.   It is quite frankly government without the consent of the
governed.   Moreover, it is likely to produce confused and uncertain administration.   Even if the powers to be exercised by city officials in adjacent

territory have been specified with great care, disputes are almost certain to arise.

Intergovernmental Arrangements

To some extent, at least, the problems of metropolitan areas can be solved by co-operative action among the several governmental units involved. This comparatively recent development has already produced significant results, though it certainly is not a complete answer to the problems of metropolitan government.

AMONG NEIGHBORING COMMUNITIES. In police work dozens of large cities maintain radio hookups with suburban communities. The Chicago police department broadcasts information that is received by radio-equipped cars in more than fifty neighboring cities. Cincinnati performs a similar function for cities, counties, and townships within its metropolitan area, and also provides training for the members of neighboring police forces. A number of states have enacted legislation permitting any city or county to contract with a neighboring unit of government for the use of its fire equipment and apparatus—usually on the basis of a stipulated price per run; and the result has been a marked increase in co-operative fire fighting. Nearly fifty Michigan cities provide fire protection to outlying communities on a contractual basis, and many municipalities in California, Pennsylvania, and Wisconsin have adopted a similar policy. Arrangements among neighboring cities for mutual aid in case of fire are becoming increasingly common. More than one hundred California cities rely on county authorities to assess and collect municipal property taxes.[5]

Regional Plan

A plan for meeting metropolitan needs that has long gripped the imagination of administrators and students of government is the creation of a new political area—the region. In many respects the metropolitan territory of every great city is already an economic unit. Its several parts are securely bound together by the forces of trade and industry. Thousands of its people are city folk by day and suburban residents by night. Yet its needs are so diverse that complete consolidation under a single government would create a host of fresh problems. Why not, therefore, retain the existing cities and townships and boroughs, with their separate mayors, their separate councils, and their separate school systems, and superimpose upon them an additional unit of local government, embracing them all, but re-

[5] See *Co-operative Administration of Property Taxes in Los Angeles County,* by J. E. Swanson, W. R. Bigger, and W. W. Crouch.

sponsible only for matters of regional importance?   The region's governing body—commission, council, or whatever it might be called—would have control over planning, traffic, transportation.   Such matters as water supply and sewage disposal might also be placed under its jurisdiction.   Other functions could be added from time to time as they acquired regional significance.   For the most part, however, the existing local units would continue as before.   The cities and towns of the region would still choose their own officials and still determine most of their own policies.

BOSTON REGION.   The Massachusetts legislature has already adopted some such plan for the Boston region.   Parks, water supply, and sewerage have been placed in charge of a metropolitan district commission, whose jurisdiction extends over Boston and all the neighboring cities and towns for a distance of about fifteen miles.   This commission is appointed by the governor, and therefore is not directly dependent on local approval. Two other regional agencies also function within the Boston area—a metropolitan transit authority, created in 1929, and a planning division of the metropolitan district commission, created in 1923.   This planning division, despite its name, is entirely separate from the district commission.

MONTREAL REGION.   In the Canadian province of Quebec the finances of the region surrounding Montreal are under the jurisdiction of a metropolitan commission of fifteen members.   The city of Montreal selects eight of the fifteen, and therefore its control of the commission is assured.   One member, who has no vote, represents the provincial government, and the remaining six are chosen by the cities and towns flanking the metropolis. The commission has broad powers over fiscal matters.   It passes upon the proposed bond issues of all the communities in the region except Montreal, and alters their property valuations when necessary.   It has no control over Montreal's fiscal policies, but it may borrow on the combined credit of all the cities and towns, including Montreal.   In recent years, when approving a loan for one of the smaller cities or towns, it has adopted the policy of issuing its own bonds and collecting the principal and interest money from the community concerned.   The commission has been markedly successful in strengthening the credit of the weaker municipalities and putting the finances of the region on a sound basis.

OTHER EXAMPLES.   There are numerous other examples of regional or district commissions in charge of metropolitan affairs.   The sanitary district of Chicago covers an area of more than four hundred square miles.   Its nine trustees are chosen by the voters of the district.   Milwaukee has a metropolitan sewerage commission.   The water supply system of the nine cities on the eastern shore of San Francisco Bay is administered by the directors of a special utility district. In the Los Angeles area a metropolitan water district serves thirteen cities and two other governmental units. The Port of New York Authority is the product of an agreement made by the states of New York and New Jersey and ratified by Congress.[6] Since 1947 the Port Authority has been responsible not only for port matters but also for the management of New York City's three major airports. It administers railroad freight, grain, truck, and bus terminals. In Europe boards and commissions with regional powers are fairly common. Neither in Europe nor in the United States, however, are these metropolitan commissions given control over all matters of regional importance. They are entrusted with sewage disposal or water supply or planning, while other functions affecting regional welfare are left in the hands of city and village officials.

SELECTION OF REGIONAL OFFICIALS. If the region is to develop as a new unit of local government in this country, a significant question must first be answered: How are its officials to be chosen? Should they be elected or appointed? If appointed, by whom?

Appointment. The Boston method of appointment of regional officials by the governor is used in some states. But the widespread adoption of this plan is unlikely, for it violates the principle of home rule. It gives to state-appointed officials control over matters that obviously are not of primary state concern.

There are other ways, of course, by which regional officials might be chosen without resorting to popular election. They might be selected by the councils of the municipalities affected, as are the members of the Montreal metropolitan commission.[7] They might, as frequently suggested, be appointed by the judges of the courts in the region—an arrangement obviously designed to keep the commission members out of politics, but likely to have the opposite effect of drawing the judiciary into the political mire.

Election. If regional commissions are to be established, there is at least one valid reason why their members should be elected. They must formulate broad policies concerning regional activities, and naturally the people desire a voice in those policies. The practical objection raised to direct election is that it usually gives complete control to the metropolis. The representatives of the outlying communities find themselves outvoted on every proposition. It is possible, of course, to provide that every city and

---

[6] Frederick L. Bird is the author of an excellent monograph, *"A Study of the Port of New York Authority,"* 1949.

[7] Except two, who serve ex officio.

town in the region, regardless of its size, shall have one vote, or that no city, however large it grows, may choose more than forty or forty-five per cent of the total membership. Yet such restrictions violate the principle of majority rule.

FAVORABLE ASPECTS: *Preservation of local self-government.* Strong arguments can be advanced in favor of creating a regional commission to solve regional problems. First, it means the preservation of local self-government. All the local units are retained, and in most matters they continue as before. The old traditions and the old loyalties remain practically unchanged. Only those functions that have outgrown city boundaries are transferred to the region. Then, too, a regional commission can be so constituted as to give proper representation to every local community. A majority of its members may be chosen by the central city, but if the central city represents seventy or eighty per cent of the population and wealth of the region, as it usually does, its predominant position certainly ought to be recognized.

Flexibility. Another important advantage of the regional plan is its flexibility. Once the new agency has been set up, it may readily be given new duties. As functions become of regional importance they may be transferred from city and town to the region. If some functions outgrow even regional boundaries they may be taken from the region and placed directly under the jurisdiction of state officials.

UNFAVORABLE ASPECTS. Objections have been raised to the creation of a regional commission, of course. No plan yet devised to meet regional needs is entirely satisfactory. One defect is that the units of government are increased. We already have too many administrative areas—counties, cities, townships, and school districts, many of them with overlapping boundaries and conflicting jurisdiction. If we make the region another unit of local government we add to the number, and we may also add to the confusion. The movement for city-county consolidation is intended to produce greater simplicity. But our government will remain as complex as ever if we abolish a large number of county offices and put in their place a complete regional government.

THE COUNTY AS THE REGIONAL UNIT. The idea of a local supergovernment, extending beyond the limits of a single city and dealing with matters of general importance, is not new. In fact, the county now serves the purposes of regional government, though rather crudely as a rule, in several metropolitan areas. Los Angeles County, which includes almost the entire Los Angeles metropolitan region, provides the best example of the expansion of county government to meet regional needs. The county's functions include regional planning and flood control, and also police and fire protection for parts of the area.   A majority of the cities and towns within the county have contracted with the county government for tax assessment and collection, and for public health service.   Some cities receive assistance from the county civil service commission in preparing and scoring examinations and handling other technical matters.   A number of municipalities pay their library tax receipts into the county treasury, in exchange for county maintenance of local library facilities.   County officials administer public charity for the city of Los Angeles.[8]

In other metropolitan areas the attempts of county governments to solve regional problems have been less ambitious.   Milwaukee County, Wisconsin, has a system of county parks and parkways.   Essex County, New Jersey, which includes Newark, also maintains a park system.   In addition, it administers all vocational schools within its boundaries.   Hamilton County, Ohio, has assumed responsibility for construction of some major highways and bridges within the city limits of Cincinnati.   But these instances of county activity serve chiefly to show that the county, with but one or two possible exceptions, is not fitted to take the place of an urgently needed new unit of government—a region, metropolitan district, or something of the sort.   The county's boundaries have been determined without reference to economic development.   Its functions have been assigned with little regard for economic needs.   But the region, if set up as a new administrative area, would presumably be designed to solve metropolitan problems.   Otherwise there would be no excuse for establishing it.

PROBLEMS

1. Study the metropolitan region in which you live, as defined by the Bureau of the Census.   How many units of local government does this region contain?
2. Prepare a brief report on Chicago's metropolitan area.
3. Write a description of New York City's government.
4. Prepare a brief report on the government of London, explaining the relations of the administrative county, the city, and the metropolitan police district.
5. Frame a model plan of regional government for the metropolitan area in which you live.

SELECTED REFERENCES

American Municipal Association, *Changes in Municipal Boundaries Through Annexation, Detachment and Consolidation*, Chicago, 1938.

[8] The Bureau of Governmental Research of the University of California at Los Angeles has issued a number of mimeographed studies of county-municipal co-operation in the Los Angeles area.

Bard, Erwin W., *The Port of New York Authority*, 1942.

Bemis, George W., and Basche, N., *Los Angeles County as an Agency of Municipal Government*, Los Angeles, 1947.

Bird, Frederick L., *A Study of the Port of New York Authority*, 1949.

Bogue, Don J., *The Structure of the Metropolitan Community: A Study of Dominance and Subdominance*, Ann Arbor, 1949.

Bollens, John C., *The Problem of Government in the San Francisco Bay Region*, Berkeley, Calif., 1949.

Carpenter, Wm. S., *Problems in Service Levels; Readjustment of Services and Areas in Local Government*, Princeton, 1940.

Cooper, Weldon, *Metropolitan County: A Study of Government in the Birmingham Area*, University, Ala., 1949.

Fairlie, J. A., and Kneier, C. M., *County Government and Administration*, 1930, Chap. XXIV.

Griffith, E. S., *Current Municipal Problems*, Boston, 1933, Chap. IX.

Haynes Foundation, *Metropolitan Los Angeles: A Study in Integration*, XVI vols., Los Angeles, 1952–1953.

Holtzman, Abraham, *Los Angeles County Administrative Officer: Ten Years' Experience*, Los Angeles, 1948.

Institute of Public Administration, *Governmental Organization Within the City of New York*, 1938.

Jones, Helen, and Wilcox, Robert F., *Metropolitan Los Angeles: Its Government*, Los Angeles, 1949.

Jones, Victor, *Metropolitan Government*, Chicago, 1942.

Landers, Frank M., *Units of Government in Michigan*, Ann Arbor, Mich., 1941.

Leonard, J. M., and Upson, L. D., *The Government of the Detroit Metropolitan Area*, Detroit, 1934.

Lipman, V. D., *Local Government Areas 1834–1945*, 1949.

McKenzie, R. D., *The Metropolitan Community*, New York, 1933.

Merriam, C. E., Parratt, S. D., and Lepawsky, Albert. *The Government of the Metropolitan Region of Chicago*, Chicago, 1933.

National Municipal League, Committee on Metropolitan Government, *The Government of Metropolitan Region of Chicago*, Chicago, 1933.

National Resources Committee, *Urban Government*, Washington, D.C., 1939, Sec. 4.

New York State Constitutional Convention Committee, *New York City Government; Functions and Problems*, 1938.

Parton, Mary Field, *Metropolis: A Study of New York*, New York, 1939.

Rankin, Rebecca B., *Guide to the Municipal Government, City of New York*, 1939.

Rush, John A., *The City-County Consolidated*, Los Angeles, 1941.

Rutherford, Geddes W., *Administrative Problems in a Metropolitan Area: The National Capital Region*, 1952.

Scott, Mel, *Metropolitan Los Angeles: One Community*, Los Angeles, 1950.

Simon, Herbert A., *Fiscal Aspects of Metropolitan Consolidations*, Berkeley, Calif., 1943.

Tableman, Betty, *Governmental Organization in Metropolitan Areas*, Ann Arbor, Mich., 1951.

University of California, Bureau of Governmental Research, *Integration of Public Library Services in the Los Angeles Area*, Los Angeles, 1942.

————, *Co-operative Health Administration in Metropolitan Los Angeles*, Los Angeles, 1949.

————, *Co-operative Administration of Property Taxes in Los Angeles County*, Los Angeles, 1949.

————, *Co-ordinated Public Planning in the Los Angeles Region*, Los Angeles, 1948.

————, *Intergovernmental Cooperation in Fire Protection in the Los Angeles Area*, Los Angeles, 1943.

————, *Intergovernmental Cooperation in the Los Angeles Area*, Los Angeles, 1940.

Wells, Roger H., *American Local Government*, 1939, Chap. III.

Woolston, Howard B., *Metropolis; A Study of Urban Communities*, 1938.

CHAPTER 12

County Government

Forty-seven of the forty-eight states are divided into smaller governmental units known as counties, and the lone exception—Louisiana —has corresponding units called parishes. The number of counties varies widely from state to state; thus Delaware has only three counties, whereas Texas has two hundred and fifty-four. Marked variations exist, also, in the area and population of counties and in the organization and functions of county government. Generalization, therefore, is difficult, but any brief description of county government and administration must necessarily be in general terms.

ORGANIZATION OF COUNTY GOVERNMENT

Its Varying Functions

Everywhere the county plays an important part in the administration of justice. Some states use it as a judicial district, with one trial court in each county. Other states combine counties to form judicial districts, which is the more common plan by a wide margin; [1] but even under such circumstances the prosecuting attorney, the sheriff, and the clerk of court are usually county officers. County courthouses expedite judicial business, and county jails hold those persons who are awaiting trial as well as those who have been sentenced to short terms of imprisonment.

Poor relief administration, also, is in the hands of county officials in most states. Highway construction and maintenance, public health work, and education, including vocational training specifically designed to improve agriculture, are generally regarded as matters in which the county should take a part. Almost everywhere the county is an important unit of fiscal administration, levying and collecting taxes for its own purposes and often for state and municipal purposes as well. The election system of the state commonly utilizes the county as a major unit.

These are the more important county functions, but if the list were ex-

[1] See page 165.

tended to include all activities performed wholly or partly by county officials in any state, it would be a most impressive enumeration. It would include the development of park systems, the establishment of other recreational facilities, such as gymnasiums, swimming pools, and public baths, the maintenance of libraries, and the development of airports. It would include, also, rural housing—a movement greatly stimulated by federal aid.

Its Chaotic Structure

The governmental structures established in the three thousand-odd [2] counties of the United States closely resemble one another in one important respect—they violate, almost without exception, every sound principle of organization. They are headless and formless. Authority is scattered among a large number of elective officers, who usually pursue their separate ways with little or no thought of effective co-operation.

No one person, corresponding to the mayor or manager of a city or the governor of a state, exercises supreme executive power. No one person can be held responsible for the lack of effective, co-ordinated administration. Even the so-called legislative body of the county has very limited legislative powers and can determine county policies only within certain narrowly limited fields. Administrative and judicial functions are often combined in the same officer or group of officers. The inevitable result of such a governmental jumble is chaos, and *chaos* accurately describes the present state of county government in the United States.

A few counties are predominantly urban, the cities within their borders having grown to metropolitan proportions. Such counties present special problems that have already received passing notice.[3] A much larger number of counties contain cities of medium size and therefore face some of the same problems. Duplication of county and city activities must be reduced or, if possible, completely eliminated; co-operation between county and city authorities must be fostered.

But these matters are not typical county problems, for the average county is still a predominantly rural area, existing as a unit of local rural government and designed, however crudely, to meet rural needs. Most of the state legislation for counties is for rural counties, and most of the proposals for the reform of county government are based on rural conditions.

[2] There are 3,049 counties, including the Louisiana parishes.
[3] See pages 232–233.

The County Board

The chief governing body of the county—or, more accurately, the body that most nearly deserves to be called *chief* among the numerous independent and unrelated agencies of county government—is the county board.[4] This body is generally known as the board of supervisors or board of county commissioners, but is sometimes called the board of revenue, fiscal court, or board of chosen freeholders.

ITS FUNCTIONS. The county board performs both legislative and executive functions, contrary to the traditional and commonly accepted doctrine of the separation of powers. Its legislative functions are narrowly restricted, covering only a few matters that the state legislature or, less commonly, the framers of the state constitution have seen fit to place under county control. The constitutions of a few states, such as California, specifically empower the county commissioners to make necessary local regulations not in conflict with the general state laws; and in a few other states, such as New York, the legislature is authorized to confer such power of local legislation as it may deem expedient. But even these narrowly restricted grants or potential grants of authority represent an attitude of extreme liberality. In most states the legislative powers of the county board, aside from its power to tax and to appropriate for specific purposes, are scarcely worthy of enumeration.

As an administrative agency the county board is more important. It manages county finances and property, supervises the construction of public works other than highways, and sometimes highway construction as well,[5] maintains courthouses and jails, administers the county poor relief program, and supervises the conduct of elections. Its financial powers generally include examination and approval of the budget, which its finance committee may prepare, and also equalization of property assessments among the townships of the county—or, in some states, among individuals.[6]

Effective management of county affairs is virtually impossible, because the county board shares responsibility with a large number of independently chosen officers, such as the sheriff, the coroner, and the assessor, whose acts are largely beyond its control. Only a few minor county officers are appointed by the county board in most states. The list usually includes the superintendent of the poor and the superintendent of the workhouse.

---

[4] Rhode Island is the only state where the county board is unknown.
[5] In most states the county boards at least locate the more important county roads.
[6] See page 608.

Sometimes, though rarely, it includes an important county officer—the treasurer.

ITS ORGANIZATION. The organization of county boards varies widely from state to state. Two general types of boards may be distinguished, however, though with many exceptions and modifications. One of these general types is the large board, ranging in size from fifteen members to one hundred or even more. The members of such a board are commonly chosen by the voters of their respective townships, and individually have supervision of township affairs; therefore the board is known as a board of supervisors. New York, Michigan, and Wisconsin make use of this plan, and Illinois has adopted it in part.

The other general type of county board is the small board, with a membership seldom in excess of seven, and more commonly three or five. This is called a board of county commissioners; its members are usually, although not invariably, elected at large from the entire county. It is popular in most of the states of the South and Far West, where township organization is unimportant or nonexistent.

Townships do not necessitate large county boards, however, as shown by the experience of a number of states. Thus Pennsylvania, Ohio, Indiana, and most of the New England states combine township or town organization with small county boards. On the other hand, large boards are found in Arkansas and Tennessee, which have no townships. Moreover, the states do not follow a consistent scheme of nomenclature. Some of them use the term *board of supervisors* for the small county board, even if there are no townships to be supervised.[7]

ATTEMPTS TO IMPROVE EFFICIENCY. Neither large nor small boards have proved wholly satisfactory because of the various—and, to some extent, conflicting—functions that county boards are called upon to perform. As legislative bodies they should be fairly large, in order to secure adequate representation for the many shades of opinion that exist in virtually every community. Three men, or five, cannot be expected to legislate with due regard for all the interests that are entitled to consideration. And yet, when county boards are enlarged to permit adequate representation, they immediately become too unwieldy for administrative bodies. The members spend their time in discussion when action is needed. They adopt formal

[7] Edward W. Weidner presents a detailed picture of the organization of county government in his article, "The Confused County Picture," which is published in three successive issues of the *National Municipal Review,* April, 1946, pp. 166–171, May, 1946, pp. 228–232, and June, 1946, pp. 288–294. See also the Census Bureau's 1946 report, *County Boards and Commissions.*

rules of procedure, and these rules delay still further the normal functioning of the administrative machinery.

Some of the large county boards in a number of states have tried to overcome the difficulty by creating small standing committees to handle the details of administration, but this plan has proved generally unsatisfactory. The committees usually show very little desire to co-operate with one another, and there is no way of compelling them to do so. The result is a still further disintegration of county administration. Moreover, all important committee actions must receive board approval, and most county boards are not disposed to accept committee recommendations, except in rare instances, without prolonged debate. Therefore the saving of time under the committee plan is more apparent than real.

Devices intended to improve the efficiency of county government by separating to some extent the functions of legislation and administration include the establishment of a county council in addition to the county board, as in Indiana, and the creation of a chief county administrative officer, as in a few counties of New Jersey and California. The chief county administrative officer possesses very limited powers, however, and cannot be considered the county equivalent of a city manager. In Los Angeles County, where a chief administrative officer was appointed in 1938, he has been entrusted with a measure of responsibility for most aspects of county administration. But department heads are still chosen by the board of supervisors, under civil service rules.[8] San Diego County makes use of a similar plan. A handful of counties have adopted the manager form of government, but these experiments are discussed in another part of this chapter.[9]

MEETINGS AND COMPENSATION. When the county board is a large body, it usually meets at infrequent intervals; in some states three or four meetings a year are the rule. The small board usually holds meetings more often —every week or every fortnight, in some of the more populous counties. Members of county boards are commonly paid by the day, the compensation ranging from five to twenty dollars, plus an allowance for mileage. This arrangement is often coupled with some sort of limitation on the number of days that the board may meet or the number of days that salary may be drawn. A few of the large counties in several states pay their board members by the year rather than by the day, thus removing the temptation to delay the public business in order to obtain a slightly larger salary.

---

[8] See Abraham Holtzman's 1948 monograph, *Los Angeles County Chief Administrative Officer: Ten Years' Experience*. See also Earl R. Strathman's article, "They Like Los Angeles Plan," in the September, 1948, issue of the *National Municipal Review*, pp. 428–432.

[9] See pages 248–250.

SHARED RESPONSIBILITY. As previously indicated, the county boards share responsibility for the management of county affairs with a large number of independently chosen officers. One of these is the sheriff, the peace officer of the county, who enforces the law, serves court processes, and keeps the county jail. Another is the coroner, whose task is to investigate cases of violent death. The public prosecutor, also, is usually although not invariably a county official. A few counties have public defenders as well as prosecutors. Since the work of these several officers is described in a later chapter,[10] nothing need be added at this point.

The Treasurer

SELECTION AND TENURE. Nearly every county has a treasurer, who receives, holds, and disburses county money according to law. Usually he is elected by the voters, but in a few states he is chosen by the county board or the governor. The term of office of the treasurer is generally fixed at two years, and in many states he is forbidden to serve two consecutive terms. Such provisions concerning tenure, though designed to insure strict examination of county funds at frequent intervals, as each new treasurer takes office, actually accomplish no useful purpose. On the contrary, they put a premium on ignorance by excluding men from office as soon as they have had an opportunity to gain experience.

PROTECTION OF COUNTY FUNDS. Virtually everywhere the treasurer is placed under heavy bond to protect the county against possible defalcation. The county is also protected against poor judgment in the selection of depositories, under the court decisions of some states, which hold that the treasurer is liable for the safe-keeping of all funds placed in his custody. The effect of these decisions is to permit the county, in the event of a bank failure, to recover directly from the treasurer to the extent of his personal resources, even though no evidence of bad faith appears.

The numerous bank failures during the years 1930, 1931, and 1932 worked serious hardship upon many honest county treasurers, and have led to a number of modifications of the rule. Eventually, in all probability, the deposit of county funds will be regarded universally as a matter to be regulated by law, and the treasurer will not be held liable unless he violates some statutory provision. This more rational plan has already been adopted by a majority of the states.

DISBURSEMENTS. With regard to disbursements the treasurer exercises but slight discretion. He must pay every lawful claim allowed by the county board and approved by the auditor. If, however, the claim is for

[10] Chapter 17, pages 354–361.

a purpose not authorized by law, he may refuse payment. In fact, it is his duty to do so. County treasurers, therefore, should know all the lawful objects of expenditure, so as to be able to pass upon the legality of claims presented to them. But in practice they seldom possess such knowledge, relying instead on the auditors or corresponding officers to reject unlawful claims.

The Auditor

Every county needs some officer to examine bills and claims and determine their validity. Even though these bills and claims are approved by the county board before payment, a separate audit by some person not a member of the board is highly desirable. Many counties, however, make no provision for such an audit. Many others assign this task to the county clerk, with reasonably satisfactory results. There is, in fact, little justification for both a county auditor and a county clerk, except in very populous counties. But separate county auditors have been established, regardless of need, in about one third of the states.

They are chosen in a variety of ways—by the county board, as in New Jersey; by the county's members of the state legislature, as in Connecticut; by the judges of the courts, as in Vermont; by the governor, with senate approval, as in South Carolina; or by the voters at the polls, as in at least ten states. One auditor to a county is the rule, but a few states prefer boards of auditors as a further check upon possible dishonesty.

In addition to passing upon bills and claims against the county, some auditors are empowered to examine the accounts of other county officers at regular intervals. Such periodic examinations are necessary, of course, though often neglected in county government. But they should be made, in the opinion of most students of public administration, by some state agency with broad powers of audit rather than by any county officer, however chosen.

Assessors

The locally elected assessors, sometimes county officers and sometimes officers of the town or township, are poorly qualified to perform the difficult task of determining the value of property for purposes of taxation. A few states have amended their constitutions to provide for assessors appointed by the governor, and this plan has usually proved more satisfactory. But some politically minded governors have used this additional appointing power to strengthen their own political machines, and these unfortunate experiences, coupled with the long-standing American fear of concentrated authority, have been sufficient to prevent widespread adoption of the appointive plan.

In Kentucky, one of the many states where assessors are still chosen by popular vote, the names of candidates are not placed upon the ballot until they have demonstrated their fitness by appearing before the state tax commission and passing an examination. This scheme, or some modification of it, has been tried by a number of metropolitan centers in several states and has proved infinitely superior to the usual method of popular election without any attempt at prequalification.

The Clerk of the Court and the County Clerk

Two other county officers whose duties are sufficiently important to deserve special mention are the clerk of the county court and the county clerk. The clerk of the county court opens court sessions and adjourns them, keeps the official record of all court proceedings, dockets all cases for trial, and issues necessary processes and writs. The county clerk acts as secretary to the county board; in addition, he has a wide variety of miscellaneous functions, ranging from the preparation of ballots to the issuance of marriage licenses. In no two states are his duties exactly the same; often they include the examination and approval of claims, in case there is no separate auditor, or the registration of voters, if no other officer has been assigned that task. The offices of clerk of the county court and county clerk have been considered jointly because in many states they are combined in one official, who usually bears the title of court clerk. Popular election and short terms are the rule, for no better reason than that most county officers are popularly elected and serve for short terms.

The Register of Deeds

In many states the clerk of court or county clerk maintains a public record of deeds, mortgages, and other documents affecting the title to real estate. More than half of the states, however, have assigned this duty to a separate officer whose title is recorder or register of deeds. This officer is elected by the voters, and as a rule his term is two years. Like other county officials, therefore, he is an amateur charged with a task requiring professional skill.

In most instances he makes use of the old-fashioned methods inherited from his predecessors in office. Documents are copied tediously in longhand—or, more rarely, on the typewriter. Only a few of the more progressive recorders' offices make full use of available printed forms, and modern photostat recording is practically unknown, except in some of the large metropolitan centers.   Filing systems are antiquated.   The inevitable re-sult, in nearly every county, is a set of records whose accuracy is open to serious question.   Private interests have taken advantage of this situation to establish companies for the purpose of searching the records and guaran-teeing the title to property.

A few states have adopted the so-called "Torrens system" [11] of land registration, which eliminates the danger of possible flaws in the title at comparatively small cost to the purchaser.   Under this system title is awarded by court decree after a public hearing, and may not be clouded by valid claims presented at a later date.   These claims are not ignored, however; instead they are settled by cash payments from an assurance fund built up from the fees charged for registration.

The Surveyor

Nearly every county has a surveyor, an elective officer whose duty is to make surveys of land upon the request of private owners or the order of the court.   He has no fixed salary, but instead receives his compensation in the form of fees.   Today his office is unimportant, because property lines have been precisely fixed in most communities.   Some surveyors still play a part in the construction of highways, and in a few states this is their prin-cipal function.   But modern road building is a task for trained engineers, and county engineers are rapidly replacing surveyors as the directors of highway construction programs.   A considerable number of states have combined the duties of the county surveyor and the county engineer, and this arrangement has generally proved satisfactory.

DEFECTS IN COUNTY ORGANIZATION AND ADMINISTRATION

This, then, is the usual form of county government: a board with limited powers, responsible in a general way for policy determination and also for the administration of county affairs, but forced to share its control over county administration with a large number of independently elected officers who follow their separate paths unchecked, utterly heedless of the need for co-ordinated action.   By every adequate theory of government such a scheme should be a complete failure—and, by every practical test, it is. All students of public affairs agree that county organization must be thor-oughly overhauled before it can function effectively under modern condi-tions.   The literature of county government is filled with recitals of in-efficiency and waste until the story becomes monotonous through repetition.

[11] Introduced in Australia by Robert Torrens.

ORGANIZATION OF AN URBAN COUNTY (ALAMEDA) IN CALIFORNIA

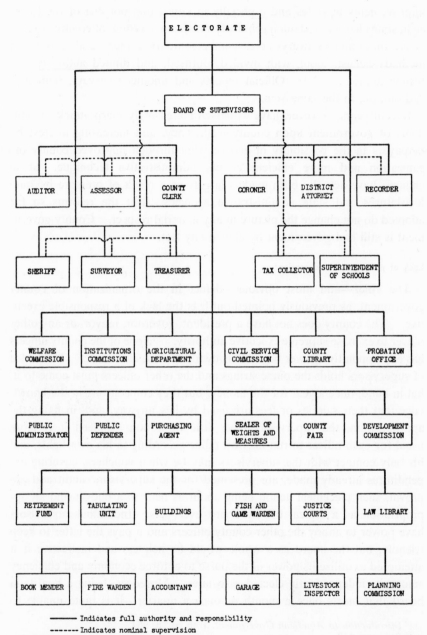

Indicates full authority and responsibility
Indicates nominal supervision

Reproduced from *Alameda County Government,* a survey prepared by the Alameda County Taxpayers Association, Inc.

Professors Ogg and Ray declare "that, in general, the county has been largely untouched by reform movements which have yielded remarkable improvements in states and especially in cities; that not one of the forty-eight states has worked out a genuinely satisfactory system of county government; that, almost everywhere, cumbersome machinery and antiquated methods persist, along with divided, diffused, and diluted authority and responsibility. . . ." [12] Official reports and unofficial surveys, both new and old, are in the same vein.

Recent years, however, have witnessed increasingly sharp attacks by students of government upon county inefficiency, and increasing interest by taxpayers in the possibility of economizing through improved county organization and more efficient county administrative technique. Some changes have actually been made—largely as a result of pressure by state legislatures and state administrative agencies. But the reforms so far adopted do not change the picture in any material respect. County government is still bad government by almost any test.

Lack of a Responsible Executive

The chief—and most obvious—defect in the organization of county government, as previously pointed out,[13] is the lack of a responsible executive. The county does not have a president, governor, mayor, or any other officer to exercise supreme executive authority. "None of the county officers has any appointive power beyond his own deputies, clerks, etc. The board of supervisors holds the purse strings and the other officers must come to it, hat in hand, once a year for the money, but they come strong in the knowledge that their salaries or fees are fixed by law anyway, and, in fixing the appropriation, the supervisors have little discretion. Indeed it is more usual for each officer to run his own office according to his own lights, and his only contact with the supervisors may be when vouchers, covering expenditures already made, are presented for the supervisors' audit and approval, such piecemeal action being about as near to a budget and an appropriation as a typical county board ever gets. Individual supervisors have power to annoy the other county officers and it pays the latter to keep friendly, but the board as a whole would be helpless and ineffective if it attempted to utilize its power of the purse to enforce economy and efficiency among its independently elected associates. Moreover, being a board—a board that meets once a month or once a quarter—it is quite unable to

---

[12] *Introduction to American Government,* 10th ed., p. 964.
[13] See page 237.

operate as an executive or follow its resolutions through to secure whole-hearted compliance. When there is a controversy between county officers, their only common superior to which appeal may be made is the remote legislature which, by special law, may for example settle the issue of what salary the sheriff may pay his wife for services as cook in the county jail." [14]

Failure to vest complete authority and responsibility in a single executive is due in part to the opposition of local politicians, who regard any proposal to change the existing governmental structure as a threat aimed directly at their freedom of action. In part, too, popular indifference is responsible. The average voter is not interested in the government of the county in which he happens to live, unless his pocketbook is directly and obviously affected.

However, other factors are also to blame. Thus the constitutions of most states indirectly prohibit the establishment of unified executive control by imposing a long ballot on all counties. In Texas, for example, the list of elective county officers—by constitutional mandate—includes the county judge, the justice of the peace, the clerk of the district court, the constable, the county commissioner, the county clerk, who serves ex officio as recorder, the county attorney, the tax collector, the assessor, the treasurer, and the surveyor.[15] And Texas is not an especially serious offender in this respect; these provisions concerning counties are typical of many state constitutions. Amendment of the constitutional clauses imposing a long ballot is possible, of course, but in most states amendment is a slow and difficult process. So those people who are interested in the reform of county government often give up the fight in despair, and the old, inefficient organization continues to function in the same old, inefficient way.

A few county governments have been altered to provide for a popularly elected executive possessing a certain general power of supervision over county administration. Thus Cook County, Illinois, has a county president, elected as a member of the county board and authorized to appoint those county officers—mostly of minor rank—who are not chosen by direct vote of the people. He exercises a limited veto over the acts of the board. In certain counties of New York, New Jersey, and Virginia a popularly chosen chief executive officer is partly responsible for the co-ordination of county administration. But such schemes are far from satisfactory. First, they go only a short distance along the path of reform. Although recognizing in

[14] Richard S. Childs, *The County Manager Plan,* pp. 3–4.
[15] Texas counties with populations in excess of sixty-two thousand may escape this arrangement, however, by adopting home-rule charters.

part the need for concentrated authority, they still diffuse power among a considerable number of independently chosen officials. Second, they rely on an elective officer, who is therefore necessarily an amateur, to direct the technical details of administration.

Need for the County Manager Plan

The next step, logically, is the adoption of the manager plan by counties. County government—perhaps even more than city government—is chiefly a matter of administration. Only occasionally does an important question of policy require consideration. Therefore the head of the county should be an administrator; he should be chosen with regard to technical qualifications and not on the basis of ability to get votes. In other words, he should be appointed, because this method of choice is much more likely to produce technical skill than any scheme of popular election. The appointing body should be the county board, representing the voters; and board members should understand clearly that they are no longer responsible for the details of administration. All officers and employees in the administrative service of the county should be appointed by the manager and hold office at his pleasure; thus the ballot for county officers would become a short ballot *par excellence*.

Despite the obvious merits of the manager plan for counties, it has made but slight progress, in marked contrast to the rapid spread of manager government in the municipal field. Only fifteen American counties [16] make use of the manager plan, and most of them still divide administrative authority between the manager and various elective officers. In Arlington County, Virginia, for example, the people still elect a clerk, sheriff, commonwealth's attorney, treasurer, and commissioner of revenue. The two so-called manager counties of North Carolina give their managers almost no appointing power, while continuing to elect a number of administrative officers. The slowness of counties to adopt the true manager plan—or, for that matter, any plan of manager government—can be explained in part by the fact that constitutional or statutory provisions quite generally prevent such a step and that these restrictions must be cleared away before the voters can indicate effectively whether they desire a change from the ramshackle form of county government that has so long served as a barrier to progress. In Ohio the state laws are so restrictive that Cuyahoga County, which includes

---

[16] Sacramento, San Mateo, and Santa Clara counties, California; Fulton County, Georgia; Anne Arundel and Montgomery counties, Maryland; Petroleum County, Montana; Monroe County, New York; Durham and Guilford counties, North Carolina; McMinn County, Tennessee; and Albemarle, Arlington, Fairfax, and Henrico counties, Virginia.

Cleveland, has been obliged to appoint its "county administrative officer" as an assistant to the clerk of the board of county commissioners.[17]

Although most qualified persons accept the point of view presented in these pages—that the manager plan is desirable for counties and should be

MODEL COUNTY GOVERNMENT

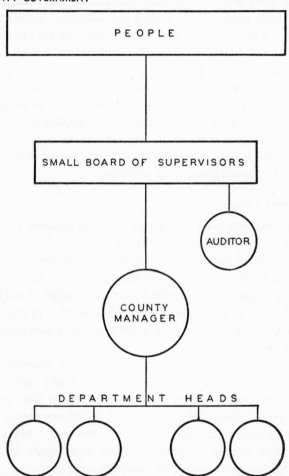

Based on Richard S. Childs' *The County Manager Plan,* with some modifications. Reprinted with the permission of the National Municipal League.

generally adopted by them—there are some who disagree.   They contend that the functions of the county are primarily matters of state concern, and should be brought under direct state control until little or nothing is left for

[17] See the note on pp. 205–206 of the April, 1952, issue of the *National Municipal Review.*

a manager to manage.   This line of reasoning is plausible, but it rests on the highly questionable assumption that expanding state control will reduce the importance of counties until they become little more than agencies for the performance of state functions.   As a matter of fact, the counties in most states have by no means reduced the number of their functions.   Loss of control of some activities has been matched by the assumption of new services.   County planning, unknown a few years ago, has already become a vital force in a number of states.   County libraries are rapidly becoming commonplace, and county recreational facilities are far from rare.   Some counties maintain airports; some accept responsibility for the prevention of forest fires; some have assumed important new obligations in the fields of education, health and housing.   Unless counties cease to function as separate agencies of government—and there is not the slightest indication that such a radical change is in prospect—they should certainly have the benefit of the best possible type of local administrative organization for the performance of their multifarious local activities.

Poor Administrative Technique

Too much emphasis must not be placed on the structure of government, however.   Good government is more than a matter of managers or supervisors; it depends in large measure on the development of adequate administrative technique—a satisfactory merit system for the recruitment and supervision of employees, a standard executive budget, a modern system of central purchasing, and effective accounting control.   In these matters, as in governmental structure, the large majority of American counties are extremely backward.

Thus the time-honored spoils system of selecting employees continues almost unchecked.   There are, however, some bright spots in the dark picture.   Nearly three hundred counties now choose their personnel by competitive examination.   The list includes all the counties of New York State, which are required by state law to follow this plan.   Many states have established merit systems for county welfare departments, in order to be eligible for federal grants under the Social Security Act.

County budgets are now required by law in more than half of the states, but many of the statutory provisions concerning county budgetary procedure are so poorly phrased as to be practically worthless.   Only about one county in ten has established a system of central purchasing, and some of these central purchasing systems are totally inadequate.   On the other hand, modern methods of keeping accounts have been adopted by many counties in recent years.   This improvement has been effected largely by changes in state laws making the use of improved, standardized accounting methods mandatory.   State supervision of county accounts, including the preparation of standard forms by the state auditor for county use, is rapidly increasing in popularity, and bids fair to solve the problem of slipshod county accounting.

COUNTY CONSOLIDATION

One of the most serious obstacles to efficient county government, in many states, is the excessive number of counties.   Poor counties, with small populations, totally unable to support expensive governmental organizations or to find a sufficient number of competent officials, are required by state law to have substantially the same form of government as wealthy counties with large populations.   In many parts of the United States the county organization exists chiefly for the benefit of empty acres.

The most obvious solution of this problem is the consolidation of counties to form units of government sufficiently rich and sufficiently populous to support adequate governmental organizations.   The pioneer in this field was Tennessee, which consolidated two counties in 1919.   More recently there have been proposals for extensive consolidation in other states, but little has been accomplished.   Local loyalties and local political pressures have generally proved too strong.

Much more popular is a plan of "county co-operation," whereby two or more counties join in the conduct of certain administrative services, though retaining their separate entities as governmental units.   In the field of poor relief, for example, the Virginia county almshouse has almost disappeared; as many as eight counties, in some instances, co-operate to main a district poor home.   Many other states have authorized similar arrangements concerning police, fire, and health protection, public utility services, construction and maintenance of public improvements, and other services.[18]

FUNCTIONAL REALIGNMENT

Some students of county government, dissatisfied with the slow progress of reform and the indifferent results achieved by many reform programs, urge the creation of special districts for the performance of certain functions now placed under county control.   These districts would not be the same for all functions; on the contrary, each separate activity would involve the division of the state into new districts, presumably on the basis of the work

[18] See Dorothy Luber's article, "Health Consolidation Works," in the March, 1951, issue of the *National Municipal Review*, pp. 141–144.

to be done. Thus, within a single state, there might be fourteen judicial districts, twenty districts for school administration, and forty districts for the assessment of property. Presumably the officers of these various districts would be state-appointed and state-controlled; any other arrangement would lead to serious complications.

The proponents of this plan are pleased to call it *functional realignment,* because they believe that the new governmental areas would be created solely on a functional basis. Whether the most suitable administrative areas could be determined with any degree of accuracy, and whether, once found, they would be utilized by politically minded state legislatures or constitutional conventions, are questions that lie within the realm of speculation.

PROBLEMS

1. Prepare a chart showing the governmental organization of your county. What changes in the present organization would you advocate?

2. Describe the organization and work of the treasurer's office in your county. What qualifications does the present treasurer possess? Note his training and previous experience.

3. What are the duties of your county clerk? How well does he perform these duties?

4. Examine the budget system of your county, or of some county in a neighboring state that requires county budgets. Does the existing budgetary procedure seem reasonably satisfactory? Are all items of county expenditure and revenue included in the budget?

5. How are your county's employees selected? Is an attempt made to secure properly trained persons? Are dismissals ever made for political reasons?

SELECTED REFERENCES

Alderfer, H. F., *Pennsylvania Local Government Survey,* 1935.

Anderson, William, *Local Government and Finance in Minnesota,* Minneapolis, 1935.

Andrews, Columbus, *Administrative County Government in South Carolina,* Chapel Hill, N.C., 1933.

Bradshaw, William L., *County Government Manual for the Missouri Constitutional Convention of 1943,* Columbia, 1943.

Bromage, Arthur W., *American County Government,* 1933.

Bureau of Governmental Research, Univ. of Calif. at Los Angeles, *County Government in California,* Sacramento, Calif., 1951.

Carleton, R. L., *Local Government and Administration in Louisiana,* University, La., 1935.

Crouch, W. W., *State Aid to Local Government in California,* Berkeley, 1939.

Duncan, John P., *County Government, An Analysis; County Government, Con-*

stitutional Data; County Government, Forms (Nos. 12, 13, and 14 of a series prepared for the Oklahoma Constitutional Survey Committee); Oklahoma City, 1948.

Euler, H. L., *County Unification in Kansas,* 1935.

Fairlie, John A., and Kneier, Charles M., *County Government and Administration,* 1930.

Ford, R. S., and Tharp, C. R., *Reorganization of Michigan's County Government,* Ann Arbor, 1946.

Georgia University Institute of Public Affairs, *Round Table on County Government,* Athens, Ga., 1934.

Hughes, Melvin C., *County Government in Georgia,* Athens, 1945.

Jay, C. A., *County Reorganization in Texas,* Dallas, 1934.

Kilpatrick, Wylie, *County Management,* Charlottesville, Va., 1929.

Lancaster, Lane W., *Government in Rural America,* rev. ed., 1952.

Manny, T. B., *Rural Municipalities,* 1930.

Murphy, W. C., *County Government and Administration in Texas,* Austin, 1934.

Porter, K. H., *County and Township Government in the United States,* 1922.

Reed, Thomas H., *Twenty Years of Government in Essex County, New Jersey,* 1938.

Rosenthal, Edgar P., *The County Unit of Local Government,* Mineral Point, Wis., 1941.

Schmit, Edward Benjamin, *County Consolidation,* Lincoln, Neb., 1934.

Snider, Clyde F., *County Government in Illinois,* Springfield, 1942.

Spicer, G. W., *Fifteen Years of County Manager Government in Virginia,* Charlottesville, 1951.

Sorrell, V. G., and Stuart, James R., *County Consolidation in New Mexico,* Albuquerque, 1934.

Tharp, C. R., *A Manual of County Administrative Organization in Michigan,* Ann Arbor, 1944.

Wager, Paul W., *County Government and Administration in North Carolina,* Chapel Hill, 1928.

Wager, Paul W., ed., *County Government Across the Nation,* Chapel Hill, North Carolina, 1950.

Wisconsin Historical Records Survey, *County Government in Wisconsin,* 3 vols., Madison, 1941.

Works, George A., and Lesser, Simon O., *Rural America Today,* 1942.

CHAPTER 13

Towns, Townships, Villages, and Special Districts

Local government in the United States presents a bewildering picture. In addition to the counties and cities, there are towns, townships, villages, and boroughs. There are also special districts of many kinds. No two states have organized their local governments in exactly the same manner. Words like *town* and *township* do not even have a uniform meaning in all parts of the nation. So the student of local government must anticipate exceptions to almost every statement. And he must be prepared to give separate consideration to different sections of the country, instead of trying to find a pattern that will fit the entire United States.

NEW ENGLAND TOWNS

Extent and Nature of Town Government

The six New England states use the town instead of the county as the primary unit of local government. Towns are normally rural or semi-rural; when they grow into populous urban centers they are commonly transformed into cities by act of the state legislature. The New England states have counties as well as towns, but the counties serve chiefly as units for the performance of certain minor functions. In Rhode Island they are merely election districts. The towns of New England are smaller than the counties. The area of Massachusetts, for example, comprises thirteen counties, which in turn are divided into three hundred and twelve towns. The New England town usually has well-defined natural boundaries—a river or a range of hills. Therefore it follows no uniform pattern as to size or shape. Originally the New England towns were church congregations as well as areas of government. They were small, compact communities, and their inhabitants could readily assemble for the worship of God, the protection of their homes against the Indians, or the consideration of any public problems that might arise. Today the problems are very different, but the general form of town government remains essentially the same.

Functions of Towns

The towns of New England perform a wide variety of functions.   They generally maintain school buildings and equipment and hire teachers. They play a major part in the complex task of safeguarding the public health. They are responsible for local parks and public buildings, sanitation, water supply, and police and fire protection.   Construction and maintenance of minor roads usually fall within their jurisdiction.   Libraries and recreational facilities, if provided at all, are usually a town responsibility.   In some matters the towns act on their own initiative, but in others they serve as agents of the state.   They may be required by law to assess and collect state taxes or to enforce state statutes concerning education, health, or other matters. Towns, like cities, are creatures of the state.   Unlike cities, however, the towns do not have their own charters setting forth their rights and liabilities. Such matters are commonly controlled by general state laws.   In most of the New England states, however, the laws regulating town affairs are reasonably generous; the towns possess approximately the same powers as full-fledged cities.   They may tax and borrow, of course, at least within reasonable limits.   They may own property, and they may sue or be sued. Lawyers say that the New England towns are *quasi*-corporations, or corporations *in a certain sense,* whereas the cities are true corporations.   But this distinction is not very important.

Organization of Town Government

THE TOWN MEETING.   The most distinctive feature of town government, today as in colonial times, is the town meeting, which is held once a year during the spring months.[1]   Special meetings may be held at other times if the pressure of public business warrants.   All the qualified voters of a town are entitled to attend the town meeting and participate in its decisions.   Therefore the town meeting is direct democracy in action— one of the very few examples of direct democracy still to be found in the United States.   Every voter has a right to be heard, no matter how mistaken his arguments or how trivial his ideas.   Every voter can identify himself directly with his government in a way that is not ordinarily possible in this modern age.   In some communities large numbers of voters habitually absent themselves from the town meeting, but in other communities the record of attendance is excellent.

The meeting is called to order by the town clerk, and those present then proceed to elect a presiding officer, who is known as the moderator.   Usu-

[1] Except in Connecticut, where the regular meeting time is October.

ally the rules require the selection of a new moderator at every meeting, but in some towns the person chosen to preside over the annual meeting also presides over any special meetings that may be called during the year. After the moderator has been installed, the officers of the town for the en-

NEW ENGLAND TOWN GOVERNMENT

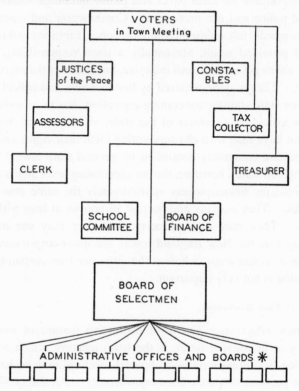

* In many towns, the selectmen may perform the functions
of at least some of these offices.

Reproduced with permission from *Government in Rural America* by Lane W. Lancaster, 2nd ed., copyright, 1952, D. Van Nostrand Company, Inc.

suing year are chosen by secret ballot.[2]   Attention is then given to the official order of business, which town officials have prepared in advance.   This order of business is certain to include necessary taxes and appropriations, and may include additional borrowing.   The range of proposals presented

[2] In some communities the town officers are chosen at a separate election before the town meeting, but this practice is not common.

for the consideration of the meeting is likely to be as broad as the scope of the town's powers.   The rules of the town meeting generally provide that no subject may be considered unless it is on the official agenda.   Voters are thus prevented from introducing dozens or even hundreds of irrelevant proposals.   But they are not stopped from interminable debate—much of it puerile—concerning matters that have been legitimately presented.   So the town meeting frequently fails to conclude its regular business in a single day, and must hold adjourned sessions on succeeding days.

Need for reform.   Statesmen and students of other days hailed the New England town meeting as a bulwark of democracy.   Alexis de Tocqueville, the French statesman who traveled extensively in the United States in 1831, regarded the town meeting as a major factor in the success of the young nation.[3]   As recently as 1907 the supreme judicial court of Massachusetts declared: "No small part of the capacity for honest and efficient local government manifested by the people of the commonwealth has been due to the training of citizens in the forum of the town meeting."[4]   In recent years, however, the town meeting has often proved a disappointment to its admirers.   Towns have grown so populous that many voters who wished to attend the meeting have been unable to crowd into the town hall.   European immigrants, legally transformed into American citizens but still unfamiliar with the ways of American democracy, have sometimes failed to adjust themselves to the spirit of the town meeting.   And the growing complexity of government has inevitably reduced the town meeting's efficiency as a forum for the consideration of public problems.   Many matters on the agenda are beyond the understanding of the average voter.

Budget committee.   In fiscal matters the inefficiency of the town meeting is especially apparent.   The meeting is supposed to make the year's appropriations and levy the year's taxes, but in most instances it has only a carelessly prepared budget to guide it.   No one person or group of persons has ever devoted sufficient thought to the relative importance of the many services that the town must perform.   When savings must be made, no one can say with any degree of assurance what activities can best be eliminated or curtailed.   Fluent speakers, entirely unhampered by facts, sometimes induce the town meeting to make large appropriations for trivial undertakings; meanwhile matters of major importance may remain neglected.   One remedy for this state of affairs is the creation of a special budget committee, composed of a certain number of voters—perhaps thirty or forty.   This committee is charged with the responsibility of preparing

[3] Alexis de Tocqueville, *Democracy in America* (Spencer ed.), Vol. I, p. 87.
[4] Wheelock *v.* Lowell, 196 Mass. 220; 81 N.E. 977 (1907).

the budget and defending it before the town meeting. The budget committee plan has been tried in many of the larger New England towns, with varying degrees of success.

Modified town meeting.   One plan for reducing the inefficiency of the town meeting, especially in more populous communities, is to restrict the number of persons entitled to full participation in the meeting's activities. Two or three hundred voters may be elected to represent all the residents of the community; these representatives then occupy the seats at the front of the town hall on meeting day, and make all final decisions on matters presented to the meeting.   Other residents of the town may attend the meeting, however, if they can crowd into the hall; and they may even participate in debate, though without the right to vote.   In this form, therefore, the town meeting is really a representative assembly, rather than an expression of direct democracy.   The modified town meeting plan is virtually unknown outside of Massachusetts.   In other parts of New England, and even in Massachusetts with increasing frequency, populous communities tend to turn to the legislature for permission to abandon their status as towns, and receive incorporation as cities.   But the inhabitants of many towns resist this change, even when common sense would seem to suggest it.   They cannot forget the town meeting, which served rural New England well for several centuries.[5]

BOARD OF SELECTMEN.   Although the town meeting is a central feature of town government, it is in session not more than a few days each year. It decides only a few of the more important questions relating to the town's business.   Obviously some officials must give more or less continuous service throughout the year, carrying out the resolutions adopted by the town meeting, making hundreds of other decisions that never came to the meeting's attention, and supervising the day-to-day routine of town business. The persons chiefly responsible for these activities are known as the board of selectmen.[6]   They are chosen by the town meeting, of course, and are accountable to it for the satisfactory performance of their duties.   The board of selectmen is a small body, poorly paid, having only three or five members in most instances, but sometimes as many as nine.   Members are generally elected for a single year,[7] though re-election is common.   The selectmen, sitting as a group, issue licenses, award contracts, provide for the maintenance of town property, conduct elections, and make necessary arrangements for town meetings.   In the smaller towns the selectmen in-

---

[5] See *Town Meeting Country*, by Clarence M. Webster.

[6] In Rhode Island the name *town council* is used.

[7] In some Massachusetts towns the term is three years, with one member of the three-member board chosen each year.

dividually assess property, arrange for the care of the poor, and perform necessary tasks in connection with health and highways; but in the more populous communities these duties are in the hands of administrators chosen by the selectmen or, in some cases, by the town meeting.

TOWN CLERK.   Every town has an official known as the town clerk, who is elected by the town meeting.   Usually his term is one year, but he is normally re-elected for as long as he wishes to serve.   In time he becomes the recognized authority on many aspects of town business; the selectmen often turn to him for guidance as to established precedents.   The clerk keeps the records of the town meeting and other information concerning town affairs, such as vital statistics and legal documents.   He issues marriage licenses; sometimes he serves as the clerk of the probate court.   Whenever a town function does not logically fit into the duties of some other officer, it is usually given to the town clerk.   In most towns he comes nearer than any other one person to being the head of the government, though he possesses neither the authority nor the prestige to make him the equivalent of a city's mayor or manager.

TOWN MANAGER.   In recent years the success of manager government in the cities of the United States has inspired some New England towns to hire managers.   Almost all the state legislatures in New England [8] have enacted laws permitting the adoption of the manager plan whenever a town meeting so desires.   Massachusetts now has a handful of town managers; so have New Hampshire and Vermont.   In Maine, where the idea has proved most popular, nearly one fifth of all the towns in the state are administered by managers.[9]   The decision to adopt the manager plan is made by the town meeting.   The board of selectmen then hires the manager and holds him responsible for the administration of town business.   He normally devotes full time to his job, and continues to serve at the board's pleasure. He hires his principal administrative assistants.   In the smaller New England towns the selectmen may still be able to manage local affairs without undue inefficiency, but in the larger communities the manager plan seems to provide the only satisfactory method of town administration.

OTHER OFFICERS.   Every town has a substantial list of other officers, chosen in different ways, who perform a great variety of duties.   The town treasurer receives public funds from taxes and other sources, deposits them in authorized banks, and pays bills and other claims that have been properly approved.   The constable is the chief law enforcement officer of the town,

---

[8] Rhode Island is the only exception.

[9] In 1953 there were one hundred and twenty-two town managers in New England, according to the directory of the International City Managers' Association.

but he spends very little time in pursuit of criminals.   Like most county sheriffs,[10] he prefers the safer and more lucrative task of serving processes issued by the courts.   He may, however, devote a number of hours each day to the enforcement of the speed laws.   The justice of the peace, whose duties have been discussed at length in an earlier chapter,[11] deals with petty civil disputes and minor offenses against the laws of the state.   He also takes the necessary preliminary steps in more serious cases, which are tried in the higher courts.   Other officers deserve at least passing mention— the members of the school board, who administer the town schools and hire the teachers, subject to such restrictions as may be imposed by state law; park trustees, if the town has any parks; library trustees, if the town has a library; sealers of weights and measures, fish and game wardens, and fire wardens.   Some of these officials—the treasurer and school trustees, for example—are almost always popularly elected.   Others may be chosen by the board of selectmen or—in manager towns—by the manager.   The salaries of town officers are almost always small.   In many cases the duties require a minimum of time.

TOWNSHIPS

Extent of Township Government

In New York, New Jersey, and Pennsylvania, and also in twelve of the North Central states, stretching from Ohio to North Dakota, the primary unit of local rural government is the township.[12]   Natural boundaries commonly separate the townships of the Atlantic coastal states from one another. West of the Alleghenies, however, most of the townships are squares on the map; government surveys first laid them out, six miles on a side, and thus fixed their present borders.[13]   Pennsylvania has more than fifteen hundred townships; so have Kansas and Minnesota.   But New Jersey has only two hundred and thirty-three.   The number changes from time to time, as townships lose their rural character and receive charters as cities.

10 See page 355.
11 See pages 161–163.
12 Townships are found also in one Washington county and part of another.   It should be noted that several of the so-called "township states" use the township plan for only part of their territory.   There are a few states that use the term "township" for judicial or other districts having no governmental powers; such states are not included in this discussion.
13 The townships thus laid out were intended to serve as congressional districts; their boundaries do not always coincide with the boundaries of the townships that now form units of local government.

Functions of Townships

There is a superficial resemblance between the towns of New England and the townships of the East and Middle West.   Both towns and townships are units of rural government; both are concerned with local problems; both try to preserve the spirit of democracy at the grass-roots level. But the towns are the _principal_ units of local rural government, far overshadowing the counties, whereas the townships are far less important than the counties of which they form a part.   At one time the townships performed a great variety of duties.   Today, however, their most important function is to maintain the minor roads.   Principal highways, of course, are a part of the state system, and are constructed and maintained by state highway departments, with a measure of federal supervision.   Even the counties may assume responsibility for the more important farm-to-market roads. But the country lanes that are too insignificant to warrant the attention of the counties usually fall within the jurisdiction of the townships.

In some states the townships assume responsibility for local school administration.   Township assessors determine the value of local real estate for purposes of taxation, not only by the township, but also by the county and sometimes by the state.   Township officials administer the election laws and certify election returns to the proper county authorities.   Township justices and constables play their small part in the general system of law enforcement.   Formerly the townships handled local poor relief, but this responsibility has now shifted almost entirely to the nation and the states, with some co-operation from the counties.

Organization of Township Government

TOWNSHIP MEETING.   About half of the township states make provision for a township meeting, modeled closely on the town meeting of New England.   All the voters—or all who care to make the effort—assemble once a year, and at such other times as may be necessary, to decide major township policies.   A presiding officer is chosen, committees present reports, and issues are debated and put to the vote.   In some states the township meeting, like the New England town meeting, selects the principal officers for the ensuing year.   But in other states township officers are chosen at regularly scheduled elections, rather than in meeting.   The present tendency is to restrict the powers of the township meeting, making it far less important than the town meeting of New England.   This tendency is logical enough, for the township meeting has not generally succeeded in capturing the popular imagination or arousing the spirit of local loyalty.   Large numbers of voters habitually ignore the annual meeting, and even larger numbers stay away from any special meetings that may be called.   So control of the township inevitably falls into the hands of those who care enough about township affairs to put in an appearance.   Many times this little group consists almost entirely of the township officials and a few of their friends.   Small wonder that township government is sometimes described as government by default!

TOWNSHIP BOARD.   The principal governing body of the township, corresponding roughly to the board of selectmen of the New England town, is generally called the township board.[14]   It usually has three members, who are popularly elected in more than half of the township states.   But sometimes the members of the board, or part of them, serve ex officio.   Thus state law may provide that the clerk or the treasurer or one of the justices of the peace, or all three of them, shall serve as board members.   The board carries out the decisions of the township meeting—in those states where a township meeting exists—and administers township affairs.   Where there is no township meeting, the board has much more power.   It levies taxes, makes appropriations, and borrows money on the township's credit.   It appoints a number of officials who might otherwise be chosen by the township meeting.

Regardless of the township meeting, the powers and duties of the board are not everywhere the same.   In about half of the township states the board handles most of the details of township administration, though its members do not necessarily act as a group.   Instead, each of the three members may serve as administrator for one third of the township.   Within this restricted area he may individually direct road repairs, supervise the local school, and assess local property.   Under this plan, therefore, no one person is responsible for any major aspect of local administration throughout the entire township.

TOWNSHIP SUPERVISOR.   In the other half of the township states administrative authority is largely centered in one official, who is known variously as the township's supervisor, trustee, or chairman.   Usually he is a member of the township board, which still possesses some important powers, especially with regard to township finance.   The supervisor generally directs local road construction and repair, manages the schools, and assesses property.   He prepares the township budget.   In many states he serves as township treasurer.   He hires minor officials and employees, and dismisses them at his pleasure.   He might almost be compared, therefore, to a city man-

---

[14] A variety of other names are used, however, such as board of supervisors, board of trustees, board of auditors, advisory board.

ager.   But there are important differences: the township supervisor is an elected official, chosen for a fixed term, almost always untrained in the techniques of public administration, and highly sensitive to the pressures of local politics.   Such a person cannot reasonably be expected to take the steps necessary for good township government.   Some writers say that better results are generally obtained by centralizing township authority in a supervisor than by diffusing responsibility among the members of a township board.   To this statement there can be no objection.   The supervisor plan is certainly the lesser of the two evils.   But to speak well of the supervisor plan because it improves upon board control is to give faint praise indeed.

OTHER OFFICERS.   Every township has a number of minor officers, but they are chosen in so many different ways and entrusted with so many different functions that any general description is extremely difficult.   There must be a clerk, of course, to keep the records, a treasurer to receive and disburse funds, an assessor to determine property values, a constable to enforce the law, and a justice of the peace to perform minor judicial duties. These persons may be popularly elected, or chosen by the township board. They may serve for one or two years, or for longer periods.   In some instances, as we have already seen, the township supervisor acts ex officio as treasurer or assessor.   There is not the slightest approach to uniformity among the township states.[15]

Decline of Township Government

One of the most obvious facts about township government in the United States is its general inefficiency.   The plain truth is that the township is too small a unit of government to give satisfactory results.   In earlier days, when pioneer conditions prevailed and inadequate means of transportation made distances seem much greater, the township served a real local need.   "Justices of the peace and constables elected from the township dispensed simple justice in neighborhood disputes and dealt with minor infractions of the criminal law.   Overseers of the poor saw to it that destitute members of the community did not go hungry.   Highway commissioners opened and maintained local roads to provide township residents with access to schools, churches and markets.   And township assessors appraised real estate and personal property for purposes of taxation." [16]   For nearly a century township government gave reasonable satisfaction.   But changing conditions

[15] See the 1952 edition of Lane W. Lancaster's *Government in Rural America*, which describes township government in considerable detail.
[16] "The Twilight of the Township," by Clyde F. Snider, in the September, 1952, issue of the *National Municipal Review*, p. 391.

have made the township virtually obsolete. Rural dwellers no longer need local government so close at hand; they can drive their automobiles over good roads to the county seat without serious inconvenience. Untrained township officials can no longer cope satisfactorily with the increasing complexities of modern public administration. And rising costs of government have emphasized the need to eliminate waste and inefficiency wherever possible.

In many states, therefore, some of the traditional township functions have been transferred to other units of government during the last two decades. Poor relief has almost ceased to be a township responsibility. Many township school systems have been taken over by the counties. Property assessment is more commonly in the hands of county officials. A movement to replace the township justices of the peace with state-appointed magistrates has had some small measure of success. Two decades ago a committee of experts recommended that the township be abolished and its functions transferred to other units of government—county, city, or state.[17] To some extent this recommendation has been adopted in a number of states. A few townships have been swept away, and in several states the laws have been amended to permit the abolition of any township whenever the local residents desire to take the step. Township elections attract less and less interest. In many instances township offices go unfilled for lack of candidates. Iowa townships have become so unimportant that the United States Bureau of the Census decided in 1952 to drop them from its list of local governments.[18] "Most students of local government agree," as one writer recently pointed out, "that under modern conditions the township is not and cannot be an effective governmental unit."[19]

VILLAGES

Nature of Village Government

The townships, and also the towns of New England, are essentially units of rural government. When they become large urban centers, they normally incorporate as cities. But there are many small communities that have outgrown their rural status, though they are still not so thickly settled as to be true cities. These semiurban centers may be parts of towns in

[17] "Recommendations on Township Government," Report No. 3 of the National Municipal League's Committee on County Government. This report was published as a supplement to the February, 1934, issue of the National Municipal Review.

[18] United States Bureau of the Census, Governments in the United States in 1952, p. 16.

[19] "Iowa Townships Still Here?" by Richard C. Spencer, National Municipal Review, September, 1952, p. 397.

New England, or of townships in the Middle West, or of counties in other parts of the country.   But in any event they require public services, such as sidewalk paving, street lighting, and fire protection, that the town or township or county authorities may not care to supply.   So these small communities take the steps necessary to secure incorporation as villages or boroughs.   The exact procedure is determined by state law; usually the prospective village must have a minimum population and a maximum area, and the question of incorporation must be submitted to the local voters for their approval.   Villages are found in every part of the United States, though they are more common in the Middle West than elsewhere.

Organization of Village Government

Villages are cities in miniature, and for that reason village government is very much like the government of cities.   There is always the equivalent of a municipal council, though its members are known by many different names—trustees, burgesses, commissioners, aldermen, bailiffs, councilmen. The village council—by whatever name it may be called—is always a small body, having three or five members as a rule, but never more than nine. These councilmen are popularly elected, of course, and usually for short terms.   They decide village policies and enact necessary ordinances.   Some villages have village meetings, like the town or township meetings, but this arrangement is not common.   The principal officer of the village is the mayor,[20] who bears a strong resemblance to the mayor of mayor-council government.   In some states the village mayor has almost full responsibility for local administration, but in other states he must share his authority with minor officials who have been popularly elected or chosen by the council. Almost everywhere the mayor presides over the council's sessions.

SPECIAL DISTRICTS

A special district is a unit of local government created to perform some specific function, or at most a small number of functions, rather than to exercise general governmental authority.   A county or city or township assumes responsibility for a wide variety of public activities; it protects the public health and safety, provides public education and recreation, and generally promotes the public welfare in such manner as its powers permit. But a special district has no such responsibility and no such authority.   It is, as its name implies, a district created for some *special* purpose—a flood control district to control floods, for example, or a mosquito abatement

[20] In some states the village mayor is called burgess or warden or intendant.

district to eliminate mosquitoes. It performs only those activities that relate directly to its principal function.

Prevalence of Special Districts

Special districts are found in every state.   They are more numerous than all the counties, cities, towns, townships, and villages combined.   Some states make very extensive use of special districts.   Nebraska, for example, has nearly seven thousand, and Minnesota has almost as many.   But states as widely separated as Maryland and Utah have kept the number of their special districts below two hundred.   In the entire United States the number of special districts is nearly eighty thousand.[21]

Types of Special Districts

Special districts have been created for a wide variety of purposes.   By far the most common, however, are the school districts; they represent about eighty-five per cent of the total.   School districts have been established in nearly all parts of the nation,[22] and are the principal units of local educational administration in twenty-six states.   Yet the number of school districts has been substantially reduced in recent years, and the states have assumed a greater measure of direct control over public education.[23]

A great many special districts deal with the conservation or development of natural resources.   Some of them reclaim swamps or deserts, take necessary precautions against floods, adopt measures for the conservation of the soil in farming areas, or bring water supplies—sometimes for great distances —to major metropolitan centers.   Other special districts are responsible for roads, street lighting, fire protection, health work, hospitals, sanitation, parks, libraries, and cemeteries.   There are special districts that operate airports and others that administer port and terminal facilities.   Almost every major function of local government has been made the basis for the creation of special districts in some states.

Reasons for Creation of Special Districts

It may seem strange that the people of the United States should go to the trouble of setting up thousands of special districts to perform dozens of local functions when they already have the regularly established units of local government, such as counties, cities, and towns.   Why, it may be

---

[21] See the previously cited 1953 publication of the Bureau of the Census, *Governments in the United States in 1952*.

[22] Only five states—Maryland, Massachusetts, North Carolina, Rhode Island, and Virginia—have no school districts.

[23] See page 433.

asked, must a special district be entrusted with the responsibility for fire protection or flood control or soil conservation when the existing local authorities are already performing duties that may not be too dissimilar? Two factors have been mainly responsible. In some cases the area requiring a special service may not correspond even roughly to any established unit of government. Perhaps half a dozen neighboring small cities lying within two or three predominantly rural counties feel the need for an improved water supply, but are unable to arouse the interest of county authorities. Perhaps the suburban corner of a rural county requires street lighting facilities that the county is unwilling to supply. Under such circumstances the residents of the area normally ask for—and normally receive—permission to create a water supply or street lighting district. This new district then provides the one service for which it was created. Most of the functions of local government within the area are handled by the county or city, as before.

Special districts are sometimes set up to avoid constitutional restrictions on taxing and borrowing. If a city needs a new junior college, but is rapidly approaching the debt limit established by the state constitution, it may decide to take advantage of the law authorizing the creation of junior college districts. The new district may have exactly the same boundaries as the city, and, therefore, exactly the same property subject to taxation. But since the district is a separate governmental unit, it is not bound by constitutional debt restrictions applying to cities, so it borrows whatever it needs. This chicanery may violate the spirit of the constitution, but it leaves the letter intact.

Forming Special Districts

The residents of a proposed district usually take the initiative in giving it life. They prepare a petition setting forth its boundaries and the function that it is supposed to perform. This petition must be signed by a certain number of residents or property owners, according to the terms of the state law. Then the petition is presented to the proper authority, which is most commonly the county board of supervisors.[24] The board sometimes has the right to approve or reject proposals for new special districts, but in most states and for most kinds of districts it is required to submit to the voters of the proposed district every petition that bears the proper number of valid signatures. The voters then decide the matter—usually by a simple majority, but sometimes by a majority of three fifths or two thirds.

[24] In some states, however, and for some types of districts, petitions must be presented to the district court or to some administrative agency of the state.

Government of Special Districts

Because a special district normally performs but one function, it does not require and does not usually have a complex administrative organization. Its governing body is a board of three or five members, commonly elected by the voters of the district.[25] This board establishes district policies, makes necessary regulations, and borrows money on the credit of the district. It also fixes the district tax rate, but as a rule it relies on the county assessor to determine the value of property and the county treasurer to collect the tax imposed for district purposes. The board frequently appoints a trained technician—a road engineer or health officer, for example—and holds him responsible for the management of district activities. State and county agencies exercise varying degrees of supervision over special districts. Within a single state the highway districts may be permitted to maintain local roads with virtually no guidance or control, while the health districts are required to conform to rigid state standards. Chance and the whims of state legislators seem to be the principal factors in determining the amount and kind of state supervision.

Future of Special Districts

The number of special districts in the United States is certainly excessive. Some districts that once served a useful purpose have long since outlived their usefulness. Some districts that borrowed extensively—on their own credit, in most cases, and not on the general credit of the state—have been unable to meet their obligations, and have become virtually bankrupt. The financial situation of many special districts was desperate during the Great Depression of the 1930's. The obvious remedy for too many special districts is to eliminate a great many of them. If their functions can be performed as well or better by some of the regular units of government, such as the county or city, or even the state, then they should certainly be abolished. The result would usually be simpler and more efficient administration. It would always be a less complicated structure of government. Though the number of school districts has been greatly reduced since 1942, the number of other types of special districts has increased fifty per cent in this short period.[26] The time has come to survey the whole problem of special districts, and to refuse petitions for additional districts unless the petitioners can fully demonstrate a genuine need. Existing districts should

[25] The members of the board of a special district are chosen in some instances by the county board of supervisors or by a judicial or administrative agency of the state.

[26] See Joseph E. McLean's article, "Use and Abuse of Authorities," in the October, 1953, issue of the *National Municipal Review*, pp. 438–444.

be subjected to much closer central supervision, especially with regard to their financial practices.

PROBLEMS

1. Prepare a brief history of the town meeting in colonial New England.

2. Study the organization of township government in your state or some neighboring state. What recommendations can you make for improvement?

3. Select some village near your home, and observe the organization and work of its government. How does its efficiency compare with the efficiency of some nearby large city?

4. How many special districts are there in your state? Is the number increasing or decreasing?

5. Study some special district in your community. Could the work of this district be performed satisfactorily by the county or one of the other units of general government?

SELECTED REFERENCES

Bradshaw, William L., and Garrison, Milton, *Township Organization in Missouri,* Columbia, Mo., 1936.

Bromage, Arthur W., *American County Government,* Chap. 9, 1933.

Fairlie, John F., and Kneier, Charles M., *County Government and Administration,* Chaps. XX–XXIII, 1930.

Gould, John, *New England Town Meetings; Safeguard of Democracy,* Brattleboro, Vt., 1940.

Guitteau, William B., *Ohio's Townships; The Grassroots of Democracy,* Toledo, Ohio, 1949.

Hicks, Granville, *Small Town,* 1947.

Hormell, Orren C., *Maine Towns,* Brunswick, Me., 1942.

Lancaster, Lane W., *Government in Rural America,* rev. ed., Chaps. 2 and 3, 1952.

Manny, Theodore B., *Rural Municipalities,* 1930.

Ogden, Jean and Jess, *Small Communities in Action,* 1947.

Rohr, C. J., and Others, *Local Government in Massachusetts,* Amherst, Mass., 1941.

Sly, J. F., *Town Government in Massachusetts,* Cambridge, Mass., 1930.

State Planning Board, *Towns of South Carolina,* rev. ed., Columbia, S.C., 1943.

Tharp, C. J., *A Manual of Township Government in Michigan,* Ann Arbor, Mich., 1948.

Wells, Roger A., *American Local Government,* Chap. III, 1939.

White, Max R., *The Connecticut Town Meeting: A Handbook for Moderators and Other Town Meeting Officials,* Storrs, Conn., 1949.

PART FOUR

The Political Process

CHAPTER 14

Nominations and Elections

The first step in the election of public officials is the nomination of candidates—usually by the regular political parties or by other organized groups. This step is very important—in part because it weeds out the candidates and eliminates from the final ballot the names of those who have no appreciable support, and in part because it enables the various groups of voters to unite in support of persons who seem best fitted to represent them.

THE CAUCUS SYSTEM

Even in the first days of American independence, when government was a far less complicated process than at present, candidates were nominated in advance of the regular election. The nominating methods of that early period conformed to no set plan, however. Most commonly a little group of community leaders would meet at some private home a short time before election day and informally indorse certain men for public office. In time this gathering of the leaders became known as the *caucus*. The word was derived from the Caucus Club of Boston, which met regularly in the garret of one Tom Dawes for the purpose of discussing public issues and nominating local candidates. Every town had its caucus—its informal conference of the "best" people.

Gradually, however, the caucus lost some of its earlier aspects. It became a meeting of the party heads, and most of its original informality disappeared. From this stage it was but a step to the legislative caucus, or gathering of the party representatives in the legislature. Because roads were poor and journeys difficult in those early days, the party leaders gave up the attempt to meet for the purpose of making nominations to state offices, and permitted the legislators to make the nominations instead. Each party would hold its caucus separately, of course; the Whig members of the legislature would unite upon Whig candidates, while the legislature's Democrats made their selections. No attempt was made to determine the wishes of the people at any time during the nominating process, and no one was greatly disturbed by the omission. Democracy was still a questionable experiment, even in the United States, during the first two decades of the nineteenth century.

THE CONVENTION SYSTEM

Increase in Democratic Control

But the period from 1820 to 1835 witnessed a widespread and constantly increasing demand for democratic control of government. The masses of the people, whose fathers had been content with the assurance that their interests were carefully safeguarded by the "governing class," now began to insist upon reversing the process and doing their own safeguarding. Democracy was in the air. It was not the polite, cultured democracy of Thomas Jefferson, but the raucous, untutored democracy of Andrew Jackson.

In 1828 Jackson was elected president, and set out to interpret literally the rhetorical statement of the Declaration of Independence that "all men are created equal." His ideas proved extremely popular. Rotation in office became the order of the day. In most states the remaining barriers against white manhood suffrage were swept away. Men became equal— politically, at least—to the extent that the law could make them so. Of course, Negroes were excluded from the benefits of this movement. Few of those who prated at great length about the equality of man ever intended to include black men or yellow men in their generalization; equality as they understood it was equality *within the white race.*

Rise of Party Conventions

One of the results of the widespread adoption of the Jacksonian creed was the general abandonment of the caucus system. The caucus did not entirely disappear; as a gathering of the party voters it is still used in Connecticut for making nominations to certain offices. But it had become generally unpopular long before 1940, and in that year it ceased to be a factor of any importance.

Its place was taken by the convention system, which was designed to vest control of the selection of candidates more securely in the hands of the people. Under the convention plan the voters of each party choose delegates to a party convention; these delegates then meet prior to the election and make the party's nominations. Thus the part played by the people is indirect; instead of naming their candidates they merely empower others to do so.

WEAKNESSES. On its face the convention system is a reasonably accurate means of gauging public opinion. It affords the voters of each party an opportunity to elect delegates who will faithfully represent their wishes. When first introduced it was hailed as a triumph of democracy—a certain way to make the people masters of their government. But the passing of years revealed unexpected weaknesses. The triumph of democracy seemed less sure.

For the professional politicians had devised and perfected means of controlling the conventions through delegates who could be counted on to vote "right." Usually they managed to have their friends and henchmen chosen as delegates; but if the voters, in an unusually independent mood, cast so many votes in opposition that even ballot box stuffing and fraudulent counting would not avail, then other methods were adopted. The unexpectedly successful delegates were exposed in turn to flattery, argument, promises of position or money, and intimidation. If, at the end of this time, some delegates still remained unmoved, their credentials were contested as soon as they arrived at the convention, and they were speedily excluded. Because practices of this sort violated no law and carried no danger of a jail sentence, they became a generally accepted part of the great game of politics.

REGULATION. It must be remembered that the convention system, as originally developed, was merely an unofficial device for securing the opinions of party members. The law did not regulate it—in fact, did not even recognize it. Therefore it became the great proving ground for all sorts of tricks and malpractices that would have been punishable with fines and imprisonment if used in regular elections.

In time arose the demand that the states regulate the party conventions in the interest of fair play, and a number of states, led by California in 1866, took this step. These early statutes were crudely drawn. They prohibited only certain glaringly unfair practices, and applied only to those parties that chose to accept their provisions. But optional laws gradually gave way to mandatory, and virtually all fundamental aspects of the convention system came under state regulation. By 1900 the plan of regulated conventions was well established. It never had a fair chance to prove its worth, however, for almost immediately it was discarded in favor of the direct primary.

The unregulated convention system had been a complete failure; on that point all fair-minded persons were agreed. So something had to be found to take its place. Some students of government devoted their time and attention to improving the convention plan and bringing it under state control. Others, however, completely abandoned their faith in conventions as a means of selecting candidates for public office, and proposed instead the use of the direct primary, a system by which the voters of each party might make their nominations directly in party elections.   Through such elections they hoped to determine accurately the wishes of the voters of each party, and secure party nominees who would represent the rank and file of the party members instead of the party leaders.   They hoped to break the strength of the party organizations.   And they hoped, too, to improve the caliber of party nominees.

THE DIRECT PRIMARY

The direct primary was certainly used as early as 1868, and perhaps even before that date.   Its spread was slow, however, and it did not become a part of a comprehensive, state-wide, mandatory system until 1903, when Wisconsin set the pace for the other states.   Oregon followed a few months later; in 1907 six states enacted reasonably satisfactory primary laws; by 1909 the total number of direct primary states had risen to eighteen.   Since that time the movement has continued to spread rapidly, and today candidates for public office are nominated by means of primary elections in forty-seven states.[1]   The sole exception—Connecticut—still relies on a combination of conventions and caucuses.

Conduct of the Primary

A primary is conducted for the most part like a general election, with the same regulations and safeguards.   The polling places are commonly the same, and the same persons usually serve as presiding officers.   The ballots are nearly always furnished by the state, and the cost of the primary is met from public funds.   The date of the primary election is fixed by state law, which generally provides that all parties must hold their contests at the same polling places as well as at the same time.[2]   Each party has a separate ballot; in nearly half of the states distinguishing colors are used.   The winners at the primary become the official nominees of their respective parties, and the candidates at the following general election.

Requirements for Nomination

The laws of the several states vary widely concerning the manner in which an aspirant for public office may have his name placed on the primary

[1] It must not be assumed, however, that the primary is the sole method of making nominations in all forty-seven states.   Five states permit the use of primaries or conventions at the discretion of the political parties, and five others retain the convention for certain offices or under certain conditions.

[2] A few of the Southern states provide exceptions to these statements.

ballot of his party. In four states [3] a simple declaration of candidacy is sufficient; ten others specify that the declaration must be accompanied by a fee. Usually the fee does not exceed twenty-five or fifty dollars, except for the most important state offices. Fees as high as two hundred dollars, even for the office of governor, are unusual.

Those states that do not make use of the declaration plan, with or without fee, rely instead on nominating petitions. Every nominating petition must be supported by the signatures of a given number or percentage of party voters. The required number or percentage varies with the importance of the office and also with the state. There is a general tendency to fix this requirement so low that it will not interfere with anyone who seriously desires to be a candidate for nomination, but this tendency has not prevented Illinois from specifying one thousand signatures as the minimum for a valid nominating petition to the office of governor. In a few states nominating petitions are combined with fees. California has an unusual arrangement whereby every petition of candidacy must be filed by a certain number of "sponsors"—the number ranging from ten to one hundred. These sponsors do not assume any responsibility for the private or public acts of their candidate, but they must swear that they know him personally and consider him "qualified mentally, morally, and physically" for the office he seeks to fill.

Many careful students of government believe that the regular party organizations, acting through committees or conferences of responsible party officials, should be permitted by law to propose candidates for public office. These candidates would not automatically receive the party nomination; on the contrary, they would be obliged to compete with other aspirants whose names had been placed on the primary ballot by means of petitions or declarations of candidacy. But the preferred status of the "official" candidates would be made known to the voters—perhaps by asterisks after their names. Four states use variations of this scheme. Three of them—Colorado, Massachusetts, and Utah—permit pre-primary conventions, at which candidates are given the official party blessing. Rhode Island authorizes party committees to make selections. The idea of allowing the regular party organizations to make known their preferences has definite merit. It strengthens party responsibility and presumably makes for better candidates. Most of the arguments against the plan are really arguments against the party system of government.[4]

[3] Delaware, Indiana, Oklahoma, West Virginia.
[4] See the National Municipal League's *Model Direct Primary Election System,* published in 1951. See also "Pre-Primary Trial Dropped," by A. C. Breckenridge, in the April, 1954, issue of the *National Municipal Review,* pp. 186–191.

Open versus Closed Primary

There is considerable discussion concerning the relative merits of the _open_ primary—which is open to all qualified voters without regard to party membership, and the _closed primary_—so called because the primary of each party is closed to everyone save the party's duly qualified members. When the open primary is used, every voter at the primary receives the ballots of all the parties.   He casts one of these ballots and deposits the others in a blank ballot box, thus escaping the necessity of revealing his party affiliation.[5]   Under the closed primary system the voter is asked to declare his party allegiance—perhaps to meet some test of party membership.   He then receives only the ballot of his own party.

The declaration of party affiliation, an essential feature of the closed primary, is objectionable to many men and women.   Some of them desire to hold aloof from partisan groups and factions, and to cast their vote with the Republicans at one election and unite with the Democrats at the next. The very thought of party organization and party discipline may be distasteful to them.   Or they may resent the necessity of stating in public how they usually vote.   Such persons naturally prefer the open primary, with the complete secrecy that it assures.   Yet the open primary system has had a very uneven history.   At one time it was used by twelve states, and seemed to be gaining in popularity; then the number gradually shrank to two.   More recently open primary legislation has been enacted by a number of other commonwealths, bringing the present total to ten.

The opponents of the open primary complain chiefly of its failure to prevent the political trick known as "raiding the primary."   When one party is united upon a single candidate, it may be able to spare the votes of hundreds or even thousands of its professional and semi-professional workers at the primary election.   These surplus votes can then be used to secure the nomination of the weakest candidate of the rival party, especially in a close contest.   One year the Republicans may "capture" the Democratic primary and dictate the selection of the Democratic nominee; the next year, under changed circumstances, the Democrats may be able to return the compliment.   This constant shifting of voters in the primary is possible under the open primary plan because every voter has the ballots of all the

[5] In Washington, where the primary is "open" to the fullest extent, the voter receives a single ballot containing the names of all candidates for all party nominations for all offices.   There is no obligation to conform to a single party throughout; therefore the voter may aid the Republicans in nominating their candidate for governor and help the Democrats to select their nominee for senator.   Some of the results of this system are described by Daniel M. Ogden, Jr., in a brief article, "Parties Survive Cross-Voting," in the May, 1950, issue of the _National Municipal Review_, pp. 237–241.

parties and is free to vote for whatever set of candidates his fancy may dictate.

The closed primary is supposed to prevent the too frequent severance of party ties, thus making primary raiding impossible. The extent to which it actually does so, however, depends upon the provisions of the primary law concerning changes in party allegiance. There are a few states whose laws are so lenient in this respect that they might almost be classed with the open primary group. In Vermont, for example, a voter need merely indicate the party ballot he desires, and this selection constitutes his declaration of party affiliation. There is nothing in law or custom to restrain him from changing his party at every primary election.

At the other extreme are several Southern states that empower the party committees to set up tests of party membership; the tests thus established are intended to discourage frequent transfers. Generally speaking, the tendency is to impose a moderate requirement of some sort—to ask the voter to declare that he habitually supports the candidates of the party in whose primary he desires to participate, or that he has not supported the candidate of any other party for at least two years. Failure to meet a test of this sort, it must be understood, does not prevent a qualified voter from casting a ballot in the final election, but merely excludes him from the party primary.

Plurality Principle Almost Universal

Plurality choice is the general rule in both primary and final elections. The candidate who receives the greatest number of votes at a primary becomes the nominee of his party, and if he receives the greatest number of votes at the final election he is declared elected, even if the combined votes of his opponents exceed his own total by a considerable margin.

Most students of government defend the plurality principle. Though admitting the desirability of securing an absolute majority whenever possible, they point out that it is usually impossible, except by artificial means, to secure an absolute majority in a field of several candidates. In most cases the voters do not prefer one candidate to all the others combined, and any attempt to create the appearance of a united majority that does not in fact exist is certain to produce disappointing results.

"RUN-OFF" PRIMARIES. Yet a number of states make use of various devices for securing majority choice. Provision is made in nine Southern states [6] and Utah for second or "run-off" primaries, involving only the two

---

[6] Alabama, Arkansas, Florida, Georgia, Louisiana, Mississippi, North Carolina, Texas, Virginia. In Virginia, however, the run-off primary is not held unless requested by the candidate who stood second in the balloting.

highest candidates, in case no one receives an absolute majority on the first balloting.   Such an arrangement adds to the expense and complexity of the election system and to the already heavy burden placed upon the voters; therefore it is scarcely known outside of the South, where the dominance of one party makes the primary more important than the final election.   Under the laws of two states—Iowa and South Dakota [7]—the highest candidate for an office must receive at least thirty-five per cent of his party's primary vote; otherwise the nomination to that office is made by a post-primary convention.

PREFERENTIAL VOTING.   It has been suggested that genuine majority choice might be obtained by some form of preferential voting, such as the Bucklin [8] plan which was used for many years by Grand Junction, Colorado. Under this scheme the voter is permitted to express one first choice, one second choice, and as many third choices as he sees fit.   If no candidate has a majority of first choices, first and second choices are added together. The election then goes to the man receiving a majority of first and second choices combined.   If necessary to secure a majority, third choices are also added.   It sometimes happens that even the addition of third choices does not establish a clear majority for any one candidate, so that the person with the largest plurality must be declared elected.

The most serious objection to the Bucklin plan, however, is not its occasional failure to establish a *nominal* majority, but its habitual failure to create a genuine majority.   For it produces results by giving second and third choices, when added, exactly the same weight as first preferences.   Obviously this is not in accord with the wishes of the voter, whose first choice indicates that he prefers one candidate to all the others.

Other forms of preferential voting vary the Bucklin formula somewhat by giving greater weight to the first choice than to second and third choices. The Ware plan, which is based on an entirely different principle, provides for the successive elimination of the lowest candidates and the transfer of their ballots to second or subsequent choices.   But no system of preferential voting can create a majority that does not exist in fact.

Inadequate Minority Representation

Probably the most serious objection to the ordinary method of selecting the members of legislative bodies is that political parties and organized groups of voters seldom receive representation in exact proportion to their numerical

---

[7] In South Dakota the law applies only to candidates for governor, United States senator, and congressman.

[8] Named for James W. Bucklin, who devised the scheme.

strength.   The minority may receive more than its share of the total number of representatives; much more commonly it receives far less than its
share.   It all depends on the distribution of party strength.

Three Proposed Electoral Remedies

A number of remedies for inadequate minority representation have been
proposed—limited voting, cumulative voting, proportional representation.
Limited voting is so called because each person's vote is limited to a number of candidates less than the full number to be elected.   If three members
of the legislature are to be elected from a given district, for example, each
voter may express his preference for but two candidates.   The obvious result
of this arrangement is to give two seats to the majority party, and one to the
strongest minority group.   Minority representation is thus assured, but
without any reference to actual party strength.   It is a crude device and has
never been tried for members of a state legislature, though it has long been
used in Pennsylvania to select certain state and county officials.

For more than three quarters of a century Illinois has made use of cumulative voting.   Three members of the lower house of the state legislature are
chosen from each assembly district.   Each elector has three votes, and may
distribute them as he sees fit.   He may give one to each of his three favorite
candidates, or he may concentrate two or even three votes on one man.
The result of this plan has been to give the two major parties legislative
representation in very close proportion to their numerical strength as indicated at the polls.   Less powerful minority groups, however, have seldom
been able to elect a single representative to the legislature.   The scheme has
strengthened party lines and has necessitated highly developed party organizations.   No other state uses the Illinois plan.[9]

The plan that seems most likely to secure representation of every shade of
public opinion in direct proportion to its numerical strength is known as proportional representation.   There are two forms of this system, but the one
that has made the stronger appeal to English-speaking people is the Hare
plan, named for the Englishman who perfected it.

Under the Hare system the voter is told to express as many choices as he
pleases.   In fact, the number of his preferences is limited only by the number of candidates.   He places a figure 1 on the ballot opposite the name of
his first choice, a 2 opposite his second, a 3 opposite his third, and so on
until he has no additional preferences to express.

When the ballots are first counted, only first choices are considered.   As

[9] See "The Case for Cumulative Voting," by George S. Blair, in the July–August,
1952, issue of the *Northwestern University Law Review*, pp. 344–357.

the count proceeds, however, it soon becomes clear that some candidates have more than the number of votes necessary for election, while others are hopelessly out of the running.   Therefore, the surplus votes cast for those elected on the first count, plus all the votes for those who have been declared defeated, are transferred to the second choices—or, if these aspirants have already been eliminated or elected, to the third choices.

So the transferring process continues, until every vote is made effective for some candidate.   The Hare plan is sometimes described as the system with the single transferable vote.   No matter how many preferences a person may express, he has only one vote, and it is transferred from candidate to candidate until it actually helps to elect someone.[10]

In the United States the Hare system has not proved very popular.   It has not been adopted by any state of the Union, and is now used by but nine American cities.[11]   It has found some favor, however, in Eire, Australia, New Zealand, and Canada.

There seems to be little doubt that the Hare system has accomplished its purpose of securing representation for every group in almost exact proportion to voting strength.   Yet its adoption by American states will doubtless come slowly, if at all, for a number of court decisions indicate that constitutional amendments would be necessary in some commonwealths to permit its use.   Moreover, it has been deliberately abandoned by a number of cities, including such metropolitan centers as New York City and Cleveland.

Another form of proportional representation, known as the "list" system because it is based on lists of candidates prepared by the political parties, has been adopted, with several variations, by many countries of Continental Europe.   Its excessive emphasis on party regularity makes it seem less desirable than the Hare plan for American use.

Non-partisanship

NOMINATION BY PETITION.   Although a candidate for public office usually tries to secure the endorsement of one of the political parties at the primary election, it is not necessary for him to do so.   Instead he may be nominated by petition, and thus have his name placed on the ballot that is presented to the voters at the final election.   The procedure is exactly the same as if he were merely a candidate for nomination, except that more

[10] By far the most thorough description of the Hare system may be found in Hoag and Hallett's *Proportional Representation*.   See also Geo. H. Hallett, Jr.'s *Proportional Representation: The Key to Democracy*.   The value of proportional representation is challenged vigorously by Prof. F. A. Hermens in his *Democracy or Anarchy?*
[11] Cambridge, Lowell, Medford, Quincy, Revere, and Worcester, Massachusetts; Cincinnati and Hamilton, Ohio; and Hopkins, Minnesota.

signatures are commonly required. An independent, unwilling to affiliate himself with any political party, commonly secures nomination in this way.

Most states require the filing of the petition at some time subsequent to the primary, and several of them attempt to prevent defeated party candidates from suddenly becoming "independents" by specifying that persons failing of nomination at the primary may not be candidates at the final election. It is also customary to prohibit voters who participated in the primary from signing any nominating petitions that may subsequently be circulated, since this form of nomination is reserved for those who are not regular party members.

RECENT ADOPTIONS OF THE PRINCIPLE. In recent years the principle of non-partisanship has been accepted for judicial, school, and local offices in a number of states. The names of all candidates for these offices are placed on the primary ballot by petition—minus party designations, of course— and the two highest candidates become the nominees. Their names then appear on the ballot at the final election.[12] A large number of cities, especially those operating under the commission or manager forms of government,[13] have adopted the non-partisan method of choosing all their elective officers. In some instances the non-partisanship is genuine; in others it is a convenient mask for party activities. But even strong party organizations often have difficulty in maintaining their full vigor when candidates are chosen by petition and party designations are omitted from the ballot.

Attacks on the Direct Primary

The direct primary has become the generally accepted method of nominating candidates for public office, yet there is no general agreement as to the desirability of retaining it. Some critics urge a return to the ordinary convention system that was commonly used before the primary came into vogue. In 1921 New York re-established the convention system for nomination to state offices. A bill that would have restored conventions in Vermont was defeated in 1925 by the deciding vote of the lieutenant-governor in the state senate, and the following year a similar measure failed of passage by a single vote in the New Jersey legislature. Proposals to repeal the primary laws have received more or less serious consideration in over half of the states. On the other hand, the people have consistently voted to retain the direct primary system whenever the question has been presented to them at the polls. Idaho, which adopted the direct primary in 1909 and

[12] A few states specify, however, that any candidate receiving an absolute majority of all the votes cast in a non-partisan primary shall be declared elected.
[13] See Chapter 10.

abandoned it in favor of the convention plan ten years later, again joined the primary states in 1931.[14]

Merits and Defects of the Direct Primary

The merits and defects of the direct primary are not easily determined. To a large extent they seem to be a matter of opinion. Thus the friends of the primary system contend that it has improved the caliber of public officials, whereas its opponents assert with equal assurance that it has had exactly the opposite effect. Yet no one has explained how it is possible to measure the relative capacities of the men nominated for public office, whether by conventions or by primaries. In many instances popular political leaders have managed to secure election under both systems.

Nor is there any satisfactory way of determining the validity of the charge that the direct primary results in larger campaign expenditures. The sums spent to secure nominations and elections are undoubtedly excessive in many instances—especially in the more populous states, where large numbers of voters must be reached. But money must be spent under the convention system also, and probably with greater likelihood that it will be spent secretly for dishonest purposes.

The direct primary tends to weaken the position of the political parties; whether this fact is an argument for or against it depends largely upon the point of view. Those who favor the primary speak of the necessity of crushing the political machines and restoring control to the people. Those who desire a return to the convention system lament the destruction of party responsibility. But both groups agree that the primary method of making nominations gives the independent—especially the wealthy independent— a somewhat better chance of success.

There is one argument in favor of the direct primary that cannot be successfully refuted: it places a powerful weapon in the hands of the voters. It enables them to secure control of their respective parties whenever they seriously desire to do so. It permits them to brush aside the secret agreements and private understandings of the professional politicians, and nominate for public office the men who hold their confidence. It makes the people the masters of their government—provided, of course, that they are sufficiently interested to assume control. Usually they are not sufficiently interested. Year after year they stay at home on the day of the primary election, thus proclaiming their complete indifference. It is a matter worthy

[14] South Carolina, which abandoned the direct primary in 1944, is not considered at this point, because its action was taken without regard to the merits of the primary system. See page 297.

of more than passing mention when one half of the men and women who are eligible to participate in a primary actually go to the polls and vote. Very seldom does a primary contest engage the attention of so large a portion of the electorate.

Occasionally, however, the people may be roused to action by some unusual circumstance, such as the exposure of widespread corruption in the state government. Their habitual apathy may be transformed into a temporary desire to act. After all, the public commonly votes its indignation rather than its approval. Under such circumstances the primary lends itself readily to the popular mood. It enables the people to name their candidates directly instead of through the complexities of party conventions.

ELECTIONS

The election machinery conforms roughly to a standard pattern in all states. Although there are numerous minor variations, the broad outline is everywhere the same. The area of a state is divided into a large number of election districts or precincts, with a polling place in each district. One district for every four or five hundred voters is a common arrangement. The number of voters is supposed to be approximately the same in every election district; actually there are wide discrepancies.

Some states use public buildings—schools, police stations, and the like— as polling places. This is a growing tendency, but has not yet been generally adopted. It saves expense, assures a proper environment, and simplifies the voter's problem of finding the building where he is to cast his ballot. When public buildings are not used, the common practice is to rent private shops, garages, or other quarters for the day of the election. The choice of the private structures to be rented for polling places rests with the agency in charge of the election—the county commissioners or board of supervisors in most cases, but a special election board in more than one of the large metropolitan centers. Since the rental paid by the county or city is generally ten or fifteen dollars a day, and sometimes even twenty-five, for each polling place, the election officials thus possess a considerable amount of petty patronage. They can rent the polling places from those faithful followers who seem most likely to yield a small harvest of votes in return. Or, if they are sufficiently unscrupulous, they can demand for themselves a share of the rental. Election investigations occasionally unearth such scandals.

Election Boards

The conduct of the election at each polling place is under the direction of a district or precinct election board. This board commonly consists of three members, though the number varies from two to four, according to the law of the state. Not more than two members—in the case of a three-member board—may belong to the same political party.[15] The obvious purpose of this provision is to prevent the dominant party from obtaining complete control of the board and manipulating the election in its own favor.

Actually, however, bipartisan boards have not been very effective in eliminating fraud. In some instances the majority party has proved so powerful that it has been able to dictate the selection of minority party representatives as well as its own board members; in other cases the two major parties have agreed to a "rational" distribution of the spoils of office on the basis of their normal voting strength and have then proceeded to declare certain candidates of each party elected in accordance with a prearranged schedule—entirely without regard for the preferences actually expressed by the voters at the polls.

The members of the district board are known as inspectors or judges of elections. Usually they are selected by the county commissioners or the municipal election board. In a few states, however, they are appointed by the judge of the county court or by the court clerk, and in one state—Pennsylvania—they are elected by the party members of the district. They are commonly assisted by poll clerks.

Since the election inspectors are generally selected from lists of persons who have applied for appointment and since the remuneration is too small to attract men and women of ability, it follows in the majority of cases that second-rate politicians—men whose honesty is questionable and whose ignorance is beyond doubt—are named. To this generalization there are many exceptions, of course—especially in the smaller communities; but it remains true none the less that most inspectors of elections are poorly fitted for their task. They are not usually required to have any special qualifications, other than the qualifications of an ordinary voter plus the ability to read and write. They should be familiar with the election laws, of course, but unfamiliarity is not usually a bar to appointment.

[15] Except in the Southern states, where the Democratic Party normally assumes complete control.

Watchers

In order to minimize the likelihood of fraud, the several political parties represented at the election—and sometimes the individual candidates—are permitted to have duly accredited watchers at the polling places. These watchers are present from the original inspection of the ballot boxes or voting machines, prior to the opening of the polls, until the counting of the votes is over. They have the right to challenge any voter and to examine all the records of the election. A great deal may depend upon their knowledge of the law, their experience, and their ability to withstand intimidation.

Corruption

It is astonishing how many ways can be devised by corrupt politicians to insure the election of their friends. "Let the boys have their fun," an old-time New York political leader once advised his followers as they watched the independent voters cast a heavy vote for independent candidates. "Let 'em cast their ballots the way they please. After all, we do the counting."

In many communities this attitude still prevails. The full extent of corruption at the polls is not known, and probably never will be known, because the heavy penalties prescribed by state law make it advisable to proceed with caution. Yet the charges of dishonesty are too common and too widespread to be entirely without foundation. Quite frequently these charges are proved in the courts, and election inspectors or other election officials are sent to the penitentiary. Every year brings fresh rumors, and sometimes fresh evidence, of election frauds in widely scattered communities.

Polling Hours

The polls usually remain open for a period of twelve hours, though there is considerable variation. The opening hour is usually early in the morning—six or seven o'clock—so as to permit laborers to vote on their way to work.

Identification of Qualified Voters

When a person appears at the polls claiming the right to vote, he is generally given a ballot and directed to one of the voting booths. Any member of the election board or any voter may challenge him, however, on the ground that he lacks the qualifications for voting established by law or that he is not the person he claims to be. The effect of such a challenge is not everywhere the same, but in most states the suspect may still cast his ballot

if he takes oath that he is legally entitled to do so.   Subsequently he may
be convicted of perjury or impersonation; it is then too late, however, to
identify his ballot and cast it out.[16]

The most effective way to identify a voter is to require him to sign the
registration record when registering, and also to sign when he receives his
ballot on election day.   The signatures can readily be compared by the
election officials.   This system is now used in a few jurisdictions.

Counting the Votes

Immediately following the closing of the polls the count begins, and frequently continues until the early hours of the following morning.[17]   It is a
complicated process, except in those communities that use voting machines,
for paper ballots give rise to all sorts of questions that must be answered
without delay.   What shall be done with ballots on which preferences are
indicated by check-marks or circles, instead of the customary crosses?   If a
cross apparently intended for one candidate sprawls partly across another
candidate's space, shall it be counted?   If a facetious voter writes in the
name of a comic strip character for one office, shall the entire ballot be
declared invalid?   Is a large ink stain across the face of the ballot sufficient
reason for refusing to count it?

One by one these questions are decided by the election board as the count
proceeds.   Eventually all the votes are counted and entered on the official
tally sheets.   The ballots are then placed once more in the boxes, which are
padlocked and taken to some central place for safekeeping.   A contested
election may necessitate a re-examination of the ballots at some subsequent
time; otherwise they are destroyed after a proper interval.

Election Results

Upon completion of the count the election officials affix their signatures
to the tally sheets—the official record of the election returns in the precinct.
From these figures the newspapers estimate the total city or state vote, so
that the final result of the election is usually known by the following morning
—or by afternoon at the latest.

Election results are not official, however, until the returns from the several
precincts have been canvassed,—that is, until the votes for each candidate
have been totaled.   The canvassing, which takes place several days or even

---

[16] Except in a very few states, where the ballots are numbered.

[17] Double election boards, which are now used in about one fourth of the states,
facilitate the process of counting the votes.   The members of the second board arrive
a few hours after the opening of the polls and maintain a continuous count of the
ballots while the election is in progress.

a week later, is done by the county commissioners, the judges of the county court, or some other agency designated by law. For officers elected on a state-wide basis there must be an additional canvass—a totaling of the county figures by the state canvassing board. Certificates of election are then issued to the successful candidates. These certificates are only *prima facie* evidence of the right to hold office, however; they do not prevent defeated candidates from contesting the election on the ground of fraud or error.

THE BALLOT

The form of the ballot deserves at least passing mention at this point. During the greater part of the nineteenth century the party organizations printed and distributed their own ballots—that is, the lists of their own candidates—and no one questioned this arrangement. Official ballots, printed by the state, were unknown; state law went no further than to provide that white paper must be used, and perhaps also to specify the size.

Because these elementary precautions were insufficient to preserve the secrecy of the ballot or to prevent wholesale ballot box stuffing, recourse eventually was had to the so-called "Australian" ballot—a blanket ballot containing the names of the candidates of all parties, printed at state expense, and distributed at the polls by state election officials. Such a ballot, which had long been used in Australia, made its first appearance in the United States at the Louisville municipal election of 1888. A few months later it was adopted by Massachusetts. Within a short time it had received general acceptance; today it is used by every state of the Union.

Present Types of Ballots

The original Australian ballot, as borrowed from Australia and first used in the United States, contained no party designations. The candidates for each office were grouped together, and a separate mark was required for each preference the voter desired to indicate.

Under American influence, however, the Australian ballot began to assume new forms. Its essential features—secrecy and official preparation and distribution—were preserved, but in other respects it differed radically from the original model. First, Massachusetts printed the party affiliation of each candidate after his name. A little later, Indiana rearranged the ballot so as to place the names of all the candidates of a party in the same column, and specified that a cross at the top of any column would be considered a vote for that party's entire slate of candidates. Although it was possible under this plan for the voter to divide his allegiance, it was much easier for him to vote a straight ticket, for splitting the ticket meant placing a cross after the name of every candidate favored, whereas straight voting necessitated only a single mark.

Indiana's party-column ballot thus encouraged party regularity, and for that reason it was enthusiastically received by the professional politicians. Today it is used—with occasional variations—in thirty states.   Most of the others have adopted the Massachusetts or office-group ballot.   Nebraska and Pennsylvania, however, have modified this type of ballot by adding the party square or circle for the benefit of those who desire to vote a straight ticket, thus offering the very inducement to party regularity that is characteristic of the Indiana plan.

Voting Machines

It has already been indicated that voting machines are now used by many communities in place of paper ballots.   These machines are operated by means of pointers and levers.   Across the face of a machine the names of the candidates are placed, each name with its separate pointer, and the voter is directed to turn down the pointers that indicate his preferences. Or, if the policy of the state is to encourage straight voting, the machine may be so arranged as to make possible a vote for all the candidates of a party by a single turn of the party's lever.

ADVANTAGES.   The voter is carefully protected against mistakes; it is mechanically impossible for him to express too many choices or turn the pointers the wrong way.   When he finally pulls the lever that records his vote, the curtain that has concealed him from the election officers and watchers is automatically drawn back, thus making it impossible for him to vote a second time without everyone's knowledge.

First introduced in 1896, voting machines have been used rather widely for several decades, and have proved markedly superior to paper ballots. They save voting time, insure absolute secrecy, eliminate the chance of error, and, despite their heavy initial cost, actually result in reduced election expenses.   Still more important, they greatly diminish the likelihood of fraud.   Successful tampering with the machines is extremely difficult, so that correct returns are assured if there is even one honest election official or watcher in the polling place.   The speed of the count is also an important factor.   Votes are automatically tabulated as they are cast; therefore the final result of an election can often be announced within one or two hours after the polls are closed.

OBJECTIONS.   Most of the arguments against voting machines are in-

A LONG, LONG BALLOT

(STUB A)

Consecutive **X 569¢**

(STUB A)

Consecutive **E 202**

OFFICIAL OFFICE TYPE BALLOT
CUYAHOGA COUNTY

a. To vote for a candidate place "X" in the rectangular space at the left of the name of such candidate.
b. If you tear, soil, or deface or erroneously mark this ballot return it to the precinct election officials and obtain another ballot.

USE **X** ONLY IN MARKING BALLOT

OFFICIAL NON-PARTISAN BALLOT
CUYAHOGA COUNTY

a. To vote for a candidate place "X" in the rectangular space at the left of the name of such candidate.
b. If you tear, soil, or deface or erroneously mark this ballot, return it to the precinct election officers and obtain another ballot.

USE **X** ONLY IN MARKING BALLOT

For Governor (Vote for not more than one)	For State Senator (Vote for not more than six)	For Representative to General Assembly (Vote for not more than seventeen)	For County Commissioner (Vote for not more than two)
CHARLES P. TAFT REPUBLICAN	MARK McELROY DEMOCRAT	JAMES F. McCAFFERY DEMOCRAT	HENRY W. SPEETH DEMOCRAT
FRANK J. LAUSCHE DEMOCRAT	JOSEPH R. NUTT, JR. REPUBLICAN	JAMES J. McGETTRICK DEMOCRAT	JOHN F. CURRY DEMOCRAT
For Lieutenant Governor (Vote for not more than one)	GERTRUDE E. POLCAR REPUBLICAN	ROY F. McMAHON REPUBLICAN	ERNEST A. GOTTERMEYER REPUBLICAN
GEORGE D. NYE DEMOCRAT	M. M. ROCKER REPUBLICAN	RALPH A. MILLER REPUBLICAN	RICHARD M. MASTERSON REPUBLICAN
JOHN W. BROWN REPUBLICAN	FRANK J. SVOBODA DEMOCRAT	RAY T. MILLER, JR. DEMOCRAT	**For Prosecuting Attorney** (Vote for not more than one)
For Secretary of State (Vote for not more than one)	JOSEPH W. BARTUNEK DEMOCRAT	JOHN F. O'BRIEN DEMOCRAT	HARRY T. MARSHALL DEMOCRAT
CHARLES F. SWEENEY DEMOCRAT	ANTHONY J. CELEBREZZE DEMOCRAT	META E. PAVLIK REPUBLICAN	FRANK T. CULLITAN DEMOCRAT
TED W. BROWN REPUBLICAN	JOHN T. CORRIGAN DEMOCRAT	ANDREW C. PUTKA DEMOCRAT	**For Clerk of Court of Common Pleas** (Vote for not more than one)
For Auditor of State (Vote for not more than one)	HARRY E. DAVIS REPUBLICAN	E. M. ROSE REPUBLICAN	WILLIAM J. REICHLE REPUBLICAN
JAMES A. RHODES REPUBLICAN	ARTHUR W. FISKE REPUBLICAN	WILLIAM B. SAUNDERS REPUBLICAN	LEONARD F. FUERST DEMOCRAT
JOSEPH T. FERGUSON DEMOCRAT	ELIZABETH F. GORMAN DEMOCRAT	EUGENE J. SAWICKI DEMOCRAT	**For Sheriff** (Vote for not more than one)
For Treasurer of State (Vote for not more than one)	FRANK C. GRISMER REPUBLICAN	FRANCIS D. SULLIVAN DEMOCRAT	JOSEPH M. SWEENEY DEMOCRAT
ROGER W. TRACY REPUBLICAN		MIKE M. SWEENEY DEMOCRAT	THOMAS F. McCAFFERTY REPUBLICAN
JOHN J. GALLAGHER DEMOCRAT		RICHARD H. WOODS DEMOCRAT	**For County Recorder** (Full Term Commencing January 5, 1953) (Vote for not more than one)
For Attorney General (Vote for not more than one)		HENRY S. ZWOLINSKI REPUBLICAN	KENNETH W. THORNTON REPUBLICAN
PAUL F. WARD DEMOCRAT		JOSEPH H. AVELLONE DEMOCRAT	FRANK S. DAY REPUBLICAN
C. WILLIAM O'NEILL REPUBLICAN		WALLACE J. BAKER, JR. REPUBLICAN	**For County Recorder** (Unexpired Term Ending January 4, 1953) (Vote for not more than one)
For United States Senator (Vote for not more than one)		JAMES J. BARTON REPUBLICAN	ALBERT B. LEMLEY DEMOCRAT
MICHAEL V. DiSALLE DEMOCRAT		HUGH P. BRENNAN DEMOCRAT	**For County Treasurer** (Vote for not more than one)
JOHN W. BRICKER REPUBLICAN		WILBUR H. BREWER REPUBLICAN	CHARLES M. PETERSEN REPUBLICAN
For Representative to Congress 22nd District (Vote for not more than one)		WILLIAM S. BURTON REPUBLICAN	LESLIE R. MONROE DEMOCRAT
CHAT PATERSON DEMOCRAT		ANTHONY O. CALABRESE DEMOCRAT	**For County Engineer** (Vote for not more than one)
FRANCES P. BOLTON REPUBLICAN		PAUL T. CARUSO REPUBLICAN	ALBERT S. PORTER DEMOCRAT
		F. WILSON CHOCKLEY, JR. REPUBLICAN	RALPH KELSEY REPUBLICAN
		JOHN V. CORRIGAN DEMOCRAT	**For Coroner** (Vote for not more than one)
		MICHAEL J. CROSSER DEMOCRAT	HERBERT W. SALTER REPUBLICAN
		CLARENCE FERGUSON REPUBLICAN	SAMUEL R. GERBER DEMOCRAT
		ADRIAN B. FINK, JR. REPUBLICAN	
		FRANK M. GORMAN DEMOCRAT	
		WILLIAM J. HART, JR. DEMOCRAT	
		JOSEPH J. HORVATH DEMOCRAT	
		GEORGE N. KALKAS DEMOCRAT	
		MOLLY B. LAFFER DEMOCRAT	
		FRANCIS V. MAY REPUBLICAN	

For Judge of the Supreme Court (Full Term Commencing January 1, 1953) (Vote for not more than one)

CHARLES B. ZIMMERMAN

FRANCIS B. DOUGLASS

For Judge of the Supreme Court (Full Term Commencing January 2, 1953) (Vote for not more than one)

JAMES GARFIELD STEWART

KENNETH B. JOHNSTON

For Judge of the Court of Appeals (Full Term Commencing January 9, 1953) (Vote for not more than one)

LEE E. SKEEL

For Judge of the Court of Appeals (Unexpired Term Ending February 9, 1957) (Vote for not more than one)

LOCKWOOD THOMPSON

JULIUS M. KOVACHY

For Judge of the Court of Common Pleas (Full Term Commencing January 1, 1953) (Vote for not more than one)

FELIX T. MATIA

For Judge of the Court of Common Pleas (Full Term Commencing January 2, 1953) (Vote for not more than one)

JOSEPH A. ARTL

For Judge of the Court of Common Pleas (Full Term Commencing January 3, 1953) (Vote for not more than one)

ANTHONY A. RUTKOWSKI

BENJAMIN D. NICOLA

For Judge of the Juvenile Court (Full Term Commencing January 1, 1953) (Vote for not more than one)

HARRY L. EASTMAN

valid, or of minor consequence. It is sometimes said, for example, that they are apt to break down—perhaps at the voting peak—thus leaving the voters without any means of expressing their preferences. Yet the dependability of the better grade of machines has been amply demonstrated over a considerable period of years. References to their unreliability are generally the result of ignorance or deliberate malice. Troubles due to defective workmanship have not been common since the experimental period at the beginning of the present century. Moreover, it is a simple matter to keep one or two machines at some central point, ready for any possible emergency.

Objection to voting machines on the ground of excessive cost can readily be met by indicating the savings made possible. Use of machines means fewer election officials, because of the automatic count; larger election precincts, as a result of quicker voting; no printing cost, through the elimination of paper ballots.

In Maryland it was argued that voting machines were a violation of the constitutional mandate that "all elections shall be by ballot." But the supreme court of the state rejected this contention, declaring that "a constitution is to be interpreted by the spirit which vivifies, and not by the letter which killeth." [18]

The only valid objection to voting machines—that they were not adapted to the requirements of proportional representation elections—has now been removed by the development of suitable instruments. Because of their numerous advantages, voting machines have been widely adopted. They are used extensively in nine states [19]—especially in the larger cities; and thirty other states also permit their use. They have been installed in several thousand communities, although not necessarily in all precincts or for all elections.

Too Many Elective Offices

Students of government agree that the most necessary reform in the election systems of the several states is a substantial reduction in the number of offices filled by popular vote. Since the days of Andrew Jackson there has been a widespread belief that popular election is the one certain cure for all the ills of government, and the complete failure of this theory has only slightly diminished its popularity. In thousands of elections the people have demonstrated conclusively that their ability to discriminate among

[18] Norris v. Mayor and City Council of Baltimore, 192 A. 531 (1937).

[19] Connecticut, Florida, Indiana, Iowa, New Jersey, New York, Pennsylvania, Rhode Island, and Washington.

candidates and select wisely is in inverse ratio to the number of choices they are required to make, yet ballots are still filled with long lists of offices and longer lists of office-seekers.

In the average state the voters are asked to choose a veritable horde of state officers—governor, lieutenant governor, secretary of state, attorney-general, treasurer, auditor, superintendent of education, legislators, and members of the judiciary, plus perhaps a few board members—in addition to such local officers as mayor, sheriff, coroner, prosecuting attorney, treasurer, recorder of deeds, registrar of wills, city clerk, and members of the city council and the county board of supervisors. Nor does this partial enumeration include the officers of school districts, park or water districts, or other special areas of local government. Likewise, it omits the elective officers of the national government—president, vice president, and members of both houses of Congress.

Small wonder, therefore, that the voter cannot make intelligent selections. He has neither the time nor the inclination to study the records of hundreds of candidates for scores of offices. Concerning a few outstanding men he may have very definite views; the other names on the ballot are meaningless to him. Yet the law specifically states that numerous minor offices are to be filled by his vote, and the societies for getting out the vote inform him that it is his patriotic duty to express preferences he does not have.

Faced with such a problem, many voters conclude that the most satisfactory solution is to remain at home on election day. Those who actually go to the polls pursue the one rational course that is open to them: they vote the straight ticket of their respective parties in the hope that the party selections have been wisely made. Thus they play directly into the hands of the boss—the man who controls the dominant party organization and dictates the selection of public officials. Their votes are merely a ratification of his choice. The fault is not with them, however, it is with the system that makes any other result impossible.

The Short Ballot as a Remedy

Fortunately, a remedy for the long lists now appearing on ballots is at hand. It is the short ballot—a ballot that contains only the names of candidates for outstanding public offices. Other offices must then be filled by appointment. In the field of state government only the governor, the lieutenant governor, and the members of the legislature should retain their elective status.[20] With this reform accomplished, the people could reason-

---

[20] If the auditor is not chosen by the legislature he should be added to this list, for it is necessary that he remain independent of the executive. See page 120.

ably be expected to shoulder their lighter burden more willingly and to exercise greater discrimination in the selection of their representatives.   And the actual choice of minor officials would be transferred from the boss—an irresponsible despot—to the governor—a responsible leader.

The short ballot movement is a product of the present century.   Prior to 1900 there had been a number of suggestions for the transfer of specific offices from the elective to the appointive class, and some of these suggestions

A SHORT, SHORT BALLOT

1	**HOGG** (Quintin McGarel Hogg of The Corner House, Heath-view Gardens, Putney Heath, London, S W 15, Barrister-at-Law.)	
2	**KEELING** (Ernest Keeling of 57 New Road, Headington, Oxford, Organiser.)	
3	**PAKENHAM** (Lady Elizabeth Pakenham of 10 Linnell Drive, Hampstead Way, London, N.W. 11, Married Woman.)	
4	**TWEDDLE** (Donald William Tweddle of 13 Scillonian Road, Guildford, Organiser.)	

Reproduced with permission from *Civic Victories,* by Richard S. Childs, Harper and Brothers, New York, 1952.

had borne fruit.   But there was no organized plan of attack on the old order until 1909, when the National Short Ballot Organization was formed, with Woodrow Wilson as its first president and Richard S. Childs, the mainspring of the movement, as secretary-treasurer.[21]

Since that time the short ballot has been endorsed by leading statesmen, publicists, and scholars.   It has received the support of every sincere friend of good government.   It has proved its effectiveness, and has not been weakened by a single valid criticism.   As Theodore Roosevelt told the Ohio Constitutional Convention of 1912: "You cannot get good service

[21] In 1921 the National Short Ballot Organization consolidated with the National Municipal League.

from the public servant if you cannot see him, and there is no more effective way of hiding him than by mixing him up with a multitude of others so that they are none of them important enough to catch the eye of the average work-a-day citizen."

Yet the progress of the short ballot movement has been slow, especially in state government. Though a few states, such as New York, New Jersey, and Virginia, have substantially shortened their ballots in recent years, most states still encumber their ballots with the names of candidates for minor offices, so that intelligent voting is impossible. In the cities of the United States the short ballot has met with greater favor. It has been adopted by a considerable number of the metropolitan centers, and by hundreds of smaller communities. Cities with commission or manager forms of government have accepted it as fundamental, and even the mayor-council cities have amended their charters in many instances for the purpose of reducing the number of elective officials. The short ballot has become a prime tenet in nearly every recent campaign for charter revision. Only the national government has remained entirely unaffected. Since the adoption of the Constitution in 1789 it has had a short ballot *par excellence,* and has served as a convenient illustration of the successful operation of the short ballot principle.

WHO MAY VOTE

Constitutional Limitations

Every state constitution prescribes the qualifications necessary for voting at state and national elections. Therefore the qualifications that are required—even to vote for the president and vice president of the United States and for members of Congress—vary with the state in which the voter has his residence. The federal Constitution imposes only two limitations upon the power of the states to establish suffrage requirements: no citizen of the United States may be deprived of the right to vote on account of race or color,[22] or on account of sex.[23]

In addition, there is an unenforced clause of the federal Constitution: "When the right to vote at any election for the choice of electors for President and Vice President of the United States, Representatives in Congress, the Executive and Judicial officers of a State, or the members of the Legislature thereof, is denied to any of the male inhabitants of such state, being twenty-one years of age, and citizens of the United States, or in any way abridged, except for participation in rebellion, or other crime, the basis of

[22] Fifteenth Amendment.
[23] Nineteenth Amendment.

representation" of the state in the federal House of Representatives "shall be reduced in the proportion which the number of such male citizens shall bear to the whole number of male citizens twenty-one years of age in such State." [24]

The political consequences of an attempt to enforce this section on reduction of representation might be serious. Moreover, it would be necessary to reduce the congressional representation of *every* state that imposed voting restrictions on its adult male citizens, regardless of the purpose of those restrictions. Therefore New York, Massachusetts, California, and other states whose literacy requirements are designed to improve the standard of intelligent voting would suffer equally with the states of the "solid South," where Negro voters are excluded *en masse*. The "reduction of representation" clause was never intended to have any such effect. Adopted in 1868, its obvious purpose was to force the extension of the suffrage to the newly enfranchised Negro population of the South. So the leaders of both major parties have tacitly agreed that the wisest course is to permit it to remain a dead letter.

State Qualifications

The voting age is twenty-one years in every state except Georgia, which lowered it to eighteen years in 1943, on the theory that "the best training in citizenship is participation in the rights and obligations of citizenship." Not long ago President Eisenhower proposed a constitutional amendment lowering the voting age to eighteen in all parts of the nation, but this suggestion was rejected by the United States Senate. Every state has residence requirements—usually one year within the state, two or three months within the county, and a shorter time within the election precinct where residence is maintained at the time of voting. Citizenship is now universally required, although this policy has been adopted by a number of states only within the last half century. Just prior to the outbreak of the First World War nine states extended the suffrage to aliens who had declared their intention of becoming American citizens. Tax-paying as a qualification for voting has lost much of its early popularity, though it is still found in a few states. Most common is the poll tax—a head tax of fifty cents or one dollar on every person, or on every person who does not meet some other requirement, such as payment of taxes on real estate. The poll tax was once widely used in the South as a device to discourage Negro voting but it has now been largely abandoned by the Southern states. Today it is found in only three states of the South—Alabama, Texas, and Virginia.

[24] Fourteenth Amendment, Sec. 2.

DISFRANCHISEMENT OF NEGROES. Of course, the poll tax has never been the sole means—or even the most important means—of disfranchising the black race. The white people of the South have displayed astonishing ingenuity in this respect. Thus at one time the constitution of many a Southern state contained a so-called "grandfather clause," which extended the suffrage to persons who lacked prescribed tax-paying or educational qualifications, *provided their fathers or grandfathers, or any of their ancestors, were voters in 1867, or had served in the Union or Confederate forces.* Obviously very few Negroes could benefit by this waiver of voting restrictions. But poor, illiterate whites could and did benefit; they lost no time in enrolling as voters. This discrimination was so obvious a violation of the federal Constitution that in 1915 the Supreme Court of the United States, considering Oklahoma's grandfather clause, declared it unconstitutional.[25]

After that time increased reliance was placed on party action prescribing the qualifications for voting at the party primaries; Negroes were then excluded by party rules from the Democratic primary, which had long been the equivalent of a final election in the far South. In 1935 the United States Supreme Court upheld this arrangement, on the ground that the discrimination was a party—not a state—action, and therefore outside the protection of the Fifteenth Amendment.[26]

Nine years later, however, the Court specifically reversed its stand, declaring that Negroes might not be excluded by party rules.[27] It pointed out that these rules were in effect state laws, since they were made with the sanction of the state, and in conformity with the procedure established by the legislature. This decision created widespread consternation throughout the South. In South Carolina the governor called a special session of the legislature, which promptly repealed all statutes concerning party primaries, and even initiated an amendment designed to remove from the state constitution all reference to primary elections. The Georgia legislature passed a somewhat similar measure, but it was vetoed by the governor. The obvious purpose of these moves was to transform the Democratic Party from a semi-official agency of the state into a private club. As such, it could make its own rules concerning membership, presumably without judicial interference.

These schemes were frustrated in 1947, however, when a federal district

[25] Guinn v. United States, 238 U.S. 347 (1915).
[26] Grovey v. Townsend, 295 U.S. 45 (1935).
[27] Smith v. Allwright, 321 U.S. 649 (1944). See also United States v. Classic, 313 U.S. 299 (1941), in which the right of Congress to regulate congressional primary elections was upheld.

court upheld the right of a South Carolina Negro to vote in the Democratic primary, despite contrary party regulations. The court took note of the fact that all the state primary laws repealed by the legislature had subsequently been adopted by the Democratic Party as its own rules, and it concluded that the alleged transformation of the Party had not really taken place. Whatever the laws might or might not say, the Democratic Party in South Carolina was the agency that determined the choice of national and state officers. Therefore it must be considered a part of the state's election machinery, and must respect the federal Constitution's prohibition of racial discrimination at the polls. "It is time," said the court in a tart postscript, "for South Carolina to rejoin the Union. It is time to fall in line with the other states and adopt the American way of conducting elections." [28] Later in 1947 this decision was approved by a higher federal court, and the following year it was sustained without comment by the Supreme Court of the United States.[29]

Even though the courts have left no doubt as to their attitude toward Negro voting, the matter is still far from settled. Other ways can be found to disfranchise colored persons. One reasonably effective device is the literacy test. The constitutions of a number of Southern states specify that every elector must be able to read and write, or read the constitution of the state, or read any portion of the constitution "and give a reasonable interpretation thereof." To give an interpretation that will satisfy the white election inspectors is not a difficult task for a white man, but may prove virtually impossible for a Negro. Other plans will doubtless be devised when necessary. Yet there is some evidence that the old order is slowly changing. Negroes are registering and voting in increasing numbers in the South, especially in states like Texas, where the colored population is relatively small. The growth in all the Southern states of politically conscious labor organizations, with their deliberate encouragement of Negro voting, may force many Southern politicians to modify their traditional point of view.[30]

LITERACY TESTS. It has already been indicated that literacy tests for voting are not confined to the South. They are now used by seventeen states, representing every section of the country. Their obvious purpose, in the North and West, is to deny the franchise to the group that is least likely to use it intelligently. The ability to read and write is not in itself an assurance of intelligent voting, but it may well be considered a prerequisite.

---

[28] Elmore v. Rice, 72 Fed. Supp. 516 (1947).
[29] Rice v. Elmore, 165 Fed. 2nd 387 (1947); 333 U.S. 875 (1948).
[30] See the significant study, *Southern Politics*, by V. O. Key, Jr.

Illiterates are not usually well informed concerning public affairs.   To them the happenings outside their own little world are necessarily a closed book.

Objection is sometimes made to literacy tests on the ground that they are "undemocratic."   It is said that they establish an aristocracy of education to replace the aristocracy of wealth that vanished with the disappearance of property requirements for voting.   But this argument is scarcely entitled to serious consideration.   It rests on the untenable premise that democracy can best be served by a multiplication of votes, regardless of the qualifications of the voters.   The real trouble is not with the theory of the literacy requirement, but with its enforcement.   Usually it is administered by local election officials, whose concept of literacy often varies with the hour of the day, the state of their digestion, and the party affiliation of prospective voters.

Only one state—New York—has taken the test out of the hands of the election officials.   Under the New York plan it is administered by the state department of education.   Persons who can give proof that they have completed the fifth grade of the grammar school receive certificates of literacy without further formality; others are required to pass the department of education's examination before they may be enrolled as voters.

REGISTRATION OF VOTERS

Fraudulent Voting

When a state prescribes qualifications for voting, it should also take steps to prevent ineligible persons from participating in elections.   Otherwise large-scale frauds are likely to result.   Aliens may cast their ballots unchallenged; the dead may come to life through the magic of unscrupulous politicians; professional "repeaters" may visit precinct after precinct, voting under a different name at each polling place.   Such practices are not common in rural communities, where every man is known and attempts at impersonation would speedily be detected.   But in the cities, with their congestion and rapidly shifting populations, another story must be told.   Men do not know even their immediate neighbors, and therefore the opportunities for election fraud are vast.

REGISTRATION LISTS.   Some means must be found of enabling the election officials to identify voters, so that persons not properly qualified may be excluded from the polls.   Years ago, when this problem first became serious, some states attempted to solve it by making provision for the preparation of lists of eligible voters, to which reference could be made when necessary. But the lists were carelessly prepared, and no effort was made to keep them up-to-date.

Therefore they proved of little value, and fraud continued to be practically as prevalent as before. "The colonization of voters was quite common. Hoodlums were rounded up and lodged for a night or so in various lodging houses and cheap hotels and then registered from all of them. On the day of the election, gangs of 'repeaters' were hauled from precinct to precinct and voted under different names. Sometimes the same persons would vote several times at each precinct, changing coats or hats between times. The early registration lists were often padded with bogus names or the names of persons who had died or moved away, and these names were voted by 'repeaters' on the day of election or were checked off and voted by the corrupt precinct election officers without the necessity of providing 're-peaters.' " [31]

PERSONAL REGISTRATION. In 1866 California and New York took an important step toward the elimination of such conditions by providing for the personal registration of voters. Every person desiring to vote was required to appear before a registration board at some time prior to election day and establish the fact that he possessed the necessary legal qualifica-tions. Failure to have his name placed on the list of eligible voters in this manner automatically operated to deprive him of the right to cast a ballot at the next election. Personal registration gradually came into popular favor; it is now used by forty-six states—either on a state-wide basis or for the larger cities only. The constitution of Arkansas prohibits registration of voters; and the Texas constitution permits it only in cities whose popula-tion exceeds ten thousand.[32]

As used in the several states, personal registration assumes a variety of forms. The most important difference is the length of time for which a voter's registration remains valid. The election laws of some states re-quire all voters—or at least all voters in the larger cities, where fraud is most likely to occur—to register every year. This arrangement is found in the cities of New York. It places a very heavy burden on the electorate, since it requires two trips to the polls—one to register and one to vote—for every election. Moreover, it adds materially to the expense of the election system. Biennial and quadrennial registration are correspondingly less expensive and less burdensome, but in the metropolitan centers, unless ex-treme care is taken to purge the voters' lists by striking out the names of

[31] Joseph P. Harris, *Registration of Voters in the United States,* p. 6. Reprinted by permission of the Institute for Government Research.

[32] See the third edition of Joseph P. Harris' *Model Registration System,* prepared for the National Municipal League.

persons who have died or moved away, they lead naturally to fraud.   Nebraska has registration every six years in certain cities, and in South Carolina decennial registration is the rule throughout the state.

PERMANENT REGISTRATION.   Most common, however, is permanent registration, which is used by forty-three states.[33]   Under this plan a voter is permitted to register at any time during the year, and is not limited to two or three registration days prior to the election.   His name, once placed on the list of qualified voters, remains there until he dies or moves to a new address.   Permanent registration has certain obvious advantages.   It is very cheap, and offers a maximum of convenience to the electorate.   Unless coupled with an effective means of revising the voters' lists at frequent intervals, however, it is an open invitation to fraud.   For this reason it was formerly regarded as unsuitable for the larger cities.   But improved means of purging the lists have been developed in recent years, and therefore the trend has been toward permanent registration—even in cities of metropolitan proportions, such as Philadelphia, Detroit, Los Angeles, Cleveland, Boston, San Francisco, Milwaukee, and Minneapolis.

By far the best way to clear the voters' lists of names that should be removed is to conduct a house-to-house canvass.   This task is performed by election officials or the police.   In addition, it is an extremely simple matter to secure a copy of the official death reports and to cancel the registration of every voter who has died.   An effective system for recording transfers of registration within a city or county is also important.   In a few cities the proprietors of lodging houses, rooming houses and hotels are required to file lists of their permanent guests.   A number of states cancel the registration of an elector who fails to vote at two or three successive elections.   This action does not disfranchise him, but merely necessitates another registration.   These various devices for purging the lists have proved so satisfactory, when given even a reasonably fair trial, that they have completely destroyed the only valid argument against the use of permanent registration in large cities—its tendency to encourage fraudulent voting.

ABSENT VOTERS

Many voters are away from home on election day, and therefore unable to go to the polls and cast their ballots.   The laws of almost all the states, however, permit them to vote *in absentia*.   Usually this is done by issuing ballots in advance to those who expect to be absent on election day; the

---

[33] Not necessarily on a state-wide basis, however.   Thus Nebraska's permanent registration applies only to Douglas County, which includes Omaha.

ballots are then mailed to the local election boards in time to be counted. A few states vary this procedure by permitting an elector who is absent from the precinct in which he resides to cast an absentee ballot in any other precinct of the state. The privilege of voting without going to the polls is most commonly extended to all voters, but a few states limit it to those who are sick or disabled, and several other states provide that it shall apply only to members of the armed forces in time of war.

In the spring of 1944, with several million young Americans in the armed services in all parts of the world, and a presidential election only a few months away, absent voting suddenly became a major issue. Some leaders of public opinion, emphasizing the inadequacy of many of the state laws, urged federal legislation guaranteeing to American troops the right to vote for president and vice president and members of Congress. Opposition to this proposal was based on the undeniable right of the states, rather than the federal government, to control elections.

Finally, after prolonged controversy, Congress passed a compromise law authorizing the preparation of a federal ballot to be used by overseas troops. This ballot might not be used by any voter, however, unless the governor of his own state certified that it was acceptable under state law. Furthermore, it might not be used unless the voter first applied for a state ballot, and failed to receive it by a given date. Only twenty states agreed to accept the federal ballot, and as a result more than half of the troops overseas were unaffected by the law of Congress.

Sound absent-voting legislation is desirable, not only in wartime, but also in days of peace. Men and women should always be encouraged in every legitimate way to express their political preferences. It must be confessed, however, that laws facilitating absent voting have had slight effect on the habits of the electorate. The overwhelming majority of persons who are ill or away from home fail to exercise their absent-voting privilege.

NONVOTERS

Far more serious, however, is the problem of the chronic nonvoter—the man who stays away from the polls, although he lacks the excuse of illness or absence from home. Just how many qualified electors habitually fail to vote cannot be stated with assurance, but it is certain that the number is excessively high. Even in a presidential year, when popular interest is usually at its peak, the total number of votes scarcely ever exceeds sixty-five per cent of the number of citizens of voting age. Usually the percentage is far lower.   Of course, some citizens are denied the franchise on account of illiteracy, failure to pay taxes, or inadequate periods of residence.   But due allowance for these factors does not change the obvious truth that a large part of the American public deliberately abstains from voting.   In state and municipal elections the citizens who vote are usually less numerous than those who do not.

There are many reasons why men and women stay away from the polls, but indifference is by far the most important.   The rank and file of the electorate, faced with the task of making an intelligent selection among hundreds of candidates for dozens of offices, in addition perhaps to passing upon constitutional amendments, charter changes, and ordinary legislative proposals, frequently become discouraged.   And their interest in public affairs is further dampened by such hurdles as rigid annual registration laws, unnecessary taxpaying requirements, frequent regular and special elections.

It may fairly be said that widespread nonvoting is the natural and almost inevitable result of our general scheme of government.   If we wish to draw larger numbers of voters to the polls, we must first simplify our election machinery and then shorten our ballots to the point where intelligent voting can reasonably be expected.   It is quite fashionable at the present time to speak of the "slacker vote," as if every person who stayed away from the polls on election day had shirked an important civic duty.

But many leading students of public affairs are of the opinion that uninformed voting is quite as dangerous as nonvoting, and that good government cannot be obtained by a mere multiplication of ballots.   They urge that the real need is for an enlightened citizenry, and that the first step is the elimination of needless complexities so as to bring government within the comprehension of the average man.

COMPULSORY VOTING

Compulsory voting is used with varying degrees of success in a number of foreign countries.   Every qualified elector is required to appear at the polls and cast a ballot on election day.   If he fails to do so and can show no good reason for his neglect of duty, he must pay a fine.   European experience has led to the suggestion that compulsory voting be adopted in the United States.   In fact, the constitutions of Massachusetts and North Dakota authorize the legislature to prescribe penalties for failure to vote. But the penalties have not been imposed, and in other states compulsory voting has received scant consideration.   It is contrary to the American political tradition.   It transforms the privilege of participating in elections—or the "right," to use the phraseology of the federal Constitution [34]—into an obligation.   And it does not in any way stimulate the public's interest or add to the public's knowledge of governmental affairs.   It increases the number of ballots, of course—but that is a matter of small consequence.

PROBLEMS

1. How are candidates nominated for public office in your state?
2. Observe the operation of the election system in your state on election day. What suggestions can you offer to—
    a. Reduce cost.
    b. Prevent fraud.
    c. Make voting easier for the average voter.
    d. Increase the speed of vote-counting?
3. Study the results of compulsory voting in Europe or Latin America.   Do you believe that the United States would be justified in adopting such a plan?
4. The State of Iowa is considering the advisability of establishing a literacy test for voting.   Prepare a paper presenting both sides of the matter, with emphasis on the experience of those states that have used literacy tests.
5. What percentage of the eligible voters in your community actually voted at the last state election?   Talk with a number of persons who did not vote, and try to learn their reasons for staying away from the polls.

SELECTED REFERENCES

Albright, S. D., *The American Ballot*, Washington, D.C., 1942.
Bernard, Bertram M., *Election Laws of the Forty-Eight States; How to Register and Vote*, 1950.
Council of State Governments, *Registration for Voting in the United States*, rev. ed., 1946.
————, *Soldier-Sailor Voting*, 2nd ed., 1944.
Ewing, Cortez A. M., *Primary Elections in the South: A Study in Uniparty Politics*, Oklahoma, 1953.
Glassman, Benjamin, *A.B.C. of the Direct Primary Law*, 3rd ed., 1938.
Gosnell, Harold F., *Democracy; The Threshold of Freedom*, Chaps. II–VI, 1948.
Harris, Joseph P., *Election Administration in the United States*, Washington, D.C., 1934.
————, *Registration of Voters in the United States*, Washington, D.C., 1929.
Holland, Lynwood M., *The Direct Primary in Georgia*, Urbana, Illinois, 1949.
Illinois Legislative Reference Bureau, *Constitutional Convention Bulletins* Nos. 2, 5, Springfield, 1920.
Johnsen, Julia E., comp., *Lowering the Voting Age*, 1945.

[34] E.g., "The *right* of citizens of the United States to vote shall not be denied or abridged by the United States or by any state on account of sex." (Nineteenth Amendment.)

Key, V. O., Jr., *Politics, Parties, and Pressure Groups*, 3rd ed., 1952.

————, *Southern Politics*, 1949.

Kies, Harry B., and McCandless, Carl A., *Manual on the Bill of Rights and Suffrage and Elections for the Missouri Constitutional Convention of 1943*, Columbia, 1943.

Luce, Robert, *Legislative Principles*, Chaps. XIII, XIV, XVIII, 1930.

McCulloch, Albert J., *Suffrage and Its Problems*, University Research Monographs, No. 9, Baltimore, 1929.

McGovney, Dudley O., *The American Suffrage Medley*, 1949.

Merriam, Charles E., and Gosnell, Harold F., *Non-Voting*, 1924.

————, *The American Party System*, 4th ed., 1949.

Merriam, Charles E., and Overacker, L., *Primary Elections*, 1928.

Miller, George F., *Absentee Voters and Suffrage Laws*, 1948.

Myrdal, Gunnar, and Others, *An American Dilemma; The Negro Problem and Modern Democracy*, Vol. I, Chaps. XX–XXIII, 1944.

National Municipal League, *Model Direct Primary Election System*, 1951.

Nelson, B. H., *The Fourteenth Amendment and the Negro in the United States*, 1946.

Odegard, Peter H., and Helms, E. A., *American Politics; A Study in Political Dynamics*, rev. ed., Chaps. XII–XIII, 1947.

Overacker, Louise, *Money in Elections*, 1932.

Penniman, Howard R., *Sait's American Parties and Elections*, 5th ed., 1952.

Perry, Jennings, *Democracy Begins at Home*, 1944.

Pollock, James K., *The Direct Primary in Michigan, 1909–1935*, Ann Arbor, 1943.

————, *Election Administration in Michigan*, 1934.

————, *Party Campaign Funds*, 1926.

————, *Permanent Registration of Voters in Michigan: An Appraisal*, Ann Arbor, 1937.

Porter, K. H., *A History of Suffrage in the United States*, 1918.

Smith, Carl O., ed., *Book of Ballots*, Detroit, Mich., 1938.

Titus, Charles H., *Voting Behavior in the United States*, Berkeley, Calif., 1935.

CHAPTER 15

Parties and Politics

Government is something more than a matter of constitutions and laws. Its length and breadth are not encompassed by the administrators, legislators, and judges who officially represent the people, for these public officials are chosen by the political parties, and must look to the parties for re-election or reappointment. Their political fate is decided by the party leaders, and only at rare intervals do the voters upset the leaders' plans. Government operates through the medium of political parties; in large measure it is what the parties wish it to be.

Therefore the political parties are an integral part of the governmental process and any discussion of government that overlooks their function and organization is necessarily incomplete. Before examining these, however, let us consider just what is a political party, and how the system of parties developed.

DEFINITIONS OF A POLITICAL PARTY

To give a satisfactory definition of the term "political party" is not easy. Edmund Burke once said that "a party is a body of men united for promoting by their joint endeavor the national interest upon some particular principle in which they are all agreed." This statement has been quoted many times—usually with approval, yet it furnishes no clear understanding of what parties are or why they exist. Political parties as we know them today—and as Burke should have known them—are seldom able to find any principle upon which a substantial number of their members can agree. The Republican Party, for example, includes within its membership conservatives like John Bricker and liberals like Earl Warren. Both the liberal Harry S. Truman and the conservative James F. Byrnes call themselves Democrats.

Some amateur students of politics are greatly distressed to find politicians of widely assorted hues wearing the same party label. "You know very well," the March Hare is reported to have said, "how the label on tomato soup must state whether preservatives or artificial coloring matter are used, mustn't it? And the label on a peroxide bottle has to say ninety-seven per cent inert matter—namely, water. And you always have to state the alcoholic contents, don't you? So it's odd that people are so particular about tomato soup and canned spinach and beer and not at all about Republicans on a Communist ticket. But if you had a law saying that a Democratic candidate for mayor must have a label saying 'Democratic Contents Not Under 23 Per Cent'—" [1]

Despite a lack of precise principles, however, both major parties continue to operate with surprising efficiency. Their leaders may not be "united for promoting by their joint endeavor the national interest," but they are held together by the hope of office and the promise of patronage. This view of political activities is less idealistic than that presented by Edmund Burke, but it conforms more closely to the facts, and for that reason is considered more satisfactory by present-day students of public affairs. It finds expression in Professor Sait's definition of a political party as "an organized group that seeks to control both the personnel and the policy of the government." [2]

There are times when it is difficult to distinguish political parties from other organized groups that also seek to control the government. Such organizations as the National Association of Manufacturers, the American Federation of Labor, the Congress of Industrial Organizations, and the American Legion have their own legislative programs, and frequently endorse or denounce candidates for public office. Their programs are usually more restricted than the platforms of the regular political parties, however, and they do not put their own slates of candidates into the field. Instead they try to win the support of the nominees of one of the major political parties— or of both major parties, if possible; and their endorsement of individuals is given without regard to party lines. [3]

Definitions of party are found, not only in the writings of statesmen and political scientists, but also in the election laws of the several states. These legal definitions are necessary, for in most states the political parties are subject to more or less thoroughgoing regulation. The organization and functions of party committees, the collection and expenditure of party funds, and the tests of party membership are all prescribed by state law. Provision is made for party nominations of candidates for public office. Therefore the exact nature of party must be determined.

---

[1] "Topics of the Times," in *New York Times,* July 25, 1937.

[2] *American Parties and Elections,* p. 141.

[3] There is an interesting article, "Pressure Groups *versus* Political Parties," in the September, 1948, issue of *The Annals* of the American Academy of Political and Social Science, pp. 17–23.

The laws of the states do not approach the question from the standpoint of principle, as did Burke, or from the point of view of function, as do the modern realists, but on the basis of demonstrated voting strength.   In New York, for example, a party is any political organization that polled at least twenty-five thousand votes for governor at the last preceding gubernatorial election.   Other states use substantially the same formula, varying the required number of votes or expressing the requirement in terms of a percentage.

Such tests of party have one obvious advantage; they are easily administered.   But they fail to square with the facts in many cases.   Thus the Socialist Party may be a legally recognized party after one election and yet sink to the level of an "independent body" two years later—merely because some of its adherents have changed their allegiance or have neglected to go to the polls.   Other minor parties may never be able to acquire the legal rank of parties under state law.

RISE OF THE PARTY SYSTEM

In the first days of American independence parties were generally regarded with disfavor.   Madison, writing in the *Federalist,* urged that the Constitution should be adopted because it would tend "to break and control the violence of faction," and Washington took occasion in his Farewell Address to warn the people "in the most solemn manner against the baneful effects of the spirit of party. . . . It serves always to distract the public councils, and enfeebles the public administration.   It agitates the community with ill-founded jealousies and false alarms, kindles the animosity of one part against another, foments occasional riot and insurrection. . . . There is an opinion that parties in free countries are useful checks upon the administration of the government, and serve to keep alive the spirit of liberty.   This within certain limits is probably true—and in governments of a monarchical cast, patriotism may look with indulgence, if not with favor, upon the spirit of party.   But in those of popular character, in governments purely elective, it is a spirit not to be encouraged. . . . A fire not to be quenched, it demands a uniform vigilance to prevent its bursting into flame, lest, instead of warning, it should consume."

But the "spirit of party" was not quenched by Washington's words.   On the contrary, it burned with greater intensity after his retirement to private life.   Democrats, or "Republicans," as they first called themselves, vied with Federalists for control of the government and eventually became the dominant party in American politics.   About 1834 their supremacy was challenged by the Whigs, who borrowed their name from England.   Then came the collapse of the Whig Party some twenty years later, the birth of the Republican Party and its rise to national power, the period of Republican supremacy, continuing until 1874, and the subsequent rivalry of Republicans and Democrats.   Throughout the history of the United States, almost from the adoption of the Constitution, there have been two major parties competing for popular favor, and occasionally the struggle has been complicated by the rise and fall of "third parties."

Yet there are still many persons who believe, like Washington, that partisanship is "a spirit not to be encouraged."   Their constant aim is to make all government *non-partisan,* despite the obvious fact that partisanship is merely a synonym for differences of opinion, which are certain to exist under any scheme for managing public affairs.

In the cities, as previously pointed out,[4] non-partisanship has met with some success.   This is not at all surprising, for good city government is largely a matter of sound administration and does not involve policy determination to any considerable extent.

But state government necessitates a much greater emphasis on politics— that is (using *politics* in its proper sense), the determination of policies— so non-partisanship has proved less popular.   There is non-partisan selection of judges in fourteen states, certain school officers in four others, and members of the legislature in Minnesota and Nebraska.   Elsewhere, when adopted for state-wide offices, the non-partisan plan has generally been abandoned after a short trial.

THE FUNCTION OF POLITICAL PARTIES

In every generation the party system has been a target for the heavy artillery of reform, yet it still flourishes.   Political parties are accepted by the people as a matter of course and supported as a matter of principle. It is reasonable to suppose, therefore, that parties serve a useful purpose in the general scheme of government.   Their function is, in fact, threefold.

Provision of a Political Creed

First, they assort the many questions of public policy and find a common ground on which large numbers of voters may unite in order to make their political beliefs effective.   In other words, they make it possible to express the will of the "people"—that mystical, composite deity of which every professional politician is the self-appointed high priest.   Without parties—

[4] See page 283.

or organized groups, whatever their name—united action would be virtually impossible; the fact that few men think exactly alike on *all* public questions would be an insurmountable obstacle.   But differences of opinion can often be reconciled.   In many instances they relate only to minor issues or matters of detail and can readily be compromised or brushed aside as inconsequential.

All that is needed, therefore, in order to present a united front, is a political creed phrased in general terms—a platform so broad that all manner of men may stand upon it without crowding.   The political parties meet this need.   Their platforms are often said to be evasive and platitudinous, and undoubtedly the description is accurate.   But it is difficult to see how the allegiance of a majority of the voters could be won and kept with a more specific declaration of principles.

Responsibility for Candidates

Second, the political parties provide continuous, collective responsibility. They are the guarantors of the integrity and efficiency of the men and women whom they present to the electorate as candidates for public office. When maladministration is prevalent and corruption is the order of the day, the party in power must take the blame; when efficient administration is firmly established and honesty is generally accepted as the best—and safest —policy, the party in power may reasonably claim the credit.

Continuous responsibility is highly important, for without it the voters are virtually powerless to express their displeasure.   They may refuse to re-elect a faithless public servant—provided, of course, that he is a candidate for re-election.   They may demand his impeachment, though they realize that impeachment is a slow and cumbersome process.   They may recall him if the laws of their state provide for the recall and apply it to his office.   Beyond that they cannot go, unless the official's acts are of such a nature as to justify criminal prosecution.   But party responsibility places a new weapon in the hands of the voters.   It enables them to vent their wrath upon the party, even if the individual dies, retires or absconds.   For a political party does not die or desert the field; it strives continuously to win public support and thus control the government.

The collective nature of party responsibility should also be emphasized. In the average state the whole structure of government has been designed with a view to preventing too much concentration of authority in any one person; therefore no one person can be blamed when promised reforms fail to materialize and old evils continue unabated.   The governor may declare that the secretary of state and the treasurer, over whom he has no control, are at fault; or he may point out that the senate has refused to confirm his appointments, or charge that the legislature has made unwise appropriations and refused to abide by his veto.   The secretary of state and the treasurer may reply that they are trying to save the state from the consequences of the governor's folly.   The members of the legislature may criticize the governor's appointments and legislative recommendations.

In this maze of charges and countercharges the voter is hopelessly bewildered.   He has no ready way of ascertaining the truth.   If he tries to select certain individuals for punishment at the next election, he is as likely to pick the innocent as the guilty.   But he can make no mistake when he places the blame on the party.   For every political party is collectively responsible for the public acts of the men chosen to office as its representatives.   If it selects its candidates unwisely, it must be prepared to pay the price of popular disfavor.

Information on Public Business

Third, the parties perform a valuable service by informing the electorate on public questions.   The information thus supplied may not always be accurate; it may be twisted and warped to meet the requirements of temporary expediency or long-established tradition.   But at least the voters are apprised that important public business awaits their consideration, and if they stay at home on election day instead of playing their part in the process of government, the political parties cannot fairly be blamed.   Moreover, the misrepresentations of one party will almost certainly be pointed out by the other.   Arguments in favor of virtually any proposal or any candidate will be met by arguments in opposition.   Thus both sides of the story are told, and the discriminating voter has an opportunity to weigh the merits of men and measures.

For these reasons the party system has become an established and essential part of democratic government.   The parties do not always perform their threefold function perfectly; sometimes they do not even perform it well. Their platforms are often unsatisfactory, and their candidates unworthy of public office.   Parties created to promote noble principles now function chiefly to control ignoble patronage.   But these abuses do not affect the fundamentals of the party system.   As long as men are permitted to express their divergent views on public questions, they will organize into political parties for the furtherance of their respective beliefs.

DOMINANCE OF NATIONAL PARTIES IN STATE AND
LOCAL ELECTIONS

The two major political parties that occupy the center of the national arena also dominate the governments of the states and of most cities. Governors and state legislators, mayors and councilmen are usually chosen on the basis of their Republican or Democratic allegiance.   To many people this merger of national and local interests seems unfortunate, since it encourages disregard of local problems.   Local issues are settled on the basis of national party platforms and candidates.

In strict logic there is no reason why the national record of a party should bear any relation to the selection of local party representatives, but the voters are not strictly logical.   They can readily be swayed by appeals to party loyalty or party prejudice, and such appeals are commonly made. Therefore mayors are elected to office because they will "support the president"—a promise they are powerless to make effective; and governors are chosen because they oppose or favor some particular variety of farm relief, although it should be obvious that their opposition or advocacy can have no effect on the policy of the national government.

But this condition of affairs should occasion no surprise.   National issues are more spectacular than local questions and make a more dramatic appeal to the voters.   The nation is big—as big as the forty-eight states combined, and its vast proportions endow it with a certain prestige that no state can share.   Moreover, the national parties find it decidedly advantageous to control state and local governments—in part because well-trained local party organizations are extremely valuable in winning national elections, and in part because local patronage provides a convenient means of rewarding zealous party workers.   It seems likely, therefore, that national affairs will continue to overshadow matters of purely local concern and that local issues will be decided along national party lines in the future, as they have been in the past.

The experience of England with separation of national and local parties may well be cited at this point.   For many decades party lines were loosely drawn in local elections, and candidates were chosen for office at municipal elections without much regard to their national party affiliations.   In London the Municipal Reform Party and the Progressive Party maintained their own organizations, quite separate from the national parties.   To a very large extent, it must be admitted, the members of the Municipal Reform Party were recruited from the ranks of the Conservatives, while the Progressive Party drew heavily on Liberal support.   There was, however, no formal alliance. But the Labor Party's rise to power completely altered the situation. Labor refused to recognize any distinction between national and local issues or national and local candidates. Thus it forced the other parties, in self-defense, to follow its lead. National and local party lines merged and have not since separated.

Nor is the English experience unique. Elsewhere the union took place long ago. In most of the countries of continental Europe everyone takes for granted that local campaigns will be conducted primarily for the benefit of the national parties.

But agitation still continues in the United States for the separation of national and local issues. Those who urge this reform propose two ways of accomplishing it. First, they suggest that state and local elections be held on a different day from the national election, or in a different year. The voters would then be free to devote their undivided attention to state and local problems. But this plan has met with little favor. The other suggestion is that state and local officials be chosen without regard to party affiliation. The spread of the non-partisan movement in cities and its limited success in state government have already been discussed.[5]

THE TWO-PARTY SYSTEM

Throughout the course of American history a number of "third" parties have been forged in a flame of revolt against the major party organizations. But in virtually every instance [6] the flame has died out, leaving the major parties still in control. Just why the two-party system should be so firmly established in the United States is a question not easily answered.

Most democratic nations make use of a multiple-party system that raises every faction to the importance of a party and makes majority control by a single party virtually impossible. Government is conducted by coalitions —combinations of political groups whose tenets are not widely divergent. In France there are about nine parties whose organizations extend beyond the confines of Parliament; the number fluctuates from time to time. Holland has eight parties, and Italy has seven.

Only in the United States, England, and some of the British dominions has the balance of power been divided between two major parties almost continuously for many years. The two-party scheme was British in its inception and became a natural part of America's political inheritance. In recent years the growth of the British Labor Party seemed for a time to

[5] See pages 282–283.
[6] The Republican Party, organized at a time when the Democrats and the Whigs controlled the political field, is the only exception.

menace the traditional two-party alignment, but the subsequent collapse of
the Liberals opened the way for the Labor Party to become the defender of
the liberal faith and thus one of the two major parties.   It has been suggested that the development of two-party government in England and
America, in contrast with world experience, is due to racial differences, to
long-established habits of thought, or to constitutional and legal provisions;
but none of these explanations is very convincing.   The problem deserves
careful investigation.

ONE-PARTY DOMINANCE IN THE SOUTH

In the Southern states, of course, the dominance of the Democratic Party
is normally taken for granted.   Victory in the Democratic primary is considered tantamount to election.   Therefore the Republican leaders do not
work very hard trying to win elections; most of them consider such efforts
a waste of time.   They strive instead to gain and retain the recognition of
the Republican Party's national leadership, for they know that without such
recognition they cannot continue to function.   Persons unfamiliar with
the ways of politics may wonder why anyone bothers to work for the Republicans in an unbreakably Democratic Southern state.   They may ask
what rewards are to be gained from laboring in a lost cause.   The rewards
are numerous and can be very substantial when a Republican president
is in the White House.   For there are many federal jobs in every state
to be filled by presidential appointment, and, of course, these jobs go to
those persons recommended by the state's regular Republican organization.   The old-time Southern Republican politicians were concerned
chiefly with questions of patronage; in fact, they actually preferred to keep
the party weak so that there would be fewer party workers clamoring for
jobs after election day.   But the picture has changed considerably in recent years.   The Republicans have won only one presidential election
in the last quarter of a century, and therefore have had little opportunity
to reward their Southern followers.   Many of the patronage politicians
have lost interest.   Their places have been taken by business and professional men who regard politics as a delightful but expensive hobby.
"Most of them are overwhelmed by the futility of it all, but they keep the
faith in a quiet spirit of dedication not unlike that of the Britisher who,
although living in the jungle surrounded by heathen, dresses for dinner." [7]
Such men are not at all interested in keeping the party small and exclusive;
on the contrary, they do their amateurish best to gain new converts and,

[7] V. O. Key, Jr., *Southern Politics,* p. 293.

if possible, to win elections. At times they make a surprisingly good showing. The Republicans of Virginia actually polled forty-five per cent of the vote for governor in the 1953 election, which suggests that Virginia may be moving toward a genuine two-party system.

When one party is in complete control, the normal pattern of politics assumes a very different aspect. The primary election is not merely a device for choosing the party's nominee; it is in effect the final election. Therefore the real battle is among the rival candidates for the majority party's nomination, and it must be fought before the primary. All the serious contenders bear the same party label, so the regular party machinery is not supposed to be used for the benefit of any one of them. This theoretical impartiality actually fits the facts in some Southern states, whereas in others it runs directly counter to the gross favoritism displayed by Democratic Party officials. But it may fairly be said that the average Southern Democratic contender for his party's nomination to public office relies largely on his own personal organization, which is almost certain to be much less durable, and much more expensive to the candidate, than the regular machinery of the party.

ORGANIZATION OF THE MAJOR PARTIES

The minor parties are so incompletely organized that they merit no more than passing mention in a discussion of party organization. In some states, or parts of states, they may establish fairly complete hierarchies of committees, from precinct committees to state governing bodies. The Socialist Party, for example, maintains its local organization in many of the larger cities, and tops this local setup with a national executive committee of nine members. But only the two major parties are completely organized on a nation-wide scale; for all practical purposes their organization is the organization of political parties in the United States.

Committees

Most important in the organization of each party is the national committee, which consists of one man and one woman from each state and territory. This committee and its work lie beyond the proper scope of a volume dealing with state government, but a few words are necessary in order to present a clear picture of party organization.

The presidential and vice-presidential nominees of a party are chosen by a national convention, which also adopts the party's national platform. Upon the national committee rests the responsibility of calling the convention, organizing it, and directing its activities along the lines desired by the party leaders. After the convention, the committee is charged with the conduct of the campaign. It raises funds and spends them as it sees fit; it prepares campaign literature; it maintains a speakers' bureau for the purpose of flooding the country with oratory.

In the intervals between national elections it keeps a watchful eye on political conditions in the states. Although it is the nominal superior of state and local committees of the party, it has no direct means of controlling their activities. Only through its prestige, its use of party funds, and its supervision over party speakers and workers can the national committee influence the local party organizations.

Both of the major parties also maintain congressional committees. These committees, composed of members of Congress, have no official connection with other party committees, but co-operate with them in furthering the party interests.

State and local committees differ from the national and congressional committees in that their organization and functions are commonly prescribed by state law. The only exceptions are found in the South, where parties are still regarded as voluntary associations, and in a scattered handful of other states that still retain the convention system for the nomination of party candidates. Elsewhere parties have been recognized as essential parts of the machinery of government, and therefore have been subjected to strict public regulation.

At the head of the party organization in each state is a central or executive committee, which ranges in size from ten or eleven members to several hundred. The members of this committee are chosen by the local committees, by conventions, or, more commonly, by direct vote of the party members. Usually they serve for two years, though longer terms are coming into favor. The powers of a state central committee are seldom clearly defined, but they relate chiefly to the management of the campaign. Funds are obtained and distributed, meetings are arranged, literature is prepared and widely circulated. Deals with the rival party or with rival candidates may be arranged if circumstances warrant. The central committee is, in fact, the party's state board of strategy. It takes whatever steps may be necessary to insure victory at the polls. To a considerable extent, especially in the collection of campaign funds and the selection of campaign speakers, it supplements the work of the national committee. In some states it exercises a measure of supervision over the local committees, but such instances are exceptional. The more common arrangement leaves the local committees free to conduct their own affairs in their own way, subject only to the necessity of maintaining harmonious party relationships.

No exact description of local committee organization can be given, because it varies so widely from state to state.   There are county committees, city committees, township committees, ward committees, precinct committees.   Each major division of local government has its party organizations representing the two dominant parties, and perhaps one or more minor parties in addition.

The local committees perform substantially the same functions as the national and state committees, though on a smaller scale.   Some of them —especially the county and city committees—usually play an important part in the management of party affairs and the distribution of local patronage.   Places are reserved for women on the party committees, or else separate women's committees are established.

The Precinct Captain

At the base of the pyramid of party organization is the precinct committee—or, much more commonly, a single individual who bears the title of precinct captain or leader.   In a few states he is known as precinct committeeman, even though he may be the sole member of the "committee."   Under state law and party rules he is generally elected by the party's voters in the precinct, but in a considerable number of states he is appointed by the ward leader or some other party officer.   Regardless of statutory and other provisions the actual choice is almost invariably made by someone high in the party councils, and this choice is ratified by the voters—should ratification be necessary—as a matter of course.   Comparatively few voters take the trouble to mark their ballots for the office of precinct captain; therefore the votes of the party workers, their friends and relatives, and others who can be depended on to "vote right" are sufficient to make the popular will, as expressed at the polls, coincide with the will of the ward or district leader.

The chief function of the precinct captain is to carry the precinct for his faction on the day of the primary election—and, if possible, for his party at the final election.   Failure to win, especially at the primary, may cost him his leadership and wreck his political career.   So he naturally regards every election as a matter of vital importance.   He tries to make as good a showing as possible, even if the final result of the city- or state-wide balloting is not in doubt, because he knows that he will be judged solely on the basis of the returns from his precinct.   His superiors—the men who control the affairs of the party—are not especially interested in his methods. They give him a free hand. They are not likely to question his political morality. But failure is one sin that they will not forgive.

In many rural districts, and in some of the smaller cities, the precinct leader devotes only a small part of his time to politics. Most of his working hours are claimed by some other vocation, and he regards politics as a pleasant, though somewhat exacting, diversion. He may be attracted by the excitement of the game, the opportunity for petty profit through appointment to some minor post, or the possibility of establishing friendships that will further his business interests. But he seldom considers politics a matter of life or death, and neither knows nor cares about the fine points of political technique. He is frankly an amateur—or, at most, a semi-professional. Of course, this description does not fit all rural precinct leaders. Some of them make politics their only business, and a very serious business indeed. Their methods are so unscrupulous as to cause city politicians to turn red with shame or green with envy. But they should not be considered typical; they are exceptions to the general rule.

In the larger cities, however, everything is different. The spoils of office are many times greater, and therefore worth a hard fight. And urban politics *is* a hard fight, from start to finish. It is a game for the professional, and not the dilettante. The precinct captain is almost invariably a full-time political worker. He has no spare hours for other business, and very few hours for pleasure, for he must be always within easy reach of the voters of his precinct, ready to serve them as occasion may arise. He must be prepared to give them help when they need it, regardless of whether that help takes the form of advice, information, money, food, coal, or political influence. His power rests on the solid foundation of service. After all, it would be foolish for him to use closely reasoned arguments in an attempt to convince the electors that they should support his ticket, for some other party or faction might have better arguments or better candidates, and then his time would be wasted. But when he asks the people to vote their gratitude, he can be certain of their support as long as he gives them cause to be thankful. The precinct captain is likely to hold some minor city or county position that pays reasonably well and does not take too much time from the main business of keeping in touch with the voters. He usually has a number of assistants—aspiring young party workers who secretly covet his position and hope to win it when he moves upward into the higher party councils or downward out of precinct leadership.

The methods of the precinct captain vary with the neighborhood that he controls. He must give service, of course; but the exact nature of that service is not everywhere the same. So he learns what the people want, and sees that they get it. As Plunkitt of Tammany Hall declared, he must "study human nature and act accordin'."

Even in a wealthy precinct the voters are quite willing to accept favors. Some complain that the assessments on their homes are too high, and regard the captain as the proper person to intercede with the assessor. Others go to the captain with their notices to appear in court to answer charges of reckless driving, because they know that a little political pressure applied at just the right spot can usually straighten out such matters. And the captain helps them all. He is an ever-present friend in time of trouble, and he asks nothing in return except a vote on election day. The vote he desires may not be for the "right" people—but, after all, a vote is a very little thing to exchange for big favors. So the people of his precinct fall into line. Their votes can be purchased, though not quite so readily as the votes of the very poor; it is merely a question of using the proper technique.

In the slums, of course, the technique is quite different. The people need the more obvious kinds of aid—food to appease their hunger, fuel to keep them warm, money to give to the landlord. They turn to their precinct captain as a matter of course, and he never fails them. To some extent, of course, the poor are less dependent on his help than they were two decades ago, before the adoption of old age pensions, unemployment compensation, and similar public services. But the precinct captain has many strings to his bow. His name heads every subscription list. He associates freely with the people and wins their confidence as a friend and neighbor. He knows the name of every man, woman, and child; he knows their hobbies and aversions, their desires and needs, and also their voting tendencies. He attends christenings, weddings, and funerals; he rejoices with those who are glad and mourns with those who are sorrowful. When any resident of his precinct gets into trouble with the police, he whispers a few well-chosen words into the ear of the desk sergeant. Or, if the matter has passed beyond that early stage, he visits the magistrate before whom the hearing is to be held. The offense may be slight—failure to procure a peddler's license, for example. So the precinct captain gets the license and pays the small fine that is imposed. But if the offense is serious and the accused is guilty beyond reasonable doubt, the precinct captain still intercedes, and his word usually carries a great deal of weight.

It is obvious that an energetic precinct captain must spend in the course of a year many times the amount of the small compensation that he may receive from some minor government position. This does not indicate, however, that he must be a man of independent means. Money—an abundant supply—will always be available for his use if he demonstrates his ability to distribute it effectively. Nor will he be questioned too closely concerning his expenditures. If some of the gold sticks to his own fingers as it passes through, that is no one's business but his own. The city and county committees, which are usually responsible for local finances, are not inclined to quarrel over a few dollars. Their task is to win elections, and they will be generous to the point of prodigality with anyone who can produce results on election day.[8]

SOURCES OF REVENUE FOR STATE AND LOCAL MACHINES

The Underworld

It may well be asked where the money comes from to finance the party machines that dominate the political life of most big cities. There are many sources of revenue. First, and among the most important, is the underworld. The gambling dens, the houses of ill repute—these places must be free from police interference if they are to survive, and they are willing to pay for "protection." Every week they turn over a portion of their profit to the policeman on the beat, or to a special agent of the police captain. The money passes through several hands on its way to the top, and some of it evaporates along the way. But a considerable part eventually finds its way into the treasury of the corrupt political machine and is ready for distribution to the ward and precinct leaders.

Public Utility Corporations

The public utility corporations also contribute large sums. In many instances their contributions are forced from them so flagrantly that the transactions can best be described as blackmail. A bill is introduced imposing unreasonable burdens upon a utility corporation, and the corporation's officials are advised to take quick action to prevent its passage. The "action" consists in writing out a check for an amount sufficient to dull the consciences of those councilmen who intended to vote in the affirmative, and delay only increases the size of the check that must be written. Some public utility officials, after a few experiences of this sort, decide that the cheapest plan is to buy the government outright—not openly, of course, but through whispered negotiations. After a time the story leaks out that the president of the street railway or the electric light and power com·pany is the real boss of the city—the man from whom all the minor poli

---

[8] For a more detailed discussion of the precinct captain and his activities, see Sonya Forthal's *Cogwheels of Democracy: A Study of the Precinct Captain.*

ticians take orders. But very few people know what to believe, and still fewer care. So "government with the consent of the governed" becomes a polite myth, and government by the utilities becomes the order of the day.

Other Businesses

It must not be assumed, however, that the utility corporations are the only businesses that contribute to the support of the political machine. They are very likely to be in the forefront, because they have special privileges from the government which must be protected. But other businesses have privileges also—alleys occupied for storage purposes contrary to law, old buildings that should have been condemned long ago by the building inspector, restaurant kitchens that are operated in an unsanitary (but cheap) manner without protest from the health department. Usually it costs less to buy from the politicians the right to keep these privileges than to comply with the law, so deals are readily arranged. State laws may— and usually do—forbid corporate contributions to political parties, but such prohibitions are easily evaded. The corporations merely pay additional compensation to their officers, who in turn contribute to various political funds.[9]

There are, of course, many business men who do not pay a single dollar to the political machine, or who pay only in order to escape petty persecution. The number of forms that such persecution may take is surprising. *No parking* regulations may be rigorously enforced against the loading and unloading trucks of the merchant who refuses to make his contribution to "the cause," although the trucks of other merchants remain unmolested. Statutes and ordinances of every description—many of them hoary with age and almost forgotten—may be unearthed and held in readiness to cause maximum annoyance. Adequate police protection may be deliberately withheld at times when it is vitally necessary. Several months of such treatment are usually sufficient to convince a business man that he should pay for the privilege of being let alone.

Public Works Construction

Contracts for the construction of public works are also a profitable source of the machine's revenue. State laws and city charters and ordinances commonly provide that every contract shall be awarded to the lowest responsible bidder, but this requirement is easily evaded. The favored con-

[9] See Dean E. McHenry's article, "Present Party Organization and Finance," in the September, 1952, issue of the *Annals of the American Academy of Political and Social Science*, pp. 122–126.

tractor's bid is almost invariably found to be the lowest, and this miracle is performed by means of a secret agreement assuring lax inspection, or by some other trick, such as the specification of patented materials that no other contractor can obtain or the omission of important features that are subsequently to be added as "extras" at excessively high prices. The contractor then shares his huge profit with the politicians who made it possible.

In the years immediately following the close of the Civil War, when the infamous Tweed Ring of New York City was at the height of its power, the construction and equipment of the county court house became a scandal of vast proportions. "When designed in 1868 its cost was estimated at $250,000. Before the end of 1871 a sum variously estimated at from $8,000,000 to $13,000,000 had been expended upon it, and it was still un-finished. This was effected, as was afterwards proved in judicial pro-ceedings, by the simple method of requiring the contractors, many of whom resisted for a time, to add large sums to their bills, sums which were then appropriated by Tweed, Connolly, and their minions or accomplices." [10] Bills submitted by contractors and approved by the city auditor included $404,347 for safes and $7,500 for thermometers. Today the corrupt poli-ticians who control the destinies of many American cities handle such mat-ters less blatantly, and somewhat less crudely. But their methods have not altered radically in more than three quarters of a century.

Political Assessments

Considerable sums are also obtained from the political assessment of officeholders. Some years ago, when the spoils system was a part of the accepted order and virtually every person in the public service held his position by reason of his ability to control votes, political assessments were accepted without question. It was considered quite proper that public officials and employees, selected through the influence of the dominant party, should show their gratitude by contributing to the party's campaign fund. Failure to contribute the required amount—two per cent of each month's salary, or four per cent, or even ten per cent, as the case might be —would result in speedy removal from office. Thus the parties used their control of government to obtain funds that could be used for the purpose of making their control of government still more secure. It was a vicious circle.

More recently the merit system has made considerable headway. The

[10] James Bryce, The American Commonwealth (1914 ed.), Vol. II, p. 390.

people have learned to regard public office as a public trust, and to demand that positions in the public service be filled without regard to party affiliation. It follows naturally, therefore, that officeholders should not be required, under pain of dismissal, to contribute to party campaign funds. In theory, at least, they have been selected because of their special fitness for the positions they hold, and not through political influence. So they owe nothing to either party. Conforming to this modern viewpoint, state statutes and city ordinances now commonly prohibit the political assessment of public officials and employees, and impose heavy penalties for violations. Yet assessments are still levied in many state and city governments, and those who are forced to pay dare not complain. Sometimes the demands of the party organization are thinly veiled as requests, but everyone understands what is meant.

BOSS CONTROL

The nominal head of the party within a state is the chairman of the state central committee. Within a city the chairman of the city committee is supposed to possess similar authority. It often happens, however, that the titular chief is not the chief in fact. Instead, actual authority may rest in someone who is merely a member of the committee, or who does not hold any party or public office. His name may not be connected with the government of state or city in any formal way; his words may have no binding effect in law. Yet he is the boss—the absolute master of the government! Like the centurion of old he is able to say: "For I am a man under authority, having soldiers under me: and I say to this man, Go, and he goeth; and to another, Come, and he cometh; and to my servant, Do this, and he doeth it." [11] Governors, mayors, state legislators, municipal councilmen, and a host of minor officers do his bidding, for they know that their political fate is in his hands.

Some years ago, when George B. Cox was asked if he were boss of Cincinnati, he unhesitatingly replied in the affirmative.

"Of course," remarked his interrogator, "you have a mayor, and a council, and judges?"

"I have," Cox admitted, "but"—he pointed with his thumb back over his shoulder to the desk—"I have a telephone, too." [12]

Usually the boss shuns important public office and even chooses a minor

[11] Matthew VIII, 9.
[12] Lincoln Steffens, *Autobiography*, pp. 483–484.

rôle in the party organization, for he knows full well that official position brings responsibility.   And he prefers, naturally, to hold the substance of power without being held accountable for its use.   His method is to arrange the election of puppet governors, mayors, and others, who will dance when he pulls the strings and take the blame when trouble arises.   Of course, there are some exceptions—some bosses whose vanity has led them to seek public office despite the obvious disadvantages of such a course.   But most bosses prefer to remain in the background.

This discussion of bosses and their habits should not lead to the assumption that every state or every city has its boss—its irresponsible despot who holds undisputed sway and is recognized by everyone as the unofficial head of the government.   There are many states that have never known the evils of bossism, or have remained unbossed for long periods.   Even in the industrial states and in the great cities, where the large spoils of office draw the corrupt politicians as sugar attracts a swarm of flies, dozens or even scores of aspiring political workers may strive in vain against one another for undisputed leadership.   There may be ward bosses, even though no one is firmly established as boss of the city; or there may be city bosses vying for state control.   Generally speaking, bossism is less prevalent in the states than in the cities.   Even a small state has a relatively large area and many diverse interests that cannot readily be reconciled.

The structure of American government—state and municipal [13]—lends itself readily to boss control.   In most instances it is still based on the theory of checks and balances; it rests on the assumption that concentration of power is dangerous and must be avoided at any cost.   Thus it virtually destroys the possibility of effective leadership under the constitution and laws.   And, since legal leadership is prohibited, extra-legal leadership takes its place.   The boss assumes the control that is denied to the governor and the mayor.   He takes the many loose ends of government and weaves them into clear design.   Scores or even hundreds of nominally independent officials acknowledge his authority.

Richard Croker, boss of New York for many years, saw very clearly the source of his power.   One day he was asked: "Why must there be a boss, when we've got a mayor and—a council and—"

"That's why," he broke in.   "It's because there's a mayor *and* a council *and* judges *and*—a hundred other men to deal with.   A government is nothing but a business, and you can't do business with a lot of officials who

---

[13] The council-manager form of government and, to some extent, the commission plan, are exceptions to this general rule.   For a discussion of these schemes of municipal government, see Chapter 10.

check and cross one another and who come and go, there this year, out the next. A business man wants to do business with one man, and one who is always there to remember and carry out the—business." [14]

The surest way to strike at bossism, therefore, is to remove the need for it. When the state constitution or the city charter provides specifically for a responsible leader, irresponsible leadership is less likely to flourish. The experience of the federal government is in point. The federal Constitution recognizes the president as the leader of the nation by placing broad authority in his hands; and it is interesting to note that *there has never been a national boss*. Similar concentration of power in the chief executives of states and cities would not work an immediate transformation. Political machines created with infinite care during a long period of years would not crumble overnight. The spoils of office—the life-blood of politics—would still attract the politicians. But bosses and their machines would no longer be an essential part of government, and thus the first step would be taken toward their ultimate elimination.

PROBLEMS

1. Study the organization of the major political parties in your community. To what extent do the rank and file of the party members participate in party affairs and influence party decisions?

2. Make the acquaintance of your precinct leader (or leaders, if both of the major parties are organized in your precinct). What methods do they employ to secure support for their candidates?

3. How many private organizations in your community are interested in influencing legislation? What methods do they employ to secure the adoption of laws that they have sponsored or indorsed?

4. Trace the newspaper accounts of some recent graft prosecution, and note the methods used by the political machine to enrich its members.

5. Who is the boss of your city or state? Study the history of his life, as far as you can obtain the facts from the newspapers or other sources, and try to learn the methods that he uses to remain in power.

SELECTED REFERENCES

Allen, Robert S., ed., *Our Sovereign State*, 1949.
Beals, Carleton, *The Story of Huey P. Long*, 1935.
Bean, Walton, *Boss Ruef's San Francisco*, Berkeley, Calif., 1952.
Binkley, Wilfred E., *American Political Parties; Their Natural History*, 1943.
Bone, Hugh A., *American Politics and the Party System*, 1950.

[14] Lincoln Steffens, *op. cit.*, p. 236. Reprinted by permission of Harcourt, Brace and Company, Inc.

Carlson, Oliver, and Blake, Aldrich, *How to Get into Politics; The Art of Winning Elections*, 1946.

Childs, Richard S., *Civic Victories*, 1952.

Cousens, Theodore, *Politics and Political Organization in America*, 1942.

Edge, Walter, *A Jerseyman's Journal; Fifty Years of American Business and Politics*, 1948.

Forthal, Sonya, *Cogwheels of Democracy: A Study of the Precinct Captain*, 1946.

Gosnell, Harold F., *Machine Politics: Chicago Model*, 1937.

Harris, Thomas O., *The Kingfish; Huey P. Long, Dictator*, New Orleans, 1938.

Key, V. O., Jr., *Politics, Parties, and Pressure Groups*, 3rd ed., Chaps. II–XII, XV, 1952.

———, *Southern Politics*, 1949.

Lynch, Denis T., *Boss Tweed*, 1927.

Mailey, Hugo V., *The Italian Vote in Philadelphia Between 1928–1946*, Philadelphia, 1950.

McKean, Dayton D., *Party and Pressure Politics*, 1949.

Merriam, C. E., and Gosnell, H. F., *The American Party System*, 4th ed., 1949.

Minault, S. Sydney, *Corrupt Practices Legislation in the Forty-Eight States*, 1942.

Moon, Henry L., *Balance of Power: The Negro Vote*, 1948.

Moscow, Warren, *Politics in the Empire State*, 1948.

Odegard, Peter H., and Helms, E. A., *American Politics; A Study in Political Dynamics*, rev. ed., 1947.

Penniman, Howard R., *Sait's American Parties and Elections*, 5th ed., 1952.

Salter, John T., *Boss Rule*, 1935.

———, *The Republican Organization of Philadelphia*, 1933.

Steffens, Lincoln, *The Autobiography of Lincoln Steffens*, 1931.

Stoddard, Theodore Lothrop, *Master of Manhattan*, 1931.

Van Riper, Paul P., *Handbook of Practical Politics*, 1952.

Walby, H. O., *The Patronage System in Oklahoma*, Norman, Okla., 1950.

Zeller, Bell, *Pressure Politics in New York*, 1937.

Zink, Harold, *City Bosses in the United States; a Study of Twenty Municipal Bosses*, North Carolina, 1930.

CHAPTER 16

Direct Legislation and the Recall

There are many times when the work of legislative bodies fails to reflect accurately the popular will.   Every session of almost every state legislature and city council provides instances of such misrepresentation. Measures that would almost certainly receive the disapproval of the voters are passed by overwhelming majorities, while other proposals that have been given many evidences of popular favor are sidetracked for indefinite periods.   In other words, elected representatives do not always represent. Sometimes downright dishonesty is responsible for their failure to respect the wishes of their constituents; much more commonly ignorance of the true state of public opinion is to blame.   But whatever the reason, no one can deny that there is often a wide gap between the popular preference and the legislative product.

Some persons contend that the best way to correct this weakness in our governmental system is to permit the voters to enact their own laws, and many states and cities have accepted this point of view.   In those jurisdictions, therefore, the voters are authorized to take matters into their own hands whenever they believe that their interests have not been properly protected.   They may veto any legislative acts of which they disapprove. They may write their own laws and put them directly on the statute books when their elected representatives prove too slow or too indifferent.   As thus stated, the theory of direct legislation is beyond reproach.   There can be no quarrel with the results it seeks to achieve.

THE INITIATIVE AND REFERENDUM

Direct legislation assumes two forms—the initiative and referendum. The initiative provides a means whereby any voter or group of voters may propose a measure and, after securing a sufficient number of endorsements, submit it to the electorate.   The first step is to put the proposal into the form of a bill, so that it may be ready for enactment; then a petition must be prepared to accompany the bill.[1]   When the petition has been signed by the requisite number of voters it is filed with the proper official.

From this point the procedure varies considerably, according to the laws of the several states.   Nine states [2] specify that the measure shall without further formality be placed on the ballot at the next regular election or at a special election; this form, which is generally favored by American cities, is known as the direct initiative.   Under the indirect initiative, as found in six states [3] and a small number of cities, a popularly proposed bill does not go to the electorate unless it fails of passage at the next session of the legislature.   Three states [4] complicate the matter still further by making provision for both the direct and indirect initiative, and requiring a larger number of signatures or earlier filing of the petition if the direct form is used.   Three other states [5] permit the legislature to submit a rival proposal to the people if it cares to do so.   Regardless of these details, the fundamental principle is the same: the fate of the measure as placed upon the ballot is determined by the voters at the polls.

The referendum is designed to secure an expression of popular opinion concerning measures that have been passed by the legislature.   In its earlier form, as applied to ordinary legislation, it merely authorized the submission to the people of such proposals as the legislature might care to place upon the ballot; it was an optional referendum—so called because the option rested with the legislature of submitting pending legislation to a popular vote or of withholding it.   More recently the obligatory referendum has become the generally accepted type; under its provisions a certain percentage of the voters—usually five per cent, but sometimes ranging as high as ten per cent—may compel the legislature or the city council to submit to the electorate any newly enacted measure.

The laws of those states and cities that have adopted the obligatory referendum provide that bills passed by the legislative body shall not go into effect immediately, under ordinary circumstances, but shall remain inoperative for a certain period—usually ninety days.   During this period of suspension the opponents of any proposal have an opportunity to draft a referendum petition and secure the requisite number of signatures; if they are successful in their efforts the measure is then placed on the ballot, and its fate is decided by the voters.

[1] In California there must also be a summary of the proposed measure prepared by the attorney-general of the state upon the written request of the measure's sponsors.

[2] Arizona, Arkansas, Colorado, Missouri, Montana, Nebraska, North Dakota, Oklahoma, Oregon.

[3] Maine, Massachusetts, Michigan, Nevada, Ohio, South Dakota.

[4] California, Utah, Washington.

[5] Maine, Michigan, Nevada.

Certain laws designed to meet specific emergencies cannot remain in-operative for ninety days, however, without entailing considerable hardship. In recognition of this obvious fact, "emergency" measures are permitted to go into effect as soon as they have been duly enacted. This provision is necessary, yet it leads to serious abuses. The legislative body has the power to determine what constitutes an emergency, so it usually places in the emergency category every enactment that is likely to arouse popular disapproval. The number of such "emergencies by definition" is aston-ishingly large. Many states and cities have tried to correct this evil, but without much success. Their constitutions and charters commonly require a three-fifths, two-thirds, or even three-fourths vote in order to make an emergency declaration valid. But an extraordinary majority for this pur-pose can usually be obtained without the slightest difficulty. Thus the legislators ignore the spirit of the fundamental law.

The initiative and the referendum are separate devices, and it is quite possible to have one without the other. In fact, there are many states that do not have the initiative, and yet regularly refer proposed constitutional amendments to the voters. Some cities also fit into this category with regard to charter amendments. Two states—Maryland and New Mexico —have adopted the referendum for ordinary legislation without making provision for the initiative. Generally speaking, however, the initiative and referendum as instruments of ordinary lawmaking go hand in hand.

The first state to authorize the initiative and referendum for ordinary legislation was South Dakota, in 1898. Other states soon followed its example—Utah in 1900, Oregon in 1902, Montana in 1906. By 1918 the total had risen to nineteen, and two other commonwealths had adopted the referendum only. In addition, the voters of Mississippi had approved a constitutional amendment directing the legislature to establish systems of direct legislation, but the state supreme court declared the amendment invalid. Since 1918 no state has been converted, and none has deserted.

San Francisco was the first large city to make provision for direct legisla-tion. It did so in 1899, but there were no additional converts among the cities of the United States until 1907, when Des Moines borrowed Galveston's commission plan, and added the initiative and referendum as "improve-ments." Since then direct legislation has generally been regarded as an integral part of commission government, and more recently it has been associated with the manager plan. Provisions for its use are almost always found in commission and manager charters, and have undoubtedly helped to popularize the newer schemes of government.

Merits and Defects of Direct Legislation

Many merits are claimed for direct legislation. According to its proponents, it takes ultimate control from the professional politicians and makes the people the real masters of their government. Certainly this is "a consummation devoutly to be wished," but there is reason to doubt that it is achieved by the initiative and the referendum. For the forces that mold public opinion—the "pressure groups" that dominate the legislative programs of state and nation—seem to operate quite as successfully in states that have direct legislation as in other commonwealths. They simply modify their technique to meet the changed situation.

After all, it is idle to speak of the people as the authors of any proposal. "The people" do not draft a measure, frame a petition, go from door to door for signatures, and stimulate the necessary enthusiasm. These things are done by organized interests—manufacturers' associations, labor federations, farm bureaus, utility corporations, war veterans' organizations. Signatures are obtained by professional canvassers; there are a number of companies that make a business of securing signatures to proposals of any sort, charging five or ten cents a name for this service. When the petition has been duly filed, more money is spent in "accelerating public opinion." And the final result, registered at the polls, is apt to be a triumph of good advertising and masterful showmanship, masquerading in the guise of self-government.

Sometimes the questions placed on the ballot by means of initiative or referendum petitions are of such a nature that the people may reasonably be expected to have intelligent opinions concerning them. Frequently, however, this is not the case. Highly technical questions are submitted to the electorate, as well as many non-technical measures of obscure purpose and uncertain result. Fortunately the voters have grown wary of such proposals. In self-defense they have generally adopted the maxim: "When in doubt, vote no!" Therefore the negative of any question enjoys a certain advantage at the polls.

It is often said that direct legislation stimulates popular interest in government. When all the laws are made by representatives who commonly misrepresent, the inevitable result is general indifference to the legislative product. The people know that their wishes will probably be ignored, regardless of the party in power, so they gradually acquire a cynical disregard for all parties and all agencies of government. They need, but do not have, some means of correcting the mistakes of the legislative body. Direct legislation supplies that need. It enables the voters to enact the laws that they desire and set aside the proposals of which they disapprove. Thus popular interest quickens, and popular enthusiasm is aroused. So runs the argument.

Unfortunately, it does not fit the facts. The people are actually less concerned with the proposals placed upon the ballot for their consideration than with the men who offer themselves as candidates for public office. As a rule the total vote for candidates exceeds the total vote for and against measures by at least twenty-five or thirty per cent—frequently by forty or fifty per cent. This means that a substantial portion of the electorate, though sufficiently interested in the choice of candidates to go to the polls and vote, is too indifferent or too uncertain of the right course to mark the part of the ballot reserved for initiative and referendum measures. Occasionally there are exceptions to this rule, but they serve only to emphasize the plain fact that the initiative and the referendum do not stimulate the interest of the people.

Other claims are also made for direct legislation—it produces more carefully drafted laws, because the sponsors of an initiative measure are more conscious of their need for trained assistance than are the almost equally ignorant legislators; it permits the proponents of a reform to go directly to the people, instead of accepting perforce the emasculating amendments of the legislative body; it eliminates the need for detailed constitutional or charter limitations upon the power of the legislative branch, and thus leads naturally to shorter constitutions and charters. But there is little reason to believe that these highly desirable results have actually been achieved.

The objections to direct legislation are numerous. It is "government by minorities," because so many important questions are decided by a minority of the voters. It weakens legislative responsibility, and thereby discourages able men from seeking election as legislators. It ignores the increasing complexity of governmental problems and the increasing difficulty of solving such problems by popular vote.

The validity of these arguments is not easily determined. Direct legislation may be minority legislation, but so is lawmaking by legislative bodies. All government is, to a large extent, the handiwork of minorities. As to the charge that direct legislation has an unfortunate effect upon the caliber of legislators, the only possible retort is that no one really knows. At every election the people select some incompetents to represent them in the state legislature or the city council, as well as some men of outstanding ability; but they did not always choose wisely before the advent of direct legislation. The initiative and the referendum were adopted because of popular dissatisfaction with the work of the legislative body. The argument that present-day legislation is often too technical for popular consideration is difficult to refute.   Many questions appear on the ballot that cannot be intelligently decided without careful investigation of intricate data—detailed information that the public does not possess and would not know how to use.   Eight states [6] attempt to overcome this objection by mailing to every voter a publicity pamphlet containing the text of each proposal plus arguments pro and con.[7]   These arguments may be officially prepared, as in California, or prepared by private persons who are sufficiently interested to pay for space in the official pamphlet, as in Oregon.   The value of the publicity pamphlet is uncertain.

By far the most serious objection to direct legislation, in the opinion of many students, is its conflict with the short ballot movement.[8]   Both reforms propose to make democratic government more effective, but they strive to reach this goal by opposite routes.   The short ballot is predicated on the theory that the voter is already overburdened, that he cannot do a great deal and do it well, and that his effective participation in government depends upon his release from the multitudinous tasks imposed upon him by a long ballot.   Direct legislation, on the other hand, postulates that the voter's capacity for participation in government is infinite, that he can and will assume other burdens in addition to those already placed upon his shoulders, and that his failure to elect suitable representatives can best be cured by permitting him to make his own laws.

Between these two points of view there seems to be no tenable middle ground.   Yet thousands of so-called liberals and progressives—many of them prominent in public life—constantly reaffirm their advocacy of direct legislation *and* the short ballot with no realization of the inconsistency of their stand.   In defense of direct legislation it is sometimes said that it is not used to excess; seldom are more than three or four proposals placed on the ballot at a single election.[9]   But there are some exceptions.   California is notorious for its excessive use of the initiative and referendum; in 1952 the people of San Francisco were asked to pass upon forty-seven questions—twenty-four constitutional amendments and twenty-three proposed changes in the city's charter—at a single election.   In 1948 the voters of Louisiana were called upon to consider forty-one proposed amendments to the state constitution.   They were asked to decide, among other things, whether

[6] Arizona, California, Massachusetts, North Dakota, Ohio, Oregon, Utah, Washington.

[7] Nebraska achieves approximately the same result by publishing this information in the newspapers.

[8] For a discussion of the short ballot movement, see pages 293–295.

[9] For a sympathetic appraisal of direct legislation, see the article by Joseph G. La Palombara and Charles B. Hagen, "Direct Legislation: An Appraisal and a Suggestion," in the June, 1951, issue of the *American Political Science Review,* pp. 400–421.

THE VOTER'S BURDEN IN CALIFORNIA: General Ballot—Alameda County—November 4, 1952 they favored "the issuance of revenue bonds by the City of New Orleans for the purpose of refinancing the mortgage indebtedness outstanding against the Upper Pontalba Building and for the purpose of constructing, acquiring, extending and improving other revenue-producing properties of the city." The people were supposed to have opinions, also, concerning the organization of sub-sewerage districts and the compensation of members of boards of supervisors of garbage districts.[10]

THE RECALL

Frequently associated with direct legislation is the recall, because these two reforms first sprang into popularity at about the same period.   Both are concerned with the improvement of government, but the specific evils they seek to correct are very different.   The recall is a device for making public officials continuously responsible to the electorate.   The first state to adopt it was Oregon, in 1908, but it had been made a part of the Los Angeles charter five years earlier.   It is now used by twelve states [11] and by most commission and manager cities.

The recall provisions of state constitutions and city charters vary somewhat in detail, but fundamentally they are much the same.   They authorize the removal of a public official by an adverse popular vote at any time after the first few months of his term.   The first step is the preparation and circulation of a petition for the officer's removal.   This petition, which states the reasons—or at least the alleged reasons—why its sponsors desire to have the officer recalled, must be signed by a certain percentage of the voters of the state.   The required percentage ranges from ten to thirty, but twenty-five is by far the most common.   To secure the signatures of twenty-five per cent of the voters of a state, or even of a large city, is no easy task; it almost invariably necessitates a substantial expenditure of money. Therefore the recall cannot be put in operation by every disgruntled group that disapproves of the management of state affairs.   When the necessary signatures have been obtained, the petition is filed with the appropriate official, who certifies that all legal requirements have been met.   The question of the officer's removal from office is then placed on the ballot for the voters to decide.   Usually their decision is registered at an election held

[10] For a good statement of California's experience with direct legislation, see Winston W. Crouch's pamphlet, *The Initiative and Referendum in California,* published by the Haynes Foundation in 1950.   See also the same author's "Direct Legislation Laboratory," an article in the February, 1951, issue of the *National Municipal Review,* pp. 81–87.

[11] Arizona, California, Colorado, Idaho, Kansas, Louisiana, Michigan, Nevada, North Dakota, Oregon, Washington, Wisconsin.

for this special purpose, but if a general election is close at nand the matter may be postponed until that time.

There is no general agreement as to the proper form of the recall. In some states and cities the two questions—whether the officer shall be removed, and who will succeed him in the event of removal—are placed side by side upon the ballot. In other jurisdictions the voters merely express their opinions on the question of recall. The officer's successor, if any, is then chosen at a subsequent election, held usually within thirty days. Some state constitutions and city charters permit the officer whose removal is sought to be a candidate for re-election. Under such circumstances it is quite possible for a public official to be recalled from office and at the same time re-elected to complete the remainder of his term. Even though a majority of the voters express their disapproval of him, their failure to agree upon his successor may enable his adherents to secure for him a substantial plurality over rival candidates, and thus return him triumphantly to power. In order to prevent such a farcical result, a number of jurisdictions exclude the name of the involved official from the list of candidates. While this arrangement accomplishes its purpose, it offers no safeguard against another danger—the possibility that an unpopular official will be replaced by someone whom the voters desire even less.

An illustration is necessary to make the matter clear. Governor A is recalled from office because fifty-five per cent of the voters express a desire to be rid of him. The other forty-five per cent of the electors may be his stanch adherents, but they cannot vote to return him to power, because his name is excluded from the ballot. So one of the rival candidates is chosen to complete the remainder of the term. The winner's plurality may be small; he may be able to secure the support of but twenty per cent of the electorate. But twenty per cent is sufficient, *if it is larger than the vote cast for any of the other aspirants.* Seventy or even eighty per cent of the voters may be definitely opposed to the successful candidate. They may consider him far less desirable than the man whom they have just voted to remove. They have no effective means of expressing their dislike, however, unless they resort to another recall election as soon as the new governor has taken office. Therefore, although a number of forms of the recall are in operation, no one of them is entirely satisfactory. The problem is not easily solved.

Merits and Defects of the Recall

The recall has been a stormy petrel of American political life ever since its introduction nearly half a century ago. It has been warmly defended and bitterly denounced. Actually it has not accomplished one tenth of the good claimed for it, nor has it produced one tenth of the evil so freely predicted. Its effect on the conduct of public affairs has been very slight. The most obvious merit of the recall is that it permits the immediate removal of unpopular or unfaithful public servants. Without it, a governor elected for four years would probably continue in office until the end of his term, even though he had completely lost the confidence of the people by repeated displays of gross inefficiency, blatant partisanship, or even downright dishonesty. Impeachment proceedings could be brought against him at any time, of course, but impeachment trials are inevitably slow, awkward, and uncertain. The recall, on the other hand, is direct and sure. It produces results when results count. It enables the people to rid themselves promptly of public officials whose popularity has waned.

It should not be forgotten, however, that the recall can be twisted and warped to serve partisan ends quite as readily as it can be used to secure higher standards of efficiency and honesty. It can be used to embarrass high-minded public officials in the proper performance of their duties. Sometimes it is so used. Bird and Ryan, in their careful monograph on *The Recall of Public Officers,* report the case of a state senator who was recalled because of his aggressive fight against the vice interests,[12] and of a city manager who lost his office by popular vote "because he was an outsider, because he stepped on the toes of certain more or less powerful men in Long Beach, and because the local populace was unenlightened as to the nature and requirements of the office." [13] Professor Barnett's *Operation of the Initiative, Referendum, and Recall in Oregon* repeats the same story with infinite variations. Only occasionally do the people know the real motives that prompted the circulation of a recall petition.

An argument commonly advanced in favor of the recall is that it forces public officials to consider the public welfare at all times, instead of just prior to election day. It is said that unless the threat of removal from office is ever present, many officials will disregard the desires and interests of their constituents, trusting to luck and their own facile tongues to justify their misconduct when the day of accounting arrives. But if they know that they may be recalled at any time, they will be much more likely to keep to the straight and narrow path. Their direct responsibility to the people is continuous, and not periodic. It might also be added that this continuous responsibility not only reduces the likelihood of improper partisanship or actual dishonesty, but at the same time compels all public officials to keep in close touch with the electorate.

[12] Pp. 275–279.
[13] Pp. 224–226.

When impeachment is the only method of removal, the honest, efficient governor who happens to be more interested in the science of administration than the art of politics may neglect to keep the public sufficiently informed concerning the work of the state. Secure in the knowledge of his own integrity and ability, he may forget that the voters will not take these qualities for granted. But if he is subject at any time to the recall, he cannot afford to wait for the ultimate justification of his policies. He must take the people into his confidence, and explain the reasons for every important decision. Thus the recall possesses a definite educational value; it increases the opportunities of the voters to learn about their government.

Of course, this is purely deductive reasoning. No one knows whether the adoption of the recall has actually reduced corruption in government. No one can say with assurance that public officials have really been forced to lay greater emphasis upon the task of informing the electorate.

In fact, it might be argued with equal plausibility that the recall has virtually destroyed the possibility of far-sighted planning in matters of state. In those commonwealths where it has not been adopted, a governor or other officer is free to use the methods that seem to him best suited to the solution of each problem, even though the reasons for his choice are not immediately apparent to the casual observer. He knows that he will not be required to give an accounting until election day, and that the intervening months or years will make the wisdom of his course apparent to all except the blindest partisans.

But the governor who is subject to the recall is not so fortunately situated. He must consider the immediate political effect of every action. He must shift his course to meet every passing gust of public fancy. His policies must be determined largely on the basis of their momentary popularity. In other words, expediency must replace constructive statesmanship. It is easy to overemphasize this danger; perhaps it has little foundation in fact. But it is doubtless quite as real as the danger that public officials will loot the public treasury or heedlessly pursue their haughty way merely because they do not have to fear a recall election.

A very strong argument in favor of the recall is that it leads naturally to longer terms for public officials. Students of government agree that terms of office are too short, generally speaking, and for many years they have constantly advocated longer tenure. But the people have been slow to sanction longer terms. They have been loath to sacrifice their opportunity of calling public officials to account at frequent intervals. They have not forgotten the old adage that unchecked power soon degenerates into tyranny. The introduction of the recall, however, has undoubtedly lessened the popular opposition to longer terms. The voters have become more willing to trust their officials with power for long periods, because they can now remove them from office at any time without waiting until some far distant regular election day.

In all fairness, however, it should be pointed out that the recall, though it leads naturally to longer terms, at the same time destroys their chief advantage. Longer tenure is desirable because it gives officeholders a fair chance to become familiar with their work and demonstrate their ability before they are forced to campaign for re-election. For a reasonable period they are placed in authority, with the understanding that at some definite time in the future they must accept full responsibility for the results of their work. But the recall robs them of any reasonable opportunity to prove the merit of their plans, free from popular interference. They must be prepared to undergo the ordeal of trial by ballot *at any time,* on the assumption that democracy is thus better served.

The original proponents of the recall advocated its adoption, in part, on the ground that it would be a weapon of last resort, to be used only in cases of extreme urgency. It would be a safety valve, they said, and not merely another fly-wheel added to the already complicated machinery of government. For the most part this prediction has proved correct. Only one governor,[14] and a mere handful of other state officers, have ever been recalled from office. Even in local elections the recall has been used sparingly. While it has "become a part of the established political technique" in some jurisdictions,[15] such instances are not typical.

One of the objections commonly raised by the foes of the recall is that it places an added burden on the voter. The average citizen already has more political obligations than he cares to assume. Therefore it would seem desirable to reduce the number of elections instead of increasing them. In this respect, at least, the recall is a step in the wrong direction. It imposes additional responsibilities. This objection is not serious, however, because recall elections are so infrequent.

Much more to the point is the contention that the recall is an unsound remedy for the political ill it seeks to cure. If the public invariably chose virtuous, efficient men for public office, recall elections would never be necessary. But everyone recognizes that some of the men chosen to public office are neither virtuous nor efficient. The public has erred; its judgment has been faulty. And in order to correct these mistakes of the people, the

[14] Governor Frazier of North Dakota, in 1921. Subsequently the people of the state elected him to the United States Senate.

[15] Bird and Ryan, *op. cit.,* p. 259.

friends of the recall propose that the people be permitted to try again.   If they guessed wrong the first time, perhaps they will guess right on the second or third attempt!   To suggest more democracy as a means of correcting the defects of democracy is like prescribing more whisky for the drunkard or gold for the spendthrift.

PROBLEMS

1. Obtain a list of the initiative and referendum measures submitted during the last five years to the people of your state—or to the people of a neighboring state, if your state does not employ the initiative and referendum for ordinary legislation.   What percentage of these measures dealt with nontechnical matters on which sound popular judgments might well have been formed?

2. Describe briefly the procedure established for direct legislation in your state or some neighboring state.

3. Contrast the California and Oregon official publicity pamphlets.   Which type do you prefer?   Defend your choice.

4. Prepare a brief history of the recall in one of the twelve recall states.

5. Draft a model state constitutional amendment authorizing the use of the recall.   Defend briefly the principal provisions of the amendment.

SELECTED REFERENCES

Barnett, J. D., *The Operation of the Initiative, Referendum, and Recall in Oregon*, 1915.

Bird, F. L., and Ryan, F. M., *The Recall of Public Officers; A Study of the Operation of the Recall in California*, 1930.

Crouch, Winston W., *The Initiative and Referendum in California*, 3rd ed., Los Angeles, 1950.

Hall, Arnold B., *Popular Government*, 1921.

King, Judson, *The American Voter as Lawmaker*, Washington, D.C., 1923.

Oberholtzer, E. P., *The Referendum in America*, 1912.

Pollock, J. K., *Direct Government in Michigan*, Ann Arbor, 1940.

———, *The Initiative and Referendum in Michigan*, Ann Arbor, 1940.

Zeitlin, J. V. P., *Initiative and Referendum; A Bibliography*, Los Angeles, 1940.

PART FIVE

The Protective Services

CHAPTER 17

Safety

The federal Constitution forbids the states to keep troops without the consent of Congress.[1] At the same time it recognizes the need for state militia forces of some sort, and authorizes Congress "to provide for organizing, arming, and disciplining the militia, . . . reserving to the States respectively, the appointment of officers, and the authority of training the militia according to the discipline prescribed by Congress."[2]

THE NATIONAL GUARD

Creation of the State Militia

The first law of Congress concerning the state militia was enacted in 1792. Its most significant clause merely provided for the enrollment of every able-bodied male citizen between the ages of eighteen and forty-five, requiring him to furnish a good musket at his own expense. The state forces originally organized under the provisions of this act were far from uniform. Training and equipment varied greatly from state to state.

Inefficiency of State Troops

The federal government made no effort to enforce minimum standards. At first it contributed nothing toward the support of the state forces, but in 1808 provision was made for an annual appropriation of two hundred thousand dollars, to be used for the purpose of arming and equipping the militia. The arms and equipment thus obtained were turned over to the states, and utilized under state rules and regulations. For nearly eighty years no significant change was made in the law. Few crises came to reveal the pitiful weakness of the state forces.

[1] Art. I, Sec. 10, Cl. 3.
[2] Art. I, Sec. 8, Cl. 16.

Federal Supervision of State Forces

Not until 1886 did Congress make even a feeble gesture in the direction of central supervision of state military activities. But in 1903 it laid the foundation of the present system. The measure adopted at this time was faulty in many respects, however, and in 1916 it was replaced by the National Defense Act, which provided in sweeping terms for federal supervision—one might almost say control—of the state militia. The word "militia" was dropped altogether, the term "National Guard" appearing in its place. The change in phraseology is significant.

In its present form the law fixes the size of the National Guard in each state, and specifies the kinds of troops that must be maintained. Air units have become important components of the Guard in recent years. The qualifications for National Guard officers are enumerated at length. Officers must be examined as to their physical, moral, and professional fitness by a federal board. Each troop, battery, and detachment of the National Guard must assemble at regular intervals for drill and inspection, and must participate in annual encampments. Federal law prescribes in detail the kind of training to be given, fixes the period of enlistment, and requires an oath of allegiance to the United States as well as to the particular state.

In order to induce the states to accept this comprehensive supervision of their militia, the federal government assumes nearly all the expenses of maintaining the National Guard. It pays the officers and men of Guard units, and issues their arms and equipment. Only the armories are provided by the states, and they are now financed in part with federal funds. The conditions imposed by Congress have been accepted by all the states, and as a result the forces of the National Guard now bear the mark of federal standardization.

Federal and State Service

In time of war or other grave emergency the National Guard may be called into the federal service. The president is not required to wait until war threatens. He may call out Guard units whenever the public order is menaced. Several presidents have, in fact, found it necessary to make use of state troops in the enforcement of federal laws. Usually, however, the National Guard has been held in reserve; its periods of peacetime duty, whether in federal or state service, have been infrequent.

Gubernatorial Control

The governor is the constitutional head of the state militia, but he does not actually assume command of his forces, as did some governors in the early days of American history.   Instead, he exercises control through an adjutant-general, who is directly responsible to him for the organization, training, and work of the state troops.   The governor selects the adjutant-general, but his choice is narrowly restricted by the necessity of securing federal approval.   Federal standards are high, and politically minded governors experience considerable difficulty in evading them.

Strike Duty

From time to time the governors of the several states call upon their National Guard troops to enforce the law.   Most commonly these calls are for the preservation of order during industrial disputes.   Troops are directed to protect private property and to prevent militant demonstrations by strikers.   Sometimes they do this work very effectively; quite often, however, they only succeed in provoking bloodshed.

Strike duty requires an excessive amount of time—an amount that the officers and men, nearly all of whom are filling positions in the business or professional world, can ill afford to spare.   It necessitates prompt action, but the National Guard is not organized to act promptly.   Valuable time is lost while the necessary units are mobilized.   Moreover, strike duty is scarcely a military function; it is more closely akin to the regular work of the police.   Small wonder, therefore, that state governors have become increasingly reluctant in recent years to call out Guard units during industrial disputes.

Service during Disasters

With regard to disasters, however, the story is very different.   State troops are commonly called into service following any great calamity, such as flood, fire, hurricane, or earthquake.   At such a time they assist in giving necessary first aid treatment, distributing food and medical supplies, constructing temporary shelters, and guarding private property.   In the event of atomic bomb attacks on the great cities of the United States, the National Guard will undoubtedly play an important part in maintaining order and caring for bomb victims.

STATE POLICE FORCES

Every state has a police force or highway patrol. Its primary purpose, in most states, is to enforce the motor vehicle laws. Usually it is empowered to compel obedience to the criminal laws of the state,[3] but in most jurisdictions it is not equipped to do a thorough job of law enforcement, and therefore limits itself almost exclusively to traffic matters. There are, however, some important exceptions. About one fourth of the states have set up police forces that systematically enforce the criminal laws in rural areas, thus supplementing the work of local sheriffs and constables. State police forces vary widely in size. Thus the Wyoming force has only thirteen police officers, while that of Pennsylvania has more than thirteen hundred.

Duties

LAW ENFORCEMENT. The state police organization is generally regarded as an agency for the enforcement of state law in the rural districts. Law enforcement in the cities is primarily a task for the municipal police. There are times, however, when this distinction cannot be strictly maintained. A state patrolman has authority to make arrests within the limits of a city as well as beyond its boundaries, and when he is in hot pursuit of a criminal he is not likely to stop at the city line. Nor is it reasonable to expect him to do so.

Yet care must be taken not to affront local pride, for the result may be the severance of friendly relationships between state and municipal authorities. If the local police find that the area within their jurisdiction is subject to "invasion" by state forces at frequent intervals, they are almost certain to show their resentment in the one way open to them—by refusing to co-operate in the detection of criminals. The state police must definitely subordinate themselves to the local police authorities when operating within the cities, or else be prepared to play a lone hand. Usually they accept the rôle of subordinates.

Thus the state policeman who enters a city on business normally reports first at city headquarters, explains his errand, and requests local assistance. Even this precaution does not invariably eliminate friction, however; the state policeman may still be considered an outsider who has exceeded the proper scope of his authority. A great deal of tact is sometimes required

---

[3] There are, however, twelve states that specifically limit their highway patrols to the enforcement of the traffic laws. These states are Arizona, Colorado, Minnesota, Mississippi, Montana, Nebraska, Nevada, North Carolina, North Dakota, Ohio, Tennessee, and West Virginia.

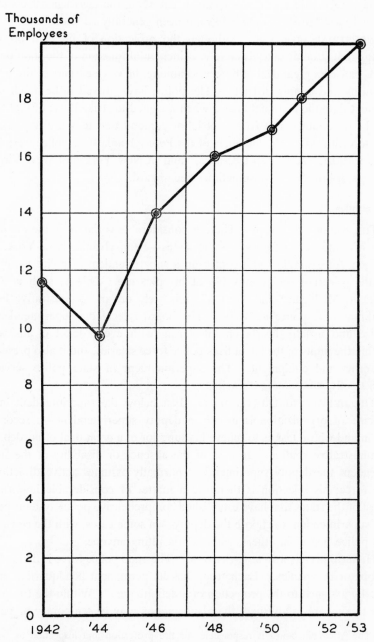

Based on figures from *The Book of the States, 1954–55,* and previous volumes.

to establish and maintain co-operation.   The police forces of a few states are sent into the larger cities without the consent or even the knowledge of the city authorities for the purpose of enforcing the laws against commercialized vice, but this practice has not been generally adopted.

INDUSTRIAL DISPUTES.   Although the protection of life and property during industrial disputes is merely an incidental function of the state police, it has caused a great deal of bitterness among the wage earners of the manufacturing and mining districts.   The police have proved to be much more efficient than the National Guard when assigned to strike duty; of that there can be no doubt.   But friends of labor contend that they are too efficient and too ruthless.   The members of the Pennsylvania state police were once known as the "American Cossacks," and in New York and West Virginia charges of brutality have sometimes been heard.

Organization

THE SUPERINTENDENT.   There is considerable variation in the organization of state police forces.   Some states—Pennsylvania, New York, and Oregon, for example—vest control in a superintendent of police appointed by the governor and removable at his pleasure.   Others, such as Connecticut, Michigan,[4] and West Virginia, rely on an administrative board to direct state police activities.   The board selects the superintendent of police and usually insists on interfering with every detail of his work. Within the limits of the law it fixes police force salaries, and it also prescribes uniforms and equipment.   The superintendent of state police serves in a distinctly subordinate capacity.

THE DEPUTY SUPERINTENDENT.   Just below the superintendent in the scheme of organization is usually a deputy superintendent—a second in command whose task is to relieve his superior of a great deal of burdensome administrative routine.   In case of the absence or disability of the superintendent the deputy superintendent normally assumes active direction of the force; his selection is therefore a matter of considerable importance. Most of the states that have established comprehensive police systems permit the superintendent to choose the deputy—in some cases, with the consent of the police board; in others, without consulting anyone.

HEADQUARTERS AND SUBSTATIONS.   The state police force is divided into troops or companies.   Each troop has its permanent headquarters and is usually assigned to the protection of a definite area.   Within the troop area substations are established; these substations may be temporary or perma-

---

[4] The Michigan board is responsible for fire protection and inspection as well as police inspection.

nent.   The advantage of temporary substations is that they may be moved from time to time to permit adequate patrol of all sections of the state, and also to facilitate concentration of state troops at any spot where trouble is anticipated.   Such substations are commonly located in private homes, boarding houses, or small hotels.

When permanent substations are used, the troops are housed in buildings owned by the state; therefore the men are less likely to become unduly familiar with any one group of persons, and less likely to display favoritism in the enforcement of the law.   On the other hand, they must of necessity neglect the more remote sections unless the force is very large or the state very small.   Reserves, if any, are quartered at the main troop stations.

Patrol of the rural sections is the regular work of the rank and file of the force.   In some states the men are assigned to definite routes that they must follow according to a prescribed time schedule; more commonly, however, they are permitted considerable discretion as to the exact roads to be covered and the time to be spent in each community.   Their work has been greatly facilitated in recent years by the equipment of patrol cars with two-way and even three-way radio facilities.

TRAINING.   The amount of training provided for new recruits is far from uniform.   Some states have established regular police schools, where new members of the state force are given systematic instruction for a period of weeks or even months.   In other states the men receive only a little superficial training and are then assigned to patrol duty, in the hope that experience will soon teach them the things they ought to know.   Formal instruction for new recruits is becoming increasingly common.   So, too, are refresher courses for experienced members of the force.   A number of the larger universities are co-operating in this work.[5]

MUNICIPAL POLICE FORCES

Agents of the State

The police forces of the cities are primarily agencies for the enforcement of state law.   They are concerned also with municipal ordinances and regulations, but the enforcement of state statutes is their most important task.   Every serious crime is defined by state law;[6] every professional

---

[5] For a brief discussion of the compensation of state police forces, see "State Police and Patrol Compensation," by Robert L. Mawhinney, in *State Government,* February, 1953, pp. 52–54.

[6] Excepting, of course, those acts that are solely offenses against the federal government.

criminal deliberately challenges the state's supremacy. Quite naturally, therefore, the courts declare that municipal policemen are agents of the state. This doctrine has been affirmed in case after case.[7]

BUT UNDER MUNICIPAL CONTROL. Yet all the judicial decisions combined do not provide the governor or any other state officer with the means of controlling local police forces. City policemen are agents of the state, of course, but they are locally chosen, locally paid, locally disciplined, and subject to local dismissal. Therefore they take orders only from their locally selected superiors, and give no heed to state policy. They enforce only those state laws that meet with local approval.

Temporary State Control

During the second half of the nineteenth century it became fashionable to transfer the control of urban police forces from municipal to state agencies. New York set an example for other states in 1857, when it created a metropolitan police district comprising New York City and surrounding territory and gave to the governor the power to appoint the members of the metropolitan police board. During the next two decades a number of other states followed suit. Most of these changes were made at the insistent demand of prominent citizens of the communities affected. Locally controlled police departments had quite generally become corrupt and inefficient, and there was a widespread belief that state control would speedily remedy this condition of affairs.

Unfortunately, however, the belief proved ill-founded. After a time, therefore, the prominent citizens who had previously urged state control of the police as a remedy for civic ills began to demand that control be returned to the cities. Local self-government became the immediate goal, and as a result of this movement the states relinquished their authority over municipal police forces. State control was retained, and has continued to the present day, in only a few cities—Boston, Baltimore, and St. Louis. To the list of municipal police forces under state jurisdiction, however, must be added the police force of Kansas City, Missouri, which was placed under a state board in 1939 after several years of corruption.

Police Department Organization

There are a number of cities that combine police and fire protection in a department of public safety, but students of public administration generally regard this arrangement with disfavor. Better results can undoubtedly be obtained by separating police and fire protection.

[7] See Buttrick v. Lowell, 1 Allen (Mass.) 172 (1861).

GROWTH OF MUNICIPAL POLICE FORCES

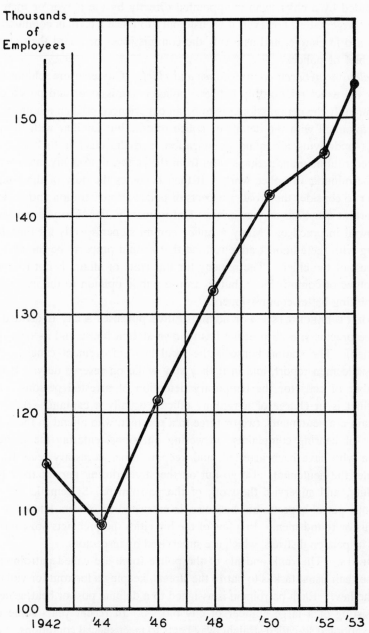

Based on figures from the Federal Bureau of Investigation's *Uniform Crime Reports, 1953,* and preceding issues.

THE HEAD OF THE POLICE DEPARTMENT. There is considerable variation in the organization of police departments. Sometimes the department
is headed by a chief, who is appointed directly by the mayor or manager.
In the larger cities, however, it is customary to place a civilian commissioner
or board in charge, and as a rule the commissioner or board then chooses
the chief of police.

Relations between commissioner and chief. City charters seldom make
clear the exact relationship between police commissioner and police chief.
Presumably the commissioner is to be an experienced civilian administrator,
unacquainted with the details of police routine but familiar with the principles underlying all sound organization, and the chief is to be a highly
trained routine man, perhaps risen from the ranks, thoroughly familiar with
all the minutiæ of police work. It then becomes the duty of the commissioner to consider the broader aspects of police administration and to decide
important questions as they arise. Unfortunately, this theory is not always
followed in practice. Many a police commissioner spends his time interfering with the administrative routine that should properly be the exclusive
interest of the chief. The remedy for this state of affairs is not to abolish
the office of commissioner, but to arouse public opinion to the necessity of
appointing better commissioners.

POLICE PRECINCTS. For administrative purposes a city is divided into
police precincts; each precinct has its own station house and its own quota
of men. The station house is the local law enforcement center. To it
the policemen report, and in it they stay while on reserve duty. It has a
number of cells for the temporary detention of arrested persons. Each
precinct is in charge of a ranking officer, usually a captain. Below the
captain are lieutenants, two or three to a precinct, who attend to the routine
work of hearing complaints, answering questions, entering the names of
those who have been arrested, and keeping other necessary records. As
a rule, the lieutenants also go out on the street during part of their hours
of duty, and supervise the work of the patrolmen. Systematic and continuous patrol supervision, however, is entrusted to officers known as ser-
geants or roundsmen. In a few of the big cities the precincts are combined
into inspection districts, which are supervised by inspectors.

BEATS. The rank and file of the police force are called patrolmen because their usual task is to patrol the streets, keeping a lookout for violations
of the law. Each patrolman is assigned to a definite post or beat, generally
consisting of a large number of city blocks. In recent years some cities
have adopted so-called straightaway beats to meet special conditions. Each
beat is laid out as nearly as possible in a straight line, extending for a certain

distance along a single street, though perhaps including side streets for half a block on either side of the main thoroughfare. The straightaway plan enables a patrolman to have a continuous view of most of his post, and also makes it easier for his superior officers and for citizens to find him.

Foot and motor patrol. Most patrolmen cover their beats on foot, especially in the larger cities. No other method of patrol would prove satisfactory in many districts—the downtown business center, for example. The foot policeman may require a long time to cover his post, but he covers it more thoroughly than does a motorized patrolman. He is able to devote his entire attention to his work, and free to investigate every suspicious occurrence. There is no doubt, however, that automobile and motorcycle patrol can be used to advantage, especially in the small communities and in the suburban districts of the metropolitan centers. More than one half of all patrol is now motorized in cities with populations of less than half a million, and complete motorization has been adopted in a few cities. The popularity of the automobile in patrol work is due in large measure to the development of the radio as an instrument of crime suppression. Several hundred police radio broadcasting systems have been installed, and many of these systems in the metropolitan centers also serve small municipalities that lack broadcasting facilities of their own.

PLATOONS. Since police duty is continuous, it becomes necessary to divide a force into shifts or platoons. Three platoons are the rule, one serving from eight A.M. until four P.M., another from four P.M. until midnight, and the third from midnight until eight in the morning. These platoons are commonly of uniform size. They should not be, however, because more men are needed for patrol duty at night than during the day hours. A certain number of policemen should always be on reserve duty, which simply means that they should sleep at their station houses, or possibly at city headquarters. In a few instances, the members of the force are shifted at regular intervals from one platoon to another, so that everyone will have his share of day, night, and reserve service. The once popular two-platoon system has now been discarded by most cities because it makes too heavy demands on the policeman's time. When only two platoons are used, every member of the force must be on active or reserve service two hours for every hour he is off duty.

THE DETECTIVE FORCE. Although the detective force is much smaller than the uniformed force, its work is very important. The chief of the detective bureau is commonly appointed by the head of the department, perhaps upon the recommendation of the chief of police. No distinction is made between detectives and uniformed policemen except that the rate of pay for detectives is sometimes slightly higher. Men are regularly shifted from patrol duty or traffic regulation to detective service, and back again to patrol or traffic duty. As a rule, no attempt is made to select detectives because of their special aptitude for the work. A policeman who has shown conspicuous bravery or has demonstrated his ability to pull the proper political wires is often assigned to the detective bureau as a relief from the monotony of street patrol.

Police Training Schools

The idea of special training for policemen, which was once considered very radical, is now generally accepted. As early as 1911 Detroit established a training school for recruits, and a few years afterward New York extended the scope of its early experiments to provide a three months' course of instruction for all new members of its force. Special classes were also formed for patrolmen and officers who expected to take promotional examinations. All the larger metropolitan centers have since followed the lead of Detroit and New York, though in many instances their schools offer less elaborate instruction, and for shorter periods. The problem of police training for smaller municipalities has been solved in large measure by the establishment of more than twelve hundred police schools or institutes throughout the United States. These institutes, sponsored by the Federal Bureau of Investigation in co-operation with city, county, and state law enforcement agencies, offer short programs of training in the essentials of police work. Reference has already been made to the work of the National Police Academy.[8] The only real objection to in-service training for policemen is that they are likely to be in the classroom when needed for active duty. Los Angeles has tried to overcome this difficulty by giving instruction to its patrolmen in short daily doses when they report for roll call. The International City Managers' Association sponsors a correspondence course in municipal police administration.

THE SHERIFF

His Duties

The peace officer of the county is the sheriff, whose office dates from Anglo-Saxon times. In those early days the "shirereeve"—the presiding officer of the shire or county—was a very important person. He was the governor of the shire, the military commander of its troops, and the president of its court. But the passing years have witnessed a constant reduction of

[8] See page 65.

the English sheriff's powers, until at the present time the office is of very little consequence. In the United States, however, no such change has occurred. In fact, the sheriff has managed to retain most of his early powers. Not only does he conserve the peace of the county, but in addition he commonly serves court processes and writs, and executes court decrees. He is the keeper of the county jail and sometimes the executioner.

His Payment from Fees

PROCESS SERVING. As a rule he performs all these functions very badly. His time and energy are devoted mostly to serving processes and managing the jail instead of conserving the peace, because the profit is greater. The sheriff is paid on a fee basis in almost all jurisdictions. He buys the automobiles needed for the work, and keeps them in running order; they are his personal property. From the county treasury he then collects his fees, and the net profit is his reward.

COUNTY JAIL MANAGEMENT. A considerable part of the income of the sheriff is derived from the management of the county jail. He is allowed a certain amount for feeding the inmates; seventy-five cents or one dollar a day for each prisoner is quite common. Since this sum is constant, regardless of the amount actually spent, it is to the interest of the sheriff to spend as little as possible for the prisoners' food. Some sheriffs have experimented with the near-starvation of jail inmates until they know exactly the minimum amount of food on which it is possible to sustain human life.

LAW ENFORCEMENT. As previously suggested, the sheriff's duty to enforce the law pales into insignificance when contrasted with the highly profitable functions of jail tending and process serving. Then, too, law enforcement is a much more dangerous undertaking. So the average sheriff spends very little time apprehending criminals and justifies this neglect of duty on the ground that he cannot afford to do otherwise.

Conflict with Municipal Police

An American city normally lies within the boundaries of a county. Thus we commonly have two independent agencies charged with the duty of maintaining municipal peace and order—the municipal police force, which operates solely within the city's boundaries, and the sheriff, whose jurisdiction extends throughout the entire county, including both urban and rural areas. A possibility of conflict thus exists. In ordinary routine police work this danger is not serious, however, because of the sheriff's tendency to abandon almost completely his function of crime repression.

His Selection

The sheriff is an elective officer almost everywhere,[9] for no good reason save that election is the traditional method of choice. Usually the constitution or statutes of the state prohibit him from serving two consecutive terms, so that he cannot possibly hope to acquire a complete understanding of the tasks entrusted to his care. He is an amateur—not a professional; and the provision that he may not succeed himself is a sure way to preserve his amateur status.

THE PUBLIC PROSECUTOR

His Selection

The public prosecutor—prosecuting attorney, district attorney, state's attorney, or whatever he may be called—is an important figure in the general scheme of law enforcement. Usually he serves a single county, but this is not invariably the case. A few states combine their counties into districts, with one prosecutor for each district. Nearly everywhere the public prosecutors are popularly chosen. They are selected by the governor in two states,[10] however, and by the judges of the superior court in one.[11] Their terms of office range from two to six years; four-year terms are most common.

His Authority in Criminal Proceedings

The importance of the prosecuting attorney arises from the powerful influence that he is able to exert over the entire course of criminal proceedings. At every step in the conduct of a case, from the preliminary search for clues to the conviction of the accused person, the public prosecutor plays a leading rôle. To some extent he derives his authority from statute, but more largely he relies on custom. This tendency is quite marked in the field of criminal investigation. The prosecutor commonly forces his leadership upon the police department—chiefly by means of the party organization and the party press.

INFLUENCE WITH THE GRAND JURY. Even more pronounced is the prosecuting attorney's influence on the grand jury, a body of persons chosen by lot and ranging in number from seven to twenty-three. Unlike the petit or trial jury, a grand jury does not decide the innocence or guilt of persons

---

[9] Rhode Island is the only exception.
[10] Georgia and New Mexico.
[11] Connecticut.

accused of crime.   Instead, it merely determines whether there is sufficient evidence against suspects to warrant holding them for trial.   Its presentation of formal charges is known as *indictment;* persons who have been indicted must then stand trial for the crimes of which they have been accused. A unanimous verdict is not necessary to indict.

Since the grand jury is picked at random, and is composed of men and women who presumably know little of the law or of the science of criminal investigation, it is poorly fitted to perform its allotted task.   Therefore it is virtually compelled to rely on the prosecutor for its facts, witnesses, and opinions.   His attitude nearly always determines what action the grand jury will take, for he is in a position to suppress vital evidence—either favorable or unfavorable to the accused; to summon witnesses or neglect to do so; to tell the whole story or only a part.

ACCUSATION BY FILING AN INFORMATION.   More than half of the states now specify that prosecution may be by *information* instead of indictment, at least for some offenses, and in a number of these states the grand jury is never called except by an occasional court order.   Information is the presentation of formal charges by a prosecuting attorney against a person suspected of crime; these charges are filed in a court of competent jurisdiction and have exactly the same effect as indictment.   The person informed against must stand trial for the crime of which he is accused.   This procedure thus places responsibility squarely on the shoulders of the prosecutor.

Information has proved quite satisfactory in those states that have given it the most thorough trial.   By saving time and money and eliminating unnecessary technicalities it has demonstrated its superiority over the older method of fact-finding by amateurs.   The mistake must not be made, however, of assuming that the grand jury has entirely outlived its usefulness.   Though unsuited to the ordinary routine of separating the obviously innocent from the probably guilty, it may still prove at times an eminently satisfactory agency for investigating the alleged inefficiency, neglect, or dishonesty of public officials.

REFUSAL TO PROSECUTE.   An important source of the prosecutor's influence is his power to refuse to proceed with the prosecution of a criminal case.   Since prosecution is commonly the result of an information that he has filed or of a grand jury indictment that he has recommended, he is not likely to take this step.   But occasionally the discovery of new facts or the pressure of influential politicians may cause the prosecutor to experience a change of heart.   Thereupon he enters a *nolle prosequi* or notice that he does not intend to prosecute; he may take this step before or after the trial has begun.   The court is free, technically, to proceed with the case even after the prosecutor's support has been withdrawn, but the probability that it will do so is very remote.

NEGOTIATIONS WITH ACCUSED.   The public prosecutor frequently bargains with persons accused of crime.   He may, for example, agree not to prosecute one member of a gang in return for a full confession that can be used against the other members.   He may even enter into informal agreements for more personal reasons if he chances to be unscrupulous.   The law makes no provision for bargaining of any sort with criminals, but public prosecutors do not wait for express authorization.   They regard the power of negotiation as one of the most important weapons in the arsenal of crime prevention.

INFLUENCE IN IMPOSING SENTENCE.   When the trial of an accused person ends in conviction, the judge then pronounces sentence.   In so doing he may impose whatever penalty, within the limits of the law, that seems to him best suited to the circumstances.   He may even suspend sentence, in many instances, and place the convicted person on probation.   His decision as to the proper measure of punishment is final, except for the possibility of appealing certain cases to the higher courts.   In practice, however, a judge does not usually rely solely on his own opinion, but turns to the prosecuting attorney for guidance, for he knows that the prosecutor or one of his assistants is supposed to have studied each case carefully and should be in possession of all the facts.   Thus the power of the prosecutor is still further increased.

FAILURE TO PROTECT THE INNOCENT.   It is a maxim of the law that the prosecutor's duty is to ascertain the truth in every case that comes within his jurisdiction.   He is legally responsible for the protection of the accused, and it is his task to make certain that no unfairness is practiced.   Therefore the acquittal of the innocent should be his goal quite as much as the conviction of the guilty.   But legal maxims cannot alter the plain fact that the prosecutor is *not* the protector of the innocent, except at rare intervals and under unusual circumstances.   His success or failure is measured in terms of convictions, and every ambitious prosecutor sets out to secure as many convictions as possible.   To save from prison those who are falsely accused is noble, but not likely to lead to political preferment.

DEFENSE COUNSEL

Public Defender

Some persons, convinced that the prosecutor's office can never be transformed into an agency for the protection of the rights of the accused as long as it performs its primary function of trying to secure convictions, urge that a separate office be established in every county or district for the defense of persons held on criminal charges.   This plan has already been adopted by thirty-eight cities and counties throughout the United States.   It is used on a state-wide basis in Connecticut and Rhode Island.[12]   The public defender, as the head of this office is called, ranks equally with the prosecutor. The facilities of the state are at his disposal for the purpose of proving men innocent, just as they are at the disposal of the prosecutor for the purpose of proving men guilty.   Thus many of the abuses common to criminal trials are curtailed, and every person is given a reasonable assurance of fair treatment.

Assigned Counsel

In those jurisdictions—the overwhelming majority—that have not provided for public defenders, it is customary for the court to assign counsel to the defense of poor people who cannot afford to hire the attorneys they need.   This plan is practically worthless, however, because the fees paid from the public treasury for the defense of accused persons are so small as to attract only recent law school graduates who are badly in need of experience and shyster lawyers who hope to augment the regular compensation by means of various unsavory tricks.

THE CORONER

His Duties

The office of coroner is also a part of the machinery of law enforcement, and therefore deserves mention at this point.   The coroner is a county officer, elected by the people in most states, and virtually free from state supervision.   His task is to investigate cases of violent death and to hold inquests to determine how death occurred.   Customarily every case of sudden death unattended by a physician also comes within his jurisdiction, even if violence is not suspected.   The coroner is empowered to call a jury whenever the circumstances surrounding a death are unusual, and this so-called *coroner's jury,* which is usually composed of six persons chosen at random, then makes the decision as to the cause of death.

His Unfitness

In the entire structure of American government—federal, state, and local —there is probably no officer who is more poorly qualified than the coroner

[12] See "The Public Defender System in Connecticut," by David Mars, in the February, 1954, issue of *State Government,* pp. 29 ff.

to perform his assigned duties. There are some outstanding exceptions, of course, but the average coroner is a political worker who has been rewarded in this manner for long years of amenability to party discipline. His methods are the layman's methods—crude, blundering, ineffective.

Qualifications Needed

Yet there is probably no phase of governmental activity that requires greater knowledge or skill in order to produce satisfactory results. Accurate determination of the causes of death is extremely difficult in many cases; it calls for highly specialized information and a carefully developed technique. The specialist in this field should have a comprehensive knowledge of medicine, surgery and law. But to ask an elected coroner to meet these requirements is virtually to ask the impossible.

In some counties it is customary to have one or more physicians attached to the coroner's staff. While the degree of M.D. does not necessarily imply a knowledge of all the specialized subjects that fall within the province of the coroner, it assures a technical training that is of considerable value. A physician on the staff of the coroner can usually make the inquest less of a guessing contest and more of a scientific inquiry. But if the physician is politically appointed, as is often the case, he is likely to take his responsibilities rather lightly.

Steps to Eliminate Weakness

A few states, impressed with the weaknesses of the coroner system, have abandoned it altogether. In place of the coroner's office they have established the office of medical examiner and vested it with responsibility for determining the causes of death. Massachusetts took this step in 1877. The law passed in that year provide that the governor should appoint as medical examiners in the several counties of the state "able and discreet men, learned in the science of medicine." The judicial functions formerly performed by the coroner were transferred to the district attorney, and the coroner's jury was abolished. Subsequently Maryland, Virginia, and Rhode Island followed Massachusetts' example; New York City has had an appointive medical examiner since 1915. A number of other states, though retaining the office of coroner, have tried to strengthen it by abolishing the coroner's jury, as in Indiana, or by specifying that the coroner must be a physician, as in Louisiana.[13]

[13] See the National Municipal League's 1951 report, *A Model State Medico-Legal Investigation System.*

THE STATE FIRE MARSHAL

Thirty-six states have state fire marshals or officers with similar titles. The functions of the fire marshal, which vary somewhat from state to state, commonly relate to the prevention of fire and the enforcement of the state's fire laws.   Every serious fire—other than a forest fire—is investigated, and an attempt made to determine its cause.   Fires that bear evidence of incendiary origin are studied with especial care for the purpose of finding clues that may lead to the guilty persons.   The fire marshal also enforces the laws of the state concerning the storage, sale, and use of combustibles and explosives, and in many states he examines buildings to make certain that they are provided with proper exits and fire escapes and contain no prohibited fire hazards.   Educational campaigns designed to reduce the fire loss are commonly directed by the fire marshal; he supervises the systematic instruction of school children in ways of preventing fire and also appeals to the adult population by means of such devices as "Fire Prevention Week."   Protection against forest fires lies beyond his jurisdiction, and is commonly assigned to the state forester.[14]   Generally speaking, the fire marshal operates in the smaller cities and the rural districts, since there is no reason to duplicate the educational and inspectional activities of the metropolitan fire departments.

MUNICIPAL FIRE DEPARTMENT ORGANIZATION

Similarity to Police Organization

Municipal fire departments are organized in much the same manner as police departments.   Sometimes there is a board of fire commissioners, but more commonly department control is vested in one person—a civilian commissioner or a professional fire chief.   If fire and police work are combined in a department of public safety, the fire chief becomes merely the head of the fire bureau.   A city is divided into fire districts, which vary in size according to the amount and value of property requiring protection, the height of buildings, the congestion of population, and other factors affecting the fire hazard.

The Fire Company

The basic fire-fighting unit is the company, a little group of men assigned to a single piece of equipment—a pumping engine or ladder truck, for example.   Each company has its captain or lieutenant, and all the com-

14 See pages 489–490.

panies in a district are under the command of a battalion chief, who reports directly to the municipal fire chief.   Scattered throughout the city are fire stations, usually four or more to a district, which house the men and equipment.   It is customary to have but one or two companies at each station.

Fire Alarm Systems

When a fire breaks out, an alarm must be sent in.   This may be done from any telephone, or from any one of the fire alarm boxes that are placed at frequent intervals throughout the city.   The alarm is first sounded at headquarters, and then relayed to the proper station.   The sounding of an alarm brings prompt action.   Within three or four minutes, at the most, at least one company is at the scene of the fire.   The amount and kind of apparatus responding to a first alarm vary with the neighborhood.   If additional alarms are sounded, other apparatus goes into action, all according to a pre-arranged schedule.   A special signal, known as a general alarm, brings out virtually every company in the city.   The two-way radio, which is rapidly becoming an indispensable part of standard fire equipment, enables headquarters to keep in close touch with all the fire companies at all times.

The Battalion Chief

The first company captain to reach a fire takes charge until the arrival of the battalion chief; he then relinquishes his authority.   The battalion chief quickly surveys the situation, and maps out a plan of action.   He determines what the firemen are to do, and how their equipment is to be used. If the fire continues to make headway, he sends for additional companies. In the larger municipalities the city fire chief responds only to the most serious fires, but when he appears, he of course assumes command.

TREATMENT OF CRIMINALS

Punishment before Modern Times

Few people realize that imprisonment is a comparatively new method of punishing criminals.   There were dungeons in Europe during the Middle Ages, but they were reserved chiefly for those who had incurred the disfavor of the king or some powerful baron.   Even the jails of eighteenth-century Europe and America were used mainly for the detention of debtors, persons awaiting trial, and those convicted persons who were about to be executed or subjected to flogging or some other form of corporal punishment.   Imprisonment as a means of punishment did not come into general use until the early part of the nineteenth century.

For thousands of years—in fact, from earliest antiquity—torture and death were customarily meted out to anyone who transgressed against the established social order. The Old Testament is filled with accounts of the brutal punishment of criminals and with exhortations to kill those guilty of wrongdoing. "He that curseth father or mother, let him die the death." [15] "And the daughter of any priest, if she profane herself by playing the harlot, she profaneth her father: she shall be burnt with fire." [16]

Even in colonial America death was the penalty decreed for scores of crimes. Minor offenses were punished less severely—with the branding iron, the whipping post, the pillory. The ducking stool and the gag were reserved chiefly for nagging women.

Capital Punishment

Reliance is now placed chiefly upon imprisonment as a means of punishing criminals, reforming them, deterring others from following their example, and protecting society against their further wrongdoing. Corporal punishment is used very little except to enforce prison discipline. Fines are reserved for minor offenses, or as a supplement to incarceration. Capital punishment is still retained for certain major crimes in forty-two states of the American Union, however,[17] and in six of these states the judge and jury have no power to substitute life imprisonment.[18] The list of offenses for which the death penalty may be imposed includes murder (in every state that makes provision for capital punishment), rape (in seventeen states), treason (in fourteen), arson (in nine), and robbery, burglary, kidnaping, and train wrecking (in a scattered handful of states).[19]

Imprisonment

UNWHOLESOME ENVIRONMENT. Within each state are a number of different kinds of penal institutions—state prisons, county and city jails, workhouses and houses of correction, and state and local reformatories. The state

[15] Exodus XXI: 17.

[16] Leviticus XXI: 9.

[17] The six states that do not have capital punishment at the present time are Maine, Michigan, Minnesota, North Dakota, Rhode Island, and Wisconsin.

[18] These six states are Connecticut, Florida, New Mexico, New York, North Carolina, and Vermont.

[19] See "Trends in the Use of Capital Punishment," by Frank E. Hartung, in the November, 1952, issue of the *Annals of the American Academy of Political and Social Science*, pp. 8–19.

prisons are reserved for those who have been convicted of serious offenses, usually involving imprisonment for more than one year. Although these prisons are generally known as penitentiaries the name is clearly a misnomer, for steel bars and brutal treatment do not make criminals penitent. Almost every aspect of the prison environment confirms the inmates in their anti-social outlook and tends to make rehabilitation a virtually impossible task, for prisons are not designed to remake men; they are designed to hold them in safety until the end of their terms.

Therefore the emphasis is placed mainly on prevention of escape. Only about one third of the criminals in a penitentiary, under normal circumstances, would take desperate chances to regain their freedom, but prison architects and prison wardens find it easier to assume that all convicts are desperate. And every aspect of prison life, from buildings to discipline, reflects this assumption. Most penitentiaries are still built on the cell block plan. Most of the rules that govern the lives of the inmates are unnecessarily severe.

IMPROVED PRISON CONDITIONS. Despite its many unsatisfactory features, however, prison life in the newer penitentiaries under the higher type of prison officials is a vast improvement over the prison life of a few decades ago. Sanitary provisions are much better. Suffering from extremities of heat and cold is less common than formerly, though even in the most modern prisons there is frequently a difference in temperatures of 10° to 15° F. between the bottom and top tiers of cells. Many prison cells now in constant use are so designed that they never receive the direct rays of the sun, but a determined effort is being made to correct this state of affairs, for sunlight and fresh air are now recognized as necessities for convicts quite as much as for other people.

In the treatment of prisoners, also, marked changes have taken place. The strict rule of early days that absolutely prohibited communication with friends and relatives has been substantially modified, though most states still limit mail privileges in various ways. Nearly every present-day prison has a fairly good library, and a number of prison newspapers have been established. Prison schools are becoming increasingly common. Interesting experiments have been made with the honor system for selected groups of prisoners, and also with various forms of prison self-government.

PRISON LABOR. Persons convicted of crime and sentenced to the state penitentiary are supposed to serve their sentences "at hard labor." The idea of putting prisoners to work was originally conceived as a means of increasing the severity of their punishment, but penologists have long understood that enforced idleness is a far more drastic penalty. They point out that idleness is subversive of discipline and that it injures both the minds and the bodies of prison inmates.   Unfortunately, however, "hard labor" is little more than a meaningless phrase in many prisons, and for large numbers of prisoners.   It is almost certainly true that at least half of our prison population lives in substantial idleness.   The attitude of organized labor is largely responsible for this state of affairs.   Union leaders resent the competition of prison-made goods with the products of union workmen, and have succeeded in securing the enactment of state laws that restrict prison labor in various ways.

LOCAL JAILS.   Although living and working conditions in the state penitentiaries are unsatisfactory in many respects, they are far superior to the conditions found in most county jails, workhouses, and houses of correction, where persons serving terms of one year or less are commonly sent.   Every careful study of these local correctional institutions has dwelt upon their filthiness, their lack of proper sanitary facilities, their failure to classify prisoners, and the almost universal absence of equipment for feeding prisoners, so that meals of none too satisfactory quality have to be brought in from the outside.   Especially regrettable is the customary lack of work, because idleness leads so readily to mental, moral, and physical deterioration.   At least seventy-five per cent of all prisoners in institutions for misdemeanants are idle.

The conditions of local jails do not seem to have improved in recent years, despite extensive discussion of their shortcomings.   Some jails are better, of course, but others are definitely worse.   Since young criminals commonly make their first contacts with the county jail, rather than the state penitentiary, they are exposed to all the worst features of our penal system at the very time when they most need protection from debauching influences. Small wonder that they drift naturally into careers of professional crime! The suggestion has been made that all institutions for misdemeanants be placed under state control, so as to secure units of sufficient size to permit the classification of prisoners according to age, type of offense, personality, and number of convictions.   Such a plan, if coupled with the establishment of district industrial farms in place of the present county jails, might well be expected to accomplish the rehabilitation of a fairly high percentage of misdemeanants—especially young offenders in whom the habit of crime has not yet become firmly fixed.

Probation

Since prison life usually has a disastrous effect upon the minds and bodies of the men who are required to undergo it, any plan that can keep some convicted criminals out of prison and yet afford a reasonable likelihood of rehabilitation, together with reasonable protection for the community, deserves a thorough trial. Such a plan is probation, which originated in Massachusetts in 1878, and has since swept the country. Today it is used in almost all the states.

As a rule, though not necessarily, probation is associated with the suspended sentence. When a person convicted of crime for the first time is brought before the court for sentence, the judge who imposes the sentence may suspend its operation for a considerable period, in order to give the offender a reasonable opportunity to demonstrate his ability and willingness to live as a law-abiding citizen. During this period the offender is said to be on probation. If he is found guilty of further anti-social conduct or violates any of the conditions that the judge may see fit to impose, he is sent to jail without additional delay. But if he successfully avoids other conflicts with the law and gives promise of having abandoned his criminal ways, he is given unconditional freedom at the end of his probationary period.

Such a scheme is excellent in principle, but its successful operation requires a large staff of thoroughly trained social workers to serve as probation officers. Without such a staff probation speedily degenerates into a farce. Probation work has been hampered more or less seriously in nearly every state of the Union by poor probation officers—politically chosen, poorly paid, overworked. Despite these handicaps it has produced good results in a surprisingly large number of cases and seems destined to become increasingly important as the personnel of probation staffs improves and the courts acquire a better understanding of the fundamental factors involved.

Parole and the Indeterminate Sentence

Parole and the indeterminate sentence are other important modern developments in the field of penology. Though not necessarily related, they usually go together and are now found side by side in most of the states. Under the laws of these states prisoners are given sentences with minimum and maximum limits instead of the fixed sentences that were so generally used a few decades ago. Any prisoner who has served his minimum term may then be released by the parole agency, provided his conduct in prison points to the likelihood of his rehabilitation.

As under the probation system, however, he is assigned to some officer and required to make reports at regular intervals, either in person or by correspondence. These reports may be the merest formality, especially if personal visits are not required.   On the other hand, they may be made the means of keeping in close touch with the paroled man and guiding him along the path of good citizenship.   Everything depends on the parole officer.   It is rather discouraging, therefore, to learn that the methods of supervision are singularly inadequate in many states.

Sometimes reliance is placed solely on the written reports of parolees. No attempt is made to check the reports, which are received by a parole officer stationed at the state penitentiary.   A few commonwealths do not even have parole officers; the letters of parolees are sent to the clerk of the state board of prison commissioners or other employee.   In some states the written reports are occasionally coupled with volunteer oversight.   Part-time paid parole agents may be used.   Only about half of the states maintain regular staffs of full-time, professional parole agents.   And even in these states the parole officers are usually underpaid and overworked.

A Sentencing Commission

The suggestion has frequently been made that sentences be imposed upon convicted criminals by an administrative commission—a commission of sentences, or something of the sort—instead of by the judges of the trial courts. Two chief advantages are claimed for this plan.   First, it would eliminate the inequalities that inevitably arise when sentences are meted out by different judges sitting in different parts of the state, each governed by his own theories of punishment and entirely independent of his colleagues.   Second, it would make possible the sentencing of prisoners by skilled specialists— psychiatrists, social workers, criminologists—whose composite judgment as to the time necessary to accomplish complete rehabilitation should be of considerable value.

Within the last few years several states have adopted modified versions of this plan, with excellent results.   California led the way in 1941, with the creation of a Youth Authority having jurisdiction over most classes of offenders under the age of twenty-one.   The Youth Authority selects the institutions in which youthful offenders are to be confined.   It may grant them varying degrees of liberty, and may even assign them to conservation work with certain agencies of the state government.   It releases young prisoners on parole when it believes that they are ready for this privilege. In 1944 California set up an Adult Authority, whose work now parallels that of the youth agency.   The Adult Authority examines most of the older prisoners, determines the nature, time, and duration of their punishment, and even modifies their terms of imprisonment at any time prior to release.

It serves as a parole board, and advises the governor concerning pardons. Somewhat similar plans, applicable only to minors, have been adopted by Louisiana, Minnesota, Wisconsin, Massachusetts, and Texas.

PROBLEMS

1. Study the organization and work of the state police in your state or a neighboring state. What suggestions can you offer for improvement?

2. Prepare a report on the employment of college graduates in municipal police departments.

3. Observe the organization and work of the coroner's office in your community. To what extent are modern scientific methods employed in the determination of the causes of death.

4. What new types of fire fighting equipment have been purchased by your city since 1940? In what way is the new equipment superior to the equipment that it replaced?

5. Visit the nearest state penitentiary and note the living and working conditions. What provision is made for the recreation of prisoners?

SELECTED REFERENCES

American Prison Association, *A Statement concerning Causes, Preventive Measures, and Methods of Controlling Prison Riots and Disturbances*, 1953.

Beckwith, Edmund R., and Others, *Lawful Action of State Military Forces*, 1944.

Elliott, Mabel A., *Crime in Modern Society*, 1952.

Glueck, Sheldon, *Delinquents in the Making: Paths to Prevention*, 1952.

———, *Unraveling Juvenile Delinquency*, 1950.

Hurwitz, Stephen, *Criminology*, London, 1952.

International City Managers' Association, *Municipal Fire Administration*, 5th ed., 1950.

———, *Municipal Police Administration*, 3rd ed., 1950.

Kreml, Franklin M., *Report on the California Highway Patrol*, Sacramento, 1946.

Leonard, V. A., *Police Organization and Management*, 1951.

National Municipal League, *A Model State Medico-Legal Investigative System*, 1951.

Pollack, Otto, *The Criminality of Women*, Philadelphia, 1950.

Puttkammer, Ernst W., *Administration of Criminal Law*, 1953.

Reckless, Walter C., *The Crime Problem*, 1950.

Soderman, Harry, and O'Connell, John J., *Modern Criminal Investigation*, 1951.

Sutherland, Edwin H., *Criminology: A Cultural Interpretation*, 1950.

———, *White Collar Crime*, 1949.

Tappan, Paul W., *Juvenile Delinquency*, 1949.

Tappan, Paul W., ed., *Contemporary Correction*, 1951.

Teeters, Negley K., and Reinemann, John Otto, *The Challenge of Delinquency*, 1950.

Wilson, O. W., *Police Administration,* 1950.

————, *Police Planning,* Springfield, Ill., 1952.

The January, 1949, issue of the *Annals of the American Academy of Political and Social Science* is entitled "Juvenile Delinquency." The November, 1952, issue is entitled "Murder and the Penalty of Death," and the May, 1954, issue is called "Prisons in Transformation."

CHAPTER 18

Welfare

The care of the poor is a social problem of the first magnitude. It cannot be solved merely by good intentions and a full purse. The poet may advise "a hand open as day for melting charity," [1] but every student of social problems knows that indiscriminate almsgiving is a sorry substitute for efficient welfare work. Generosity is not enough; there must be a highly developed organization, trained personnel, and skilful technique. In other words, guesswork must be eliminated. The problem requires a scientific approach.

SUBSTANDARD INCOMES

Extent

The extent of poverty cannot be determined with any degree of exactness. No one knows how many people are trying to subsist on incomes that are insufficient to maintain even a minimum standard of decent living. But extensive surveys are not necessary to show that poverty is widespread. Evidence of dire need appears on every hand, even in prosperous times; and in periods of depression the proofs of poverty multiply with startling rapidity.

Social workers used to speak of the poor as "the submerged tenth," and many writers of a few decades ago estimated that ten per cent of the people of the United States were wholly or partly dependent on public or private charity. But these figures have undoubtedly been much higher within the last twenty years. As recently as 1939, just before the preparations for the Second World War created new jobs and sharply reduced the relief rolls, more than twenty million people—fifteen per cent of the people of the nation—were on public relief. More recently employment has been at a fairly high level, but no one can say with certainty when the conditions of 1939, or the more serious conditions of the earlier depression years, may return. Obviously, therefore, poverty is a serious problem demanding serious consideration.

[1] Shakespeare's *King Henry IV*, Pt. II, Act IV, Scene 4.

Causes

Many factors predispose to poverty. To determine their relative importance in any given case, however, is extremely difficult—sometimes almost impossible. Yet little can be accomplished without an understanding of fundamental causes and a determined effort to remove them. To give poor people money, food, or shelter without at least trying to correct their social maladjustment is strongly suggestive of bailing a tub of water without turning off the faucet that constantly brings a fresh supply. Temporary relief may be accomplished, but something more is needed for permanent results.

Among the factors that tend to produce poverty, some lie wholly within the individual. Feeble-mindedness, for example, or low normal mentality, may prevent steady employment at any regular trade. Mental instability may have the same effect. Sickness, especially for long periods, may dissipate savings and also reduce earning capacity. Physical handicaps of any sort may play a part. So, too, may an improper diet or an abuse of stimulants and narcotics.

Frequently several of these factors combine to produce that condition of mind and body known—for lack of a more precise term—as shiftlessness. The person so afflicted is in need of charity more or less constantly. Any small savings that he may manage to accumulate soon disappear as a result of extravagance, or lack of sound judgment in business matters, or "unforeseen" emergencies for which provision should have been made long in advance. Every step forward is followed by a loss of the ground gained. Poverty becomes chronic. Welfare agencies are well acquainted with such persons and families, but have found no way to effect a solution of their problems. Against stupidity, it is said, the gods themselves are powerless.

Not all the factors that predispose to poverty, however, lie within the individual. Inadequate natural resources or bad climatic conditions may affect whole communities. Changes in manufacturing processes or in the popular demand for certain products may throw entire groups of workers into the ranks of the unemployed and force them below the level of self-support. Periods of depression may have a nation-wide or even world-wide effect.

Obviously, therefore, no simple remedy will cure such a complex social disease as poverty. Every one of the factors involved, of which only a few have been suggested above, must be given separate consideration. Some factors can be completely eliminated or substantially modified by careful planning and proper treatment; others seem to defy solution. Whether poverty can be wiped out is a moot question; that it can be greatly reduced is beyond doubt.

THE FORCED SHIFT FROM PRIVATE TO PUBLIC POOR RELIEF

Until a quarter of a century ago poor relief was largely in private hands, although the part played by the state was increasing in importance. Some persons urged that the government should assume primary responsibility for the care of the poor, but their proposals were met with numerous objections. The depression of 1930, however, compelled government to take a hand. Poverty had increased rapidly, and many self-supporting persons had suffered such drastic reductions in income that they were no longer able to carry their normal share of the burden of poor relief. Government action meant action at the national level, for many states, counties, and cities were fast approaching the limit of their resources. At first the federal government adopted the theory that recovery would be rapid and permanent, and it took steps to speed the process. There was to be a national business survey; industry should be asked to increase production; and "the spirit of voluntary service" should be encouraged. But these measures were of no avail, and even a marked increase in federal public works took care of but a small part of the unemployed.

The Reconstruction Finance Corporation

In 1932, therefore, the Reconstruction Finance Corporation was set up, with power to lend large sums to the states "to be used in furnishing relief and work relief to needy and distressed people and in relieving the hardships resulting from unemployment." The states were to receive these federal loans with virtually no strings attached; their own officials were to determine the exact nature of relief plans. In few cases was the money spent with maximum efficiency—a not unnatural condition of affairs, for state officials were totally unprepared to meet the crisis. Suitable agencies had to be set up, and suitable personnel had to be obtained. But relief could not await the refinement of administrative processes; it demanded immediate attention. So the money was spent, and the states thus indebted themselves to the federal government to the extent of several hundred millions of dollars. Later, however, an act of Congress waived the earlier provisions for repayment, and the loans became gifts.

Social Security Legislation

When President Roosevelt took office, in 1933, the unemployment situation was acute. At least fifteen million men were out of work, and most of them had exhausted their meager savings. Many states and cities lacked available funds for relief purposes. Federal grants had proved insufficient by a wide margin. A more comprehensive federal relief program was urgently required, and one was speedily adopted. This program had three major parts: (1) employment of young men in forest camps maintained by the federal government, (2) large direct grants (not loans) to the states, and (3) employment of large numbers of persons on federal work projects. Thus the emergency situation was met.

But something more was needed: a permanent program that would insure workers against poverty and provide systematic care for all persons in need. A Committee on Economic Security was created, and for more than a year it dealt with every aspect of the problem. In the early days of 1935 it presented its report, and seven months later Congress enacted its recommendations into law—though with substantial modifications. Thus the United States achieved a form of "social security."

Many criticisms have been directed at the program. Some persons declare that it is totally inadequate. It excludes certain groups from unemployment benefits; it fixes maximum benefits for many classes—dependent children, for example—at a very low level; and it makes no direct attack on the problem of poverty through illness. Then there are other persons who criticize the program for a very different reason. They say that its cost is excessive and must somehow be reduced. To these complaints others are added: the present methods of financing the plan are economically or socially unsound; the lack of proper federal supervision over related state activities is a serious weakness; numerous administrative difficulties interfere with the prompt granting of relief. Some of these objections still have a certain validity, despite important changes in the system by Congress and the state legislatures since 1950. But no one can deny that the people of the United States now have a substantial measure of social security.

State and Federal Responsibility

The social security program is essentially a co-operative affair, involving both the states and the federal government. Some phases of the plan, such as old age insurance, are handled directly by the nation, but most aspects are administered by the states with the aid of federal funds and a small measure of federal supervision.   Each state prepares its own program—within broad limits fixed by Congress—and uses its own staff of administrators.

Subordination of Private Agencies

Private charitable organizations still function, of course, and play an important part in the relief of human misery.   The Red Cross maintains an organization, even in peacetime, that permits prompt action at the scene of every major disaster, such as earthquake, flood, or fire.   The Salvation Army cares for homeless persons and attempts to rehabilitate them.   In many cases it successfully bridges the gap between private need and available public funds.   Dozens of other private welfare agencies still perform useful services.   The annual Community Chest drive provides an excellent means of financing this private work.   But private activity has been definitely subordinated to public in the field of poor relief.   The old argument concerning the desirability of public participation has been settled for all time.

INDOOR VERSUS OUTDOOR RELIEF

Outdoor Relief—Pro and Con

The relief of the poor assumes two general forms—indoor relief, or the care of poor persons in institutions, and outdoor relief, or the care of poor persons in their own homes.   Both forms of charity are used in present-day American communities.   The outdoor principle has many advantages.   It enables the unfortunate to receive assistance without suffering the inevitable humiliation of life in a charitable institution.   It avoids the necessity of severing family ties or separating friends.   It is frequently urged as an economical solution of the problem of poor relief, on the ground that a great deal of the cost of indoor relief can be saved.   Many families are only a little below the level of self-support and could maintain themselves with a minimum of assistance.   To insist that they abandon their family life and go to an institution, at greatly increased public expense, may sometimes be the height of folly.

But other factors, which must not be overlooked, present outdoor relief in a less favorable light.   For one thing, the absence of humiliation that is advanced as a merit of the system often proves to be a serious disadvantage, since it greatly increases the number of applicants.   Men and women who managed to live without charity when charity meant the poorhouse suddenly discover that they can no longer support themselves, but must have food, fuel, or money at public expense.   Because outdoor relief is more pleasant,

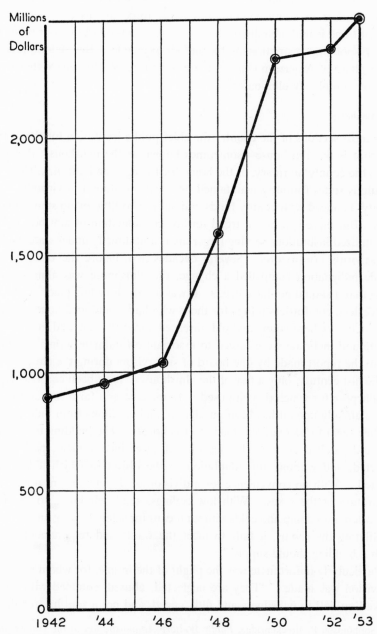

Based on figures of the United States Bureau of the Census.

it is very much more popular.   Thus the savings effected in the care of each family must be used to provide for additional families, and still larger appropriations may become necessary.   The experience of public officials with outdoor relief in many communities lends force to this argument.   The present trend is undoubtedly toward marked expansion of outdoor relief and a corresponding restriction of the indoor principle.   But indoor relief is still a phase of American charity; there is little reason to believe that it will ever be completely eliminated.

The Almshouse

In most sections of the country the chief public institution for the care of the poor is the almshouse—sometimes known as the poorhouse, the poorfarm, the county infirmary, or the home for the aged and infirm.   The more populous states formerly maintained one such institution in virtually every county, financed with county funds and subject to little or no state supervision.   But there is a recent trend toward consolidation of almshouses into hospitalized institutions serving larger areas and directly under state control.

PREVIOUS CONDITIONS.   Several decades ago, before the rising tide of public indignation compelled a change, the almshouse was almost everything that it should not have been.   It was a filthy breeding place of disease; a cheerless, comfortless refuge for those who had abandoned hope; a veritable catch-all where young and old, diseased and well, sane and insane, temperate and inebriate were forced to associate on intimate terms.   According to the report made by one board of supervisors during the closing years of the last century, only a few of the almshouses "have been constructed for the purpose for which they are used.   In most cases a farm with a dwelling house already upon it has been purchased, and additions from time to time, as they seem to be required, made to the house.   The building thus pieced out and patched up is in the majority of cases inconvenient, poorly constructed, and without any adaptation to the object to which it is appropriated.   With no convenience for a division of the inmates, or a complete separation of the sexes.   With low ceilings, small windows, no drainage, and oftentimes damp and cold, without means for safely heating and properly ventilating the rooms, it fails to meet the wants and requirements which such a building should supply." [2]

Particularly unfortunate was the plight of the insane, for whom no special provision was made.   "They are neglected, abused, confined with chains, locked up, left in nakedness and filth, caged, and not a soul has for them a

[2] Sophonisba P. Breckenridge, *Public Welfare Administration in the United States*, p. 630.

friendly word. The medical supervision of them is wholly inadequate; they have no proper personal attendance; they are without amusement or occupation of any sort. Some of them are taken out at long intervals for an airing or to be washed, possibly by standing them naked in a corner and throwing water upon them with a hose pipe. Others remain in their cells or dens from one end of the year to the other. Their mental malady is aggravated by neglect and cruelty, and their only hope is in death." [3]

RECENT IMPROVEMENTS. In recent years, however, conditions in the county almshouses have been vastly improved. This improvement has been made possible, in part, by the transfer of groups requiring special care to separate institutions. The sick poor are sent to hospitals where their maladies may be treated; the feeble-minded and insane are placed in hospitals for mental diseases. Children are placed in separately maintained orphanages or in private homes. Cripples are given highly specialized vocational training whenever such instruction seems likely to make them wholly or partly self-supporting. Therefore the almshouse is largely an institution for the care of the aged, although other groups have not been completely weeded out. Almshouse construction, also, has received greater attention. First, large, dormitory-type buildings took the place of makeshift farmhouses, and these, in turn, are now being replaced, in at least a few jurisdictions, by poor homes of the cottage variety.

NEED FOR CONTINUANCE. The introduction of old-age pension systems and other forms of social security has led to the widespread belief that public homes need no longer be maintained. Why, it is asked, should aged men and women be sent to institutions when they can receive from the government sufficient funds to enable them to live comfortably in their own homes? The obvious answer—entirely aside from the frequent inadequacy of public pensions—is that many old people require institutional care. Thousands of them must have almost constant medical and nursing services that cannot be provided adequately in their own homes or the homes of relatives. Although many institutions have closed their doors since the enactment of the Social Security Act, many others are operating at or near capacity.

PROVISION FOR ACTIVITY. Some form of activity should be provided for the old people living in institutions. This aspect of the care of inmates is often neglected, largely because the aged cannot engage in many forms of diversion that are open to younger men and women. But it is a vital factor in making institutional life bearable for those who are obliged to accept its inevitable monotony. Equally important is the assignment of light daily tasks to all inmates—except, of course, the incapacitated—for idleness is

[3] Sophonisba P. Breckenridge, *op. cit.*, p. 640.

quite as harmful to the able-bodied inmates of homes as to the prisoners in jails and penitentiaries.   The women can assist in the housework; the men can engage in agricultural or industrial work suited to their physical condition.   Small savings in the operation of the home usually result from the adoption of such schemes of general employment.   Far more significant, however, is the effect upon the workers.   In most instances they acquire a fresh interest in life, and delight in the realization that their usefulness is not entirely past.

THE OLD-AGE PROBLEM

In the United States, according to the most recent census figures, there are more than twelve million men and women who have passed their sixty-fifth birthdays.   This group comprises over eight per cent of the total population.   Their earnings power has dropped practically to the vanishing point, yet most of them have not saved enough to buy even the barest necessities for the remainder of their lives.   Many have children or other close relatives who are willing to assume the burden of support, or can be made to do so.   But many others do not have relatives or friends to help them and must inevitably turn to charity.   Some provision must be made for their care.

Assignment to institutions was, until recently, the plan most commonly adopted.   Privately managed homes for the aged supplemented the public homes and almshouses in many communities.   These private institutions aided in reducing the burden of public charity, but their usefulness was lessened by the restrictions that they imposed upon would-be inmates. Sometimes they required a flat payment of several hundred or even several thousand dollars, in addition to the deeding of any real property that the applicant might own.   Quite commonly they imposed religious or racial restrictions, or accepted only persons belonging to certain fraternal groups.

Most of the responsibility of caring for the aged, therefore, rested upon public institutions.   And every study of this phase of poor relief emphasized the fact that public institutions—or public and private institutions combined, for that matter—were too few and too small to meet the needs of the aged poor.   Moreover, the situation was constantly becoming more acute.   The high cost of living was making it increasingly difficult for the average wage earner to save any substantial sum during his working years despite reasonably good wages; and medical science was rapidly augmenting the proportion of old people in the general population.   Recent trends in birth and death rates have by no means relieved this situation; on the contrary, they

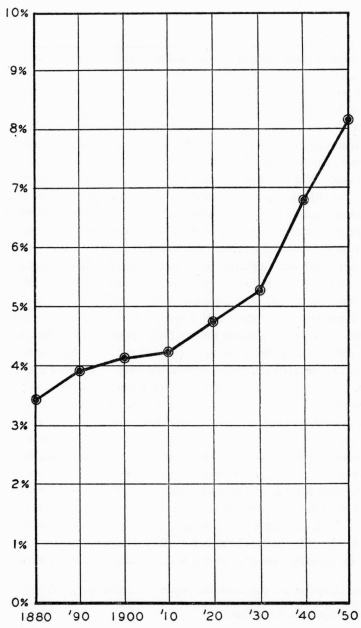

Based on figures of the United States Bureau of the Census.

have accentuated it.   The proportion of aged persons continues to increase. By 1980, according to the estimates of the National Resources Committee, 14.4 per cent of the population of the United States will be sixty-five years of age or over.

Old-age Insurance

When the federal government decided to establish a permanent scheme of social security in 1935, it recognized that the ultimate solution of the problem of poverty in old age must be a nation-wide retirement system.   Similar systems had long been maintained by leading private corporations for the benefit of their employees, but they applied only to employees who had been in their service for twenty or twenty-five years.   At most they applied to not over five million workers—a small percentage of the total number requiring protection.   Nor could private industry extend the system very greatly.

But the federal government, with its nation-wide jurisdiction and broad powers of taxation and control, encountered no substantial difficulties.   Its old-age insurance plan was applied to all workers—with the exception of certain groups [4]—who had been employed at least five years (though not necessarily with one employer, or for any specified minimum period during each year).   A tax, beginning at one per cent and rising gradually to three per cent—was placed on the payroll of each employer, and a similar tax was imposed on the wages of each employee.   From these revenues a huge reserve—reaching an ultimate total of forty-seven billion dollars, according to government actuaries—was to be created; and from this reserve workers were to receive, after retirement, regular payments that would continue until death.   The amount of each worker's pension would depend in part upon the length of his service, and in part upon the amount of his earnings.

As might have been anticipated, numerous objections were raised.   The new taxes were too heavy; the number of beneficiaries was too few.   Most serious of the plan's weaknesses, however, was the contemplated forty-seven-billion-dollar reserve.   No government in the world's history had ever created such a fund, and no one could say with certainty what its effects would be.   But most students believed that it would unsettle the investment market and that it might readily be used for purposes not originally contemplated.   In order to avoid these difficulties, Congress amended the law in 1939 by advancing the year for the first payment of benefits, increasing the

---

[4] The exceptions are now much less important than formerly.   In 1950 regularly employed agricultural workers and domestic servants were brought within the scope of the old-age insurance system.

number of beneficiaries, holding the tax at one per cent for a number of years, and limiting the size of the reserve to three times the maximum yearly benefit payments expected in the next five years. More recently, on several occasions, Congress has continued to postpone some of the scheduled increases in the rate of the tax. Since 1950 self-employed persons—with certain exceptions—have been covered by the federal government's old age insurance plan, and have been required to meet the cost by paying a certain percentage of their earnings into the federal treasury.

Old-age Assistance

Old-age insurance does not completely solve the problem, however. It has no value for aged persons who never earned wages, or who retired before the insurance plan was adopted. Even today it fails to cover at least forty per cent of the old people who need some form of financial assistance. These indigent men and women cannot be permitted to starve. Some provision must be made for their care, despite the fact that they fall outside the scope of an insurance system. The establishment of public almshouses was one of the earliest recognitions of this obligation.

Later a number of the states granted relief to the aged poor in their own homes. Small sums, contributed regularly from state or county treasuries on the basis of need, often supplemented the money earned by the old people themselves or contributed by relatives or friends. In California, where this scheme was in operation for a number of years prior to the adoption of a regular pension system, public contributions of ten or fifteen dollars a month enabled the beneficiaries to live semi-independently in many instances, and thus retain their self-respect and escape the odium of becoming poorhouse inmates.

From this form of poor relief it was but a step to the establishment of old-age pensions, available on equal terms to all poor persons who had reached a certain age. Pension systems for the aged had long been a part of the social insurance schemes of European nations, but had received little serious consideration in the United States. An old-age pension law had indeed been enacted by Arizona in 1914, but had been declared unconstitutional by the state supreme court because of ambiguous phraseology. Then came the Montana law of 1923—the first valid old-age pension statute. Nevada followed a few months later, and Wisconsin fell into line in 1925. By 1935 the number of states with pension laws had risen to thirty, though some of the state statutes were virtually inoperative because they permitted each county to determine whether it would accept the plan contemplated by the legislature's action, at the same time placing the financial burden upon the county treasury.   Most of the state laws required fifteen years of uninterrupted residence, and specified a minimum age of seventy years.

At this point the federal government entered the picture.   In addition to providing old-age insurance for workers, it brought great pressure to bear on the states to set up adequate pension systems for the aged poor.   The federal offer consisted in matching state funds for old-age pensions, up to fifteen dollars a month.   Later Congress changed the method of apportionment, and also the amounts available to the states.   At present the national government offers to pay four fifths of the first twenty-five dollars a month, plus one half of the remainder, up to fifty-five dollars.   The obvious effect of this arrangement is to favor the low-income states.   In Alabama, for example, where average monthly payments for old age assistance are only twenty-five dollars, most of the money comes from the federal treasury.   In Colorado, on the other hand, where payments average nearly eighty dollars a month, the federal government bears only a little over one third of the cost of the pension program.

In every state certain conditions are attached to the federal grant: every plan submitted for federal approval must be state-wide in operation; it must provide a fair hearing for any person denied assistance; the age limit must not be higher than sixty-five years; the residence requirement must not exceed five years in the last ten.   But no provision is made for federal supervision of state administrative activities; on the contrary, the Social Security Board is specifically directed not to interfere with state affairs.   All forty-eight states have accepted the federal offer, and have established more or less satisfactory pension schemes.   Pensions have been generally increased since 1940, as a result of higher living costs and improved state finances. But there are many variations in the terms of state laws and also in their administration.   Many common weaknesses must be eliminated.

THE CARE OF HOMELESS CHILDREN

Not only the very old, but also the very young, are likely to require the special consideration of the state.   When parents die without making adequate provision for their dependent children; when broken homes leave the children without proper care; whenever, for any reason, young boys and girls lack the bare necessities of life—then public or private charity must assume the responsibility that the parents have failed to meet.

Children's Homes

For many years it was believed that homeless children should be placed in institutions, where their training could be closely supervised, their habits carefully regulated, and their playtime activities guided into useful channels. Children's homes were established by public authorities, religious denominations, and fraternal orders. Today, however, most students of social problems vigorously challenge the old assumption that institutions furnish a

DISTRIBUTION OF STATE PUBLIC WELFARE EXPENDITURES, 1953

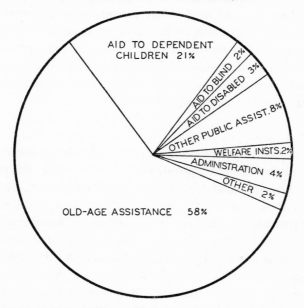

AID TO DEPENDENT CHILDREN 21%

AID TO BLIND 2%

AID TO DISABLED 3%

OTHER PUBLIC ASSIST. 8%

WELFARE INSTS. 2%

ADMINISTRATION 4%

OTHER 2%

OLD-AGE ASSISTANCE 58%

Based on figures from *Compendium of State Government Finances in 1953.*

proper environment for growing boys and girls. In large measure they have convinced the public that institutional life retards initiative, produces undesirable uniformity, and tends to unfit children to take their places as normal men and women in the outside world. The result has been an increased emphasis on placement in private homes.

But the "orphanage"—usually so-called regardless of whether the children in it are actually orphans—has by no means outlived its usefulness. It provides a temporary shelter for children whose normal family relationships have recently been severed. Moreover, it is still considered the proper place to rear certain kinds of children—those whose chronic physical disabilities require highly specialized training, for example, or those whose emotional reactions suggest the need of institutional discipline. Even normal children, under some circumstances, may fare better in orphanages than in private foster homes. Thus if the mother is dead and the father, although anxious to maintain affectionate relationships, is unable to make suitable provision in his own home for the children's care, an institution may be the means of preserving family ties and eventually reuniting the family when the children have reached the age of self-support.

A number of different types of institutions for the care of children have been established. In addition to the usual orphanages or children's homes, which formerly sheltered all kinds of young people without regard to their individual differences and needs, there are now industrial schools for the delinquent, special institutions for the blind, the deaf, the crippled and the feeble-minded, and receiving homes where boys and girls may be kept and studied pending final disposition of their cases. Day nurseries and nursery schools, where working mothers may leave their very young children during the day, are becoming increasingly common.

Foster Homes

A significant development in the care of the homeless young is the growing practice of placement with private families. Sometimes this plan is used not only for homeless children, but also for children whose homes are badly disrupted or whose parents are habitually so cruel or neglectful as to forfeit the right of parental control. As a rule, children are placed in foster homes with the understanding that they will be formally adopted at some later time if the arrangement proves satisfactory to all concerned. But there are many exceptions. Some families willingly take boys or girls for long periods without any expectation of adopting them—perhaps requiring a certain amount of work as the children grow older. Other families, in exchange for regular payments by public or private agencies, assume the responsibility of caring for children who are to be returned eventually to parents or relatives.

PROPER PLACEMENT. Whatever the basis of placement, it is important to select for each child a foster home suited to his individual needs. Therefore the first step in placement proceedings is a careful investigation of the families that are applying for children. The intelligence, training, ability, and character of the would-be foster parents should be considered, as well as their financial status, home life, and attitude toward children's problems. Any adverse factors that might make the process of adjustment difficult should be brought to light by means of questionnaires and personal interviews.

It must not be forgotten, however, that the placement of children in permanent foster homes creates mutual relationships.   Not only must the home be good; it must be good for the child who is to become a member of the family circle.   Therefore the agency responsible for selecting homes must have an intimate understanding of every child's character and a full appreciation of his needs.   Proper consideration should be given to his health, habits, intelligence, family history, and early environment.   Provision should be made for curing any disease and correcting any remediable physical defect.

SUPERVISION AFTER PLACEMENT.   Quite as important as proper placement is careful follow-up work.   There should be a staff of trained social workers whose duty is to exercise watchful supervision over the children after they have been placed in foster homes, and make certain that the experiments are turning out as planned.   During the first few months, especially, misunderstandings are likely to arise.   Children may feel that they are unfairly treated, and foster parents may conclude that their efforts are wasted. Under such circumstances a skilful supervisor can often straighten out apparently irreconcilable differences by bridging the gap between the viewpoints of youth and age.   Periodic visits are necessary to determine also whether the children's interests are being properly safeguarded—whether health and education, for example, are receiving the attention they deserve. The foster parents may require some training in the fundamentals of their new work.   After the children have been legally adopted, of course, the jurisdiction of the placement agency is at an end, although friendly relationships may still be maintained.   It is important, therefore, to be quite sure that the experiment is well on the road to success before custody is judicially awarded.

Every public or private agency that places homeless children with private families admits the necessity of close supervision after placement, but only a few maintain supervisory staffs that could be called adequate by any stretch of the imagination.   Frequently the visitors are untrained and have no real understanding of their duties.   In almost all cases they are underpaid and overworked.   Thus supervision becomes largely nominal, and the success of placement becomes a matter of choice.   While this is not an argument against the placement system, it is a serious criticism of the manner in which placement is being conducted in nearly every state of the American Union.

AID FOR MOTHERS OF DEPENDENT CHILDREN

It requires no elaborate discussion to show that children should be reared by their own mothers wherever possible, and not by foster mothers or workers in institutions.   The home should not be disrupted if it can be held together.   This principle is fundamental in social work, yet it was virtually ignored until 1911, when Missouri enacted a law authorizing regular payments from the public treasury to indigent mothers of dependent children. Illinois followed with similar legislation a few months afterward, and in 1913 mothers' aid laws were adopted by eighteen states.   The movement continued to spread, and by 1934 there were but three states that made no provision of any kind for assistance to mothers.

Many of the laws were practically worthless, however.   They relied solely on county initiative, as in Indiana and Oregon, or authorized state appropriations that were never made, as in Virginia.   The early statutes applied only to *widows* with dependent children, but most of the later laws granted financial assistance to poor mothers who were dependent on their own efforts to support their children, regardless of whether the fathers were dead, deserting, imprisoned, or incapacitated.   American citizenship was not usually made a prerequisite, but residence in the state for a given period—one to five years—was almost invariably required.   Moreover, nearly all the states relied on county officials to administer the mothers' aid laws, and made little attempt to supervise county activities.

But the situation changed rapidly when the federal government entered the field in 1935.   Federal funds were made available to the states for mothers' aid, but with conditions that entailed liberalization of most state laws.   No child might be excluded for lack of county or city residence, nor might the state residence requirement exceed one year.   Assistance should be granted until children were at least sixteen years of age, and might extend to children living with close relatives other than mothers.   Administration must be directly in the hands of the state.

The federal funds originally granted under this statute were limited to one half of the amount appropriated by states and cities; and there was a further restriction that they might not exceed eighteen dollars per month for the first child in a family, and twelve dollars for each additional child. Today, however, the federal government pays considerably more than half of the cost of the program in the poorer states.   Maximum allotments have been substantially increased, although social workers still complain that they are unreasonably low.   Every state except Nevada has accepted the federal offer, and has prepared plans meeting federal approval.   Nevada makes some provision for the support of dependent children, but not in accord with federal policies.

HELP FOR THE BLIND AND THE DISABLED

The federal Social Security Act also makes provision for federal participation in state programs of financial assistance to needy blind persons. The usual conditions are attached to the federal offer: the states must participate financially; they must submit work plans acceptable to the federal government; and they must make regular reports. When this grant was first offered to the states, in 1935, only two states were able to qualify. But state laws were speedily changed in conformity with federal standards. Today, all the states co-operate with the federal government in aid for the blind. In 1950 Congress amended the Social Security Act to permit federal-state participation in a program of financial assistance to needy persons who were permanently and totally disabled. Thirty-nine states have accepted the federal offer, either by amending their own laws or by applying laws already in force.

THE ABLE-BODIED UNEMPLOYED

The problem of poverty is accentuated by the fact that many able-bodied adults are unable or unwilling to find employment. Some of the members of this group are professional or semi-professional vagrants—homeless wanderers who seldom or never work because they have reached the conclusion that charity will meet all their needs. Such men constitute a class of unemployables. Closely allied to these shirkers is a second group, occasional workers, whose periods of employment are likely to become less frequent as the lure of vagabondage proves increasingly difficult to resist. Then there is still a third group, made up of men and women who genuinely desire work but can find none. In periods of depression the number of such persons is very large, but even in prosperous times, when employment is at or near its peak, there are still some who cannot find jobs—perhaps because of changes in popular taste or the adoption of new manufacturing processes. Obviously all three classes of persons cannot be treated alike.

Just what should be done with those who seem to prefer unemployment and charity to steady work and independence is still a moot question. In some counties they are arrested as vagrants and committed to jail for a term of days or months. Other communities simply order them to leave town within twenty-four hours—a method that does not solve the problem but shifts it to other shoulders. Police stations are often used as lodgings for the homeless. A few of the more progressive communities have established public lodging houses, where destitute men may receive temporary shelter and perhaps one or two meals in exchange for a few hours' work on the wood pile.

Modern society is less concerned with the unemployable and semi-unemployable, however, than with those self-respecting men and women who have been forced into idleness by the pressure of economic forces. Their right to a job or public support can no longer be questioned. Federal work relief took care of several million such persons until the spring of 1943, when the federal program was temporarily abandoned because of the tremendous increase in private employment. But the long-run need of these jobless men and women is not relief: it is some form of job insurance, so that they will be guaranteed a means of self-support when they are thrown out of work. Unemployment insurance has long been accepted by European nations as a matter of course, but it was not generally adopted in the United States until 1935. Now it has become a major factor in the fight against poverty. Its main features are discussed in a subsequent chapter.[5]

ADMINISTRATIVE ORGANIZATION

Movement toward State Control

In the early days of American history the care of the poor was entrusted solely to the local units of government—chiefly the counties. State authorities did not attempt to exercise even a cursory supervision. The results were highly unsatisfactory. Diverse practices, competitive relationships, and wasteful methods characterized local poor relief. Unsuitable buildings and inadequate equipment were found almost everywhere. A demand for some measure of state supervision naturally arose, therefore, and in 1863 Massachusetts led the way by creating a state board of charities. Ohio and New York followed in 1867; then came Illinois, North Carolina, Pennsylvania, and Rhode Island in 1869. By 1913, just half a century after the establishment of the first state board of charities, thirty-eight states had set up similar agencies, and during the next twenty years the number increased to forty-five.

There was a definite tendency to make the board or department of charities responsible for the administration or supervision of all state charity. But depression set in motion a countertrend. Separate agencies were created in some commonwealths for the administration of unemployment relief, children's services, old-age pensions, and other phases of the social security program. Today [6] only about one half of the states vest responsibility for all

[5] See pages 559–561.
[6] 1954.

forms of assistance in a single department or board. The state agency or agencies responsible for the various aspects of public charity usually possess a considerable measure of control over local activities. Sometimes they inspect all local charitable institutions and approve plans and specifications for new buildings, in addition to supervising the administration of local charity. Usually, however, state jurisdiction is not so extensive.

UNIFIED CONTROL. In 1917 Illinois departed from the traditional plan of board control and established the first single-headed state department responsible for charity administration. The head of the department, selected by the governor and responsible solely to him, was made a member of the newly created executive cabinet. Provision was also made for a board of public welfare commissioners, but the functions of this board were purely advisory. It was given no voice in rule-making or the preparation of department estimates; these matters, as well as general supervision of the department's work, were entrusted to the director. The Illinois department was called the *department of public welfare,* and its authority was made sufficiently broad to justify this new name. In addition to poor relief it assumed supervision over the treatment of criminals, administering the penal institutions of the state, directing parole work, and investigating applications for pardons.

Establishment of single-headed departments has been opposed by many students of social problems on the ground that political influences might interfere more readily with efficient administration. The plan has made considerable headway, however, despite this stock argument against every form of unified control. At the present time it is used, at least for some aspects of charity, by nearly two thirds of the states. Almost all the newer plans of reorganization substitute *welfare* for *charities,* but this change in nomenclature does not always indicate a regrouping of functions.

BOARD CONTROL. Among those states that still rely on the board plan of charity control, there is no general agreement as to the size of the board, its powers or duties, or the terms or salaries of its members. In many cases the board is composed of laymen whose principal function is to select an executive officer to handle the actual details of administration. Some states have established ex officio boards of charities or welfare.

Boards of control have been established, at least for certain aspects of charity administration, in about one fourth of the states. These boards usually have from three to five members, appointed for long terms by the governor with senate approval. Since the members receive full-time salaries they are expected to devote full time to their official duties. Individually they administer various phases of the work; as a group they formulate policies and establish rules of procedure.   They are presumed to possess special technical fitness, though sometimes their chief qualification is an ability to control votes.

Local Organization

In each county there is usually a welfare director chosen by the county board of supervisors and approved by the state department of welfare. Municipal welfare activities are sometimes directed by a board, and sometimes by a single commissioner.   Under the board plan, the members may be paid or unpaid, elected or appointed.   The tendency in the larger cities is to rely on a single welfare director, appointed by the mayor or manager. Sometimes poor relief is assigned to a separate department; sometimes it is placed in a department that includes a number of other activities, such as parks, playgrounds, and legal aid.   Social welfare directors and their staffs must possess qualifications that are acceptable to the federal Social Security Board.

PROBLEMS

1. Describe briefly the organization and administration of the Community Chest in your city.
2. Visit your county almshouse, and observe how it is managed.   Is work provided for those inmates who are capable of working?   What recreational facilities are furnished?
3. Study the operation of your state's old age pension law.   What agency is responsible for its administration?   Are pension allowances adequate?   What methods are used to detect impostors?
4. Describe the system of placing homeless children in private homes, as it operates in your community.   How many families eventually return the children instead of adopting them?   How thoroughly are families examined before children are entrusted to their care?   How carefully are families and children supervised after placement?
5. Examine the mothers' aid law of your state, and note the manner in which it is administered.   What defects do you observe in the law or its administration?
6. Describe the organization and activities of the state agency or agencies administering charity in your state.

SELECTED REFERENCES

Abbott, Edith, *Public Assistance,* 1940.
Abbott, Grace, *From Relief to Social Security,* 1941.
Atwater, Pierce, *Problems of Administration in Social Work,* 1940.
Becker, Joseph M., *The Problem of Abuse in Unemployment Benefits,* 1953.

Breckenridge, Sophonisba P., *Public Welfare Administration in the United States; Select Documents,* 2nd ed., 1938.

Brown, Josephine C., *Public Relief, 1929–1939,* 1940.

Burns, Eveline M., *The American Social Security System,* Boston, 1949.

Clarke, Helen I., *Principles and Practice of Social Work,* 1947.

———, *Social Legislation,* 1940.

Council of State Governments, *Social Security Revision,* 1946.

Glueck, Sheldon and Eleanor, *Delinquents in the Making,* 1952.

Haber, William, and Cohen, Wilbur J., eds., *Readings in Social Security,* 1948.

Harris, Seymour E., *Economics of Social Security,* 1941.

Hopkirk, Howard W., *Institutions Serving Children,* 1944.

James, Arthur W., *The State Becomes a Social Worker,* Richmond, Va., 1942.

Klein, Alice C., *Civil Service in Public Welfare,* 1940.

Landsdale, Robert T., and Others, *The Administration of Old-Age Assistance,* 1939.

Meriam, Lewis, *Relief and Social Security,* 1946.

Muntz, Earl E., *Growth and Trends in Social Security,* 1949.

National Resources Planning Board, *Security, Work, and Relief Policies,* Washington, D.C., 1942.

Odum, Howard W., *American Social Problems,* 1945.

Riesenfeld, Stefen A., and Richard C. Maxwell, *Modern Social Legislation,* 1950.

Stevenson, Marietta, *Public Welfare Administration,* 1938.

———, and MacDonald, Alice, *State and Local Public Welfare Agencies,* 1939.

Stewart, Bryce M., and Others, *Planning and Administration of Unemployment Compensation in the United States,* 1938.

Street, Elwood, *The Public Welfare Administrator,* 1940.

Stroup, Herbert H., *Community Welfare Organization,* 1952.

Tharp, Claude R., *Social Security and Related Services in Michigan, Their Administration and Functioning,* Ann Arbor, 1946.

White, R. Clyde, *Administration of Public Welfare,* 2nd ed., 1950.

Woytinsky, Waldimir S., *Earnings and Social Security in the United States,* Washington, D.C., 1943.

Wright, Helen R., ed., *Social Service in Wartime,* 1944.

The January, 1952, issue of the *Annals of the American Academy of Political and Social Science* is entitled "Social Contribution by the Aging."

Every student of welfare problems should be familiar with the *Social Work Year Book,* published by the Russell Sage Foundation.

CHAPTER 19

Health

Public health work is of comparatively recent origin. The first state board of health—in the modern use of the term—was established by Massachusetts in 1869. Fourteen years previously Louisiana had created a health board with state-wide powers, but this body had been concerned chiefly with the enforcement of quarantine regulations arising from a severe epidemic of yellow fever. It may seem surprising that the public health should have been so generally neglected for so long a time, yet the explanation is simple.

No one knew what health measures should be employed. The causes of disease were not understood, and therefore public officials were virtually powerless to prevent the spread of many virulent diseases that have since been brought under control. Smallpox, the worse scourge, was combated with quarantine and with valueless sanitary ordinances. In 1866, however, Louis Pasteur laid the foundation for the germ theory of disease and the modern science of preventive medicine. His investigations made possible, for the first time, the development of effective public health work based on disease prevention instead of disease suppression.

ESTABLISHMENT OF STATE HEALTH ORGANIZATIONS

The example of Massachusetts in setting up a state board of health was soon followed by other states. California set up a state health organization in 1870, and Minnesota and Virginia fell into line two years later. Then came Michigan in 1873, Maryland in 1874, and Alabama in 1875. By 1881 twenty-five states had assumed direct responsibility for the public health. Fifteen other states created health departments before the close of the century, and in 1909 the list was made complete. This universal recognition of public health protection as a state function has not led, however, to the establishment of uniform standards of public health organization. The effectiveness of the several state health organizations varies widely.

STATE EXPENDITURES FOR HEALTH

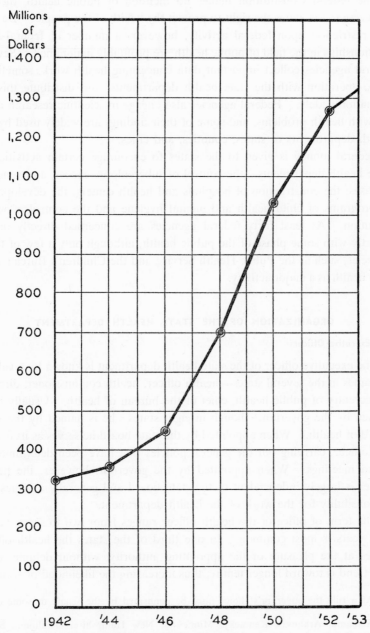

Based on figures of the United States Bureau of the Census.

FEDERAL PARTICIPATION IN PUBLIC HEALTH ACTIVITIES

The federal Constitution makes no mention of public health, thereby reserving to the states the right to protect the health of the people. Despite this restriction upon federal activity, however, a number of federal-state relationships in the field of public health are profitably maintained. Several federal agencies collect important data concerning health work, sometimes in co-operation with the state health departments, and distribute this information widely. Federal agencies also engage in scientific research dealing with health problems, and some of their findings are widely used by the health departments of states, counties, and cities.

Federal money is given to the states to encourage certain activities of state health departments—the control of tuberculosis, cancer, and venereal diseases, the construction of hospitals and health centers, the development of programs of child health and mental hygiene and the control of water pollution. At least forty federal agencies are concerned directly or indirectly with some phase of the public health, although only a few of these agencies, such as the Public Health Service and the Children's Bureau, deal with health as a major activity.

ORGANIZATION OF THE STATE HEALTH DEPARTMENT

The Executive Officer

The executive officer of the state health department is known by a variety of names in the several states—health officer, health commissioner, director or secretary of public health, chief of the bureau of health. Usually he is chosen by the governor,[1] though in eight states [2] he is named by the state board of health. When appointed by the state board he serves as its executive officer, carrying out the general policies that have been determined at board meetings. When appointed by the governor, however, the health officer is largely independent of the state board and generally assumes full responsibility for the work of the health department.

The term of office of the health officer ranges from two to seven years; four years is most common. In one third of the states the health officer serves at the pleasure of the appointing authority, without definite term. The trend is toward longer tenure, thus increasing the likelihood of securing

---

[1] As a rule the governor's choice must be confirmed by the senate or some other body.

[2] Alabama, Arkansas, Kentucky, Minnesota, New Hampshire, Oklahoma, South Dakota, Texas. In Arkansas the board's selection must be approved by the governor.

professional service.   Salaries, though low, have been materially increased in recent years.   They now compare not unfavorably with the salaries paid to other state officials of corresponding rank.

The legal qualifications of the health officer vary considerably, from the Colorado requirement that he must be a "citizen and a voter" to the New York specification that he must be a "physician with ten years' experience, skilled in sanitary science and public health work."   Six of the forty-eight states omit the essential requirement that he be a doctor of medicine, but physicians are commonly chosen in these states despite the lack of constitutional or statutory provisions.

The State Board of Health

Nearly every state has created a state board of health, public health council, or similar agency.   Sometimes it is an ex officio body, but much more commonly the members are appointed by the governor, usually without the necessity of securing senate approval.   The state medical association plays a part in the selection of health board members in a few states.

Members usually hold office for four, five, or six years, with overlapping terms to insure reasonable continuity of policy and experience in handling board business.   They are paid by the day in about half of the states and serve without compensation in the others.   Regular meetings are held three or four times a year except in a few states, where monthly meetings are the rule.

Most of the state health boards have authority to make and enforce necessary rules and regulations concerning public health and sanitation, including proper sewage disposal, prevention of water pollution, and prevention and treatment of communicable diseases.   Less frequently their jurisdiction extends to such matters as the practice of medicine, the practice of midwifery, or the sale of foods and drugs.

LOCAL HEALTH ORGANIZATION

Although public health work is generally conceded to be a state function, many health activities are commonly performed by the local units of government.   The local unit exercising principal jurisdiction over health matters is not everywhere the same.   In some states it is the township or—in New England—the town.   More often it is the county.   A few states have adopted the district plan.   Just as the township has proved unsatisfactory as a unit for school administration,[3] so it has produced undesirable results

[3] See page 434.

in the field of public health.   The average township is too small and too poor to employ full-time professional personnel; therefore it relies on a part-time health officer, who in some instances is not even a physician.

County Health Activities

As recently as 1915 there were only thirteen counties in the United States that had created effective public health organizations.   Elsewhere, under the county plan, health work was generally restricted to the occasional services of a physician whose chief interest was his private practice.   Thus county health work differed from township health work only in the size of the administrative unit.

During the last few decades, however, more than nineteen hundred county health departments have been organized for full-time service.   These departments, with trained medical health officers in charge, employ public health nurses and sanitary inspectors, in addition to necessary office assistants.   Part of the cost is commonly borne by the state, which also provides consultant service in laboratory diagnosis, sanitary engineering, child hygiene, and a number of other fields.

City Health Activities

Almost every city has a health organization of some kind.   The board system is still very popular.   Board members are commonly chosen by the chief executive, with the consent of the council.   The law frequently provides that one or two members of the board must be physicians; occasionally this requirement applies to all members.   Terms of office range from one year to six years or more; board members are commonly unpaid.   The president of the board, chosen by the other members, is nearly always a physician.

The city health officer is in direct charge of municipal health activities. If there is also a board of health, he is chosen by that board; otherwise he is usually selected by the city's chief executive.   Almost invariably he is a physician, and quite commonly he is a part-time man with a private practice.   In the very small cities a part-time arrangement may be necessary, but after a municipality acquires a population of twenty-five thousand it needs the full-time services of a competent physician.

Consolidation of City-County Health Services

A trend toward city-county consolidation of public health services has developed in the last few years.   The result has been the elimination of a great deal of unnecessary duplication, and also the adoption of higher

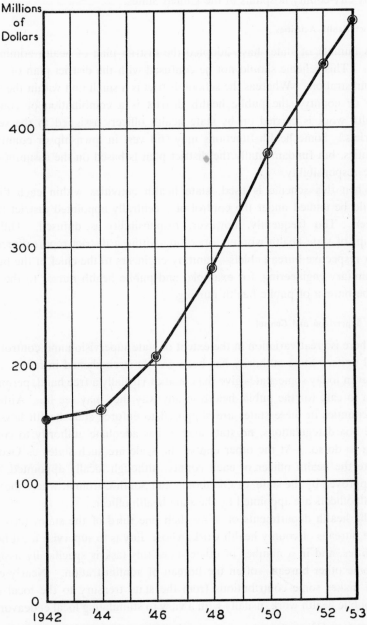

Based on figures from *Compendium of City Government Finances in 1953,* a publication of the United States Bureau of the Census.

standards, especially for the suburban areas. The total number of joint city-county health units is now well in excess of three hundred. There are many city-county hospitals in the United States.

District Health Activities

A number of states have adopted the district plan of health administration. This scheme should not be confused with the district plan of school administration. Whereas the school district is a small unit within the township or county,[4] the public health district is a combination of counties. Health work is carried on by state health officers assigned to the several districts. Some health functions may still vest in township or county authorities, but fundamentally the district plan is based on the assumption of state responsibility.

When this scheme is used, state health activities within each district should be unified under the control of a centrally appointed district health officer. Too frequently, however, responsibility is diffused. Different groups of state health workers operating within a district report directly to their respective bureau chiefs—sanitary engineers to the chief of the bureau of sanitary engineering, for example, and public health nurses to the chief of the bureau of public health nursing.

State Supervision and Control

There is great variation in the extent of state supervision and control over local units. State authority has been greatly strengthened in recent years, but even today some states give the counties virtually a free hand, permitting them to care for the public health in any way they may see fit. Although the counties in these states are supposed to enforce state health laws and state board regulations, no state agency has adequate authority to compel them to do so. At the other end of the scale are such states as Georgia, where the health officer of each county, although locally appointed, must be approved by the state, or Oklahoma and South Carolina, where the local health officers are appointed by the state health officer.

The health departments of more than one third of the states have separate bureaus of county health work, whose duty is to supervise local health activities, and in a number of other states this task is specifically assigned to some other bureau—often the bureau of administration. Nearly every state makes some contributions from the state treasury to the local units for public health work, usually with a view to stimulating local endeavor and

[4] See page 433.

raising local standards.   Delaware and Rhode Island pay the entire cost of full-time county health service.

COMMUNICABLE DISEASE CONTROL

The first state health departments were organized to prevent the spread of communicable diseases.   Their principal function was to fight epidemic with quarantine regulations.   The value of vaccination as a means of preventing smallpox was known, but compulsory vaccination was prevented by the opposition of various ill-informed groups.   Gradually, as medical science developed effective means of combating a number of major diseases, quarantine assumed a less important position in the public health program. But attention still centered on a few communicable diseases, such as tuberculosis, typhoid fever, malaria, diphtheria, syphilis, and gonorrhea.

Within the last few decades, however, public health work has undergone a virtual transformation.   The emphasis has shifted from communicable disease control to public health education, maternal and child hygiene, the detection and removal of physical defects, and the development in the general population of sound habits of living.   Yet this change has not involved an abandonment of the fight against communicable diseases.   On the contrary, most states are spending considerably more money today for the purpose of controlling these diseases than they did in 1915, though a smaller percentage of the total appropriation for public health.   In a number of states communicable disease work receives less than three per cent of the health appropriation; in other commonwealths the percentage ranges as high as thirty.   Virtually all state health departments have separate bureaus or divisions of communicable diseases or epidemiology, usually headed by full-time epidemiologists.

Reports by Physicians

The first step in the fight against communicable diseases is to make certain that they are promptly and accurately reported.   This principle is recognized in the laws of every state, but unfortunately these laws are far from satisfactory.   Sometimes they are carelessly phrased, making evasion easy.   Sometimes they omit reference to diseases that should be on the notifiable list.   Even more serious, they are negligently enforced in the rural sections of nearly all the states and in every section of some states. In some commonwealths, however, physicians are required to report to the state health department at regular intervals.

Quarantine

Although quarantine is relatively less important than in the early days of state health activity, it still remains a vital part of public health routine. In most states, however, quarantine regulations are enforced by the local health authorities. Nearly three fourths of the states have created special funds for emergencies. The use of these funds may be limited to public health emergencies—principally epidemics—or may be permitted for emergencies of any sort. In some states the emergency fund is administered by the state board of health or some other board or commission, but more often it is placed at the discretion of the governor.

Immunization

Smallpox vaccination is now compulsory—usually for school children —under the laws of about one fourth of the states. Many other states permit local authorities to provide for compulsory vaccination at their discretion, or under certain prescribed circumstances. Elsewhere free vaccination is generally provided by state or local health departments, and the people are taught the value of this protection against smallpox.

In recent years the development of antityphoid vaccine and diphtheria toxin-antitoxin has made possible the further immunization of large groups of persons in many states. The Southern states, especially, have waged active campaigns against typhoid fever and have immunized virtually the entire populations of many communities. Immunization against diphtheria has become an important part of the public health program in many sections of the country. Several states have separate appropriations for the purchase of antitoxins, vaccines, and serums. Malaria control, in those states where malaria is a problem, is frequently under a separate division or bureau, although sometimes it is entrusted to the state sanitary engineer.

Venereal Diseases

The growth of great urban centers has made venereal disease control a problem of the first magnitude. More than three fourths of the states have bureaus, divisions, or sections of venereal diseases, and the remaining commonwealths carry on the work through their bureaus of communicable diseases or central administrative staffs. Federal funds have greatly stimulated this activity.

Venereal disease clinics are maintained by state or local health authorities, or through state-local co-operation. Tests are made without charge or at nominal cost, and fees for treatment are reduced to a minimum. Free treatment is almost invariably provided for the indigent.   Revolutionary new methods of treating venereal diseases have greatly simplified the problem.   Syphilis and gonorrhea are now universally declared to be reportable diseases, most states having added them to the list during the last three decades.   Within the last twenty years most of the states have enacted laws requiring a premarital health examination, including a blood test for syphilis.

Tuberculosis

At the beginning of the present century the state health departments were just beginning antituberculosis work.   Methods of combating the disease and preventing its spread were known, but not widely used.   In 1904 the National Tuberculosis Association was formed, and through its efforts hundreds of local private organizations were established.   Today forty-four states have separate divisions or bureaus of tuberculosis in their health departments, and practically all the commonwealths maintain public tuberculosis clinics or leave this work to their cities and counties.   The technique of mass X rays has been developed as a means of detecting the disease in its early stages.   Public sanitariums, also, have become a feature of public health programs.   State, county, and municipal sanitariums, as well as private and semiprivate sanitariums, often function within a single state. Some local sanitariums receive subsidies from state treasuries.

Other Health Activities

Activities for the prevention of trachoma and various forms of blindness are carried on by a number of states.   Other minor communicable diseases, as they occasionally acquire local significance, receive the attention of state or county health departments.

MENTAL DISEASES

Many persons in the United States suffer from mental disorders.   The Second World War focused attention on this problem.   Mental and nervous diseases were the most important single reason for the rejection of young men about to be inducted into the armed services, and by far the most important reason for medical discharges from the military forces.

Hospitalization of the Mentally Ill

Long before the Second World War, however, there was widespread recognition of the need for public care of those persons so seriously deranged as to require hospitalization. The states long ago accepted this responsibility. Every state now maintains at least one institution for persons who are mentally ill, and nearly ninety per cent of all mental hospital cases are in state hospitals. Patients are commonly accepted on a part-pay basis, or even without charge, if necessary. Unfortunately, however, the facilities provided by these public institutions are often inadequate. There is widespread overcrowding, neglect, and sometimes even a lack of simple decencies. Many attendants are not trained, and many patients are treated as prisoners. Yet there has been vast improvement in the last few years. In 1949 the Governors' Conference directed the Council of State Governments to make a comprehensive survey of existing facilities for the care of the mentally ill. That survey was published in 1950.[5] Together with earlier reports from other sources,[6] it led to remarkable improvement in the mental health facilities of the states. The Council of State Governments was able to report in 1954 that "practically every state passed legislation and appropriated funds for the construction of whole new hospitals, buildings, wings, units or wards, or for remodeling antiquated buildings and facilities. About three quarters of the states raised salaries, provided better employee housing, improved working conditions, shortened hours or expanded professional opportunities, thus encouraging better qualified employees to join or remain with the staffs. Many states employed special personnel to improve hospital and treatment programs." [7]

Early Diagnosis and Treatment

Fully as important as the care of mentally ill persons requiring hospitalization is the early diagnosis and treatment of children and adults whose psychiatric disturbances have not yet reached serious proportions. One half of the states had established mental hygiene clinics by 1946. In that year Congress enacted a National Mental Health Act, which provided, among other things, for grants to the states to develop adequate mental health programs, with emphasis on the prevention and early treatment of mental disorders. Almost all the states have accepted the federal offer, and have begun mental health services or expanded those services already in operation. The federal authorities believe that the states should establish at least one mental health clinic for every one hundred thousand persons, but this goal is not yet attainable, partly because of the shortage of trained personnel.

[5] Council of State Governments, *The Mental Health Programs of the Forty-Eight States.*

[6] See, for example, Albert Deutsch's 1949 study of state mental hospitals, published under the title *The Shame of the States.*

[7] "Progress in Mental Health, 1952–1953," *Book of the States, 1954–1955,* p. 298.

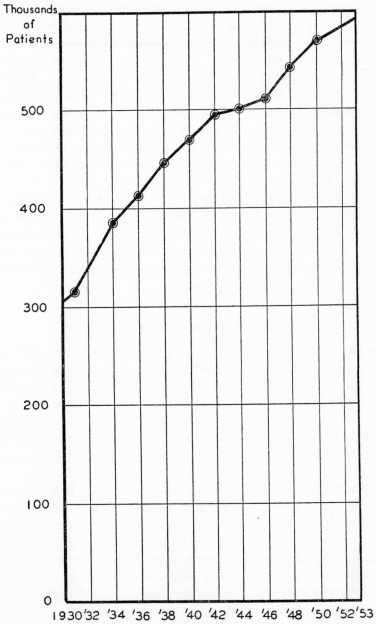

Based on reports of the United States Bureau of the Census.

VITAL STATISTICS

One of the most important phases of public health work is the collection of vital statistics. These statistics—the "bookkeeping" of public health—provide the only effective means of measuring health department success or failure. They point the way to future health department activities. A complete record of deaths, and of the various causes of death, serves as a crude index of the effectiveness of the several aspects of health work. Communicable disease reports furnish the basis for community health plans and forewarn against impending epidemics. Birth records enable the health department to keep in close contact with mothers during the crucial first year of their children's lives. In large part because of the efforts of the federal government, more or less complete vital statistics are now kept in all the states.

A bureau or division of vital statistics in the state department of health usually supervises the collection of records. The primary registration unit, however, is the county, city, town, township, or election district. Within each unit is a registrar of vital statistics, who is generally paid a small fee for each birth and death entered on the records. There is no uniform method of selecting these local registrars.

PUBLIC HEALTH LABORATORIES

In 1890 Minnesota made provision for a smallpox vaccine laboratory. Four years later Rhode Island established a public health laboratory for the diagnosis of communicable diseases. From these early beginnings have developed the modern public health laboratories, now operating in every state. Sometimes the state laboratory is connected with the state university, but this arrangement is less common than formerly and is now found in only a few states.

Diagnosis of communicable diseases—the *raison d'être* of the early public health laboratories—is still one of their major activities. In addition, however, they perform a number of other functions, such as the examination of water supplies, sewage, and milk. They also manufacture or purchase biological products—antitoxins, vaccines, and the like—and distribute them to the local health departments free or at cost. The Kentucky laboratory conducts a school for laboratory technicians. In Michigan the health laboratory does technical work for the state police and the state bureau of education. More than half of the state public health laboratories de-

vote some of their appropriations to research activities; the others are prevented from engaging in research by limited funds and personnel.

Within recent years has developed a movement for branch laboratories
conveniently located throughout the state, in addition to the central state
laboratory.   These branches, though equipped to perform only the simpler
laboratory functions, have rendered a valuable service to many outlying
sections.   In emergencies, especially, their prompt diagnosis has sometimes
prevented the spread of epidemics.

SANITARY ENGINEERING

Nearly every state health department employs a sanitary engineer and
generally places its sanitary engineering functions in a separate division or
bureau.   These functions have become much more numerous and important
during the last two decades; they now consume ten per cent or more of the
total state health appropriation in more than half of the states.

The work of the bureau of sanitary engineering is not everywhere the
same, although it commonly includes the examination of water and milk
supplies and the protection of lakes, streams, and harbors against pollution.
State health department approval is generally required for all plans for
the construction, alteration, or extension of public water supplies and
sewerage systems, and these plans go to the sanitary engineer, who determines whether they meet minimum state requirements.   His analysis
of public water supplies is made at regular intervals—monthly, quarterly, or
annually—in some states, and irregularly in others.

A number of states have enacted laws requiring inspection of bottled
waters offered for sale.   This inspection is commonly made by the bureau
of sanitary engineering, though sometimes by the food and drug division.
In those states that have sanitary regulations concerning the ice industry,
enforcement is uniformly entrusted to the bureau of sanitary engineering.
Water supplies to be used in the production of ice are analyzed, and on the
basis of this analysis permission to make ice is granted or withheld.   Since
1948 federal funds have been available to the states for more thorough campaigns against water pollution.

Camp sanitation has become a matter of considerable importance in
recent years, largely as a result of the increased use of camps by motorists,
and is now generally regulated by state law.   In many states the camps
are required to secure health department licenses, which are granted only
after inspection by the bureau of sanitary engineering.   The health depart-

ments of a few states, however, act merely in an advisory capacity regarding camp sanitation.

Varying degrees of control over swimming pools are exercised by the sanitary engineers of the several states. In some states swimming pool plans must be approved; in others operating permits are required. Roadside water supplies, also, are frequently subject to health department examination. Satisfactory supplies are marked with "safe water" placards. In some sections of the county shellfish sanitation has recently acquired considerable importance.

CHILD HYGIENE

In 1921, when a federal subsidy was offered to the states for child hygiene, only a few state health departments were carrying on extensive child hygiene activities. The federal grant proved a powerful stimulus, however, and before long nearly every state had adopted a reasonably adequate program. Later, when the federal government withdrew its support, many state appropriations for child hygiene decreased, and many child hygiene activities were abandoned. But no state entirely deserted the field; and when federal funds again became available, as part of the social security program, state interest quickly revived. All the states now have separate bureaus of child hygiene or bureaus that combine child hygiene with public health nursing or other related activities.

Prenatal Care and Advice

Under the head of maternal and child hygiene, prenatal work is an important phase of public health in many states. Large numbers of permanent prenatal clinics have been established, and at these clinics expectant mothers are supplied with necessary information. Some states rely on temporary or itinerant clinics, whereas in a number of instances the permanent clinics are conducted by the counties or other local units as part of their general health programs.

An alternative to the clinic, less effective but also less expensive, is the prenatal "conference"—a public meeting under the direction of state doctors and nurses at which questions concerning mothers and babies are asked and answered. Women who attend prenatal conferences and leave their names are placed on the mailing list of the state bureau of child hygiene, which sends out monthly letters as well as educational pamphlets and leaflets. Many—perhaps most—women reached by the health department's clinics or conferences receive no regular medical care during the prenatal period, and have no other way of learning how to care for themselves and their babies.

Midwifery

In certain sections of the country the supervision and training of midwives is a serious problem.   Although midwifery is not recognized in Massachusetts and is steadily decreasing in a number of other states, it is still very important in the South and some parts of the West.   The Southern midwives, chiefly Negroes, are sadly in need of even the most elementary instruction. Their practices are often reminiscent of the days before the Civil War, when semisavage prayers to unknown spirits were a part of the established ritual.

Because of the vast differences among midwives in the several states, radically different standards have been adopted.   Thus New York provides instruction through lectures and letters, and subjects all its midwives to rigid state inspection, whereas some commonwealths, although supplying short courses of training, ignore the legal requirements that all midwives must be licensed and thus permit hundreds of midwives to practice without training of any sort.

Care of Premature Infants

Nearly all the states now make some provision for the protection of children born prematurely.   The most advanced plans include the establishment of hospital facilities to meet the special needs of such infants.   But some jurisdictions rely on graduate training for physicians, plus demonstrations for the mothers of the prematurely born.   A few states furnish home nursing services.

Eye Treatment for the New-born

Legislation concerning eye treatment of the new-born for the purpose of guarding against gonorrheal infection has been enacted everywhere. Usually the law specifies that a one per cent solution of silver nitrate must be used, although in some instances a "comparable antiseptic" is permitted. Most of the states provide for free distribution of silver nitrate to physicians. Infant and preschool clinics, corresponding to the prenatal clinics already described, are maintained by the state health department in nearly three fourths of the states.   In some of the remaining states infant and preschool clinics are directed by the local health organizations.

Crippled Children

In 1935 the federal government offered to pay a part of the cost of medical care for crippled children, and all the states accepted the subsidy. The result has been a marked expansion in state programs, which now include diagnosis, treatment, and convalescent care. Permanent clinics for crippled children have been established in the larger population centers; elsewhere the work is carried on by itinerant staffs, which make a complete circuit of the state once or twice a year. Nurses attached to the clinics assume responsibility for finding cases, stimulating clinic attendance, and following up clinic work with home visits. Braces and other orthopedic appliances are furnished by the state if they are not available from any other source. About one fourth of the states maintain their own orthopedic hospitals; the others rely on local hospital facilities.

Dental Inspection and Care

Nearly all the states are concerned with the possibility of improving the dental health of children. Boys and girls in the schools are taught the importance of caring for their teeth, and these lessons may be followed by regular dental inspection. Teeth found to be defective are not usually treated by the school dentist, however. Instead, the condition is called to the attention of the parents, who are urged to take their children to the family dentist at the earliest opportunity. But treatment at public expense may be provided for the indigent, or for those in the first two or three years of school. Increasing emphasis has recently been placed on practices designed to retard the decay of teeth. Nearly eight hundred communities in the United States now add small quantities of fluorine to their water supplies.

PUBLIC HEALTH NURSING

Public health nursing, stimulated by federal funds, has become an important phase of health work. In most states it developed under local control and marked an expansion of local health activities. Most state health departments, however, have now assumed responsibility for public health nursing programs and have created separate bureaus to deal with this work.

Public health nursing is closely related to child hygiene, and the two activities are often carried on by the same nurses. In many instances women seeking information concerning the care of their babies are taught valuable lessons in health protection for the entire family. Home visits as well as public demonstrations serve to emphasize the importance of health and the necessity of obeying the simple rules of personal hygiene.

The eligibility requirements for public health nurses vary considerably. Usually they must be registered nurses with a certain amount of experience in general nursing or public health work, but some states specify merely that they must be registered nurses or even omit this basic requirement; whereas some states at the other extreme demand postgraduate training in public health nursing and extensive experience under supervision. Political considerations do not usually play a part in the selection of public health nurses, although there have been a few flagrant examples of partisan interference in this field.

INDUSTRIAL HYGIENE

Almost all the states have now established bureaus or divisions of industrial hygiene, whose task is to promote the health of workers in industry. Occupational diseases are studied, and the causes removed wherever possible.[8] Efforts are made to improve the working environment by encouraging better lighting and ventilation. Workers are given medical examinations at regular intervals, and in many instances physical defects are corrected. Instruction is provided for factory employees concerning such diverse matters as nutrition, personal hygiene, and methods of avoiding industrial accidents. Sometimes the state health department co-operates with the department of labor—especially in accident prevention. Federal funds have been granted to the states for the development of industrial hygiene programs, and most of the nation's factory workers now receive some services in this field.

EDUCATIONAL ACTIVITIES OF THE STATE HEALTH DEPARTMENT

It has already been indicated that nearly all the state health departments carry on educational activities. In some states these activities are widely scattered, each bureau preparing and distributing its own literature, designing and displaying its own exhibits, and making its own arrangements for radio broadcasts, without regard for the plans of other bureaus. Much more commonly, however, responsibility for health education vests in a single division—either a separate division of public health instruction or the office of the head of the department. Not all the details of the depart-

[8] See pages 538–539.

ment's educational campaigns are centrally administered, but a general oversight is exercised and an attempt is made to prevent unnecessary duplication and other forms of wasted effort.

Types of Publicity

The educational programs of the state health departments assume a
variety of forms.   Newspaper publicity is nearly always important, because
it provides a means of reaching a maximum number of people at minimum
expense.   About one third of the state health departments maintain regular
newspaper service, with department employees assigned to the task of finding newsworthy incidents and putting them in proper form for publication.
In most of the other states news stories and articles are released from time
to time.

Another common form of publicity is the health department bulletin,
published at regular intervals in most states.   Some of the more progressive health departments issue their bulletins every week or every month;
others provide for quarterly or semiannual publications.   Radio talks are
given on health topics.   Motion picture films and projecting machines are
often a part of the equipment of the state health department; in some instances the projecting machines are mounted on trucks that tour the rural
sections.

Co-operation of State Department of Education

Many phases of public health education require the co-operation of the
state department of education, and in most instances this co-operation is
freely given.   In fact, more than half of the states report some co-operative
activities involving the department of education and the health department.
Among the co-operative features of public health programs may be mentioned the joint management of courses in public health at teachers' institutes, the preparation by the health department of the hygiene textbook
for the public schools, and the promotion of teacher training in health subjects.

Miscellaneous Duties

A number of miscellaneous duties occupy the attention of many state
health departments.   Most important is the enforcement of the food and
drug laws—a task entrusted to the health department in one third of the
states.   Nearly all the other states place food and drug inspection in the
department of agriculture.   Among the other functions occasionally performed by the health department are plumbing inspection, inspection of

weights and measures, and enforcement of sanitary regulations concerning hotels and restaurants.

SOCIALIZED MEDICINE

One of the most marked characteristics of public health work has been its tendency to include an ever-expanding list of functions. From its early beginning in the field of communicable disease control it has grown to comprise child hygiene, public health nursing, sanitary engineering, and a surprisingly long list of additional activities. It goes far beyond the original concept of disease suppression.

From time to time the proposal has been made that public health go still further, and take as its province practically the entire field of medicine, including the suppression, prevention, and treatment of disease. Necessary medical attention might be supplied directly by the state to all the people, or to all in the lower income brackets; or, as an alternative, such attention might be supplied by quasi-public groups of physicians, who would be closely regulated by the state as to charges and quality of service.

Private Studies and Legislative Proposals

This suggestion for public medicine, in whatever form, was formerly brushed aside with scant consideration. But in 1932 the Committee on the Costs of Medical Care, a committee of eminent physicians, social scientists, and laymen whose investigations were financed by the Rockefeller Foundation, the Russell Sage Foundation, and a number of other foundations and funds, indorsed the idea of quasi-public medical service under state control.

At once socialization of medicine became a live issue, and its importance was emphasized still further by the enactment in 1935 of the federal social security program, which sought to eliminate most of the major causes of economic insecurity *except illness*. Many persons contended that this omission was serious—that it weakened the entire program. Bills providing for some form of public medicine were introduced from time to time in Congress and in a number of state legislatures. These bills were sponsored by the governors of several states, and in 1949 one congressional proposal received the endorsement of President Truman. Today, however, the attitude of the Republican administration is very different. President Eisenhower has spoken strongly against socialized medicine, and has urged instead a larger measure of voluntary health insurance. Medicine has not yet been socialized in any state of the American Union.

Health Insurance

In Europe, where the masses of the people have long been supplied with free medical services at public expense, weekly benefits are regularly paid by the government to persons incapacitated by illness. Four states of the American Union—California, New Jersey, New York, and Rhode Island —now pay sickness benefits, and a number of other states have considered the plan. But it must be understood that health insurance is not necessarily a companion of public medicine. The state may compensate its citizens for loss of earnings during illness without assuming the responsibility of trying to restore their health. Yet the arguments in favor of both schemes are much the same.

Arguments for Socialized Medicine

The basic argument of those who favor socialized medicine is that it would produce a marked improvement in the health of the American people. Every year, it is said, there are hundreds of thousands of deaths that modern medical science has the knowledge and skill to prevent. These deaths occur because people do not have the money to pay for necessary medical services, or because they live in areas where such services are not available. There are, of course, privately financed and operated hospital plans in the United States, and also privately financed systems of medical care. Some of these schemes have the active support of the American Medical Association, and have enrolled millions of subscribers. But the proponents of public medicine declare that such plans are not enough, because they fail to reach the very groups that need them most.

Arguments against Socialized Medicine

Thus stated, the merits of socialized medicine seem to exceed its defects by a wide margin. But there are a number of arguments against socialized medicine that must not be overlooked. The opponents of the scheme contend that it would lead to the establishment of a medical hierarchy in every community, without whose consent medicine could not be practiced. Arbitrary discriminations would result, and the situation might be complicated still further by the intrusion of partisan politics. Then, too, the expense of administering great medical centers and of assigning patients would be so great as to increase, instead of decrease, the cost of medical care. Wastefulness and inefficiency, so often associated with public and quasi-public undertakings, at least in the public mind, would characterize this newest enterprise. And the final result would be a triumph of bureaucracy, to the infinite detriment of American medicine. Perhaps most serious of all, the continuous personal relationship of physician and patient, involving understanding on the part of the physician and confidence on the part of the patient, would be destroyed. The proponents of socialized medicine usually recognize this danger, and declare that a personal relationship must be preserved. But any comprehensive scheme of public medicine, according to its opponents, would make such preservation impossible.

Conclusions

Here, then, are both sides of a bitter controversy. The arguments against socialized medicine are potent, yet it must be admitted that they closely resemble the objections once raised against "socialized" education—that is, a system of free schools with compulsory attendance. Perhaps some day the public will decide that health, like education, is so closely related to the general welfare that it should not be left in private hands. Perhaps on the other hand, it will find that a system of voluntary or compulsory health insurance, backed by generous federal grants, will substantially solve the problem. No one can safely predict the future of socialized medicine in the United States.

PROBLEMS

1. Study the organization of your state health department. Enumerate the services that it performs, and note the date that each of these services was added to the list.

2. Trace the relations of state and local health authorities in your state. Has state supervision resulted in higher standards of local health work?

3. Should smallpox vaccination be made compulsory? What proposals for compulsory vaccination have been made in your community? What groups have opposed the movement?

4. Study the relations of public and private agencies in the control of tuberculosis. Have these relations proved entirely satisfactory?

5. Visit your state public health laboratory, and write a brief description of its organization and work.

6. Prepare a summary of the proposals for socialized medicine that have been made in Congress and in various state legislatures.

SELECTED REFERENCES

American Public Health Association, *Control of Communicable Diseases,* 1943.
American Public Health Association, *Committee on Administrative Practices,* 1944.
Anderson, Gaylord W., and Arnstein, Margaret G., *Communicable Disease Control; A Volume for the Health Officer and Public Health Nurse,* 1941.

Anderson, H. B., *Public Health the American Way*, 1945.

Bachman, George W., and Associates, *Health Resources in the United States*, Washington, D.C., 1952.

Bachman, George W., and Meriam, Lewis, *The Issue of Compulsory Health Insurance*, 1948.

Bolduan, C. F. and N. W., *Public Health and Hygiene*, 2nd ed., 1936.

Corwin, E. H. L., *The American Hospital*, 1946.

Council of State Governments, *The Mental Health Programs of the Forty-Eight States*, 1950.

Currie, J. R., *Manual of Public Health Hygiene*, Baltimore, 1938.

Davis, Michael M., *America Organizes Medicine*, 1941.

————, *Public Medical Services*, 1937.

Deutsch, Albert, *The Shame of the States*, 1949.

Dodd, Paul A., and Penrose, E. F., *Economic Aspects of Medical Services*, Washington, D.C., 1939.

Federal Security Agency, *The Nation's Health*, 1948.

Goldmann, Franz, *Voluntary Medical Care Insurance in the United States*, 1948.

Levy, Herman, *National Health Insurance; A Critical Study*, 1945.

Millis, H. A., *Sickness and Insurance*, 1937.

Mountin, Joseph W., and Flook, Evelyn, *Distribution of Health Services in the Structure of State Government*, Public Health Bulletin No. 184, 3rd ed., U.S. Public Health Service, Washington. D.C., 1943.

————, *Guide to Health Organizations in the United States*, U.S. Public Health Service, Washington, D.C., 1953.

Mustard, H. S., *Government in Public Health*, 1945.

New York Academy of Medicine, *Medicine in the Changing Order*, 1947.

Simpson, Herbert D., *Compulsory Health Insurance in the United States*, Evanston, Ill., 1943.

Sinai, Nathan, and Others, *Health Insurance in the United States*, 1946.

Smilie, W. G., *Public Health Administration in the United States*, rev. ed., 1940.

Stern, Bernard J., *Medical Services by Government—Local, State, and Federal*, 1946.

Tobey, J. A., *Public Health Law*, 3rd ed., 1947.

United States Public Health Service, *Public Health Personnel, Facilities and Services in Local Areas*, 1953.

White House Conference on Child Health and Protection, *Hospitals and Child Health*, 1932.

————, *Public Health Organization*, 1932.

The March, 1953, issue of the *Annals of the American Academy of Political and Social Science* is entitled "Mental Health in the United States."

CHAPTER 20

Housing

The health of a nation's inhabitants is closely related to the homes in which they live. Every study of housing conditions in America and Europe, especially in the cities, discloses an astonishingly high death rate and an almost unbelievably large amount of sickness in houses—especially of the tenement variety—where men, women, and children are herded together like cattle, and where fresh air and sunlight are at a premium. Contagious diseases spread most rapidly in the congested areas. Tuberculosis is rapidly becoming a slum disease. A survey made in Buffalo some years ago showed that public health costs were three times as high per family in slum areas as in other parts of the city.[1] The slum is a breeder of disease, a destroyer of vitality, an arch-enemy of health.

Bad housing is an acute menace to family life, breaking down established moral standards and leading naturally to sexual perversion. When a family of five or six persons, including perhaps older children of different sexes, is housed in one or two rooms, making it impossible to have even the slightest degree of privacy, and when the meager family income is augmented, as it frequently is, by taking in a lodger or two, the result is very likely to be moral deterioration. Very young boys and girls acquire a morbid knowledge of sexual matters, and older children are subjected to temptations that many of them cannot resist.

UNSATISFACTORY HOUSING CONDITIONS

Magnitude of Metropolitan Problems

The housing problem is especially serious in the great cities—New York, Chicago, Philadelphia, Boston, and perhaps two dozen other metropolitan centers. In these municipalities the need for decent living accommodations is acute, and the problem of providing them is very difficult of solution. New York, especially, faces a task of stupendous magnitude in its efforts

[1] See the Federal Public Housing Authority's pamphlet, *Reference and Source Material on Housing and Housing Needs* (1947).

to improve housing conditions. It has accomplished some important results in the last few years, yet it still permits the existence of miles of unsanitary tenement houses. Living conditions in slum areas are appalling.
Congestion and overcrowding are almost beyond belief.

Backward Conditions in Smaller Cities and Rural Areas

It must not be assumed, however, that even the smaller cities have satisfactory housing conditions. They have their overcrowded lots and overcrowded rooms, dark rooms and damp rooms, lack of water, lack of sanitary
conveniences, houses in every state of decay, with fire hazards that are excessive. Cellar dwellings are still sometimes permitted, and though a relatively
few cellars are fit for human habitation, the large majority are not. The
ideal of running water in every separate apartment is still a long way from
realization, and even today some persons seriously contend that bathtubs
are luxuries instead of necessities. In the rural areas housing conditions
are even worse than in the cities, but at least everyone can secure his fair
share of fresh air and sunlight.

Decentralization of Industry

A major cause of housing congestion is the natural desire of workers to
be near their places of employment. Most men and women, especially of
the poorer classes, are unwilling to spend a great deal of time and money
traveling between their homes and the factories, warehouses, and other
places where they work. Some of them could undoubtedly be tempted to
move into the suburbs, where land is cheaper and housing problems are relatively simple, by means of high speed transit lines and lower fares. But
the only way—aside from expensive slum clearance—to get the majority
of the slum dwellers out of their present environment would be to uproot
bodily the factories and warehouses where they are employed. The tendency of certain types of industry to desert the downtown section of high
land values for outlying districts where land is relatively cheap is already
quite marked in many communities, but no one knows whether it will continue. One thing is obvious, however: every city should at once make
certain that the congested housing conditions of its present slum district
will never be duplicated in the communities of workers' homes that may
some day spring up in its suburbs alongside suburban factories. This it
can do by means of a carefully prepared plan and a comprehensive zoning
law.

MUNICIPAL HOUSING LAWS

Prevalence of Housing Codes

It has been estimated that the homes of over one third of the people of the United States fail to measure up to minimum standards of health and decency.   It is necessary, therefore, for government to take a hand.   Nearly every city has a code that specifies minimum standards of building construction.   This code applies, of course, to stores and factories as well as to homes, but its provisions may be so framed as to produce vastly improved housing conditions.   For example, it may prohibit windowless rooms, uncemented cellars, wooden tenements.   In addition to these minimum building specifications, the average municipality has a series of regulations concerning the equipment of buildings, and imposing conditions under which they may be occupied as homes.   These regulations may be made a part of the building code, incorporated in a separate housing code, or merely added to the health ordinance.

Construction Provisions of Laws

The housing law of a city—using this term to cover all its housing rules except the zoning ordinance, whether or not they have been brought together in a single code—is a very comprehensive affair.   It deals both with construction and with maintenance.   The provisions concerning construction are commonly grouped under three heads: light and ventilation, sanitation, fire protection.

LIGHT AND VENTILATION.   Under the title of light and ventilation are usually found limitations on the amount of lot space that may be used for building purposes, unless this matter has already been covered by zoning. Here, too, are placed requirements concerning minimum height and floor space of rooms, and minimum window space.   Some cities stipulate that every room in a dwelling must have at least one window opening to the outer air, but a great many municipalities are still unwilling to go so far.

SANITATION.   The sanitation requirements of the housing law deal with such matters as water supply, toilet facilities, sewer connections, drainage of yards and courts.   Sometimes running water in every apartment of a tenement house is made mandatory, but frequently the law merely provides that there must be running water on every floor, accessible to all families.

FIRE PROTECTION.   The provisions of the building code designed to prevent fires are usually very comprehensive.   Wooden tenements are commonly prohibited, and there are clauses concerning fire escapes, stairs, elevator and dumb-waiter shafts.   There are also miscellaneous safety requirements, covering excavations and foundations, use of steel, timber, concrete and the like, and specifying the exact procedure in building operations.

NEW CONSTRUCTION TECHNIQUES AND MATERIALS.   Many present-day building codes are unsatisfactory, because they fail to recognize recent developments in construction techniques and the use of new materials.   Prefabricated houses, for example, cannot be erected in many communities, merely because the men who drafted the building code a number of years ago never heard of them.   Plaster must still be used, because plywood and wallboard have been developed too recently to secure recognition as suitable wall materials.   Not all cities are so completely bound by tradition, however.   Several hundred of them have recently revised their building codes, or are in process of doing so.   The modern tendency is to emphasize performance.   The new codes will accept any material that meets proper standards of structural strength and fire resistance, even though it may not conform to preconceived notions of weight and thickness.

Maintenance Provisions

The maintenance provisions of municipal housing codes are designed to insure the proper upkeep and use of properly constructed homes.   They commonly stipulate that cellars must be whitewashed, roofs kept in repair, and fire escapes unencumbered at all times.   In addition, they usually prohibit the keeping of horses, cows, swine, and poultry in tenements.   Such a prohibition has been found necessary.   With respect to air space, a minimum number of cubic feet per person is generally required—perhaps four or five hundred for every adult, and two or three hundred for every child. These air space provisions are essential,[2] yet the difficulty of enforcing them is obvious.   If a family of four lives in a single room, the enforcement officer can readily take the dimensions of the room and find whether it contains a sufficient number of cubic feet of air.   But how can he tell whether one or two lodgers also use the room at night?

The Lodger Evil

The practice of taking lodgers has become very widespread among the tenement dwellers of the large cities.   Rents are so high that in many cases there seems to be no other way of balancing the family budget.   Needless to say, this "lodger evil," as it is generally called, presents a serious social

[2] It must be admitted, however, that the flat air space requirement is a very crude way of providing for an adequate air supply. A small room opening directly on a broad street may make a much more satisfactory bedroom than a larger room opening on a narrow court. But it is difficult to devise a better standard.

problem. It destroys the privacy of the home, and makes normal family life virtually impossible. It leads naturally to the violation of accepted standards. Thousands of young women are degraded every year in their own homes by male lodgers, with whom they must necessarily associate on terms of enforced intimacy.

One of the worst aspects of the lodger evil is the difficulty of curbing it. It is a simple matter to enact drastic legislation, but the adequate enforcement of such legislation is an almost impossible task. If inspections are made, they must be carried on at night. A veritable army of inspectors is needed. And even then it is very difficult to detect violators, for lodgers soon learn the trick of moving out on the fire escapes while inspections are in progress. Better results could doubtless be obtained by abandoning such inspections altogether and holding the landlords directly responsible for any overcrowding.

Enforcement of Housing Laws

DIFFICULTIES. With regard to new buildings, the construction clauses of the housing code can be enforced readily enough by securing adequate inspection. Already existing buildings, however, present a more difficult problem—especially the overcrowded tenements built three or four decades ago, when people had a very different concept of what constituted a minimum standard of decent living. There are tenements in almost every large city so far below the minimum requirements for new construction that the expense of putting them in proper condition would be prohibitive. The only proper way to treat such buildings is to prohibit their use as dwellings. In many cities, however, the housing laws are unduly lenient. The New York tenement house law, for example, permits an inside room to be used as a bedroom if it is connected by a window with a room that opens to the outer air. As a result of this provision, thousands of windows have been cut through thousands of room partitions, making the inside rooms legally light, but leaving them actually almost as dark as before.

ENFORCEMENT AGENCIES. Two or three separate agencies of the city government are usually charged with the task of enforcing the different sections of the housing law. Those provisions that refer to construction and fire protection are commonly placed under the care of a bureau or division of building inspection. Matters of a sanitary nature, such as light and ventilation, water supply and plumbing, are generally entrusted to the health department. These two agencies sometimes share the responsibility for enforcement with the police department or the fire department, or both. New York has concentrated most of its supervisory and inspectional activities concerning tenements in a single division of the city government known as the Tenement House Department.   This plan gives reasonable satisfaction, and might well be copied by other metropolitan centers.   Housing authorities are generally agreed, however, that unless a city has a great many tenements there is no need for it to increase the complexity of its administrative organization by adding a separate tenement house department.   The average city can secure best results by providing for the co-operation of the bureau of building inspection and the health department.

Nonuniformity of Codes

One of the most serious defects of municipal building codes is their lack of uniformity.   Some are long; others are short.   Some are indexed; others are not.   Some are needlessly complex; others attain simplicity by omitting essential provisions.   Some are expressed in general terms; others are very specific.   Equally unfortunate, there is no uniformity of arrangement.   The result is that an architect or engineer finds himself greatly handicapped when he tries to expand his activities beyond his own city.   No matter how small or unimportant the building, he must spend long hours studying new legal provisions that are likely to be classified according to some plan with which he is unfamiliar.

Necessity of Compromises

Every housing law presents a twofold problem.   It must be sufficiently strict to prevent the building of homes that are structurally unsafe, poorly ventilated and lighted, unsanitary, and veritable firetraps.   On the other hand, it must not be so drastic that it virtually puts a stop to the building of low-cost housing.   It must of necessity be a compromise between what is desirable and what is practicable.   It must be based on a recognition of the obvious fact that a considerable percentage of the people of every city are but little above the borderline of poverty and greatly prefer low rentals to vastly improved living conditions.   The chief result of an unduly stringent housing law may be a housing shortage.

THE SLUM PROBLEM AND LOW-COST HOUSING

Many of the dwellings in the slums of every large city are so dilapidated and unsanitary that there is no likelihood of ever transforming them into suitable places for human habitation.   Their decay and squalor may be kept within reasonable limits by strict enforcement of the housing code, but at best they will continue to be breeding places of disease and vice.   One way to treat such sore spots is to eliminate them.   Buildings may be torn down and new buildings erected in their stead.   In the meantime, provision must be made for housing the families that have been forced to vacate their homes.

Slum Clearance through Private Initiative

New York City pioneered in the field of low-cost housing in the early 1920's, placing its reliance chiefly on private initiative.   During the next few years a number of other cities and several of the states experimented with somewhat similar plans, and in 1933 the federal government offered substantial loans for limited-dividend, low-cost private housing projects.   Within a few months it had received more than five hundred applications, but subsequent investigation revealed that only seven of these requests could meet federal requirements.   Thereupon the federal government abandoned its attempt to solve the problem by stimulating private enterprise.   Not all the states were discouraged, however.   A number of them subsequently enacted laws granting to private "urban redevelopment corporations" the right to condemn and clear slum areas, and use the land for low-cost housing projects. Some states offered the inducement of partial tax exemption; others did not. But their plans produced paltry results.[3]

The truth was that low-cost housing seldom provided an adequate return on the money invested.   Millions of workers could not afford to pay for decent housing out of their meager earnings.   Therefore they were obliged to accept substandard accommodations unless the government somehow bridged the gap between their incomes and their needs.

Urban Redevelopment with Federal Assistance

In 1949 Congress enacted a comprehensive housing law, which attacked the problem on several fronts.   Among other things, this law and its subsequent amendments offer federal assistance to cities in clearing blighted areas. Every city receiving federal funds must have a suitable housing agency, with full power to direct the work.   It must have a detailed plan for redevelopment of the slum area, and also for the development of the entire community. Even though a city lacks specific redevelopment plans, however, it may borrow federal money to cover the cost of making necessary surveys.   Eventually it submits its finished plans, and receives federal approval.   Then it becomes eligible for a substantial grant of federal funds.   With this money, plus smaller sums from its own treasury, a city buys the land in the designated

---

[3] There were some examples, however, of successful private ventures in the low-cost housing field.   The Metropolitan Life Insurance Company invested considerable sums in such housing.

slum area, using its power of eminent domain when private owners are not willing to sell. The land is then cleared of its dilapidated buildings, and assembled in tracts suitable for new construction. At this point the project loses most of its public character. The land is sold or leased to private builders, who agree to construct apartments or single-family houses for persons of low income, all in accordance with the city's master plan.

One of the most serious objections to slum clearance is that it dispossesses the slum families, sometimes leaving them without any living quarters until the new housing has been completed. In order to avoid this difficulty, the Housing Act of 1949 provides that every city receiving federal funds for slum clearance must make suitable provision for the housing needs of families affected by its projects. In some cases, of course, cities may desire to encourage private low-rent housing on vacant land. They may receive federal loans for this purpose, but not outright grants.

Even before the passage of the Federal Housing Act of 1949, half of the states had authorized the redevelopment of slum areas in their larger cities. Ten other states have since enacted similar legislation. More than one hundred projects have received federal approval, and in many instances the work of clearing blighted areas has begun. Philadelphia completed the nation's first federally subsidized redevelopment project in 1952.

Federal Mortgage Insurance

The federal government stimulates private home building, not only for the very poor but also for persons of moderate means, by offering to guarantee a substantial part of the mortgage—as much as ninety-five per cent, in many cases—on any moderately priced two-bedroom house. For veterans it even agrees to underwrite second mortgages, thus enabling them to buy houses with almost no outlay of their own. Or, if the veterans find that the rate of interest charged by private mortgage companies is too high, they may borrow directly from the federal treasury. These policies of the federal government undoubtedly have played a part in the building boom of the last five years. More private homes have been built in these years than in any other equal period of American history. But the needs of the very poor have received relatively little attention.

Public Housing

LARGE-SCALE EUROPEAN PROJECTS. The most obvious answer to the problem of providing low-cost housing is public housing, which has become commonplace in Europe. The cities of England, Holland, Sweden, and other European nations have systematically undertaken large-scale housing

CONSTRUCTION OF NONFARM HOMES

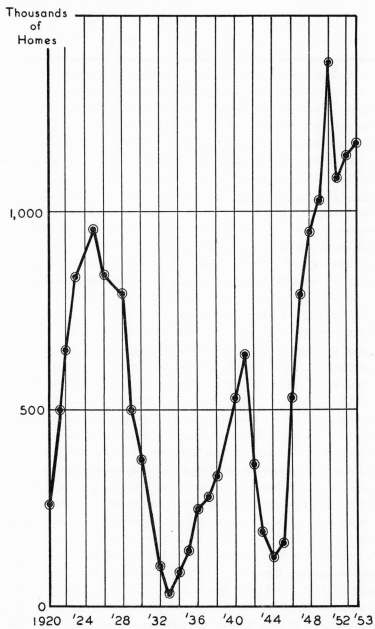

Based on information from reports of the United States Housing and Home Finance Agency.

projects, using their own funds to build small houses for working people. When the houses are completed they may be sold on easy terms, or perhaps rented. Such schemes were not seriously considered in the cities of the United States before the depression of the 1930's. Nor was anything of importance accomplished until the federal government took a hand.

FEDERAL HOUSING SCHEMES: *Public Works Administration.* The first federal housing projects were regarded primarily as a means of reducing unemployment; the improvement of housing conditions was a secondary consideration. The Housing Division of the Public Works Administration constructed more than fifty housing projects in thirty-six cities, at a cost of one hundred and thirty-six million dollars. Rentals were fixed so low that they covered only a part of construction and maintenance costs; the difference represented a direct federal subsidy for low-cost housing.

Federal Housing Act of 1937. The federal housing program struck an unexpected snag when a United States district court ruled that the national government's power of eminent domain might not be used to take land for slum clearance and low-cost housing projects. This decision was affirmed by a circuit court of appeals.[4] Before it could be carried to the Supreme Court of the United States, however, Congress decided upon another housing policy that would avoid constitutional difficulties and at the same time stimulate local interest in the housing problem.

This new policy took legislative form in the Housing Act of 1937, which placed on state and local authorities the primary responsibility for adequate housing facilities, but authorized substantial federal loans and grants for low-cost dwellings. Any local public housing agency might apply to the United States Housing Authority for financial assistance in the development of low-rent housing or slum clearance projects. If these projects met certain federal specifications, the federal government agreed to lend up to ninety per cent of the total cost, at a low rate of interest and for a long term of years. It also provided outright grants for the purpose of keeping rentals at a low level. Tenants were to be selected from low-income families; they had to be persons who would otherwise be obliged to accept substandard accommodations.

The law required the elimination of one slum dwelling for every new dwelling constructed with federal aid. There were, of course, some exceptions: slum buildings might be improved instead of demolished, if circumstances seemed to warrant; demolition might be postponed in the face of a real housing shortage. But the fundamental principle—the linking together of slum clearance and low-cost housing—remained unaltered. Many housing experts objected to this mixture of purposes. They contended that the

[4] United States *v.* Certain Lands in the City of Louisville, 78 Fed. (2nd) 684 (1935).

excessive cost of slum clearance (because of the high value of the land) made such areas unsuitable for low-cost housing. Their arguments had no effect on federal policy, however.

Acceptance by local housing agencies. The federal offer of assistance was accepted eagerly by the states and the local communities. More than three fourths of the state legislatures specifically authorized the cities to engage in public housing, and several hundred municipal housing authorities were set up. By the end of 1941 virtually all available federal money had been lent to local housing agencies, and 137,000 family units were under construction or occupied. In Ohio the public housing program encountered unexpected difficulties when the state supreme court refused to permit tax exemption of municipal housing, on the theory that housing funds were not devoted exclusively to a public purpose.[5] But elsewhere the courts were virtually unanimous in upholding the constitutionality of all phases of the housing program.[6]

War housing. Something should be said concerning the housing problems created by the Second World War. Four million war workers and their families—nine million persons in all—left their homes and migrated to the communities where war industries were booming. Nearly half a million men, women, and children moved into the Los Angeles area; as many came to the metropolitan region of San Francisco. Baltimore, Detroit, Norfolk, and Seattle gained ten to forty per cent in population within a few months. And living quarters had to be found for all these newcomers. More than 165,000 permanent dwellings were built, most of them by private contractors whose costs were virtually guaranteed by the federal government. About 75,000 demountable houses were built, also, and some were removed from their original sites, where they were no longer required, to areas suffering from housing shortages. Temporary homes and dormitories for nearly 300,000 workers were hastily thrown up. Much of the housing constructed under the terrible urgency of war proved totally valueless for permanent peacetime living. Some of it, however, became a part of the postwar public housing program.

Federal Housing Act of 1949. After the war Congress debated housing legislation for several years without finding any acceptable formula. Finally, however, it passed the Housing Act of 1949, to which reference has already been made. This law does not neglect public housing. On the contrary, it

[5] Columbus Metropolitan Housing Authority *v.* Thatcher *et al.,* 42 N.E. (2nd) 432 (1942).

[6] See, for example, Benjamin *v.* Housing Authority of Darlington County *et al.,* 15 S.E. (2nd) 737 (1941); and State *ex rel.* Grubstein *v.* Cambell, Tax Assessor, 1 So. (2nd) 483 (1941).

greatly increases federal subsidies to cities for public housing projects. The principles of the 1937 law have been left substantially unchanged, but there are certain differences. For one thing, the 1949 statute is more specific than its predecessor in determining the basis on which families may become eligible to live in public housing projects. All applicants must be American citizens, and occupants of substandard homes. And, of course, they must have low incomes. The law specifies in addition that preference must be given to veterans and to persons displaced by slum clearance projects.

PRESENT STATUS OF PUBLIC HOUSING. Forty-three states [7] have enacted laws authorizing their local communities to participate in the federal public housing program, and more than one thousand communities have accepted the federal government's terms. Four hundred and fifty thousand units of low-rental housing for poor families have now been completed or are under construction. A few states have made their own funds available for public housing, and in some instances have specified that a part of the housing must be available for war veterans or for the aged. Almost all public housing projects are located in the cities, but federal aid is not restricted to urban areas. On the contrary, it is available for any counties that desire to construct low-cost farm dwellings. Only a handful of rural counties, however, have shown the slightest interest in public housing.

PROBLEMS

1. Summarize the provisions of your city's housing law. What changes would you recommend?

2. Write a brief history of rent control in the United States.

3. Prepare a concise account of public housing activities in London or Stockholm.

4. Write a brief description of federal-municipal relationships in the field of housing since 1933.

5. Describe and analyze New York's experience with limited dividend housing companies.

SELECTED REFERENCES

Abrams, Charles, *The Future of Housing*, 1946.

American Public Health Association, *Standards of Healthful Housing: Planning the Neighborhood*, Chicago, 1948.

Angell, P. D., *Case for Slum Clearance by Private Enterprise*, Chicago, 1939.

Aronovici, Carol, *Housing the Masses*, 1939.

Carlson, Eric, *Co-operative Housing in Urban Redevelopment*, 1951.

[7] The five exceptions are farm states—Iowa, Kansas, Oklahoma, Utah, and Wyoming.

Colean, Miles L., *American Housing*, 1944.

Colean, Miles L., and Davis, Arthur P., *Cost Measurement in Urban Redevelopment*, 1945.

Comer, John, *New York City Building Control, 1800–1941*, 1942.

Fitch, James M., *American Building, The Forces that Shape It*, Boston, 1948.

Gray, George H., *Housing and Citizenship*, 1946.

Hillman, Arthur, and Robert J. Casey, *Tomorrow's Chicago*, 1953.

Housing and Home Finance Agency, *A Handbook of Information on Provisions of the Housing Act of 1949*, Washington, D.C., 1949.

Hunter, Carrie E., *State Rent Control Laws; An Analysis of the Statutory Provisions*, Washington, D.C., 1948.

McGeary, M. Nelson, *The Pittsburgh Housing Authority*, State College, Penna., 1943.

McGoldrick, Jos. D., and Others, *Building Regulation in New York City: A Study in Administrative Law and Procedure*, 1944.

National Association of Housing Officials, *A Housing Program—For Now and Later*, Washington, D.C., 1948.

———, *Community Services and Public Housing*, Chicago, 1947.

National Housing Agency, *Housing Costs*, Washington, D.C., 1945.

National Housing Policy Conference, *A Report to the Nation: Housing in Peace and War*, 1951.

Perry, Clarence A., *Housing for the Machine Age*, 1939.

Reed, W. V., and Ogg, E., *New Homes for Old*, 1940.

Rosenmann, Dorothy, *A Million Homes a Year*, 1945.

Russell, Horace, and Keyserling, Leon H., *Legal Problems in the Housing Field*, Washington, D.C., 1939.

Stein, Clarence S., *Toward New Towns for America*, 1951.

Straus, Nathan, *The Seven Myths of Housing*, 1944.

———, *Two Thirds of a Nation: A Housing Program*, 1952.

Walker, Mabel L., *Urban Blight and Slums*, Cambridge, Mass., 1938.

Weimer, Arthur M., and Hoyt, Homer, *Principles of Urban Real Estate*, 1948.

Wickens, David L., *Differentials in Housing Costs*, 1939.

Zisman, S. B., *The General Plan in the Redevelopment Program*, 1952.

PART SIX

Education and Development

CHAPTER 21

Education

During the early period of American history, and even in the first years of the nineteenth century, education was generally considered a private matter. Except in New England, where public schools early made their appearance because of the close connection between church and state, free education was reserved almost exclusively for the children of paupers. It was, in fact, a form of poor relief. As one writer declares, the masses made no distinction "between putting a coat on a child's back, food into his stomach, and knowledge into his head." [1]

SHIFT FROM PRIVATE TO PUBLIC EDUCATION

A few persons, like Thomas Jefferson in Virginia, favored universal elementary education at state expense, but they were shouted down. They were many years ahead of their time. As late as 1850, when the proposal for a system of free schools received final approval in New York State, most rural voters expressed themselves in opposition. A similar plan for Pennsylvania proved unpopular in the farming sections until the Civil War.

Many persons argued vehemently that public education would foment social unrest and perhaps lead to revolution, since the poor would gain a better understanding of their burdens. It was said, also, that taxation for school purposes was a gross violation of private property rights. Why should a man be compelled to support a public school system if he chose to send his children to a private sectarian academy? But these arguments were of no avail against the trend of the times. The ideal of free, universal, compulsory education was rapidly gaining general acceptance. Today it is no longer questioned; it is a foundation of the American social structure.

DIVISION OF RESPONSIBILITY FOR PUBLIC EDUCATION

Responsibility for financing and directing public education is divided among the nation, the states, and the local units of government. The na-

[1] Wm. A. Cook, *Federal and State School Administration*, p. 35.

tion's part is narrowly restricted by the federal Constitution, which makes no mention of educational matters, thus reserving control of education to the states.[2]   Yet the federal government has appropriated hundreds of millions of dollars for educational purposes.   It has turned over to the states more than seventy million acres of the national domain in furtherance of public education.   And it has even secured the right to supervise certain phases of the state educational systems by means of conditional grants from the federal treasury.[3]   It maintains an Office of Education that collects educational statistics, conducts educational surveys, and furnishes advice to state and local school officials concerning educational problems.

During the depression years of the 1930's its Civilian Conservation Corps operated an elaborate educational program; its Works Progress Administration maintained many educational projects; and its National Youth Administration provided part-time employment for hundreds of thousands of young people enrolled in high schools and colleges.   At the close of the Second World War Congress enacted legislation permitting many returned war veterans to complete their education at federal expense.[4]   For the most part, however, education still remains outside the sphere of federal control. Though the federal government is much more than a mere spectator of educational progress, it plays no important part in the administration of public education.

A vast number of court decisions have established beyond reasonable doubt the fact that education is primarily a matter of state concern.[5]   Even in those states that have accepted the principle of municipal home rule,[6] education remains under state control unless specifically assigned by the state to the local units of government.   In nearly every state, however, the actual management of the school system rests with locally chosen officials.   School expenses are met chiefly from local taxes.   The state, though supreme in matters of education, generally prefers to exercise its authority through local channels.   Therefore the local units of government properly come first in any discussion of school administration.

[2] By the Tenth Amendment.   See page 6.
[3] See pages 11–16.
[4] The states also provided educational opportunities for veterans.
[5] See, for example, Louisville v. Board of Education, 154 Ky. 316; 157 S.W. 379 (1913); Associated Schools v. School District, 122 Minn. 254; 142 N.W. 325 (1913); MacQueen v. Port Huron, 194 Mich. 328; 160 N.W. 627, 630 (1916).
[6] See pages 51–56.

LOCAL UNITS OF SCHOOL ADMINISTRATION

The School District Plan

The local unit responsible for directing the school system is not everywhere the same. It may be the school district, the town, the township, or the county. The school district plan of organization has several features worthy of mention: it was one of the earliest schemes of school management; it is unquestionably the worst; it is still the most widely used; but it is rapidly losing much of its former popularity. In early times, and under more primitive conditions, the district plan was reasonably satisfactory. But as educational standards rose and it became increasingly evident that small districts—especially districts of the "little red schoolhouse" variety—could not meet present-day requirements, a determined movement began in many states for the elimination of the school districts and the transfer of their functions to larger units of government, such as the townships or counties.

OBJECTIONS. In opposition to the district system it was pointed out that most districts were too poor to warrant the employment of suitable teachers and too small to permit the division of the student body into grades; that schools were unwisely distributed; that educational facilities varied widely from district to district because of unequal wealth and uneven interest in education; that so many school trustees—often five hundred or more in a single county—were required by the plan as to make the selection of many mediocre persons almost inevitable; and that in practice the scheme had proved inefficient, wasteful, and a barrier to educational advancement. The result of this crusade, which is still in progress, has been the abandonment of the district system in many states and its modification in a number of others. The total number of school districts in the United States has been reduced one third in the last ten years. Illinois, an outstanding example of this reform, had nearly twelve thousand school districts in 1945; it now has about thirty-four hundred.[7] The district plan is still used extensively in twenty-seven states, however. But the district trustees have generally been deprived of several important functions, including the certification of teachers, the selection of textbooks, and the distribution of school funds.[8]

LARGE URBAN DISTRICTS. It should be pointed out that a municipality, from the standpoint of educational administration, is simply a single school district. Even a large metropolitan center occupies this legal position. It

[7] See "School District Reorganization in Illinois," by Harlan Beem, in *State Government*, July, 1951, pp. 178–181.

[8] See "School District Reorganization Today," by Leslie L. Chisholm, in *State Government*, September, 1952, pp. 197–199.

has its own board of trustees (or board of education, as it is more commonly known) and its own teachers and schools.   Usually the board of education is independent of the municipal government.   It levies a separate tax for the support of the schools [9] and makes rules and regulations concerning school policy without consulting the mayor or council.   Its powers are much broader than the powers of a rural board of trustees.   Obviously the usual objections to the district system do not apply to the large urban districts, which maintain high standards and generally lead in educational matters.

The Township Plan

Three states [10] have tried to escape the disadvantages of the district plan by adopting the township as the chief unit of school administration.   Several other commonwealths, though still retaining their school districts, have entrusted the township with authority to supervise district educational activities. Because a township is many times larger than the average rural district, this change has usually produced reasonably good results.   Better teachers have been employed in many instances.   Better buildings and equipment have been made possible.   Township high schools have been established without the delays incident to separate district action.   The merit of the township as the unit of school control is that it is large enough to wipe out some of the more glaring district inequalities.   Properly applied, the township plan tends to equalize educational cost and educational opportunity *within each township*.

Results have not always been good, however.   They have been especially unsatisfactory in those states that have permitted the township trustees to exercise only a small measure of control over school affairs, leaving the districts within the townships virtually undisturbed as the primary units of educational administration.   Such an arrangement does not deserve to be called a township plan, although it sometimes assumes that name; it is more nearly the district scheme behind a thin disguise.   Moreover, even with a genuine township plan, inequalities continue undisturbed among the several townships of a county.

The County Plan

Quite natural, therefore, is the proposal to abolish township as well as district control of education and make the county the primary administrative unit.   This plan or its equivalent is now in state-wide use in twelve states,

---

[9] In Baltimore, Buffalo, Detroit, New York, and a number of other cities, however, the school system is dependent upon the city government for financial support.

[10] Indiana, New Jersey, and Pennsylvania.

NUMBER OF SCHOOL DISTRICTS, 1932-1952

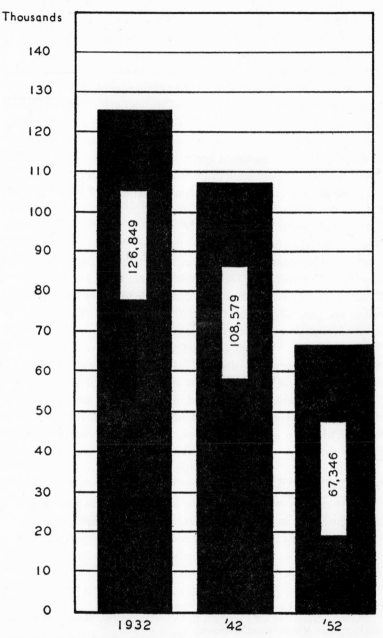

The 1932 figure is from William Anderson's *The Units of Government in the United States,* and the 1942 and 1952 figures are from the reports of the United States Bureau of the Census.

mostly in the South.[11]   Control vests in a board of education chosen by the people of the county or appointed by the governor.   This board supervises all the county schools; appoints all supervisors, principals, and teachers; fixes salary schedules; and determines all questions of policy concerning courses of instruction, textbooks, and other school matters, except so far as state law requires uniformity.

THE SCHOOL SUPERINTENDENT.   Most important of all, the county board of education selects a school superintendent who acts as the administrative officer of the school system.   The list of his duties commonly includes the co-ordination of the work of the schools, the approval of plans for new schoolhouses, the examination of applicants for teaching positions, the supervision of teachers, the direction of institutes for further teacher training, and the settlement of disputes that arise among members of the teaching force. As a rule the school superintendent also acts as the business officer of the county school system.

Thus all the educational activities of the county are brought under a single executive.   The county plan eliminates a great deal of unnecessary duplication and makes possible the use of county school funds for the benefit of all the county schools without regard to district or township boundaries.   Authorities are generally agreed that its universal adoption would be an important advance along the path of educational progress.

MODIFICATIONS.   Though only a few states look with favor upon the county as the primary unit of school administration, nearly all have established some form of county control over educational matters.   County school superintendents are now found in forty states,[12] and in most of these states there are also county boards of education,[13] usually in addition to the district or township school authorities.   The superintendent is commonly elected by the people of the county, although he may be chosen by the judges of the county courts, as in some counties of Tennessee, or by the state board of education, as in Virginia.

His powers vary widely from state to state.   In Iowa he is little more than a figurehead; in California he exercises considerable authority.   The functions commonly assigned to him include general supervision of district or township school activities and auditing of local accounts.   He keeps necessary records, collects and reports statistical information, and acts as

[11] Alabama, Florida, Georgia, Kentucky, Louisiana, Maryland, New Mexico, North Carolina, Tennessee, Utah, Virginia, and West Virginia.

[12] The only exceptions are Connecticut, Delaware, Maine, Massachusetts, Nevada, New Hampshire, Rhode Island, Vermont.

[13] Ten states do not have county boards of education, although they have county school superintendents.   These ten states are Arizona, Colorado, Illinois, Kansas, Missouri, Montana, North Dakota, Oklahoma, South Dakota, Wyoming.

intermediary between state and local officials. He is supposed to be a professional educator and an expert in school administration. All too often, however, his selection is due to partisan considerations. Popular election is a poor way to choose any technician, and county superintendents are no exception to the rule.

County boards of education also assume a variety of forms in the several states. Some of them exercise scarcely more than nominal authority. In New York, for example, each county board meets but once in five years, and its sole function is the selection of the school superintendent. The Mississippi county school board, whose members are appointed by the county superintendent, holds annual meetings but possesses no important powers. In Virginia, however, the county board apportions the school fund among the districts, audits the district accounts, prepares a county school budget, and makes rules governing a number of minor matters. Reference has already been made to the broad powers of the county school boards in those states that have abolished districts and townships, and adopted the true county plan of school administration.[14]

The New England Town Plan

In New England, where the county has never possessed important governmental functions, the town remains the primary unit of school administration. There is usually a town school committee, which decides questions of policy and selects a superintendent to handle the actual details of administration. In recent years, as a result of state insistence upon proper standards, it has become common practice in some of the New England states for two or more towns to join in choosing a school superintendent, whose jurisdiction extends over the "superintendency union" thus formed.

Gradual Shift to Larger Units

For many years the trend toward larger units of school administration has been manifest in every part of the United States. The transfer of school control from district to township and from township to county has seldom been matched by a countermovement favoring a return to the smaller units. School consolidation, proposed and debated in virtually every state and used effectively in many, is a reflection of the general tendency. In New England, the impracticability of developing county administration has led to closer state supervision and control. State control has been strengthened in other sections of the country, also.

[14] See page 436.

UNIFIED STATE SCHOOL ADMINISTRATION

The arguments for a county system of school administration apply with
equal force to a state system of school administration.   If a large unit is
good, a larger unit should be better.   If inequalities of educational opportunities within a county should be removed, then similar inequalities among
counties should also be eliminated.   The logic of this position is unassailable.

The Delaware Plan

To date, however, only one state—Delaware—has attempted to organize
its schools into a single, centrally administered unit, and this attempt has not
been completely successful.   By an act of 1921 the counties were deprived of
all control over educational matters, and their powers transferred to the state
board of education.   School districts were retained, but only for administrative purposes.   The state assumed the responsibility of financing the system.
The City of Wilmington and the larger towns, however, were specifically exempted from the provisions of the law.   In Wilmington and these towns the
schools are now managed by specially created local boards, subject to general state oversight.   The remainder of the state is under direct central control.

Partial State Control

In 1931 the state government of North Carolina accepted complete financial responsibility for the maintenance and support of the public schools for
the six months' term guaranteed by the constitution, and later lengthened this
term to eight months.   The county boards of education have been retained,
however, and in some respects their authority has actually been increased.
They still select superintendents and teachers, and exercise considerable
discretion over the business affairs of the schools.

New Hampshire, though still retaining the town form of school administration, has greatly strengthened state control within recent years.   Minimum
local standards are fixed by the state board of education, and maintained by
contributions from the state treasury wherever necessary.   Local school
revenues in excess of local needs are paid into the state fund.   Nearly half
of the area of Maine lies within territory unorganized for school purposes,
and the administration of this area is under the immediate direction of the
state superintendent.   The laws of Rhode Island authorize the state board
of education to assume control of the schools of any town, upon request of the
town school committee, if satisfied that local revenues are insufficient.   Apparently, therefore, a number of states are well on the road to unified state

control.   Other states, also, have gestured in the direction of state unification, but their gestures are scarcely worth recording.

Inequalities in Educational Facilities

During the past half century surveys of school finance have been conducted
in every section of the United States.   Every major fiscal problem of school
administration has been considered from many standpoints.   These investigations differ in many respects, but they invariably reach the conclusion that
*wealth is so unevenly distributed among the local units of school administra-
tion as to preclude the possibility of maintaining reasonably uniform—or
even reasonably adequate—standards without some form of state support.*
Even assuming equal willingness, it would be utterly impossible for the poorer
districts to support schools equal to the schools found in some of the richer
sections.   Taxes sufficient to provide satisfactory educational facilities would
impose a very light burden on some communities but would prove virtually
confiscatory if applied to others.

The inequalities resulting from this uneven distribution of wealth are so
glaring that they cannot be brushed aside or condoned by any person interested in the establishment of a sound educational system.   In the rural sections, which are chiefly affected, and also many poor industrial areas, boys and
girls are taught for shorter periods by teachers of inferior training and experience.   Equipment is inadequate or obsolete.[15]

State Financial Support

Such inequalities in educational facilities cannot be permitted to continue
indefinitely.   Reform comes slowly, however, because it necessarily involves
larger contributions from the state treasury—a policy at variance with the
widespread idea that education is purely a matter of local concern.   For
many years the states have contributed to the support of the public schools,
but until recently these payments never represented more than a small part of
the total cost except in a very few states.   Even today the local units of government—school districts, towns, townships, cities, counties—bear more
than sixty per cent of the burden in twenty-five of the states.

STATE SUBSIDIES.   A number of states have recently moved in the direction of increased state support, however.   Delaware provides the most conspicuous example of state-financed education; its establishment of a state-
managed school system has necessitated virtually complete state support.   In
eleven other states at least sixty per cent of the cost of local school systems is

[15] One of the best surveys of school administration and finance is *The Forty-Eight
State School Systems,* published in 1949 by the Council of State Governments.

paid with state subsidies.   In 1953 the states paid more than two and one half billion dollars to their minor civil subdivisions for school purposes—an increase of three hundred per cent in fifteen years.[16]   A great deal of this money was distributed on the basis of the school census, each governmental unit receiving state aid in proportion to the number of children of school age resident within its borders.   But many other bases were used also, such as the number of children actually enrolled in school, the number of children attending for fixed periods, the average daily school attendance.   Some states paid a fixed sum for each teacher; others graduated their teacher grants according to experience, training, and salary.   Still other plans were in operation—a flat sum to each school or each district; a grant to each district proportional to its ability to finance a minimum educational program; a subsidy applying only to the poorer units.   These schemes, and others, were combined by many states in various ways, with interesting but sometimes confusing results.

One of the chief reasons for the faulty operation of these subsidy laws is that most of them have been enacted and are now being administered without any clear understanding of what they are supposed to achieve.   Relief of the poorer districts is undoubtedly a factor, at least in many of the laws, but this purpose is often defeated by the very statutes that seek to accomplish it.   Almost all the states now use at least a portion of their school funds for a broader purpose than mere haphazard relief—namely, equalization of the financial burden of education among all the local units.   Some states apportion all their distributive school funds with this end in view, while others devote only nominal sums to equalization.   But the large majority of states lie somewhere between these two extremes.

A number of different equalization schemes have been devised.   Thus Michigan apportions certain funds among school districts whose property valuation per child in average school membership is less than the state average; New York grants money to cover deficits in approved local budgets; and Mississippi employs a complicated formula involving three factors—need as measured in terms of cost per teaching unit, effort as measured by the local tax rate and average daily attendance, and ability to finance a school system as measured by the taxable wealth per teaching unit.   Most of these so-called "equalization" plans do not equalize, or do so only to a very limited extent. Some actually work against the poorer districts.   No entirely satisfactory plan has yet been formulated, although several of the newer equalization schemes are reasonably acceptable.

[16] See "State Aid and the Support of Our Public Schools," by Roger A. Freeman, in the October, 1953, issue of *State Government,* pp. 237–240.

CONDITIONS ATTACHED TO APPORTIONMENTS. Nearly every state apportions some of its school money to local units with certain conditions attached —conditions that must be met as a prerequisite to state aid. In Massachusetts, where this policy of stimulation has been highly developed, the local communities receive money from the state treasury in proportion to the caliber of their teachers and other school officers, as determined by salary, professional preparation, and teaching experience. Thus every town is encouraged by the prospect of state aid to employ properly qualified teachers and pay them adequate salaries. The weakness of this plan is that it tends to foster inequalities. The wealthy communities, which least need state money, are best able to meet minimum state requirements.

Proposals for Federal Support

Uneven distribution of wealth, which so hampers the poorest sections in their efforts to provide a decent minimum of educational opportunity, occurs not only within the boundaries of each state, but also among the several states of the American Union. Recently prepared statistics show that the income per school child in some states is four or five times as high as in others.[17] Not unnaturally, therefore, many persons contend that the federal government should assume a large measure of responsibility for general education, and that it should distribute to the several states, on the basis of educational need, a reasonable part of the funds collected, presumably on the basis of ability to pay, from the people of the several states. Such a proposal presents numerous technical and administrative difficulties, but it has been warmly supported, nonetheless, by many professional educators. Bills authorizing large grants from the federal treasury to the states in support of general education have been introduced at every session of Congress for many years—sometimes with presidential approval—but have invariably lacked sufficient support.[18]

STATE ADMINISTRATIVE ORGANIZATION

The State Superintendent

In the first period of American independence not a single state had a superintendent of public instruction or corresponding officer. Nor was any such officer needed, since education rested so largely in private hands. But

[17] The most recent figures are readily available in the 1954–1955 edition of the *Book of the States*, pp. 244–248.

[18] See Charles A. Quattlebaum's 1949 monograph, *Federal Aid to Elementary and Secondary Education*. See also *How Shall We Pay for Education?* by Seymour E. Harris, published in 1948.

as the emphasis shifted from private to public education, and local school activities began to assume more than purely local importance, the need for some state agency vested with supervisory powers over the local units in matters relating to education became increasingly clear.

In 1812 New York took the first step by appointing a superintendent of public schools. Other states followed slowly—Maryland in 1826, Vermont in 1827, and Michigan in 1829. Several of these states temporarily abandoned the office after experimenting with it a few years, but in the meantime the movement was growing, and before the end of the nineteenth century the office of superintendent of public instruction had been established in every state.

At first the superintendent's duties were light and his powers few. He apportioned the state school grants to local communities in the manner prescribed by law, prepared rudimentary educational statistics, and furnished legal advice on educational questions. Other duties and powers were added from time to time, however, as the state's part in the general scheme of education became increasingly important. In many states the superintendent acquired considerable authority over the local school units—the power to supervise local finances, to issue and revoke teachers' certificates, and to control a number of other matters that will be considered at greater length in the remaining pages of this chapter. The recent trend has been to increase still further the superintendent's powers.

Little has been done, however, to attract able men. As previously pointed out, the superintendent of public instruction is still chosen by popular vote in more than half of the states.[19] His salary is small—often much smaller than that paid to school superintendents of the larger cities. In New York, however, he receives twenty thousand dollars a year, and in Texas his salary is seventeen thousand, five hundred. At the other end of the scale, six states have fixed the salary of the superintendent of education at less than seven thousand dollars a year. His term of office is short—seldom more than four years, and frequently only two years. In those states that retain popular election as the method of choosing the superintendent, re-election is the exception rather than the rule. Quite naturally, therefore, professional educators of proved ability commonly refuse to become candidates for the post of state superintendent of public instruction, and the professional politicians gladly include it among the spoils.

[19] See page 121.

State Boards of Education

State boards of education, exercising varying degrees of control over general educational policy, have been created in forty-two states.[20]   Sometimes these boards are composed solely of state officers serving ex officio, as in Colorado, Florida, and Mississippi.   Sometimes they are made up of persons appointed by the governor, as in California, Connecticut, and Maryland. A number of states—Montana and Tennessee, for example—combine ex officio and appointed members.

Usually the state board of education plays a minor part in the general scheme of educational administration.   This is especially true in the case of the ex officio board,[21] which in some states does little more than administer certain school funds, formulate general policies on minor educational matters, and give the superintendent of public instruction advice that he is free to accept or reject.

For many years, however, the tendency has been to increase the board's powers, at the same time ridding it of ex officio members.   In the sixteen states [22] that provide for the selection of the superintendent of public instruction by the board of education, the board is the dominant force in the administration of the school system.   It exercises broad powers of supervision and control, although presumably leaving to its agent, the superintendent, the task of enforcing the policies upon which it has agreed.

IMPROVED STANDARDS FOR TEACHERS

Original Plan of Local Certification

Many matters formerly left to the discretion of the local administrative units have been brought under state control in recent years.   One such matter is the certification of teachers.   The necessity of determining whether prospective teachers were properly qualified was recognized as soon as education became a public function.   In each community the local authorities examined applicants and issued teaching certificates to those who passed with satisfactory grades.   This plan was defective in many respects.   It permitted each local unit to fix the standards of its own teaching force, regardless of how low those standards might be; it left the preparation of examination

---

[20] In most of the remaining states—Illinois, Maine, North Dakota, Rhode Island, South Dakota, Wisconsin—there are boards that exercise control over certain specific aspects of education, such as normal schools or vocational training.

[21] Ex officio boards have proved unsatisfactory in all fields of government.

[22] Arkansas, Colorado, Connecticut, Delaware, Idaho, Iowa, Maine, Maryland, Massachusetts, Minnesota, Missouri, Nebraska, New Hamphire, New York, Ohio, Vermont.

questions and the grading of papers to laymen whose fitness to serve as examiners might well have been questioned; and it limited the supply of teachers in each community to residents of that community because certificates granted elsewhere were not accepted.

Gradual Change to State Certification

Gradually, however, important changes were made in the system of certification—if the plan first adopted can be called a "system." The right to certify teachers passed from the districts and townships to the counties and from the lay officials to the county superintendents of education, who presumably were better informed concerning the maintenance of proper educational standards. Inter-county recognition of the higher grades of certificates was first made optional, and then compulsory. A little later, in the more progressive states, the lower grades of certificates were abolished by state law. The next step was state preparation of examination questions, to be used in all counties. Then some states authorized the counties to forward the papers to the state office for grading. About this time state certificates began to make their appearance, though certificates were also issued by those counties not operating under the state system. From this point it was but a step to a complete system of state certification of teachers, with the counties completely eliminated from the picture. Not all states have passed through these several stages, however. The counties still play a part in the issuance of teachers' certificates in some of the states. They grant certificates in direct competition with the state authorities, or use questions prepared by the state, or, in some jurisdictions, merely act as state agents in giving examinations.

Quite frequently cities are exempted from the operation of a state certification system on the assumption that their standards are higher than the minimum prescribed by state law. But this assumption is not always justified. In some small municipalities the exemption from state supervision merely affords a welcome opportunity to avoid reasonable requirements. With the possible exception of a few great metropolitan centers, therefore, all municipalities should be compelled to conform to the state certification system. Those cities desiring to maintain still higher standards should be permitted to do so, of course; but their special requirements should be in addition to, and not in lieu of, the state certificate.

Teacher Training and Salary Schedules

At one time certificates were granted to teachers solely on the basis of examinations, but the modern tendency is to place emphasis chiefly on recognized academic and professional training. Graduates of normal schools need not further demonstrate their fitness by passing formal tests.   At least one year of college or normal school has now been made a prerequisite to certification for elementary and high school teachers in almost every state. It must be understood, however, that these requirements apply only to new teachers.   A substantial part of all the persons now teaching in the public schools have never received any training above the high school level.

Not only by certification, but by other plans as well, the states try to secure competent teachers for the public schools.   State normal schools and teachers' colleges have become commonplaces.[23]   Some states have established general plans for teacher training in the high schools, the last year of the high school course or, less commonly, a fifth graduate year being set aside for this work.   Although high school teacher training is objectionable in many respects, it has undoubtedly improved the quality of rural teaching.

In about half of the states minimum salary laws have been enacted.   Most of these laws have proved practically worthless, partly because the minimum has been placed very low and partly because the districts unable to pay even the minimum have defeated the purpose of the higher-salary-per-month requirement by keeping their schools open fewer months each year.   A few states, however, have adopted carefully prepared state-wide salary schedules based on advanced teaching preparation and maintained by heavy state subsidies.   Teacher pension systems have been almost universally accepted as a means of making the teaching profession more attractive to able men and women.

COMPULSORY SCHOOL ATTENDANCE LAWS

Nation-wide Adoption

Compulsory school attendance laws are now found in every state, but their adoption was attended with a number of difficulties and opposition from many sources.   When Massachusetts in 1852 declared that all children between the ages of eight and fourteen must attend school for twelve weeks each year, "if public schools so long continued," thus initiating the compulsory attendance movement in the United States,[24] a veritable storm of adverse criticism broke loose.   Such legislation was declared to be un-American, an unreasonable violation of the rights of parents, a gross disregard of the sanc-

[23] These state schools have been supplemented by county normal schools in a number of states.   Municipal normal schools are less common than formerly, but are still maintained by a number of cities.

[24] During the early colonial period Massachusetts and Connecticut had compulsory school attendance laws, but these statutes had become dead letters long before the Revolution.

tity of the home, and an unnecessary interference with business.   Even many
teachers and many county superintendents voiced their disapproval.

But the principle of compulsory attendance slowly gained popular support
despite widespread opposition.   New York followed the example of Massachusetts in 1853, and Vermont in 1867.   By the end of the nineteenth century thirty-one states had enacted some sort of compulsory school attendance
legislation, and the number was finally increased to forty-eight in 1918 when
Mississippi, the last to fall into line, adopted a weak county-option scheme.

Provisions

The provisions of these laws are by no means uniform.   Some fix the age
limits of compulsory attendance within a narrow range; the Georgia statute,
for example, applies only to children between the ages of eight and fourteen.
The laws of other states fix much broader age limits, as in Nevada, where the
span is from seven to eighteen years.

Wide variations are found, also, in the length of the required annual period
of school attendance.   While more than half of the state laws now require
attendance for the full school term, others specify merely that children must
attend school for a fraction of the term—often two thirds, or for a minimum
number of days, the minimum sometimes being placed as low as forty or fifty.

In some states many classes of children are exempted from the provisions
of the law for no good reason.   Certain exceptions are necessary, of course,
and have become a universal feature of compulsory school attendance statutes.   But the undue multiplication of exempted groups is contrary to the
spirit of compulsory attendance and leads inevitably to a breakdown of the
compulsory feature of public education.

EXCEPTION OF PRIVATE SCHOOL STUDENTS.   The exemption from public
school attendance of children who are receiving equivalent instruction in
private or parochial schools is generally recognized as proper.   Proposals to
abolish private education, aimed chiefly at parochial and other sectarian
schools, have been made from time to time, but have won popular favor in
only one state.   That state—Oregon—adopted a 1922 initiative measure requiring private and parochial school children to attend public schools
throughout the entire school term.

The law was promptly attacked in the courts, however, and in 1925 was set
aside by the Supreme Court of the United States as an unconstitutional interference with the right of parents and guardians to direct the upbringing of
their children.   "Rights guaranteed by the Constitution," declared the Court,
"may not be abridged by legislation which has no reasonable relation to some
purpose within the competency of the state.   The fundamental theory of

liberty upon which all governments in this Union repose excludes any general power of the state to standardize its children by forcing them to accept instruction from public teachers only. The child is not the mere creature of the state; those who nurture him and direct his destiny have the right, coupled with the high duty, to recognize and prepare him for additional obligations." [25]

Enforcement

Quite as important as the text of a compulsory school attendance law is the manner of its enforcement. In many states, however, enforcement is limited to occasional feeble gestures. This is true especially in the rural districts, where reliance is often placed on the sporadic efforts of constables or deputy sheriffs. Even the appointment of regular compulsory-attendance officers does not always solve the problem. These officers are commonly overworked; in some jurisdictions they receive from the school authorities reports of far more cases than they can possibly find time to investigate. Salaries are low, and appointments are often made for partisan reasons. Provision is scarcely ever made for an accurate census of school children, with the result that the compulsory-attendance officers commonly lack the information necessary for a proper performance of their duties. Small wonder, therefore, that thoroughly satisfactory enforcement of the compulsory school attendance law is a matter worthy of special comment!

STATE CONTROL OF OTHER EDUCATIONAL MATTERS

Courses of Study

The state legislature usually specifies in considerable detail the subjects to be taught in the public schools. Sometimes it goes still further and prohibits the teaching of certain subjects or certain theories that are considered undesirable. Thus the schools may be required to give instruction in American and local history, or forbidden to teach the theory of evolution. A certain amount of state control over courses of instruction is justifiable, especially if it assumes the form of general requirements, leaving sufficient discretion to the teachers and the local school authorities.

Too often, however, the value of local initiative is forgotten, state regulations even going so far as to establish uniform courses of study, with uniform textbooks and uniform assignments. While such detailed central control may at times raise the standards of instruction in the least progressive rural communities, its general effect is to prevent desirable experi-

[25] Pierce v. Society of the Sisters, etc., 268 U.S. 510 (1925).

ments and set the curriculum of the public schools in a hard, unyielding mold.

Textbooks

State-wide uniformity of textbooks is the practice in twenty-four states of the South and West. A few Western states make provisions for county-wide uniformity; elsewhere the district or township is the unit for textbook adoption. In those commonwealths having state uniformity the adopting body may be the state board of education, a separate textbook board, or the board of education plus other persons designated to sit with it when textbook adoption is being considered.

There are a number of arguments in favor of state-wide uniformity, most of them centering around the factor of lower cost, but experts in educational administration generally consider such uniformity unwise. They point out that the use of uniform textbooks hampers local initiative in curriculum con-struction, prevents proper recognition of differences among the school sys-tems of the state, and often leads to the corruption of the state board by text-book publishers whose scruples have melted away in the heat of the fight for a large contract.[26]

At one time pupils were generally required to pay for the textbooks they used, but in recent years the trend has been toward free distribution. Twenty-one states now specify by law that free textbooks must be supplied, and most of the others make free distribution optional with the local com-munities. California and Kansas have tried to reduce textbook costs by establishing their own printing plants and publishing the textbooks used in their schools, but the experience of these two states should not lead others to adopt the plan.

Building Construction; Pupils' Medical Inspection

The physical environment of the school is regulated by the state to some extent. A few states have enacted elaborate codes that deal with virtually every phase of schoolhouse construction, including such matters as gross structure, lighting, air supply, heating system, fire protection, cleaning sys-tem, water supply, toilet facilities, and arrangement and equipment of class and play rooms, gymnasium, and offices. Only a few of these subjects are covered by the code of the average state, however, and in many states school-house construction is still considered a purely local function. Medical in-

[26] In some states the adopting body prepares a list of four or five acceptable books for each high school course, and permits the schools to make the final selections. Such a plan avoids some of the most serious objections to state-wide uniformity, but unfortunately it lacks some of the advantages.

spection of school children is generally optional with the local communities, but a few states require every local unit to arrange for periodic physical examination of all school children by qualified physicians.

Rural School Supervision

More than three fourths of the states exercise some degree of supervision over the work of the rural schools.   This supervision may be simply a device for enforcing some of the specific state requirements already described, or it may be made an effective means of promoting desirable educational policies and inducing backward communities to adopt improved practices.   Inspirational professional guidance has largely taken the place of routine inspection in the more progressive states, and this trend will doubtless become more pronounced during the next decade.

SPECIAL SCHOOLS AND CLASSES

State schools are maintained in nearly all the states for the training of handicapped children—the blind, the deaf and the dumb, the feeble-minded.   Sometimes blind children and deaf and dumb children are educated at the same institution, although this arrangement is not common. Special day-class instruction for these several groups has recently been made a feature of the school systems of the larger cities.   This instruction, which supplements the work of the state institutions, is usually financed in part with grants from the state treasury.

The larger cities now commonly maintain schools, or classes in schools, for other special groups.   There are open-air schools for tubercular and anemic children, and classes for children with speech defects.   Separate classes are often maintained for especially gifted children.   To this list must be added over-age classes, non-English-speaking classes, ungraded classes.   Many cities have special art classes.   The problems of adult education now receive widespread attention.   And there are night schools appealing to students of all ages.

HIGHER EDUCATION

All the states make some provision for higher education.   Forty-three of them support state universities, twenty-four of these states have agricultural colleges as divisions of the state universities, and nineteen have separate colleges of agriculture and mechanical arts.   Of the remaining five states, two [27] have so-called state "colleges" which are, in effect, universi-

[27] Massachusetts and Rhode Island.

ties.[28]   Reference has already been made to the state normal schools and teachers' colleges.[29]   The junior college movement, now rapidly gaining favor in many parts of the country, is bringing a form of higher education within the reach of many persons who could not afford to attend a distant state university.

The several public institutions of higher learning within a state may be placed under the control of a single board, as in Kansas; they may have their individual presidents and boards of trustees, although functioning as parts of a unified administrative organization, as in Montana; or they may be permitted to act with almost complete disregard of one another, even competing for legislative appropriations, as in most of the states.   The modern trend is toward some form of unified control, but this movement is progressing slowly.

Regional Co-operation

It has long been apparent that many of the states are too small or too poor to provide adequate university instruction in all subjects that might properly interest considerable numbers of students.   There is, however, no valid reason why a state specializing in certain phases of education, such as veterinary medicine or dentistry or social work, might not make its facilities readily available to students from other states.   When this is done reciprocally, important advantages are gained.   State governments are saved the expense of duplicating costly facilities, and students are given much wider opportunities in choosing their careers.   Only recently, however, have the states begun to establish higher education on a co-operative basis.   In 1948 eleven Southern states signed a formal compact for reciprocal acceptance of one another's students, on a quota basis, without payment of out-of-state fees.   Each state agreed to reimburse the other compact states for expenses incurred in training its students.   Fourteen Southern states have now accepted this plan.   In the Far West five states signed a similar agreement in 1951, and three other commonwealths have since ratified it.

[28] Every state receives a grant from the federal government for the benefit of a college of agricultural and mechanical arts, but three states—New Jersey, New York, and Vermont—give this money to privately endowed institutions.   In 1948 New York enacted a law establishing a so-called "state university," but what this statute actually accomplished was to create central administrative control for a number of state colleges located in different parts of the state.   See Daniel E. Button's article, "State University of New York," in the April, 1953, issue of *State Government,* pp. 123–124.

[29] See page 445.

PROBLEMS

1. Study the relations of state and local school authorities in your state. Do you favor a further extension of state control, or do you believe that the local school officials should be protected from additional encroachments on their authority?

2. What are the relations of the county school superintendent and the county school board in your state? Do you think that the present arrangement is satisfactory? If not, what changes would you suggest?

3. Enumerate the powers and duties of your state superintendent of public instruction. How is his office organized to carry on its various activities?

4. What provisions for teacher training have been made by your state government? Has a minimum salary law applying to teachers been enacted? Is it enforced in all sections of the state?

5. What public supervision over private schools is exercised in your state? Is a serious attempt made to insure the proper training of private school teachers?

6. Visit a state school for handicapped children. What methods are employed in training these children? What are the subjects of instruction?

SELECTED REFERENCES

Allen, Hollis P., *The Federal Government and Education*, 1950.

Axt, Richard G., *The Federal Government and Financing Higher Education*, 1952.

Beach, Fred F., and Hutchins, Clayton D., *The Financing of State Departments of Education*, Washington, D.C., 1949.

Beach, Fred F., and Gibbs, A. H., *The Structure of State Departments of Education*, Washington, D.C., 1949.

———, *Functions of State Departments of Education*, Washington, D.C., 1950.

Burke, Arvid J., *Financing Public Schools in the United States*, 1951.

Chism, Leslie L., *The Economic Ability of the States to Finance Public Schools*, 1936.

Council of State Governments, *The Forty-Eight State School Systems*, 1949.

———, *Higher Education in the Forty-Eight States*, 1952.

Epsy, H. G., *Public Secondary School*, Cambridge, Mass., 1939.

Garvey, Neil F., *Financial Problems Arising from Changes in School District Boundaries*, Urbana, Ill., 1946.

Hagman, Harlan L., *Administration of American Public Schools*, 1951.

Hamilton, Robert R., and Mort, Paul R., *The Law and Public Education*, 1941.

Harris, Seymour E., *How Shall We Pay for Education?*, 1948.

Jaggers, R. E., *Administering the County School System*, 1934.

Macdonald, Mary E., *Federal Grants for Vocational Rehabilitation*, 1944.

Merrill, Julia W., *State Grants to Public Libraries*, 1942.

Millett, John D., *Financing Higher Education in the United States*, 1952.

Morlan, Robert L., *Intergovernmental Relations in Education*, Minneapolis, 1950.

National Education Association, *Efforts of the States to Support Education,* Washington, D.C., 1936.

————, *Federal Aid for Education,* Research Bulletin, Vol. XX, No. 4, September, 1942.

————, *Financing Public Education,* 1936.

————, *State School Finance Systems,* Research Bulletin, Vol. XX, No. 5, November, 1942.

————, *Statutory Provisions for Statewide Retirement Systems,* 1946.

————, *Your School District,* 1948.

New Jersey Education Association, *A Plan for State School Aid,* Trenton, 1946.

Norton, John K., and Lawler, Eugene S., *Unfinished Business in American Education; An Inventory of Public School Expenditures in the United States,* 1946.

Norton, T. L., *Public Education and Economic Trends,* Cambridge, Mass., 1939.

Quattlebaum, Charles A., *Federal Aid to Elementary and Secondary Education,* 1949.

Reeder, Ward G., *Fundamentals of Public School Administration,* rev. ed., 1941.

Shepard, E. F., and Wood, W. B., *The Financing of Public Schools in Michigan,* Ann Arbor, 1943.

Thayer, V. T., *The Attack upon the American Secular School,* Boston, 1951.

Wahlquist, John T., and Others, *Administration of Public Education,* 1952.

CHAPTER 22

Recreation

Many years ago it was generally assumed that private initiative could be trusted to provide suitable recreational facilities.   In rural areas that idea is still widely accepted, and not without some reason.   But in the cities a very different situation prevails.   City life has destroyed many of the attractions of a more primitive civilization.   It has reduced the number and size of open spaces, put trees and flowers at a premium, transformed the quiet woodland and the old swimming hole into mere memories, and placed hunting and fishing beyond the reach of the average boy or man.   In their stead it offers street fights, police raids, fires, stolen rides on trucks and passenger automobiles.   Small wonder that the cities have a serious problem of juvenile delinquency!   For delinquency is the direct result of unguided spare time in a vast number of cases.   Every city must face the task of making it easy for both children and adults to spend their spare time pleasantly and to advantage.

Public recreation costs from two to five times as much as it did a quarter of a century ago, even after discounting the lower value of the dollar.   This rising cost is readily explained in terms of increased service.   The progressive city of today meets the playtime needs of its children and adults by providing parks, playgrounds, athletic fields, tennis courts, golf courses, ice skating rinks, bathing beaches, bath houses, boulevards, gardens, concerts, art exhibits, competitive athletic events, and colorful spectacles.   It inspires community interest in dancing and games, debating and dramatic entertainments, group singing, manual arts, sewing and knitting.   It furnishes the leadership and the meeting places.

PARKS

Neighborhood Parks

The need for parks and open spaces has long been recognized.   Nearly every city has small islands of grass and trees dotting the sea of tall buildings that constitutes its downtown business district.   Even more generous provision for small open spaces at frequent intervals is commonly made in the suburbs. Odd-shaped remnants of land are often converted into parks at low cost. Sometimes these small neighborhood parks are partly converted into playgrounds, with a certain amount of special equipment for the use of children. Sometimes they are provided with bandstands, and free concerts are given during the summer months.[1] Parks of this kind, with areas ranging from a few thousand square feet to perhaps an acre or more, should be numerous and widely scattered. They should be selected with reference to some general plan, so as to afford maximum convenience to all the people. Too often, however, their location is determined by the cheapness of certain land or the political influence of the persons who wish to sell it.

Larger Park Areas

In addition to widely scattered neighborhood parks, a city should make provision in advance of actual need for a number of larger park areas—ranging in size from fifty acres to five hundred acres or more. Many an American city has seven or eight such parks, or an even greater number.[2] There should be, also, at least one vast wooded area devoted to park purposes. A natural beauty spot should be chosen if possible—a narrow river valley, perhaps, or a stretch of hilly countryside. Fortunately, such land is poorly adapted to ordinary residential or commercial development, and for that reason it can generally be purchased by the municipal authorities at a moderate price. It may be situated in an outlying suburb, at some distance from the homes of most of the people. Usually it is. It may be beyond the city limits. But accessibility is less important than in the case of smaller parks. Moreover, the widespread use of passenger automobiles has helped to solve the park transportation problem. Most people are willing to travel a reasonable distance in order to spend a few hours in the woods.

Need for Park System

In virtually every city the assortment of open spaces maintained by the municipal authorities is known as the park system. Sometimes the name is deserved. All too frequently, however, the word *system* is used as a matter of courtesy. Park sites are often selected without reference to one another, and in many instances no attempt is made to link the principal parks together by means of parkways or boulevards. A number of parks may properly be called a park system only when they are the product of co-ordinated planning, and when they are joined together by streets that retain some park features.

[1] Miami and some other cities furnish year-'round concerts.
[2] For example, Boston, Chicago, Los Angeles.

Based on figures of the United States Bureau of the Census.

If a motorist or pedestrian leaves one park, he should be able to tell by the general appearance of the street whether he is on his way to another. He should be able to recognize a parkway by certain distinguishing characteristics —unusual width, well-planted trees and shrubs, a section of roadway devoted to restricted traffic.

There is no great danger that stores or factories will be erected along a parkway, even in the absence of suitable zoning regulations, for when a street is given a width in excess of one hundred feet, business usually shuns it. Chicago furnishes a good example of a genuine park system. Its famous lake front parks are connected by broad boulevards, so that it is possible for the motorist to drive for miles without ever losing the impression that he is still within a park area. The park systems of Boston, Kansas City, and Minneapolis are also well planned.

County Parks

As might well be expected, the large majority of county governments do not maintain public parks. There are, however, nearly two hundred counties that have established park areas, and their total holdings are in excess of two hundred thousand acres. For the most part these county parks are adjacent to large cities, and supplement urban park facilities. Unfortunately, however, they do not always form a part of a co-ordinated metropolitan park system.

State Parks

The principal part played by the states in public recreation is through the maintenance of park areas. The first state park was created in 1865, when the federal government gave the Yosemite Valley to California for recreational purposes. Yosemite has since been returned to the federal government and is now a national park, but numerous other tracts of land have been set aside by California as state parks, and a comprehensive park system has been developed.

In 1885 the second state park was established, when Niagara Falls and a small strip of surrounding territory were set aside by the State of New York. Once again the primary object was the preservation of a great natural wonder. Other states followed slowly until about 1910, when the state park movement received fresh impetus from the increasing use of automobiles. State parks, created specifically for recreational purposes or for the preservation of places of natural beauty, were established in twenty-eight states by 1933. Then the federal government entered the picture, offering to aid the states in the development of their park areas by furnishing the labor of thousands of young men from the Civilian Conservation Corps. Financial assistance from the federal treasury was also provided. And as a result, the acreage of state parks doubled in five years. Today there are more than eighteen hundred state parks, historic sites, and similar recreation areas, with a total area of nearly five million acres.

PLAYGROUNDS

The Need for Playgrounds

Every city finds it necessary to meet the play needs of its children by setting aside some land for playgrounds. A few decades ago the playground was generally regarded as a haven for slum children. It was assumed that the children who lived in better neighborhoods could find adequate play space near their own homes. In the large cities, at least, that assumption is no longer justified. Suitable open spaces of sufficient size have almost disappeared, even in the better residential neighborhoods, and in many sections the number of children per block has been multiplied many-fold by the substitution of apartment houses for private homes. Urban boys and girls, the rich as well as the poor, find that they have no natural play places. The streets, filled with swift-moving traffic, can no longer be used in safety. So playgrounds must be provided. They should be as near the schools as possible; under ideal conditions the neighborhood playground is the school yard. This fact is now generally recognized, and when a new school is built it is commonly placed upon a tract of ground sufficiently large to provide adequate play space. Many of the older schools have very small yards, however, and nearby land must be purchased for playground purposes.

Desirable Characteristics

SIZE. The size of a playground should depend, of course, upon the number of children who may reasonably be expected to use it. But this does not mean that so many square feet of play space should be provided for every child in a community. There will never be a time, in all probability, when all the children will be on the playground at exactly the same moment. Hence a neighborhood playground may safely be designed to accommodate simultaneously but forty or fifty per cent of the neighborhood's children. Some writers, in fact, place the estimate as low as twenty per cent, but their views are not shared by most students of playground administration. In any event, there should be about two hundred square feet for every child using the playground at peak load. And under no circumstances should the minimum area be less than four acres for playgrounds adjacent to elementary schools, or six acres for high school playgrounds, for a school with a small enrollment needs just as large a football gridiron or baseball field as a school with many students.

OTHER FEATURES.   If possible, the playground should be square or nearly so.   It should be drained and graded, fenced, and provided with drinking fountains.   Apparatus and equipment should be placed around the sides, leaving the center for group activities.

Makeshifts

When playgrounds are scarce and not easily provided, a number of cities resort to novel makeshifts.   Some of them rope off certain sections of little-used streets for several hours every day, perhaps making provision for games conducted under leadership.   When snow is on the ground, coasting may be made safe by this method.   Sometimes the roofs of schools, tenement houses, hotels, and apartments are so equipped as to make them suitable for children's play.   Baltimore, Chicago, New York, and some other cities construct piers especially for recreational purposes, or use existing piers.

Pre-school-age Playgrounds

The play needs of pre-school children can best be met in the backyards of their own homes, for they are too young to travel several blocks unescorted to neighborhood playgrounds without danger of mishap, and too immature to join in the highly organized play of older boys and girls.   Most American families, even in the larger cities, still have backyards that could readily be adapted to the requirements of small children by the addition of sandboxes, improvised swings, or other simple equipment.   Of course, there are some residential sections of great metropolitan communities where backyards have disappeared, and in such neighborhoods the play space problem of the pre-school child is not easily solved.   In New York there is an organized movement to create so-called backyard playgrounds by tearing down the fences between tenement houses or other residences.   Some cities set aside special areas of playgrounds and neighborhood parks for the use of pre-school children, under the care of their nurses, mothers, or older brothers or sisters.

Playground Leaders

Some years ago the idea was prevalent that the chief function of playground leaders was to act as law enforcement officers.   If they put a stop to free-for-all fights, and prevented the bad boys of the neighborhood from carrying off the fences, nothing more was asked of them.   Today, however, a totally different principle prevails.   Playground workers—directors, play leaders, supervisors—are expected to be thoroughly trained for their jobs. It is now understood that expert playground workers are quite as essential as adequate space and equipment.   The unsupervised playground is apt to degenerate into a hangout for all the rowdies and bullies of the neighborhood. Two persons, a man and a woman, can handle a small playground.   If motives of economy suggest a reduction of the staff to one person, that one should be a woman, for a woman is far more effective with small children and girls, and can usually obtain quite satisfactory results from boys until they have reached the age of eleven or twelve.   A large playground with diversified areas requires a number of workers.   There must be play leaders and assistants to organize games and guide the children in their play activities. The director must be a man of administrative ability, trained to deal with recreational problems.   He must know how to inspire as well as control. Special activities, such as music, drama, handcrafts, storytelling, should be in charge of supervising specialists.

COMMUNITY CENTERS

Community Recreational Activities

Only recently has the importance of providing wholesome recreation for adults as well as children been generally recognized.   Within the last few years the community center idea has made rapid headway.   In some cities it takes the form of merely providing suitable space where self-organized groups may meet and carry on their activities.   Clubs and associations may be permitted to use the school auditorium, the playground gymnasium, or the library club room without charge or upon payment of a small fee to cover janitor service, heat, and light.

A number of municipalities have gone still further and undertaken the responsibility of initiating complete community recreation programs.   Such programs may include classes in public speaking, dramatics, china painting, cooking, home nursing, lamp shade making, needlework, millinery, gymnastics.   The people of a community are encouraged to form their own organizations—bands, orchestras, glee and mandolin clubs, minstrel troupes, mothers' clubs, men's community clubs, parent-teacher associations.   For the children there are local divisions of the boy and girl scouts and camp fire girls.   Indoor games are commonly provided—not only table games, but basketball, volleyball, indoor baseball.   At the community center there may be special features, such as Wednesday evening entertainments and Saturday evening neighborhood socials. Tuesday and Thursday evenings may be reserved for dancing. Even motion pictures may be shown occasionally.

Leadership by Group Members

When the activities of a community center become extensive, they should be in charge of a full-time, well-trained, and well-paid recreation director. The assistance of volunteers should be welcomed, however, for a community program is most likely to succeed if it has the hearty support of local residents who are willing to undertake responsibility for certain phases of the work in which they are especially interested. The old notion that recreational activities should be organized for the people but not at all by the people has been largely discarded. Today it is freely admitted that best results can be obtained by stimulating the residents of a community to take an active part in the development of their community center.

Facilities

USE OF EXISTING BUILDINGS. A few cities have constructed buildings especially designed and equipped to meet neighborhood recreational needs. For the average municipality, however, this plan is needlessly expensive. Satisfactory results can be obtained by utilizing existing buildings, notably the school houses. Community center activities are carried on for the most part in the evenings, when the large majority of school houses would otherwise be idle. Some of the rooms of branch libraries can usually be pressed into service. Churches, fraternal organizations, and civic clubs often have buildings that are well adapted to recreational purposes, and city authorities may find it possible to arrange for the use of these buildings by the public at certain times. Greater use of existing facilities, rather than the creation of new facilities, should be the aim of those responsible for public recreation.

ATHLETIC FIELDS. The outdoor play needs of adults can be met in part by athletic fields conveniently distributed throughout the city. These fields should be large enough to permit baseball, football, soccer, hockey, and similar sports, and to provide ample space for everyone who cares to use them. Though designed primarily for persons of post-school age, they should be made available to persons of all ages. It is important that they be kept open on Sunday, the one day of the week when nearly everyone has free time for wholesome outdoor recreation.

MUNICIPAL CAMPS

Vacation Camps

Many cities now have municipal camps, often situated several miles beyond their boundaries.   These camps provide opportunity for families to live out of doors for two or three weeks in the summer under rather primitive conditions at surprisingly low cost.   Campers keep their own tents or cabins in order, and make their own beds.   They take their turns at preparing the food, waiting on table, stacking the dishes.   Only a few paid workers are necessary—a director, a nurse, a supervisor of hikes, a supervisor of campfire social activities, a cook, and perhaps five or six others.

Tourist Camps

Camps are frequently provided for tourists at a city's edge.   Motorists may park their automobiles under the trees, and secure overnight lodging in tents or log shelters for fifty cents or one dollar.   Breakfast is sometimes served in a community house at slight additional cost.   Strictly speaking, a tourist camp is not a recreation center.   It is a sort of municipal hotel.   But it helps to bring a splendid form of recreation—long-distance travel—within reach of great numbers of people.

DIVIDED CONTROL OF RECREATIONAL POLICIES

State parks are administered by a variety of agencies—the conservation commission, as in Iowa, the park commission, as in Delaware, or the forestry and recreation department, as in New Hampshire.   In 1937 the states of New York and New Jersey created a joint commission to manage the Palisades Interstate Park, which parallels the Hudson River.

In the average city, responsibility for preparing and carrying out recreational policies is hopelessly divided.   Parks, picnic grounds, camp sites, golf courses may be in charge of the park department.   Playgrounds, athletic fields, swimming pools, community centers may come under the jurisdiction of the department of playgrounds.   The board of education may be conducting a vast number of play activities for school children.   Such divided responsibility almost inevitably entails wasteful duplication and makes it impossible to apportion praise or blame fairly.

It is desirable, therefore, to place all phases of municipal recreation, except perhaps the play activities of school children, under the direct control of a single bureau or department of the city government.   A number of the more progressive cities have already taken this step.   In the life of the school child, play and study are so interlocked that many careful students believe the board of education should assume responsibility for both.   In that case, however, close co-operation between the board of education and the department of recreation is essential.

PROBLEMS

1. What park areas are maintained by the government of your state?   When were these areas acquired?
2. Trace briefly the growth of your city's park system.   Are the present park facilities adequate?
3. What forms of public recreation are provided in your city?   What additional forms of public recreation should be provided?
4. Describe the organization of the agency chiefly responsible for recreation in your community.
5. Write a brief description of the summer camps maintained by your city or some neighboring city.

SELECTED REFERENCES

Allen, H. K., *Camps and Their Modern Administration,* rev. ed., 1938.
American Youth Congress, *Case for the Use of Schools as Recreation Centers,* 1939.
Butler, Geo. D., ed., *Introduction to Community Recreation,* 1949.
————, *Playgrounds: Their Administration and Operation,* 1950.
————, *Recreation Areas: Their Design and Equipment,* 1946.
Cline, Dorothy I., *Training for Recreation,* Chicago, 1939.
Dyer, Donald B., and Lichtig, J. G., *Liability in Public Recreation,* Appleton, Wis., 1949.
Fietz, L. A., *The Role of the State in Recreation,* Berkeley, Calif., 1947.
Fitzgerald, Gerald B., *Leadership in Recreation,* 1951.
Hjelte, Geo., *The Administration of Public Recreation,* 1940.
Hutchinson, John L., *Principles of Recreation,* 1951.
Institute for Training in Municipal Administration, *Municipal Recreation Administration,* rev. ed., Chicago, 1948.
Meyer, Harold D., and Brightbill, Charles K., *Community Recreation,* 1948.
National Housing Agency, *Planning and Operating the Playground Program,* Washington, D.C., 1943.
National Recreation Association, *Municipal and County Parks in the United States,* 1942.
Shanas, Ethel, *Recreation and Delinquency,* Chicago, 1942.
Symons, Farrell G. H., *Municipal Auditoriums,* 1950.

CHAPTER 23

Highways

The early American roads were chiefly from farm to market. Designed primarily to serve local needs, they were controlled by the local road districts into which the counties and townships were commonly divided. At best these roads were rutted and dusty; at worst, during the rainy months, they were virtually impassable bogs. Such road maintenance as might prove indispensable was entrusted to the residents of the district, and each man was required by law to devote a portion of his time—perhaps one or two days a year—to road work. In farming communities this requirement was not unreasonable, yet it was evaded whenever possible. Later, as trade and commerce became more important, and many men found it increasingly inconvenient to devote even a small portion of their time to road maintenance, the early laws were modified to permit the hiring of substitutes, or even the payment of cash in lieu of labor.

ROAD BUILDING IN THE UNITED STATES

Early Federal Construction

Road building was not limited entirely to the local units of government, however, for at an early date the federal government took a hand. In 1806 Congress made an initial appropriation of thirty thousand dollars for a national road to connect Cumberland, Maryland, with Steubenville, Ohio, and this Cumberland Road, as it was generally known, eventually became an important artery of traffic. Total appropriations for its construction ultimately reached nearly seven million dollars, and the road extended as far as southern Illinois.[1]

But the successful development of railroad transportation about 1840 marked the end of national highway construction, and for more than half a century the railroad was unchallenged as the principal means of long-distance travel. Wagon roads served the local communities, and the federal government did nothing to further highway construction except to continue

[1] See page 6, n. 5.

its well-established practice of granting to the newly created states a portion of the receipts from the sale of public land within their borders, directing that this money be used for "highways or other internal improvements."

Influence of the Bicycle

About 1890 a definite movement for good roads began to take form. This movement was given impetus by the widespread popularity of the bicycle, which had just been improved by the addition of the safety brake and the newly invented pneumatic tire. A number of large bicycle factories were established during the nineties, and "wheel clubs" with large memberships functioned in all the principal cities. The national organization known as the League of American Wheelmen devoted its attention largely to the task of rousing popular sentiment in favor of improved highways; its official magazine carried the good roads gospel everywhere. While many persons, especially in the rural sections, considered well-paved roads a needless luxury, the trend of the times was definitely toward better road construction and systematic road maintenance.

Influence of the Automobile

It was not until the advent of the automobile, however, that the phrase "good roads" began to acquire its present significance. Motor vehicles, with their greater weight and higher speed, necessitated a more substantial type of road construction, and hard surfaces replaced sand-clay and gravel along the main lines of travel. Then came the surfacing of even the secondary roads. Highways became more durable and more expensive. A major revolution in methods of road building was well under way.

In the four decades following 1900, as motor car registration increased from four thousand to thirty-three million, more than one and one-half million miles of American roads were surfaced in varying degrees. Highway construction became a task for skilled engineers instead of a neighborhood job dependent upon the skill and energy of the residents of each community. And highway expenditures, mounting at an astonishing rate, became one of the major expenditures of government.

Toll Roads

Toll roads, which existed in the United States in great numbers prior to the era of railroad building, eventually ceased to be profitable undertakings and were abandoned or taken over by the state. The twentieth-century renaissance in highway construction did not lead at once to a return of the toll road, even on a small scale, for the public had learned to regard high-

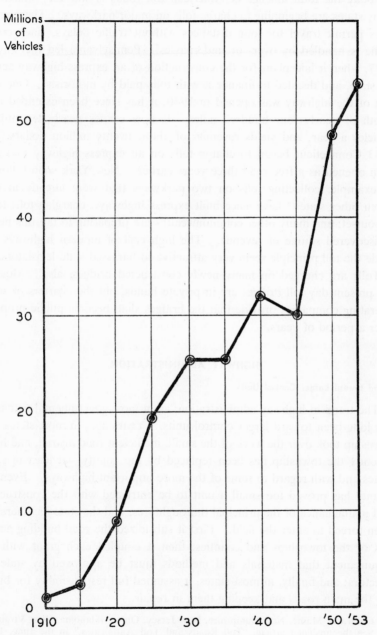

Based on figures of the United States Bureau of the Census.

ways as a free means of communication and looked with disfavor upon the toll-road principle.

Today the total mileage of American toll roads is still very small, but many states are beginning to charge tolls on major parkways. These parkways permit travel for long distances without traffic delays, since cross-traffic is handled by over- or underpasses. Pennsylvania led the way in 1937, when it laid plans for the construction of an express highway across the state, and decided to finance it with tolls paid by motorists. One section of the highway was opened in 1940; it has since been extended to a length of nearly four hundred miles. It now carries nearly ten million vehicles a year, and yields revenues of about twenty million dollars. In 1943 Connecticut began to charge tolls on an express highway that had been opened as a free road three years earlier. New York soon followed its example, collecting tolls on two parkways that were already in use. Seven other states [2] have since built express highways, charging tolls from the outset; and many other commonwealths are preparing to tap this newly rediscovered source of revenue. The high cost of modern highways has made the toll principle seem very attractive to harassed state legislators.[3]

Tolls are charged on many newly constructed bridges, also. Most of the present-day toll bridges are in private hands, but the charters of some operating companies provide that the bridges shall become public property after a period of years.

HIGHWAY ADMINISTRATION

Trend toward Larger Control Units

The trend in highway administration, as in most governmental activities, has long been toward larger control units. Years ago, in most states, the township took over the work of the small, inefficient road district, and more recently the township has been replaced by the county—at least in some states and with regard to some of the more important highways. Even the county has proved too small a unit to be entrusted with the construction and maintenance of the principal thoroughfares, and the state has therefore been forced to enter the field. First it subsidized the road-building activities of the townships and counties; then it coupled each grant with the requirement that materials and methods must be approved by state inspectors; and finally, in most states, it assumed full responsibility for building the main roads and keeping them in repair.

[2] Colorado, Maine, New Hampshire, New Jersey, Ohio, Oklahoma, West Virginia.
[3] See the unsigned article, "Toll Roads and Toll Authorities," in the June, 1953, issue of *State Government*, pp. 157 ff.

State Highways

The first state-aid highway law was enacted by New Jersey in 1891. This statute solemnly recited that "public roads in this state have heretofore been built and maintained solely at the expense of the respective townships in which they are located," although "such roads are for the convenience of the citizens of the counties in which they are located, and of the entire state as well as of said townships"; and then made provisions for payment from the state treasury of one third of the cost of road construction.   The following year Massachusetts also accepted the state-aid principle for main highways connecting the cities of the state.   Then came California and Connecticut in 1895, Maryland, Vermont, and New York in 1898, and North Carolina and Maine in 1901.   Thirty-six states had fallen into line by 1911, and in 1917 the list was made complete.

The condition of the roads had ceased to be a matter of purely local concern.   As early as 1894 Massachusetts amended its state-aid law to provide for the construction and maintenance of state-aid roads by the state highway commission, the counties being required to bear their share of the total cost.   This increase of state authority and responsibility was generally regarded with suspicion at the outset, but the results were so satisfactory that eventually all the other states followed Massachusetts' example and established state highway systems—usually under complete state control.   In 1916 the federal government assumed a portion of the cost of road construction in exchange for a measure of supervision and control over the main roads, and a national system of highways speedily developed from the highway systems of the several states.

Township and County Road Administration

This gradual transition to larger control units has not involved all roads, however.   In fact, nearly four fifths of the rural road mileage in the United States is still under county or township control, although the other one fifth includes virtually all the main highways and most of the hard surfacing, and bears most of the motor vehicle traffic.   The township is the primary unit of road administration in the states of the North and East, while the county generally serves in this capacity in the South and West.

TOWNSHIP CONTROL. Under the township plan one or more road commissioners are elected or appointed—election being the more common method—in each township.   Popular favor seems to incline toward single-headed rather than group administration.   Since the road commissioner is not required to possess any special qualifications for his office, he is seldom a trained engineer. Frequently he lacks even a practical working knowledge of road-building methods and is forced to rely on such gratuitous information as he can secure from various sources. He employs the road gangs who do the actual work of construction, and the foremen who supervise them. If plans and specifications are required, they are secured from private contractors on a competitive basis. Bridge and culvert work, also, may be entrusted to contractors, or may be placed under the jurisdiction of the county authorities.

Thus township road construction is essentially construction by amateurs, and township road policies are merely a phase of township politics. Small wonder that the township plan is marked by waste and inefficiency in every state where it still exists! Its continuance is due in part to the insistent demand of local politicians that government be kept "close to the people," but more largely to the relative unimportance of township roads. These roads comprise no system; they are merely the residue after national, state, and county systems have been selected. They serve only to connect the farms with the main highways. Since they are worth building and repairing, however, the way in which this work is done should not be a matter of complete indifference.

Efficient administrative methods should be adopted wherever possible, and the first step in this direction should be the abolition of the township plan of road administration. The township is too small a unit to obtain competent engineering services, except in rare instances. Its amateur government is not competent to deal with the technical problems of road construction. Its financial resources are usually too limited to permit any large expenditures, even with a view to ultimate savings. The change from township to county road administration has already been made in some states, but there is little likelihood that all the states will fall into line, at least for some years to come.

COUNTY CONTROL. The extent of county control over highways is not everywhere the same. In those states where the township still assumes responsibility for local roads, the county's part is usually limited to construction and repair of some of the more important thoroughfares that have been designated as county highways. There may be a certain amount of county supervision over township activities, however. The laws of a few states specify that all township road expenditures, or township contracts for road construction and maintenance, must be approved by the county authorities. Where the county is the primary unit of road administration, it usually exercises complete control over all roads within its boundaries, with the exception of a few main highways that comprise the state system.

In a number of states even these principal thoroughfares are entrusted to the counties, subject to state supervision.

Responsibility for county road work may be vested in the county board of supervisors or in a special county highway commission. In either case the actual direction of road building and repair is generally entrusted to a single official, who is variously known as road supervisor, road overseer, or road engineer. This official is usually appointed, although sometimes chosen by the voters of the county. In most cases he is a politician with little or no knowledge of road-building methods.

Several states have tried to insure the selection of more competent persons by providing that every road supervisor must be "a practical road builder" or "a man well versed in practical road building," while a few states have declared that only civil engineers may be chosen. Engineering training is highly desirable, and should be required wherever practicable. In most states, however, there are poor counties that cannot afford to pay for skilled engineering services and must accept whatever measure of practical experience their meager salaries will attract. One way to solve the problem of the poor county is to provide that two or more counties may join to form a highway district, although continuing to function independently in other matters. This plan has been adopted in California, Michigan, Oregon, Pennsylvania, South Dakota, and a number of other states.

The State Highway Departments

THE COMMISSION PLAN. The state plays a dual rôle in highway administration. On the one hand it constructs and maintains a system of main state highways; on the other it exercises supervision over county road building and repair. Every state now has a department of highways, traditionally headed by a commission of three, five, or seven members. The single-headed department has won considerable favor, but highway commissions are still found in a majority of the states. The members of the commission serve only part-time; in a few states they serve ex officio. Meetings are held at infrequent intervals to consider matters of policy—especially the designation of highway routes, the approval of contracts, and the preparation of financial plans for legislative consideration. The most important task of the highway commission, however, is to select a state highway engineer, who directs the actual work of road building and repair.

THE SINGLE-HEADED DEPARTMENT PLAN. Under the single-headed department plan the highway engineer has the title of director of highways and combines the functions of engineer and commission. He is responsible solely to the governor—or, in some states, to a director of public works whom the governor has appointed. Single-headed control has generally proved more satisfactory than control by a commission because it has tended to emphasize the importance of the technical factors in highway work. In many of the states where the commission plan is used there are frequent disagreements between politically minded commissioners and professionally minded engineers. Commissioners at times interfere with the selection of department personnel, and even go so far as to override the engineer's decisions concerning the location of new roads.

Although such practices may be the exception rather than the rule and are no longer attempted on projects built in part with federal money, they occur with sufficient regularity in certain states to constitute a serious objection to commission control of highways. The single-headed department plan furnishes no guarantee that highway administration will escape the blighting effect of partisan politics, but experience shows that this result is more likely to ensue. The argument that a highway commission is necessary to determine policies need not be given serious consideration, for policy determination is an infinitesimal part of the work of a state highway department.

THE HIGHWAY AUTHORITY. Regardless of the manner in which the state highway department is organized, it should certainly have full responsibility for all state highway construction and maintenance within the state's borders. Unfortunately, however, many a state has placed its toll-financed express highways in the care of a specially created highway authority while permitting the highway department to control all other parts of the state road system. The evils of this arrangement have already been noted.[4]

SUPERVISION AND CONTROL OF COUNTY CONSTRUCTION. State-county relations in the field of highway administration assume a variety of forms. The laws of a number of states provide that the state highway department shall furnish advice and assistance upon the request of the county authorities. This advice and assistance may be limited to the examination of general plans prepared by county road officials, or it may include the preparation of actual specifications for county roads by the state's engineering staff.

In Massachusetts the state division of highways compiles statistics concerning the public roads of counties, cities, and towns, and makes such investigations as it deems advisable, in addition to maintaining a free consulting service for local highway officials. A few states have established road schools or institutes, where those in charge of local road building may

4 See page 105.

receive practical instruction under the direction of the state highway engineer. Annual sessions are held in the several counties or at convenient places scattered throughout the state, and county road commissioners, supervisors, and overseers are required to attend.

Some measure of supervision over county road-building activities is maintained by the provision that county road officials must submit annual reports to the state. A few commonwealths have gone much further along the path of state control by requiring state approval of locally chosen highway officials. Thus Illinois specifies that persons selected by the county boards must pass competitive state examinations, and West Virginia provides that county road engineers must hold certificates of efficiency from the state road commission. A few states give the state highway department broad powers with regard to the selection of county highway systems. At least partial state supervision usually accompanies state aid to counties for road construction. In exchange for state financial assistance, amounting generally to one half of the total construction cost of approved projects, the counties are required to build their main roads according to state specifications—or at least to secure state approval of the specifications that have been prepared by county engineers. Some states restrict county authority even more narrowly by directing the state highway department to construct all roads financed in part with state funds.

In 1931 North Carolina tried a new and interesting experiment. The state government assumed full responsibility for the construction and maintenance of all roads, thus taking from the counties one of their most important functions. This transfer of authority followed the publication of a careful survey that showed widely varying results in county highway administration. The state legislature dissolved all local road districts and road boards and reorganized the state highway department to enable it to perform its new duties efficiently. The following year the state government of Virginia also assumed responsibility for virtually all roads, and some time later this plan was adopted by West Virginia and Delaware. But no other states have yet abandoned the historic division of responsibility between state and county road authorities.

THE STATE HIGHWAY SYSTEM. The state highway system, which generally comprises about ten per cent of the total road mileage of the state and bears from one half to three fourths of the volume of traffic, is under the direct control of the state highway department in most states, though occasionally built and maintained by the counties under close state supervision. The trunk highways forming this system were tentatively selected

after many preliminary hearings, and then definitely chosen after additional hearings and intensive surveys by members of the state highway department's staff.

FEDERAL AID FOR HIGHWAYS

In 1916, when the federal government renewed its early interest in good
roads, there were a number of states that had no functioning highway departments. But the act offering federal funds for highway construction
directed the federal secretary of agriculture to co-operate with the *state
highway departments,* and a subsequent statute specified that these departments must have "adequate powers" and be "suitably equipped and
organized." Thus the federal government did its share to develop in every
state a strong central road authority capable of dealing with the problem
of main highways.

Appropriations

For a number of years the federal subsidy to the states for road building
amounted to seventy-five million dollars a year. In 1931 the annual
grant was increased to one hundred and twenty-five millions, and in 1933
an additional sum of four hundred millions was appropriated under the
National Industrial Recovery Act. The 1938 grant was in excess of three
hundred million dollars, but by 1941 it had dropped to one hundred and
twenty-five millions. Then came the war, and the virtual suspension of
the federal-aid program. Congress made no additional appropriations for
this purpose, and funds available from previous years were used only for
improvements having direct war significance. With the end of hostilities,
however, the road-building program went forward at an accelerated pace.
Federal grants to the states for highway construction were raised to five
hundred million dollars a year, and have now been increased to five hundred and seventy-five million.

Conditions of Grants

Let us see how the federal highway program functions. A somewhat
complicated basis of apportionment is used, involving population, area,
and mileage of rural mail delivery routes. The usual conditions are attached to the federal grant: the state legislature must specifically accept the
federal government's offer; federal funds must be matched—dollar for
dollar—from state or county sources; and federal approval must be given
to every project before payment is made. When a state desires to improve

a section of highway or construct a new road it submits to the federal district engineer [5] a project statement containing all necessary information, such as the exact route to be followed, the nature of the proposed construction, the type of paving, the grades, and the estimated cost.   Federal approval of this project statement enables a state to begin construction with the assurance that it will be partially reimbursed from federal funds after the job has been finished and inspected by a federal representative. Although federal money may not be used for road repairs, the federal government insists upon proper maintenance as a prerequisite to continued federal aid.   Completed projects are inspected twice a year by the federal field forces, and any state failing to keep its federal aid highways in good condition is notified that it must make necessary repairs promptly or forfeit its claim to further federal funds.

The Federal-aid System of Highways

In 1921 Congress specified that subsequent federal road subsidies, and also the state money used to match them, must be expended upon a connected highway system limited originally to seven per cent of the total road mileage in each state, but with additions of one per cent permitted as the accepted program neared completion.   The result has been the development of a network of main roads touching practically every city with a population in excess of five thousand.   This network—the federal-aid system, as it is generally known—is composed of roads originally selected by the highway engineers of the several states and subsequently co-ordinated by the federal government.   Standard route numbers, and also uniform guide and warning signs, are used on important highways comprising more than half of the system.

The National System of Interstate Highways

In 1944 Congress directed the Public Roads Administration, in cooperation with the state highway departments, to select the principal routes connecting the chief metropolitan areas of the United States.   These routes, totaling approximately forty thousand miles, have now been chosen, and are known as the national system of interstate highways.   They reach forty-two of the state capitals, and over ninety per cent of the cities with populations in excess of fifty thousand.   The new system has an important relation to the defense of the nation.   It is rapidly being improved to meet the highest modern standards.

[5] The United States has been divided into ten districts for the purpose of administering the federal road subsidy, and each district has an engineer authorized to deal with the state highway departments.

Secondary Road Building

During the depression years of the early 1930's highway construction was used as a device for relieving unemployment. Congress appropriated several hundred millions of dollars to aid the states in building secondary roads, on which large quantities of relief labor could readily be employed. The program of federal grants for main highways was not abandoned, but it was definitely subordinated to the new policy.

Most students of highway administration assumed that this change was temporary. They reasoned that local road construction was scarcely a matter of federal concern and that congressional interest would wane as soon as the unemployment crisis had passed. But Congress showed no sign of losing interest. On the contrary, it incorporated into the regular federal aid program a provision for continued support to secondary road building. In 1944 it directed the Public Roads Administration to combine the principal secondary and feeder roads, rural free delivery mail routes, and public school bus routes into a secondary highway system. At present this system includes four hundred and sixty thousand miles. Thus Congress has modified considerably the original purpose of the federal highway subsidy.

Federal and State Control of Municipal Construction

Some years ago city streets that formed connecting links in the state highway systems were generally permitted to remain completely under municipal control, but this policy has now been virtually abandoned—largely because of congressional legislation providing for the use of federal highway funds within city boundaries. The laws of a number of states now authorize state control of trunk highways within the boundaries of all cities or all small cities and towns, and in most of the other commonwealths the grants from the state treasury to the municipalities are conditioned upon the adoption of certain types of paving material or the establishment of certain minimum pavement widths. Proper maintenance, also, is sometimes required. More than half of the states subsidize municipal street construction, but some of them distribute their funds unconditionally instead of using state aid to secure state control.

MEANS OF FINANCING HIGHWAY CONSTRUCTION

Increased Expenditures

The rapid increase in road mileage and the marked trend toward high-type construction, with some of the major trunk highways costing almost one million dollars a mile, have created a serious financial problem. The magnitude of this problem can best be appreciated by a comparison of highway expenditures in 1903 and 1953, the most recent year for which figures are available. The states and their local units spent about fifty million dollars for highways in 1903, this sum including the cost of construction and repair, and also payments for equipment, interest on highway bonds, and administration. By 1953 the annual state and local expenditures for highways were about three and one half billion—an increase of seven thousand per cent. This stupendous increase represents in part the needs of a growing population, but chiefly it indicates the growth of highway mileage. Small wonder, therefore, that legislators have many times been hard pressed to find revenues sufficient to meet the cost of such a vastly expanded government activity!

License Fees

Highway tolls represent only a tiny fraction of what is needed. Nonetheless, most of the burden of paying for the highways has been placed on the motorist, who is generally recognized as the chief beneficiary. This result has been accomplished by means of license fees and taxes of various kinds. The first state to license motor vehicles was New York, in 1901. Its fees for that year amounted to nine hundred and fifty-four dollars. By 1909 the licensing of automobiles had become general, and state revenues from this source had increased to nearly one hundred thousand dollars. Subsequent increases in motor vehicle registration and in the amount charged per vehicle have raised the total to nearly nine hundred million dollars a year. Some states have established flat rates for all pleasure cars, but the more common practice is to vary the license fee according to weight, horse-power, or value. Higher rates are generally charged for trucks than for pleasure vehicles. In a few states the counties are permitted to collect license fees in addition to the fees imposed by the state government.

The Gasoline Tax

Among the taxes imposed on motorists, the gasoline tax is of prime importance. First adopted by Oregon in 1919, it spread rapidly and within a decade had been adopted by every state of the Union. At the outset the rate was one cent a gallon, but higher rates have now become universal. Louisiana collects nine cents a gallon, and rates of five or six cents are common. The federal government also imposes a tax of one and one-half cents a gallon on gasoline sales, and a few states permit counties or cities, or both, to make additional levies. The highest rate is found in some of the cities of Alabama, where combined federal, state, county, and municipal taxes amount to twelve cents a gallon.

Throughout the United States the state gasoline tax yields almost one billion, nine hundred million dollars a year. The tax is collected easily and cheaply, especially if no serious attempt is made to prevent evasion; and, within reasonable limits, it has no marked effect upon the consumption of gasoline. State officials are now beginning to learn, however, that the rate cannot be increased beyond five or six cents a gallon without creating serious problems.

APPORTIONMENT TO LOCAL UNITS. More than half of the states distribute some part of their gasoline tax receipts among the local units of government—usually the counties, although the cities are gradually establishing their claim to a share for the paving of their streets. No uniformity exists as to the basis of distribution. Some states divide the money equally among the counties; some return to each county a fixed percentage of the amount collected within its borders; while others apportion the fund on the basis of area, population, highway mileage, motor car registration or assessed valuation.

USE OF GASOLINE TAX RECEIPTS. The original purpose of the gasoline tax was to defray at least a part of the cost of building and maintaining highways, and revenue obtained from this source is still commonly used for highway improvements. A few states, however, now devote a portion of the gasoline tax receipts to various activities, such as schools or poor relief, that yield motorists, as a class, no special benefits. On the other hand, proposals to divert gasoline tax money from its chief purpose of highway improvement have been severely defeated in a number of commonwealths, and about one fourth of the states have gone so far as to write into their constitutions the provision that gasoline tax receipts may be used only for highways. Congress has entered the lists with a statutory provision withholding a part of federal aid from any state using motor vehicle tax revenues for other than highway purposes.

It was once thought that the gradual completion of the main highway systems might lead to a reduction of gasoline tax rates or to a continuance of present rates and a more general use of this revenue for other purposes.

STATE EXPENDITURES FOR HIGHWAYS

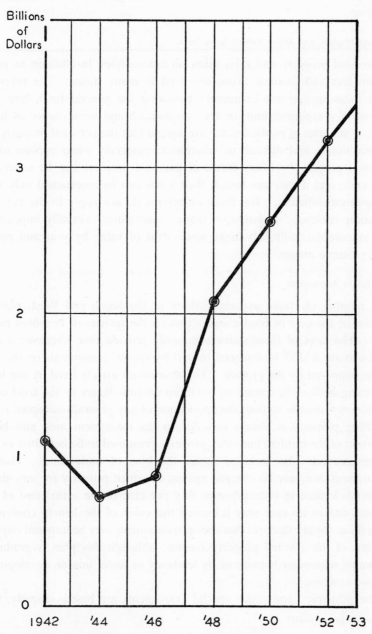

Based on figures of the United States Bureau of the Census.

But more recent increases in the potential speed of motor cars, plus the adoption of expensive highway construction methods for greater safety, seem to have destroyed the likelihood of reducing the total outlay for road building.

Personal Property and Motor Vehicle Sales Taxes

Personal property and sales taxes on automobiles, in addition to registration fees and gasoline taxes, are used in many states. The revenues from these sources are commonly paid into the general fund, however, instead of a separate fund for the construction and maintenance of highways. Students of public finance are agreed that the personal property tax is unequitable and difficult to administer, especially when applied to *all* personal property.[6] Many forms of personal property can be concealed with ease; and if they are found, their value can be ascertained only with the greatest difficulty. But these objections do not apply to the taxation of motor vehicles. Registration makes concealment virtually impossible, and automobile trade lists make assessment of value by year and model a very simple matter.

Real Estate Assessments

A number of states, especially those of the South and West, place a portion of the cost of road construction on the owners of benefited property. The laws of these states commonly provide that whenever a new road is built, it shall be financed in part by special assessments on the real estate improved by the project. The assessment area is fixed by the local governing body—the county or township commissioners or the road commissioners—usually without the application of any generally accepted rules. Abutting property is always included in the assessment area and bears the brunt of the burden, but other property presumed to be benefited by the improvement is also included under the laws of most states. Usually the amount that may be charged against benefited property for any single project is limited to twenty-five or fifty per cent of the actual cost of the project, and in no case may it exceed the value of the benefit conferred. Sometimes the law declares that special assessments may be imposed only on petition of the affected property owners, although this plan is gradually becoming unpopular because of its tendency to foster uneven development of road systems.

The principle upon which special assessments are based—namely, that

6 See pages 604–607.

persons receiving special benefits from government should contribute in proportion to their gain—is unquestionably sound. But the application of this principle presents a number of problems.[7] The most serious objection to the special assessment method of financing highways, aside from the difficulty of determining the assessment area, is that this method may be used to justify amateur interference in the selection of paving materials. When property owners know that they must pay a considerable part of the construction cost of a new road, they frequently demand and receive the right to specify the type of roadway. Usually their intentions are good, but their knowledge of the characteristics of paving materials is lamentably slight, and the result is likely to be more or less haphazard selection, with reference chiefly to the element of cost. It should be obvious that the choice of roadway types is a technical matter unsuited to the capacity of the rank and file of property owners, but Americans are loath to admit that any function of government is beyond the comprehension of the average man. Special assessments have lost considerable popularity in recent years, because of the default of many special assessment districts during the depression.

Borrowing

Nearly three fourths of the states and many of their civil subdivisions have resorted to borrowing in order to finance the construction of their highway systems. The long-term debt of all the states, according to the most recent census figures, is well above the six billion dollar mark, and thirty-five per cent of this total represents indebtedness incurred for highways. Moreover, the states are still borrowing for the purpose of building more miles of expensive roads. The end is not in sight.

MEASURES TO DECREASE MOTOR CAR ACCIDENTS

An unfortunate result of increased highway travel and increased highway speeds has been the rapid multiplication of highway accidents. During the two decades from 1921 to 1941 the number of fatalities due to motor car accidents rose from twelve thousand to nearly forty thousand a year. Gasoline and tire rationing during the Second World War caused a substantial reduction from the high mark of 1941, but more recently the annual motor vehicle death toll has again approached the forty thousand mark. Nonfatal traffic accidents, of course, are many times as numerous

[7] See pages 618–619.

as fatalities. Accurate information concerning the value of property damaged by motor cars is not available, but there is no doubt that this annual property loss amounts to many millions of dollars.

Every state has taken some steps to reduce the number of motor car accidents, or at least to prevent further increases; and the more progressive commonwealths have approached the problem in a number of different ways—for example, by limiting the speed of motor vehicles and in other ways regulating their operation, by testing the fitness of drivers, by inspecting motor vehicles at periodic intervals, and by constructing highways with greater regard to the factor of safety.

Speed Laws

Laws governing the speed of automobiles have been enacted in all states. These laws usually fix maximum open-road driving speeds and also maximum speeds for residence districts, business districts, and curves and intersections.

THE PRIMA FACIE MODIFYING CLAUSE. In some states the maximum speed limitation is modified by a so-called prima facie clause, which specifies that a driver exceeding the speed limit is only prima facie guilty of law violation and that he may introduce evidence, if arrested and brought to trial, to show the reasonableness of his speed under the road conditions existing at the time. Unfortunately, however, this plan has worked poorly. Most drivers are too busy to contest the charges brought against them, and most courts are loath to accept refutatory evidence.

THE RULE OF REASONABLE AND PROPER SPEED. Many of the states, dissatisfied with the customary methods of speed regulation, have abolished fixed limits for open-road driving—and, in some instances, for driving in cities and towns. In place of the fixed limit has been substituted the rule that operators of motor vehicles must at all times drive at a reasonable and proper speed. This rule is a recognition of the obvious fact that safe driving is not merely a question of miles per hour, but of miles per hour in relation to driving conditions—the road surface, the weather, the volume of traffic, and a dozen other factors. At first glance, therefore, the requirement of "reasonable and proper" driving may seem to be the fairest way to limit motor car speed. But there is a practical objection—the difficulty of enforcement. The rule provides no guide for motorists or law-enforcement officers, with the inevitable result that the phrase "reasonable and proper" receives many different interpretations.

Other State Motor Vehicle Laws

State laws concerning the operation of motor vehicles cover a great many matters in addition to speed. Nearly all require the use of hand signals for stopping and turning, and declare that cars must not stop on the highway. The passing of street cars on the left, or when taking on or discharging passengers, is generally prohibited. Most of the states forbid drivers to overtake and pass on hills or curves if the view is obstructed. The use of stickers on windshields or rear windows is forbidden in more than half of the states, and prohibitions against coasting in neutral are quite common. Other regulations concerning motor car operation, such as requirements that headlights be dimmed for approaching vehicles or that a full stop be made at railway grade crossings, have been adopted less widely. The enforcement of the motor vehicle laws by state highway patrols has previously been noted.[8]

Drivers' Examinations

In recent years increasing emphasis has been placed upon the fitness of motor car operators. The first state to require applicants for drivers' licenses to pass a test was Rhode Island, in 1908. For two decades other states followed slowly, but after 1928 the scheme became increasingly popular. It has now been adopted by all the states.

The examination for prospective motor car operators is generally divided into four parts: physical test, literacy test, test of knowledge of state laws, and road test. The physical examination deals chiefly with eyesight and hearing, although an attempt is made in some jurisdictions to discover any physical defects that might interfere with efficient driving. Frequently the literacy test is combined with the examination on the state motor vehicle law, the applicant being required to write answers to printed questions dealing with the provisions of the state code. The road test, involving a demonstration by the applicant of his ability to handle an automobile on the open road, is by far the most important part of the examination, and some states use it in lieu of written questions. A few states, however, go to the other extreme, relying solely on written questions—plus, perhaps, a physical examination.

The value of a road test depends in large measure on its administration. Some states entrust the administration of the test to the state police, without giving them any special training for the work, while others give their inspectors—police or civilians—thorough courses of training and complete

[8] See page 346.

instructions before assigning them to road test duty. In a few states the road test is administered by county officials who are not subject to state supervision or control, with the result that widely varying standards are found. The test means much or little, according to the diverse concepts of county inspectors.

In recent years psychologists have devised numerous tests for measuring driving ability. Some of these tests are conducted in the laboratory; others simulate actual road conditions and measure the skill of motor vehicle operators in backing, turning, giving signals, and the like while they drive through a labyrinth of paths and lanes. These tests have been adopted by several large industrial establishments in the selection of their truck drivers, but state officials have evinced slight interest.

Motor Vehicle Inspection

The laws of more than half of the states [9] require the periodic inspection of all motor vehicles for the purpose of eliminating serious mechanical defects that might cause accidents. Most of these laws are far from satisfactory, however. They commonly apply only to brakes or headlights, or both, instead of including such important additional factors of automobile safety as wheel alignment, steering wheel, horn, rear-view mirror, windshield cleaner, parking lights, tail light, and stop light. Moreover, inspection is not generally required once a year, as it should be, but biennially, triennially, or at infrequent intervals determined by the whim of the legislature. Still more serious, most state laws fail to make adequate provision for supplementary road examinations by members of the highway patrol, with the result that mechanical defects multiply unchecked after the formal biennial or triennial inspection.

Elimination or Protection of Grade Crossings

Railway grade crossings have long created a serious traffic accident problem, and in recent years the more dangerous crossings have been steadily eliminated. Until 1935 the cost of this work was borne by the railway, the state, and, as a rule, the benefited county or township, but since that year Congress has granted several hundred million dollars to the states for grade-crossing elimination. Yet the problem is by no means solved, for new highways are constructed and new railway grade crossings created almost as rapidly as the old crossings are removed. A great deal has been done to reduce the element of danger by protecting grade crossings. Nearly nine tenths of all crossings are now marked by fixed

[9] In some states, however, the law applies only to certain cities.

signs, and most of the others—especially those located on the main arteries of traffic—are protected by crossing gates, watchmen, or warning devices that indicate the approach of trains.

Need for Other Safety Steps in Highway Construction

During the last quarter of a century the state highway departments have increasingly emphasized the factor of safety in their road-building programs, yet much remains to be accomplished. Highways should be wider, in many cases, with medial strips to separate traffic flowing in opposite directions and distinct footways for pedestrian traffic. Parking space off the traveled portion of rural highways should be provided—either continuously or at reasonable intervals. Grades should be reasonable and curves should be banked. Heavy guard rails should protect embankments, and all necessary steps should be taken to insure a clear view of approaching vehicles for several hundred yards. And adequate night lighting of highways, despite its heavy cost, should be seriously considered as an important means of reducing after-dark accidents.

Safety Education

Nearly all the state highway departments devote some attention to educational campaigns. The need for caution on the highways is explained and emphasized by means of posters in public places, motion pictures, lantern slides, radio talks, newspaper and magazine publicity, mass meetings, and special campaigns. Schools for motorists are maintained in a few states, and privately organized safe drivers' clubs are encouraged. A number of states place strong emphasis on safety education in the schools. The task of educating the public in matters of highway safety was first undertaken by the motor clubs and later developed by safety councils and other private or semi-private groups. These various organizations are still functioning very efficiently and doing their full share to reduce the traffic accident rate, but state activity has made possible the distribution of safety propaganda among many groups not reached by private agencies.

Accident Reports and Investigation

The importance of adequate statistics concerning motor car accidents has long been recognized, and the laws of most of the states now provide a means of securing such statistics by specifying that accidents must be reported to some state agency—usually the agency vested with power to revoke operators' licenses. The law may apply only to accidents causing injury to persons, or it may specifically exempt accidents involving only property damage below a certain amount—often twenty-five or fifty dollars. Prompt investigation of accident reports enables the police to determine accurately the causes of most accidents and to fix the blame in many cases.

Financial Responsibility of Drivers

All the states now have laws designed to protect the public from financially irresponsible motorists. These laws usually specify that every driver of a motor vehicle involved in a serious accident must furnish evidence that he carries adequate insurance against damage to person and property —or, failing to do so, must deposit with the state suitable security in cash, bonds or the like, from which legitimate damage claims may be paid. If a driver fails to meet these requirements, his license is suspended.

A Uniform Motor Vehicle Code

In 1926 the National Conference on Street and Highway Safety, meeting at the national capital, prepared a draft of a so-called "uniform vehicle code" and offered it for the consideration of the forty-eight state legislatures. This uniform code has been revised five times. In its present form it comprises five acts, covering major phases of motor vehicle regulation: (1) the registration of automobiles, and the prevention of theft; (2) the issuance of drivers' licenses; (3) civil liability for motor car accidents; (4) responsibility for highway safety; and (5) the regulation of highway traffic. Every state has adopted one or more of these five acts, at least in part or in modified form, but the goal of virtual uniformity in all vital matters of motor vehicle regulation has not been reached.

PROBLEMS

1. Write a brief history of the good highway movement in your state.

2. Study the relations of the federal government, your state, and its local subdivisions in highway construction and maintenance.

3. Prepare a report on the proposals that have been made in Congress and elsewhere for expanded programs of highway construction in the postwar era.

4. Trace the history of the movement to transfer a portion of gasoline tax receipts from highways to other activities. What groups favor this change and what groups oppose it? In your judgment, would such a change be desirable?

5. What steps have been taken by your state highway department to reduce automobile accidents?

SELECTED REFERENCES

American Association of Motor Vehicle Administrators, *Procedure for the Minimum Standard Examination for Drivers,* 1939.

————, *Standards and Procedures for the Examination of Applicants for Drivers' Licenses*, 1947.

American Association of State Highway Officers, *Manual on Uniform Control Devices for Streets and Highways*, 1948.

Bateman, J. H., *Introduction to Highway Engineering*, 3rd ed., 1939.

Council of State Governments, *Highway Safety-Motor Truck Regulation*, 1950.

Crawford, F. G., *The Administration of the Gasoline Tax in the United States*, 4th ed., 1936.

Dearing, Charles L., *American Highway Policy*, Washington, D.C., 1942.

De Silva, H. R., *Mechanical Tests for Drivers*, Cambridge, Mass., 1938.

Ford, Robert S., and Bacon, Marvin A., *Michigan Highway Finance*, Ann Arbor, 1943.

Gomez, R. A., *Intergovernmental Relations in Highways*, Minneapolis, 1950.

Hewes, Laurence I., *American Highway Practice*, 1942.

Hoffman, P. G., and Clark, N. M., *Several Roads to Safety: A Program to Reduce Automobile Accidents*, 1939.

Kennedy, G. D., *Modern Urban Highways*, Washington, D.C., 1944.

Key, V. O., Jr., *The Administration of Federal Grants of the States*, 1937.

Labatut, Jean, and Lane, W. J., *Highways in Our National Life, a Symposium*, Princeton, New Jersey, 1950.

Macdonald, Austin F., *Federal Aid*, 1928.

McGalliard, H. W., *Guides to Highway Safety*, Chapel Hill, N.C., 1935.

National Conference on Street and Highway Safety, *Uniform Act Regulating Traffic on Highways*, 1943 and 1944.

Owen, Wilfred, and Dearing, Charles L., *Toll Roads and the Problem of Highway Modernization*, Washington, D.C., 1951.

Owens, W., *A Study in Highway Economics*, Cambridge, Mass., 1934.

Smith, Wilbur, and LeGrew, Charles S., *Traffic Speed Enforcement Policies*, 1948.

Stocker, H. E., *Motor Traffic Management*, 1938.

Tripp, H. A., *Road Traffic and Its Control*, 1938.

Trull, E., *Borrowing for Highways*, 1937.

Tucker, Harry, and Leager, Marc C., *Highway Economics*, Scranton, Pa., 1942.

United States Bureau of Public Roads, *Uniform Vehicle Code*, Washington, D.C., 1952.

Walker, J. E., *Highway Tax Costs*, Washington, D.C., 1938.

CHAPTER 24

Natural Resources

Until almost the beginning of the present century the natural resources of the United States were considered practically inexhaustible. They were exploited as rapidly as possible without the slightest attempt to prevent waste; in fact, many resources were wantonly destroyed in the process of facilitating the nation's development. By 1895, however, a number of scientists and statesmen were pointing out the folly of heedless waste, and gradually during the next two decades conservation became a national slogan.

The masses of the people realized for the first time that gas, oil, and coal supplies were rapidly diminishing and could not be replaced. They began to understand the relationship between forest lands and a constant water supply. So they demanded legislation that would encourage the proper utilization of the nation's wealth and prevent careless or extravagant methods of development. As a result, every state now devotes some attention to the conservation and development of its natural resources.

Generally speaking, state programs are far from adequate. The conservation laws are sometimes needlessly repressive or, much more commonly, needlessly lenient. Enforcement is often lax. Resources that should be included are frequently omitted. But public responsibility for the public's natural wealth is universally recognized, and sound principles of conservation have been developed by the more progressive commonwealths.

STATE CONSERVATION AGENCIES

Nearly three fourths of the states have created conservation commissions or departments, whose official task, phrased in slightly varying terms, is "to protect, conserve, and replenish the natural resources of the state." In this field the commission (properly, board) form of administration is popular. Usually the members are appointed by the governor for overlapping terms and serve without pay.

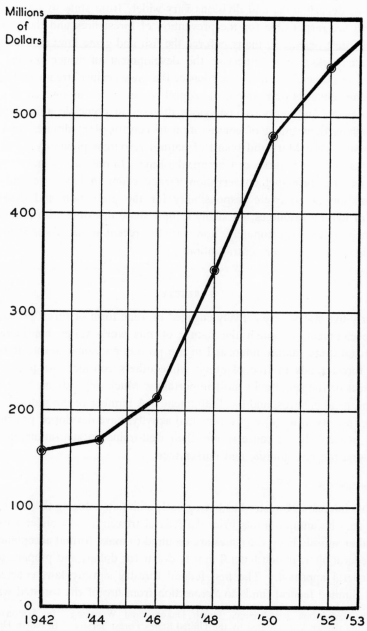

Based on figures of the United States Bureau of the Census.

Their principal duty is to select an executive officer to handle the actual details of administration.   Matters of policy are decided at regular monthly or quarterly meetings.   The functions of the several conservation commissions, departments, and divisions vary widely from state to state.   Almost all are responsible for the prevention of forest fires and the protection of forest resources; many enforce the fish and game laws and manage the state parks; some supervise the development of water power and mineral resources; and a few administer the laws against stream pollution. The Massachusetts department of natural resources is empowered to control, prevent, and suppress contagious diseases in domestic animals, and the Indiana department of conservation to control plant diseases and insect pests.   The Maryland board of natural resources plants oyster shells on rocks in the tributaries of Chesapeake Bay.   In only a few states, however, can the principal conservation agency claim to have even an approximation of complete responsibility for the protection and development of natural resources.   Usually it must share this duty with a number of other bodies.   Fortunately, however, the recent trend seems to be in the direction of greater centralization.

FORESTRY

Forty-five states [1] are actively engaged in some form of forest protection or development, although the nature of this work varies considerably. Some states are mainly interested in fire prevention; some devote most of their forest funds to tree planting; while others consider the prevention of insect or fungus attacks most important.   Much depends on local conditions, local finances, and local sentiment.   A number of the states, recognizing forestry as a major governmental activity, have developed practically every phase of forest conservation; their well-trained organizations include foresters, rangers, guards, and nurserymen.

Federal Subsidies

State interest in forestry has been greatly stimulated during the last forty-five years by annual grants from the federal treasury.   As under most of the other subsidy laws, the states are required to make formal acceptance of the federal offer, match federal money dollar for dollar, and prepare plans for federal approval.   The first federal forestry subsidy law, enacted in 1911, limited federal funds to "protection from fire of the forested water-

[1] The exceptions are Arizona, North Dakota, and Wyoming.   In Arizona and Wyoming the work is handled by the United States Forest Service.   In North Dakota the president of the school of forestry has the title of state forester.

sheds of navigable streams," but subsequent legislation has broadened materially the scope of federal aid. All "timbered and forest-producing lands" have been brought within the terms of the federal offer; moreover, additional federal funds have been appropriated to aid the states in growing and distributing trees, suppressing forest insects and diseases, and stimulating popular interest in tree growing. Nearly all the states have accepted the federal government's terms and now co-operate with the United States Forest Service.

Fire Protection

ORGANIZATION. Nearly three hundred and seventy-five million acres of state and private forest lands are afforded more or less systematic protection from fire. Unfortunately, another fifty-eight million acres are practically without protection, although this state of affairs is being corrected gradually. State organization for forest fire protection has assumed three main forms, with a number of variations. Most common is the scheme of centralized administration, which vests complete authority and responsibility in the state forester. This officer selects his staff of fire fighters, and directs their work. Another plan is generally used in New England; there each town assumes the obligation of protecting its own forests. The town fire wardens are locally chosen, with the almost inevitable result that wardens from neighboring towns often fail to co-operate in fighting serious conflagrations. The situation has improved greatly in recent years, however. In 1950 the New England states and New York signed an agreement to prepare a regional fire plan and to provide mutual aid in time of catastrophe. In the heavily forested states of the Northwest, where the large timber owners had developed efficient private fire-fighting organizations before the state governments became interested in forest protection, the work of the states centers around this private activity. Some states entrust the entire task of fire protection and fire fighting to the private associations, paying them with public funds and supervising their work closely.

LEGISLATION. Most states have enacted legislation designed to reduce the forest fire hazard. The burning of brush in or near woodland is generally prohibited, or at least restricted in various ways. Some state laws specify that a permit must first be secured. Penalties are provided for lack of proper care in handling camp fires and for carelessness or malicious intent in starting fires on public or private property. The laws of a few Western states declare that any person burning brush or grass on his own land during the dry summer months must notify his neighbors some time in advance. The timber companies and others engaged in logging operations are required to dispose of slash—that is, the leftover tops and limbs of trees —before a sufficient quantity accumulates to constitute a serious fire risk. Spark-arresting devices are commonly prescribed for locomotives and other engines operating near forest land. In recent years the work of forest fire control has been facilitated by the use of modern devices, such as airplanes and radios to detect and report fires, and bulldozers and pumper trucks to fight them.

Educational Programs

The federal government's offer to aid in financing educational field work in forestry has been accepted by more than three fourths of the states. This field work consists of practical demonstrations and projects conducted on the farmers' own land. The importance of timber is emphasized, and farmers are shown how their woodlands can be made to yield increased returns. Boys and girls are taught the essentials of forest planting, woods care and management, and fire protection. The federal appropriation for this activity is so small that most of the cost is necessarily borne by the states, yet state programs are regularly submitted to the federal government under the terms of the co-operative agreements.

State Forests

Laws providing for the permanent retention of state forest lands as state forests have been enacted in forty-one states. These forest areas vary greatly in size. Thus Georgia has only a few acres, while the area of Michigan's state forests totals more than five thousand square miles. Most of the large state forest areas are found in the Western states because these commonwealths originally received substantial grants of timberland from the national government. In many cases, however, this land was given for the purpose of resale—the money thus obtained to be used for specific purposes, such as common schools, institutions of higher learning, penal and charitable institutions, or public buildings. Moreover, the bulk of the land, even if free from such restrictions, was in widely scattered sections that could not readily be administered as state forests.

In recent years, however, the federal government has encouraged consolidation of state forest holdings by offering to exchange timberland with the states, and many exchanges have been effected. Federal funds have recently been made available to help complete state forest systems, the states agreeing to repay these loans as they derive revenue from the sale of forest products and the use of forest lands. A number of states have formulated the general policy that all state lands chiefly valuable for timber or for watershed protection shall be "forever dedicated to the public welfare." Large bond issues have been floated in some states for the acquisition of wooded areas suitable for state forests, whereas in other states bond issues for this purpose are prohibited.

Reforestation

More than five sixths of the states, under co-operative agreements with the United States Forest Service, maintain nurseries for the production of planting stock. Three hundred million young trees are distributed to private landowners each year. Usually a nominal charge is made, but the laws of a few states provide for free distribution. This activity is so closely related to other phases of forestry that it is generally administered by the state forester. In some states, however, the growth and distribution of forest trees have been entrusted to the state agricultural colleges, whose numerous contacts with the farmers through the county agents [2] greatly simplify the task of arousing popular interest in reforestation.

Most of the timberland of the United States is in private ownership. When it is cut over its immediate commercial value is destroyed, and its owners usually abandon it. Taxes on the land become delinquent, and after a time the state or county comes into possession of cut-over forest areas that have become a liability instead of an asset. Of course, the private owners are not to blame. Their sole interest is in the timber, and after that is gone they cannot afford to pay heavy taxes for many years while slow-growing crops of fresh timber replace the trees that have been cut down. Yet some way must be found to reforest these areas, for the forests of the United States are being cut four times as fast as they are grown.

It is obvious, therefore, that if private owners could be induced to retain their cut-over land and grow new timber, and to pay taxes and contribute to the cost of fire protection during the years required for the new crop to mature, the states would be spared the necessity of undertaking reforestation at public expense. More than half of the states have offered the inducement of materially lower taxes, or even tax exemption, on cut-over lands devoted to new forest crops. On the other hand, a number of states have been prevented from granting preferential treatment by "uniform tax" clauses in their constitutions. Whether the inducement of a lower tax—

[2] See pages 497–498.

or no tax at all—will lead to widespread reforestation of private lands is a question not yet decided. Some states seem to have obtained fairly satisfactory results, but others have been less fortunate.

Forest Experiment Stations

The movement for conservation of the nation's forest resources has suffered a severe setback in the last few years because of vastly increased wartime and peacetime demands for lumber. Present production is fifty-five per cent higher than in 1936, and large quantities of young seed growth are being cut prematurely. But public interest in the problems of forest conservation has not waned. In fact, increased appropriations have been made for the eleven forest experiment stations that have been established in various parts of the United States.

These stations are administered by the federal government, but close relationships are maintained with the state foresters and the state agricultural colleges. Many of the experiments are made co-operatively, the states supplying money, equipment, or personnel, and sharing in the results. These experiments include nursery and planting investigations, studies of the best methods of forest cutting, studies of forest growth and productivity, and investigations of forest relationships to climate, grazing, and fire. Tree insects and diseases are studied, these inquiries necessitating the assistance of specialists in entomology and plant pathology. A few experimental forests are being developed in connection with some of the stations.

FISH AND GAME

Protective Legislation

Every state has enacted more or less complete legislation designed to protect its wild life. The federal government, also, has acted to safeguard wild animals and birds, and its laws supplement the state statutes. While there is considerable variation in detail from state to state, the general principles of all the state fish and game laws are substantially the same. Open and closed seasons are fixed, with perhaps no open season for certain kinds of game that seem threatened with extinction or no closed season for other kinds that have proved too prolific. Hunting and fishing licenses are required, usually with higher fees for nonresidents. Bag and possession limits are established. Prohibitions are generally placed on the sale of protected game and also on its exportation from the state except under certain specified conditions.   Certain methods of killing fur animals, such as the use of poison or of traps that unnecessarily inflict torture, are forbidden.

Commissions

These fish and game laws, which far antedate the modern conservation movement, were originally enforced by the local sheriffs and constables as a part of their general duties of law enforcement.   But this arrangement never produced satisfactory results, and during the latter half of the nineteenth century it was abandoned by most of the states in favor of the appointment of special officers.   The first state to take this step was Maine, and it made the change even before the middle of the century—in 1843. The government was authorized to appoint three county fish wardens and also, a few years later, a number of county moose wardens.   Fish commissions were established in Massachusetts and New Hampshire in 1865, and shortly afterward in Connecticut and Vermont.   Other states fell into line rapidly, creating agencies for the protection of fish or game. After the reorganization in 1878 of the New Hampshire fish commission as the board of fish and game commissioners, it soon became customary to place fish and game protection under a single agency.

Commissions, boards, departments, bureaus, or divisions of fish and game are now found in every state, although under a variety of names and with a variety of functions.   The commission or board may have jurisdiction over parks, as in Nebraska.   It has already been indicated that in some states the department of conservation enforces the fish and game laws.[3]

The fish and game agency—by whatever name it may be called—ranges in size from three members in Arizona and eight other states to nine members in New Jersey.   Usually the members are unsalaried, although there are some exceptions.   The executive officer, chosen by the agency, directs the daily administrative routine.   He selects a number of wardens, whose primary duty is to police the state and apprehend violators of the fish and game laws.   In the more progressive states the wardens perform a number of other important functions also.   They aid in solving the conservation problems of their respective districts, and in planning and constructing fish ponds.   They lead many local movements for the conservation of wild life.

Although the state fish and game agencies were created merely for purposes of law enforcement, their activities now include virtually every

[3] See page 488.

phase of wild life conservation. Most of them carry on extensive programs of propagation and restocking that involve the operation of fish
hatcheries and rearing ponds, from which various species of fish are distributed to the public lakes and streams, and game farms where birds and
animals are reared and kept until ready for distribution. In addition,
game refuges are maintained by more than one third of the states. They
furnish sure rest and feeding grounds for protected birds and animals, and
thus play an important part in the general plan to increase the game supply.
Predatory animal control is also an important function. Most of the
states try to secure the protection of game by offering bounties for the
skins of such predatory animals as wolves or mountain lions. In addition,
a few states employ trained hunters whose task is to trap and kill these
beasts of prey. The federal government bears a part of the cost of state
programs of wild life protection and predatory animal control.

Educational work is almost invariably a part of the fish and game
agency's program. Motion pictures of wild life are prepared and distributed, lecturers are provided at the request of many organizations, and
schools are aided in their conservation studies and exhibits. Other common methods of arousing popular interest, such as newspaper publicity and
the publication of reports and bulletins, are regularly used. Some states
issue periodicals devoted to fish and game, distributing them without charge
or at the cost of printing.

Within the last few years many of the states have made co-operative
agreements with their neighbors, or have adopted uniform regulations, concerning the conservation of wild life. Co-operative agreements usually
cover such matters as hunting and fishing seasons, bag and possession limits,
issuance of reciprocal licenses, and joint policies of stocking and policing
wild life areas.

Relief from Wild Life Overpopulation

The movement for the protection of our wild animals and birds has been
so successful that many states are now faced with the problem of wild
life overpopulation. Deer and elk are so numerous in some sections that
they seriously damage crops. Pheasants, also, have multiplied so rapidly
in many areas that they present a grave menace to agriculture. Today the
United States has more bears, rabbits, ducks, and other forms of wild
life than it has had in many decades. The bison is no longer in danger of
extinction.

Today, therefore, even the most ardent conservationists are willing to
concede that wild game might be made a valuable supplementary source of

food.   Many states have recognized this fact by occasionally permitting longer hunting seasons, increasing bag and possession limits, and otherwise relaxing the game laws.   There seems to be little danger that these changes will impair the long-run policy of protection.

SOIL CONSERVATION

Soil erosion is one of the nation's most destructive enemies.   It has caused serious damage to hundreds of thousands of acres of land, making them virtually useless for crops or grazing.   In 1935, after a careful sur-

DISTRIBUTION OF STATE EXPENDITURES FOR NATURAL RESOURCES, 1953

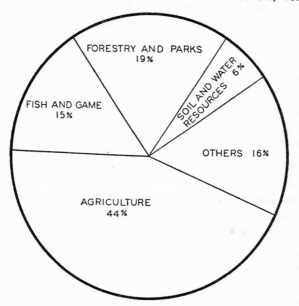

Based on figures from *Compendium of State Government Finances in 1953,* a publication of the United States Bureau of the Census.

vey had revealed the full extent of the problem, Congress established a national Soil Conservation Service, authorizing it to co-operate with appropriate state and local agencies in the protection of their soil resources. Between 1937 and 1945 all the states accepted the federal offer and established soil conservation committees or similar agencies.   The work of these state committees is largely supervisory, however.   Direct responsibility for obtaining results is assumed by local soil conservation districts.   More than twenty-five hundred such districts have been created.

The initiative for forming a soil conservation district is taken by the residents of a locality. They prepare a petition and, after obtaining a certain number of signatures, submit it to the state committee, which holds public hearings to determine the feasibility of the proposal. If satisfied, it then calls for a popular referendum. The voters of the community decide the matter, and, if they have voted in favor of a special district, proceed to elect its officers. The governing body is usually a three- or five-member board. It prepares a plan of soil conservation, which must be approved by the federal authorities before federal assistance can be made available. Federal agents give technical advice, not only to the officials of the district, but also directly to farmers and ranchers whose lands lie within district boundaries. Proper methods of crop use and conservation farming are taught. Trees and grasses are planted in those areas where the problem of erosion is acute. Thousands of acres have already been restored to normal use. During 1951 and 1952 the soil conservation program was expanded to include rehabilitation of midwestern farms damaged by the major floods of those years.

AGRICULTURAL EXTENSION WORK

Farmers' Institute

The states have long recognized their obligation to improve the standards of American farming by acquainting the people of the rural sections with the best farming methods. As early as 1852, when the Massachusetts state board of agriculture was established, the secretary was directed to "visit the various agricultural districts of the state and deliver lectures on the practice and science of agriculture." Eleven years later the board made provision for annual meetings of the leading agriculturalists of every farming community for the purpose of discussing common problems. Other states followed with so-called "farmers' institutes," and before 1890 the movement had spread to more than half of the states. By 1910 practically every state was included, the one- or two-day sessions of the institutes drawing hundreds of thousands of people. The railroads ran special trains to all the more important institutes.

In 1914, when the institute movement was at its peak, the total attendance in all states exceeded three million. Farmers were vitally interested in the discussion of their problems by experts. About this time, however, it became clear that a still better way of reaching the rural population of the United States had been found, and after 1914 the farmers' institutes declined rapidly in importance. Today their influence is negligible.

County Agents

A better way to reach farmers is the county agent system, now employed by every state. This system had its inception in Texas in 1906. The federal government had established a number of demonstration farms in various parts of the South for the purpose of teaching better methods of crop production and had succeeded in persuading many farmers to cultivate some of their own land under government supervision. Federal agents were assigned to the task of supervising these co-operative enterprises and pointing out mistakes. Pleased with the results obtained, the farmers in one Texas county requested the full-time services of a federal agent, offering to pay part of his salary. Their request was granted, and the county's share of the agent's salary was raised by popular subscription. Other counties soon made similar arrangements, and by 1914 the number of "county agents," as these men were generally called, had risen to nine hundred.

In that year Congress recognized the importance of the work by making a grant of several million dollars to the states for the purpose of providing "instruction and practical demonstrations in agriculture and home economics to persons not attending" the state agricultural colleges. This statute was a typical piece of subsidy legislation, including the usual stipulations that the state must formally accept the federal offer, that it must match federal money with money from state or local sources, and that it must submit plans acceptable to the federal administrative officials. The state agricultural colleges direct the work of the county agents, and assume responsibility for the effectiveness of extension work.

Although the county agent is paid from federal and state sources as well as from county funds and must possess the qualifications established by the state with federal approval, he is primarily a county employee. His title clearly indicates that he is chiefly responsible to the county he serves. He is chosen by the county supervisors, though usually from a list of names submitted by the state director of extension work, and in most states he may be dismissed by the supervisors for any reason that they deem adequate. Dismissal from a county does not necessarily involve dismissal from the extension service, for the state director who wishes to place a dismissed agent in another county can usually do so without difficulty. But chronic inability to give satisfaction is certain to destroy an agent's usefulness and force him from the service after a period of years.

The county agents carry their message to the farmers by means of actual demonstrations on the farmers' own land wherever this method of instruction is practicable.   Their activities are numerous and varied.   They teach soil improvement through the increased use of fertilizers and the introduction of nitrogenous crops such as sweet clover, soybeans, and cow peas.   They emphasize the use of higher grade seed.   The importance of tree crops is a part of their message.   They encourage the breeding of better live stock and lead the fight on animal diseases.   Land improvement is a part of their program, whether the land needs terracing, draining, irrigating, or clearing.   They teach the use of dynamite.

Nor is the work of the county agents restricted to improving methods of production.   Better marketing is emphasized.   The farmer who keeps bees, for example, is shown how to grade his honey and how to pack it attractively.   In many states, emphasis is placed on co-operative marketing. Through another important phase of the work—instruction in farm management—farmers are taught how to keep accurate records of their transactions.   As a result, cost accounting is becoming more generally understood and used.

Although some of the poorer rural counties, unable to bear the financial burden of extension work, have never had county agents, or have abandoned extension activities after a short trial, many a county has two or more agents.   The work of the male county agent is often supplemented by the work of a female home economics agent, whose task is to teach farm women how to make their homes more attractive, how to use time- and labor-saving devices, and how to safeguard the health of their families. Club agents, who deal exclusively with children, helping them to form pig clubs, cotton clubs, or other juvenile organizations where the use of proper farming methods can be stressed, are found in some of the wealthier counties. Usually, however, boys' and girls' clubs are developed and supervised by the county agricultural agents, who accept this task as a part of their regular duties.   A few Southern counties employ Negro extension agents to carry the message of improved agriculture to the members of their own race, but in most cases the white agents serve all the families in their respective counties, without regard to race or color.

The federal government prescribes minimum educational standards for county agents, including successful completion of a four-year college course in agriculture and practical farming experience.   Some states, however, have gone considerably beyond the federal minimum, and have thus been able to secure agents of unusually high caliber.   It need scarcely be added that the salaries paid by these states are well above the average.

AGRICULTURAL AND MINING EXPERIMENT STATIONS

Every state maintains an agricultural experiment station in connection with its agricultural college. These experiment stations were originally established as a direct result of a federal subsidy, but state appropriations now amount to three times the federal grant. Most of the customary conditions have been omitted from the federal offer, so that the states are free to conduct their stations without federal supervision or control.

The experiments carried on at the stations cover a wide range—soils and fertilizers, field crops, horticulture, plant diseases, animal production, dairying, animal diseases, foods and human nutrition, rural home management, agricultural engineering and economics, and rural sociology. Numerous reports, bulletins, and miscellaneous publications of the experiment stations contain the results of experiments, and thus make this information available to the public.

A number of the states also maintain mining experiment stations, engineering experiment stations, or divisions of engineering research. This work is usually administered by the state university or the agricultural college. Studies are made of the origin and occurrence of minerals, methods of prospecting and mining, mineral analyses and tests, extraction and refining, properties and utilization of minerals, and preservation of safety and health in mining. Many experiments are conducted co-operatively with the federal Bureau of Mines. As in the case of agricultural experiments, results are published at frequent intervals.

OIL AND GAS

Conservation Legislation

The states have done very little to prevent wasteful exploitation of most of their mineral resources. Oil and gas, however, are exceptions to this general rule. Every state possessing substantial known deposits of oil and gas has enacted legislation to reduce waste. The first oil conservation measure was adopted by Pennsylvania more than half a century ago; a short time afterward New York and Ohio followed. These early laws were designed to protect oil- and gas-bearing sands from the infiltration of salt water. They provided merely that water should be cast off, that wells should be plugged in a specific manner when abandoned, and that the owners of adjacent land, in case of the failure of well owners to plug properly, might remedy the deficiency.

A little later, as it became evident that generally accepted methods of oil production were causing the loss of immense quantities of natural gas, other laws were enacted for the specific purpose of preventing this waste. An Indiana statute of 1893, for example, provided that neither oil nor gas should be permitted to flow or escape into the open air for a period longer than two days after discovery. The constitutionality of this act was promptly attacked by one of the oil companies of the state, as contrary to the Fourteenth Amendment's due process clause. The company said, in effect, that it was interested only in the production of oil and that it could not produce oil without wasting gas. But the Supreme Court of the United States upheld the state's power of regulation, though upon rather narrow grounds.[4]

Somewhat later the oil-producing states enacted laws dealing with virtually every phase of oil and gas conservation, and establishing administrative agencies to make supplementary regulations and secure proper enforcement. It was found that unnecessary waste in the production of oil and gas could be prevented most readily by restricting production to the current market demand. Fair treatment of all the operators in a field was assured by prorating production among them. Voluntary proration agreements were encouraged in California for several years, but without substantial success.

The other leading oil-producing states went still further and enforced production limits established by administrative decree. The validity of the Oklahoma law authorizing the corporation commission to restrict total production and to establish production limits for each operator was challenged by one of the affected companies as a violation of the due process and equal protection clauses of the Fourteenth Amendment to the federal Constitution. But the Supreme Court of the United States upheld the statute. "Every person has the right to drill wells on his own land and take from the pools below all the gas and oil that he may be able to reduce to possession including that coming from land belonging to others," declared Mr. Justice Butler, speaking for the Court, "but the right to take and thus to acquire ownership is subject to the reasonable exertion of the power of the state to prevent unnecessary loss, destruction, or waste."[5] Restrictions on the production of oil and gas are now made effective by co-operative arrangements involving most of the important oil-producing states. Congress has done its part by prohibiting the shipment in interstate commerce of oil produced in excess of quotas fixed by state laws.

4 Ohio Oil Co. *v.* Indiana, 177 U.S. 190 (1900).
5 Champlin Refining Company *v.* Corporation Commission of Oklahoma, 286 U.S. 210 (1932).

Tidelands Oil

Some of the richest oil deposits in the United States lie in coastal areas, between the shore line and the three-mile limit of American jurisdiction. Since these deposits are under the sea, it may well be argued that they belong to the national government, and not to any of the states. The question of title has aroused many bitter controversies, although the oil-producing states long acted on the assumption that they were the rightful owners. They granted permission to private oil companies to exploit the coastal strip, imposing such conditions as seemed desirable in the public interest. Finally, as some federal officials declared with increasing insistence that the tidelands really belonged to the nation, Congress tried to settle the matter by giving clear title to the states. President Truman vetoed this bill, however, and his veto was sustained. That was in 1946. The next year, in a test case, the Supreme Court ruled that the nation, rather than the states, owned the three-mile coastal belt.[6] The obvious effect of this decision was to invalidate the leases of all the private oil companies operating in tideland areas of California and other states, and to deprive such states of a part of their tax revenue. A number of bills were promptly introduced in Congress, though without success, to restore the tidelands to the states. Meanwhile private oil companies were permitted to continue operations on a temporary basis. By 1952 the tidelands oil controversy had become a political issue. Congress again approved a proposal to give the tidelands to the states, and President Truman once more vetoed it. Dwight Eisenhower, then campaigning for the presidency, spoke out in support of state claims to the submerged lands beneath their coasts, and promised that as president he would sign an act of Congress abandoning federal title to the lands. Early in 1953 Congress did pass this measure, and it became law with President Eisenhower's signature.

WATER POWER

Absolute Federal Control

The federal government has taken the lead in the conservation of water power. Its control extends to water-power developments on navigable streams (through the right to regulate interstate commerce) and also to projects on the national domain. Since the justification for federal control

[6] United States v. California, 332 U.S. 19 (1947). The claims of Louisiana and Texas were subsequently rejected by the Supreme Court in other suits. United States v. Louisiana, 339 U.S. 232 (1950); and United States v. Texas, 339 U.S. 707 (1950).

in most instances is that streams are navigable, it becomes important to have a test of navigability.   Such a test was established by the United States Supreme Court in 1871: "Those rivers must be regarded as public navigable rivers in law which are navigable in fact.   And they are navigable in fact when they are used, or are susceptible of being used, in their ordinary condition, as highways for commerce. . . ." [7]

This ruling stood for nearly three quarters of a century, but it was modified in 1940 by the Supreme Court, when it was called upon to determine the navigability of the New River.   It held that the river was navigable, in spite of existing rapids, shallows, gorges, and other obstructions, because these barriers could be removed and the river made navigable in fact by the expenditure of a not unreasonable sum of money.   "To appraise the evidence of navigability on the natural conditions only of the waterway is erroneous," said the Court.   "Its availability for navigation must also be considered." [8]

This new criterion was attacked by Mr. Justice Roberts in a vigorous dissenting opinion.   "If this test be adopted," he declared, "then every creek in every state in the Union which has enough water, when conserved by dams and locks or channelled by wing dams and sluices, to draw a boat drawing two feet of water, may be pronounced navigable because, by the expenditure of some enormous sum, such a project would be possible of execution.   In other words, Congress can create navigability by determining to improve a non-navigable stream."   And that is exactly what Congress can do, in the view of the Supreme Court, despite Mr. Justice Roberts' protest. [9]   The effect of this decision has been to insure absolute federal control over all the water-power resources of the nation.

State Participation in Conservation

As early as 1920 a Federal Power Commission was established.   In 1930 it was reorganized with additional powers, and five years later its authority was still further expanded.   It now passes upon applications to construct power plants and grants licenses to responsible persons for periods not exceeding fifty years.   It supervises the design, construction, and operation of each project; regulates the financial policy of each operating company; and controls such important matters as rates and services.

The Federal Power Act does not, however, exclude the states from participation in the program of conserving water power.   On the contrary, it recognizes the desirability of federal-state co-operation.   No federal license

[7] Daniel Ball Case, 10 Wallace 557 (1871).
[8] United States v. Appalachian Electric Power Co., 311 U.S. 377 (1940).
[9] Mr. Justice McReynolds joined Mr. Justice Roberts in his dissent.

is granted until the applicant has met all the requirements of state law. No federal regulation of rates, services, or financial policy is attempted if there is a state commission possessing adequate authority. The right of the state to acquire federally licensed projects upon payment of just compensation is expressly reserved. Until a state acts, however, the federal government continues to occupy the entire field of water-power regulation. In certain areas the federal government has undertaken direct construction and management of vast hydroelectric power projects, of which the best known is the Tennessee Valley development.

Unfortunately, very few of the states have formulated any definite policies for conserving and developing their water-power resources. State public service commissions generally exercise a measure of control over companies that sell electricity developed from water power, but this control is merely a phase of public utility regulation, not directly related to water-power development.[10] There are, however, a few exceptions to the general rule of state inaction. Most notable is California, whose division of water resources in the department of public works prepared a comprehensive state water plan as early as 1931.

PROBLEMS

1. Describe the forest fire prevention work of your state or a neighboring state. What part is played by the federal government and by private agencies in protecting forests against fire?

2. Summarize the fish and game laws of your state. By whom are these laws administered?

3. Observe the work of the county agent in your county or a neighboring county. Write a brief description of his principal duties and the manner in which he performs them.

4. Visit your state agricultural experiment station. What are its principal activities?

5. Write the recent history of public control of the petroleum industry.

6. Study federal-state relations in the development of water power. What has been done by your state to conserve its water-power resources?

SELECTED REFERENCES

Baker, G., *County Agent*, 1939.

Brinser, A., and Shepard, W., *Our Use of the Land*, 1939.

Briscoe, Vera, Martin, James W., and Reeves, J. E. *Safeguarding Kentucky's Natural Resources*, Lexington, 1948.

Bruner, H. B., and Smith, C. M., *Conserving Our Natural Resources*, 1938.

[10] See Albert Lepawsky's article, "Water Resources and American Federalism," in the September, 1950, issue of the *American Political Science Review*, pp. 631–649.

Council of State Governments, *Postwar Problems of Agriculture*, 1944.

Dahlberg, E. M., *Conservation of Renewable Resources*, Appleton, Wis., 1939.

DeRoos, Robert W., *The Thirsty Land; The Story of the Central Valley Project*, Palo Alto, Calif., 1948.

Durisch, Lawrence L., and Macon, Hershal L., *Upon Its Own Resources: Conservation and State Administration*, University, Alabama, 1951.

Fietz, L. A., *The Role of the State in Recreation*, Berkeley, Calif., 1947.

Flynn, Harry E., and Perkins, Floyd E., *Conservation of the Nation's Resources*, 1941.

Gabrielson, Ira N., *Wild Life Refuges*, 1943.

Galloway, George B., *Postwar Planning in the United States*, 1942.

———, and Others, *Planning for America*, 1941.

Glover, K., *America Begins Again: The Conquest of Waste in Our Natural Resources*, 1939.

Greene, Lee S.; Brown, Virginia H., and Iverson, Evan A., *Rescued Earth*, Knoxville, Tenn., 1948.

Greene, Lee S., and Williamson, Rene de Visme, *Resources and Policy: Current Issues in Conservation*, Gainesville, Florida, 1951.

Gulick, Luther Halsey, *American Forest Policy: A Study of Government Administration and Economic Control*, 1951.

Gustafson, Axel F., and Others, *Conservation in the United States*, Ithaca, N.Y., 1944.

Highsaw, Robert B., *Mississippi's Wealth*, Oxford, 1947.

Hynning, C. J., *State Conservation of Resources*, Washington, D.C., 1939.

Larsen, Christian L., *South Carolina's Natural Resources*, Columbia, 1947.

National Resources Planning Board, *Human Conservation; The Story of Our Wasted Resources*, Washington, D.C., 1943.

———, *National Resources Development, Report for 1943, Part I: Postwar Plan and Program*, 1943.

———, *National Resources Development, Report for 1943, Part II: Wartime Planning for War and Postwar*, 1943.

———, *State Conservation of Resources*, 1942.

———, *The States and Planning*, 1942.

Parks, Robert W., *Soil Conservation Districts in Action*, Ames, Iowa, 1952.

President's Water Resources Policy Commission, *Report:* Vol. 1, *A Water Policy for the American People;* Vol. 2, *Ten Rivers in America's Future;* Vol. 3, *Water Resources Law*, Washington, D.C., 1950.

Pryor, W. C. and H. S., *Water—Wealth or Waste*, 1939.

Ray, Joseph M., and Worley, Lillian, *Alabama's Heritage*, University, 1947.

Renner, George T., *Conservation of National Resources; An Educational Approach to the Problem*, 1942.

Troup, R. S., *Forestry and State Control*, 1939.

Wager, Paul, and Hayman, Donald B., *Resource Management in North Carolina*, Chapel Hill, 1947.

The May, 1952, issue of the *Annals of the American Academy of Political and Social Science* is entitled "The Future of Our Natural Resources."

PART SEVEN

Business and Labor

CHAPTER 25

Regulation of Business

It was long accepted as axiomatic by most Americans that business should be free from governmental supervision and control to the fullest possible extent. In recent years, however, this *laissez-faire* theory has been substantially modified—to some extent, even discarded. Twentieth-century business has outgrown eighteenth-century philosophy; depression and war have further emphasized the need for public control; and the result has been a rapid multiplication of governmental regulations, extending to every phase of business and professional activity.

These regulations range from comparatively simple statutes or administrative decrees prohibiting the sale of adulterated foods and drugs to complex codes fixing the rates that may be charged by utility companies, prescribing the quantity and quality of service that must be rendered to the public, and establishing uniform accounting methods that must be adopted. Four main purposes underlie the control of business by the state: (1) production of revenue, (2) maintenance of free competition, (3) protection of public health and safety, and prevention of fraud, and (4) assurance of adequate service at reasonable rates in those businesses that are deemed essential to the public welfare.

CORPORATION CHARTERS

Abolition of Legislative Grants

When several persons unite to form a business corporation, they must secure a charter from the state. At one time these charters were granted in every instance by special act of the legislature, with very unsatisfactory results. Valuable legislative time was wasted in discussion of matters that were essentially private—or at least of no great public importance; favoritism was shown in granting or withholding requested powers; and charges of bribery were common.

So constitutional amendments were generally adopted to insure uniform and impartial treatment in granting charters. Ohio led the way in 1851, with the provision that "the general assembly shall pass no special act conferring corporate powers." Other states followed slowly; by the end of the century this clause or its equivalent had become a part of most state constitutions. Today, therefore, the legislature merely establishes a general policy for chartering corporations, and the details of the law are administered by the secretary of state or some other appropriate officer.

Ineffectiveness of Restrictions

Numerous restrictive provisions, designed to protect the public interest, are found in the charter laws of the several states. These provisions are far from uniform, but they commonly deal with such matters as the purposes of incorporation, the minimum number of incorporators, the residence of incorporators, and the holding of corporation stock by other corporations. Approximately half of the states have requirements concerning paid-in capital and a few states prescribe the minimum amount of capital necessary to begin business.

But evasion of these restrictions is comparatively easy in most jurisdictions. Thus, if a statute specifies that incorporators must be residents of the state, nonresidents desiring to form a corporation need only secure the services of *bona fide* residents to act in their stead until the charter has been granted. The stock, once issued, can then be transferred to its real owners without violating the letter of the law. Or, to use another example, the requirement that every charter must state the purpose or purposes of incorporation can be nullified by including in the list of purposes almost every conceivable legitimate business activity.

Most of the states view these evasions with equanimity, for they have discovered that lenient corporation laws attract would-be incorporators and thus swell the volume of state revenue from the granting of charters. A few commonwealths, following the early example of New Jersey, have deliberately adopted the policy of attracting incorporation business by lowering their standards almost to the vanishing point. Thus the need for protection of the public interest is sometimes subordinated to the need for additional state income.

Regulation of Local versus Interstate Commerce

Incorporation in one state does not confer the right to enter other states for the purpose of doing a local business. In this respect a corporation receives less protection than an individual, who may move freely across state boundaries without thought of interference. The federal Constitution declares that "The citizens of each State shall be entitled to all privileges and immunities of citizens in the several States," and the United States Supreme Court has ruled that these privileges and immunities include the right "to pass into any other State of the Union, for the purpose of engaging in lawful commerce, trade, or business, without molestation . . ." [1] But this protection, enjoyed by every natural person who is a citizen, may not be shared by the corporation, an artificial person.

As previously noted,[2] a corporation is not a "citizen," as the term is used in the Fourteenth Amendment. "The corporation, being the mere creation of local law, can have no legal existence beyond the limits of the sovereignty where created. . . . Having no absolute right of recognition in other states, but depending for such recognition and the enforcement of its contracts upon their assent, it follows, as a matter of course, that such assent may be granted upon such terms and conditions as those states may think proper to impose." [3]

It should be pointed out, however, that a corporation engaged solely in interstate commerce may enter any state of the Union at will and escape state interference with its affairs by incorporating in a state that imposes no restrictions. Regardless of its domicile, it may seek business through the mails. Or it may send salesmen from state to state for the purpose of procuring orders, provided that such orders are subject to validation at the home office. The matter of validation at the home office may seem unimportant, but it is sufficient to mark the difference between interstate and local commerce—and, therefore, between immunity from state control and complete subjection to state regulation.

It is becoming increasingly difficult for great corporations, with representatives in every state in the Union, to avoid "doing a local business" in the legalistic sense of the term. Modern methods of distribution necessitate the concentration of goods at strategic points in many states, so as to facilitate prompt delivery. Modern sales and service policies frequently involve the maintenance of local factory-controlled agencies. To an increasing extent, therefore, business is assuming a "local" character as it expands to national proportions. This paradox is the source of complex legal problems, for problems inevitably arise when corporations doing business on a nation-wide scale are subjected to forty-eight different kinds of regulation.

And, in fact, forty-eight different kinds of regulation really exist. No two states have identical requirements for admitting foreign corporations to do business within their boundaries, and few states have policies that even remotely resemble the policies of their neighbors. Some states admit for-

[1] Ward v. Maryland, 12 Wallace 418 (1871).
[2] See page 24.
[3] Paul v. Virginia, 8 Wallace 168 (1868).

eign corporations on terms more favorable than those afforded to corporations of their own creation; some permit foreign and domestic corporations to do business on equal terms; while others impose on foreign corporations heavy burdens from which domestic corporations are exempt. There is no general agreement among the states as to whether foreign corporations should be encouraged or repressed, and this diversity of purpose naturally prevents unity of action. But every state is supreme in the regulation of business within its own boundaries, and those corporations that cannot remain beneath the sheltering cloak of interstate commerce must be prepared to accept the vagaries and uncertainties of state control.

ANTI-TRUST LAWS

National Legislation

The prevention of monopolies and combinations in restraint of trade has become chiefly a function of the federal government. In 1890 Congress enacted the Sherman Anti-Trust Act, which prohibits combinations in restraint of interstate trade. In 1914 it enacted two other important statutes: the Clayton Act, which defines certain abuses and restraints of trade more clearly than the Sherman Act; and the Trade Commission Act, which established an administrative agency—the Federal Trade Commission—to investigate alleged abuses and enforce the anti-trust laws. Since virtually all large business enterprises enter the field of interstate commerce, they come under federal jurisdiction. It is the Federal Trade Commission, therefore, that scrutinizes business practices most closely and displays greatest activity in combating monopolistic combinations.

State Legislation

The prevention of unfair monopolies is not solely a federal responsibility, however. The states also have acted to insure free competition. Many of them had constitutional or statutory provisions directed against trusts and monopolies before the passage of the Sherman Act, and many others subsequently followed the example of the federal government by enacting anti-trust laws. Today laws relating to monopolies and restraints of competition or trade are found in nearly all the states. These laws display wide variations. Some of them in sweeping terms prohibit trusts, monopolies, and all combinations that restrain trade or injuriously affect the public welfare. Others are directed against monopolies in special fields, such as the production and marketing of foodstuffs. Certain business practices tending to restrain competition are sometimes specifically forbidden.

Fair Trade Laws

In recent years, however, the states have tended to look with favor upon business practices once regarded as highly undesirable.   Price maintenance, for example, which was formerly a punishable offense in many jurisdictions, is now almost universally permitted under certain conditions.   A law of Congress enacted in 1937 permitted contracts fixing minimum prices for the resale of commodities, provided such contracts were in accordance with state law.   All but three of the states [4] subsequently enacted so-called "fair trade" laws, which authorized manufacturers to make agreements with retailers as to the minimum prices at which products might be sold.   Most of these laws applied not only to retailers who were willing to sign the free trade contracts, but—once an agreement had been signed between a producer and a single retailer—to all nonsigners as well.   In 1951 the Supreme Court of the United States invalidated the conviction of a Louisiana liquor dealer who had refused to sign a fair trade contract, and had thereupon sold his wares below the prices fixed by the manufacturer.   Since he was a nonsigner, said the Court, he could not be bound by the agreements of others.[5] But this decision was based solely upon a literal and rather narrow interpretation of the federal law, which of course could be changed by Congress whenever it so desired.   In 1952 Congress did, in fact, legalize the price control practices of the states, thus generally preventing the sale of goods below manufacturers' minimum prices.[6]

PURE FOOD AND DRUG ACTS

Laws to promote public health and safety are numerous and varied.   In this category are the pure food and drug acts, now found on the statute books of every state, which prohibit the sale of diseased or adulterated food products, establish standards of purity for drugs, and specify that medicines containing dangerous ingredients shall be plainly marked.   In 1906 the federal government entered this field with the enactment of a law prohibiting the shipment in interstate commerce of adulterated or misbranded foods or drugs.

The federal statute was more comprehensive than most of the state laws adopted prior to that time, and within a year twenty-one states had modified

---

[4] Missouri, Texas, Vermont.   In Georgia and Michigan, however, the courts have ruled that the fair trade laws are in violation of state constitutional provisions.

[5] Schwegmann Brothers v. Calvert Distillers Corp., 341 U.S. 384 (1951).

[6] For a brief discussion of the ethics of fair trade laws, see the article by J. C. Furnas, "Are Fair Trade Laws Fair?" in the *Reader's Digest,* February, 1954, pp. 39–44.

their requirements to conform more nearly to federal standards. Most of the other states, in amending their food and drug laws from time to time, have been influenced to some extent by the federal statutes of 1906 and 1938. But diversity in state legislation has never been eliminated.

Federal-state co-operation has been fostered by the establishment of an office of co-operation in the federal enforcement agency, and state-local co-operation is no longer merely the expression of a fond hope. The general plan of co-operative activity involves the inspection of factories and the control of intrastate trade by the states, the regulation of interstate and foreign shipments by the national government, and the examination of markets and local deliveries by the cities. The tendency in recent years has been to vest the state food and drug law administrators with considerable power to issue necessary regulations, and the result has been the steady growth of a body of administrative decrees supplementing and interpreting the provisions of the laws.

PROTECTION FROM FRAUD

Misrepresentation

The states have enacted many laws designed to protect the public from fraud. Nearly every state has a statute directed at fraud in advertising; this statute commonly prohibits the circulation of any advertisement containing "an assertion, representation, or statement of fact that is untrue, deceptive, or misleading." Certain specific trade practices, such as the imitation of competitors' products or the sale of rebuilt machines as new products, are often declared to be misdemeanors. Sales contracts are generally regulated by state law, partly to prevent deception and partly to eliminate unnecessary misunderstandings.

Securities Regulation

STATE BLUE-SKY LAWS. Among the most important statutory provisions aimed at fraud are the so-called "blue-sky" laws, now found in every state except Nevada. In 1911 a Kansas legislator, pointing out that the people of his state were losing millions of dollars each year through the purchase of worthless stocks and bonds, declared that some dishonest promoters would sell shares "in the bright blue sky itself." The statute that he sponsored, intended to protect the purchasers of securities, was speedily dubbed a blue-sky law, and the name is now applied to all similar legislation.

At first the Kansas plan did not prove very popular. It was copied by a few states, but the others held aloof. The old common law principle of *caveat emptor*—let the buyer beware—was still the order of the day. Following the First World War, however, the rapid increase in national wealth and the boundless enthusiasm of the American people combined to make an especially fertile field for the operations of stock swindlers, and public opinion forced the general adoption of protective legislation. Not all the blue-sky laws are equally effective, however; some of them contain so many exemptions as to be practically worthless.

The state blue-sky laws originally assumed several forms. Some of them applied only to the securities offered for sale, without attempting to regulate the dealers. Every security issue, or every issue of "speculative" securities, had to be approved by the state securities commission or other administrative agency before it might lawfully be sold within the state. Those states that limited the requirement of commission approval to speculative issues generally adopted complete though by no means uniform definitions of "speculative." Another type of blue-sky law was concerned only with dealers, on the assumption that honest men would not try to sell worthless stocks or bonds. Under the provisions of such a law dealers in securities had to be registered or licensed and were required to present evidence of good character and of an equitable plan of business.

Nearly all the states now combine these two types of legislation by controlling both the securities and the dealers. Some states have established securities commissions or other separate agencies to administer the blue-sky laws, whereas others have relied on previously existing agencies, such as the railroad commission, the bank commissioner, the insurance commissioner, the secretary of state, or the attorney-general.[7]

The blue-sky laws of four states—Delaware, Maryland, New Jersey, and New York—differ so radically from all other state legislation on the subject that they cannot be placed in any of the usual categories. Under these laws no attempt is made to register dealers or to examine securities in advance of sale, but appropriate court action is instituted by the attorney-general whenever it appears to him that fraud has been perpetrated. The protection thus afforded to purchasers of securities is sometimes known as "locking the stable door," because the administrative mechanism begins to operate after the damage has been done. In New York, however, where enforcement has been particularly rigorous, fairly satisfactory results have been obtained.

THE SECURITIES AND EXCHANGE COMMISSION. In 1933 and 1934 the federal government assumed a considerable part of the responsibility for regulating security issues. It established a Securities and Exchange Com-

---

[7] See the articles entitled "State Regulation of Securities," in recent volumes of *The Book of the States*.

mission and prohibited the circulation in interstate commerce or through
the mails of any prospectus advertising a security not listed with the commission.   Every detail of new stock issues must be declared under oath;
this information must include such matters as the company's financial condition, its purposes and business, its principal operators and owners, under-
writing costs, commissions, and bonuses.   Company directors are made
civilly and criminally liable for any misrepresentation to investors.   Moreover, the stock exchanges of the nation are brought directly under federal
control.

FEDERAL-STATE CO-OPERATION.   The federal regulation of securities
through the Securities and Exchange Commission has no relation to purely
local transactions, which remain within the jurisdiction of the states.   In
fact, the Commission has repeatedly made clear that it wishes to co-operate
with the state commissions, instead of trying to put them out of business.
Such co-operation has now been achieved to a considerable degree.   Federal
and state officials confer frequently concerning applications for registration,
and they exchange information with regard to violations of the securities laws.

REGULATION OF INTEREST RATES ON LOANS

Usury Laws

Every one of the forty-eight states has established by statute a so-called
legal rate of interest, which applies to certain contracts when the parties have
failed to specify a particular rate.   This rate ranges from five to eight per
cent a year; usually it is six per cent.   In addition to the "legal" rate, nearly
every state prescribes a maximum rate for interest on loans.   This maximum rate may be the same as the legal rate; usually, however, it is somewhat higher, varying from six to twelve per cent.   Interest charged in excess
of the maximum lawful limit is declared to be usury, and usurious practices
are punished by the forfeiture of all interest, as in Florida, the forfeiture of
the principal, as in Oregon, or even by imprisonment under certain circumstances, as in California.

Small-loan Acts

The theory that the borrower should be protected from excessive charges
is by no means new; all the American colonies had usury laws, with heavier
penalties than at present.   In recent years, however, it has become evident
that the usury laws frequently do more harm than good through their failure
to recognize differences in risks, types of loans, costs, and security.   Small
loans to persons in dire need, often without security or with security of

doubtful worth, cannot possibly be made by professional money-lenders at the legal maximum limit, even when the limit is twelve per cent.   The cost of their business is too high, and the risk too great.   A usury law that ignores this fundamental fact inevitably produces one of two results: either it drives professional money-lenders from the small-loan field, thus multiplying the problems of the poor persons whose protection is sought, or else it draws into the field a group of unscrupulous Shylocks who willingly violate the law and charge exorbitant rates as compensation for the added risks they must assume.

More than three fourths of the states, therefore, have supplemented their usury laws with small-loan acts, applying usually to loans of three hundred dollars or less.   For such loans the lawful maximum rate is fixed sufficiently high to permit a reasonable return on invested capital even after the necessarily heavy losses have been deducted.   Three per cent a month is the most common limit.   The small-loan laws are further strengthened by unusually heavy penalties for loans at rates in excess of the maximum and also by provisions concerning the periodic examination of money-lenders' records by state officials.

REGULATION OF BUSINESSES AFFECTED WITH A PUBLIC INTEREST

Certain businesses, such as banks, insurance companies, electric light and power companies, gas companies, and common carriers, are subject not only to ordinary governmental regulations designed to prevent unfair trade practices, promote the public health and safety, and prevent fraud, but also to special governmental control affecting every detail of their affairs—their accounting methods, the quality of their service, and, in most instances, their rate schedules.

In wartime, of course, this distinction among different types of businesses may virtually disappear.   Public control of prices, as well as quality and quantity of both goods and services, may be extended to all businesses that are even remotely connected with the war effort.   In peacetime, however, such far-reaching control would not be accepted by the people or by the courts.   Extensive public regulation has always been reserved for the banks, the common carriers, and the like.

Definition

The question may well be asked, therefore, why these businesses may be so closely supervised.   What characteristics do they possess that ordinary businesses lack?   The generally accepted answer is that they are affected with a public interest. But that statement is not an explanation. As Justice Stone declared in his cogent dissent from the majority opinion in the case of Tyson *v*. Banton,[8] "the phrase 'business affected with a public interest' seems to me to be too vague and illusory to carry us very far on the way to a solution. It tends in use to become only a convenient expression for describing those businesses, regulation of which has been permitted in the past. To say that only businesses affected with a public interest may be regulated is but another way of stating that all those businesses which may be regulated are affected with a public interest."

SUPREME COURT DECISIONS. The Supreme Court of the United States has attempted a definition of public interest enterprises,[9] but its classification is so broad as to include every business that the courts have ever regarded as affected with a public interest, and so vague as to permit the inclusion of other enterprises from time to time, should changing conditions seem to warrant additions to the present list. It is, therefore, utterly worthless as a guide to underlying principles. The truth of the matter seems to be that no underlying principles exist.

For many years the United States Supreme Court seemed willing to accept as binding practically every legislative declaration that a business was affected with a public interest. Legislative regulation, whenever attempted, was approved almost as a matter of course. Later, however, the Court refused to sanction a number of state laws extending the public interest principle. Thus it held in 1927, in the case of Tyson *v*. Banton,[10] that the fees charged by theater ticket agencies might not be fixed by statute. The next year it invalidated a New Jersey statute requiring private employment agencies to charge no higher fees than those deemed reasonable by the state commissioner of labor, on the ground that "an employment agency is essentially a private business." [11] Then, a few months later, came the decision that the business of selling gasoline was not affected with a public interest to the extent of permitting public regulation of rates.[12] In 1932 it was held that the business of manufacturing and selling ice was essentially private, and that the number of those engaging in it might not be limited by legislative action.[13]

On the other hand, the Supreme Court adopted a liberal attitude in 1934 by upholding state regulation of milk prices.[14] Earlier decisions were not

[8] 273 U.S. 418 (1927).
[9] Wolff Packing Company *v*. Court of Industrial Relations, 262 U.S. 522 (1923).
[10] 273 U.S. 418 (1927).
[11] Ribnik *v*. McBride, 277 U.S. 350 (1928).
[12] Williams *v*. Standard Oil Co. of Louisiana, 278 U.S. 235 (1929).
[13] New State Ice Co. *v*. Liebmann, 285 U.S. 262 (1932).
[14] Nebbia *v*. New York, 291 U.S. 502 (1934).

expressly overruled by this case, yet there seems to be no escape from the conclusion that the Supreme Court changed its attitude after it had invalidated public regulation of the fees charged by employment agencies and theater ticket brokers.

VARIATIONS IN PERMISSIBLE REGULATION. Even judicial determination of the fact that a business is affected with a public interest does not necessarily indicate the extent of public regulation that will be permitted. For businesses affected with a public interest may be affected in varying degrees, and therefore subject to varying types of supervision and control. Banks and telephone companies, for example, are both public interest enterprises, but the state's regulation of telephone companies is much more extensive than its regulation of banks.[15]

Banking

SUPERVISION FOR SECURITY. Every state exercises strict supervision over the banks that it has chartered to do business within its borders. This supervision does not extend to the charges made for bank services, but is aimed solely at greater security for depositors. Thus the state law commonly includes provisions concerning the minimum amount of capital stock for banks and the manner in which such stock must be subscribed; restrictions on the purposes for which bank loans may be made; requirements as to the amount and form of reserves; and definition of the obligations of bank stockholders. Half of the states permit branch banking, although branches are usually limited to the city or county in which the head office is located.

THE BANKING COMMISSIONER. The banking laws are enforced by a banking commissioner or other officer—sometimes known as the bank examiner, bank supervisor, or secretary of banking. This officer is commonly appointed by the governor, although he is chosen by the banking board in Oregon and by the corporation commission in Virginia. Two states—Mississippi and Tennessee—give the banks a voice in the selection of the chief banking officer. Florida vests the duties of banking commissioner in the state treasurer, who is chosen by the voters, and Illinois assigns these tasks to the popularly elected auditor. Banking boards are found in but one third of the states; their functions are chiefly advisory.

Important powers are vested in the banking commissioner. He selects a staff of bank examiners who visit the banking institutions of the state and make such periodic investigations as are deemed necessary. In most states he is authorized to take charge of closed banks, liquidate their assets, and

---

[15] Wolff Packing Co. *v.* Court of Industrial Relations, 262 U.S. 522 (1923).

pay depositors. Usually he possesses a discretionary power to grant or refuse charters to new banks, although a number of states permit appeal from the banking commissioner to a board of review or to the courts.

A STATE-OWNED BANK. One state—North Dakota—has gone directly into the banking business in competition with private institutions. The state bank, established in 1919, is supervised by a three-member ex officio board which hires a full-time manager. Most of the deposits are from the state and its civil subdivisions, but many individual accounts are also maintained. The bank serves as fiscal agent for the state, frequently advancing the funds necessary to carry on various public activities and thus eliminating the need for short-term borrowing. It also supervises the management of several thousand farms acquired by the state as a result of foreclosures in the 1930's, during the depth of the depression.

DEPOSIT GUARANTEES. During the decade prior to the First World War a number of states passed laws guaranteeing bank deposits. The customary procedure was to levy an assessment upon every bank operating under state law and to establish a depositors' guarantee fund with the money thus obtained. These laws were upheld by the courts, but they failed to meet the test of financial depression in 1929 and subsequent years. Guarantee funds were speedily exhausted, and several states were obliged to issue scrip in temporary payment of their obligations. The result was the repeal of every state law guaranteeing deposits.

In 1933, however, the financial panic created widespread agitation for some form of insurance against loss of bank deposits, with the result that the federal government enacted a statute guaranteeing deposits, with maximum limits, in all member banks of the Federal Reserve System, as well as other banks accepting the provisions of the law. Whether the federal deposit guarantee system can withstand financial crisis more successfully than the guarantee systems of the states is not certain.

EXTENSION OF FEDERAL CONTROL. The federal government has long exercised a considerable measure of control over banking. In 1863, largely because of the difficulty of selling war bonds on reasonable terms, it established a national banking system and issued charters to approved banks applying for membership. These banks, therefore, came under national instead of state supervision. With the establishment of the Federal Reserve System in 1914, federal control became even more extensive. National banks were required to join the system, and state banks were permitted to do so if they conformed to federal standards. The nation's banking system was still further centralized by laws enacted in 1933 and 1935.

Insurance

THE INSURANCE COMMISSIONER. Insurance, also, is a business subject to strict public regulation. Every state except Louisiana has an officer known as insurance commissioner, superintendent of insurance, or something of the sort; Louisiana vests the duty of enforcing the insurance laws in the secretary of state. The insurance commissioner is appointed by the governor in most states, although a few commonwealths specify election by the legislature or by the people. Technical qualifications are seldom prescribed.

The duties of the commissioner are numerous and far-reaching. Usually he exercises a measure of control over the incorporation of domestic insurance companies and the licensing of insurance companies from other states. Agents and brokers are subject to his supervision. From time to time he examines the records of all domestic companies for the purpose of determining the state of their finances. His powers in this respect are usually very broad. He may revoke a company's license to do business for unsound financing, violation of visitorial requirements, or a number of other reasons. The body of legislation that he is required to enforce generally includes statutes regulating the investment of insurance company funds, prescribing the procedure in the event that capital is impaired, specifying the forms of policies, prohibiting certain methods of getting business, requiring equitable treatment of policy holders, and assuring reasonable rates.

RATE REGULATION. Public regulation of the rates charged by insurance companies is an indication of the extent to which the insurance business is clothed with a public interest. Rates for fire, industrial compensation, and some other forms of insurance are commonly fixed by the companies through the rating bureaus of which they are members, but the rate schedules thus privately prepared must be submitted to the state insurance commissioner, who has the power to prevent discriminations and, in some jurisdictions, the power to order a general reduction if the level of rates seems too high. Life insurance rates are automatically controlled within narrow limits by statutes prescribing the mortality table and rate of interest upon which reserves must be based.

The Supreme Court of the United States has held that insurance is a business sufficiently affected with a public interest to justify public price fixing.[16] In 1944 the Court ruled that insurance companies doing business across state lines were engaged in interstate commerce, and therefore subject to federal

[16] German Alliance Insurance Company v. Lewis, 233 U.S. 389 (1914).

control.[17]   Shortly afterward, however, Congress nullified this decision by expressly renouncing its right to regulate the insurance industry.   "The business of insurance . . ." declared the law of Congress, "shall be subject to the laws of the several states which relate to the regulation or taxation of such business."

Liquor Industry

The need for strict public regulation of the liquor industry arises from the fact that liquor is a product inherently susceptible of abuse.   Many persons will use it immoderately, to their own detriment, if given the opportunity. Therefore the state should restrict consumption within the narrowest possible limits—though bearing in mind, of course, that too great restriction tends to encourage law violation.   The liquor policies adopted by the several states since the repeal of the prohibition amendment in 1933 fall into three general categories: (1) sale by private persons, under a state licensing system; (2) sale by the state, through state-operated stores; and (3) prohibition of liquor sales throughout the state, or in those communities desiring such an arrangement.

Complete prohibition has become increasingly unpopular during recent years, even in the small group of states that originally elected to remain "dry" after the repeal of national prohibition; therefore it requires no more than passing mention.   The state store system has been adopted by seventeen states.[18]   Its essential feature is the establishment of a chain of retail stores [19] for the package sale of liquor, under the management of a liquor control board or some similar agency.   The state thus holds a monopoly of package liquor sales.   But sales by the drink require separate regulation. Some of the so-called "monopoly" states permit licensed hotels and restaurants to sell intoxicants by the drink; others prohibit by-the-drink sales of all intoxicants, except light beer or beer and wine.

Under the license plan, which most states have adopted, the sale of intoxicants is a private matter, but is restricted to those persons who have been granted permits by the state liquor authority.   State laws regulate the hours of sale, the physical features of sale places, and the like.   Although one of the chief reasons for state control of intoxicants is supposed to be the restriction of consumption, this purpose is often forgotten by state legislators

---

[17] United States v. Southeastern Underwriters' Association, 322 U.S. 533 (1944).

[18] Alabama, Idaho, Iowa, Maine, Michigan, Montana, New Hampshire, North Carolina, Ohio, Oregon, Pennsylvania, Utah, Vermont, Virginia, Washington, West Virginia, Wyoming.

[19] In Wyoming the state liquor stores operate on a wholesale basis.

and administrators, who tend to encourage the expansion of the liquor industry because it means additional tax revenue. This conflict of purposes is reflected in many state laws.

Public Utilities

Public control of business assumes its most complete form in the regulation of public utilities. These businesses, which are said to be essentially public in character though owned and operated by private persons, differ from other enterprises affected with a public interest in that they enjoy special privileges such as the use of public property or the right of eminent domain. Not only may they be regulated, like banks, as to their financial structure; not only may they be supervised, like insurance companies, as to rates and quality of service; but in addition they may be compelled to serve all persons without discrimination. The list of utility enterprises is long and imposing. It includes wharves, docks, and bridges; telephone, telegraph, and power transmission lines; water, gas, and electric service; and transportation facilities such as car, bus, cab, and airplane lines, gas and oil pipelines, and railroads. Nor does this enumeration make any pretense at completeness.

THE STATE REGULATORY AGENCY. The state agency created to supervise public utility affairs is variously known as public service commission, public utilities commission, or railroad commission. The early commissions were concerned solely with railroad control, and this fact explains the occasional survival of the name "railroad commission," despite the expansion of commission activity.

Except in Oregon and Rhode Island, where the public service commission has been replaced by a single commissioner of utilities, the commissions range in size from three members—the usual number—to seven members in South Carolina. Appointment by the governor is the most common method of selecting the commissioner, although popular election is still widely used in the South and Middle West. South Carolina and Virginia vest the power of selection in the legislature. Terms of office are long, averaging about six years. But there are many contrasts, such as the ten-year term in New York and Pennsylvania and the two-year term in South Carolina.

Technical qualifications for commissioners are seldom prescribed, either by law or custom. The inevitable result is that very few public service commissioners possess an adequate understanding of the complicated engineering and accounting problems they are called upon to solve. Therefore these problems are left to the technical staff, and commissioners busy themselves with "broad questions of public policy"—an euphemism for the repair of broken-down political fences.

Extent of control. Commission control usually extends to the approval of utility rates, the establishment of standards of service, the examination of financial practices for the purpose of preventing mismanagement, and the prescribing of uniform accounting methods. Rate control, of course, is most important. The fundamental purpose of utility regulation is to insure reasonable service at a reasonable price; therefore every public service commission possesses power to pass upon the charges made by the utility companies operating within its jurisdiction. Sometimes this power is limited to the fixing of maximum charges, but more commonly complete rate schedules are set up. Appeals from the commission's decisions may be taken to the courts, and such appeals are frequent. But every request for permission to charge a higher rate must first go to the public service commission, which makes a detailed study of all the facts involved.

Service standards, also, are important. A fair rate cannot be determined unless some agreement has been reached as to the quantity and quality of service to be given. Therefore the commissions are obliged to formulate and publish regulations covering these matters in great detail. Electric light and power companies, for example, are controlled by commission orders so numerous and so complete that their enforcement virtually necessitates a measure of commission participation in the management of the companies.

These orders specify the conditions under which service may be secured, the aid that must be given to customers in selecting appliances best suited to their needs, the charges, if any, that may be made for extensions and service connections, the contents and form of bills, the deposits that may be required, the information that must be supplied to customers, and the manner in which complaints must be handled. Provision is made, also, for securing efficient service through the establishment of frequency requirements, together with statements of allowable voltage fluctuations. Other regulations deal with service interruptions, the location and testing of meters, and the prevention of accidents.

Commission rules for other utilities are equally detailed, although necessarily covering other matters to some extent. Thus they deal with the installation of specified heating, ventilating, and safety devices on street cars, buses, and subway and elevated trains. Most commissions, though not all, possess the right to order service extensions. This power is important because it assures adequate service for newly developed areas, even though the amount of paying business may be comparatively small.

IMPORTANCE OF EFFECTIVE UTILITY REGULATION. The total investments in privately owned and operated public utilities amount to many billions of dollars. Some authorities believe that these investments represent one fifth of the entire productive wealth of the nation. When it is realized that the utility business is largely monopolistic, and therefore able to charge whatever the traffic will bear unless restrained from making exorbitant charges by the public service commission, the importance of effective utility regulation becomes apparent.

An alert, honest commission, composed of competent technicians possessing adequate authority, can save huge sums that would otherwise swell the profits of the utilities. A commission that deviates from some of these specifications can transform regulation into a farce—or a tragedy. Unfortunately, most public service commissions have proved defective in one or more respects. And, in some states, it cannot be denied that public utility regulation has long hovered between tragedy and farce.

HANDICAPS TO EFFECTIVE UTILITY REGULATION

Poorly Qualified Commissioners

Partisan politics often plays a part in the selection of commissioners, even in those states that vest the power of appointment in the governor. When the commissioners are popularly elected, of course, only an accident or a miracle can lead to the choice of properly qualified technicians. So the commissioners take office with political favors to be granted and political debts to be repaid. They cannot consider the public welfare until the welfare of their friends and followers has received due consideration.

Even when commissioners are chosen solely on the basis of merit, it is usually well-nigh impossible to obtain outstanding men. For one thing, salaries are too low and tenure is too uncertain. Then, too, most of the leading technicians in the field are associated, quite naturally, with the utility companies. They can see no reason to jeopardize their future by accepting appointment to positions that will make them the guardians of the public interest against the interest of their former and probable future employers. Small appropriations, also, handicap most of the public service commissions. Technical staffs are undermanned and equipment is inadequate.

Incomplete Jurisdiction of Commission

Public service commissions are seriously handicapped by inept and out-worn legislation. In some states their authority does not extend to electric light and power lines. In others, although applying to all utilities, it does not include the right to prescribe uniform systems of accounting. The rules of commission procedure established by law are generally unsatisfactory and badly in need of revision.

As recently as 1930 virtually all the public service commissions were without jurisdiction over holding companies. This denial of holding company control proved especially unfortunate, for it enabled the public utilities to escape effective regulation in a number of different ways. Within the last few years, however, this weakness has been recognized, and nearly all the state legislatures have enacted suitable statutes. Even more effective has been an act of Congress extending federal control over utility holding companies engaged in interstate commerce.

The Courts' Theory of Rate-making

Fully as important as any other factor in weakening the effectiveness of utility regulation has been the attitude of the courts. For many years the federal and state courts, led by the Supreme Court of the United States, developed and applied a theory of rate-making that placed serious obstacles in the path of the commissions and virtually reduced valuation proceedings to a dignified and highly expensive game of blind man's buff.

In 1898, in the case of Smyth v. Ames,[20] the Supreme Court gave the first adequate statement of this theory. "We hold," it said, "that the basis of all calculations as to the reasonableness of rates to be charged . . . must be the fair value of the property being used by it for the convenience of the public." At first glance this statement seems entirely satisfactory. Certainly there must be some basis for determining the reasonableness of rates. When a public utility company applies for permission to increase its charges, the public service commission to which application is made must decide whether the present rates are unreasonably low. For if it does not permit the utility company to earn a reasonable return, it will deprive the company of its property without due process of law, in violation of the Fourteenth Amendment to the federal Constitution. A reasonable return must be allowed, therefore, and this return must be upon the "fair value of the property."

FAIR VALUE OF PROPERTY. But how is fair value to be determined?

[20] 169 U.S. 466 (1898).

The ordinary test of value, as applied to most goods and services, is selling price. An article or a service is worth exactly what it can be sold for. But this test is worthless in determining the value of public utilities, for utility properties are not daily bought and sold like clothing or foodstuffs. A few shares of utility stock or a few bonds may change hands, but these transactions cannot be accepted as an accurate index of the value of the entire property.

Is it possible, then, to determine a public utility's value by capitalizing its earnings? This method of finding value, or selling price, is common in the field of competitive business. It cannot be used to ascertain the value of a public utility for rate-making purposes, however, because utility earnings are so closely related to the rates whose reasonableness is to be determined. The most obvious circular reasoning is involved in the statement that a public utility should be permitted to earn, say, six million dollars a year because this sum is a reasonable return upon its fair value of one hundred millions, and that the property is worth one hundred million dollars because it is capable of earning six million dollars annually. Such logic would make possible a complete justification of any rate, however large it might be.

DIFFICULTIES OF APPLICATION. If fair value is to be accepted as the basis for determining the reasonableness of utility rates, the usual tests of value cannot be applied. The "value" of a public utility must be something different from the value of a motor car or a pair of shoes. The Supreme Court realized this difficulty when it first enunciated the principle of a reasonable return upon the fair value of the property, and in the same case it established a formula of its own for finding value. This formula, as amended by subsequent court decisions, remained the basic principle of all valuation proceedings for nearly half a century. It was the starting point for every consideration of the reasonableness of rates by public service commissions.

"In order to ascertain . . . value," said the Court, "the original cost of construction, the amount in permanent improvements, the amount and market value of bonds and stocks, the present as compared with the original cost of construction, the probable earning capacity of the property under particular rates prescribed by statute, and the sum required to meet operating expenses, are all matters for consideration." [21]

Here, certainly, were enough factors to occupy the time and attention of the public service commissions. But how much weight should each factor receive? The Supreme Court answered that question by stating that

[21] Smyth v. Ames, 169 U.S. 466 (1898).

each of these elements of value should be given such consideration "as may be just and right in each case." Beyond that meaningless generalization it did not commit itself.

Over a period of years, however, and with the aid of subsequent court decisions, the public service commissions of the several states were able to gain some knowledge of the relative importance of the various elements of value as defined by the Supreme Court. They learned that certain factors, such as the amount and market value of bonds and stocks and the probable earning capacity of the property, might safely be accorded little more than lip worship. Other factors, such as the original cost of construction and the amount expended in permanent improvements, were deemed highly important.

PRUDENT INVESTMENT OR REPRODUCTION COST? Gradually two theories emerged as to the proper basis of utility valuation. One of these was the "prudent investment" theory; its advocates believed that the value on which a reasonable return should be allowed was the amount actually and prudently invested, including any additions to the original investment, with proper deductions for depreciation. The "reproduction cost" theory, on the other hand, was not concerned with the amount actually invested. Its proponents contended that the only true test of utility value was the cost of re-creating plant and equipment at present prices and with modern methods. Between these two theories yawned a wide gulf—as wide as the difference between the prices at the time of valuation and the prices at the time of original construction.

Let us suppose that a valuation for rate-making purposes was made in 1950. Most public utility companies were developed much earlier, during the days of relatively low price levels. It is easy to understand, therefore, why they heartily favored the reproduction cost theory. For under this theory a public utility's properties erected in 1910 at a cost of twelve million dollars might be worth seventeen millions in 1950, without regard to subsequent improvements, merely because of a change in the value of the dollar.

If the theory of prudent investment were accepted instead, this company's properties would still be worth twelve million dollars in 1950—that is, omitting all consideration of depreciation and subsequent improvements in order to avoid unnecessary complications. In this instance, therefore, five million dollars would represent the difference between prudent investment and reproduction cost. Small wonder that the representatives of the utilities and of the public seldom agreed as to the proper basis of valuation!

The Supreme Court of the United States lent aid and comfort to both camps at different times.   In Smyth v. Ames it mentioned both actual investment ("the original cost of construction, the amount expended in permanent improvements") and reproduction cost ("the present as compared with the original cost of construction") as factors to which just and proper weight should be given.   Later it appeared to accept the theory of reproduction cost without qualification.   Thus it said in 1909: "If the property . . . has increased in value since it was acquired, the company is entitled to the benefit of such increase." [22]   But in 1923 it declared: "The refusal of the commission and of the lower court to hold that . . . the physical properties of a utility must be valued at the replacement cost less depreciation was clearly correct." [23]   In 1937 it seemed to place considerable emphasis on prudent investment,[24] and five years later it even went so far as to hint its willingness to abandon the theory of reproduction cost.[25]

REJECTION OF REPRODUCTION COST THEORY.   Not until 1944, however, was the traditional doctrine of Smyth v. Ames definitely thrown into the discard.   The Federal Power Commission had ordered the Hope Natural Gas Company to reduce its rates, basing its order on a finding that the company was receiving an excessive return on the "actual legitimate cost" of its properties—in other words, the amount prudently invested.   The company contended that its properties were worth nearly three times the actual investment because of changes in the price level, and it challenged the Federal Power Commission's right to ignore reproduction cost.   But the Supreme Court upheld the Commission in a sweeping decision, making clear that rates based upon prudent investment would be upheld.[26]

Unfortunately, however, the Court did not accept the prudent investment theory in so many words, thus establishing a clear and workable theory of utility valuation.   Instead, it declared itself willing to accept any theory that would produce reasonable results.   "It is not theory but the impact of the rate order which counts," declared the Court, speaking through Mr. Justice Douglas.   "If the total effect of the rate order cannot be said to be unjust and unreasonable, judicial inquiry under the act is at an end.   The fact that the method employed to reach that result may contain infirmities is not then important."

Such broad tolerance would undoubtedly be commendable, if it did not leave so many vital questions unanswered.   Public service commissions are

[22] Wilcox v. Consolidated Gas Co., 212 U.S. 19 (1909).
[23] Georgia Railway and Power Co. et al. v. Railroad Commission of Georgia et al., 262 U.S. 625 (1923).
[24] Railroad Commission of California et al. v. Pacific Gas and Electric Co., 302 U.S. 388 (1937).
[25] Federal Power Commission v. Natural Gas Pipeline Co., 315 U.S. 575 (1942).
[26] Federal Power Commission v. Hope Natural Gas Co., 320 U.S. 591 (1944).

constantly engaged in the task of determining the value of utilities for rate-making purposes, and they must know what standards to use. For if they fail to use standards acceptable to the Supreme Court their findings will be declared invalid. But the Court itself refuses to give a direct answer. "Employ whatever methods you think best," it tells the commissioners. "We shall accept any standards that you may care to use, *provided the result is just and reasonable.*" And the members of regulatory commissions, both state and federal, can only shake their heads in bewilderment and ask: "How can we tell whether our findings are just and reasonable?" Surely the question of method is not unimportant, when different standards produce widely different results.

Mr. Justice Jackson, in a dissenting opinion, makes clear the dilemma in these words: "I must admit that I possess no instinct by which to know the 'reasonable' from the 'unreasonable' in prices and must seek some conscious design for decision. The Court sustains this order as reasonable, but what makes it so or what could possibly make it otherwise, I cannot learn." [27]

Too much weight must not be given, however, to the confusion of thought evident in the majority opinion. One important fact stands out in this case: the willingness of the United States Supreme Court to accept utility valuations based solely on prudent investment. The long fight to eliminate reproduction cost from the rate base has been won, at least so far as the highest court of the land is concerned.

PUBLIC OWNERSHIP OF UTILITIES

Unless public regulation of the privately owned and operated utility companies can be made effective, the only practicable alternative seems to be public ownership. But public ownership of utilities has not proved very popular in the United States, except as applied to a few enterprises, such as roads, the post office, water supply, and garbage collection, which are now generally considered governmental functions. State ownership, especially, as distinguished from federal or municipal ownership, has made but slight progress.

There are, however, some examples of state ownership. A number of states own and operate grain elevators. State printing plants have been established in California and Kansas.[28] Several states own and operate extensive systems of wharves and warehouses. The State of Louisiana, for example, has constructed more than seven miles of wharves, and vast stor-

[27] Federal Power Commission *v.* Hope Natural Gas Co., 320 U.S. 645 (1944).
[28] See page 448.

age facilities for grain and cotton. The Port of New York Authority is responsible for the operation of state-owned railroad, truck and bus terminals, as well as the major airports serving New York City. There is also a New York Power Authority, which controls the development of hydroelectric power on the St. Lawrence River. In Massachusetts the Port of Boston Authority, a state agency, is directing a vast program for the improvement of the port's cargo terminal facilities.

In the municipal field, American experience with public ownership of transportation lines and gas and electric plants is rather limited. Only forty-two cities in the United States own and operate their street transportation systems, though the list is headed by such large urban centers as New York,[29] Chicago, Detroit, Cleveland, San Francisco, and Seattle. About one hundred gas plants are municipally owned, as compared with nearly seventeen hundred in private hands. Practically all the larger cities rely on privately owned gas plants for their supply. In the field of electric light and power municipal ownership has made the greatest gains. More than two thousand municipal electric plants are now in active operation, though they serve chiefly the smaller cities,[30] many of them with populations of less than five thousand, and provide but a small part of the total electricity sold to ultimate consumers. The movement for municipal ownership of electric plants has recently been stimulated by federal grants and loans to cities for this purpose, and by the development of vast federal hydroelectric projects which offer current to nearby cities at very low cost. But it must still be recorded that municipal ownership of such utilities as electricity, gas, and street transportation has had no widespread vogue in the cities of the United States.[31]

REGULATION OF PROFESSIONS AND TRADES

The practice of certain professions and trades is restricted by state law to those persons who have satisfactorily demonstrated their proficiency. Examinations are held at stated intervals, and successful applicants are licensed to pursue their respective vocations. Restrictions of this sort, designed to protect the health or safety of the people, or protect them against

[29] New York owns and operates all its subway and elevated lines, and some of its street railway and bus lines.

[30] The municipal plants of Cleveland, Columbus, Los Angeles, Memphis, San Antonio, and Seattle are important exceptions.

[31] A few words should be added about other municipal services. A great many cities, including most of the large urban centers, own and operate airports, markets, auditoriums. There are also municipally owned and operated fuel yards, ice plants, laundries, and central heating systems.

fraud, are applied in different states and in varying degrees to physicians, dentists, osteopaths, chiropractors, optometrists, chiropodists, cosmetologists, pharmacists, veterinarians, nurses, embalmers, lawyers, accountants, engineers, architects, brokers, barbers, and plumbers, among others. At least seventy-five different occupations are affected.

The right of the state to fix the qualifications for persons engaged in some of these vocations has been established beyond doubt. The practice of medicine, for example, is subject to complete public control, and any regulations that the state may impose, short of mere arbitrary enactments, will be upheld by the courts.[32] Regulations concerning other professions and trades, also, are upheld under most circumstances and in most jurisdictions.

Occasionally, however, a law providing for the examination and licensing of persons engaged in some vocation is set aside as bearing no reasonable relationship to the public welfare. Thus the Supreme Court of Maryland invalidated the state's 1935 barber act, because it imposed "requirements entirely out of proportion with the character and purposes of this trade. . . . In order to obtain a license, one must have had ten years of educational preparation." Such a standard indicated "an apparent design, although indefensible and unreasonable, to give to this simple and useful trade the characteristics and standards of a highly technical profession." [33] Despite occasional adverse court decisions, however, the list of professions and trades subject to examination and license requirements is constantly growing, and state standards of technical proficiency are constantly being raised.

The question may well be asked, however, whether standards have not been made too high in some instances. The story is told of a group of men who desired to enlist the governor's support for a new law licensing their trade. "Governor," the men said, "passage of this licensing act will ensure that only qualified persons will practice this occupation; it will eliminate charlatans, incompetents, or frauds; and it will therefore protect the safety and welfare of the people of this state." The governor, from long experience, was somewhat skeptical. "Gentlemen," he asked, "are you concerned with advancing the health, safety and welfare of the people under the police power of this state, or are you primarily interested in creating a monopoly situation to eliminate competition and raise prices?" The spokesman for the occupational group smiled and said: "Governor, we're interested in a little of each." [34]

Separate boards of examiners for the several vocations conduct exam-

[32] Dent v. West Virginia, 129 U.S. 114 (1889).
[33] Schneider v. Duer, 184 A. 914 (1936).
[34] Council of State Governments, *Occupational Licensing Legislation in the States,* 1952, p. 1.

inations and, in most states, issue licenses. In more than half of the states these boards go their separate ways with virtually no supervision. In eighteen states, however, steps have been taken to centralize control of the various examining boards. Illinois, for example, has a department of registration and education which issues all professional and occupational licenses, though upon the recommendation of examining committees responsible to the department's director. In some of the other states that are supposed to have centralized their licensing activities, the department performs only routine functions while the examining boards continue to operate in much the same manner as before.

PROBLEMS

1. Summarize the laws of your state concerning the incorporation of business enterprises.

2. Study the operation of the small-loan act of your state or a neighboring state. What defects has it revealed in practice? What agency administers it?

3. What effect did the financial panic of 1933 have upon the banking laws of the several states? Describe the work of the banking commissioner of your state.

4. What service standards have been established by the public service commission of your state for electric light and power companies? For street railway companies? What penalties are provided for failure to comply with these standards?

5. Make a list of all the publicly owned and operated utilities in your community. Are they self-supporting?

6. How many agencies in your state government are responsible for examining and licensing persons who desire to practice professions and trades? Describe the organization and work of these agencies.

SELECTED REFERENCES

Bauer, John, *The Public Utility Franchise, Its Function and Terms under State Regulation,* 1946.

————, *Transforming Public Utility Regulation,* 1950.

Bauer, John, and Peter Costello, *Public Organization of Electric Power: Conditions, Policies, and Program,* 1949.

Bauer, John, and Nathaniel Gold, *The Electric Power Industry,* 1939.

Baum, Robert, *The Federal Power Commission and State Utility Regulation,* Washington, D.C., rev. ed., 1946.

Bonbright, James C., *Public Utilities and the National Power Policies,* 1940.

Bryant, John M., and Hermann, R. R., *Elements of Utility Rate Determination,* 1940.

Council of State Governments, *Aviation and the States,* 1944.

————, *Federal Action with Respect to Regulation of Insurance,* 1945.

Council of State Governments, *Occupational Licensing Legislation in the States,* 1952.

————, *Securities Regulation in the Forty-Eight States,* 1942.

Dimock, Marshall E., *Business and Government,* 1949.

Fesler, James W., *Independence of State Regulatory Agencies,* 1942.

Froesch, Charles, and Prokosch, Walther, *Airport Planning,* 1946.

Grether, Ewald T., *Price Control under Fair Trade Legislation,* 1939.

Hall, Ford P., *The Concept of a Business Affected with a Public Interest,* Bloomington, Ind., 1942.

————, *Government and Business,* 3rd ed., 1949.

Hunt, Edward E., ed., *The Power Industry and the Public Interest,* 1944.

Joint Committee of the States to Study Alcoholic Beverage Laws, *Alcoholic Beverage Control,* 1950.

Koontz, H. D., *Government Control of Business,* 1941.

McGeary, M. Nelson, *Pennsylvania and the Liquor Business,* State College, 1948.

Mund, Vernon A., *Government and Business,* 1950.

Nau, Carlton L., *Public Power Pays!,* 1948.

New York Public Service Commission, *Regulation of Public Utilities during the War,* 1943.

Pegrum, Dudley F., *Regulation of Industry,* 1949.

Robinson, Louis N., and Nugent, Rolf, *Regulation of the Small-Loan Business,* Russell Sage Foundation, 1935.

Rohfing, C. C., and Others, *Business and Government,* 5th ed., 1949.

Scharff, M. R., and Others, *Depreciation of Public Utility Property,* 1941.

Stone, Harlan F., *Public Control of Business,* 1940.

Taylor, Jack, *Business and Government; An Introduction,* 1952.

Thomas, Robert W., *Workmen's Compensation in New Mexico,* Albuquerque, New Mexico, 1950.

Thompson, C. Woody, and Smith, Wendell R., *Public Utility Economics,* 1941.

Wilson, Stephen, *Food and Drug Regulation,* Washington, D.C., 1942.

CHAPTER 26

Regulation of Labor

The *labor problem* is more than a phrase. Labor presents a most serious problem—or, more accurately, a large number of serious problems, including strikes, industrial accidents, and unemployment. The attempt to solve these problems has already produced a vast mass of legislation, and new labor laws are constantly swelling the total. Five main purposes underlie the labor legislation of the several states: (1) the protection of the safety and health of the workers, (2) the promotion of reasonable working periods and wage scales, (3) the prevention of racial discrimination in employment, (4) the settlement of industrial disputes, and (5) the reduction of unemployment.

PROMOTION OF SAFETY IN INDUSTRY

Prevention of Industrial Accidents

The total number of persons injured in industry is appallingly high. In every state measures have been adopted to reduce industrial dangers, although these laws differ materially in scope and effect. Usually they prescribe minimum conditions of safety that must be maintained in every factory. Active parts of machines, such as saws, mangles, and emery wheels, must be screened or otherwise guarded. All mechanism for transmitting power must be equipped with adequate safety devices. Fire escapes must be installed, and safe exits must be provided.

Safety requirements applicable to mines are common in the mining states. In some respects these requirements are even more important than the factory safety laws, for mining is an especially hazardous occupation. This fact is generally recognized, and the state mining codes are usually long and complex. Railroads, street car lines, and subway and elevated lines also come within the scope of governmental safety regulations. Such matters as track clearance, headlight power, and brakes are controlled by action of the state—or, in the case of interstate lines, the federal government. State laws frequently require railroad employees to pass tests of vision, including tests for color blindness. A number of states have enacted legislation designed to secure a greater measure of safety for workers engaged in the construction or repair of buildings. These laws relate to scaffolds, hoisting apparatus, signal systems, and inspection.

Despite the rapid spread of the movement for industrial safety during the last few years, state laws on the subject are still far from satisfactory. As a rule they apply only to certain specified occupations or processes, completely ignoring others that are equally dangerous but have escaped the legislature's attention. Lacking definite standards in many instances, they cannot readily be enforced. The more progressive states have obtained satisfactory results by passing outline laws [1] designed merely to express the legislative will in general terms, leaving the determination of specific rules to the industrial commission or similar agency. In this way the necessary element of flexibility is added to safety regulations. Desirable modifications need not await the next session of the legislature.

Exclusion from Certain Industries

CHILDREN. The prevention of industrial accidents is more than a matter of safety devices. It requires also the exclusion from certain industries of persons whose age, sex, or inexperience makes them especially susceptible to the hazards involved. Every state has enacted legislation prohibiting children from engaging in various kinds of labor before they reach a certain age, and some states extend this prohibition to include "any gainful occupation." Fourteen or sixteen is usually the minimum age for general factory work, and eighteen is often fixed as the minimum for industries with a high accident rate.

The contention has frequently been raised that child labor laws are an unreasonable and unconstitutional interference with individual liberty. Minors, it is said, share with adults the inalienable right to engage in any lawful occupation. But the courts have refused to admit the validity of this reasoning. In a long line of decisions they have established the principle that children are "wards of the state," and subject to special protective measures that might be unconstitutional if applied to the entire population.[2]

WOMEN. Women, also, are generally excluded from certain occupations, the list of occupations varying from state to state, but often including the cleaning of moving machinery and the operation of emery wheels. Manual labor by women in mines is forbidden in more than one third of the states. Even more general are the prohibitions against the employment of women

---

[1] See pages 112–113.
[2] See, for example, *In re* Spencer, 149 Cal. 396 (1906).

in occupations requiring constant standing.   Some of these restrictions obviously aim to protect health quite as much as to prevent accidents.   The
courts uniformly uphold reasonable state laws restricting women's occupations, for women, like children, are deemed in need of special protection.[3]

MEN.   Because the special protection of women and children cannot be
extended to adult males without the risk of a judicial veto, laws excluding
men from dangerous occupations are not of universal application.   Instead
they apply only to men whose inadequate physical or technical qualifications
apparently unfit them for the proper performance of certain duties.   State
laws frequently prescribe rigid physical examinations for persons engaged
in such dangerous occupations as mining, and forbid the employment of
those who cannot meet the established standard of health.

Even more important and far-reaching are the technical qualifications.
Persons are not permitted to serve as railroad engineers, motion picture
machine operators, elevator operators, or electricians—to mention but a
few of the employments affected—unless they can demonstrate sufficient
technical skill, and, in addition, present evidence of sobriety and good
character.   The elaborate qualifications prescribed for physicians, lawyers, architects, engineers, and others, sometimes in the interest of safety
but more commonly for the protection of health or the prevention of fraud,
have already been mentioned.[4]

WORKMEN'S COMPENSATION

Accident Reports

Virtually all the states require industrial accidents to be reported to some
state authority.   Massachusetts enacted such a law as early as 1886, and
a number of other commonwealths followed its example before the end of
the century, but these early statutes were poorly enforced.   Injured employees had nothing to gain by supplying the necessary information; employers were reluctant to disclose facts that might indicate unsatisfactory
working conditions; and state officials seldom bothered to prosecute.

Thus the factual basis for a systematic plan of accident prevention was
lacking.   But conditions have materially improved since the adoption of
workmen's compensation laws.   The injured workman now has a definite
pecuniary interest in reporting his case, and may reasonably be expected
to do so promptly.   Even today, however, thousands of industrial accidents

[3] The 1954–1955 edition of the *Book of the States,* pp. 397–401, presents a good
summary of recent state labor legislation affecting women.
[4] See pages 529–531.

are not reported—chiefly because they are not covered by the compensation laws.

Accident Compensation under Common Law

The movement for workmen's compensation legislation arose from the unsatisfactory state of the common law concerning the liability of employers. Under common law this liability was narrowly restricted. It did not extend to injuries arising from the ordinary risks of the occupation, the extraordinary dangers of employment, the carelessness or negligence of the workman receiving the injury, or the carelessness or negligence of fellow workmen.

Whenever an accident occurred, the injured employee had to institute a lawsuit in order to recover damages. At the outset he was handicapped by the law's delays. Lacking funds, he was seldom able to secure the best legal talent. At best he could hope for the payment of his claim only after a period of several years. At worst he would find his claim set aside because the employer had been able to establish some legal defense, such as the negligence of a fellow employee. Thousands of injured workmen learned from bitter experience the truth of the old maxim that delayed relief is no relief. Thousands of others accepted ludicrously small sums in full settlement of their claims rather than face the prospect of protracted litigation, with uncertainty as to the final outcome.

Compensation Laws

Students of the problem of accident compensation became convinced that substantial justice could not be obtained under common law rules, or any mere modification of them. The remedy, they urged, was a system of compensation that would extend to all injured employees without regard to the relatively trivial matter of fixing the blame. Accidents were an inevitable accompaniment of modern industry; therefore industry should be made to bear the cost of providing proper medical treatment for disabled employees and caring for them and their families while disability continued. At first this reasoning was bitterly opposed, and some of the early compensation laws were declared unconstitutional. In 1911, however, four states [5] enacted workmen's compensation statutes that subsequently met the approval of the courts, and thus the movement was firmly established. It has since spread to all the states, although Mississippi did not make it unanimous until 1948. The early statutes applied only to industrial accidents, but to-

[5] California, New Jersey, Washington, Wisconsin.

day the laws of forty-six states [6] also require compensation for occupational disease.

PROVISIONS. Compensation laws provide for payments to injured or sick workers according to some established scale, the amount varying with the seriousness of the injury and the wage earned. The question of blame does not affect the payments, except that a certain percentage may be added if the employer violated the safety laws or deducted if the employee failed to avail himself of safety devices or received his injury while under the influence of liquor. Usually there is a short waiting period before payments begin.

The compensation prescribed for various injuries varies widely from state to state. For temporary total disability, for example, maximum weekly payments range from twenty-three dollars in Alabama to one hundred and fifty in Arizona. Some states require continuing benefits to dependents in the event of a workman's death, but such provisions are far from universal. Although the compensation laws of most states are optional, the option is more apparent than real, for employers who refuse to accept statutory liability are specifically deprived of their traditional common law defenses.

INSURANCE REQUIREMENTS. The additional liability imposed upon employers by the workmen's compensation laws necessitates some form of insurance. Recognizing that the cost of this insurance is high even under the most favorable circumstances, many states have endeavored to keep it at a minimum by establishing state compensation insurance funds. In some of these states the employer is compelled to insure through the state fund; in others he is permitted to choose between state insurance and insurance with a private company. So-called "self-insurance" is permitted in some jurisdictions; in other words, the employer is permitted to assume his own risk under the compensation laws upon furnishing adequate proof of solvency.

LIMITED COVERAGE. One of the most serious defects of workmen's compensation legislation, as found in most states, is its limited scope. Usually it covers the range of industrial employment rather thoroughly, but sometimes it applies only to occupations that have been designated as especially hazardous. Domestic service and agricultural work are almost always excluded, as are all casual employments. Liability under the compensation laws of seventeen states does not extend to those employers who have only a few workmen. In two states it does not relate to disability caused by occupational diseases, and in many of the others it covers only disability

---

[6] In twenty-six states the laws refer to all occupational diseases, whereas in the remaining twenty states only certain listed diseases are covered.

from a few specified diseases.   Such restrictions have the effect of denying
prompt and adequate relief to thousands of injured workers who happen
to belong to the less favored groups.

CONSTITUTIONALITY.   The constitutionality of the principle of workmen's compensation legislation was determined beyond question in 1917,
when the Supreme Court of the United States upheld the compensation laws
of three states in a series of important decisions.[7]   "It is evident," said the
Court in the New York Central Railway case,[8] answering the argument that
the law was unreasonable because it imposed liability on the employer even
if the employee were at fault, "that the consequences of a disabling or fatal
injury are precisely the same to the parties immediately affected, and to the
community, whether the proximate cause be culpable or innocent.   Viewing
the entire matter, it cannot be pronounced arbitrary and unreasonable for
the state to impose upon the employer the absolute duty of making a moderate and definite compensation in money to every disabled employee, or,
in case of his death, to those who were entitled to look to him for support, in
lieu of the common law liability confined to cases of negligence."

PROTECTION OF HEALTH

Regulations to Decrease Occupational Diseases

Many state laws have been enacted for the purpose of protecting the
health of workers.   These laws are concerned in part with preventing, or at
least retarding, the spread of occupational diseases.   Some substances regularly used in industry are poisonous, and only the greatest care can protect the workmen who are required to handle them.   Lead, for example,
may cause lead colic or paralysis of the wrists.   Sometimes long-continued
contact with it is fatal.   Radium, also, produces physical deterioration if not
properly controlled.   Many radioactive substances, products of the atomic
age, must be handled with the greatest care to prevent disastrous consequences.   There are other occupational diseases produced, not by poisonous
substances, but by unhealthful working conditions.   Miners' hookworm,
for example, is a constant menace in certain types of mining operations.
Caisson disease, caused by breathing compressed air for long periods, often
affects underwater workers.   These are but a few of the many diseases traceable to specific occupations.

Some poisonous substances once widely used in industry are now pro-

---

[7] New York Central Railway Co. v. White, 243 U.S. 188 (1917); Hawkins v. Bleakly,
243 U.S. 210 (1917); Mountain Timber Co. v. Washington, 243 U.S. 219 (1917).
    [8] 243 U.S. 188 (1917).

hibited.   More commonly, however, the states rely on regulation instead of prohibition to check the spread of occupational diseases.   Factories are required to be properly ventilated, so as to reduce the hazard from dust and fumes.   Wet cleaning methods, respirators, special work clothes, and wash and lunch rooms separate from the place of work are all important means of decreasing the danger from such diseases as lead poisoning, and are commonly required.   Most of the states, led by California in 1911, have made provision for the reporting of occupational diseases, but as a rule these laws are poorly enforced.

Exclusion from Certain Industries

Reference has already been made to the exclusion of children from dangerous industries for the purpose of promoting industrial safety.   On the ground of health, also, child labor is prohibited or narrowly restricted. Restrictions applying to women are found in most states.   Men are excluded from certain occupations only if they cannot pass prescribed physical examinations.   The object of these examinations is to weed out various groups of persons—those who are especially susceptible to particular trade maladies, those whose physical defects might interfere with the proper performance of their duties, and those suffering from contagious diseases that might be passed on to other workmen or to the purchasing public.

RESTRICTION OF HOURS OF LABOR

Another matter that has attracted the attention of labor leaders, social workers, and statesmen is the length of the working day.   Long hours destroy health, increase the likelihood of accidents, and leave insufficient time for recreation and mental improvement.   There is a great deal of evidence to show that in certain occupations, at least, shorter hours actually result in increased output.   In recent years, therefore, the trend has been definitely toward shorter hours of labor.

Children

STATE LEGISLATION.   Every state has enacted some laws concerning the length of the working day.   Children, especially, are afforded a measure of protection against exploitation.   Their working hours are generally limited to eight a day, and forty-eight a week, although four states still permit work for longer periods.   Wisconsin, on the other hand, has established a twenty-four hour work week for children under the age of sixteen.   The first state laws restricting the hours of children's labor were promptly challenged by employers as a violation of their rights under the Fourteenth Amendment to the federal Constitution, but the courts again declared what they had previously said in another connection—that children were poorly qualified to protect their own interests and therefore were entitled to receive the special protection of the state.[9]

FEDERAL LEGISLATION. Because many of the state child labor laws were improperly drafted, poorly enforced, or unduly lenient as to hours of work, the federal government entered the field in 1916. Direct regulation of industrial conditions was beyond the scope of its authority, so it attempted to accomplish the desired result by indirection. Utilizing its power to regulate commerce, it prohibited the shipment in foreign and interstate commerce of goods produced in factories where children under fourteen were employed, or where children between the ages of fourteen and sixteen were employed more than eight hours a day. But this act was set aside by the courts as an unconstitutional invasion of the reserved sphere of state authority,[10] so Congress tried to accomplish its purpose in another way.

This time it turned to the taxing power, and levied a tax of ten per cent on the net profits of factories employing child labor in violation of the conditions imposed. Once again, however, the Supreme Court interposed its judicial veto. "Grant the validity of this law," it said, "and all that Congress would need to do, hereafter, in seeking to take over to its control any one of the great number of subjects of public interest, jurisdiction of which the states have never parted with, and which are reserved to them by the Tenth Amendment, would be to enact a detailed measure of complete regulation of the subject and enforce it by a so-called tax upon departures from it. To give such magic to the word 'tax' would be to break down all constitutional limitation of the powers of Congress and completely wipe out the sovereignty of the states." [11]

After this decision the federal government abandoned its attempt to regulate child labor until 1933, when it insisted upon the inclusion of anti-child labor clauses in most of the "codes of fair competition" established under the National Industrial Recovery Act. The subsequent collapse of the act, following another unfavorable court decision, marked the failure of this attempt at child labor control. A proposed amendment to the federal Constitution, authorizing Congress to limit, regulate, and prohibit the labor of persons under eighteen years of age, was placed before the states in 1924,

---

[9] Inland Steel Co. v. Yedinak, 172 Ind. 423 (1909).
[10] Hammer v. Dagenhart, 247 U.S. 251 (1918).
[11] Bailey v. Drexel Furniture Company, 259 U.S. 20 (1922).

but never received the approval of more than twenty-eight state legislatures —eight short of the necessary three fourths.

Finally, in 1938, Congress once more attempted to regulate child labor through its control of interstate commerce. It prohibited industries engaged in interstate commerce from employing children under sixteen years of age. Certain exceptions were permitted, however, such as boys and girls "employed in agriculture while not legally required to attend school." The Supreme Court upheld the law,[12] and thus an important victory was gained in the long fight against the evils of child labor. Much remains to be accomplished, however. Large numbers of children are engaged in agriculture—sometimes for long hours. Others work in a wide variety of businesses not affected by the federal law, such as retail stores, restaurants, hotels, repair shops, and bowling alleys.

Women

Laws restricting the hours of labor of women in specified employments, or in general factory work, have been enacted by forty-three states.[13] Most of these states fix the maximum at eight or nine hours a day, but many states still permit ten hours or even more. Weekly as well as daily limits, ranging from forty-four to sixty hours, are commonly established. When laws of this type first reached the courts they were declared unconstitutional,[14] but public opinion has long since compelled a reversal of this early judicial attitude.

The Supreme Court of the United States has accepted the obvious fact that "woman's physical structure and the performance of maternal functions place her at a disadvantage in the struggle for subsistence. . . . This is especially true when the burdens of motherhood are upon her. Even when they are not, by abundant testimony of the medical fraternity, continuance for a long time on her feet at work, repeating this from day to day, tends to injurious effects upon the body, and, as healthy mothers are essential to vigorous offspring, the physical well-being of woman becomes an object of public interest and care in order to preserve the strength and vigor of the race." [15] The constitutionality of legislation reasonably limiting the hours of labor of women is, therefore, no longer in doubt.

[12] United States v. Darby Lumber Co., 312 U.S. 100 (1941).
[13] The only exceptions are Alabama, Florida, Indiana, Iowa and West Virginia.
[14] See, for example, Ritchie v. Illinois, 155 Ill. 98 (1895).
[15] Müller v. Oregon, 208 U.S. 412 (1908).

Men

Most state laws restricting the hours of labor of men apply only to public work, or to certain occupations that are considered especially dangerous or unhealthful, such as mining, smelting, or railroading. It has long been recognized that such laws are within the sphere of state power.[16] But what of maximum-hours legislation applying to all classes of workers in general manufacturing establishments, or to workers in occupations that create no special hazard to life or health?

Constitutionality

STATE LAWS. The constitutionality of such legislation was long in doubt. In 1902 the State of New York enacted a law limiting the hours of labor of workmen in bakeries to ten a day, and three years later, when this statute was challenged before the Supreme Court of the United States in the important case of Lochner v. New York,[17] it was declared unconstitutional. The Court took the position that hours of labor were a matter of private bargaining between employer and employed and that the state might not interfere with this bargaining process except in the case of businesses particularly affecting the public health or safety. But this decision did not prevent further legislative attempts to fix maximum hours of labor for men in industry. Mississippi enacted a ten-hour day for all factory workers in 1912; Oregon followed with a somewhat similar statute the next year; and in 1915 North Carolina's general law fixed a limit of eleven hours.

The Oregon law, which permitted three hours of overtime work in emergencies at one and one half times the normal rate of pay, came before the United States Supreme Court in the case of Bunting v. Oregon,[18] and was declared valid. Without expressly reversing its opinion in Lochner v. New York, the Court quietly abandoned the doctrine of the Lochner case and accepted instead the proposition that hours of labor in all occupations were a matter of public concern, to be regulated by the legislature in such manner as it might see fit—subject, of course, to judicial review for the purpose of preventing mere arbitrary enactments.

Six years later, however, the United States Supreme Court created widespread consternation by casting doubt once more upon the validity of all comprehensive maximum-hours legislation. Referring to Lochner v. New York, the early case in which a ten-hour day for bakers was declared un-

---

[16] See, for example, Holden v. Hardy, 169 U.S. 366 (1898).
[17] 198 U.S. 45 (1905).
[18] 243 U.S. 426 (1917).

constitutional, Justice Sutherland said for the Court: "Subsequent cases in this Court have been distinguished from this decision, but the principles therein stated have never been disapproved." [19]   This was news to most students of constitutional law.   "I have always supposed," declared Chief Justice Taft in a noteworthy dissenting opinion, "that the Lochner case was . . . overruled *sub silentio*. . . . In Bunting *v*. Oregon . . . this Court sustained a law limiting the hours of labor of any person, whether man or woman, working in any mill, factory, or manufacturing establishment to ten hours a day with a proviso as to further hours. . . . The law covered the whole field of industrial employment and certainly covered the case of persons employed in bakeries.   Yet the opinion in the Bunting case does not mention the Lochner case.   No one can suggest any constitutional distinction between employment in a bakery and one in any other kind of a manufacturing establishment which should make a limit of hours in the one invalid, and the same limit in the other permissible.   It is impossible for me to reconcile the Bunting case and the Lochner case."   For a time, therefore, two apparently inconsistent Supreme Court decisions delimited the power of the state to prescribe maximum hours of labor for all industrial workers.

FEDERAL STATUTES.   In 1933 hours of labor in industry became a matter of federal concern when Congress enacted the National Industrial Recovery Act, designed in part to increase employment by narrowly restricting the hours of work of mercantile and clerical workers, artisans, mechanics, and laborers, and thus indirectly compelling the hiring of additional workmen. The "codes of fair competition" established under this act were declared unconstitutional by the Supreme Court of the United States, not only because they exceeded the scope of national authority but also because they represented an improper delegation of legislative power.[20]

But Congress was not discouraged.   In 1938 it enacted a general law applying to all employees of firms whose products were shipped in interstate commerce.   Maximum daily hours were fixed at eight, and maximum weekly hours at forty.   Longer hours were permitted, however, but only when compensated with overtime pay at one and one half times the regular rate. Once again Congress was attempting to regulate labor conditions through its control of interstate commerce, as it had done when it enacted the first federal child labor law.   That law had been declared unconstitutional in the case of Hammer *v*. Dagenhart,[21] but in the intervening years the Supreme

[19] Adkins *v*. Children's Hospital, 261 U.S. 525 (1923).   For a consideration of the facts involved in this case, see pages 545–546.
[20] Schechter *v*. United States, 295 U.S. 495 (1935).
[21] See page 540.

Court's personnel had changed almost completely, and labor's need for protection had received increased public recognition.

Astute observers were not surprised, therefore, when the Court upheld the law, and declared that Hammer v. Dagenhart "should be and now is overruled." [22] The Court went on to declare that reasonable hours of labor might be fixed by statute and that such legislation would not deprive employers of their property without due process of law. Thus the right of Congress to safeguard the vast majority of American workmen against excessive working hours was established beyond the shadow of a doubt.

WAGE LEGISLATION

Payment of Wages

Wages, like hours of labor, are a matter of utmost importance to workers and have been made the subject of legislation in every state. Some of these laws attempt to prevent unnecessary delays in payment of wages by specifying that payment must be made at regular intervals—usually two weeks. Others provide for payment in cash, rather than scrip or orders on the company store. If a worker is discharged, he is permitted to collect his wages at once under the laws of many states. Fines for breaches of shop discipline, bad work, or the like, which are widely used to reduce the real wage, are often subjected to state regulation or even prohibition. These laws, unless purely arbitrary, receive the approval of the courts as a valid exercise of the police power.[23]

Mechanic's lien

Another type of wage legislation, also accepted by the courts, is the so-called "mechanic's lien," which has long been recognized in every state. Mechanics and other classes of workers engaged in the construction of buildings are permitted to bring suit for their wages against the value of the buildings or land on which they have been employed; thus they are protected against irresponsible contractors who cannot meet their payrolls. The types of property to which the lien applies vary from state to state. Public buildings and railroad properties are often exempted on the ground of public policy.

[22] United States v. Darby Lumber Co., 312 U.S. 100 (1941).

[23] See, for example, McLean v. Arkansas, 211 U.S. 539 (1909); Knoxville Iron Co. v. Harbison, 183 U.S. 13 (1901); and Erie Railway Co. v. Williams, 233 U.S. 685 (1914).

Minimum Wages

WOMEN AND CHILDREN. In 1896 the Australian state of Victoria took a bold step by fixing minimum wages for workers in certain industries where the wage scales were known to be particularly low. The movement spread to other occupations and to other states. Today minimum wage legislation, applicable to practically all workers except farm laborers, is in force in nearly every nation of Europe.

The first American state to enact a minimum wage law was Massachusetts, in 1912. Other states followed, until the total had reached fifteen. Unlike the European laws, however, the American statutes applied only to women and children, on the theory that men could sufficiently protect their own interests in a living wage. In fact, the labor unions endorsed this attitude, for they believed that men could accomplish more by organization.

In a few states the minimum wage for women and children was fixed by law. But this crude method of approximating a reasonable minimum proved unsatisfactory everywhere that it was tried, and most states adopted the more satisfactory plan of establishing wage boards to determine the proper minimum for each industry. These boards, composed of representatives of the employers, the employees, and the public, were usually voluntary bodies exercising only advisory functions, but their decisions as to minimum wages were generally accepted and enforced by the state commission or other administrative agency—subject, of course, to appeal to the courts.

CONSTITUTIONALITY. It was inevitable that social legislation of this sort should be challenged as a violation of the freedom of contract guaranteed by federal and state constitutions. Both employee and employer, it was said, had an absolute right to obtain the best possible terms from each other as the result of private bargaining; and any legislation interfering with that right must be declared unreasonable and therefore void. At the outset this logic was lightly regarded by the courts. The Oregon minimum wage law was sustained by the state supreme court,[24] and this decision was affirmed by the Supreme Court of the United States by an even vote of four to four, without opinion filed.[25]

But in 1923 came an authoritative statement of Supreme Court opinion, this time by a five-to-four vote, in the case of Adkins v. Children's Hospital.[26] The law under consideration, enacted by Congress for the District of Co-

[24] Stettler v. O'Hara, 69 Ore. 519 (1914).
[25] 243 U.S. 629 (1917).
[26] 261 U.S. 525 (1923).

lumbia, authorized a commission to fix minimum wage standards for women in all occupations. In sweeping language the Court declared this act unconstitutional and even branded it as potentially a great menace to employees. "If, in the interest of the public welfare, the police power may be invoked to justify the fixing of a minimum wage, it may, when the public welfare is thought to require it, be invoked to justify a maximum wage. . . . The same argument which has been used here to strip the employer of his constitutional liberty of contract in one direction will be utilized to strip the employee of his constitutional liberty of contract in the opposite direction."

This decision was bitterly criticized by persons in all walks of life. Some characterized it as "a constitutional guarantee of the right to starve." But the Supreme Court held resolutely to its position for more than a decade, voiding the minimum wage laws of Arizona, Arkansas, and New York. In 1937, however, it specifically reversed its stand, overruling the Adkins case and upholding the minimum wage act of the State of Washington. Chief Justice Hughes, speaking for the Court, declared that the protection of women and minors from the evils of starvation wages was an object closely related to the public welfare and that it might properly be promoted through the police power.[27] Thus was won the long fight to legalize the minimum wage for women and children. Minimum wage statutes, applying both to women and minors—or, in some instances, only to women—have now been adopted by twenty-six states.

ALL WORKERS. But what of statutory minimum wages for all workers? The argument used to justify such legislation for women and children—that they are "wards of the state" requiring special protection—can scarcely be applied to adult men. Yet Congress has enacted a number of laws establishing minimum wage scales for men. In 1917 it temporarily regulated the wage schedules of interstate railroads in order to prevent a national calamity—a nation-wide strike of railroad labor; and the Supreme Court of the United States upheld the law as a proper emergency measure.[28]

The attempt to enforce minimum wage requirements in the so-called "codes of fair competition" prepared under the National Industrial Recovery Act of 1933 was necessarily abandoned when the Supreme Court invalidated the entire statute. In 1935 the Guffey Coal Act attempted comprehensive regulation of the bituminous coal industry and, among other things, made provision for minimum wages. It was declared unconstitutional on several grounds.[29]

[27] West Coast Hotel Co. v. Parrish et al., 300 U.S. 379 (1937).
[28] Wilson v. New, 243 U.S. 332 (1917).
[29] Carter v. Carter Coal Co., 298 U.S. 238 (1936).

There were two other congressional enactments, limited to agencies or groups more or less directly under federal control, and then came the most comprehensive of all national attempts at wage legislation—the Fair Labor Standards Act of 1938, fixing minimum wages for all workers employed by firms engaged in, or shipping their products in, interstate commerce. This statute went far beyond the traditional concept of minimum wage regulation, but it was upheld by the Supreme Court in United States v. Darby Lumber Co.,[30] the case that also established the right of Congress to enact comprehensive legislation concerning hours of labor.[31]   In 1944 New York took advantage of this new attitude of the highest court of the land and amended its minimum wage law to include men as well as women and children.   Four states [32] have since followed New York's example, and twenty-one others have accomplished the same result inadvertently by prohibiting discrimination in wages on account of sex.

PREVENTION OF RACIAL DISCRIMINATION

A comparatively recent development in labor legislation has been the attempt to prevent discriminatory practices against minority groups, either by employers or by labor unions.   New York took the lead in 1945 with a statute that forbade employers to show discrimination in hiring practices or working conditions "because of race, creed, color, or national origin." The law also prohibited such discrimination by labor unions in their membership requirements or treatment of members.   Employers and employment agencies were forbidden to "print any statement, or use any form, or make any inquiry which imposes a limitation" because of race or color.   A state commission against discrimination was created by the act, and charged with the responsibility of establishing suitable policies and hearing complaints.

Within a few months New Jersey enacted a similar law, and six other states [33] have since fallen into line.   In addition, four states [34] have adopted anti-discrimination statutes that place reliance chiefly on education and persuasion, rather than compulsion.

The compulsory-type laws all follow the same general pattern.   They authorize the commission to receive complaints from the attorney-general or other state officials, or from persons who claim to be victims of discriminatory practices.   Each complaint is carefully investigated and discussed

[30] 312 U.S. 100 (1941).
[31] See page 544.
[32] Connecticut, Massachusetts, New Hampshire, and Rhode Island.
[33] Connecticut, Massachusetts, New Mexico, Oregon, Rhode Island, Washington.
[34] Colorado, Indiana, Kansas, Wisconsin.

with the responsible employer or union official.   A few words of caution may be sufficient.   If not, there is a formal hearing, which may be followed by a commission order to end the objectionable practice.   However, this order may be challenged in the courts.

Most of the complaints lodged with state anti-discrimination commissions are dismissed eventually for lack of evidence.   Yet there seems to be little doubt that the enactment of legislation and the establishment of administrative machinery to prevent discrimination has had a marked deterrent effect upon the practices of race-conscious employers and union officials.[35]

COLLECTIVE BARGAINING

Virtually every student of labor problems emphasizes the important fact that the individual worker is at a serious disadvantage when bargaining with the individual employer.   The worker does not know the condition of the labor market; in many instances he must accept a proffered job on the employer's terms or face the alternative of starvation.   He cannot afford to wait, for he has no reserve of wealth.   Moreover, he lacks experience in making contracts and driving bargains.   At all times he faces the prospect of replacement by another worker or by a machine, and this danger tends to reduce him to a state of subservience.   By organizing with his fellows, however, the worker can overcome many of these handicaps and put himself more nearly on the level of the employer in bargaining power.   Quite naturally, therefore, the movement for collective bargaining has made tremendous strides, especially among the more highly skilled laborers, and is manifested chiefly in formal workers' organizations known as labor unions.

For many years the labor unions had to overcome a series of legal handicaps.   At first the courts took the view that unions were combinations to restrain trade and, therefore, unlawful organizations.   Thus, in the early case of The People v. Fisher,[36] when the supreme court of the State of New York was called upon to consider an agreement among journeymen shoemakers not to make boots for less than one dollar per pair, it promptly branded the loosely knit shoemakers' organization as an unlawful conspiracy.   A number of similar decisions in other states reflected the sentiment of the period.

In 1842, however, the supreme court of Massachusetts sustained the legality of labor organizations in an opinion so cogent that it had far-reaching influence upon the development of labor law in other states.   "We

[35] See Morroe Berger's provocative monograph, *Equality by Statute: Legal Controls over Group Discrimination.*
[36] 14 Wend. (N.Y.) 9 (1835).

think," said the court, "that associations may be entered into, the object of which is to adopt measures that may have a tendency to impoverish another, that is, to diminish his gains and profits, and yet so far from being criminal or unlawful, the object may be highly meritorious and public spirited. The legality of such an association will therefore depend upon the means to be used for its accomplishment. If it is to be carried into effect by fair or honorable and lawful means, it is, to say the least, innocent. . . ." [37] Today the right of labor to organize is no longer questioned.

THE RIGHT TO STRIKE

The strike is labor's most powerful weapon, and any restriction of the right to strike necessarily weakens the bargaining power of the unions. Quite naturally, therefore, the representatives of organized labor contend that the right to strike is fundamental and may not be abridged by judicial action. Only the California courts accept this viewpoint, however; elsewhere the doctrine has been definitely established that a strike is lawful only if instituted for a proper purpose and conducted in a proper manner.

Approved Reasons for Striking

There are, then, some objects that may lawfully be sought through the medium of a strike, and some that may not be sought in this manner. Strikes for higher wages or shorter hours almost invariably meet the approval of the courts—provided, of course, that unlawful methods are not adopted. Dissatisfaction with sanitary or safety conditions, or with shop rules or apprentice regulations, is also considered a proper reason for striking. On the other hand, strikes to compel employers to hire more men than they require, or to continue certain plant operations, are generally regarded with judicial disfavor.

THE CLOSED SHOP. For many years the courts were sharply divided concerning the propriety of strikes to force employers to adopt the "closed shop" —that is, a shop closed to all except union workmen. Many state courts followed the lead of Massachusetts in holding such strikes an unreasonable interference with the rights of employers and nonunion workmen; many other state tribunals accepted instead the New York doctrine that workmen might legally strike for a closed shop, even though acceptance of their demands involved the dismissal of nonunion laborers.

In recent years public opinion concerning the desirability of the closed shop has fluctuated sharply, and these fluctuations have been reflected in

[37] Commonwealth v. Hunt, 4 Met. 45 (Mass.) 111 (1842).

federal and state laws.   The National Labor Relations Act of 1935 specifically authorized agreements requiring union membership as a condition of employment; the Labor Management Relations Act of 1947, commonly known as the Taft-Hartley Law, prohibits such agreements; and
state laws follow no uniform pattern.[38]   Today, therefore, before passing
upon the legality of a strike to force the adoption of the closed shop, one
must first ask whether the strike affects interstate commerce (and therefore
comes within the authority of Congress) or whether it is a matter of state
concern.   And in the latter case, one must know which state is involved.

SYMPATHY STRIKES.   But what shall we say of sympathetic strikes, carried on by the workmen of one employer or the members of one union to
aid the workmen of another employer or the members of another union?
Such strikes are prohibited by the laws of the nation and of many states,
on the ground that the participants do not have a sufficiently direct interest.
Some persons have claimed that these laws were an interference with the
right of free speech, but the Supreme Court of the United States has rejected this point of view.   In several cases it has declared that Congress
and the state legislatures may prohibit picketing, however peaceful, if conducted for unlawful ends.[39]

Disapproved Practices

COERCION AND INTIMIDATION.   A strike may be outlawed, even though
called for a legitimate purpose, if the workers engage in improper tactics.
It is obvious that a strike cannot succeed if the striking workmen are immediately replaced by other workmen of approximately equal skill; nor is
it likely to succeed if customers continue to patronize the employer against
whom it is directed.   The natural tendency of strikers, therefore, is to attempt to persuade other workmen from taking their places, and to induce
customers to withdraw their patronage.   If persuasion fails, stronger arguments may follow.   Pleading may give way to intimidation.   It is at this
point that the courts draw the line between proper and improper means of
conducting a strike.   They hold that persuasion of employees, prospective
employees, and customers is lawful, whereas threats, coercion, and intimidation are unlawful.

SIT-DOWN STRIKES.   One of the most effective means of preventing employers from continuing operations with nonstriking employees is to remain
on the job, but with folded arms.   This tactic is the "sit-down" strike—a

[38] See pages 554–555.

[39] Giboney v. Empire Storage and Ice Co., 336 U.S. 490 (1949); International
Brotherhood of Electrical Workers v. National Labor Relations Board, 341 U.S. 694
(1951).

virtual seizure of the plant by striking employees, who refuse to work and also refuse to vacate their posts. Such strikes were widespread in the United States during the late 1930's, and were justified by some persons as a legitimate means of protecting the laborer's vested interest in his job. But public opinion generally disapproved of the practice, and it received judicial condemnation from the Supreme Court of the United States in the important Fansteel case of 1939.[40]

STRIKES IN ESSENTIAL INDUSTRIES. Uninterrupted operation of some industries is essential to the public welfare. If the trains stop running, for example, or the coal mines are shut down for a long period, the resultant disruption of industry may imperil the national health or safety. For this reason Congress has set up elaborate arbitration machinery designed to keep workers on the job in such industries as steadily as possible, and to permit strikes only after every attempt at settlement has failed. There must be a thorough investigation by a presidential board of inquiry, and meanwhile the workers may be enjoined from striking for eighty days. Later, if the dispute is still unsettled, the employees must decide by secret ballot whether they wish to accept the employer's final offer. Should they vote against acceptance, after nearly three months of enforced negotiations, they may then go on strike. But the law assumes that some settlement will almost certainly be reached during the long waiting period. A number of state statutes have been patterned after this federal legislation, which is a part of the Taft-Hartley Law.

Remedies for Unlawful Strikes

THE INJUNCTION. We have seen that the right to strike is not absolute; it must be exercised in a proper manner and for justifiable ends. So the question naturally arises: What remedies for unlawful strikes may be obtained by injured parties? Three distinct remedies are provided. One of these is the injunction, a court order forbidding the performance of certain specified acts. An employer who fears that the acts of his striking employees, or of their union, may result in "serious and irreparable" damage to his property has the right of appeal to the courts for protection; and the courts, if they agree that serious and irreparable damage may be done, will issue an injunction against the persons complained of, ordering them not to engage in one or more specified practices. If, despite this judicial warning, strikers do engage in prohibited practices, they are guilty of contempt of court and liable to summary punishment.

[40] National Labor Relations Board v. Fansteel Metallurgical Corp., 306 U.S. 240 (1939).

At one time the courts had virtually unlimited discretion as to the acts that might be forbidden, and they frequently used this power to restrict union activities.   Not unnaturally, therefore, the unions brought pressure to bear on state legislatures to restrict the use of injunctions in labor disputes, and such laws were enacted in a number of states.   The Arizona statute—the most drastic of the entire crop—went so far as to impose an absolute prohibition on the granting of injunctions "in any dispute concerning terms or conditions of employment," but this law was voided by the Supreme Court of the United States as "a wrongful and highly injurious invasion of property rights" whereby "the owner is stripped of all real remedy." [41]

In 1914 Congress withdrew the right of federal courts to grant injunctions in labor disputes "unless necessary to prevent irreparable injury to property or to a property right, . . . for which injury there is no adequate remedy at law."   This statute was received with jubilation by the labor unions, but it was interpreted so narrowly by the courts as to add little to the rights that labor already possessed.[42]

Thus the law stood, nonetheless, until 1932.   In that year Congress enacted the sweeping Norris–La Guardia Act, which specified in great detail the conditions under which federal injunctions might or might not be granted and even listed eight specific acts, common to labor disputes, that might not be judicially restrained.   The Supreme Court of the United States upheld the provisions of this statute in a number of important cases.[43]

Later, however, Congress decided that it had gone too far in its desire to protect labor, so it removed some of the restrictions on the use of injunctions in industrial disputes.   More than half of the states have enacted anti-injunction legislation, but these laws vary considerably as to details, and even as to basic intent.   Today, under some circumstances, the injunction still has a certain value for employers.   They can no longer regard it, however, as a major source of protection.

THE CIVIL SUIT FOR DAMAGES.   The second remedy provided by law for the employer whose business or property has been injured by an unlawful strike is a suit for damages against the persons responsible.   In one case,[44] decided more than forty years ago, a hat manufacturing company received a judgment of more than three hundred thousand dollars against the members of a union and succeeded in collecting most of the award.   But the litigation

---

[41] Truax v. Corrigan, 257 U.S. 312 (1921).

[42] Duplex Printing Press Co. v. Deering, 254 U.S. 443 (1921).

[43] Lauf v. E. G. Skinner and Co., Inc., 303 U.S. 323 (1938); United States v. Hutcheson, 312 U.S. 219 (1941); Milk Wagon Drivers' Union v. Lake Valley Farm Products, Inc., 311 U.S. 91 (1940).

[44] Loewe v. Lawlor, 208 U.S. 274 (1908).

required seven years, and at the end of the period the company was bankrupt. Most employers believe that the possibility of a civil suit against unions or their members provides little real protection because of the difficulty of establishing union responsibility for unlawful acts.

CRIMINAL PROSECUTION. Still another remedy exists: the arrest and prosecution of persons responsible for criminal acts arising out of strikes. Almost every long-continued strike involves many arrests—usually for such petty offenses as disorderly conduct, obstruction of traffic, disturbance of the peace, or trespass, but sometimes for serious crimes such as extortion, rioting, assault, or even kidnaping or murder. The public authorities are seldom neutral during a strike, and in many instances they permit their sympathies to influence their conduct. Sometimes striking workers are arrested on flimsy evidence and convicted without adequate proof; sometimes they are allowed to commit acts of violence with the tacit approval of the police. The effectiveness of criminal prosecution as a remedy for unlawful strikes varies widely, therefore, with the time, the place, and the circumstances.

OPEN VERSUS CLOSED SHOP

The "Yellow-dog" Contract

One of the devices long used by union-smashing employers was the so-called "yellow-dog" contract, which bound the worker, as a condition of his employment, not to join a labor union. Such contracts were bitterly opposed, of course, by organized labor, and in a number of states they were prohibited by law. But the Kansas statute, which provided heavy penalties for employers who attempted to force nonunion contracts upon their employees, was declared unconstitutional by the Supreme Court of the United States in 1915. "Conceding the full right of the individual to join the union," said the Court, "he has no inherent right to do this and still remain in the employ of one who is unwilling to employ a union man, any more than the same individual has a right to join the union without the consent of that organization." [45]

This decision was a blow at organized labor, but at first employers found it of little value in fighting the unions, for it merely authorized employers to insist upon "yellow-dog" contracts, without providing any real remedy if the workers joined the union despite their nonunion agreements. True, an employer could sue his employees for breach of contract if he could prove damages; but in practice he could never obtain such proof. His real grievance was against the labor unions, which often continued to proselyte among

[45] Coppage v. Kansas, 236 U.S. 1 (1915).

the workers despite their contracts of employment forbidding union membership.

Prohibition of the Nonunion Shop

In one important case a coal company sought an injunction to restrain the United Mine Workers of America from attempting to unionize laborers who had signed "yellow-dog" contracts, and the injunction was approved by the Supreme Court of the United States on the ground that union organizers were committing an actionable wrong by inducing breach of contract.[46]   That decision came in 1917, and its immediate result was the widespread adoption of nonunion contracts by employers in all parts of the United States.   Subsequent court rulings somewhat restricted the scope of the original decision,[47] but did not seriously injure the favorable position of employers.

So the unions set out to overcome their judicial defeats with legislative victories.   They brought strong pressure to bear on the state legislatures and Congress, and after 1930 they began to reap the reward of persistent, effective lobbying.   More than one third of the states enacted laws declaring nonunion contracts to be contrary to public policy, and therefore unenforceable by injunction.   The Norris–La Guardia Act of 1932, to which reference has already been made,[48] contained a similar clause.

The 1935 National Labor Relations Act went still further by specifying that "it shall be an unlawful labor practice for an employer . . . by discrimination in regard to hire or tenure of employment or any term or condition of employment to encourage or discourage membership in any labor organization."   The United States Supreme Court upheld this provision of the law; [49] in fact, it even went so far as to hold that an employer who refused to hire workmen because of their union affiliations, although he had never employed them before, was guilty of an unfair labor practice.[50]   Therefore it may fairly be said that in three decades the United States had swung from protection to virtual prohibition of the nonunion shop.   A number of states enacted statutes modeled after the National Labor Relations Act.

[46] Hitchman Coal and Coke Co. *v.* Mitchell, 245 U.S. 229 (1917).
[47] See, for example, American Steel Foundries *v.* Tri-City Central Trades Council, 257 U.S. 184 (1921).
[48] See page 552.
[49] National Labor Relations Board *v.* Jones and Laughlin Steel Corp., 301 U.S. 1 (1937).
[50] Phelps Dodge Corporation *v.* National Labor Relations Board, 313 U.S. 177 (1941).

Prohibition of the Closed Shop

Since 1947, however, public policy has been less favorable to labor. Congress has enacted the Labor Management Relations Act, which expressly rejects the principle of the closed shop. Many state legislatures have passed somewhat similar laws. Most of these statutes follow the same formula. They provide, in nearly identical language, that no person may be denied an opportunity to obtain or retain employment because of membership or non-membership in a labor organization. The constitutionality of two of these statutes (and one amendment to a state constitution) was upheld by the Supreme Court of the United States in two important decisions.[51] "Just as we have held that the due process clause creates no obstacle to block legislative protection of union members," said the Court, "we now hold that legislative protection can be afforded non-union workers."

Extent of Federal Control

Congress plays a major role in the protection and regulation of labor. Its authority over labor matters is derived chiefly from its control of interstate commerce. Therefore the exact meaning of the term *interstate commerce* is exceedingly important to both employees and employers. The Supreme Court of the United States has interpreted the term broadly when applied to labor legislation, just as it has done in other connections.[52] When, in 1937, an order of a federal agency directed the Jones and Laughlin Steel Corporation to reinstate some workers who had been dismissed for union activities, the company contended that it was engaged primarily in manufacturing—a local enterprise—and that its affairs were therefore beyond federal control. But the Supreme Court of the United States, in a five-to-four decision, thought otherwise. "In view of the respondent's far-flung activities, it is idle to say that the effect" of a plant shutdown on interstate commerce "would be indirect or remote. It is obvious that it would be immediate and might be catastrophic."[53] Thus manufacturing is brought within the sphere of federal authority, provided the raw materials are brought from other states or the finished product is sold across state boundaries.

[51] American Federation of Labor *et al. v.* American Sash and Door Co. *et al.*, 335 U.S. 538 (1949); Lincoln Federal Labor Union *et al. v.* Northwestern Iron and Metal Co. *et al.*, 335 U.S. 525 (1949).

[52] See pages 9–11.

[53] National Labor Relations Board *v.* Jones and Laughlin Steel Corp., 301 U.S. 1 (1937).

COMPULSORY SETTLEMENT OF INDUSTRIAL DISPUTES

It is obvious that strikes create serious industrial and social problems. Most of the states, therefore, have attempted to insure speedy and peaceful settlement of industrial disputes by establishing public boards of arbitration or conciliation. But the results have not been very satisfactory. In 1920 Kansas adopted the radical plan of prohibiting strikes, lockouts, picketing, and boycotting in certain essential industries, including not only the public utilities and other businesses generally said to be affected with a public interest, but also the coal, food, and clothing industries. A court of industrial relations was established, with full power to fix wages and prescribe working conditions in these businesses, and its decisions were made binding upon all parties concerned. Workers might quit their jobs as individuals, but they were forbidden to leave as a group for the purpose of bringing an employer to terms; and employers might close their plants, but they were restrained from locking out employees to gain some advantage in a trade dispute.

From the outset this plan was bitterly opposed by organized labor, and many employers also regarded it with disfavor. In 1923, only three years after its adoption, it was greatly weakened by an adverse United States Supreme Court decision,[54] and two years later the entire scheme of compulsory arbitration, as applied to businesses not affected with a public interest, was declared unconstitutional by the Supreme Court.[55] Thereupon Kansas abolished the court of industrial relations. Between 1947 and 1951 the legislatures of eight states set up machinery for compulsory arbitration of industrial disputes, but only in businesses affected with a public interest—in other words, the public utilities. In 1951 the Supreme Court of the United States invalidated the Wisconsin compulsory arbitration law on the ground that it interfered with the established policy of Congress.[56] The reasonable assumption, therefore, is that similar statutes in other states are also invalid.

REGULATION OF UNION ACTIVITIES

The Position of the Employer

For many years the labor laws enacted by the nation and the states were designed primarily to overcome the serious handicaps imposed upon workers

[54] Wolff Packing Co. *v.* Court of Industrial Relations, 262 U.S. 522 (1923).

[55] *Ibid.*, 267 U.S. 552 (1925). It was in the first Wolff Packing Co. case that the Supreme Court attempted the classification of public interest enterprises to which reference was made in the preceding chapter. See page 516.

[56] Amalgamated Association *v.* Wisconsin Employment Relations Board, 340 U.S. 383 (1951).

by common law and statute. But these handicaps were removed in such a manner that eventually many employers complained of the unfairness of public policy. They pointed out that the "unfair labor practices" forbidden by state and federal acts were, almost without exception, directed at employer activities, and they asked why certain union practices, such as the use of force or threats of force against nonstrikers, should not also be labeled "unfair."

Another grievance arose from the inability of employers to enforce collective bargaining agreements. Employers who agreed with the union to maintain a specified scale of wages and hours could be called promptly to account for failure to keep any part of their bargain. But the union would never contract to maintain a steady labor supply; therefore if union workers, as individuals, subsequently quit their jobs because of dissatisfaction with the agreements made in their behalf, the union could not be held responsible.

In many jurisdictions the law concerning the suability of unions reflected the common law doctrine that union funds were the property of the members and therefore could not be reached except by judicial action against the individuals involved. These doctrines, and others of a similar nature, enabled the unions to grow great and powerful. Some labor leaders used their new power to cause serious inconvenience to the public. Some insisted on demands that were generally regarded as unreasonable.

Federal Regulation of Unions

By 1947 the tide of public opinion had set strongly against these abuses of power. The result was a new labor law in Congress, and similar legislation in many of the states. The federal statute, officially entitled the Labor Management Relations Act of 1947, but more commonly known as the Taft-Hartley Law, tried to restore the balance of power between employers and employees, taking into account the newly won strength of the unions. In part it sought to accomplish this end by removing certain restrictions on employers' activities.

But one very important section of the act introduced the new principle that labor unions, as well as employers, might be guilty of unfair labor practices, and should be held accountable to the public for their misdeeds. A number of these practices were listed and specifically prohibited. Unions must not coerce workers who refused to join; they must not bring pressure to bear on employers to discriminate against such workers; they must not refuse to bargain collectively; they must not collect exorbitant membership fees.

In addition, there were a number of other restrictions on union activity. Some of these restrictions were clearly in the public interest; others were more difficult to justify.   The unions, as might well have been anticipated, objected strenuously to these new limitations on their power.   They nicknamed the Taft-Hartley Law the "Tough-Heartless" Law, and bent every effort to secure its repeal, as well as the repeal of similar state legislation.   At present the fight continues.   The Eisenhower administration endorses the general principle of the Taft-Hartley Law, but with certain modifications.

State Regulation of Unions

Postwar state legislation has generally reflected the trend toward stricter regulation of unions.   Many states now prohibit certain unfair labor practices by employees and labor organizations.   Nearly one third of the states require labor unions to register and submit financial reports.   The manner of selecting union officers is regulated by law in some commonwealths, and communists are forbidden to serve as union officers or organizers.   At least one fourth of the states now permit labor unions to sue and be sued.

PUBLIC AND PRIVATE EMPLOYMENT AGENCIES

Employment agencies have long been maintained by most of the state governments and also by the governments of many cities.   These public agencies, which generally operate without charge, serve a useful purpose in bringing together those who desire work and those who desire workers. Until the depression year of 1933, however, they were seriously handicapped by inadequate appropriations and untrained personnel; and they did not co-operate in any permanent nation-wide scheme of job-finding.

In that year the federal government, which had successfully co-ordinated state and municipal employment agencies during the First World War, again entered the field, offering substantial grants to those states that would maintain employment offices in conformity with the standards prescribed by the United States Employment Service.   The states were required to match federal funds dollar for dollar.   Within a short time every state accepted the federal offer, and a nation-wide system of employment offices—totaling about three thousand—was established.   The work of these offices has been greatly increased, and the scope of their usefulness correspondingly extended, by the provision of the 1935 Social Security Act requiring all applicants for unemployment compensation to register at public employment offices.   During the Second World War the state employment services were merged with the United States Employment Service at the request of the President, but they have since been returned to state control.

The multiplication of public employment offices has by no means caused the elimination of private agencies.   Nearly one thousand private employment offices are now functioning in New York City, and the number in other metropolitan centers is very large.   Some of these offices perform a useful service in supplementing public activities—particularly in specialized fields; but in the absence of public regulation they may engage in unethical practices. They may, for example, charge exorbitant fees, or give preference to applicants who pay extra fees; they may send applicants to distant points where no work exists or working conditions are unsatisfactory; or they may conspire with employers to split the fees obtained by hiring workers who are then discharged after a few days to make room for other workers.   In some instances they may send women applicants to houses of ill fame.

While such abuses may be confined to a comparatively small number of agencies, it has been found that they occur with sufficient frequency to necessitate strict public regulation of all private employment agencies.   Most of the state regulatory laws follow the same general plan.   They provide that private agencies must be licensed and bonded, and must use a specified form of register.   The use of lodging and gambling houses as agency offices is forbidden.   In some states the fees of private agencies are fixed by law.

UNEMPLOYMENT INSURANCE

The Social Security Act

The most far-reaching plan for the solution of the unemployment problem is unemployment insurance.   This device has been widely used in Europe during most of the present century, but it did not meet with popular favor in the United States until the crisis of post-1929 depression had forced millions of persons out of work.   Then the President appointed a committee to study the entire problem of social security, and its recommendations became the basis for the Social Security Act of 1935, which establishes unemployment compensation on a nation-wide scale.

The states actually impose the payroll taxes and administer the payment of benefits, but they have been forced into line by the action of Congress in imposing a tax on the payrolls of employers and simultaneously offering to credit against the federal tax any amounts paid to the states for unemployment insurance, up to ninety per cent of the total.   The states do not retain the money collected in payroll taxes; instead they deposit it in an unemployment trust fund administered by the federal government.   Costs of administration are met by a grant to the states from the federal treasury.

Some states might perhaps prefer to omit such taxes from their revenue systems in order to attract employers and build up their industries.   But no employer, unless he belongs to one of the specifically exempted groups, can escape payment of the tax; he must make payment to the federal treasury if his own state has not seen fit to act. So state inaction benefits neither the employer nor the state; and as a result every one of the forty-eight commonwealths has enacted legislation acceptable to the federal government's Social Security Board.

STATE PLANS. The several state plans differ somewhat in minor details, but all conform to the same general set of specifications. Under their terms, any unemployed worker covered by the law may apply for compensation from public funds unless his unemployment is due to some improper cause, such as voluntary quitting or discharge for misconduct. Benefits may not be paid, however, during a preliminary period—usually two weeks; and after that their duration is strictly limited—most commonly to twenty or twenty-six weeks in any fifty-two. The laws of the several states adjust benefits with reference to past earnings; usually they specify fifty per cent of full-time weekly wages, with a weekly maximum ranging from twenty to thirty-five dollars.[57]

Under the terms of the federal act employers of fewer than eight persons are exempt. Some states have followed the federal lead in this respect, but sixteen commonwealths have applied their insurance schemes to every employer of one or more persons, and thirteen others have specified every employer of four or more. Other common exemptions include farm and domestic laborers, government employees, and workers in nonprofit organizations. Only four commonwealths pay benefits for sickness as well as unemployment.[58]

CRITICISMS. The American version of unemployment insurance, as thus outlined, has been criticized by many persons, for a variety of reasons. Employers contend that it imposes too heavy a burden on industry. Workers complain that benefits are too low. Social workers declare that the number of exempted groups is too large, and students of government indicate that the supervisory powers of the federal government are too restricted. Most of these complaints have at least a partial basis in fact, and some of them will doubtless be corrected in the light of further experience. But at least a reasonable attempt has been made to protect the nation's workers against the more serious economic effects of unemployment.

The restriction of benefit payments to a limited period in each year is, of

[57] In some states the maximum is higher than thirty-five dollars a week for persons with dependents.
[58] See page 412.

course, a necessary feature of the insurance plan.   Otherwise a serious depression might speedily deplete reserves and leave public authorities without funds for benefit payments.   But government does not thereby limit its responsibility for the alleviation of human misery.   It must still care for unemployed persons after benefit payments have ceased and their own funds have been exhausted.   That is not an insurance matter, however; it is a problem of relief.

CONSTITUTIONALITY.   The constitutionality of the unemployment compensation section of the Social Security Act was speedily challenged on a number of grounds: it involved federal coercion of the states; it made unreasonable discriminations, since it exempted some employers; it attempted to bring unemployment within the scope of congressional authority, contrary to the intent—and even the letter—of the federal Constitution.   These contentions were considered by the Supreme Court of the United States and rejected in a sweeping decision that upheld the entire system of unemployment insurance.[59]   The five majority members of the Court were unimpressed with Justice McReynolds' argument that the scheme interfered with the orderly processes of state government through "offers of seductive favors."

PROBLEMS

1. Examine the system of workmen's compensation in your state.   Are the rates of compensation adequate?   What provision, if any, is made in the law for the compensation of persons affected by industrial diseases?

2. Write a brief history of the growth of the labor union movement in your state.

3. Prepare a comprehensive account of a strike in your state or a neighboring state—the issues involved; the steps taken by the strikers and by the employers to gain their respective ends; the attitude of the public authorities; the final settlement.

4. Describe the organization and work of public employment offices in your state.

5. Talk with a number of employers in your community, and learn their criticisms of existing labor laws.   Do you think that these criticisms are justified?

SELECTED REFERENCES

Berger, Morroe, *Equality by Statute: Legal Controls over Group Discrimination,* 1952.

Bowman, D. O., *Public Control of Labor Relations,* 1942.

[59] Steward Machine Co. *v.* Davis, 301 U.S. 548 (1937).

Braun, Kurt, *The Settlement of Industrial Disputes*, 1944.

Council of State Governments, *Unemployment Compensation in the Postwar Period*, 1944.

Dankert, Clyde E., *Contemporary Unionism in the United States*, 1948.

Daugherty, C. R., *Labor Problems in American Industry*, 5th ed. rev., 1941.

Davey, Harold W., *Contemporary Collective Bargaining*, 1951.

Dawson, Marshall, *Problems of Workmen's Compensation Administration in the United States and Canada*, Washington, D.C., 1940.

Dulles, Foster Rhea, *Labor in America*, 1949.

Faulkner, Harold W., and Starr, Mark, *Labor in America*, 1944.

Gregory, Charles O., *Labor and the Law*, 1946.

Hartley, Fred A., *Our New National Labor Policy*, 1948.

Hopkins, William S., *Labor in the American Economy*, 1948.

Kaltenborn, Howard S., *Governmental Adjustment of Labor Disputes*, 1943.

Leek, John H., *Government and Labor in the United States*, 1952.

Leiserson, W. M., *Right and Wrong in Labor Relations*, Berkeley, Calif., 1942.

Lentz, Gilbert G., *Enforcement of the Orders of State Public Service Commissions*, Urbana, Ill., 1940.

Levenstein, Aaron, *Labor Today and Tomorrow*, 1945.

Lindblom, Charles E., *Unions and Capitalism*, New Haven, Connecticut, 1949.

Merritt, Walter Gordon, *Destination Unknown: Fifty Years of Labor Relations*, 1951.

Miller, Glenn W., *American Labor and the Government*, 1948.

———, *Problems of Labor*, 1951.

Millholland, Ray, *Pay Day; Labor and Management in the American System of Free Enterprise*, 1946.

Millis, H. A., *Labor's Risks and Social Insurance*, 2 vols., 1938.

———, and Brown, Emily Clarke, *From the Wagner Act to Taft Hartley*, 1950.

———, and Montgomery, R. E., *Organized Labor*, 1945.

———, and Others, *How Collective Bargaining Works*, 1942.

Moore, W. E., *Industrial Relations and the Social Order*, 1946.

Morris, Richard B., *Government and Labor in Early America*, 1946.

New York State Joint Legislative Committee on Industrial Relations, *The American Story of Industrial and Labor Relations*, Albany, 1943.

Owen, W. V., *Labor Problems*, 1946.

Peterson, Florence, *American Labor Unions; What They Are and How They Work*, 1945.

Pierson, Frank C., *Collective Bargaining Systems*, Washington, D.C., 1942.

Reed, George L., *Law of Labor Relations*, Newark, N.J., 1942.

Reede, Arthur H., *Adequacy of Workmen's Compensation*, Cambridge, Mass., 1947.

Spero, Sterling, *Government as Employer*, 1948.

Taylor, George W., *Government Regulation of Industrial Relations*, 1948.

Toner, Jerome L., *The Closed Shop*, Washington, D.C., 1942.

Warne, Colston E., ed., *Labor in Postwar America*, 1949.

Witney, Fred, *Government and Collective Bargaining*, Philadelphia, 1951.

PART EIGHT

Staff Activities

CHAPTER 27

Personnel

The number of full-time state and local government employees, exclusive of teachers, is slightly in excess of two and one half million, according to a recent estimate carefully prepared by the Bureau of the Census. This figure represents an increase of two hundred per cent in thirty-five years. The combined annual payrolls of the state and local governments are more than four and one half billion dollars.[1]

The states and their local units, therefore, are employers of labor on a very large scale, and the efficiency of their labor forces determines in large measure the efficiency of their administrative systems. Unfortunately the methods used by some states and cities, and by almost all counties, townships, and special districts, for the recruitment, supervision, promotion, and dismissal of their employees do not differ radically from the methods of a century ago, when positions in the public service were quite frankly distributed among the faithful after each election as a reward for services to the victorious political party.

GRADUAL ABOLITION OF SPOILS SYSTEM

Until the latter part of the nineteenth century the spoilsmen completely dominated every phase of governmental activity. Few persons dared to make the radical suggestion that the public's business should be conducted for the benefit of the public, instead of serving as a means of strengthening party organizations. But the last sixty years have witnessed a remarkable change in public sentiment. The spoils system is now quite generally regarded as an evil to be uprooted and cast aside. Civil service reform is a part of practically every general program for the improvement of state and local government.

Yet thousands of public employees are still selected with but scant regard for their special fitness. Administration is definitely subordinated to politics. Some technical positions are given to technically trained experts, because

[1] See the Census Bureau's report, *State Employment in 1953.*

government has become so highly specialized that the amateurs cannot control it without the aid of the specialists.   But in all too many states the professional administrators take orders from the professional politicians, even in such matters as the selection of their subordinates.

Beginnings of National Merit System

The first victory of the friends of the merit system was won in 1883, when Congress passed an act providing for the selection of some federal employees by means of competitive examinations.   This law was inadequate; it applied to but a small percentage of the total number of persons in the federal service. But it was the beginning of an important movement, and its influence was destined to be far-reaching.

State and Local Civil Service Laws

A few months after the passage of the federal act the State of New York established a civil service commission, with authority to prepare and administer tests for the selection of persons in the state service.   Massachusetts followed in 1884.   After that, for more than twenty years, these two states were the sole exemplars of the merit principle in state government.   Elsewhere the spoils system continued unchecked.

Early in the present century, however, a new era of civil service reform began.   In 1905 Wisconsin and Illinois set up civil service commissions, and provided for the selection of state employees on a merit basis.   Colorado and New Jersey did likewise two years later.   Subsequently other states fell into line—Connecticut, California, and Ohio in 1913, Kansas in 1915, and Maryland in 1920.   After that there were no further converts for nearly two decades, although California and Wisconsin materially strengthened their civil service laws in 1929.

But in 1937 interest in the merit system suddenly revived.   Four states— Arkansas, Maine, Michigan, and Tennessee—enacted statutes placing their administrative services on a merit basis; and Connecticut, which had repealed its earlier law in 1921, again adopted the merit principle.   Between 1939 and 1950 thirteen states—Alabama, Arizona, Georgia, Indiana, Louisiana, Minnesota, Missouri, Nebraska, New Hampshire, Oregon, Rhode Island, Vermont, and Virginia—joined the ranks.   Kansas, which had returned to the spoils system, was reconverted to the merit principle in 1941.   But Arkansas and Louisiana repealed their civil service laws, and the Arizona statute, enacted in 1948, was declared unconstitutional the following year. Thus twenty-five states now specifically provide for the recruitment of all, or substantially all, their employees on a formal merit basis.   Moreover, the other twenty-three states have enacted civil service laws applying to workers in certain departments.[2]

In 1884 the state legislature of New York passed a law requiring all cities in the state to select their employees by means of formal examinations. Massachusetts cities were put under similar regulations before the end of the year, and from that time the spread of the merit system in American municipalities was rapid. Eventually civil service commissions were established in nearly all the larger cities. County governments have been more reluctant to accept the merit principle.

Even the states and cities, however, often accept the merit principle in name only. Interference with the intent of the civil service law takes a wide variety of forms, ranging all the way from crude tampering with examination scores to "refined" devices, such as the inclusion in examinations of questions so highly specialized as to baffle those who have not been told in advance what to expect. Temporary appointments without examination, which are regularly permitted, are used to draw political favorites into the service of the state, and the "temporary" appointees soon become permanent fixtures, notwithstanding express provisions of the law to the contrary. On the other hand, a number of state and local governments that have no civil service laws have succeeded fairly well in establishing the custom of making appointments on a merit basis.[3]

PREFERENCE LAWS FOR VETERANS. In recent years the task of selecting and retaining efficient employees has been made more difficult by the widespread enactment of laws giving preference to war veterans. Some states and cities had legislation of this type at the beginning of the present century, but the trend did not become widespread until after the First World War. The Second World War complicated the problem still further by increasing greatly the number of persons entitled to receive preference. Under the laws of nearly half of the states, and of many local governments, veterans are favored in various ways. Thus in Massachusetts they need only receive a passing grade in examinations to have their names placed above all other candidates on the eligible list, and in a number of other jurisdictions their earned ratings are increased five or ten per cent—a bonus that gives them a marked advantage over competitors.

DISREGARD OF MERIT. Those persons who advocate such preference

[2] In 1939 Congress adopted an amendment to the Social Security Act, requiring all state departments co-operating under the act to recruit their employees on a merit basis. For this reason nearly all the state welfare agencies now function under civil service rules.

[3] See William Seal Carpenter's 1952 work, *The Unfinished Business of Civil Service Reform*.

legislation obviously ignore the merit principle in government. They regard public employment as a reward for services already performed; and, to that extent, they reason in exactly the same manner as the professional politicians. Their purpose, of course, is to reward service to the state, whereas the politicians' purpose is to reward service to the party or faction; but in either case the result is the same. Men are placed on the public payroll for reasons that bear little or no relation to their training, skill, or experience, and the efficiency of public administration is thereby reduced.[4]

CIVIL SERVICE COMMISSIONS

Supervision of Local Governments

Ten states—California, Colorado, Georgia, Kansas, Louisiana, Michigan, Missouri, New Jersey, New York, and Ohio—have written the merit principle into their constitutions; the civil service systems of the other fifteen states are based on statute. There is no general agreement as to the desirability of extending state jurisdiction in personnel matters over the local units of government—the cities, counties, towns, and villages. A few states restrict the activities of the civil service commission to the personnel of the state service, but most of them permit a certain amount of supervision or control over their civil subdivisions, although the extent of this supervision or control is not the same in any two states.

In Massachusetts the state commission handles the recruitment of both municipal and state employees. The New Jersey commission also conducts examinations for the municipal service, but only in those cities that have voted to accept its jurisdiction. Maryland has a similar plan. The cities of New York and Ohio have their local civil service commissions; in each of these states, however, the state commission has a measure of authority over local activities. The New York commission may, by a unanimous vote and with the governor's approval, remove a local civil service commissioner for incompetence, neglect of duties, or other sufficient cause. It may also amend or rescind any rule made by a local commission. In Ohio the state civil service commission may direct the mayor of any city to remove one or more members of the municipal civil service commission, subject to an appeal to the courts. Four states—Alabama, California, Connecticut, and Minnesota—make the technical services of the state personnel agency available to local communities but require the communities to bear the cost.

[4] Recommendations designed to reduce the evil effects of preference laws for veterans have been made by the Civil Service Assembly of the United States and Canada. See its report entitled: *The Employment of Veterans in the Public Service in the United States.*

Administration of Laws

The civil service law of a state is usually administered by a three-member commission appointed by the governor. In Ohio, however, a commission of two members has been established; New Jersey and Massachusetts have five-member commissions; and two states—Maryland and Rhode Island—have adopted the interesting experiment of vesting control in the hands of one person—a state personnel director.[5]

Most cities follow the plan of entrusting the merit system to a three-member commission, usually appointed by the chief executive but sometimes named by the council. The members of a municipal commission commonly serve only part time and receive only part-time pay. They then employ a full-time secretary or chief examiner, who has charge of the daily routine.

Although most of the states and cities cling to the idea of a plural executive for personnel matters, they are beginning to recognize the rather obvious fact that most of the work of the personnel agency is detailed administration, rather than rule-making. Such work can be done much more effectively by one person than by a group. For this reason California has created the office of director of personnel, and retains its civil service commission only as a rule-making and disciplinary body. Somewhat similar arrangements are found in Wisconsin, New York, Connecticut, and Vermont, and in a number of cities.

Selection of Employees

By far the most important task of the civil service commissions is the recruitment of persons for the public service. Examinations must be prepared for different types of positions and administered to applicants as the need arises. An alert civil service commission usually keeps on hand lists of eligibles who have passed previous examinations but failed of appointment, so that it can submit suitable names to the appointing authority promptly whenever a vacancy occurs. It also takes care to obtain due publicity for its examinations by such means as bulletin board notices, news stories to newspapers and trade journals, occasional advertisements, and circular letters to carefully selected groups. Otherwise it might fail to reach the very persons who were best fitted for the jobs to be filled.

EXTENSION AND IMPROVEMENT OF EXAMINATIONS. Formerly large numbers of state and local employees were outside the classified service—that is, they were appointed without examinations of any sort. Some of them, such

[5] California adopted the one-man plan in 1925, but re-established a commission of three members in 1927.

as private secretaries, were placed in the unclassified group on the ground
that their work was confidential.   Every important public officer, it was said,
should be permitted to have one or more employees chosen without restrictions—men or women in whom he had complete confidence.   Other employees, especially those holding high-salaried positions in the public service,
escaped the necessity of passing examinations because of the widespread
belief that no examination questions could be devised to measure with any
degree of accuracy their fitness for important posts.   Still others were placed
in the unclassified service for lack of suitable examinations or because tests
were deemed unnecessary; skilled and unskilled laborers were in this group.

FUNCTIONAL DISTRIBUTION OF STATE EMPLOYEES, 1953

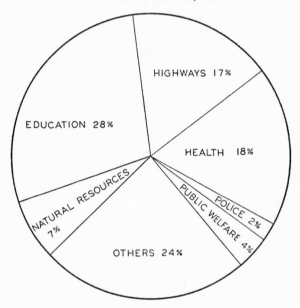

Based on figures from *State Distribution of Public Employment in 1953,* a publication
of the United States Bureau of the Census.

The passing years have witnessed a great improvement, however, in the
technique of the merit system.   Trade tests now determine with accuracy the
fitness of skilled laborers such as plumbers, bricklayers, and electricians.
Even more important, ways have been found to measure the suitability of
applicants for high-salaried positions.   Of course, the examinations given
to these candidates differ radically from the tests used in selecting clerks or
typists.   Much greater emphasis is placed on training and experience, and
personal fitness as determined by interviews may be a factor of considerable

importance.   An examination for an important public position is likely to be of the *non-assembled* variety—in other words, an examination in which the applicants are not required to assemble at one time and place.   It may even be a *non-competitive* examination, designed merely to ascertain whether the person selected for the post by higher officials has the necessary qualifications.[6]

POLITICAL OPPOSITION.   Although the development of civil service technique has made possible the extension of the merit principle to nearly everyone in the administrative service, this extension has been delayed by the professional politicians.   Loath to relinquish the patronage that has helped to maintain their power and prestige, they have fought the merit system at every turn—secretly, in most cases, but desperately.   Despite their efforts thousands of state and local employees have been transferred from the unclassified to the classified service; but thousands of others who should also be chosen on a merit basis are still selected without examinations of any sort.[7]

CERTIFICATION FOR APPOINTMENT.   While the civil service commission administers the examinations to applicants for positions in the public service, it does not make appointments.   Instead, in most jurisdictions that have adopted the merit system, it certifies to the appointing authority the names of the three persons who stood highest in the examination, and from these three the appointing authority makes his selection.   Thus it frequently happens that the candidate with the highest score is brushed aside, and one of the others chosen in his place.   This arrangement is justified on the ground that it provides the appointing authority with necessary discretion.   If the highest person on the list possesses undesirable traits not revealed by the examination —anything from a bad temper to a habit of wearing soiled linen—he may be kept out of the state service despite his arithmetical average.

The professional proponents of the merit system have frequently pointed out, however, that the certification of three names opens the door to partisan interference.   They contend, with reason, that if the highest candidate may be refused appointment because of his bad temper, then he may also be ignored because he does not possess sufficient political influence.   For this reason they constantly urge that the law be changed in every state to provide for the appointment of the highest person on the eligible list.   Their proposal is based on distrust of public officials, but in all fairness it must be admitted that many public officials have done very little to justify confidence

[6] See the interesting article by Walter Gellhorn and William Brody, "Selecting Supervisory Mediators through Trial by Combat," in the Autumn, 1948, issue of the *Public Administration Review*, pp. 259–266.

[7] See William Seal Carpenter's article, "Reformer's Task Never Done," in the July, 1952, issue of the National Municipal Review, pp. 339–345.

in their impartial administration of the civil service laws.   A few states and cities require the appointment of the candidate receiving the highest grade. Some jurisdictions, at the other extreme, permit the certification of the five highest names to the appointing authority.

CLASSIFICATION OF POSITIONS.   The civil service system cannot produce satisfactory results unless a classification has been made of the positions in the public service.   Without such a classification, persons performing the same work in different departments will inevitably have different titles and widely varying salaries.   The first step in the preparation of such a classification is the collection of all necessary information concerning the duties of each position.   Then the positions with similar duties must be grouped together, and each group given an appropriate title, an accurate description, and a suitable compensation schedule.   Only in this way is it possible to prevent gross salary discriminations, with resultant dissatisfaction throughout the entire administrative service.

Supervision of Employees

Most civil service commissions devote their time and attention chiefly to the task of *selecting* employees for the public service.   It is natural that they should do so, for the civil service movement had its inception in a desire to "keep the rascals out of office."   Honest and efficient men must be chosen for positions in the public service, it was said; once chosen, there was nothing more to be done.

In recent years, however, the leaders of the civil service movement have stressed the important fact that selection of employees is only one of the duties of the civil service commission, and should not receive disproportionate emphasis.   Quite as important as selection is adequate supervision. Efficiency ratings should be kept; a sound system of promotions should be established; salaries, hours of employment, and working conditions should be standardized; training facilities for new employees should be provided; research programs should be planned and executed.

Very few civil service commissions are in a position to perform all these functions.   They are handicapped by inadequate appropriations, by constitutional and legal provisions, by the baneful influence of partisanship, by the ignorance of commissioners, and by the inefficiency of subordinates.   Sometimes they are even handicapped by a hostile public opinion, as in their attempts to maintain efficiency ratings.   Nor is it surprising that the use of such ratings should arouse widespread cynicism.   Some experts have tended to regard their rating systems as infallible, despite the obvious fact that all such systems are based on human judgment, and therefore produce varying results according to the diverse and frequently changing opinions of the rating officers.   This does not mean, of course, that efficiency records are valueless. It does mean, however, that such records should merely provide a basis for mature judgment—not a substitute for it.   Fortunately, a few civil service commissions have learned this important lesson.

FUNCTIONAL DISTRIBUTION OF CITY EMPLOYEES

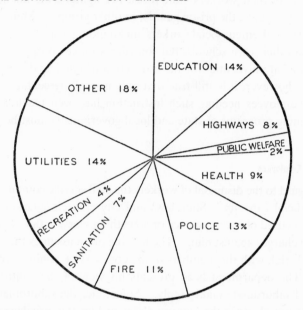

Based on figures from *City Employment in 1953,* a publication of the United States Bureau of the Census.

Training of Employees

The need for some sort of training to keep public employees abreast of the latest developments in their respective fields has long been recognized by progressive students of government.   New tools and new techniques are constantly being developed in almost every phase of public life, and public servants cannot be expected to do their work properly unless they are familiar with these changes.   Government must assume the responsibility for keeping them up to date by providing the necessary courses of instruction and making them widely available.

This "in-service" training—so called because it is designed for those who are already in the public service—has long been used by some jurisdictions for some jobs, but its widespread development is quite recent.   The Second World War was responsible in no small measure for this important change.

Trained public employees were drawn into the armed services, and in many cases their places were taken by persons of limited training and experience. Some of these new workers had to be taught the very essentials of their jobs. The end of the war witnessed the return of most of the experienced employees, but many of the in-service training programs were still retained. Today, therefore, nearly all the states have vocational programs covering at least some of their workers—the forest fire fighters, the finance officers, the purchasing agents, the prison guards, or other groups.   Many cities train their policemen, firemen, social workers, and building inspectors.   They usually maintain their own schools, but sometimes make co-operative arrangements with local universities for the instruction of municipal workers.   Unfortunately, however, it is still true that only a small percentage of the state and local employees needing such instruction has been reached.   The in-service training programs of state and local governments must be greatly expanded.

Dismissal of Employees

With regard to the dismissal of workers the civil service commission acts in a quasi-judicial capacity.   State laws and city charters guarantee to every employee accused of incompetence or something worse a full opportunity to answer the charges against him.   The hearing often assumes the appearance of a formal trial, with the members of the civil service commission sitting as a court.   The department head presents his view of the controversy, and the accused subordinate makes reply.   Sometimes the subordinate is represented by counsel, since the law usually gives him this privilege.   With all the evidence before it, the civil service commission then passes judgment.

This elaborate procedure is generally considered necessary to protect employees from unwarranted dismissal—perhaps for political or personal reasons.   It compels department heads to retain their subordinates unless there are sound reasons for removal.   Some persons believe, however, that so much "red tape" protects state employees at the expense of administrative efficiency.   They contend that it weakens discipline.   And in many cases their belief is confirmed by experience.

For the department head who has had two or three unpleasant sessions with the civil service commission, trying to prove charges that by their very nature are largely matters of opinion and therefore difficult to prove—carelessness or indifference, for example—is not anxious to stir up further trouble. After hearing department secrets dragged into the open and alleged department scandals given unwelcome publicity, he is likely to decide that a repetition of such happenings must not be permitted to occur.   So he accepts the course of least resistance and retains all his subordinates indefinitely, regardless of the quality of their work. Under such circumstances it may well be asked whether the protection of employees by means of trials before the civil service commission is worth what it costs the taxpayers. Massachusetts, especially solicitous for the welfare of accused employees, permits them to appeal to the courts.

STRIKES BY PUBLIC EMPLOYEES

For many years it was generally assumed that government employees did not share with their fellow workers in industry the fundamental right to go on strike. "You can't strike against the government," workers were told. They were assured that the functions of the state and its local units were too essential to permit interruption for whatever reason. In their relation to the government they were not only employees, but also citizens; and as citizens they could not be permitted to challenge the state's sovereign power. At first this point of view was not seriously questioned, for only a small fraction of public workers belonged to trade unions, whose leaders might plan and execute strikes. Even when the unions began to invade the field of government employment with conspicuous success, most of them took care to repudiate the strike as an instrument of union policy. They declared instead that they would advance their programs by publicity and the promotion of suitable legislation.

Since the end of the Second World War, however, the tendency of living costs to rise much more rapidly than government salaries has produced general dissatisfaction in the public service. Many workers have gone on strike, with or without the blessing of their local unions. Even policemen and firemen, in some instances, have refused to work until their demands were met. Legislators have answered this threat to the public security with a series of statutes prohibiting strikes in the public service, and imposing such penalties as dismissal from the service and loss of retirement benefits.

Some writers tend to minimize the generally accepted differences between public and private employment. They contend that strikes of private workers, such as milkmen or telephone operators, can disturb the state's economy quite as much as work stoppages by public employees, and they urge the abandonment of any general prohibition against strikes in the public service.[8] But if the prohibition is to be retained, and even extended to jurisdictions that have not yet adopted it, some provision must be made for adjusting the legitimate grievances of public employees. As the National Civil Service

[8] See, for example, Sterling D. Spero's *Government as Employer.*

League pointed out a few years ago: "It is unrealistic to expect public employees, however devoted and patriotic, to foreswear the practices so readily available to workers in private industry in the face of indifference or neglect of what they believe to be their just demands and grievances. . . . Adequate grievance machinery should be established in justice to those in the civil service and to protect the public which depends upon uninterrupted service for its essential needs." [9]   Provision should be made for examination by impartial arbiters of every complaint by a substantial number of public employees.

PENSION SYSTEMS

Benefits

One of the most effective ways to raise the standard of efficiency in the public service is to establish a sound pension system.   This truth has long been recognized by careful students of public administration.   A pension system is desirable, in part, because it facilitates the retirement of employees whose efficiency has been materially reduced by disease, accident, or old age. There is a natural tendency among administrative officials, in the absence of some sort of pension scheme, to keep such employees on the public payroll indefinitely.   The only alternative would be to dismiss them, and peremptory dismissal is scarcely a fitting way to reward years of faithful work.   So the payrolls of the state gradually become clogged with the sick and the decrepit—men and women who are permitted to remain in the service long after their period of maximum usefulness has passed—solely because the state owes them a debt of gratitude and is not permitted by law to pay its debt in any other way.   This condition of affairs can only be remedied by the establishment of a pension system.   Then the employees who have outlived their ability to serve may be retired with the assurance that they will be properly cared for, and their places may be taken by younger, more active persons.   Such an arrangement is desirable from the standpoint of the superannuated workers, of course; but it is much more important as a means of improving the personnel of the administrative service of state and local governments.

The improvement in personnel that follows the adoption of a pension system is due not only to the clearing away of human debris, but also to the recruitment of better equipped men and women.   Pensions for employees increase the attractiveness of the public service.   They provide a protection against the danger of an impoverished old age.   Thus they make it possible

[9] *Annual Report,* 1947, pp. 14–15.

to attract persons of considerable ability who would not otherwise accept the low salaries that notoriously accompany public service.

Incomplete Application of Pension Laws

Despite the obvious advantages of pensions, ten of the states have failed to adopt comprehensive pension systems applying to all state employees.[10] Most of these ten states, however, maintain pension funds for certain favored groups—teachers or state police or health department employees, for example. There is no logic in such an arrangement; it is simply an indication of the political influence of the groups that are benefited. In all probability it does more harm than good, for it breeds a rankling feeling of injustice among the less fortunate employees.

Local Participation in State Systems

More than half of the states with complete pension systems make some provision for participation by the employees of municipalities. Sometimes county and school-district workers are included also. For small units of local government, which have difficulty in financing a pension plan covering only a few employees, this arrangement is particularly advantageous. Ohio makes local participation compulsory, but elsewhere the cities, counties, and school districts are permitted to decide for themselves whether to join the state system.

State and Local Participation in the Federal System

The old age retirement pension plan established by Congress in 1935 for the benefit of the nation's workers specifically excluded the employees of state and local governments. In 1950, however, Congress amended the law to permit these groups to enjoy the benefits of the federal system, provided they were not already protected by public retirement plans. More than three fourths of the states soon accepted the federal offer—for all their employees, if no state retirement system had been established, or for those workers not included in the state system. Nearly half a million employees of state and local governments now participate in the federal government's retirement plan.

Eligibility Requirements

Retirement should be based on age rather than years of service, even if employees are required to serve ten or some other number of years before

---

[10] The ten exceptions are Arizona, Arkansas, Idaho, Kansas, Kentucky, Missouri, Nebraska, Oklahoma, South Dakota, and West Virginia.

becoming eligible for retirement benefits.   The earlier pension systems regularly provided for retirement at the end of a specified period of years, with the
result that some persons were able to leave the public service with comfortable pensions when still in their prime, while others who had entered the
service comparatively late in life necessarily remained in the public employ
long after their days of usefulness had passed because they had no other
means of support.

Commenting on the evils of time-limit pension systems, Professor White
once cited the case of a man who entered the employ of the City of Chicago
at the age of twenty-two, and retired twenty years later with a pension for the
rest of his life.   Because of the obvious disadvantages of using years of
service as the basis for retirement, this plan has now been generally
abandoned.

Methods of Financing

THE CASH DISBURSEMENT PLAN.   Some of the state and local pension
systems are financially unsound because the reserves established by law bear
but slight relation to the obligations that are certain to arise.   A great deal
of improvement has been made in some jurisdictions since the days of the
first pension plans, which entirely ignored the question of reserves or else
merely provided that the revenues from certain licenses and permits should
be paid into a pension fund.   But even today several states and cities with
pension systems applying to all employees make no attempt to establish
adequate, scientifically determined reserves.   Instead they treat all payments
into the pension fund as current revenue, and all payments of pension benefits as current expenses.   Those who favor this so-called "cash disbursement" plan contend that it is simple, because it requires no elaborate computation of reserves, and safe, because it leaves the money with the taxpayers
until needed, instead of piling up large sums in the public treasury and thus
tempting loose-moraled politicians.

But such arguments cannot conceal the obvious fact that the cash disbursement plan is unbusinesslike and unscientific.   Though it may work fairly
well during the early years of a pension system, when relatively few employees
are entitled to benefits, it usually encounters serious difficulties as the number
of pensioners increases and the burden on the taxpayers becomes noticeably
heavier.   When the situation is further complicated by periods of economic
depression, there is a strong likelihood that pensions will be reduced, or even
that the pension system will be abandoned.   A number of public retirement
systems based on the cash disbursement plan have become insolvent in various parts of the United States during the last four decades, and their reor-

ganization has usually worked serious hardship on pensioned employees.

THE ACTUARIAL PLAN.   The only proper way to finance a pension system is to put it on an actuarial basis.   The life insurance companies have statistical information concerning the expectation of life at various ages, and this information can be used by the state to determine exactly what its obligations will be.   It can calculate accurately how long its employees will live after retirement, and how many of them will be incapacitated before they reach the normal retirement age.   These matters can be taken completely out of the realm of guesswork.

With all the necessary information at hand a state or local government can then establish a pension fund and provide for regular payments sufficient with compound interest to cover the benefits anticipated for each employee.   Suitable provision is thus made at the outset for the heavier obligations sure to come as the pension system and the pensioners both grow older.   Acceptance of the actuarial principle by the more progressive states and cities has placed the retirement systems of these jurisdictions on a firm foundation.

COMPULSORY EMPLOYEE CONTRIBUTIONS.   Most persons who have studied the operation of public pension systems agree that pension funds should be supported by the contributions of the employees as well as by legislative appropriations.   The employees should be required by law to contribute, and the amount of their payments should be deducted from their salary checks.   Compulsory contributions are sometimes opposed on the ground that they infringe the right of every worker to be as improvident as his fancy may dictate, but they are desirable for a number of reasons.

First, they reduce the likelihood that the employees will make extravagant demands.   Every additional benefit means additional cost, and when the workers are required to bear a portion of that cost their viewpoint is considerably modified.   Then, too, compulsory contributions lead naturally to employee representation on the pension board, though they do not always produce this result.   It might also be added that simple justice would suggest the partial support of the pension fund by those who are the direct beneficiaries.   Today employee contributions are generally required.

PROBLEMS

1. Study the operation of the merit system in some state that has adopted it.
   a. To what extent are appointments actually made on a merit basis?
   b. Are formal examinations used for the selection of high-salaried technicians in the administrative service?
   c. What has been the practical effect of legislation giving preference to veterans?

     d. What procedure is followed in dismissing employees?

     e. Is a system of efficiency records maintained?

    2. Study the operation of the pension system in one of the states that has adopted a comprehensive system applying to all employees.

SELECTED REFERENCES

Benson, G. C. S., *Administration of Civil Service in Massachusetts*, Cambridge, 1935.

Beyer, William C., *Limited Term and Excepted Appointments in the Civil Service*, Philadelphia, 1953.

Carpenter, William Seal, *The Unfinished Business of Civil Service Reform*, Princeton, New Jersey, 1952.

Civil Service Assembly of the United States and Canada, *Employee Relations in the Public Service*, 1942.

————, *Employee Training in the Public Service*, 1941.

————, *The Employment of Veterans in the Public Service in the United States*, 1944.

————, *A Model State Civil Service Law*, 1946.

————, *Placement and Probation in the Public Service*, 1946.

————, *Policies and Practices in Public Personnel Administration*, 1942.

————, *Position-Classification in the Public Service*, 1942.

————, *Public Relations of Public Personnel Agencies*, 1941.

————, *Readings in Public Personnel Administration*, 1943.

————, *Recruiting Applicants for the Public Service*, 1942.

Commission of Inquiry on Public Service Personnel, *Better Government Personnel*, 1935.

Cooper, Alfred M., *Supervision of Governmental Employees*, 1943.

Halsey, George D., *Making and Using Industrial Service Ratings*, 1944.

Legislative Reference Service, Library of Congress, *Efficiency Rating Systems*, 1947.

Marx, Fritz M., and Others, *Public Management in the New Democracy*, 1940.

Meriam, Lewis, *Public Personnel Problems from the Standpoint of the Operating Officer*, Washington, D.C., 1938.

————, *Public Service and Special Training*, 1936.

Mosher, William E.; Kingsley, J. Donald, and Stahl, O. Glenn, *Public Personnel Administration*, 3rd ed., 1950.

National Civil Service League, *Employee Organizations in the Public Service*, 1946.

Probst, John B., *Measuring and Rating Employee Value*, 1947.

Torpey, William O., *Public Personnel Administration*, 1953.

Uhl, Raymond, *State Personnel Administration in South Carolina*, Columbia, S.C., 1950.

White, Leonard D., *Civil Service in Wartime*, 1945.

————, *Government Career Service*, 1935.

————, and Smith, T. V., *Politics and Public Service*, 1939.

Wilmerding, Lucius, *Government by Merit*, 1935.

CHAPTER 28

Expenditures

For many years state expenditures have been mounting at a rapid rate. In 1915 the cost of state government for all forty-eight states was slightly less than half a billion dollars; by 1930 this cost had mounted to more than two and one half billions—an increase of over four hundred per cent. Then came industrial depression, with a corresponding reduction in the taxpaying capacity of the nation. But state expenditures did not decrease; on the contrary they continued to mount by leaps and bounds. By 1937 they had climbed to three and one half billions—a six hundred per cent increase over 1915.

During the first years of the subsequent war era they still rose rapidly, and by 1943 they had reached the staggering total of almost six billion dollars. Then came a slight decline during the last years of the war, but by 1947 state expenditures had resumed their upward course, rising to a new high of eight billion dollars. Even that figure was dwarfed, however, by 1953's total of nearly seventeen billions. Present state expenditures are about six times as high as in 1930, and more than thirty times the 1915 figure.

In local government the story is much the same. The cities of the United States spent only about three quarters of a billion dollars in 1915; by 1953 this figure had risen to seven billion. County expenditures, also, have increased several hundred per cent in the last few decades. The trend continues steadily upward.

CAUSES OF UPWARD TREND

A number of factors have combined to produce these tremendous increases in the annual totals. First, the level of prices has moved generally upward; since 1915 wholesale prices have risen nearly one hundred and fifty per cent. Second, the population of the nation is now about sixty per cent larger than in 1915. Third, and most important by a wide margin, the state and local governments have assumed a great variety of new functions, and at the same time they have adopted higher standards of performance for functions already undertaken.

Highways—a notable example—have represented huge additional outlays. The cost of public welfare has increased more than twentyfold within the past fifteen years. Public health work has expanded rapidly. The importance of public conservation and development of natural resources has become generally recognized. In the field of education new and expensive ex-

HOW THE STATES SPEND THE PUBLIC'S DOLLAR

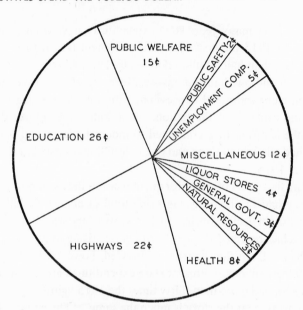

Based on figures from *Compendium of State Government Finances in 1953,* a publication of the United States Bureau of the Census.

periments have been tried, and higher standards of teacher training have been established. In fact, virtually every phase of governmental activity has felt the effect of the demand for improved services involving, in most instances, the expenditure of considerably larger sums. Students of government may reasonably assume, therefore, that the tax rate will continue to rise—at least for another decade. There is no sign of a countertrend.

MAJOR ITEMS OF EXPENDITURE

The three most important items of state expenditure are education, highways, and welfare. Together they account for more than sixty per cent of the total. Smaller sums are spent for hospitals, protection of person and property, development and conservation of natural resources, debt redemption and interest on outstanding indebtedness, and general government.

Nearly one half of city expenditure goes for education, police and fire protection, streets and highways, and health and sanitation. But there are other important items, such as welfare, recreation—and, of course, municipal indebtedness.

HOW THE CITIES SPEND THE PUBLIC'S DOLLAR

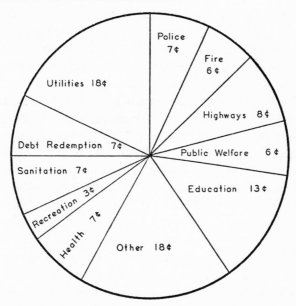

Based on figures from *Compendium of City Government Finances in 1953,* a publication of the United States Bureau of the Census.

The counties concentrate their expenditure largely on highways, health, and welfare. More than seventy per cent of their total outlay is for these purposes.

STATE PAYMENTS TO LOCAL GOVERNMENTS

Nearly one third of the money received by the states from all sources is paid to local units—chiefly the counties—in the form of subsidies or grants-in-aid. These subsidies have increased sharply in recent years. Since 1940 they have more than tripled, in order to compensate the counties and cities for the growing inadequacy of their own revenues. The largest payments are made for education, welfare, and highways, but health and other functions are also subsidized in many of the states.   Usually this money is apportioned on the basis of need.   The various states have their own peculiar methods of measuring need, however, and most of the methods now used are very crude. Some subsidies are conditioned upon the adoption of minimum standards established by state officials, and thus provide a means of improving governmental services in the less progressive communities.

Other money is paid from the state treasury to the counties and cities—not as a subsidy, but as the local share of taxes that have been imposed, assessed, and collected—or at least directly controlled—by state officials.   This money may be apportioned on the basis of need or on the basis of the tax yield in each local district; it may be given with or without conditions; but in any event it differs from a subsidy in that it varies with the amount of tax collections.   It is not a definite sum fixed by legislative action.   An illustration may serve to make clear this distinction.   When the legislature appropriates one million dollars to be apportioned among the counties of the state for the purpose of developing community health centers, it grants a subsidy; but when it specifies that the counties shall receive twenty per cent of income tax revenues, even if the money must be used for health centers, it merely shares a tax with its local subdivisions.   Many state-administered taxes are thus distributed among the counties and cities of the several states.

Every one of the forty-eight commonwealths now distributes some state-administered taxes among its counties and cities.   Gasoline tax receipts are commonly paid in part to the local communities; so, too, are motor vehicle license revenues and the receipts from various corporation taxes.   Other taxes, involving smaller sums, are apportioned in many states.   The practice of sharing state tax money with counties and cities is becoming increasingly common; it has, in fact, been growing constantly since the beginning of the present century.

BUDGET SYSTEMS

The vast sums collected and spent by state and local governments make necessary some kind of fiscal plan—in other words, a budget system that will correlate expenditures and revenues.   Fifty years ago not a single state or local government in the United States had a budget system.   Comprehensive planning of expenditures and revenues was unknown.   There was no way of telling in advance whether a fiscal year would end with a surplus or a deficit.   Former Governor Young of California has drawn a typical picture of conditions in pre-budget days: "When I first entered the legislature in 1909, there was little short of chaos as far as any orderly provisions for state

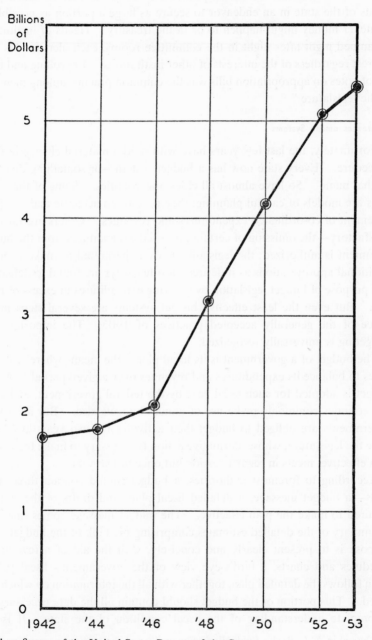

Based on figures of the United States Bureau of the Census.

expenditures were concerned.   There had been no audit of the state finances for over twenty years.   The finance committees of the two houses were scenes of a blind scramble on the part of the various institutions and departments of the state in an endeavor to secure as large a portion as possible of whatever money might happen to be in the treasury.   Heads of institutions encamped night after night in the committee rooms, each alert for his own interest regardless of the interests of other institutions.   Logrolling and trading of votes on appropriation bills was the common practice among members of the legislature." [1]

Differences among Systems

Fortunately, the last few years have witnessed a material change in fiscal procedure.   Every state now has a budget system—or something that goes by that name.   So have almost all cities and counties.   Some of these systems are models of careful planning; they present an accurate and complete statement of co-ordinated expenditures and revenues.   Others are far from satisfactory—the omission of certain proposed expenditures from the budget document is authorized; the legislative body is permitted to make as many additional appropriations as it desires; or other ways are found to defeat the real purpose of budget legislation by allowing expenditures in excess of revenue.   But even the least effective budget systems are several steps in advance of the generally accepted practices of 1905.   The importance of budgeting is universally recognized.

The budget of a government is its fiscal plan—the means whereby it proposes to balance its expenditures and revenues over a given period.   A new budget is adopted for each fiscal year by the federal government, and cities and counties commonly make use of annual budgets also.   But most state governments are obliged to budget their activities for two years at a time, since the legislature, whose affirmative action is necessary to make the budget plan effective, meets in regular session but once in two years.

According to foremost authorities, a budget should contain three main parts—a budget message, a detailed fiscal plan, and drafts of the statutes required to make the plan effective.   The budget message comes first; it is a summary of the detailed estimates comprising the bulk of the budget.   Its purpose is to present clearly and concisely, with the aid of a few simple schedules and charts, a bird's-eye view of the government's fiscal policy.   Then follows the detailed plan, together with all the information on which it is based.   This portion of the budget should contain all the data necessary for a complete understanding of the fiscal condition of the state.   It is not

[1] Quoted in A. E. Buck's *Public Budgeting*, p. 12.

enough, however, merely to present a program for the consideration of legislators and the public.   That program can only be put into effect by the
passage of appropriation and revenue acts; therefore carefully prepared
drafts of these acts should be included.

Unfortunately, not many budgets contain all these features.   Many of
them omit the budget message altogether, substituting for it a letter of trans-
mittal from the budget-making authority that neither summarizes nor inter-
prets the detailed estimates, and therefore permits them to remain a mystify-
ing mass of apparently unrelated figures.   Many budgets also omit the drafts
of necessary legislation.   These bills, if prepared by the budget-making authority, are separately submitted and are referred to appropriate committees
for separate consideration.

A Gradual Development

It is difficult to fix an exact date as marking the beginning of state and local
budgetary legislation.   Some of the first statutes that might conceivably be
called "budget laws" were so crudely drawn and so deficient in the fundamentals of sound budget procedure that they scarcely deserve the name.
Public budgeting has been a gradual growth.   But if a date is desired, 1906
is probably as good as any.   In that year the newly created New York Bureau of Municipal Research suggested that city finances should be planned
well in advance, and that estimated expenditures should be kept within the
limit of estimated receipts—in other words, that there should be a definite
budget plan.   This proposal struck a new note.   There had been no previous recognition of the importance of financial planning.   But New York
City soon made the experiment, and within a few years the budget principle
was adopted by many other municipalities in every section of the country.
Today it is accepted, at least nominally, by virtually every large urban center
in the United States and by most of the smaller communities.

The states were somewhat slower than the cities in accepting the budget
principle, but in 1911 California and Wisconsin established fiscal agencies—
the board of control in California and the board of public affairs in Wisconsin
—that were charged with the duty of making certain estimates of expenditures in advance of the legislative session.   The following year Massachusetts
passed a law containing some provisions that were preliminary to budget procedure.   In 1913 budget legislation was enacted in three states—Arkansas,
Ohio, and Oregon.   Seven other states fell into line in 1915.   By the end of
1919 forty-four states had set up budget systems of some sort.   Then came
Indiana and Florida in 1921, and Pennsylvania in 1923.   Rhode Island, displaying once more the conservatism that had made it the last to ratify the

federal Constitution, was the last to adopt a budget plan.   In 1926 it made the list of states complete.

Most of the state budget systems have been established by legislative action.   But in seven states, beginning with Maryland in 1916, and subsequently including West Virginia, Massachusetts, Nebraska, Missouri, California, and New York, the budget systems are based on constitutional amendments.   Most of these amendments are brief and are supplemented by detailed legislation.

More than three fourths of the states require all their counties to prepare annual budgets.   This requirement is usually phrased in general terms, however, and—even worse—it is not commonly enforced.   Therefore county budget practices usually leave a great deal to be desired.

PREPARATION OF THE BUDGET

Students of government are generally agreed that the chief executive should be vested with complete responsibility for the preparation of the budget.   The people look to him for leadership, and in the shaping of the government's fiscal policy leadership is especially important.   The need for executive control was not clearly recognized at first, however; seven of the first twelve state budget laws placed control in the legislature or, more commonly, in a board.   But shortly afterward came a pronounced swing toward budget systems of the executive type.   Most of the states and cities that enacted budget legislation after 1915 accepted the theory of executive responsibility.

The Executive Budget

Today forty-one states vest budget responsibility in the governor.   In six states [2] the budget is prepared by a board, whose membership usually includes the governor and the more important state administrative officers, especially the treasurer and the auditor.   Members of the legislature are also included in three states.[3]

In manager cities the manager almost invariably has responsibility for preparing the budget.   Mayor-council cities usually entrust this task to the mayor, but there are still many exceptions.   In cities retaining the commission plan the preparation of the budget is a joint responsibility of the members of the commission.   Counties similarly rely on their boards of supervisors, in most cases, though the laws of a few states assign the task

[2] Florida, Indiana, Montana, North Dakota, South Carolina, West Virginia.
[3] Indiana, North Dakota and South Carolina.

of formulating the county budget to the county clerk, the auditor, or some other officer.   Such innovations in county government have not generally made the budget system more effective, because county clerks and auditors have not been given any general authority over the administrative departments.   Therefore they merely receive the estimates from department heads, and assemble this information for the consideration of the county board.

Assistance of Staff Agencies

Although the chief executive is responsible for the preparation of the budget in most states and in most of the larger cities, it must not be assumed that he actually administers all the details of budgetary procedure.   His time and attention are inevitably divided among a great variety of activities, and the only part he can reasonably be expected to play in budget-making is to decide important questions concerning the general scheme of the fiscal plan.   Moreover, he seldom possesses the technical training necessary to enable him to prepare the budget document properly.   He must have expert assistance, and this assistance should take the form of a permanent staff agency.   In nearly one third of the states, however, and even in some metropolitan communities, no such agencies exist; the chief executives of these jurisdictions are obliged to rely on such temporary help as they can obtain at budget-making time from the several administrative departments or from private sources.

The permanent staff agencies that have been created assume a variety of forms.   In some states they are known as departments of finance or departments of administration and finance, and exercise broad powers of supervision over the accounts and expenditures of the other administrative departments.   Budget-making, therefore, is but one of their functions.   Much more common are budget bureaus or offices charged solely with the preparation of the budget, or perhaps made responsible also for the administration of the budget plan.   This is a common arrangement in the cities.   The head of such a bureau or office is generally appointed by the chief executive and reports directly to him.

Collection of Estimates

The first step in the preparation of the budget is the collection of the estimates of expenditure for the ensuing year or biennium.   These estimates, based on actual expenditures of previous years, are made on standard forms by the heads of the several departments and agencies of the government. From the heads of departments they go to the budget officer, whose task is to harmonize them with the estimate of revenue furnished by the auditor, the treasurer, or some other officer or group of officers. Almost invariably the department estimates of expenditure exceed the amount of anticipated income—sometimes by a wide margin.

Harmonizing Estimates of Expenditures and Receipts

After estimates of expenditures are collected, unless the chief executive is willing to propose new means of raising revenue, some way must be found to cut down the department requests. The simplest way to bring proposed expenditures within the limit of probable revenue is to slice a uniform percentage from all department estimates, regardless of conditions or needs.

This method produces grossly unfair treatment of some departments, of course; it illustrates the old maxim that equality may be the worst form of discrimination. But it can be done quickly and requires no highly specialized knowledge of budgetary procedure or intimate acquaintance with the details of state administration. Quite naturally, therefore, it appeals to the busy administrator who has been designated as ex officio budget officer in addition to filling the post of auditor, examiner of accounts, or purchasing officer. If no adequate staff of assistants is provided, the temptation to rely on a scheme of uniform cuts—tempered only by political expediency—is all the stronger. No state or city that has established a permanent budget staff agency, with proper personnel and equipment, makes use of such a slipshod method.

The only way a budget officer can hope to produce satisfactory results is to subject each department's estimates of expenditure to an item-by-item scrutiny. Many department requests will doubtless seem excessive; their propriety must be determined by interviews with department heads. After all, the heads of the several departments are more familiar than the budget officer with their respective projects and needs, and they can best indicate where necessary reductions will cause the least harm.

They cannot measure the needs of their own departments in relation to the needs of other agencies of the government; that is a task primarily for the budget officer and ultimately for the legislative body and the chief executive. But they possess information that the budget must have, and any budget scheme that neglects to secure their co-operation is foredoomed to failure. There is no simple formula for reducing department estimates and harmonizing their total with the total of expected revenues. The task is extremely difficult and quite delicate; its proper performance requires extensive experience, broad knowledge, and infinite tact.

Performance Budgeting

The large majority of state and local budgets explain the financial needs of each department in terms of items of expenditure—so much equipment, so many supplies, so much in salaries of employees of different grades. In recent years, however, many students of budget procedure have suggested that a much clearer picture could be obtained by presenting the needs of each department in terms of services to be performed—so many miles of streets to be paved, so many buildings to be inspected, so many acres of forest land to be protected against fire. The idea of using the budget to portray the tasks of each department was discussed by fiscal experts at least thirty years ago, but it never received much attention until 1949, when the widely publicized Hoover Report accepted the plan and gave it a popular name—performance budgeting. Today the principle of performance budgeting has received at least partial acceptance by several states, and also by such great cities as New York, Philadelphia, and Los Angeles.[4]

LEGISLATIVE BUDGETARY APPROPRIATION AND REVENUE BILLS

When the budget has been nicely balanced and arranged in a form satisfactory to the governor or mayor or other budget-making authority, it is submitted to the legislative branch, where it is referred to the appropriate committee—or, in the case of the state legislature, the appropriate committees of each house. Two or more committees in the state senate usually consider separate portions of the budget plan, and the work of these senate committees is duplicated by two or more committees of the house of representatives. Attempts to co-ordinate the work of these several committees have generally proved ineffective, although a few states have obtained satisfactory results by establishing joint committees or by providing for joint sessions of corresponding committees.[5] Committee meetings on the budget are generally held behind closed doors, but in a few states and in many cities open sessions are required.

Disregard of Executive Recommendations

When a committee has finished its work, it reports its recommendations to the entire legislative body. Early consideration is assured. In the over-

[4] See *Program Budgeting: Theory and Practice,* by Frederick C. Mosher. See also Frank Sherwood's article, "Some Non-Cost Accounting Approaches to Performance Budgeting," in the January, 1954, issue of *Public Management,* pp. 9–12.
[5] For a discussion of joint committee systems, see page 146.

whelming majority of states and cities the legislative branch is free to amend
the budget plan according to its desires.   It may strike out, increase, or reduce items of expenditure recommended by the governor or the mayor, or it
may add new items.   But there are some exceptions.   In Maryland, New
York,[6] Nevada,[7] and West Virginia, and in a number of cities, of which New
York and Boston are conspicuous examples, the appropriation recommendations of the budget may only be reduced or struck out; they may not be increased, nor may new items be added.   Separate appropriations not contemplated in the budget plan may be made in these states and cities, but such
appropriations are hedged about with numerous restrictions.

The Budget Bills

The budget, as such, has no binding effect.   It is merely a series of proposals that require legislative action to give them the force of law.   So when the
legislative branch has concluded its budget debates and has agreed upon all
changes that are deemed necessary it makes the budget effective by passing
the necessary appropriation and revenue measures.

LUMP SUM AND SEGREGATED APPROPRIATIONS.   There is considerable
difference of opinion among public officials as to whether the appropriation
bill should merely provide for lump sum payments to the several departments
and independent spending agencies or should specify instead in exact and
very minute detail just how every appropriation is to be spent.   The "lump
sum" plan is based on the assumption that the heads of departments will
allocate their appropriations to the bureaus and divisions under their control
according to some carefully devised work program.   The so-called "segregated" plan, on the other hand, is dedicated to the belief that department
heads cannot be trusted, and that the only way to prevent them from squandering public money is to state in the appropriation act exactly how every
dollar is to be spent.

Some years ago nearly all state and local appropriations were of the lump
sum variety.   Department heads were given a large measure of discretion,
and many of them abused it.   In conformity with the spirit of the times
they made contracts with professional politicians for work that was not
needed and used unexpended balances to hire their partisan followers just
before election day.   The most obvious way to prevent abuses of this sort
was to limit the discretionary power of all spending officers.   So many states
and cities abandoned the lump sum plan of making appropriations, and pro-

   [6] In New York items may be added under some circumstances, however.
   [7] The Nevada restriction is imposed by statute, and therefore may be amended or
abolished by the legislature at any time.   In practice, however, the legislature has
been careful to respect its self-imposed rule.

ceeded to enact appropriation laws that set forth minutely the purposes for which public funds were to be used.

These segregated appropriation acts put a stop to the worst abuses of administrative discretion. On the other hand, they introduced a new and undesirable element of rigidity into the administrative system. They made it impossible for unused surpluses in one bureau to be transferred to other bureaus. They prevented department heads who were honest and efficient from using their money to the best advantage. They fixed the exact mold of state or local administration for at least one year without providing an opportunity to make changes in accord with changing conditions and changing needs.

ALLOTMENT METHOD OF APPROPRIATIONS. Careful students of government were not slow to recognize these serious defects of the segregated appropriation plan. They soon came to the conclusion that the proper way to prevent abuses of the lump sum method was not to abolish the method but to provide effective supervision and control of all administrative activities by the chief executive. Therefore they urged the adoption of a scheme that has now become generally known as the allotment method.

This method is merely the lump sum system plus direct control by the chief executive. The fiscal year is usually divided into four quarters, and at the beginning of the year each department head is required to submit to the chief executive or to the budget agency a work program showing just what is to be done during each quarter and the probable cost of each operation. This work program, when approved, becomes the basis of allotments to the several departments.

Appropriations are made by the legislative branch on a lump sum basis, but the heads of departments receive their funds in quarterly allotments according to their scheduled needs. Each new quarter provides an opportunity to revise the work programs of the several departments, to examine the condition of department finances and to make certain that deficits will not occur. A few states and cities make allotments monthly instead of quarterly.

The allotment method is vastly superior to the segregated appropriation plan, because it permits the exercise of necessary administrative discretion; it is preferable to the original lump sum method because it places squarely on the executive the responsibility for preventing the abuses that are likely to accompany unsupervised lump sum appropriations. Only about one third of the states, however, led by Illinois in 1917, use the allotment plan. It has proved even less popular in the cities. Most state and local governments still cling to the system of segregated appropriations that has long hampered the development of efficient administration.

TIME OF PASSAGE.   The appropriation and revenue bills necessary to make the budget effective are usually passed by the legislative body prior to the beginning of the fiscal year or biennium to which they apply.   Occasionally, however, the failure of the majority to agree upon a budget program or the obstructive tactics of an obstinate minority may prevent the enactment of necessary legislation.   In some states the budget bills are chronically late because the legislatures do not meet until the fiscal period has begun.   The situations thus created prove serious at times.   Failure to vote the regular appropriations may render the administrative departments virtually impotent.

Some jurisdictions solve the problem very simply by refusing to make payments of any sort—even for salaries—during the period between the beginning of the fiscal year and the passage of the appropriation acts.   But there are other ways of overcoming the difficulty that are more satisfactory. The administrative departments may be authorized to continue spending money on the basis of their old appropriations until such time as the legislature may act; or they may be permitted to spend temporarily at the rate provided in the budget in case legislative action is delayed.

CENTRAL PURCHASING

Hand in hand with the development of budgetary reform has gone the movement for centralized purchasing.   At the beginning of the present century it was the almost universal practice for every agency of a state or local government to buy its own supplies.   Virtually no attempt was made to exercise central supervision of any sort over the method of making purchases or the prices paid.   The results may be imagined.   Goods of standard quality were obtained by different departments at prices that varied as much as three or four hundred per cent.   Favoritism was rife, and matériel for state service was commonly bought from those who possessed the strongest political influence.   Even the few officials who refused to respect the open alliance of business and politics and insisted upon trying to obtain maximum value with the public's money seldom knew how to achieve their desire.   Frequently they purchased at needlessly high prices through sheer ignorance. Moreover, departments competed against one another, and the advantages of large-scale purchasing were lost.

In 1897 Iowa established a board of control with power to supervise all purchases for the state's penal and charitable institutions, and two years later Texas adopted a somewhat similar plan.   But no other state recognized the principle of central purchasing until 1910, when Oklahoma established a state board of affairs and authorized it to buy the supplies of most of the state departments, boards, and agencies. This was the first instance of a fairly complete central purchasing system in state government. Soon afterward, however, the movement gained considerable popularity. Vermont fell into line in 1912, New Hampshire in 1913, and Alabama, California, and West Virginia in 1915. Forty-six states now make use of central purchasing systems to obtain all or a considerable part of their materials, supplies, and equipment.[8]

Central purchasing has made slower progress in municipal government, though it is now used by several hundred American cities. In the counties it is still generally regarded with indifference; not more than one county in twenty-five has established a central purchasing agency.

Exemptions

Some kinds of supplies are commonly exempted from the jurisdiction of the purchasing officer. Perishable goods are placed in this group as a rule, and also certain technical apparatus and equipment. To such exceptions there can be no legitimate objection. All too frequently, however, the principle of exemption is carried still further to include *all* the purchases of those agencies whose political influence is sufficient to keep them clear of the general purchasing scheme. Educational institutions are frequently permitted to do their own buying; so, too, are highway departments. In many jurisdictions the exempted agencies are so numerous that the value of central purchasing is seriously impaired.

Standardization

One of the most perplexing problems of central purchasing arises in connection with the standardization of supplies and equipment. Every department, board, and commission demands its own particular grade of paper, its own favorite brand of automobile tire, its own accustomed quality of soap. Reasons for insisting upon one grade or brand or quality are always forthcoming, but the real reason in many cases is simply the unwillingness of department heads to break away from old habits. Under such circumstances the purchasing officer is unable to secure the lower prices that accompany large-scale purchasing. Usually he is without authority to override the judgment of department heads as to the needs of their respective departments; and if they will not agree upon a small number of brands and grades, he cannot compel them to do so.

There are a few exceptions, however. In Massachusetts, for example, the

---

[8] The only exceptions are Delaware and Mississippi.

purchasing agency formulates and adopts standard specifications that become binding upon all departments when approved by the governor and council.   Nearly all the states and cities that have adopted central purchasing

THE STATE PURCHASING AGENCY
(As organized in many states)

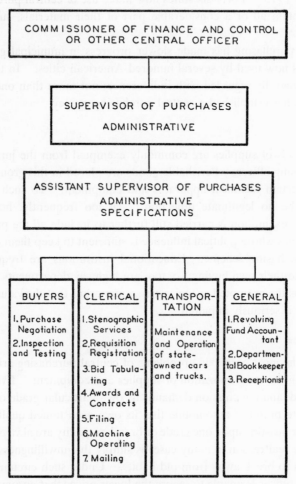

Reproduced with permission from *The Book of the States, 1948–49.*

systems have given some attention to the matter of standardization.   Many of them have created standardization committees, composed of the heads of the administrative departments; usually these committees are merely advisory bodies.

Advantages

Central purchasing has a number of advantages. In addition to saving public funds, it provides an opportunity to obtain central supervision of delivery, storage and distribution of supplies. It tends to eliminate graft and favoritism. It makes possible closer accounting control of expenditures. Unfortunately, however, not all these advantages accrue to every jurisdiction that has adopted a central purchasing system. The public systems are all defective in one or more respects; they do not provide for sufficient standardization, or they fail to insure prompt payments, or they apply only to certain departments. In some instances graft and favoritism have not been eliminated. Even at its worst, however, central purchasing is an improvement over the old methods of buying supplies. At its best it is a highly important phase of efficient public administration.[9]

PROBLEMS

1. Trace the growth of expenditures by your state government from 1915 to the present, and note the changes in the relative importance of the several items. The necessary data can readily be found in the annual reports published by the United States Bureau of the Census.

2. For what purposes are payments made from the state treasury of your state to local units of government? What conditions, if any, are attached to these grants? Is a serious effort made to enforce the conditions imposed?

3. What items of state and local expenditure are likely to increase most rapidly during the next decade? Why?

4. Study the budget procedure of your state or your city. Can you offer any suggestions for improvement?

5. How are supplies and equipment purchased in your state or in your city? Is the present arrangement satisfactory?

SELECTED REFERENCES

Buck, A. E., *Public Budgeting*, 1929.
————, *The Budget in Governments of Today*, 1934.
Buehler, Alfred G., *Public Finance*, 3rd ed., 1948.
Cline, D. C., *Executive Control over State Expenditures in New Jersey*, Princeton, 1934.
Forbes, Russell, *Government Purchasing*, 1929.

[9] See the Council of State Governments' 1947 publication, *Purchasing by the States*. The 1954–1955 edition of the *Book of the States*, pp. 174–176, contains a brief article, "Recent Developments in State Purchasing," by William E. Stevenson. See also "Public Purchasing," by Albert H. Hall, in the 1953 edition of the *Municipal Year Book*, pp. 207–210.

Forbes, Russell, *Purchasing for Small Cities*, rev. ed., 1951.

Groves, H. M., *Financing Government*, rev. ed., 1945.

Hansen, Alvin H., and Perloff, Harvey S., *State and Local Finance in the National Economy*, 1944.

Hutchinson, Ruth G., *State Administered Locally-Shared Taxes*, 1931.

Kilpatrick, W., *State Supervision of Local Budgeting*, 1940.

———, *State Supervision of Local Finance*, 1941.

Lutz, H. L., *Public Finance*, 4th ed., 1947.

Martin, James W., and Briscoe, Vera, *The Kentucky State Budget System*, Lexington, 1945.

Mosher, Frederick C., *Program Budgeting: Theory and Practice*, 1953.

Porter, Kirk H., *State Administration*, Chap. VI, 1938.

Reed, Thomas H., *Federal-State-Local Fiscal Relations*, 1942.

Schultz, William J., *American Public Finance*, 3rd ed., 1942.

Snavely, Tipton R.; Hyde, Duncan C.; and Biscoe, Alvin B., *State Grants-in-Aid in Virginia*, 1933.

Sundelson, J. Wilner, *Budgetary Methods in National and State Governments*, Albany, N.Y., 1938.

Tax Foundation, *Recent Trends in State Expenditures, 1942–1947*, 1949.

Tharp, C. R., *State Aid in Michigan*, Ann Arbor, 1942.

Van de Woestyne, Royal Stewart, *State Control of Local Finance in Massachusetts*, Cambridge, 1935.

Vickrey, William, *Agenda for Progressive Taxation*, 1947.

Williams, John H., *The Flexible Budget: How to Use It*, 1934.

Williams, Mrs. Juanita K., *Grants-in-Aid Under the Public Works Administration*, 1939.

Withers, William, *Public Finance*, 1948.

CHAPTER 29

Revenues

State revenues, like state expenditures, have risen rapidly. They amounted to four dollars and sixty-six cents per capita in 1915; by 1932 they exceeded seventeen dollars. By the war year of 1943 they had increased to more than forty-three dollars, and by 1953—the most recent year for which complete figures are available—they were slightly in excess of one hundred and sixteen dollars per capita. Gasoline taxes and motor vehicle license fees together represented sixteen per cent of the 1953 total; general sales taxes represented thirteen per cent; and unemployment compensation and income taxes each accounted for about ten per cent.

City and county revenues, also, have increased manyfold in the last few decades. In 1915 the cities of the United States had revenues of about thirty dollars per capita; by 1932 this figure had more than doubled, to sixty-nine dollars; and by 1953 it had risen well above the one-hundred-dollar mark. The increase in county revenues has been almost as spectacular.

The 1953 state revenues differ widely from those of 1932, not only in their total amount, but also in the relative importance of specific sources. General sales taxes have been widely adopted and now play an important part in state revenue systems. Payroll taxes to cover the cost of unemployment insurance have become one of the largest state taxes. New kinds of business taxes have been widely imposed. The gasoline sales tax rates have been sharply increased in many states. Individual income taxes have been adopted quite generally. And grants from the federal treasury have grown more than sevenfold within the brief span of twenty years.

In the field of municipal revenue, also, there have been significant changes since 1932. Most important has been the development of new sources of income to replace that old stand-by, the general property tax. City taxes on amusements, cigarettes, and the like are becoming increasingly common. Many municipalities have recently begun to make service charges for the collection of garbage. Others have increased their reliance on license fees. Many have installed parking meters and thus obtained revenue from motorists for the privilege of parking. Municipal sales taxes, often in addition to the sales taxes of the states, have been widely adopted.   The general property tax is still the principal source of income for cities, by a wide margin, but its relative significance has diminished.   Twenty years ago it brought in more than ninety per cent of all municipal tax revenue; today its share is less than seventy-five per cent.   The municipal trend away from utter dependence on the general property tax is unmistakable.   The counties, however, still rely on the property tax almost completely, as they have always done.

TAX CONFLICTS BETWEEN THE FEDERAL GOVERNMENT AND THE STATES

One of the most unfortunate effects of the rising cost of government, with its resultant demand for increased revenues, is the frantic attempt of both the nation and the states to collect maximum taxes from every possible source—frequently from the same source.   Congress imposes taxes on personal incomes or liquor sales or motor vehicles, and state legislatures follow a similar course, usually with little or no regard for what Congress has already done; the result is often a pyramiding of the tax burden until it becomes almost unbearable.

In some cases, to be sure, Congress deliberately imposes a light tax in order to leave a specific source of revenue primarily for the use of the states. It has adopted this policy with regard to gasoline sales taxes.   But some states take full advantage of this arrangement, while others do not.   Therefore the price of gasoline varies widely from state to state—a situation that inevitably encourages gasoline bootlegging and greatly increases the cost of efficient tax administration.

The competition between the federal government and the states for additional revenue works serious hardship upon the states, because of their smaller areas and more limited jurisdiction.   Commonwealths maintaining relatively high levels of taxation have found no effective way to prevent the emigration of persons and corporations to other states that collect less revenue and provide fewer or poorer services.

TAXES—THE CHIEF SOURCE OF REVENUE

The income of state and local governments is derived chiefly from taxes. Fines, permits, and private donations are of relatively minor importance as revenue producers.   This chapter, therefore, will deal largely with the problems of taxation.   At the outset it must be confessed that these problems cannot be solved by the adoption of a few obvious reforms.   Certain reforms are very obvious and very necessary, but even their general acceptance would by no means guarantee an equitable tax system.

Wide divergence of thought exists concerning the exact meaning of "equitable" as applied to taxes.   Every person tends to view new tax proposals in the light of their effect upon his individual interests or the interests

SOURCES OF STATE REVENUE

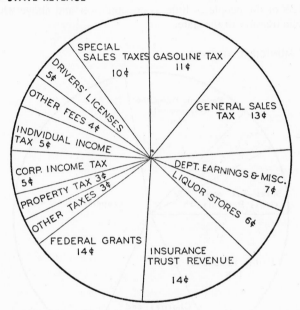

Based on figures from *Compendium of State Government Finances in 1953,* a publication of the United States Bureau of the Census.

of his group.   Moreover, there is considerable uncertainty as to the true incidence of certain taxes, so that legislators do not know, in many instances, who will actually bear the burden of the taxes they impose.   Under the circumstances, no system of taxation is likely to command the allegiance of all classes.

THE CANONS OF SOUND TAXATION

Adam Smith, a famous English economist of the eighteenth century, set forth certain principles that he deemed essential to the establishment of a sound tax system, namely: [1]

[1] *The Wealth of Nations,* Book V, Chap. 11, Part II.

1. The subjects of every state ought to contribute towards the support of the government, as nearly as possible, in proportion to their respective abilities; that is, in proportion to the revenue which they respectively enjoy under the protection of the state.

2. The tax which each individual is bound to pay ought to be certain, and not arbitrary.

3. Every tax ought to be levied at the time, or in the manner, in which it is most likely to be convenient for the contributor to pay it.

4. Every tax ought to be so contrived as both to take out and to keep out of the pockets of the people as little as possible over and above what it brings into the public treasury of the state.

SOURCES OF MUNICIPAL REVENUE

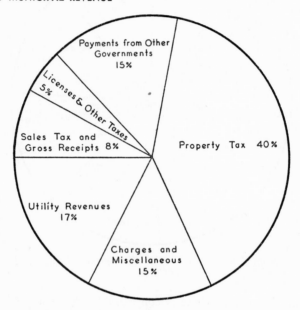

Based on figures from *Compendium of City Government Finances in 1953,* a publication of the United States Bureau of the Census.

These four principles—equality, certainty, convenience, and economy—are generally accepted as axiomatic.   They form the usual point of departure for studies of tax revision, even if those making the studies do not always depart in the same direction.   The real difficulty arises when Adam Smith's maxims are applied to specific tax proposals.   Does a given tax—the gasoline tax, for example—conform sufficiently to the principle of ability to pay? And, in the last analysis, who really bears the tax?   Is it borne by the dealers who originally pay it, or passed on to the consumers of the product?   Concrete evidence on these points is seldom available, and the whole problem is complicated by the fact that every new tax is superimposed upon an already complicated network of taxes whose incidence can be determined only with the greatest difficulty, if at all.

Moreover, even if it could be demonstrated beyond a shadow of doubt that the gasoline tax bears no relation to ability to pay, would that fact be sufficient to justify the states in abandoning its use?   Or should they be influenced instead by the fact that the gasoline tax possesses other highly desirable characteristics, such as ease of collection and economy of administration?   After all, there is probably no tax that conforms exactly to all four of Adam Smith's maxims.   Convenience must be sacrificed to economy, or equality to certainty.   Every tax system is a compromise.

THE GENERAL PROPERTY TAX

During the nineteenth century the general property tax was the main source of state revenue.   As recently as 1902 it represented more than half of the state income from taxes.   But almost every year since 1902 has witnessed a steady decline in its relative importance; in 1953 it accounted for not much more than two per cent of the tax revenue of the several states. But this does not mean that property owners are escaping their fair share of taxes, or even that they have found substantial relief from a heavy tax burden. Far from it.

State governments have largely abandoned this source of revenue for just one reason: to clear the field for the counties, cities, and other local units of government, which have relatively few available tax sources.   So property owners still pay their taxes and still complain about excessively high rates. But the money goes chiefly into local treasuries.   Today, therefore, the general property tax retains its importance in the American tax scheme because it is the mainstay of local government, despite the recent adoption of supplementary taxes by many cities.

Wasteful Duplication of Assessments

The first step in the taxation of property is to determine its value by means of assessments at regular or irregular intervals.   Most assessments are in the hands of local officials.   In twenty-four states assessment is regarded as a county function; in seventeen it is entrusted to the towns, townships, or districts; while in the others the counties and towns make separate assessments, thus duplicating a vast amount of work.   Cities frequently possess the power to make separate valuations and usually insist upon doing so instead of accepting county assessment figures.   There is no logical reason why two sets of officials, working independently of each other, should place their separate valuations upon thousands or hundreds of thousands of pieces of property merely because the property is to be taxed by state, county, and town or city.   One valuation should serve for all purposes of taxation.[2]

Some of the evils of local assessment of real estate are avoided by placing the assessment of certain realty in the hands of state officials.   Most states follow this plan with regard to the property of all public utilities, but a few states, such as Nebraska and Texas, limit its application to railroads, while a number of others, including Kansas, Mississippi, and North Dakota, use it only for railroads and telephone and telegraph companies.   The state agency charged with the task of making these assessments is the state tax commission or board of equalization.   In those states that still rely upon local assessors to value the property of state-wide utility corporations, every tax district is virtually free to follow its own whims, and the widest variations inevitably result.

Incompetence of Assessors

Local assessors—the officers who determine the value of property for purposes of taxation—are commonly chosen by popular vote.   Except in a few of the more progressive metropolitan centers, technical qualifications are neither required nor expected.   The inevitable result is that property valuations are made largely on the basis of political influence or guesswork.   A few jurisdictions have made the office of assessor appointive, and this plan has usually produced better results.   But the voters of most communities still seem to prefer the elective plan; there is a widespread feeling that such an important matter as property assessment, which directly affects the pocketbook of every property owner, should not be entrusted to persons who are one step removed from direct popular control, however competent they may be.   So the inherent popular distrust of appointive officers is made to serve the interests of the professional politicians, and the farce of popular election of incompetents to important technical positions continues.

Personal Property

TANGIBLE PERSONALTY.   One of the most serious defects of the general property tax arises from the attempt to tax personal property.   The attempt is foredoomed to failure in large measure, for no known method exists of measuring tangible personalty with even approximate accuracy, and intangi-

---

[2] Cities sometimes insist upon separate valuations because their tax and debt limits are based upon the assessed value of property within their borders, and county valuations would fix these limits too low.   If all property were assessed at full value instead of a fraction of actual value, this difficulty would disappear.

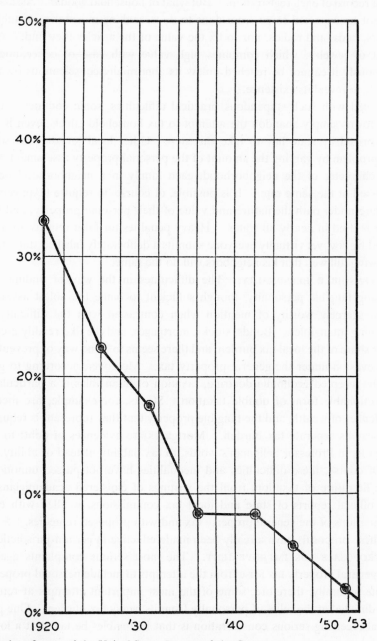

Based on figures of the United States Bureau of the Census.

bles escape detection almost completely.   Certain kinds of tangible personal property, such as automobiles, may be assessed rather easily, since the state has a record of each registration.   But what of household goods?   Assessors cannot be expected to go from door to door, making inventories of tables, chairs, beds, and radios, nor to fix the value of the articles they find.   And what of jewelry, which combines high value with ease of concealment? Obviously it cannot be reached unless its abnormally conscientious owners decide to reveal its existence.

Faced with such stupendous practical difficulties, some counties, cities, and towns simply abandon the attempt to tax household effects, even if not authorized by state law to take this step.   Other local jurisdictions solve the problem by varying the amount of the personal property assessment with the character of the neighborhood, each family in a neighborhood being assessed at the same rate.   It is possible, of course, to require taxpayers to declare under oath the nature and value of their personal property; and this plan is used in nearly all states.   Heavy penalties for false returns are provided by law, yet virtually everyone submits a deliberately falsified statement, knowing full well that his neighbors will do the same.

INTANGIBLE PERSONALTY.   The difficulties in the way of finding and valuing tangible personalty, though sufficient to baffle the ablest assessor, seem scarcely worthy of mention when contrasted with the difficulty of reaching intangibles.   Bonds, stocks, mortgages, and the like readily escape their share of the local tax burden, and there seems to be no way of preventing this evasion under the general property tax.   Moreover, according to generally accepted economic doctrine, taxation of intangibles is a particularly objectionable form of double taxation.   Stocks, for example, are merely evidences of wealth, and the tangible property that they represent is required to bear its separate tax burden.   Mortgages are evidences of debt; to tax them is, in Professor Seligman's words, to tax liability instead of ability.

Of course, these difficulties and inequalities have not passed unnoticed. The literature of taxation, from the writings of cloistered academicians to the official reports of state and local tax commissions, is filled with condemnations of the general property tax and with proposed remedies.   Some of these proposals have already been made effective in certain jurisdictions.

PROPOSALS FOR IMPROVEMENT.   The most serious complaints against the general property tax arise from the attempts to include personal property. Quite naturally, therefore, some of the most important attempts at reform are directed at the relief of personalty from its heavy tax burden.   One proposal receiving serious consideration is that intangibles be taxed at a lower rate than other property, on the optimistic theory that taxpayers will thereby be induced to declare their intangible wealth. This plan has been adopted more or less completely by more than half of the states, but the results have been generally disappointing.

Apparently the only satisfactory way to solve the problem, therefore, is to grant complete exemption from the general property tax to all the more important forms of intangible personalty, relying on other taxes to reach this wealth. A few of the more progressive states have adopted this scheme *in toto,* and a number of others have accepted it in part.

Real Estate

Even as applied to real estate, the general property tax is far from satisfactory. It does not conform to the cardinal principle of taxation—that the tax burden should fall on all members of the commonwealth in proportion to their ability to contribute to the cost of government. For the extent and nature of a man's real estate holdings are at best a poor indication of his net income.

Although the real estate tax is admittedly an inequitable tax and could not under any circumstances be made to conform to a sound theory of taxation, some of its worst features could be eliminated by the adoption of proper administrative methods. The methods now used in most American cities to determine the value of real property are thoroughly bad and lead inevitably to glaring inequalities.

For one thing, real estate is generally assessed at a fraction of its actual worth, as measured by selling price. This fact would be of little importance if all property within a state were assessed at some uniform percentage, whether thirty, fifty, or one hundred. Actually, however, the greatest variations exist among the counties, cities, towns, or other assessment areas. Some communities habitually value real estate at one half of its actual worth, while others use one fourth or three fourths of fair value as the basis of their assessments. These local assessments, with or without some attempt at equalization by the central authorities, then become the basis of a state tax. Equalization is seldom completely effective, and thus the communities whose assessments are nearest actual value make the heaviest proportional contributions to the cost of state government.

Even within a single county or city, wide variations appear. The tax burdens of some property owners are shifted to other property owners— sometimes inadvertently and sometimes as the result of political pressure— through a process of unequal assessments. Although the general level of assessments may be fixed at fifty per cent of full value, the variations on individual pieces of property may range from twenty to one hundred per cent, or even higher.

Some of the larger cities, including New York, Cleveland, Detroit, Baltimore, and Newark, have developed systems of so-called "scientific" or "mechanical" valuation of real estate. These systems are mechanical in the sense that they involve the application of certain definite rules to all pieces of property, but they do not in any way eliminate the factor of human judgment.

Land and buildings are valued separately. Front foot values are obtained for all land within the city limits; and, with this information at hand, the assessed value of any piece of ground can be obtained simply by multiplying its front foot value by the number of front feet—assuming, of course, a lot of standard depths. Special rules must be applied to lots that are longer or shorter than the accepted standard, as well as to irregularly shaped lots. Corner lots, of course, also present special problems. The assessment of buildings is based upon a number of factors, of which the cost of construction is most important, though not controlling in every instance. Depreciation tables for different types of structures have been prepared by a number of authorities.

Mechanical valuation is unquestionably the most satisfactory plan yet devised for assessing real estate. In the hands of competent assessors it can be made to produce highly satisfactory results. If administered by persons who are politically minded or feeble-minded, it is no more likely to give satisfaction than the methods now in general use. But every administrative device depends for its success upon able administrators.

Review and Equalization of Assessments

After the assessments of property have been completed, opportunity must be provided for persons who think that they have been unjustly treated to seek redress. For this purpose boards of review or equalization are maintained by the towns or counties, or both. If the original assessments have been prepared by town officials, appeals usually go to a town board of review, and from that body to a county board. Under such circumstances the county board may perform two separate functions: the hearing of individual appeals and the equalization of town assessment rates. From the decisions of the county board appeals are sometimes permitted to the state tax commission, but more commonly to the courts. The state commission is generally concerned with the equalization of assessments among counties rather than the examination of individual property owners' complaints.

Other duties of the state tax commission are considered in a later part of this chapter.[3]

The most significant aspect of the entire process of review of assessments is its almost universal failure to accomplish any worthwhile result. No effort is made to secure specially qualified persons as members of the local boards of review; in fact, most of these boards are composed of ex officio members, who devote only a small part of their time to assessment hearings. Since these men know virtually nothing about the valuation of property, they are forced to rely for their opinions almost entirely upon the judgment of the assessors whose work they are reviewing—unless they substitute partisan considerations or personal caprice. Occasionally an honest, intelligent board of review makes a determined and successful effort to judge each case on its merits and correct injustices that have developed during the process of preparing the assessment rolls, but such cases are exceptional.

Exemptions from Tax

PREFERENTIAL TREATMENT OF REAL ESTATE. Many persons have long believed that too much property is exempted from the operation of the general property tax. Despite this widespread belief the list of exemptions constantly grows longer. In nearly all jurisdictions it includes real estate used for religious, educational, or charitable purposes. Federal property cannot be taxed by the states or their civil subdivisions because of the implied prohibition in the federal Constitution, as interpreted by the United States Supreme Court.[4] State property is commonly exempted from local taxation. More than one third of the states exempt growing crops or the products of domestic agriculture. Exemption is sometimes granted to factories that produce farm machinery, and a few states exempt all manufacturing establishments.

In recent years there has been a growing tendency to grant complete or partial tax exemption to "homesteads," or private homes. Texas set the example in 1933 by exempting from state taxation the first three thousand dollars of assessed value of homes, and shortly afterward West Virginia made provision for preferential treatment, though not complete exemption. Then, in 1935, Florida exempted homesteads, to the assessed value of five thousand dollars, from all *state and local* taxation. Thirteen states [5] now grant

---

[3] See page 169.

[4] McCulloch *v.* Maryland, 4 Wheaton 316 (1819). It might perhaps be argued, however, that the United States Supreme Court's decision in Graves *v.* New York, 306 U.S. 466 (1939), opens the door for state taxation of federal property and federal taxation of property owned by the states. See page 27.

[5] Alabama, Arkansas, Florida, Georgia, Iowa, Louisiana, Minnesota, Mississippi, Oklahoma, South Dakota, Texas, West Virginia, Wyoming.

more or less complete exemption—or at least special consideration—to private homes.

The inescapable effect of such preferential treatment is to narrow the tax base and shift the burden of taxation to those whose property has not been placed in the exempt class. Thousands of property owners are thus compelled by constitution or statute to pay the taxes on their neighbors' homes; or to contribute to the support of churches they do not attend, manufacturing establishments whose products they do not buy, and private schools whose very existence is unknown to them.

Even though it be granted that religious, educational, and charitable institutions are performing valuable community services, or that agricultural and manufacturing development is essential to community welfare, the propriety of this particular form of encouragement is open to serious question. Certain property must remain exempt from the operation of the general property tax because of constitutional limitations or administrative difficulties, but the quantity of tax-exempt property in virtually every community could be materially reduced.

THE INCOME TAX

Almost three fourths of the states have enacted income tax legislation.[6] This action represents a comparatively new movement. Virginia had an income tax as early as 1843, but no general interest was manifested in this form of taxation until Wisconsin, by its law of 1911, demonstrated that the most serious administrative difficulties could be removed. The severe industrial depression following the stock market crash of 1929 caused a frantic search by state legislatures for new sources of revenue and added fresh impetus to the income tax movement. During 1931, 1932, and 1933 the tax was adopted by thirteen states, and during the next four years it was accepted by eight others.

As a rule the income tax covers both individual and corporation incomes, but two states [7] limit its application to incomes of individuals, whereas four others [8] apply it only to incomes of corporations. In the computation of the net income subject to taxation, certain deductions and exemptions are always permitted. Individual incomes are usually taxed at progressive rates—that

[6] The thirteen exceptions are Florida, Illinois, Indiana, Maine, Michigan, Nebraska, Nevada, New Jersey, Ohio, Texas, Washington, West Virginia, and Wyoming. It should be noted, however, that Michigan and Ohio tax the income from intangibles.

[7] Delaware and New Hampshire.

[8] Connecticut, Pennsylvania, Rhode Island, and South Dakota. The South Dakota law applies only to banks.

is, at rates that increase with the amount of the income.   Thus persons in the large-income brackets pay more—proportionately as well as absolutely—than persons in the small-income groups, in recognition of the generally accepted theory that proportionately greater contributions from the rich involve no greater sacrifice.   The rates of the federal government's income tax are much more steeply progressive than state rates, and this feature has been especially noticeable in recent years; but there is a tendency to strengthen the progressive feature of state income taxation.

In 1934 New York City imposed an income tax, but soon abandoned it because of jurisdictional difficulties.   Five years later, however, Philadelphia levied a tax of one and one-half per cent on all income earned within the city limits.   It now obtains about one fourth of its entire revenue from this source.   More than thirty other cities have followed its example.

THE INHERITANCE TAX

General State Acceptance

Inheritance taxes have long played a part in the general scheme of state finance, though yielding a comparatively small revenue.   Pennsylvania taxed inheritances as long ago as 1826, and Virginia and Maryland enacted similar legislation before 1850.   These early laws, however, were aimed at collateral inheritance; not until 1891, when New York set the fashion, did any state levy a tax upon direct heirs.   In recent years the inheritance tax principle has been greatly extended, and direct as well as collateral heirs have been made subject to taxation in most states, though direct heirs are commonly given the benefit of a lower rate.[9]   The inheritance tax is now used by every state except Nevada and includes direct heirs in every state except Maryland, New Hampshire, and Texas.

The rates adopted by most commonwealths are mildly progressive.   In 1925 New York modified its inheritance tax law to provide for the exemption of intangible personality belonging to residents of other states, but only on condition that other states grant a similar exemption to the estates of New York residents.   This reciprocal provision, which has since been written into the laws of nearly all the other commonwealths, has virtually solved a serious problem of double taxation that formerly caused gross injustice in many instances.

[9] The only states that make no distinction between direct and collateral heirs are Georgia, North Dakota, and Utah.

Congressional Action to Force Tax Uniformity

For many years the wide variations in the inheritance tax laws of the several states, coupled with the failure of some states to make provision for inheritance taxation of any sort, aroused unfavorable comment from many quarters.   It was pointed out that wealthy men could establish their legal residence in some commonwealth, such as Florida, that did not tax inheritances, and that in this way they could escape death levies upon their estates.

In 1926 Congress set out to remedy this situation by enacting a federal inheritance tax law, and including a proviso that any inheritance tax paid to a state government might be credited against the federal tax, up to eighty per cent of the total.   The obvious intent of this statute was to secure some degree of uniformity in the taxation of inheritances.   It was a plain announcement to the states that they must tax the estates of decedents, or have the federal government impose the tax instead.   And, obviously, if the tax were levied by the federal government, all money collected would be paid into the federal treasury.

The State of Florida promptly brought suit to have this law set aside on the ground that it was an unconstitutional interference with state affairs, but the Supreme Court of the United States refused to accept its point of view.   "The contention that the federal tax is not uniform because other states impose inheritance taxes while Florida does not," said the Supreme Court, in upholding the federal statute, "is without merit.   Congress cannot accommodate its legislation to the conflicting or dissimilar laws of the several states nor control the diverse conditions to be found in the various states which necessarily work unlike results from the enforcement of the same tax." [10]   As a direct result of this decision Florida levied an estate tax in 1930, including in the law a provision that limited the tax in all cases to the amount of the federal exemption.

BUSINESS TAXES

Special Corporation Levies

A considerable part of the total state tax revenue is derived from taxes on business corporations.   For the most part these taxes are special levies imposed upon corporations *per se,* and separate from the property taxes that corporations must pay as owners of real estate.   The justification commonly given for such special taxation is that the corporate form of business organization confers special privileges denied to individuals: corporations have per-

[10] Florida *v.* Mellon, 273 U.S. 12 (1927).

petual or long-term existence; their stock may be transferred at will; and their stockholders enjoy a limited liability fixed by law. These privileges have been created by state law; therefore they may reasonably be made the basis for special taxation. In recent years, however, corporation taxes have become increasingly heavy, and many persons believe that this form of taxation has been carried to excess.

The state usually imposes one tax for the privilege of becoming a corporation—or, in the case of a foreign corporation, the privilege of coming within state boundaries. Another levy is made for the privilege of doing business as a corporation. Other special taxes are placed on utility corporations for the privilege of doing business in a special way—in many instances, making use of public property. Banks and insurance companies are also subject to heavy taxation. These taxes on corporate enterprise assume a variety of forms—taxes on capital stock, taxes on gross earnings, taxes on net earnings (already considered under the head of income taxation), and "corporate excess" taxes.

The theory of the corporate excess tax is that every profitable business undertaking has a going value higher than the appraisal value of its property assets—a value created by the union of these property assets under a single effective management. The problem is to measure this going value for purposes of taxation. Most of the states that impose corporate excess taxes solve this problem by ascertaining the market value of each corporation's capital stock and then subtracting the value of its property already reached by the general property tax. The difference between these two figures is supposed to be the corporate excess. Thus the corporate excess tax is really an extension of the general property tax, designed to uncover the residuum of value that the general property tax fails to touch.

Municipal Business Taxes

Most cities levy taxes on various businesses and occupations. Sometimes these taxes are levied primarily for regulatory purposes, and the sum collected is just sufficient to cover costs of inspection. Every dealer in inflammables and explosives, for example, may be required to procure a license in order to prevent these substances from falling into improper hands. The cost of inspecting the place of storage may then determine the amount of the license. Sometimes business taxes are levied entirely for revenue. In that case it is customary to tax virtually every business and profession, from abstracting to zinc plate production. The amount of the levy varies from business to business, but as a rule all persons having the same occupation are taxed alike. The lawyers, for example, are taxed at one rate, and the barbers at another.

A considerable number of cities, however, attempt in a rough way to apply the principle of ability to pay.   They proportion the amount of each man's business tax to the number of his employees, the value of his stock, the quantity of his production, his gross receipts, or the length of time he has been in business.   In a great many instances, of course, it is impossible to determine whether a tax has been imposed for regulation or for revenue.   Both elements seem to enter.

Unemployment Insurance Taxes

Every state now imposes a payroll tax on employers in order to permit regular payments, for a limited period, to workers who have lost their jobs. Wisconsin adopted this plan in 1932, but no state followed its example until 1935, when the national Congress virtually compelled state action by levying a three per cent payroll tax and simultaneously offering to credit against the federal tax any amounts paid to the states for unemployment insurance, up to ninety per cent of the total.   Congress also offered to provide federal funds to cover the cost of administering the state laws.

The immediate result was a flood of state legislation.   Five states accepted the federal government's terms in 1935; twenty-eight others enacted suitable laws in 1936; and all the other commonwealths fell into line before the end of the summer of 1937.   Although the states must meet certain conditions imposed by Congress, they are still free to establish, within broad limits, the kind of job insurance that seems best suited to their individual needs.

Sales Taxes

TAXES ON SPECIFIC COMMODITIES.   Among the more common business taxes are the so-called sales taxes—levies on the sale of specific commodities and also general sales taxes affecting virtually all goods.   Taxes on the sale of specific articles are by far the more common form.   Thus the gasoline tax, which has already been discussed in some detail,[11] has been adopted by every state.   So have taxes on liquor.   Forty-one states levy taxes on the sale of cigars, cigarettes, and other forms of tobacco.[12]   Other specific commodities are singled out for "honorable mention" in certain state tax lists.   There seems to be a definite trend toward this form of taxation.

GENERAL SALES TAX.   Equally significant, in view of the widespread discussion that it has aroused, is the general sales tax, which is a tax at uniform

[11] See pages 475–478.
[12] The only exceptions are California, Colorado, Maryland, Missouri, North Carolina, Oregon, and Virginia.

rates upon the sale of all commodities, or a wide variety of selected commodities, as well as the sale of property and the use of personal services. Strictly speaking, a "general" sales tax should apply to every business transaction, but the name is used to describe a broad tax on sales, even if some specific exemptions are authorized. Thus the West Virginia business and occupation tax is commonly accepted as a good example of a general sales tax, though it does not apply to the sale of professional services. The general sales tax may be levied upon all sales—that is, upon sales by manufacturers, wholesalers, and retailers, with the effect of taxing most commodities a number of times before they reach the ultimate consumers; or it may be levied only upon sales by manufacturers or retailers.

The first state to adopt the general sales tax as an important part of its fiscal scheme was West Virginia, in 1921. Several other states had long made use of levies that might be classed as general sales taxes—for example, Pennsylvania, with its mercantile license tax of 1821, and Virginia, with its merchants' license tax of 1887. But the rates of these older taxes were very low, and it was not until West Virginia had demonstrated the feasibility of the general sales tax as a substantial producer of revenue that other states fell into line. Even then they were forced to act by the serious crisis in state finance resulting from the industrial depression of the 1930's, and in several states the general sales tax was treated strictly as an emergency measure. Thus Georgia enacted an "occupation privilege sales tax" in 1929, but did not re-enact it two years later.

Opposition to the tax is intense and comes from many sources. Manufacturers and merchants insist that it imposes an unreasonable and well-nigh intolerable burden upon industry and, in fact, upon every form of human activity; that it is a "tax upon the swaddling clothes of the newborn infant; upon the medicine that alleviates human suffering; upon the instruments of surgery and the bandages that bind its wounds; upon the plow that furrows the field; upon the pot that boils the mid-day meal; upon the coffins that encase our dead; and upon the spades that dig their graves." [13] Economists agree, for the most part, that the general sales tax is regressive, since it imposes a heavier burden upon the poor than it places upon the rich.

Nevertheless this tax has been accepted by thirty-one states, and by more than three hundred cities, as an established feature of their revenue systems; and it has received serious consideration in many states that have not yet adopted it, because it has been found to yield a large and reasonably certain revenue even in periods of economic depression. Professor Alfred D. Bueh-

[13] *Congressional Record,* 72nd Congress, 1st Session, v. 75, p. 6332.

ler, whose careful study of general sales taxation is an important contribution to the literature of the subject,[14] accepts the usual theory that the tax is regressive and unfair, at least when considered by itself; but he believes that in times of emergency, when revenue is the primary consideration, the general sales tax may properly have a place in state tax programs.

Severance Taxes

One half of the states impose so-called severance taxes—that is, taxes upon the utilization of natural resources. As these resources are severed from the land they cease to be a part of the natural wealth of the state; therefore it is not at all surprising that the state should levy a tax upon the process. In some states the tax applies only to coal or to coal and iron ore; in others it affects only oil and gas or only forest products. The severance taxes of Arkansas and Louisiana are designed to reach all natural resources.

OTHER TAXES

The Poll Tax

The poll tax, an arbitrary annual levy of a flat sum—usually one, two, or three dollars—on all persons, all able-bodied persons, all males, or all males between certain age limits, such as twenty-one and seventy, is still used in nine states.[15] Usually it is levied and collected by local officials, and paid into local treasuries. Under no circumstances can it be made a satisfactory tax, and its evils are accentuated when payment is made a prerequisite to voting.[16]

License Fees

Motor vehicle license fees are an important source of state revenue. Hunting and fishing licenses, dog licenses, and other miscellaneous license fees yield additional small sums. The money obtained from these various license fees is commonly placed in special funds, to be used exclusively for the support of the various licensed activities. Thus motor vehicle license revenues are generally devoted to road construction and maintenance, and hunting and fishing license fees defray the cost of wild life conservation.

[14] *General Sales Taxation.*
[15] Alabama, Indiana, Maine, Nebraska, New Hampshire, Texas, Vermont, Virginia, West Virginia.
[16] The relationship between poll taxes and voting has already been discussed. See page 296.

USE OF TAXATION FOR REGULATORY PURPOSES

The state's power of taxation is used chiefly to provide revenue.   There are many instances, however, of state taxation with the primary intent of regulation, and many businesses or types of business organization are encouraged or restricted by the use of the taxing power.   An excellent example of state regulation under the guise of taxation arises in connection with the development of chain stores.   Many persons, especially the independent merchants, are opposed to this type of selling.   They contend that it amounts to unfair competition, because the chain stores secure the business as long as purchasers are able to pay cash, whereas the independents secure their turn after the customers' supply of cash has been exhausted and credit must be extended.

The legislatures of eighteen states [17]—more than half of them in the South —have decided that chain-store selling is undesirable and have attempted to discourage it by especially heavy taxation from which single-unit stores are exempt.   Thus the Indiana statute, which is typical, forbids the operation of any store in the state without a license and fixes steeply progressive fees for stores operating "under the same general management, supervision, or ownership."   The fee for one store is three dollars; for two to five stores it is ten dollars for each additional store; and so the fee mounts until it becomes twenty-five dollars for each store in excess of twenty.

Shortly after the enactment of this law the owner of a chain of grocery stores in Indianapolis sought an injunction to restrain its operation, on the ground that it arbitrarily discriminated against him and thus deprived him of the equal protection of the laws guaranteed by the federal Constitution. Though admitting that the state legislature might establish classifications for taxing purposes, he urged that chain stores did not differ from independent single-unit stores in any way that would warrant proportionately heavier taxation.   The state board of tax commissioners, in arguing for the validity of the statute, tried to show that important differences between chain stores and independents did actually exist.

When the case reached the Supreme Court of the United States, the law was upheld.   "It is not the function of this court in cases like the present to consider the propriety or justness of the tax, to seek for the motives or to criticize the public policy which prompted the adoption of the legislation," said Justice Roberts, speaking for the Court.   "Our duty is to sustain the classification adopted by the legislature if there are substantial differences

[17] Alabama, Colorado, Delaware, Florida, Georgia, Indiana, Iowa, Louisiana, Maryland, Michigan, Mississippi, Montana, North Carolina, South Carolina, South Dakota, Tennessee, Texas, West Virginia. The list originally included seven other states.

between the occupations separately classified.   Such differences need not be great." [18]

SPECIAL ASSESSMENTS

A small part of state and local revenue is derived from special assessments —that is, special charges levied against the owners of real estate on the assumption that some special benefit has been derived from services performed by the state government.   Thus, when a new highway is built, there is certainly reason to believe that the owners of abutting property receive a special benefit in the form of higher property values.   Why, then, should they not be made to bear all or a portion of the construction cost?

In theory there is no valid objection to the principle of special assessments. Certain practical administrative difficulties sometimes arise, however.   One of these is the difficulty of measuring the area of benefit and determining the exact extent to which benefit has been conferred.   Should special assessments be levied only against the owners of abutting property, or also against other neighboring property owners who secure an advantage?   Should property owners bear the entire cost of permanent improvements involving the use of special assessments—assuming, of course, that the cost does not exceed the benefit actually conferred—or should a part of the burden be borne by the entire taxpaying public?

These questions have been answered in a variety of ways by the state and local governments that have accepted the special assessment principle. Some governments levy assessments up to the full value of the property; others fix the limit for special assessments at fifty per cent.   The assessments for certain types of permanent improvements, such as highways, are commonly restricted to abutting property, but some other special assessments are spread over a considerably wider area.   Almost never, however, is any attempt made to employ scientific principles in determining just how far benefit actually extends.   Guesswork is the rule, and one man's guess is as good as another's.   Nearly three fifths of the states make use of special assessments, but only about a dozen obtain any substantial revenue from this source.   Cities, on the other hand, use special assessments extensively for a great variety of purposes—chiefly sewers, paving, curbing, and sidewalks, but also street widening and grading, development of parks and playgrounds, and installation of ornamental lighting and high pressure fire fighting systems. Some cities even make use of the special assessment principle for current

[18] State Board of Tax Commissioners *v.* Jackson, 283 U.S. 527 (1931).   For a careful study of the economic effects of chain-store taxation, see *The Chain Store Problem*, by T. N. Beckman and H. C. Nolen.

services, such as street cleaning and lighting, snow removal, park maintenance; but they are in the minority. In the scheme of county finance special
assessments are not very important, though they are sometimes used for
highway improvements.

STATE TAX COMMISSIONS

The agency chiefly concerned with the administration of the state tax laws
is the tax commission. Iowa was the first state to establish such a commission, in 1851. But other states followed slowly, and by the beginning of
the present century only ten tax commissions had been set up. More
recently, however, the need for central control of local assessments and the
rapid multiplication of separate state taxes have combined to make some central agency virtually a necessity, with the result that every state except Florida
now has a tax commission or similar agency.

Nearly half of the states have adopted the plan of vesting control in a single
officer, whose title is commissioner of taxes, superintendent of taxation, or
director of finance; the other commonwealths still cling to the commission
plan. The membership of the commissions ranges from three in twenty-
seven states to six in Nevada. Terms of office are rather long—rarely less
than four years, and six or eight years in many states. Appointment by the
governor is the most common method of selection, though popular election
has not been entirely abandoned.

As previously indicated,[19] the state tax commission plays an important part
in the supervision and equalization of local assessments and usually assumes
direct responsibility for the assessment of public utility properties. In addition, it administers a wide variety of state taxes; sometimes the list includes
inheritance and income taxes, gasoline and tobacco taxes, motor vehicle
license taxes, and taxes on incorporated and unincorporated business enterprises. Efficient administration of the state tax program can best be served
by placing the state tax commission—or, preferably, the director of finance—
in charge of all state tax collections. Most of the states, however, still divide
responsibility for the collection of taxes between the tax commission and
other agencies.

PROBLEMS

1. Trace the growth of the revenues of your state government from 1915 to
the present, and note the changes in the relative importance of the several sources
of revenue.

[19] See pages 604 and 608–609.

2. What classes of property are exempt from payment of the general property tax in your state? What changes, if any, would you advocate in the present policy of exemptions?

3. Make a study of the methods of assessing real estate in your community. Note the assessment procedure, and compare the assessed value of a number of properties (if the assessment records are public) with the selling price of those properties, as obtained from the records of a title insurance company or a real estate agency.

4. What is the method of taxing personal property in your community? What classes of personal property are taxed?

5. What were the effects of the industrial depression of the 1930's and the war of the 1940's upon the state and local tax systems? See the annual reports of the United States Bureau of the Census, *Compendium of State Government Finances* and *Compendium of City Government Finances*.

6. What taxes are imposed upon corporations, foreign and domestic, by your state government?

SELECTED REFERENCES

Altman, George T., and Keesling, Frank M., *Allocation of Income in State Taxation*, 1946.

Anderson, Lynn F., *The State Property Tax in Texas*, Austin, 1948.

Beckman, Theodore N., and Nolen, Herman C., *The Chain Store Problem; A Critical Analysis*, 1938.

Blakey, Roy G., and Johnson, Violet, *Sales Taxes and Other Excises*, 1945.

————, *State Income Taxes*, 1942.

Buehler, Alfred G., *General Sales Taxation, Its History and Development*, 1932.

————, *Public Finance*, 3rd ed., 1948.

Clark, Kenneth R., *Inheritance and Estate Taxes on Life Insurance*, 1935.

Council of State Governments, *Federal Grants-in-Aid*, 1949.

————, *Postwar State Taxation and Finance*, 1947.

Crawford, Finla G., *The Gasoline Tax in the United States*, 4th ed., 1937.

Critz, Maurice, *The Use Tax; Its History, Administration, and Economic Effects*, 1941.

Federation of Tax Administrators, *Recent Trends in State Revenues*, 1943.

Hansen, Alvin H., and Perloff, Harvey S., *State and Local Finance in the National Economy*, 1944.

Jacoby, Neil H., *Retail Sales Taxation*, 1938.

Lee, Maurice W., *Anti-Chain Store Tax Legislation*, 1939.

Leonard, J. M., and Mohaupt, Rosina, *Exemption of Homesteads from Taxation*, Detroit, 1937.

Lutz, H. L., *Public Finance*, 4th ed., 1947.

National Association of Assessing Officers, *Exemption of Institutional Real Property from Taxation*, 1939.

New Jersey Commission on State Tax Policy, Sixth Report, *The General Property Tax in New Jersey*, Trenton, 1953.

Nichols, E. R., and Others, *The State Sales Tax*, 1938.

Roberts, Warren A., *State Taxation of Metallic Deposits,* Cambridge, Mass., 1944.

Simpson, Herbert D., *Effects of a Property Tax Off-set Under an Income Tax,* 1932.

————, *Tax Racket and Tax Reform in Chicago,* 1930.

————, *The Tax Situation in Illinois,* 1929.

South Carolina State Planning Board, *Is New Industry Tax Exemption Effective?,* Columbia, 1943.

Tax Foundation, *Recent Trends in Major State Taxes, 1941–1947,* 1948.

Tax Institute, *Wartime Problems of State and Local Finance,* 1943.

————, *Income Tax Administration,* 1949.

Tax Policy League, Inc., *Tax Exemptions,* 1939.

————, *Tax Relations among Governmental Units,* 1938.

Tobin, Charles J.; Hannan, W. E.; and Tolman, L. L., *Exemption from Taxation of Privately Owned Real Property Used for Religious, Charitable, and Educational Purposes in New York State,* Albany, 1934.

Tuller, Walter K., *Treatise on the Taxing Power with Particular Application to State Income Tax,* 1937.

Twentieth Century Fund, Committee on Taxation, *Facing the Tax Problem: A Survey of Taxation in the United States and a Program for the Future,* 1937.

Withers, William, *Public Finance,* 1948.

Woodworth, L. D., *Shared Taxes,* 1944.

Woolsey, John B., *State Taxation of Banks,* Chapel Hill, N.C., 1935.

CHAPTER 30

Indebtedness

Most state programs are financed in part by borrowing. Some temporary indebtedness is incurred to cover unforeseen shortages arising from emergencies or to tide over the period between the beginning of the fiscal year and the date for the payment of taxes, but this form of borrowing is relatively unimportant. The bulk of state indebtedness is represented by long-term bonds, issued to cover the cost of permanent improvements.

In the early days of American history borrowing was unpopular except for war purposes. The functions of government were few and comparatively simple. Needed funds were often obtained from the sale of public lands. In 1820 the expenditures of Pennsylvania's state government amounted to only four hundred and forty thousand dollars—not quite enough to meet its present-day expenses for four hours. Yet Pennsylvania spent considerably more than the average state. It is easy to understand, therefore, that the states had no real need to borrow substantial sums. Their modest tax revenues were quite adequate.

THE NINETEENTH CENTURY TO THE CIVIL WAR

Reckless Borrowing

Shortly after 1820, however, the picture began to change. More extensive public improvements were undertaken, and their cost could not be borne out of current revenues. So the states began to borrow extensively—almost lavishly. They turned their attention particularly to means of transportation between the established East and the newly settled Middle West. Canals and roads were built at a rapid rate, and sometimes without sufficient regard to the costs involved. The success of the Erie Canal, which was completed in 1825 at a cost of seven million dollars, inspired similar projects in a number of states. Nearly all the money came from borrowing. Pennsylvania, whose debt had been nominal in 1820, issued ten million dollars' worth of bonds during the next ten years. New York borrowed even more, and Ohio was not far behind. A little later the development of the railroads necessitated additional capital outlays. It was uncertain for a time whether the railroads would take the place of the canals, and some states made large expenditures for both purposes, increasing their indebtedness accordingly.

Between 1835 and 1838 the states borrowed more than one hundred million dollars—a very substantial sum, in terms of their revenues at that time. Such reckless financing would have been bad enough, if the money had been spent wisely and the debt had been properly administered. Unfortunately, however, neither of these conditions generally prevailed. "Loans were incurred for questionable purposes, money was spent without restraint, and there was much downright fraud. Frequently no provision was made for the payment of interest and principal of the loan; but, instead, new loans were incurred for their payment. Thus debt was pyramided upon debt." [1]

The prevailing interest rate was five per cent in some states, and six per cent in most of the others. As a rule no attempt was made to adjust the official rate to market conditions. The legislature would decide—perhaps six months in advance of the actual sale—that a new issue of bonds should be offered at six per cent. And as a result the bonds might command a handsome premium or might have to be sold instead at a substantial discount. Seldom did the official rate correspond to the market rate. If the bonds yielded a premium, state officials frequently used this surplus to make interest payments, thus concealing the real burden of the debt that had been incurred. Prosperity was in the air, and few persons questioned the wisdom of further borrowing.

Results of Business Depressions

It should have been obvious, however, that there must be a day of reckoning. The first sign of impending disaster was the severe panic of 1837. But this warning had little effect on state borrowing. Between 1838 and 1841, when borrowing should have been sharply curtailed, the total of state indebtedness actually increased ten per cent.

Then came another financial crisis and severe industrial depression. Some of the states lost heavily through bank failures, and their tax revenues declined sharply. State legislators had little inclination to improve the situation by imposing heavier taxes; on the contrary, many of them actually yielded to the demand for tax reduction, in order to relieve the financial burden on the masses of the people. Under such circumstances, it is not surprising that some of the states could find no better way to solve their difficulties than to stop paying the interest on their outstanding bonds. Be-

[1] Paul Studensky, *Public Borrowing*, p. 37.

fore the end of 1842 nine states [2] had defaulted on their interest payments. One of them—Mississippi—eventually repudiated a large part of its indebtedness.

Constitutional Restrictions on Borrowing

Public confidence in the integrity of the state governments was badly shaken, as well it might have been.   The voters of many states came to the conclusion that they could not trust their representatives in the legislature to use the borrowing power wisely and moderately, and so they took steps to check further abuses.   Constitutional limitations on borrowing were quite generally written into state constitutions.   Rhode Island was the first state to take this step; it amended its constitution in 1842 to prohibit the legislature from incurring debts in excess of fifty thousand dollars, without the consent of the voters, "except in time of war, insurrection, or invasion."

Within the next decade and a half eighteen other states followed Rhode Island's example, and eventually similar restrictions on borrowing were written into nearly all the state constitutions.   These limitations have proved singularly ineffective, however, in checking unwise borrowing.   For they operate as a restriction only upon the legislature—not upon the voters.   And whenever public opinion regards large-scale borrowing as a desirable method of financing permanent improvements, nothing can prevent a substantial increase in indebtedness.

Continued Debt Increases

It might be supposed that the unhappy experiences of the 1840's would have had a sobering effect upon the American public and would have prevented further large-scale borrowing, at least for several decades.   But the memory of a democratic people is notoriously short, and so it proved in this case.   Business conditions improved after 1845, the credit of many states was restored, and soon there was a determined demand for improved railroad facilities, to be financed largely through the use of state credit.

The pressure was strongest, of course, in those states that had not borrowed in the earlier period and had thus kept their credit unimpaired.   But New York, which had indebted itself almost to the point of repudiation between 1820 and 1840, increased its debt another fifty per cent before the outbreak of the Civil War.   Total state indebtedness, for all thirty-three states of the Union, soared to a quarter of a billion.

[2] Arkansas, Florida, Illinois, Indiana, Louisiana, Maryland, Michigan, Mississippi, Pennsylvania.

THE CIVIL WAR AND RECONSTRUCTION

War Financing

The Civil War forced new financial burdens upon the states, and most of them resorted to additional borrowing.   Some issued bonds in the early days of the war for the purpose of equipping troops.   Some borrowed in order to supplement the pay of soldiers and aid in the care of their families.   Money was needed, also, to stimulate enlistments by the payment of bounties.   Later, when Congress decided to draft the men needed for the army, the states continued to pay bounties to substitutes and even to those who were drafted.   Many years afterward Congress reimbursed the state governments for a considerable part of these expenditures, but in the meantime state indebtedness continued to grow.

The Confederate states, of course, were in a particularly difficult position. At the outset they had to shoulder most of the financial responsibility for the war, because their central government was in process of organization.   Even after it had been firmly established, it lacked both the power and the will to tax extensively.   Nor did the states increase their taxes to any appreciable extent.   They obtained necessary funds by issuing paper money and by floating long-term bonds.   The central government followed their example. The war ended with both the paper money and the bonds worthless.

Postwar Borrowing in the Confederate States

In the period immediately following the Civil War the plight of the former Confederate states was desperate.   Their governments were practically without funds and unable to pay for badly needed public improvements.   Negroes and "carpetbaggers" from the North were in control of the state governments, and they permitted or encouraged systematic looting of state treasuries.   Under such conditions large new bond issues, totaling more than one hundred million dollars, were floated by the Southern states in the decade after 1865.   The ostensible purpose of most of this borrowing was to aid the railroads; its real purpose was to line the pockets of the crooked manipulators.   Most of the white people of the South were outraged, and many leading citizens declared in no uncertain terms that the new debts would never be honored.   The men who uttered these warnings had been disfranchised, and they were powerless to stop the borrowing orgy, but they could still raise their voices in protest.

REPUDIATION OF DEBTS.   Under such circumstances it is surprising that purchasers could be found for the new bond issues.   Unusual inducements were necessary.   Some of the bonds were offered at sixty cents on the dollar or even less, but they speedily declined to thirty or forty, despite interest rates of seven or eight per cent.   Professor Ratchford tells how North Carolina bonds taken to New York were "hawked about the streets like stale fish from the market." [3]   Eventually, of course, the Southern whites regained control of their state governments, and one of their first acts was to repudiate—at least in part—the debts incurred by carpetbagger administrations.   In some instances they even extended the principle of repudiation to certain debts incurred before the Civil War, but this was not a common practice.

Debt Reduction up to 1900

During the latter part of the nineteenth century state borrowing was generally unpopular.   Most of the states of the North and West financed their activities from current revenues and even managed to reduce the amount of their indebtedness.   In the South the borrowing habit persisted, for the most part, but there were some exceptions.[4]   The net result, for all parts of the United States, was an actual reduction in the total of state debt between 1860 and 1900, despite the admission of fifteen additional states and an increase of one hundred and fifty per cent in the nation's population.

THE TWENTIETH CENTURY

Resumption of Borrowing

At the beginning of the present century came the automobile, bringing with it an urgent demand for the construction of good—and expensive—roads. The states began to borrow once more, and on a scale that made previous borrowing seem extremely modest.   Within a dozen years after the turn of the century state indebtedness had increased forty-two per cent.   It rose another twenty-seven per cent within the next three years.   But that was only a beginning.   The per capita net debt of the forty-eight states was three dollars and seventy-five cents in 1915; in 1930 it stood at sixteen dollars—an increase of three hundred and twenty-five per cent.   The states borrowed and borrowed, using their credit freely to obtain the funds for the permanent improvements demanded by the voters.   Most of the money, as previously indicated,[5] was spent on highways, but substantial sums were used to pay bonuses to veterans of the First World War and to aid them in a variety of other ways.

[3] B. U. Ratchford, *History of North Carolina Debt*, p. 190.
[4] Louisiana paid off a substantial part of its state debt before 1900; so did North Carolina.
[5] See page 479.

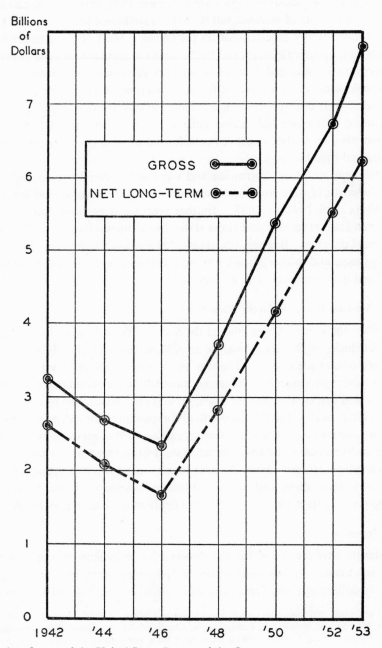

Based on figures of the United States Bureau of the Census.

Mounting Indebtedness

The years of industrial depression following 1930 witnessed some deceleration in the rate of increase, but state debts continued to mount. In 1937 they totaled nearly nineteen dollars per capita. Most of these newer bond issues were specifically approved by the voters at regular or special elections; otherwise constitutional debt limits would have been exceeded many times. Unemployment relief was one of the major reasons for borrowing during this period. Only fifteen states [6] incurred indebtedness for this purpose, but they borrowed nearly one half billion dollars. Large quantities of bonds were issued, also, for harbor improvements, for aid to local governments, and for additional road building.

Although excessive borrowing and inept debt administration had been characteristic of state government for many years, the situation did not reach a climax until 1932 or 1933. By that time the depression had seriously affected state revenues, and some states found themselves on the brink of financial disaster. But only one state—Arkansas—actually defaulted on its obligations, and it later resumed interest payments after refunding some of its bond issues at lower rates of interest.

Debt Reduction During the Second World War

When the United States entered the Second World War in 1941, the net indebtedness of the states was at an all-time high of slightly more than twenty dollars per capita. The war years brought unparalleled prosperity to the state governments. Revenues mounted by leaps and bounds. Individual and corporation income taxes, general sales levies, and business taxes of all kinds swelled the total, more than compensating for a drop in the yield of the gasoline tax. The states took advantage of this opportunity to reduce their indebtedness. In 1942 the net state debt dropped to nineteen dollars and seventy cents per capita, the next year it went down to seventeen dollars and forty-three cents, and by 1946 it had plummeted to twelve dollars and forty-seven cents per capita—the lowest figure in more than two decades.

The Postwar Era

Shortly after the end of the war, however, state indebtedness resumed its upward trend. In two years it rose sixty-four per cent, to a new high of twenty dollars and fifty cents per capita. And by 1953 it had reached the

---

[6] California, Illinois, Maryland, Massachusetts, Minnesota, Nevada, New Hampshire, New Jersey, New York, Pennsylvania, Rhode Island, Tennessee, Texas, Vermont, Washington. New York borrowed more than forty per cent of the total.

TREND OF MUNICIPAL INDEBTEDNESS

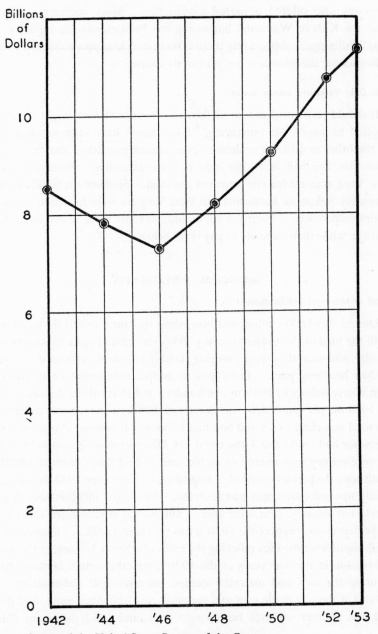

Based on figures of the United States Bureau of the Census.

breathtaking per capita figure of fifty dollars.   Immediately after the Second World War various forms of aid to returning war veterans were chiefly responsible for the increase, though the resumption of war-deferred building programs also offered a partial explanation.   More recently—especially since the Korean War—the borrowing has been chiefly for highways and school buildings.   Apparently there is no reason to suppose that the new era of large-scale indebtedness has yet run its course.

Wide Debt Variations among States

It should be pointed out, in all fairness, that not all forty-eight states have resorted to large-scale borrowing.   Some states have only nominal debts. At the other end of the scale are seven commonwealths [7] that have issued more than one half of all the state bonds outstanding.   Pennsylvania and New York account for one fourth of the total.   Some of the Southern states —notably Arkansas, Louisiana and West Virginia—are in a particularly unfavorable position.   Their per capita indebtedness is far above the national average, while their capacity to pay is far below.

MUNICIPAL INDEBTEDNESS

Trend of Municipal Indebtedness

During the 1800's municipal borrowing was on a relatively small scale. With the turn of the present century, however, cities began to borrow more heavily, and soon they were plunging steadily into debt, without ever a pause in their headlong pace.   Per capita municipal indebtedness rose from less than ninety dollars in 1919 to one hundred and thirty-three dollars in 1926. By 1934 the per capita debt was nearly one hundred and seventy dollars, and the total was close to six and one-half billions.   It seemed that neither good times nor bad could check the trend.   Cities borrowed in prosperous times because money was readily available, and in bad times because additional funds were desperately needed.   Beginning with the year 1934, however, the steady upward movement was reversed.   Municipal indebtedness dropped slowly but steadily, year after year.   The principal reason for this change, in the depression years of the 1930's, was the federal policy of financing many local improvements, thus relieving the cities of a heavy burden.   The principal reason, in the war years of the 1940's, was the virtual impossibility of securing the men and materials needed for municipal construction.   But the end of the war made men and materials available once more, and the result was another wave of borrowing.   Not until 1952, however, did the

[7] California, Illinois, Massachusetts, Michigan, New Jersey, New York, Pennsylvania.

cities of the United States finally exceed the per capita debt total that they had reached in 1934.   Today their indebtedness is at a record high point, and is still rising.

State Limitations on Municipal Borrowing Capacity

Virtually every state has attempted, through its constitution or laws, to check the growth of city indebtedness.   The usual method is to place a limit on the city's borrowing capacity, the limit being commonly fixed as a percentage of the assessed value of property subject to municipal taxation.   In some states the debt limit is as low as one and one-half per cent; in others it runs as high as twenty-five.   "Five per cent of the assessed value of taxable property" is a common maximum; ten per cent is also widely used.   But there are other ways of fixing a city's debt limit.   Sometimes the charter mentions a specific sum that may not be exceeded; sometimes the debt must not be greater than the city's annual current revenue.   It is customary, however, to make certain exceptions.   Thus the charter may provide that bonds may be issued without regard to the legal debt limit for school purposes, since the public school system is generally separate from the rest of the city government, or to meet the needs of city-owned public utilities, because the utilities are supposed to be self-supporting.   In many cities, additional bonds may be issued if approved by the voters.

BORROWING PRACTICES

Terms of Bonds

One of the worst features of state and local borrowing is the long terms for which bonds are issued.   Twenty-five- and thirty-year bonds are common, and fifty-year bonds are by no means rare.   The excesses of the past have led to the adoption of numerous constitutional provisions concerning the term of loans; these clauses are designed, for the most part, to restrict the term of each loan to the probable life of the improvement for which it is issued. Some states go even further; the constitution of Maryland, for example, specifies that no indebtedness may be incurred for a longer period than fifteen years.

PROMPT PAYMENT OF DEBT.   Many students of public finance look with disfavor upon the widely accepted theory that the terms of loans should be related directly to the estimated life of improvements.   Admitting that this test might be acceptable if each government were faced with the necessity of financing but one permanent improvement, they contend that it breaks down when applied to vast and varied construction programs.   Total indebtedness, they point out, rises rapidly in peace years; interest charges become increasingly burdensome; and eventually the state and local governments may be confronted with such a mountain of debt that they will be almost compelled to repudiate their obligations.   The only escape from this dilemma, therefore, is to pay off debts as rapidly as possible, and well within the limit of the probable life of improvements.   At the same time, attention should be given to the possibility of financing a considerable part of the construction program by means of taxes instead of relying solely on borrowing.

Inclusion of Call Feature

It is important that states and cities issuing new bonds reserve the option of calling them at or slightly above par after an initial period of perhaps five years.   More than half of the states, and a vast majority of the cities, failed to take advantage of this elementary principle during the era of heavy borrowing that followed the First World War, and as a result they found themselves saddled with long-term obligations on which they had agreed to pay interest of four or four and one-half per cent, while the interest rate on new issues was dropping steadily.   By 1936 any state or city that had maintained sound credit could borrow at two and one-half per cent.   So the jurisdictions that had been sufficiently foresighted to include the call feature in their earlier bond issues simply floated new loans at the new low interest rates, and used the proceeds to pay off the older bonds.   Thus they made substantial reductions in their interest charges, to the benefit of the taxpayers.

Redemption of Bonds

When a government issues bonds it must make some provision for redeeming them at maturity.   In the past the generally accepted method was to establish a sinking fund, paying into the fund each year from current revenue a sum which, together with earned interest, would be sufficient to meet the principal when it came due.   But this plan has fallen into disfavor in recent years because of the difficulty of preventing political manipulations of the sinking fund.   Neither constitutional limitations nor statutory restrictions seem to offer a sufficient guarantee that the fund will be honestly and efficiently administered.   So sinking fund bonds are gradually disappearing, and serial bonds are taking their place.   Under the serial bond plan there is no need for a fund.   A certain number of the bonds mature each year, in equal or practically equal instalments, until at the end of the period they have all been paid off.

Importance of a Capital Budget

Students of government have long emphasized that state and local borrowing should follow some consistent plan, carefully considered and prepared well in advance.   Budgeting is just as important for capital outlays as for operating expenditures.   Therefore every government should prepare a capital budget, showing what permanent improvements it plans to make during the next six or eight years and how it proposes to finance them.

This capital budget should be revised annually or biennially in order to keep it up to date, for modifications will be necessary regardless of the care with which the original plans are laid.   No person or group of persons can say with absolute certainty what the needs of a state or locality will be after six or eight years.   No person or group of persons can foresee the changes that may be wrought by war or industrial depression or population movements.   But everyone understands that modifications will be made from time to time.   Every new group of legislators will insist upon the right to revise the plans of its predecessors.

This fact does not lessen the importance of a capital budget.   Without such a plan, borrowing is likely to be haphazard; with it, borrowing can be orderly.   The proper place of any one bond issue in the whole fiscal picture can readily be understood.   A number of the more progressive states and cities fully realize the importance of long-term financial planning and have entrusted the task of preparing and maintaining capital budgets to their planning commissions or other agencies.

PROBLEMS

1. Trace the growth of the debt of your state or city government.   What are the principal purposes for which bonds have been issued since 1900?

2. Prepare a brief history of the state debts incurred during the Revolution, and immediately afterward.

3. Compare the provisions of your state constitution concerning indebtedness with the corresponding provisions of the Model State Constitution.   Can you account for their differences on the ground that the clauses of your state constitution are made necessary by local conditions?

4. Trace the fluctuations in the interest rates of municipal bonds during the last half-century.   Do you observe a long-range trend?   If so, how do you account for it?

5. Obtain copies of the capital budgets of a number of states and cities.   What similarities and differences do you observe?

SELECTED REFERENCES

Buehler, Alfred G., *Public Finance,* 3rd ed., 1948.

Fitch, Lyle C., *Taxing Municipal Bond Income,* Berkeley, Calif., 1950.

Fowler, John F., *Revenue Bonds,* 1938.

Groves, Harold M., *Financing Government,* rev. ed., 1945.

Hansen, Alvin H., and Perloff, Harvey S., *State and Local Finance in the National Economy,* 1944.

Horton, Donald C., *Long-Term Debts in the United States,* Washington, D.C., 1937.

Knappen, Laurence S., *Revenue Bonds and the Investor,* 1939.

Lutz, H. L., *Public Finance,* 4th ed., 1947.

McGrane, Reginald C., *Foreign Bondholders and American State Debts,* 1935.

Porter, Kirk H., *State Administration,* Chap. VI, 1938.

Ratchford, B. U., *American State Debts,* Durham, N.C., 1941.

Raymond, Wm. L., *State and Municipal Bonds,* rev. ed., 1932.

Schultz, Wm. J., *American Public Finance,* 3rd ed., 1942.

Studensky, Paul, *Public Borrowing,* 1930.

Taber, Norman S., and Co., *Report on a Survey of the Highway Indebtedness of Texas,* 1937.

Tax Institute, *Wartime Problems of State and Local Finance,* 1943.

Trull, Edna, *Borrowing for Highways,* 1937.

Withers, William, *Public Finance,* 1948.

CHAPTER 31

Planning

Every agency of government, like every private business, should give careful thought to the future. Care should be taken to decide what needs to be done, and how it can best be accomplished. Every major decision should be taken with reference to goals that have already been established. Moreover, the aims of every state agency should be harmonized with the aims of other state agencies, so as to reduce conflicting activities to the absolute minimum. State officials in charge of the principal operating departments are not unaware of the need for some form of planning, but in many cases they are too busy with day-to-day routine to give much time or attention to future needs. And even when they conduct the affairs of their own departments with vision and foresight, they almost invariably fail to see their own activities and needs in relation to the activities and needs of the entire state government. What is needed, obviously, is some agency that will have the primary responsibility for thinking about future state needs *as a whole,* and co-ordinating the programs of the many state departments into a unified plan. The state planning commission is the natural agency to assume this important responsibility. Not without reason has a state planner been defined as "a man who injects orderly thinking into a chaotic future." [1]

GROWTH OF THE STATE PLANNING MOVEMENT

The Early Years

The idea of planning as a separate function of state government is comparatively new, though, of course, statesmen and administrators have given at least some thought to future state needs since the first days of the Republic. Perhaps the modern state planning movement may be said to date from 1926, when the New York state commission on housing and regional planning published a comprehensive report on the planning of the state's major

---

[1] Quoted by F. A. Pitkin in "State Planning and Development," *State Government,* April, 1950, p. 73.

activities.   Thereupon three other states [2] established planning agencies, giving them authority to consider future needs and make suitable recommendations.

Planning in the 1930's

During the first years of the 1930's, when the nation was in the throes of the Great Depression and the tendency was to turn to government for a solution of all economic problems, the state planning movement made rapid strides. The national government gave spiritual aid by establishing a National Planning Board.   It also gave material assistance by offering to allot federal funds to state planning agencies, provided certain conditions were met.   And as a result the number of state planning agencies increased from four in 1931 to forty-seven in 1936.[3]   Nearly eighty per cent of the money to finance these state agencies came from the federal treasury.

Decline of Planning

As prosperity gradually returned to the nation, interest in planning steadily declined.   State after state reduced its planning appropriation or even abolished the agency.   By 1943 most of the remaining state planning commissions were thankful to be still in existence, even with limited funds at their disposal.   In that year the federal government abolished its planning board. The Second World War largely diverted men's minds from the problem of long-range planning, and compelled full-time consideration of the need for an early victory.

From "Planning" to "Development"

The problems of the postwar era once again emphasized the need for effective planning, but state officials showed very little interest.   Indeed, their attitude reflected the indifference—or even open hostility—of the general public to the planning movement.   There can be no doubt that the term "planning" had fallen into disrepute.   It had come to be associated with the socialism of Great Britain or even the "planned economy" of the Soviet Union.   And for that reason it invited the opposition of all who objected to excessive state intervention in private affairs.   Many state planners, in self-defense, tried to find other words to describe their activities.   "Planning" disappeared from the titles of most of the planning agencies.   It was widely replaced by "development."   Today, therefore, such titles are used for planning agencies as department of economic development (Michigan), depart-

[2] New Jersey, Wisconsin, Illinois.
[3] Delaware was the only exception.

ment of business development (Minnesota), development and publicity commission (Ohio). Only one fourth of the states still use the word "planning" to describe their planning commissions.

ACTIVITIES OF STATE PLANNING AGENCIES

Most of the state planning agencies are not doing a comprehensive job of forecasting future state needs and translating them into specific programs. Instead they occupy their time with small parts of the total task, meanwhile performing such routine chores as may have been assigned to them. The truth is that they have little choice in the matter. In the face of limited appropriations and public skepticism, most state planners are scarcely able to plan for their own immediate future.

The activities of the planning agencies vary considerably from state to state. No two commissions seem to be performing exactly the same duties. There are, however, some activities that have been recognized by many states as a proper part of the planning function.

Fact Finding and Analysis

One of the most important activities of the state planning agencies seems to be the collection and analysis of information concerning business conditions. Planning commissions are directed by law to "collect, compile, and distribute data concerning the state and its resources" (Alabama), to "collect factual information on the state's special resources and advantages" (Connecticut), or to "make available information on subjects affecting the health and welfare of the people" (Maryland). Almost all the state planning and development agencies engage in activities of this type. They make surveys of natural resources, transportation facilities, industrial and agricultural development, labor supplies, and the like. Most of these surveys are published —often in pamphlet form—and are made available to other state agencies and also to the general public. The Tennessee state planning commission, for example, which unashamedly calls itself what it really is, publishes periodicals dealing with public works planning, as well as special studies devoted to community, school, and recreational planning. Until recently it also concerned itself with industrial planning and the availability of manufacturing facilities, but these functions have now been transferred to the newly established Tennessee industrial and agricultural development commission.

Promotional Activities

Almost every state planning agency is expected to assume responsibility for publicizing the state's special attractions for tourists and new industries. States like Maine, Florida, and California welcome great numbers of tourists every year. Indeed, there are many other states that rely heavily on the tourist trade and try to encourage an ever-increasing number of visitors. Some state planning agencies have been given substantial appropriations for

advertising. Frequently, the advertising is directed at business executives who might be considering the opening of new factories or the transfer of established enterprises to new locations. Nearly one third of the states have recently enacted laws authorizing various forms of financial aid for new industries.

Co-ordination of Conservation and Public Works Programs

The major programs of the states with regard to their land, mineral, and water resources are sometimes brought within the jurisdiction of the state planning commissions, which try to co-ordinate the activities of the various operating departments. At times the forest service, the park commission, and the soil conservation service may all have their separate and conflicting ideas as to the proper utilization of land; the state planning agency may then be given the opportunity to make recommendations that will prove generally acceptable. Some of the planning agencies are charged with the task of planning state public works programs, including even financial aspects. The Indiana economic council has been directed by law to make plans and present recommendations for the further development of the state's resources, bearing in mind the needs of "agriculture, mining, labor, manufacturing, industry, the transportation of persons and goods, the conservation of forests, soils, stream flow, parks and parkways, game preserves, and other resources and activities in the state, and making adequate provision for the future population."

It must be understood, of course, that the sweeping terminology of this and similar statutes really confers very little authority on state planning agencies. They are told to formulate plans and make recommendations, but other state agencies are not usually obliged to study their plans or do what they recommend. The effectiveness of the planning agency depends in large measure on its powers of persuasion and the hard common sense of its suggestions. State planners do not usually ask for more power. They understand quite well that any attempt to strengthen their hand might only lead to the loss of their jobs.

Assistance to Local Planning Boards

Almost all the state planning agencies co-operate with city and county planning boards to some extent in solving local problems, and about one fourth of the state planning agencies devote a large part of their time and appropriations to this work. Technical aid is given at the request of local officials, and sometimes state planning employees are assigned to local planning agencies for extended periods. Some years ago this activity was an important phase of state planning, but it now receives much less attention than formerly.

ORGANIZATION OF STATE PLANNING AGENCIES

The state planning agency is usually a board or commission. Occasionally it is a department or bureau with one person at its head, but even then a board generally serves in an advisory capacity. State planning boards vary in size from three members to twenty; the average is about twelve. Terms of office vary widely, with many states specifying merely that members shall serve at the pleasure of the governor. Some states require board members to have special qualifications, which are related to knowledge or background or occupation; but most states do not attempt to establish qualifications of any kind. At least half of the planning boards have several ex officio members. The executive head of the planning agency is a director, who normally receives his appointment from the board and serves at its pleasure. Sometimes, however, the director is chosen by the governor. In any case, the director's powers are narrowly limited by the restrictions that have been placed on state planning agencies. Yet it cannot be denied that an able and enthusiastic planning director can accomplish a great deal by forceful leadership. He is in a strategic position to give direction to the whole planning and development movement in his state.[4]

GROWTH OF THE CITY PLANNING MOVEMENT

City planning is older than state planning, and it has been much more generally accepted. Perhaps it has escaped some public hostility because of its comparatively modest beginnings. At first it was widely confused with city beautification, and many persons regarded it as primarily a job for landscape architects. Today its more ambitious scope is better understood, but it still seems to present no threat to free enterprise. It is concerned chiefly with local matters—street layout, location of buildings, traffic, transportation facilities, playgrounds, water supply, and sanitation.

Until the beginning of the present century city planning was almost entirely a matter of private initiative. Groups of public-spirited citizens organized and financed commissions to study the problems of municipal growth and prepare plans for councilmanic approval. After a time city officials manifested interest in the movement. The public commission became the vogue —usually appointed by the mayor, though not infrequently composed of ex officio members. Its task was to frame a satisfactory city plan for the consideration of the council. Having prepared such a plan, it immediately passed out of existence. As a result no agency was specifically charged with the duty of enforcement. In the average city private property owners completely ignored the plan, and lukewarm city officials paid scant attention to it. The need for a permanent body to supervise the city plan, and to modify it from time to time in the light of changing conditions, became apparent.

In 1907 Hartford led the way by creating a permanent, official planning commission of eight members, who served without pay and utilized the staff of the municipal engineering department. Other cities soon fell into line.

[4] See Albert Lepawsky's able monograph, *State Planning and Economic Development in the South.*

Within a decade at least three dozen of the larger cities had set up permanent public planning commissions, and today such commissions are found in more than four fifths of the cities whose populations exceed fifty thousand.

ACTIVITIES OF CITY PLANNING AGENCIES

Street Layout

The first matter to receive consideration in any city is usually the street layout. When the first cluster of houses marks the site of a city in embryo, important decisions must be made. Shall all street intersections be at right angles? Or shall radial thoroughfares be used to break the monotony and decrease the inconvenience of the conventional gridiron plan? What shall be the width of the streets? These questions are answered at the outset by public officials. After that, until recently, street development has been left to the real estate promoters. Private interest instead of public welfare has largely determined the location, direction, and width of streets. The inevitable result has been dead ends, streets too narrow or too wide, main thoroughfares too far apart or too close together, and inadequate opportunities for through traffic to escape local congestion. These difficulties could have been avoided by continuous public control over the street plan. Realization of this fact has been partly responsible for the widespread adoption of city planning.

Location and Design of Public Buildings

Sound principles should underlie the situation and architectural design of public buildings, but in most cities the determining factor has been ward politics. There has been an almost universal tendency to follow ward lines instead of population needs in locating such neighborhood necessities as schools, police stations, fire houses, and branch libraries. Each section of the city has demanded what it conceived to be its share of these facilities, without attempting to consider its needs.

There are, of course, certain buildings in every city that must be centrally located. The city hall, the post office, the court house, the main public library, and the municipal auditorium are included in this group. They are the show places among the city's public buildings, and it is an excellent plan to group them together in a civic center, with sufficient surrounding open space to let them be seen to advantage. Their architecture is a matter of considerable importance. Then, too, there are the pariahs among public buildings—unwanted but essential. Cities must have their prisons, poor-

houses, garbage disposal plants. Some provision must be made for unpleasant sights, disagreeable odors, objectionable sounds. The tracts selected should be of sufficient size to insure permanent isolation.

Regulation of Private Property

In recent years cities have found it increasingly necessary to regulate private property, in order to prevent practices generally regarded as detrimental
to the interests of the public. They have limited the height of buildings, to
insure sufficient light and air, and to reduce the fire hazard. They have
restricted the area that might be built upon, so as to prevent undue congestion. They have fixed by law the uses to which private property might be
put, for the purpose of securing well-rounded development. These regulations, known as zoning restrictions, should be adopted with a clear understanding of the complex problems involved. City planning can provide the
factual background necessary for such an understanding.

Mass Transportation

LOCAL TRANSIT FACILITIES. It is especially important that careful attention be given to the problems of mass transportation. Every morning thousands—perhaps millions—of people travel from their homes in the outskirts
to their places of employment in the center of the city. Every evening they
reverse the process. After the evening meal comes another hegira of suburban folk on pleasure bent, and as the theaters and cafés close for the night
there follows another exodus from the downtown section. At every hour
of the day and night there is some cross-town travel. How can a city best
meet the need for local transportation facilities? Should it rely solely on
street car lines? Or should it supplement street cars with motor buses?
Should it use buses to the exclusion of street cars wherever possible? When
should it provide rapid transit facilities—elevated and subway lines? Should
the cheap but noisy and unsightly elevated be preferred to the expensive but
unobtrusive subway?

STEAM RAILROADS. What of the steam railroad? Originally the steam
lines were used almost exclusively for city-to-city journeys, but in recent years
they have handled an increasing amount of city-suburban travel. Always
they have created serious problems—most serious of all, the problem of
securing access to the city's center. A railroad terminal situated in the heart
of the downtown business district used to mean a long succession of dangerous grade crossings where tracks intersected city streets. Today it is more
likely to mean a series of tracks elevated safely above the street level, but
forming an unsightly barrier to normal city growth. The city with two or

three terminals instead of one has additional difficulties. Any satisfactory solution of the problems presented by the steam railroads must be based upon an intimate knowledge of local conditions.

The Traffic Problem

The relation of the city planner to the traffic problem is obvious. He can suggest immediate relief in the form of alternate traffic routes and downtown storage garages and parking areas. He can point out the need for widening some existing thoroughfares and building some new ones. He can furnish detailed studies to serve as a basis for the co-ordination of existing transportation facilities. Most important of all, he can direct the movement to prevent still further congestion in the great metropolitan areas. Many persons believe that if the cities are permitted to grow unchecked and unguided, rearing their skyscrapers so high that the streets become mere canyons of darkness, the traffic problem will eventually defy solution.

Airports

In recent years the rapid growth of air transportation has made necessary the development of air terminal facilities in every large city. Even the smaller municipalities have hastened to construct airports, hoping that their promptness would give them an advantage over rival communities. And the result has been a host of new planning problems. What kind of land is best suited to airport purposes? How many acres are required? What should be the number and design of airport buildings? Wrong answers to these questions have already caused the wasteful expenditure of huge sums in many cities. But many of these mistakes have been corrected and other mistakes avoided through the establishment of federal standards for airports and the grant of federal funds to cities meeting these standards.

ORGANIZATION OF CITY PLANNING AGENCIES

As might be expected, there is no uniformity in the organization of the planning commissions. They vary in size from three members to forty. Five is the most common number, though there are a great many seven-member planning bodies. Usually the commission is composed of private citizens appointed by the mayor, but occasionally appointment is vested in the council, the manager, or—if the city uses the commission plan—in the city commission. In some cities certain officials, such as the mayor, the municipal engineer, and the director of parks and playgrounds, serve with the appointed members, and in a few instances the entire membership is ex officio.   As a rule, the men and women appointed to city planning boards serve without compensation.   Terms of office vary from one year to seven. Five-year terms are most common.   Frequently the terms of office are over-lapping, one vacancy occurring every year.   It is customary to employ a city planning expert to serve with the commission either as a full-time executive or a part-time consultant, but some cities place the entire burden on the lay commissioners with such help as can be secured from the engineering depart-ment.

REGIONAL PLANNING

A Modern Necessity

Four decades ago the city planning movement was just beginning to gather momentum.   Men were thinking in terms of guided, coherent city growth almost for the first time.   Today it is quite generally recognized that the origi-nal concept of *city* planning was too narrow, too restricted, to accomplish maximum results.   After all, cities are nothing more than municipal corpora-tions whose boundaries have been fixed by the state legislature; as a rule they are merely the cores of encircling regions.   Economically city and region are one, even though artificial distinctions are established and maintained by state laws.   The proper unit for planning, therefore, is not the city but the region.   Transportation, water supply, sewage disposal, fire prevention— virtually all the problems of the city are equally the problems of the territory that lies just beyond its borders.   It will not do to plan highways, land devel-opment, or recreation facilities within the municipal limits only, leaving the solution of these problems just beyond the boundary line to the gods of chance.   For purposes of planning, city and region must be treated as an integrated whole.

Difficulty of Application

State legislators are not slow to recognize this principle of regional plan-ning, but they find difficulty in applying it.   As soon as they begin to con-sider the possibility of a planning commission for an entire region, they are confronted with a host of new and perplexing problems.   For example, what shall the boundaries of the region be?   How shall the various political units within its borders—cities, towns, boroughs, perhaps counties—be repre-sented on the commission?   Shall the city, with its larger population, be permitted to dictate the commission's policies?   Or shall every town within the region be given equal representation?   How shall the regional plan be carried out?   Shall the regional commission be transformed into a board of public works, and authorized to execute every detail?   Or shall the ultimate decision as to the commission's proposals rest with the local legislative bodies?   Presumably the several councils operating within the region must pass final judgment.   But suppose they disagree, as in all probability they will?   How shall such disputes be reconciled?

Growth of Regional Planning

These practical obstacles to regional planning long delayed its official recognition.   For many years the typical official planning commission was a city commission, often exercising limited jurisdiction for a distance of three miles or slightly more beyond the municipal boundaries, but making no attempt to deal with the economic region.   There were some exceptions, of course, such as the planning commission of Los Angeles County and the planning division of the Boston metropolitan district commission, but these exceptions served only to emphasize the general lack of official regional planning boards.

Within the last three decades, however, regional planning has received wider official recognition.   Even within the last twelve or thirteen years the movement has acquired fresh momentum.   Most of the official regional planning commissions are county agencies, but some of them are the product of joint city-county activity.   Louisville led the way in 1942 by co-operating with Jefferson County to establish a joint planning commission.   At least a dozen other official joint planning agencies have since been established.   But most of the great metropolitan centers still rely on private initiative to meet their regional planning needs.   A considerable number of comprehensive regional surveys have been privately directed and financed.

CIVIL DEFENSE

Importance of Civil Defense

For many years the people of the United States have been accustomed to think of war as only remotely related to the civilian population.   Our northern and southern neighbors are friendly—and, in any event, not very strong. To the east and west we are protected by several thousand miles of ocean. For more than a century, therefore, our wars with foreign nations have been fought on foreign soil, and our homes have not been even remotely menaced. But the last ten years have brought radical changes.   They have witnessed the development of airplanes that can fly faster than the speed of sound and atomic weapons that can destroy whole cities with a few swift blows.   Our cities and their civilian populations are no longer safe from enemy attack.

They may be the first to feel the force of an enemy's military power. So steps must be taken to deal with such possible disasters in a prompt and efficient manner.

Uncertain Objectives

One of the principal deterrents to efficient civil defense is the widespread uncertainty as to what should be done. Can enemy bombers be prevented from penetrating our defenses? If not, can they be kept from wiping out the large cities of the United States before we have a chance to retaliate? Can the civilian population be warned of attacks with atomic weapons in time to take shelter? What kind of shelter should be provided, and in what quantities? What should be done for those who survive? No simple, clear-cut answers are readily available. The Federal Civil Defense Administration has issued a formidable array of books and pamphlets by various experts— *Determining Civil Defense Training Needs, Setting Up Your Civil Defense Training Program, Evaluating the Local Civil Defense Training Program,* and the like, but no one can be quite certain that these answers will prove correct when the disaster of war strikes home. Even high officials of the government contradict one another as to the merits of various aspects of the civil defense program. By the latter part of 1953 the confusion had grown so great that President Eisenhower felt obliged to issue an order directing all federal officials to clear with him their remarks concerning civil defense. Such a procedure is not guaranteed to reduce the number of wrong answers to civil defense questions, but at least it should produce a substantial reduction in the number of conflicting answers. Uncertainty as to proper procedure in many aspects of civil defense is likely to persist. The inevitable result of such a state of affairs is widespread public apathy. Men and women ask themselves whether they should really participate actively in a community civil defense program without authoritative assurance that they are accomplishing something of value. And sometimes they decide that the result is so uncertain as to be scarcely worth the effort.

Peacetime Disaster Relief

There can be no question, however, that a civilian organization built primarily to meet the supreme catastrophe of war can render effective service in combating natural disasters, such as floods, conflagrations, tornadoes, and major train or bus crashes. In February of 1951 a commuter train left the tracks while crossing a temporary wooden trestle in northern New Jersey, killing eighty-three persons and injuring more than three hundred others. Volunteer first aid and rescue squads of the local civil defense organization were on the job within a few minutes. Later, of course, ambulances and medical aid arrived, but there seems to be general agreement that the local volunteers saved many lives. The story has been repeated, with infinite variations, in many parts of the United States.[5]

Role of the Federal Government

The federal government has taken the lead in organizing civil defense. Through the Federal Civil Defense Administration it prepares civil defense programs on a nationwide scale, co-ordinates the civil defense plans of all federal agencies, provides for training programs, and gives financial aid to the states in developing their civil defense activities. Somewhat less than fifty million dollars a year is appropriated by Congress to cover these grants, which the states must match with their own funds. Some persons have objected to the "niggardly" policy of Congress in not appropriating larger sums for state civil defense activities; they contend that many times fifty million dollars would scarcely be sufficient to cover all the costs of an adequate program in every state. Undoubtedly they are right, but they overlook the important principle of self-help on which the federal government's civil defense activities are based. Every person should learn how to take care of himself in case of enemy attack, and every community should prepare for its own protection. Financially and otherwise, the defense of the civilian population is largely a local responsibility.

Role of the States

Mutual aid in time of attack is also very important, however. The great industrial centers are almost certain to be the first targets, and they must have the active support of neighboring communities. Moreover, the state governments should have mobile units ready to converge on any area that needs help. After the fires have been extinguished and the medical aid has been supplied, arrangements must be made to house and care for homeless survivors. The state can best perform these functions, and of course it should lay its plans long in advance. All the states have, in fact, enacted basic civil defense laws, and more than half of them have followed the so-called "model act" developed in 1950 by the Council of State Governments and the National Security Resources Board. This act makes provision for training state and local employees in civil defense, and for assigning to them the tasks that they must perform in time of disaster. It contemplates an educated and well-trained public. It lays the basis for an adequate system

[5] See "Volunteer Rescuers on Guard," by Glendon A. Schubert, Jr., and Major R. Marling, in the November, 1951, issue of the *National Municipal Review,* pp. 527–532.

of warning signals and shelters, and it recognizes the need for a plan of emergency mobilization of all available resources. Most of the state plans, however, have not yet been fully prepared, and most of the state organizations are still in skeleton form.

Civil defense planning may well be regarded as one aspect of the state planning movement. Only one state,[6] however, has entrusted its regular planning officials with the responsibility for civilian defense. Most of the others have created separate defense agencies. About one third of the states have assigned defense activities to their adjutants general, who command state troops.

Interstate Agreements

It is obvious that the efficient defense of any state's civilian population cannot stop at the state border. A state that has been attacked must be able to call on neighboring commonwealths for aid, and must be sure of a prompt and adequate response. The only way to be sure is to arrange every aspect of interstate co-operation well in advance. Nearly all the states have already taken steps in this direction. Two thirds of them have entered into formal agreements for mutual aid in case of foreign attack, and most of the others now have enabling legislation, though they have not yet worked out the details.

Role of the Cities

The cities of the United States—especially the principal industrial centers —play a principal role in civilian defense. Their high priority on the list of enemy targets increases their vulnerability, and also increases the importance of every step that they take to protect their inhabitants. Present plans contemplate the establishment of ward, precinct, and even block organization, with a large part of the civilian population participating in the task of preparing for immediate action when disaster strikes. To date, however, most cities have not advanced beyond the stage of preliminary discussions. They seem to be waiting for stronger leadership at the higher levels of government.[7]

PROBLEMS

1. Trace briefly the history of the state planning movement in your state.
2. Describe the organization and work of your city's planning commission.
3. Examine the city plan of your community. What are its main features?

[6] Iowa.

[7] See Val Peterson's article, "Co-ordinating Disaster Relief," in the October, 1953, issue of the *National Municipal Review*, pp. 445–449.

4. What steps have been taken to plan the metropolitan area in which you live? What factors have retarded the planning movement in this area?

5. Write a brief description of the organization and work of the civil defense agencies in your state.

SELECTED REFERENCES

American Association of Planning Officials, *The Role of the Planning Commission in Civil Defense*, 1950.

————, *Current Problems in State Planning and Development*, 1951.

Breese, Gerald, and Whiteman, Dorothy E., eds., *An Approach to Urban Planning*, Princeton, N.J., 1953.

Brewer, Carey, *Civil Defense in the United States: Federal, State and Local*, Library of Congress, Washington, D.C., 1951.

Colean, Miles L., *Renewing Our Cities*, 1953.

Comey, A. C., and Others, *State and National Planning*, Cambridge, Mass., 1937.

Devan, Arthur, *Planning National Defense, 1950 to 1970*, Library of Congress, Washington, D.C., 1949.

Gallion, Arthur B., and Eisner, Simon, *The Urban Pattern: City Planning and Design*, 1950.

Hillman, Arthur, *Community Organization and Planning*, 1950.

Jamison, Judith N., *Regional Planning*, Los Angeles, 1952.

Lewis, Harold M., *Planning the Modern City*, 2 Vols., 1949.

Tompkins, Dorothy, *Civil Defense in the States*, Berkeley, Calif., 1953.

United States, Federal Civil Defense Administration, *Civil Defense in Industry and Institutions*, 1951.

————, *Fire Services*, 1951.

————, *Health Services and Special Weapons Defense*, 1950.

————, *Police Services*, 1951.

————, *Principles of Civil Defense Operations*, 1951.

————, *The Rescue Service*, 1951.

————, *This Is Civil Defense*, 1951.

————, *The Warden Service*, 1951.

United States, National Resources Committee, *The Future of State Planning*, Washington, D.C., 1938.

United States, Natural Resources Planning Board, *The States and Planning*, Washington, D.C., 1942.

Walker, Robert A., *The Planning Function in Urban Government*, 2nd ed., 1950.

Woodbury, Coleman, *The Future of Cities and Urban Redevelopment*, 1953.

Table of Cases and Index

Table of Cases

Adkins v. Children's Hospital, **261 U.S. 525 (1923)**, 543, 545–546

Allgeyer v. Louisiana, **165 U.S. 578 (1897)**, 22

Amalgamated Association v. Wisconsin Employment Relations Board, **340 U.S. 383 (1951)**, 556

American Federation of Labor et al. v. American Sash and Door Co. et al., **335 U.S. 538 (1949)**, 555

American Steel Foundries v. Tri-City Central Trades Council, **257 U.S. 184 (1921)**, 554

Ashton v. Cameron County Water Improvement District, **298 U.S. 513 (1936)**, 68

Associated Schools v. School District, **122 Minn. 254; 142 N.W. 325 (1913)**, 432

Bailey v. Drexel Furniture Co., **259 U.S. 20 (1922)**, 540

Barbier v. Connolly, **113 U.S. 27, 31 (1885)**, 24

Beauharnais v. Illinois, **343 U.S. 250 (1952)**, 82

Benjamin v. Housing Authority of Darlington County et al., **15 S.E. (2nd) 737 (1941)**, 425

Brown v. Board of Education of Topeka, **347 U.S. 442 (1954)**, 25

Bunting v. Oregon, **243 U.S. 426 (1917)**, 542

Buttrick v. City of Lowell, **1 Allen (Mass.) 172 (1861)**, 349

Carter v. Carter Coal Co., **298 U.S. 238 (1936)**, 546

Champlin Refining Co. v. Corporation Commission of Oklahoma, **286 U.S. 210 (1932)**, 500

Chisholm v. Georgia, **2 Dallas 419 (1793)**, 42

City of Boston v. Treasurer and Receiver-General, **237 Mass. 403; 130 N.E. 390 (1921); affirmed, 260 U.S. 309 (1922)**, 72

Colgate v. Harvey, **296 U.S. 404 (1935)**, 24

Collector v. Day, **11 Wallace 113 (1870)**, 27

Columbus Metropolitan Housing Authority v. Thatcher et al., **42 N.E. (2nd) 432 (1942)**, 425

Commonwealth v. Hunt, **4 Met. 45 (Mass.) 111 (1842)**, 549

Commonwealth v. O'Keefe, **298 Penna. 169; 148 Atl. 73 (1929)**, 171

Conner v. Elliott, **18 Howard 591, 593 (1856)**, 24

Cook County v. City of Chicago, **142 N.E. 512 (1924)**, 47

Cooley v. Port Wardens of Philadelphia, **12 Howard 299 (1851)**, 20

Coppage v. Kansas, **236 U.S. 1 (1915)**, 553

Coyle v. Smith, **221 U.S. 559 (1911)**, 28

Daniel Ball Case, **10 Wallace 557 (1871)**, 502

Dent v. West Virginia, **129 U.S. 114 (1889)**, 530

Duplex Printing Press Co. v. Deering, **254 U.S. 443 (1921)**, 552

Dyer v. Sims, **58 S.E. (2nd) 766 (1950); 341 U.S. 22 (1951)**, 39, 40

Elliott v. City of Detroit, **121 Mich. 611 (1899)**, 53

Elmore v. Rice, **72 Fed. Supp. 516 (1947)**, 298

Ervien v. United States, **251 U.S. 41 (1919)**, 29

Erie Railway Co. v. Williams, **233 U.S. 685 (1914)**, 544

Everson v. Board of Education of the Township of Ewing et al., **330 U.S. 1 (1947)**, 80

Federal Power Commission v. Hope Natural Gas Co., **320 U.S. 591, 645 (1944)**, 527, 528

Federal Power Commission v. Natural Gas Pipeline Co., **315 U.S. 575 (1942)**, 527

Ferguson v. Wilcox et al., **28 S.W. (2nd) 526 (1930)**, 108

Florida v. Mellon, **273 U.S. 12 (1927)**, 612

Frothingham v. Mellon, **262 U.S. 447 (1923)**, 16

Georgia Railway and Power Co. et al. v. Railroad Commission of Georgia et al., **262 U.S. 625 (1923)**, 527

German Alliance Insurance Co. v. Lewis, **233 U.S. 389 (1914)**, 519

Gibbons v. Ogden, **9 Wheaton 1 (1824)**, 9

Giboney v. Empire Storage and Ice Co., **336 U.S. 490 (1949)**, 550

Gloucester Ferry Co. v. Pennsylvania, **114 U.S. 196, 203 (1885)**, 10

Graves v. New York, **306 U.S. 466 (1939)**, 27, 609

Grovey v. Townsend, **295 U.S. 45 (1935)**, 297

Grubstein v. Cambell, Tax Assessor, **1 So. (2nd) 483 (1941)**, 425

Guinn v. United States, **238 U.S. 347 (1915)**, 297

A. B. Hale et al. v. Binco Trading Co., Inc., **306 U.S. 466 (1939)**, 33, 34

Haley v. Cochran, **31 Ky. L. Rep. 505; 102 S.W. 852 (1907)**, 113

Hammer v. Dagenhart, **247 U.S. 251 (1918)**, 7, 540, 543–544

Hans v. Louisiana, **134 U.S. 1 (1890)**, 42

Hawkins v. Bleakly, **243 U.S. 210 (1917)**, 538

Henderson v. United States, **39 U.S. 816 (1950)**, 25

Hitchman Coal and Coke Co. v. Mitchell, **245 U.S. 229 (1917)**, 554

Hoke v. United States, **227 U.S. 308, 320 (1913)**, 10

Holden v. Hardy, **169 U.S. 366 (1898)**, 542

Hooper v. California, **155 U.S. 648, 652 (1895)**, 24

Hurtado v. California, **110 U.S. 515, 535 (1884)**, 21

Illinois ex rel. McCollum v. Board of Education of School District No. 71, Champaign County, Ill., **333 U.S. 203 (1948)**, 80

In re Moyer, **35 Colo. 159; 85 Pac. 190 (1904)**, 113

In re Spencer, **149 Cal. 396 (1906)**, 534

Inland Steel Co. v. Yedinak, **172 Ind. 423 (1909)**, 540

International Brotherhood of Electrical Workers v. National Labor Relations Board, **341 U.S. 694 (1951)**, 550

Kansas v. United States, **204 U.S. 331 (1907)**, 43

Kentucky v. Dennison, **24 Howard 66 (1861)**, 26

Knoxville Iron Co. v. Harbison, **183 U.S. 13 (1901)**, 544

Lauf v. E. G. Skinner and Co., Inc., **303 U.S. 323 (1938)**, 552

Lincoln Federal Labor Union et al. v. Northwestern Iron and Metal Co. et al., **335 U.S. 525 (1949)**, 555

Lochner v. New York, **198 U.S. 45 (1905)**, 542–543

Loewe v. Lawlor, **208 U.S. 274 (1908)**, 552

Louisville v. Board of Education, **154 Ky. 316; 157 S.W. 379 (1913)**, 432

MacQueen v. Port Huron, **194 Mich. 328; 160 N.W. 627, 630 (1916)**, 432

Mahoney v. Joseph Triner Corp., **304 U.S. 401 (1938)**, 34

Mason v. Missouri, **179 U.S. 328 (1900)**, 72

Massachusetts v. Mellon, **262 U.S. 447 (1923)**, 16

McCollum v. Board of Education of

School District No. 71, Champaign County, Ill., **333 U.S. 203 (1948),** 80

McCulloch v. Maryland, **4 Wheaton 316, 407 (1819),** 27, 92, 609

McLean v. Arkansas, **211 U.S. 539 (1909),** 544

Milk Wagon Drivers' Union v. Lake Valley Farm Products, Inc., **311 U.S. 91 (1940),** 552

Mt. Pleasant v. Beckwith, **100 U.S. 514 (1880),** 70

Mountain Timber Co. v. Washington, **243 U.S. 219, 234 (1917),** 26, 538

Moyer, In re, **35 Colo. 159; 85 Pac. 190 (1904),** 113

Mueller v. Thompson, **149 Wis. 488 (1912),** 53

Müller v. Oregon, **208 U.S. 412 (1908),** 541

National Labor Relations Board v. Fansteel Metallurgical Corps., **306 U.S. 240 (1939),** 551

National Labor Relations Board v. Jones and Laughlin Steel Corp., **301 U.S. 1 (1937),** 554, 555

National Prohibition Cases, **253 U.S. 350 (1920),** 8

Nebbia v. New York, **291 U.S. 502 (1934),** 516

New State Ice Co. v. Liebmann, **285 U.S. 262 (1932),** 516

New York v. Miln, **11 Peters 102 (1837),** 10

New York Central Railway Co. v. White, **243 U.S. 188 (1917),** 538

New York, New Haven and Hartford Railroad v. New York, **165 U.S. 628 (1897),** 20

Norris v. Mayor and City Council of Baltimore, **192 A. 531 (1937),** 292

Ohio Oil Co. v. Indiana, **177 U.S. 190 (1900),** 500

Pacific States Telephone Co. v. Oregon, **223 U.S. 118 (1912),** 26

Panhandle Oil Co. v. Knox, **277 U.S. 218 (1927),** 27

Paul v. Virginia, **8 Wallace 168, 178 (1868),** 10, 24, 509

Pembina Mining Co. v. Pennsylvania, **125 U.S. 181, 189 (1888),** 24

Pennsylvania Railroad v. Pennsylvania, **250 U.S. 566 (1919),** 20

Pensacola Telegraph Co. v. Western Union Telegraph Co., **96 U.S. 1 (1877),** 10

People v. Fisher, **14 Wend. (N.Y.) 9 (1835),** 548

People v. Max, **70 Colo. 100 (1921),** 181

People v. Western Union Telegraph Co., **70 Colo. 90 (1921),** 181

Phelps Dodge Corp. v. National Labor Relations Board, **313 U.S. 177 (1941),** 554

Pierce v. Society of the Sisters, etc., **268 U.S. 510 (1925),** 447

Railroad Commission of California et al. v. Pacific Gas and Electric Co., **302 U.S. 388 (1937),** 527

Ribnik v. McBride, **277 U.S. 350 (1928),** 516

Rice v. Elmore, **165 Fed. 2nd 387 (1947); 333 U.S. 875 (1948),** 298

Ritchie v. Ill., **155 Ill. 98 (1895),** 541

Santa Clara County v. Southern Pacific Railway Co., **118 U.S. 394, 396 (1886),** 24

Schechter v. United States, **295 U.S. 495 (1935),** 543

Schenck v. United States, **249 U.S. 47 (1919),** 82

Schneider v. Duer, **184 A. 914 (1936),** 530

Schwegmann Brothers v. Calvert Distillers Corp., **341 U.S. 384 (1951),** 511

Shelley v. Kraemer, **334 U.S. 816 (1950),** 25

Smith v. Allwright, **321 U.S. 649 (1944),** 297

Smyth v. Ames, **169 U.S. 466 (1898),** 524, 525, 527

Spencer, In re, **149 Cal. 396 (1906),** 534

State v. Cunningham, **81 Wis. 400 (1892),** 129

State v. Hale, **129 Fla. 588 (1937),** 33

State Board of Tax Commissioners v. Jackson, **283 U.S. 527 (1931),** 618

State el rel. Dyer v. Sims, **58 S.E. (2nd) 766 (1950); 341 U.S. 22 (1951),** 39, 40

State el rel. Grubstein v. Cambell, Tax Assessor, **1 So. (2nd) 483 (1941),** 425

State el rel. Mueller v. Thompson, **149 Wis. 488 (1912)**, 53

Sterling et al. v. Constantin et al., **287 U.S. 378 (1932)**, 114

Stettler v. O'Hara, **69 Ore. 519 (1914)**; affirmed, 243 U.S. 629 (1917), 545

Steward Machine Co. v. Davis, **301 U.S. 548 (1937)**, 561

Terminiello v. Chicago, **337 U.S. 1 (1949)**, 82

Truax v. Corrigan, **257 U.S. 312 (1921)**, 552

Tyson v. Banton, **273 U.S. 418 (1927)**, 516

United States v. Appalachian Electric Power Co., **311 U.S. 377 (1940)**, 502

United States v. Bekins, **304 U.S. 27 (1938)**, 68

United States v. California, **332 U.S. 19 (1947)**, 501

United States v. Certain Lands in the City of Louisville, **78 Fed. (2nd) 684 (1935)**, 424

United States v. Classic, **313 U.S. 299 (1941)**, 297

United States v. Darby Lumber Co., **312 U.S. 100 (1941)**, 7, 541, 544, 547

United States v. Hutcheson, **312 U.S. 219 (1941)**, 552

United States v. Louisiana, **339 U.S. 232 (1950)**, 501

United States v. Southeastern Under-

writers' Association, **322 U.S. 533 (1944)**, 11, 520

United States v. Texas, **339 U.S. 707 (1950)**, 501

Virginia v. Tennessee, **148 U.S. 503 (1893)**, 26, 39

Ward v. Maryland, **12 Wallace 418, 430 (1871)**, 24, 509

West Coast Hotel Co. v. Parrish et al., **300 U.S. 379 (1937)**, 546

West Virginia ex rel. Dyer v. Sims, **58 S.E. (2nd) 766 (1950)**; **341 U.S. 22 (1951)**, 39, 40

Wheelock v. Lowell, **196 Mass. 220; 81 N.E. 977 (1907)**, 257

Wilcox v. Consolidated Gas Go., **212 U.S. 19 (1909)**, 527

Williams v. Eggleston, **170 U.S. 304 (1898)**, 72

Williams v. Standard Oil Co. of Louisiana, **278 U.S. 235 (1929)**, 516

Wilson v. New, **243 U.S. 332 (1917)**, 546

Wolff Packing Co. v. Court of Industrial Relations, **262 U.S. 522 (1923)**, 516, 517, 556

Wolff Packing Co. v. Court of Industrial Relations (second case), **267 U.S. 552 (1925)**, 556

Zorach v. Clauson, **343 U.S. 306 (1952)**, 80

Index

absent voting, 301-302
accidents
  industrial, 533-538, 539
  motor vehicle, 479-484
admission of new states, 28-29
Adult Authority, 367-368
advisory judicial opinions, 181
agricultural clubs, 498
agricultural experiment stations, 499
agricultural extension work, 496-498
airports, 69-70, 643
Alabama, 115-116, 568
allotment method of appropriation, 593-594
almshouses, 376-378
amendment, constitutional, 8-9, 84-88
American Federation of Labor, 307
American Legion, 307
American Legislators' Association, 35, 37-38, 40, 41
American Public Welfare Association, 41
American Society of Planning Officials, 41
anti-trust laws, 510-511
appellate courts, 166
appointing power
  of city council, 200, 210, 211
  of civil service commissions, 571
  of governor, 97, 109
  of lieutenant governor, 141
  of mayor, 190, 195
  of state legislature, 139
appropriations, budget, 592-594
arbitration, 178-179, 556
assessment
  political, 322-323
  of property, 603-604, 608-609
  special, 478-479, 618-619
assessors, 242-243, 604
athletic fields, 460
attorney-general, state, 118-119
auditors, 120-121, 242
automobiles, *see* motor vehicles

ballot for elections, 289-295
Baltimore, 225

banking, regulation of, 517-518
banking commissioner, 517-518
Baton Rouge, 225
bicameralism, 131-132, 199
biennial sessions, 133-134
bill
  drafting of, by reference bureaus, 153, 154
  history of a, 147-151
  speaker's power over, 143
Bill of Rights, states, 79
blind, 383, 387
blue-sky laws, 512-513
board of selectmen, 258-259
bonds, 606, 631-633
Book of the States, 42
borough plan, 226-227
borrowing, *see* indebtedness
boss control, 323-325
Boston, 225, 230, 231
Bucklin plan of preferential voting, 280
budget
  legislative appropriation for, 591-594
  preparation of, 588-591
  systems of, 584-588
Buehler, Alfred D., 615-616
buildings, public, 641-642
Bureau of Dairy Industry, 63
Bureau of Fisheries, 63
Bureau of Mines, 63
Burke, Edmund, 306
business (*see also* interstate commerce)
  depressions of, 623-624
  regulation of, 507-531, 617, 637-638
  taxes on, 612-616, 617

California
  administrative reorganization of, 102
  civil service commission of, 568, 569
  and direct legislation, 332, 333
  election of judges in, 169
  organization chart of an urban county in, 243
  and sentencing commission, 367
  State Capitol building of, 145

camps, municipal, 461
capital budget, 633
capital punishment, 363
Cardozo, Benjamin, 68
caucus
    for legislative action, 148-149
    for nominating candidates, 273-274
central purchasing, 594-597
chain store and taxation, 617
charity
    administrative organization for, 388-390
    for children, 382
    private organizations for, 374
Chicago, 456
child labor laws, 534, 539-541
children
    care of homeless, 382-385
    exclusion from certain industries of,
        534, 539
    hours of labor for, 539-541
    hygiene for, 406-408
    minimum wages for, 545
circuit courts, see district courts
city councils, 197-201
city government (see also metropolitan
        area government)
    budget for, 586-591
    central purchasing in, 594-597
    and civil defense, 648
    commission form of, 203-208
    direct federal aid to, 68-70
    federal adjustment of debts of, 67-68
    functional distribution chart of employ-
        ees in, 573
    indebtedness of, 629, 630-631
    manager plan for, 208-217
    mayor and council plan for, 187-201
    planning by, 641-644
    public health activities of, 396, 397
    revenues of, 599-600, 602, 603, 613
    state relations with, 46-60
city-manager plan, 208-217
Civil Aeronautics Administration, 69
civil defense, 66, 645-648
Civil Service Assembly, 41
civil service commissions, state, 568-575
civil service laws, 566-568
Civil War and reconstruction, 625-626
Clayton Act, 510
"clean politics" law, 65-66
clerk of the county court, 243
closed primary, 278-279
closed shop, 549-550, 553-554
collective bargaining, 548-549
colleges, see education
Colorado, 568
Colorado River Compact, 38, 39

commission government, 203-208
Committee on Legislative Processes and
    Procedures, 157-158
committees
    in constitutional conventions, 89-90
    legislative, 143-147
    in political parties, 315-317
communicable disease control, 399-401
community centers, 459-460
Community Chest, 374
compacts, interstate, 38-40
Compendium of City Government Fi-
    nances, 62
compensation, workmen's, 535-538
competition, 510, 617
compulsory education, 445-447
conciliation, 178-179, 556
Confederate states, 625-626
conference committees, of state legisla-
    ture, 151
Congress of Industrial Organizations, 307
Connecticut, 146, 568, 569
conservation, see natural resources
conservation agencies, state, 486-488
constable, 259-260
Constitution, federal
    and admission of new states, 28
    amending, 8-9
    and interstate relations, 2, 9-11
    limitation on state powers by, 22-23
    and state legislature, 137-138
    and voting, 295-296
constitution, state, see state constitutions
constitutional amendments, 8-9, 84-88
constitutional conventions, see conven-
    tions
contested elections, 130, 288
continuous sessions of state legislature,
    137
conventions
    constitutional, 84-85, 88-91
    party, 274-276
Cook County, Illinois, 3, 247
coroner, 359-360
corporations
    charters for, 507-510
    "foreign," 33
    municipal, 46-47, 71-72
    regulation of, 507-511
    taxation of, 612-613
corruption
    of party machines, 320-323
    at the polls, 287
Council of State Governments, 40-42,
    157-158
county assessors, 242-243
county auditor, 242

county board, 238-241
county clerk, 243
county court clerk, 243
county courts, *see* district courts
county government (*see also* town government)
    budget for, 586-591
    central purchasing in, 594-597
    consolidation of, 251
    defects in organization and administration of, 244-251
    diagram of model, 249
    federal restrictions on state's power over, 70-72
    functional realignment of, 251-252
    home rule for, 55-56, 57
    organization of, 236-244
    and public education plan, 434, 436
    public health organization in, 395-398
    revenues of, 599, 619
    and state authority, 46-47, 58
county manager plan, 248-250
county register of deeds, 243-244
county surveyor, 244
county treasurer, 241-242
courts, state
    advisory judicial opinions of, 181
    and civil and criminal cases, 161
    and judicial review, 179-181
    need for reform of, 171-179
    organization of, 161-167
    removal of judges from, 169-170
    selection of judges for, 167-169
courts of appeal, 166
Cox, George B., 323
crime, 172
criminals, treatment of, 362-368
Croker, Richard, 324-325
cumulative voting, 281

Dayton, Ohio, 208
declaratory judgments, 177-178
Deepwater Commission, 203
defense counsel, 358-359
Delaware, 38, 236, 438-439, 513
delegated powers, 6
Democratic Party, 306, 308-309, 314-315
Denver, 225
deposit guarantees, bank, 518
depressions, 7, 623-624
direct initiative, 328
direct legislation, *see* initiative; referendum
direct primary, 276-285, 297-298
disabled, 383, 387
disasters, 345
district attorney, 356-358

district courts, 165-166
district courts of appeal, *see* appellate courts
districts, 398, 433-434
divorce, 32
drivers, 481-482, 484
drivers' licenses, 475, 599, 601, 616
due process of law, 21-22, 71-72

education
    building construction for, 448
    city expenditures for, 583
    compulsory school attendance laws for, 445-447
    courses of study in, 447-448
    division of responsibility for, 431-432
    equal protection of the laws for, 25
    federal forestry field work in, 490
    federal grants-in-aid for, 15
    higher, 449-450
    for highway safety, 483
    and improved teacher standards, 443-445
    local units of school administration for, 433-441
    from private to public, 431
    for public health, 409-411
    special schools and classes for, 449
    state administrative organization for, 441-443
    state control of other matters of, 447-449
    state expenditures for, 582
    textbooks for, 448
Eisenhower, Dwight D., 8, 501
election (*see also* voting), 129-130, 285-289
election boards, 286
election districts, 285
employees, state, 565-579
employer, attitudes on labor, 556-557
employment agencies, 558-559
enabling act, 28
England, 5, 312-313, 315-316
equal protection of the laws, 24-25, 72
Europe, 422, 424
executive cabinet, 122
executives, state, *see* state executives
expenditures, 581-597
extramural jurisdiction, 227-229

fact finding and analysis, 637
Fair Labor Standards Act, 7, 547
fair trade laws, 511
farmers' institutes, 496
federal aid, *see* federal grants-in-aid
Federal Airport Act, 69

Federal Bureau of Investigation, 63
Federal Civil Defense Administration, 647
federal government
  and admission of new states, 28
  and civil defense, 647
  direct services of, 63-68
  forestry subsidies of, 488-489
  and grants-in-aid to states, 11-16, 472-474, 601
  and indirect services, 62-63
  power expansion of, 5-20
  and public education, 431-432, 441
  and public health activities, 15, 394
  and tax conflicts with states, 600
federal grants-in-aid, 11-16, 472-474, 601
Federal Housing Act of 1937, 424-425
Federal Housing Act of 1949, 425-426
federal-local relations, 62-72
federal mortgage insurance, 422
Federal Power Act, 502-503
Federal Power Commission, 502, 527-528
Federal Reserve System, 518
federal-state relations, 4-29
Federal Trade Commission, 510
federal training program, 65
Federalist Party, 308
federated city plan, 226-227
finance (see also expenditures; revenues), 58-59, 138
fire department, municipal, 361-362
fire marshal, state, 361
First Interstate Legislative Assembly, 37
fish and game conservation, 492-495
Florida, 33-34
"foreign" corporations, 33
forestry, 488-492
foster homes, 384-385
Fourteenth Amendment, 21-22, 27, 71-72
France, 5, 193, 313
Frankfurter, Felix, 33-34
fraud, protection from, 512-514, 530
fugitives, 26
full faith and credit, 25-26
functional realignment, 251-252
"fundamental laws," 86, 92

Galveston, Texas, 203
gasoline tax, 475-478, 599, 601
general property tax, 58, 600, 603-610
Georgia, 568
Gerrymandering, 129
Governmental Research Association, 41
governor
  legislative recommendations by, 156-157
  and National Guard, 345
  in present-day government, 106-115

restrictions on, 96-98
terms and salaries chart, by state, 1953, 107
Governors' Conference, 41, 402
governor's council, 115
grand jury, 356-357
"grandfather clause," 297
Great Britain, see England
Greater New York, 226-227
Guffey Coal Act, 546

habeas corpus, writ of, 81
Hare plan of proportional representation, 281-282
health, see public health
highways
  administration of, 466-472
  city expenditures for, 583
  construction financing methods for, 475-479
  federal grants-in-aid for, 15, 472-474
  history of, 463-466
  safety on, 479-484
  state expenditures for, 477, 582
  and state police, 346-349
Holland, 313
home rule, 51-56
Hoover, Herbert, 102
Hoover Report, 591
hours of labor, 7, 539-544, 547
housing
  low-cost, 420-426
  municipal laws for, 417-420
  nonfarm, construction chart, 423
  slum problem and, 420-426
  unsatisfactory conditions of, 415-517
housing codes, 417
housing laws, 417-420

Idaho, 102
Illinois, 100-102, 281, 389
immunization, 400
impeachment
  of governor, 108-109
  of judges, 169-170
  and recall, 336, 337
  state legislature power for, 140
implied powers of federal government, 6-7
imprisonment, see prisons
income, substandard, 370-372
income taxes, 599, 601, 610-611
indebtedness, state, 479, 622-633
independent candidate, 283
indeterminate sentence, 366-367
indictment, 357
indirect initiative, 328
industrial accidents, 533-538, 539

industrial disputes
    collective bargaining in, 548-549
    compulsory settlement of, 556
    strikes in, 549-553, 575-576
industrial hygiene, 409, 538-539
information, prosecution by, 357
inheritance tax, 611-612
initiative, 87, 327-334
injunction, 551-552
"in-service" training, 573-574
institutions
    for children, 383-384
    for mental patients, 401-402, 403
    for poor, 374, 376-378
    state aid to welfare, 383
insurance business regulation, 10-11, 519-
    520
insurance commissioner, 519
insurance trust revenue, 601
interest rates, 514-515
interstate commerce
    and "commerce" defined by Supreme
        Court, 9-11
    and labor, 555
    regulation of corporations in, 508-510
Interstate Commission on the Delaware
    River Basin, 38
Interstate Oil Compact, 38
Interstate Reference Bureau, 154
Interstate relations, 32-44
Italy, 313

jails, see prisons
Japanese-Americans, 8
Jefferson, Thomas, 431
joint address, 169-170
joint committees, 146
judges, 139, 140, 167-170
judicial council movement, 173-174
judicial interpretation, 9-11
judicial review, 179-181
judicial system, state, see courts, state
jury system, 175-177
justice of the peace, 161-163, 260

Kansas
    civil service commission of, 568
    legislative council of, 134, 136
    number of townships in, 260
    State Capitol building of, 145
Kentucky, 243

labor, 7, 533-561
Labor Management Relations Act, 550,
    551, 555, 557-558
Labor Party of England, 313, 315-316
labor unions
    and collective bargaining, 548-549

and open vs. closed shop, 553-555
    regulation of activities of, 556-558
    strike right of, 549-553
laboratories, public health, 404-405
law enforcement, 343-368
legislation
    administration measures recommended
        for, 156-157
    congestion of, at end of session, 151-
        152
    direct, 327-334
    diversity of, 32-34
    history of a bill in, 147-151
    special, 48-51, 57, 138
    uniform state laws chart, 36
legislative councils, 134-136
legislative reference bureaus, 153-154
legislature, state, see state legislature
Library of Congress, 64
licenses
    fees for, 475, 599, 601, 616
    for liquor industry, 520
    motor-vehicle, 475, 599, 601, 616
    for professions and trades, 529, 530-
        531
    as source of revenue, 599, 601, 602, 613
lieutenant governor, 115-118, 141
limited voting, 281
liquor industry regulation, 520-521
liquor tax, 601
literacy tests for voting, 298-299
loans, 514-515
lobbies, 154-156
local-federal relations, 62-72
local-state relations, 46-60
logrolling, 588
Los Angeles, 232-233
Louisiana, 145, 332, 334, 568
low-cost housing, 420-426
lump-sum appropriations, 592

machines, political, 320-323
magistrates' courts, 163
Maine, 115, 146
manager plan
    city, 208-217
    county, 248-250
Marshall, Chief Justice, 9
Maryland, 266, 513, 568
Massachusetts
    and administrative reorganization, 102
    civil service of, 566, 567, 568
    governor's council of, 115
    and joint committees, 146
    rules of procedure for legislation in,
        152
    town government plan of, 254

mayor
  history of, 187-189
  powers of, 194-196
  and public relations, 196-197
  qualifications for, 193
  salaries of, 194
  selection of, 193
  terms of office of, 193-194
  and types of mayor-council plan, 189-
    192
mayor-council plan, 189-192
mechanic's lien, 544
medical examiner, 360
medicine, socialized, 411-413
mental disorders, 376-377, 401-403
merit system, 566-568
metropolitan area government
  city-county consolidation or separation
    of, 225
  and congestion problem, 219-220
  and extramural jurisdiction, 227-229
  federated city plan for, 226-227
  and intergovernmental arrangements,
    229
  regional plan for, 229-233
  and service coordination, 220-222
  and territorial annexation, 223-225
Michigan, 102, 568
mineral resources, see oil and gas
minimum wages, 7, 545-547
mining experiment stations, 499
Minnesota
  administrative reorganization of, 104-
    105
  civil service commission in, 568
  local governments, number of, in, 3
  non-registered liquors in, 34
  special districts in, 266
  townships, number of, in, 260
minority representation in elections, 280-
    282
misrepresentation, 512
Missouri, 51, 169, 568
Model State Constitution, 137
monopolies, 510
Montreal, Que., Canada, 230
mortgages, 422, 606
mothers of dependent children aid, 385-
    386
motor vehicles
  and accidents, 479-484
  license fees for, 475, 599, 601, 616
  number of, registered in U.S., 465
  and road construction, 464
  sales taxes on, 478
"municipal bankruptcy" act, 67-68
municipal camps, 461
municipal corporation, 46-47, 71-72

municipal court, unified, 165
municipal home rule, 51-56
Municipal Reform Party of England, 312

National Association of Attorney-Gen-
    erals, 41
National Association of Manufacturers,
    307
National Association of Secretaries of
    State, 41
National Civil Service League, 575-576
national committees, political, 315-317
National Conference of Commissioners
    on Uniform State Laws, 34-35
National Conference on Street and High-
    way Safety, 484
National Guard, 67, 113, 343-345
National Industrial Recovery Act, 472,
    540, 543, 546
National Labor Relations Act, 550, 554
National Mental Health Act, 402
National Municipal League, 137
National Planning Board, 636
National Police Academy, 65
natural resources
  agricultural and mining experiment sta-
    tions, 499
  agricultural extension work, 496-498
  federal grants-in-aid for, 15
  fish and game, 492-495
  forestry, 488-492
  oil and gas, 499-501
  soil conservation, 495-496
  state conservation agencies, 486-488
  state expenditures for, 487, 495, 582
  and state planning commissions, 638-
    639
  taxation, 616
  water power, 501-503
Nebraska
  administrative reorganization of, 102
  special districts of, 266
  unicameralism in, 132
Negroes
  disfranchisement of, 297-298
  and equal protection of the law, 25
New England town government, 254-260,
    437
New Hampshire, 115, 166
New Jersey
  administrative reorganization of, 102,
    104
  blue-sky laws in, 513
  civil service commission in, 568, 569
  townships in, 260
New Orleans, 225
New York City
  budget principle of, 587

city-county consolidation in, 225
Greater New York, 226-227
housing conditions in, 415-416
playgrounds in, 458
police of, 350
New York State
blue-sky laws of, 513
civil service in, 566, 567, 568, 569
discrimination law, 547
literacy tests in, 299
taxation in, 611
nolle prosequi, 357-358
nomination of candidates, 273-285
non-partisanship and primary elections, 282-283
non-suability doctrine, 42-43
Norris–La Guardia Act, 552, 554
North Carolina, 115, 471
nursing, public health, 408-409

obligatory referendum, 328
occupational diseases, 409, 537-539
Office of Education, 63
Ohio
administrative reorganization of, 102
civil service commission in, 568, 569
special legislation prohibition in, 49
Ohio River Valley Sanitation Compact, 38
oil and gas conservation, 499-501
old-age assistance, 381-382, 383
old-age insurance, 380-381, 577
old-age problem, 378-382
open primary, 278-279
open shop, 553-555
optional referendum, 328
ordinances, governor's, 112
Oregon, 98, 100, 145
orphanage, 383-384
Our State Legislatures, 157-158

pardons, 114, 368
parish government, *see* county government
parishes, 236
parks, 453-457, 461
paroles, 366-367
parties, political
boss control in, 323-325
caucus on legislation by, 148-149
control of majority, in state legislature, 146
conventions of, 274-276
definitions of, 306-308
dominance of national, in state and local elections, 312-313
and elections, 285-295
function of, 309-311

nomination of candidates by, 273-285
one-party dominance in south, 314-315
organization of major, 315-320
ruse of systems of, 308-309
sources of revenue for state and local machines of, 320-323
two-party system, 313-314
payroll tax, 559, 599, 614
Pennsylvania, 260, 281
Pennsylvania–New Jersey Toll Bridge Authority, 38
Pensacola Telegraph Co., 10
pensions
old-age, 380-382, 577
for state employees, 576-579
for state legislators, 128
People's Power League, 98
performance budgeting, 591
personal property tax, 478, 604, 606-607
petition
for initiative, 327-328
for nomination, 282-283
for recall, 334
Philadelphia, 225
planning agencies, state, 637-640
playgrounds, 457-459, 461
plurality principle in elections, 279-280
"pocket" veto, 110
police courts, special, 164-165
police forces
municipal, 349-354, 355
state, 346-349
political assessments, 322-323
political creed, 309-310
political machines, 320-323
political parties, *see* parties, political
poll tax, 296-297, 616
polling places, 285
poor relief, 372-378, 381-382
population in metropolitan areas, 221
Port of New York Authority, 38, 231
poverty, 370-372
preamble to state constitution, 79
precinct captain, 317-320
preferential voting, 280
press, freedom of, 82
price control (*see also* rates), 511
primary elections, 276-285, 297-298
prisons, 355, 363-368
private property, 81-82, 609-610, 642
privileges and immunities, 23-27
probation, 365-366
Probation and Parole Compact, 39
process serving, 355
professions, regulation of, 529-531
Progressive Party of England, 312
property
protection of, 81-82

property (*continued*)
   regulation of, 642
   taxes on, 58, 478, 600, 601, 602, 603-
      610
proportional representation, 281-282
prosecuting attorney, 356-358
protection of life and liberty, 81
public authorities, 105-106
public defender, 358-359
public health
   child hygiene, 406-408
   city expenditures for, 583
   communicable disease control, 399-401
   educational activities of, 409-411
   establishment of organizations for, 392-
      394
   federal participation in, 15, 394
   industrial hygiene, 409
   laboratories for, 404-405
   local organization of, 395-399
   mental disorders, 401-404
   nursing, 408-409
   organization of state department of,
      394-395
   protection of, in industry, 538-539
   and regulation of business, 511-512,
      529
   sanitary engineering and, 405-406
   socialized medicine and, 411-413
   state expenditures for, 393, 582
   vital statistics on, 404
Public Health Service, 63, 64
public-interest businesses, 515-523
public personnel, 64-66, 565-579
public prosecutor, 356-358
Public Roads Administration, 63, 64-65,
   473, 474
public safety, *see* safety
public schools, *see* education
public utilities
   contributions of, to political parties,
      320-321
   public ownership of, 528-529
   regulation of, 521-528
   revenues from, 602
public welfare, 15, 370-390, 582, 583
Public Works Administration, 424
public works programs, 321-322, 638-639
purchasing, central, 594-597
pure food and drug acts, 511-512

quarantine, 400

racial discrimination, 547-548
rates
   insurance, 519-520
   interest, 514-515
   public utility, 522, 524-528

real estate
   special assessments on, 478-479
   taxation on, 607-610
recall
   in Arizona, 28
   of judges, 170
   in New Mexico, 28
   of public officials, 334-339
Reconstruction Finance Corporation, 372
recreation, 453-462, 583
Red Cross, 374
reduction of representation clause, 27, 295-
   296
referendum, 327-334
reforestation, 491-492
regional planning, 644-645
register of deeds, 243-244
registration of voters, 299-301
relief, 372-378, 381-382
religion, freedom of, 79-81
representation
   and Fourteenth Amendment, 27, 295-
      296
   minority, in elections, 280-282
   in state legislature, 130-131
republican form of government, 26-27
Republican Party, 306, 309, 314-315
revenue bills, 591-594
revenues (*see also* special assessment; taxation), 599-619
Rhode Island, 254
roads (*see also* highways), 463-464
Roosevelt, Theodore, 35, 181
"run-off" primaries, 279-280
rural government, *see* county government;
   town government; township government

safety
   education for, 483
   on highways, 346, 479-484
   in industry, 533-535
   protective services for, 343-368
   and regulation of business, 511-512,
      530
   state expenditures for, 582
St. Louis, 225
sales tax, 478, 599, 601, 602, 614-616
Salvation Army, 374
San Francisco, 225
sanitary engineering, 405-406
sanitation, 583
school district plan, 433-434
school districts, chart, 435
school lunch program, 67
school superintendent, 436
schools, *see* education
secretary of state, 116-118

securities, 512-514

Securities and Exchange Commission, 513-514

segregated appropriations, 592

select committees of state legislature, 146-147

self-determination principle, 55

sentencing commission, 367-368

"separate but equal" doctrine, 25

separation of powers, 83-84

sessions of the state legislature, 126, 132-137

severance taxes, 616

sheriff, 354-356

Sherman Anti-Trust Act, 510

short ballot, 293-295, 332

Sixteenth Amendment, 8-9

slum problem, 420-426

small-loan acts, 514-515

Smith, Adam, 601-603

Social Security Act, 387, 558, 559-561

social security program, 373-374, 380-381, 387, 577, 558, 559-561

Socialist Party, 308, 315

socialized medicine, 411-413

soil conservation, 495-496

Soil Conservation Service, 495

speaker of lower house, 141-143

special assessments, 478-479, 618-619

special districts, 51, 265-269

special legislation
    cities reaction against, 48-49
    constitutional limitations on, 138
    prohibition of, 49-51
    veto by cities of, 57

special sessions of state legislatures, 134

speech, freedom of, 82

speed laws, 480

split session of state legislature, 136-137

spoils system, 250, 322, 565-566

standing committees of state legislature, 142, 144

state board of education, 443

state board of health, 395

state constitutions
    borrowing restrictions in, 624
    conventions for, 88-91
    increasing length of, 92-94
    organization and subject matter of, 77-88
    restrictions on state legislature by, 137-138
    revision commissions for, 91-92
    table of, 93

state courts, see courts, state

state executives
    attorney-general, 118-119
    auditor, 120-121
    cabinet of, needed, 122
    governor, 96-98, 106-115
    legislative recommendations by, 156-157
    lieutenant governor, 115-118, 141
    secretary of state, 116-118
    superintendent of public instruction, 121, 441-443
    treasurer, 119-120

state-federal relations, 4-29

state forests, 490-491

state government
    administrative reorganization movement in, 98-106
    boards of education of, 443
    budget for, 584-591
    central purchasing of, 594-597
    civil defense and, 647-648
    civil service commissions of, 569-575
    conservation agencies of, 486-488
    employees of, 565-579
    executive department of, chart, 99
    expenditures by, 581-597
    federal restrictions on power of, over local government, 70-72
    grants-in-aid of, to local government, 583-584, 585
    indebtedness of, 622-630, 631-633
    planning by, 635-640
    powers of, 20-27
    public health in, 393, 394-395, 409-410
    purchasing by, 596
    revenues of, 599, 600-601, 603, 605, 612-613, 614-616, 617, 618, 619
    suits against, 42-44
    superintendent of education, 441-443

State Government, 37

state highways (see also highways), 467, 468-472

state legislation, see legislation

state legislatures
    bicameralism in, 131-132
    city underrepresentation in, 130-131
    committee system in, 143-147
    constitutional amendments by, 85-86
    constitutional restrictions on power of, 137-139
    control of local government by, 47-48
    and lobbies, 154-156
    members of, 125-130
    nonlegislative functions of, 139-140
    presiding officers of, 140-143
    and reference bureaus, 153-154
    reform of, 157-158
    sessions of, 126, 132-137
    size of, 124
    unicameralism in, 132

state-local relations, 46-60

state militia, see National Guard

state parks, 456-457, 461
state superintendent of education, 441-443
state's attorney, 356-358
stocks, 606
street construction, 66
streets, 66, 641
strike
    law enforcement during, 345, 348
    by public employees, 575-576
    right to, 549-553
suffrage (see also voting), 27, 295-299
superintendent of public instruction, 121,
    441-443
superior courts, see appellate courts
Supreme Court of the United States
    admission of new states by, 28-29
    on commerce, 9
    on interstate commerce, 33-34
    on interstate compacts, 39-40
    labor decisions of, 540, 541, 542-544,
        545-547, 550, 551, 552, 553, 554, 555,
        556, 561
    on "municipal bankruptcy" act, 67-68
    public interest enterprise decisions, 516-
        517, 519-520, 524-528
    "separate but equal" doctrine of, 25
    tax decisions of, 609, 612, 617
supreme courts, state, 166-168
surveyor, county, 244

Taft-Hartley Law, see Labor Management
    Relations Act
tax commissions, state, 619
taxation (see also specific taxes)
    canon of sound, 601-603
    and federal government, 27, 600
    for highway construction, 475-478
    for old-age insurance, 380-381
    for regulatory purposes, 617-618
    for revenue, 600-601
    sources for, 599-601, 602
    for unemployment, 599, 614
teachers, 443-445
Tennessee Valley development, 503
Texas
    agricultural extension work in, 497
    city commission government in, 203-204
    number of counties in, 236
textbooks, 448
tidelands oil, 501
Toll, Henry W., 35, 37
toll roads, 464, 466
town clerk, 259
town government, 254-260, 395-398, 437
town manager, 259
town meeting, 255-258
township board, 262

township government, 46-47, 260-264, 434
township meeting, 261-262
township supervisor, 262-263
Trade Commission Act, 510
trade restrictions, 32, 510-511
trade unions, see labor unions
trades, regulation of, 529-531
traffic problem, 643
transfer of power to federal government,
    7-16
transportation, mass, 642-643
treasurer, state, 119-120
trial by grand jury, 357
Tri-State Pollution Compact, 38
Truman, Harry S., 501
tuberculosis, 401
Tweed Ring, 322
Twenty-first Amendment, 34
two-party system, 313-314

underworld, 320
unemployment compensation, 15, 388,
    559-561, 582, 599, 614
unemployment problem, 387-388
unicameralism, 132
unions, see labor unions
United Mine Workers of America, 554
United States Civil Service Commission,
    64
United States Employment Service, 558-
    559
United States Forest Service, 489, 491
universities, see education
usury laws, 514
Utah, 266
utilities, see public utilities

venereal diseases, 400-401
Vermont, 569
veterans' preference laws, 567-568
veto
    by governor, 110-111, 151
    by mayor, 194-195
village government, 264-265
Virginia
    city-county separation in, 225
    county board of education of, 437
    number of local governments of, 3
vital statistics, 404
voting
    absent, 301-302
    ballot for, 289-295
    compulsory, 303-304
    constitutional provisions for, 27, 295-
        296
    and nonvoters, 284-285, 302-303
    primary, 276-285, 297-298

qualifications for, 287-288, 295-301
  in recall, 334-335
  registration for, 299-301
voting machine, 290, 292

wages, 7, 544-547
Waite, Chief Justice, 10
Ware plan, 280
Washington, George, 308
Washington State, 102
watchers, election, 287
water power, 501-503
welfare, public, 15, 370-390, 582, 583
West Virginia, 615
Whig Party, 309
wild life, see fish and game conservation
Wisconsin, 569
women

exclusion of, from certain industries,
    534-535, 539
  hours of labor for, 541-542
  minimum wages for, 545
workmen's compensation, 535-538
World War II
  defense activities and congestion during,
    68-69
  and equal protection of the laws, 25
  federal action in, 7-8
  housing affected by, 425
  and "in-service" training, 573-574
  state competition and, 33
  state debt reduction during, 628
  and veterans' preference laws, 567

"yellow-dog" contract, 553-554
Youth Authority, 367

Friday 1:00 go to court